# LIVING WITH CONTRADICTIONS

.D

# LIVING WITH CONTRADICTIONS

## Controversies in Feminist Social Ethics

edited by

## Alison M. Jaggar

*University of Colorado–Boulder*

## Westview Press

*Boulder • San Francisco • Oxford*

WITHDRAWN

Copyright © 1994 by Westview Press, Inc.

Published in 1994 in the United States of America by Westview Press, Inc., 5500 Central Avenue, Boulder, Colorado 80301-2877, and in the United Kingdom by Westview Press, 36 Lonsdale Road, Summertown, Oxford OX2 7EW

Library of Congress Cataloging-in-Publication Data
Living with contradictions : controversies in feminist social ethics /
    edited by Alison M. Jaggar.
      p.   cm.
    Includes bibliographical references.
    ISBN 0-8133-1775-4.—ISBN 0-8133-1776-2 (pbk.)
    1. Feminist theory.   2. Social ethics.   3. Feminism—North
America.   I. Jaggar, Alison M.
HQ1190.L58   1994
301'.01—dc20                                                    93-29466
                                                                    CIP

396

J17

Printed and bound in the United States of America

The paper used in this publication meets the requirements
of the American National Standard for Permanence of Paper
for Printed Library Materials Z39.48-1984.

10    9    8    7    6    5    4    3    2

# Contents

## PART I: Equality

## PART II: Women Working

### A. Affirmative Action and Comparable Worth

### B. Sex Work

# PART III: Marketing Femininity

## A. Representing Women:
## Pornography, Art, and Popular Culture

## B. Presenting Women: Fashion and Beauty

# PART IV: Women's Fertility—
# Individual Choices and Social Constraints

## A. Abortion

# Acknowledgments

Many people have been involved in making this book possible. First among them of course are the authors and their publishers; they graciously permitted me to reprint their work, often in a drastically edited form. My students in "Feminist Practical Ethics" at the University of Colorado–Boulder made it clear that their course experience would be vastly improved if a real textbook were available to replace their unwieldy packets of photocopied material, and they commented vigorously, sometimes ruthlessly, on the readings used in classes in 1991 and 1992. Joan Callahan, Claudia Card, Virginia Held, Mary Mahowald, Kathryn Morgan, Christine Overall, Anne Seller, Rosemarie Tong, and Joyce Trebilcot were all kind enough to look at my original table of contents; in addition to offering suggestions for specific readings, they made a number of extremely useful comments about the general conceptualization of the book. When I had difficulty rounding out particular sections, I consulted Alison Bailey, Nilak Butler, Ward Churchill, Janet Jacobs, Andy Smith, Karen Warren, and Kathryn White; they were generous with their expertise and came up with some excellent ideas. Don Barnes, Victoria Davion, Ynestra King, Gretchen Legler, and Anne Maloney all rushed manuscripts to me for consideration. I received willing clerical assistance from Marilyn McDowell and Maureen McFeeley, and Martha Leahy was generous beyond the call of duty in spending hours slaving over a hot photocopying machine. Amy Wagner's enormous contribution to this project was motivated only partly by the realization that once it was complete, she would no longer have to prepare photocopied packets for "Feminist Practical Ethics." Her willingness to track down references in the library and make innumerable copies was outstanding, and during the months of preparing this manuscript, Amy's cheerful "Absolutely!" became my favorite word.

It was a pleasure to work with the people at Westview, who remained enthusiastic and dedicated throughout a production process that turned out to be extremely arduous. Spencer Carr was constantly encouraging—though he did call my first manuscript a "monster" and send it back for drastic cutting. Martha Robbins and Connie Oehring, my first and second project editors, were friendly as well as extremely competent. Marykay Scott, helped by Elissa Braunstein, was persevering, resourceful, and good-humored over months of pursuing permissions from authors and publishers who were sometimes elusive or unresponsive.

David Jaggar supported my work on this project, as he has all my previous ones, and our children were tolerant as usual. Special thanks go to Lori Gruen, who offered invaluable help ranging from creative manuscript suggestions to chocolate in moments of crisis. When the manuscript had to be cut by one-third, she edited it with care and flair. In the absence of of Lori's energy, knowledge, and skill, this book would be a vastly inferior product.

*Alison M. Jaggar*

## B. Environmentalism

# Credits

## Part I: Equality

ALISON M. JAGGAR, "Sexual Difference and Sexual Equality," in *Theoretical Perspectives on Sexual Difference*, Deborah L. Rhode, ed. (New Haven: Yale University Press, 1990), pp. 239–254, 302–303. Copyright © 1990 by Yale University Press. Reprinted by permission of Yale University Press.

CHRISTINE A. LITTLETON, "Reconstructing Sexual Equality," *California Law Review* 1279: 75, 4 (1987). Reprinted by permission of University of California Press and the author.

CATHARINE A. MACKINNON, "Toward Feminist Jurisprudence," reprinted by permission of the publishers, from Catharine A. MacKinnon, *Toward a Feminist Theory of the State* (Cambridge, MA: Harvard University Press, 1989), pp. 242–249. Copyright © 1989 by Catharine A. MacKinnon.

KIMBERLE CRENSHAW, "Demarginalizing the Intersection of Race and Sex: A Black Feminist Critique of Antidiscrimination Doctrine, Feminist Theory, and Antiracist Politics," *University of Chicago Legal Forum* (1989): 139–167. Reprinted by permission.

## Part II: Women Working

### A. Affirmative Action and Comparable Worth

LISA H. NEWTON, "Reverse Discrimination as Unjustified," *Ethics* 83, 4 (July 1973): 374–378. Published by The University of Chicago Press. Copyright © 1973 by The University of Chicago. Reprinted by permission.

HARDY JONES, excerpts from "Fairness, Meritocracy, and Reverse Discrimination," *Journal of Social Theory and Practice* 4, 2 (Spring 1977): 211–226. Copyright © 1977 by *Journal of Social Theory and Practice*. Reprinted by permission.

NATIONAL COMMITTEE ON PAY EQUITY, "The Wage Gap: Myths and Facts." Reprinted by permission.

JUNE O'NEILL, "An Argument Against Comparable Worth," in *Comparable Worth: An Issue for the 80's*, Vol. 1 (U.S. Commission on Civil Rights, 1984).

LAURIE SHRAGE, "Some Implications of Comparable Worth," *Journal of Social Theory and Practice* 13, 1 (Spring 1987): 77–102. Copyright © 1987 by *Journal of Social Theory and Practice*. Reprinted by permission.

## B. Sex Work

ALISON M. JAGGAR, "Prostitution," in Alan Soble, ed., *Philosophy of Sex* (Lanham, MD: Littlefield Adams, 1980), pp. 348–368. Reprinted by permission of Rowman & Littlefield Publishers, Inc.

SUNNY CARTER, "A Most Useful Tool," in Frederique Delacoste and Priscilla Alexander, eds., *Sex Work: Writings by Women in the Sex Industry* (Pittsburgh: Cleis Press, 1987), pp. 159–165. Reprinted by permission of Cleis Press.

DEBI SUNDAHL, "Stripper," in Frederique Delacoste and Priscilla Alexander, eds., *Sex Work: Writings by Women in the Sex Industry* (Pittsburgh: Cleis Press, 1987), pp. 175–180. Reprinted by permission of Cleis Press.

EVELINA GIOBBE, "Confronting the Liberal Lies About Prostitution," in Dorchen Leidholdt and Janice G. Raymond, eds., *The Sexual Liberals and the Attack on Feminism* (Tarrytown, NY: Pergamon Press, 1990), pp. 67–81. Reprinted by permission of the author.

CAROLE PATEMAN, "What's Wrong with Prostitution?" excerpted from Carole Pateman, *The Sexual Contract* (Cambridge: Polity Press, 1988), pp. 189–209, 256–259. Reprinted by permission of Blackwell Publishers and Stanford University Press. Copyright © 1988 by Carole Pateman.

INTERNATIONAL COMMITTEE FOR PROSTITUTES' RIGHTS, "International Committee for Prostitutes' Rights World Charter and World Whores' Congress Statements," in Frederique Delacoste and Priscilla Alexander, eds., *Sex Work: Writings by Women in the Sex Industry* (Pittsburgh: Cleis Press, 1987), pp. 305–321. Reprinted by permission of Cleis Press.

## Part III: Marketing Femininity

### A. Representing Women: Pornography, Art, and Popular Culture

ANDREA DWORKIN, "Why Pornography Matters to Feminists," from Andrea Dworkin, *Letters to a War Zone* (New York: Dutton/New America Library, 1988), pp. 203–205. Copyright © 1988 by Andrea Dworkin. Reprinted by permission of Elaine Markson Literary Agency and Dutton Signet, a division of Penguin Books USA Inc.

HELEN E. LONGINO, "Pornography, Oppression, and Freedom: A Closer Look," in Laura Lederer, ed., *Take Back the Night: Women on Pornography* (New York: William Morrow, 1980), pp. 40–54. Reprinted by permission of the author.

## B. Presenting Women: Fashion and Beauty

JANET RADCLIFFE RICHARDS, "The Unadorned Feminist," from Janet Radcliffe Richards, *The Sceptical Feminist* (London: Routledge & Kegan Paul, 1980), pp. 181–206. Reprinted by permission of David Higham Associates.

ANDREA DWORKIN, "Gynocide: Chinese Footbinding," from Andrea Dworkin, *Woman Hating* (New York: Dutton/New American Library, 1974). Copyright © 1974 by Andrea Dworkin. Reprinted by permission of Elaine Markson Literary Agency and Dutton Signet, a division of Penguin Books USA Inc.

CAROL SCHMIDT, "'Do Something About Your Weight,'" in Susan E. Browne, Debra Connors, and Nancy Stern, eds., *With the Power of Each Breath: A Disabled Women's Anthology* (Pittsburgh: Cleis Press, 1985), pp. 248–252. Reprinted by permission of Cleis Press.

NAOMI WOLF, "Hunger," from Naomi Wolf, *The Beauty Myth: How Images of Beauty Are Used Against Women* (New York: William Morrow & Co., 1991), pp. 181–197, 334. Copyright © 1991 by Naomi Wolf. Reprinted by permission of William Morrow & Company, Inc.; Chatto & Windus, London; and Random House of Canada Limited, Toronto.

WENDY CHAPKIS, "Skin Deep," from Wendy Chapkis, *Beauty Secrets* (Boston: South End Press, 1986), pp. 37–44, 201. Reprinted by permission.

WENDY CHAPKIS, "Marieme," interview, from Wendy Chapkis, *Beauty Secrets* (Boston: South End Press, 1986), pp. 71–73. Reprinted by permission.

ROBERTA GALLER, "The Myth of the Perfect Body," in Carole S. Vance, ed., *Pleasure and Danger: Exploring Female Sexuality* (Hammersmith, England: Pandora Press, 1984), pp. 165–172. Reprinted by permission of the author.

KATHRYN PAULY MORGAN, "Women and the Knife: Cosmetic Surgery and the Colonization of Women's Bodies," *Hypatia* 6, 3 (Fall 1991): 25–53. Reprinted by permission of the author.

ALICE WALKER, "Beauty: When the Other Dancer Is the Self," from Alice Walker, *In Search of Our Mothers' Gardens: Womanist Prose* (New York: Harcourt Brace Jovanovich, 1983), pp. 384–393. Reprinted by permission of Harcourt Brace and David Higham Associates.

## Part IV: Women's Fertility—Individual Choice and Social Constraints

### A. Abortion

NINIA BAEHR, "Deregulating Abortion," from Ninia Baehr, *Abortion Without Apology* (Boston: South End Press, 1990), p. 33. Reprinted by permission.

ANNE M. MALONEY, "Women and Children First?", original chapter.

CATHARINE A. MACKINNON, "Abortion: On Public and Private," reprinted by permission of the publishers, from Catharine A. MacKinnon, *Toward a Feminist Theory of the State* (Cambridge, MA: Harvard University Press, 1989), pp. 184–194. Copyright © 1989 by Catharine A. MacKinnon.

ALISON M. JAGGAR, "Abortion and a Woman's Right to Decide," *The Philosophical Forum* 5, 1/2 (Fall/Winter 1973–1974): 184–194. Reprinted by permission.

MIKE MALES, "Parental Consent Laws: Are They a 'Reasonable Compromise'?" In *These Times* (July 22–August 24, 1992): 17. Reprinted by permission of *In These Times*, Institute for Public Affairs, Chicago, IL.

BEVERLY SMITH, "Choosing Ourselves: Black Women and Abortion," *Gay Community News* (Boston), February 19–25, 1989.

KATHRYN KOLBERT, "A Reproductive Rights Agenda for the 1990s," in Marlene Gerber Fried, ed., *From Abortion to Reproductive Freedom: Transforming a Movement* (Boston: South End Press, 1990). Copyright © 1988, Rutgers The State University. Reprinted by permission.

JODI L. JACOBSON, "The Global Politics of Abortion," from Jodi L. Jacobson, *The Global Politics of Abortion* (Washington, DC: Worldwatch Institute, 1990), pp. 37–45, 51–58. Reprinted by permission.

HELEN B. HOLMES AND BETTY B. HOSKINS, "Prenatal and Preconception Sex Choice Technologies: A Path to Femicide?" in Gena Corea et al., eds., *Man Made Woman: How New Reproductive Technologies Affect Women* (Bloomington: Indiana University Press, 1987), pp. 15–29. Reprinted by permission of the authors and Indiana University Press.

DEBORAH KAPLAN, "Disability Rights Perspectives on Reproductive Technologies and Public Policy," in Sherrill Cohen and Nadine Taub, eds., *Reproductive Laws for the 1990s* (Totowa, NJ: Humana Press, 1989), pp. 241–247. Reprinted by permission.

SUSAN SHERWIN, "Abortion Through a Feminist Ethics Lens," *Dialogue* 30 (1991): 327–342. Reprinted by permission of *Dialogue*, Canadian Philosophical Review.

## B. Procreative Technology and Procreative Freedom

BARBARA KATZ ROTHMAN, "The Meanings of Choice in Reproductive Technology," in Rita Arditti, Renate Duelli Klein, and Shelley Minden, eds., *Test-Tube Women: What Future for Motherhood* (Hammersmith, England: Pandora Press, 1984), pp. 23–33.

BETSY HARTMANN, "Reproductive Rights and Wrongs," excerpts from Betsy Hartmann, *Reproductive Rights and Wrongs: The Global Politics of Population Control* (New York: Harper & Row, 1987), pp. 38–52, 161–175, 303–307, 322–325. Copyright © 1987 by Betsy Hartmann. Reprinted by permission of HarperCollins Publishers, Inc.

ADELE CLARK, "Subtle Forms of Sterilization Abuse: A Reproductive Rights Analysis," in Rita Arditti, Renate Duelli Klein, and Shelley Minden, eds., *Test-Tube Women: What Future for Motherhood* (Hammersmith, England: Pandora Press, 1984), pp. 188–212.

GENA COREA, "'Informed Consent': The Myth of Voluntarism," excerpts from Chapter 9 of Gena Corea, *The Mother Machine: Reproductive Technologies from Artificial Insemination to Artificial Wombs* (New York: Harper & Row, 1985), pp. 166–185, 332–355. Copyright © 1985 by Gena Corea. Reprinted by permission of HarperCollins Publishers, Inc.

IRENE DIAMOND, "Babies, Heroic Experts, and a Poisoned Earth," in Irene Diamond and Gloria Feman Orenstein, eds., *Reweaving the World: The Emergence of Ecofeminism* (San Francisco: Sierra Club Books, 1990), pp. 201–210, 301–303. Reprinted by permission.

CHRISTINE OVERALL, "Access to In Vitro Fertilization: Costs, Care, and Consent," *Dialogue* 30 (1991): 383–397. Reprinted by permission of *Dialogue*, Canadian Philosophical Review.

## Part V: Family Values

### A. Contract Child Production

SUSAN INCE, "Inside the Surrogate Industry," in Rita Arditti, Renate Duelli Klein, and Shelley Minden, eds., *Test-Tube Women: What Future for Motherhood* (Hammersmith, England: Pandora Press, 1984), pp. 99–116.

CHRISTINE T. SISTARE, "Reproductive Freedom and Women's Freedom: Surrogacy and Autonomy," *The Philosophical Forum* 19, 4 (Summer 1988): 227–240. Reprinted by permission.

MARY GIBSON, "Contract Motherhood: Social Practice in Social Context," in Clarice Feinman, ed., *The Criminalization of a Woman's Body* (Binghamton, NY: The Haworth Press, Inc., 1992), pp. 55–99. Reprinted by permission of The Haworth Press, Inc.

FRANCIE HORNSTEIN, "Children by Donor Insemination: A New Choice for Lesbians," in Rita Arditti, Renate Duelli Klein, and Shelley Minden, eds., *Test-Tube Women: What Future for Motherhood* (Hammersmith, England: Pandora Press, 1984), pp. 373–381.

THOMAS W. LAQUEUR, "The Facts of Fatherhood," in Marianne Hirsch and Evelyn Fox Keller, eds., *Conflicts in Feminism* (New York: Routledge, 1990), pp. 205–221. Reprinted by permission of the publisher and the author.

## B. Valuing Alternative Families

KAREN LINDSEY, "The Politics of Childlessness," *the second wave* (Summer 1974): 12–13. Reprinted by permission of the author.

DIANE EHRENSAFT, "When Women and Men Mother," *Socialist Review* 49 (Jan.-Feb. 1980): 37–73 (Durham, NC: Duke University Press). Reprinted with permission of the publisher.

BABA COPPER, "The Radical Potential in Lesbian Mothering of Daughters," in Sandra Pollack and Jeanne Vaughn, eds., *Politics of the Heart: A Lesbian Parenting Anthology* (Ithaca, NY: Firebrand Books, 1987), pp. 233–240. Copyright © 1987 by Baba Copper. Reprinted by permission of Firebrand Books.

LINDSY VAN GELDER, "A Lesbian Family," *Ms.*, March/April 1991, pp. 44–47. Reprinted by permission of the author.

PATRICIA HILL COLLINS, "Black Women and Motherhood," from Patricia Hill Collins, *Black Feminist Thought* (New York: Unwin Hyman, 1990), pp. 115–137, 239–255. Reprinted by permission of Routledge, Chapman & Hall and the author.

ANN FERGUSON, "The Che-Lumumba School: Creating a Revolutionary Family Community," *Quest* 5, 3: 13–26. Reprinted by permission of the author.

KAREN LINDSEY, "Friends as Family: No One Said It Would Be Easy," from Karen Lindsey, *Friends as Family* (Boston: Beacon Press, 1981), pp. 257–268. Copyright © 1981 by Karen Lindsey. Reprinted by permission of Beacon Press.

## Part VI: The Personal as Political

### A. Sexual Practice

ANNE KOEDT, "The Myth of the Vaginal Orgasm," in Anne Koedt, Ellen Levine, and Anita Rapone, eds., *Radical Feminism* (New York: Quadrangle/New York Times Book Company, 1973), pp. 198–207. Copyright © 1970 by Anne Koedt. Reprinted by permission.

ADRIENNE RICH, excerpt from "Compulsory Heterosexuality and Lesbian Existence," is reprinted from Adrienne Rich, *Blood, Bread, and Poetry: Selected Prose 1979–1985* (New York: W. W. Norton & Company, 1986), pp. 23–75, by permission of the author, W. W. Norton & Company, Inc., and Virago Press Ltd. Copyright © 1986 by Adrienne Rich.

AUDRE LORDE, "Scratching the Surface: Some Notes on Barriers to Women and Loving," *The Black Scholar* 9, 7 (1978).

MARILYN FRYE, "Virgin Women," excerpt from "Willful Virgin *or* Do You Have to Be a Lesbian to Be a Feminist?" from Marilyn Frye, *Willful Virgin: Essays in Feminism, 1976–1992* (Freedom, CA: The Crossing Press, 1992), pp. 124–137. Copyright © 1992 by The Crossing Press. Reprinted by permission of The Crossing Press.

CHRISTINE OVERALL, "Heterosexuality and Choice," (originally titled "Heterosexuality and Feminist Theory") *Canadian Journal of Philosophy* 20, 1 (March 1990): 9–17.

KARIN BAKER, "Bisexual Feminist Politics: Because Bisexuality Is Not Enough," in Elizabeth Reba Wise, ed., *Closer to Home: Bisexuality and Feminism* (Seattle: Seal Press, 1992), pp. 255–267. Reprinted by permission.

ANNIE SPRINKLE, "Beyond Bisexual," in Loraine Hutchins and Lani Kaahumanu, eds., *Bi Any Other Name: Bisexual People Speak Out* (Boston: Alyson Publications, 1991), pp. 103–107. Reprinted by permission.

A SOUTHERN WOMEN'S WRITING COLLECTIVE, "Sex Resistance in Heterosexual Arrangements," in Dorchen Leidholdt and Janice G. Raymond, eds., *The Sexual Liberals and the Attack on Feminism* (Tarrytown, NY: Pergamon Press, 1990), pp. 140–147. Copyright © 1990 by A Southern Women's Writing Collective. Reprinted by permission of A Southern Women's Writing Collective.

SANDRA LEE BARTKY, "Feminine Masochism and the Politics of Personal Transformation," greatly abridged chapter from Sandra Lee Bartky, *Femininity and Domination* (New York: Routledge, 1990), pp. 45–62, 126–129. Reprinted by permission of the publisher and the author.

SHANNON BELL, "Feminist Ejaculations," in Arthur Kroker and Marilouise Kroker, eds., *The Hysterical Male: New Feminist Theory* (New York: St. Martin's Press, 1991), pp. 155–169. Reprinted by permission of The Macmillan Press Ltd.; St. Martin's Press; and New World Perspectives, Montréal.

## B. Consuming Animals

LORI GRUEN, "Dismantling Oppression: An Analysis of the Connection Between Women and Animals," in Greta Gaard, ed., *Ecofeminism: Women, Animals, Nature* (Philadelphia: Temple University Press, 1993), pp. 60–90. Reprinted by permission.

CAROL J. ADAMS, "The Sexual Politics of Meat," from Carol J. Adams, *The Sexual Politics of Meat: A Feminist-Vegetarian Critical Theory* (New York: The Continuum Publishing Company, 1990), pp. 24–38, 192–194. Copyright © 1990 by Carol J. Adams. Reprinted by permission of The Continuum Publishing Company.

LISA MARTIN, "Feminism and Vegetarianism," original chapter.

GRETCHEN LEGLER, "Hunting: A Woman's Perspective," *Northland Outdoors*, September 17, 1992. Reprinted by permission of *Northland Outdoors*, published by the *Grand Forks Herald*, Grand Forks, North Dakota.

ANDRÉE COLLARD WITH JOYCE CONTRUCCI, "Shots in the Dark," excerpted from Andrée Collard with Joyce Contrucci, *Rape of the Wild: Man's Violence Against Animals* (Bloomington: Indiana University Press, 1989), pp. 45–56. Reprinted by permission of Indiana University Press. The extract, first published by The Women's Press Ltd., 1988, 34 Great Sutton Street, London EC1V 0DX, is also used by permission of The Women's Press Ltd.

SLAVENKA DRAKULIC, "Some Doubts About Fur Coats," from Slavenka Drakulic, *How We Survived Communism and Even Laughed* (New York: W. W. Norton, 1991), pp. 133–142. Reprinted by permission of the author, W. W. Norton & Company, Inc., and Hutchinson Publishers Network (Random Century Group).

## Part VII: Feminists Changing the World

### A. Militarism

JUDITH HICKS STIEHM, "The Protected, the Protector, the Defender," *Women's Studies International Forum* 5, 3/4 (1982): 367–376. Reprinted by permission of the author.

HELEN MICHALOWSKI, "The Army Will Make a 'Man' Out of You," in Pam McAllister, ed., *Reweaving the Web of Life* (Philadelphia: New Society Publishers, 1982), pp. 326–335. Originally published in *WIN Magazine*, March 1, 1980 (War Resisters' League, 339 Lafayette St., New York, NY 10012). Reprinted by permission of the author.

CYNTHIA ENLOE, " 'Some of the Best Soldiers Wear Lipstick,' " from Cynthia Enloe, *Does Khaki Become You? The Militarization of Women's Lives* (Hammersmith, England: Pandora Press, 1988), pp. 117–155, 235–239.

"Surprise! Rape in the Army," *Off Our Backs* (March 1993): 6. Originally published by *The Orange County Register*. Reprinted with permission of The Orange County Register, copyright © 1993.

GWYN KIRK, "Our Greenham Common: Feminism and Nonviolence," in Adrienne Harris and Ynestra King, eds., *Rocking the Ship of State: Toward a Feminist Peace Politics* (Boulder: Westview Press, 1989), pp. 115–130. Copyright © 1989 by Gwyn Kirk. Reprinted by permission.

LYNN ALDERSON, "Greenham Common and All That ... A Radical Feminist View," from Lynn Alderson, *Breaching the Peace* (London: Onlywomen Press, 1983), pp. 11–15. Reprinted by permission.

SARA RUDDICK, "Notes Toward a Feminist Maternal Peace Politics," from Sara Ruddick, *Maternal Thinking: Toward a Politics of Peace* (Boston: Beacon Press, 1989), pp. 219–251, 278–280. Copyright © 1989 by Sara Ruddick. Reprinted by permission of Beacon Press.

EUGENIA, " 'They Won't Take Me Alive,' " in New Americas Press, ed., *A Dream Compels Us: Voices of Salvadoran Women* (Boston: South End Press, 1989), pp. 137–143. Reprinted by permission.

BARBARA OMOLADE, "We Speak for the Planet," in Adrienne Harris and Ynestra King, eds., *Rocking the Ship of State: Toward a Feminist Peace Politics* (Boulder: Westview Press, 1989), pp. 171–189. Reprinted by permission.

## B. Environmentalism

KAREN J. WARREN, "Taking Empirical Data Seriously: An Ecofeminist Philosophical Perspective," in *Human Values and the Environment,* Report 140 (The Wisconsin Academy of Science, Arts, and Letters, 1993), pp. 32–40. Copyright © 1993 by Karen J. Warren. Reprinted by permission of the author.

MARTI KHEEL, "From Healing Drugs to Deadly Drugs: Western Medicine's War Against the Natural World," in Judith Plant, ed., *Healing the Wounds: The Promise of Ecofeminism* (Philadelphia: New Society Publishers, 1990), pp. 96–111. Reprinted by permission of New Society Publishers and Between the Lines, Toronto.

VANDANA SHIVA, "Development, Ecology, and Women," from Vandana Shiva, *Staying Alive: Women, Ecology, and Development* (London: Zed Books Ltd., 1988), pp. 1–13. Originally published in 1988 by Kali for Women, New Delhi, India. Reprinted by permission of Zed Books Ltd. and Kali for Women.

VAL PLUMWOOD, "Conversations with Gaia," *APA Newsletter on Feminism and Philosophy* 91, 1 (Spring 1992): 61–66.

JUDITH PLANT, "Searching for Common Ground: Ecofeminism and Bioregionalism," in Irene Diamond and Gloria Feman Orenstein, eds., *Reweaving the World: The Emergence of Ecofeminism* (San Francisco: Sierra Club Books, 1990), pp. 155–161. Reprinted by permission.

CYNTHIA HAMILTON, "Women, Home, and Community: The Struggle in an Urban Environment," in Irene Diamond and Gloria Feman Orenstein, eds., *Reweaving the World: The Emergence of Ecofeminism* (San Francisco: Sierra Club Books, 1990), pp. 215–222, 303–304. Reprinted by permission.

ELLEN O´LOUGHLIN, "Questioning Sour Grapes: Ecofeminism and the United Farm Workers Grape Boycott," in Greta Gaard, ed., *Ecofeminism: Women, Animals, Nature* (Philadelphia: Temple University Press, 1993), pp. 146–166. Reprinted by permission.

JO WHITEHORSE COCHRAN, "Stealing the Planet," from Jo Whitehorse Cochran, Donna Langston, and Carolyn Woodward, eds., *Changing Our Power: An Introduction to Women Studies,* second edition (Dubuque, IA: Kendall/Hunt Publishing Co., 1991), p. 301. Copyright © 1991 by Kendall/Hunt Publishing Company, Dubuque IA. Reprinted with permission.

RONNIE ZOE HAWKINS, "Reproductive Choices: The Ecological Dimension," *APA Newsletter on Feminism and Philosophy* 91, 1 (Spring 1992): 66–73.

THE COMMITTEE ON WOMEN, POPULATION, AND THE ENVIRONMENT, "Women, Population, and the Environment: Call for a New Approach," *Radical America* (1990). Reprinted by permission of The Committee on Woman, Population, and the Environment.

# Introduction:
# Living with Contradictions

## Alison M. Jaggar

Feminist ideas, and even the word *feminism,* have always been controversial. For at least one hundred fifty years, political life in Western Europe and North America has been marked by conflict between those who seek to improve the status of women and those who assert that it needs no such improvement. Today, while feminists challenge both the blatant and subtle forms of violence and injustice that we see as inherent in many contemporary practices, others criticize what they take to be feminist proposals on the grounds that they are unnecessary, unrealistic, subversive, and/or immoral.

It would not be difficult to put together a collection of readings exploring conflicts between feminist and antifeminist views; a number of such collections already exist. This book, however, is different. Rather than exploring conflicts between feminists and antifeminists, it explores conflicts that presently occur *within* Western, primarily North American, feminism. It thus represents an in-house discussion among feminists. Rather than continuing to debate whether feminist approaches in general are justified, this book explores in detail what may be involved in a genuine commitment to feminism.

### What Is Feminism?

*Feminism* is a term that carries a potent emotional charge. To be a feminist is a badge of pride for some people, central to their sense of identity; for others, "feminist" is a label to be repudiated at all costs, a code representing whatever they fear or hate. At the extreme, feminists may be caricatured as Western bourgeois man-hating separatists! Because "feminism" is used as both an honorific title and a term of abuse, some try to deny the title "feminist" to those who would claim it, and others seek to fix it on those who would reject it. In consequence of the importance often attached to being or not being a feminist, the meaning of feminism is hotly contested not only between feminists and antifeminists but also among feminists.

In making commitment to feminism a condition for inclusion, this collection obviously presupposes a working definition of feminism independent of the more elaborate

1

understandings developed in the various selections. The working definition assumed here identifies feminism with the various social movements dedicated to ending the subordination of women. For the purposes of this collection, people, male or female, count as feminist if and only if they are sincerely committed to this goal—however they conceive it.

This working definition of feminism is not only extremely broad; it also departs from the original meaning of the term. When the word feminism was first introduced into the United States from France in the early twentieth century, it referred only to one particular group within what in the nineteenth century was called "the woman movement": a diverse collection of groups all dedicated in one way or another to "advancing" the position of women. The feminists were the "romantic" group of women's rights advocates, those who asserted the uniqueness of women, the mystical experience of motherhood, and women's special purity; by contrast, the "sexual rationalists" argued that the subordination of women was irrational, not because women were purer than men, but because women and men were basically similar.

There are several reasons for using a definition of "feminism" that is broader and more minimal than the original one. First, it makes political sense to employ a definition that is as uncontroversial and widely acceptable as possible—though it would be presumptuous to insist that people who were uncomfortable for one reason or another with identifying themselves as feminists were "really" part of the feminist community. Second, a definition must prejudge as few questions as possible about what feminism entails and also avoid framing disputes about the subordination of women in terms that encourage sectarianism. Rather than debate which ideas and practices are "truly" feminist, it is more productive as well as less divisive to recognize that people who are sincerely committed to ending the subordination of women may have genuine disagreements about what that involves and how it may be accomplished. Third, a definition that reduces possible fears of exclusion from the feminist community lowers the political and emotional stakes of feminist debates and allows substantive issues to be discussed with less acrimony and polarization.

Creating a safe space for in-house discussion among feminists is necessary because, though feminists are united by a conscious commitment to ending women's subordination, we are divided about much else. Not only do we disagree about issues apparently unrelated to gender, which is only to be expected, since feminists are different individuals from a wide variety of backgrounds; we also often disagree, perhaps less predictably, over what should be done to end women's subordination and even over how to identify its various manifestations. Thus, feminist disputes are not restricted to strategic disagreement about the best means for achieving our long-term goals; we also sometimes differ about our goals. Our visions are not all alike.

Disagreement among Western feminists is not a new phenomenon. Feminists of the nineteenth and early twentieth centuries debated with each other not only over women's special purity but also over practical issues such as temperance, how far feminism should involve itself with seemingly nongendered working-class or antiracist struggles, whether feminists should support World War I, and how important the vote was. Many of those early disagreements still echo through present-day feminist debates. Over the course of the twentieth century, however, world historical changes, including technological developments, have added new dimensions to old issues and have raised new questions that were quite unforeseeable at the beginning of the century. Thus, for example, feminist discussions of the treatment of animals or of war and peace have been transformed by the advent of factory farming and weapons of mass destruction; and we now debate the custody of frozen embryos and the selective abortion of female fetuses.

This book explores some of the moral and public policy issues that divide Western, especially North American, feminists as the twentieth century ends and the twenty-first century begins. Obviously, the issues we confront today are identical neither with the issues faced by North American feminists a hundred years ago nor with those currently faced by movements against women's subordination in Latin America, Asia, northern and southern Africa, or Eastern Europe. The diversity of issues addressed by feminists in different places at different times raises the general question of what makes an issue feminist. Is it only the contingent fact that some feminists somewhere have been concerned about it, or can feminist issues be characterized in some more general or principled way?

## What Makes Something an Issue for Feminism?

Since feminists are distinguished by our commitment to ending women's subordination, institutions, values, practices, and ways of thinking or speaking become problematic for us whenever they seem to cause, perpetuate, intensify, or rationalize the subordination of women. Feminist issues may be identified, therefore, as concerns about anything perceived to contribute to women's subordination. Such concerns may be raised about any aspect of social life, from daily practices, to cultural and religious values, to legal and political institutions, to the so-called master categories through which we conceptualize human and nonhuman nature, knowledge, and value. This book explores questions feminists have raised about specific public policies and personal practices, focusing on possible relationships between these policies and practices, on the one hand, and the subordination of women, on the other.

Identifying feminist issues in terms of their salience to women's subordination obviously leaves room for debate as to whether some issue is properly a matter of feminist concern. It opens the possibilities both that some legitimately feminist issue may not yet be acknowledged as such because its connection with women's subordination remains unnoticed and that feminists may be concerned about issues that have little bearing on women's subordination. Feminists indeed have often disputed whether certain issues should fall within the scope of feminist concern. In the late 1960s, for example, some feminists denied that lesbianism was a feminist issue. One of the selections in this book argues that feminists should not concern ourselves with militarism. I have often been uncertain whether the treatment of animals is properly an issue for feminism.

Although not all moral or political issues may have feminist dimensions, a striking feature of Western feminism's recent history has been the progressive enlargement of its moral and political concerns. Twenty years ago, it was common to conceptualize so-called women's issues as a limited and, some thought, relatively unimportant subset of more general "human" issues. As late as 1980, for instance, the New Zealand representative to a U.N. conference on women asserted that "to talk feminism to a woman who has no water, home or food is to talk nonsense." This New Zealander was making the seemingly commonsense assertion that what she saw as women's basic and presumably nongender-specific "human" needs should be addressed before our supposedly "special" needs as women. This assertion assumes not only that issues of subordination are secondary to issues of housing, nutrition, and disease but also that each can be addressed independently of the other.

Feminists today are increasingly rejecting this way of thinking, recognizing that, as I have argued elsewhere, moral or public policy issues cannot be separated cleanly into those that are and those that are not of special concern to women. On the one hand, since men's and women's lives are inextricably intertwined, there are no women's issues that are not also men's issues. The availability or otherwise of child care and abortion, for instance, has significant consequences for the lives of men as well as women, affecting, among other matters, women's dependence on men and men's power over women. On the other hand, since men and women typically are not what lawyers call "similarly situated" relative to each other, there is a gendered aspect to virtually all moral and public policy issues. Thus, to take the New Zealand representative's 1980 example, access to the necessities of water, home, and food is often more difficult for women than for men precisely because of women's subordinate status—and the availability of these necessities typically has different meanings for men's and women's lives. For instance, when drinking water is carried by women for long distances, the advent of piped water has more immediate and dramatic consequences for women than for men because women can now spend less time carrying water and because children's mortality resulting from waterborne diseases is reduced. As long as infant mortality rates are high, birth rates are also high—with deleterious consequences for women's health and opportunities for a life that goes beyond childbearing and childrearing. Similarly, malnutrition and starvation affect women and girls worldwide far more severely than men and boys because more of the available food is given to males. Thus, feminist issues often cannot be contrasted with such supposedly general or human issues as housing, nutrition, and disease because these are themselves feminist issues. For this reason, it is usually incoherent to assert that feminist issues are more or less urgent than human issues: feminist issues are obviously human issues, and "human" issues invariably turn out to have a feminist dimension.

## Feminist Issues in North America Today

Since the revival of Western feminism in the late 1960s, the situation of most women in North America has changed dramatically. Whether you regard women's present situation as better or worse than it used to be depends in part on your personal values: on whether, for instance, you think it is better to live alone on a limited income or to enjoy more material security while serving a man whose comfort and convenience must come before your own. It also depends on which group of women you take as representative.

Generally speaking, the situation of younger middle-class women today seems to be better than that of their mothers a generation ago. College-educated women today have many more career opportunities open to them than their mothers did; they also have a greater degree of reproductive freedom, they experience less pressure to marry or to be heterosexual, and if they choose to live with a male partner, he is more likely than their fathers to take some responsibility for day-to-day child care. By contrast, the situation of many working-class women, including many women of color, has deteriorated. Fewer working-class women have the option of staying at home with their young children than they did a generation ago, and the jobs open to them are typically low paying, insecure, and often hazardous. Abortion is legally available to all adult women, but in a number of U.S. states it is unobtainable in practice, and in many other states there are considerable obstacles to abortion access. Thus, young and/or working-class women often have much greater difficulty in securing abortions than do adult women who are middle class. In all classes and age groups, rates of reported battery, rape, and incest are rising, though it is unknown how much, if at all, the actual incidence of these assaults is increasing.

If it is difficult to generalize about women's contemporary situation in North America, it is still more difficult to estimate how far feminism should be credited with recent improvements—or perhaps blamed for recent deteriorations—when so much else has changed in women's economic and social environment. These concurrent changes include overall declines for all workers in real wages, in social services, and in full-time, as opposed to part-time, employment—all of which provide economic incentives for women to enter the paid labor force that are independent of any feminist motivations. Similarly, though antifeminists often blame feminism for a supposed breakdown in family values, including the rise in children born outside marriage (now a quarter of all U.S. births), changes in U.S. families since the early 1970s have occurred in a context in which the gap between rich and poor has widened dramatically and the cities have disintegrated, especially those areas inhabited by people of color. In such a context, it is understandable that some mothers, exhausted by the combination of financial and domestic responsibilities, should challenge what they take to be feminist dogma by seeking a reliable man to take care of them.

In spite of the unevenness in contemporary women's situations and the uncertainty over just how much has been achieved by a quarter-century of feminist activism, some things are clear. Women are still evaluated primarily by a standard of sexual attractiveness that prizes youth, slenderness, blondness, and the absence of visible disabilities. We are stigmatized if we are not perceived as heterosexual and, to a lesser extent, if we lack a male partner. A substantial gap between the earnings of full-time male and female workers remains, though it has diminished on average since the early 1970s and is much wider at the lower end of the educational spectrum. Women (and our children) predominate in the increasing ranks of the poor. Reproductive freedom is incomplete and even more limited for poor women. Child care facilities have spread rapidly, sometimes franchised, but they receive relatively little public subsidy. Women, including full-time employed women, still do most of the necessary work involved in childrearing and household maintenance. Many older women live in poverty, many girls are subjected to incest, and many women of all ages are beaten, harassed, and raped.

North American feminists are virtually unanimous in their agreement that all these represent important problems that contemporary feminism must continue to address. Many of these issues are absent from this collection, however. This is not because they are any less urgent than those on which this book focuses; they are omitted merely because they are less controversial among feminists.

As noted already, disagreement is endemic to feminism. Some of the debates in which Western feminists have engaged have been quite theoretical, even esoteric. In addition to the perennial question of whether women are the same as or different from men, feminists in the 1970s disputed the "ultimate" causes of women's subordination, and in the 1980s they argued about how the concept "woman" should be deconstructed and whether it could survive its deconstruction. Although the answers given to these broad theoretical questions certainly have practical implications, such issues nevertheless often seemed remote from the daily concerns of nonacademic feminists. By contrast, the controversies explored in this book focus much more directly on issues of immediate concern to all contemporary feminists as we reflect on our political agendas and our daily practices. Most of them address issues of public policy. Should violent pornography be banned? Should so-called surrogacy contracts be enforced? Should sex work be regulated by law? Many of these controversies, however, also involve questions of personal responsibility and individual choice. Even if I have a legal right to do so, should I abort my female fetus? Should I eat meat or join the military or put my limited political energies into working against nuclear weapons rather than providing shelters for battered women?

Even though these issues are debated in many contexts, the discussions in this book are distinguished by the fact that they address the issues in the light of an explicit commitment to ending women's subordination. As they debate specific moral and political controversies, they simultaneously explore how this distinctively feminist commitment intersects with other ideals and values, such as freedom, equality, and community. Thus, the discussions in this book not only clarify the feminist implications of certain concrete social issues; at a more philosophical level they also enrich our understanding of the ways in which a principled commitment to feminism may influence as well as be influenced by prevailing interpretations of contemporary ideals and values.

## Feminist Contradictions

Why do some issues arouse more controversy than others among feminists? Answering this question by identifying some of the underlying sources of feminist disagreement may clarify what is really at stake in some controversial issues and even contribute to resolving them.

One factor contributing to the problematic status within feminism of some public policies and personal practices is our ignorance of certain matters of fact, which hinders our evaluation of the impact on women of some of the institutions and practices discussed in this book. Psychologists and social scientists disagree, for instance, about the significance of violent pornography in causing sexual assault; similarly, the causal relationships between women's subordination, on the one hand, and the mistreatment of animals or the degradation of the environment, on the other, remain insufficiently explored. Although the incompleteness of relevant data may partially explain the existence of controversy among feminists, it fails to explain the intensity with which feminists dispute many of these issues. This intensity is more likely the result of conflicts among the deeply held values and even metaphysical attitudes to which feminists are committed.

A striking feature of most of the issues addressed in this book is that they involve a sexual and often a procreative dimension. For instance, though at first sight militarism appears to involve women primarily as fighters or taxpayers, it turns out to include such questions as whether the values of militarism are compatible with those of mothering and whether women soldiers may be sufficiently or, alternatively, too sexually attractive to men. Because the Western tradition has consistently regarded women primarily as mothers and as sexual objects, it is not surprising that procreative and sexual issues have always been prominent among feminist concerns, and it is only to be expected that many feminists should experience contradictory feelings about these issues. For instance, we may internalize dominant views of mothering and/or sexual attractiveness as central to women's identities even while opposing the reduction of women to mothers and sexual objects. When these factors are supplemented with the general North American preoccupation with and anxiety about sexuality, recently expressed in terms of "family values," it is inevitable that feminist discussions about issues involving sexuality and mothering should acquire an intense emotional charge. Given our present cultural context as well as our history, it is quite predictable that advocacy of lesbian sadomasochism, for instance, will precipitate acute moral distress among feminists as we seek to balance our commitments to opposing, on the one hand, the sexual repression of women and, on the other hand, the eroticization of women's subordination.

Many of the issues currently dividing North American feminists involve conflicts of value that go beyond mothering and sexuality. For instance, the issue of pornography certainly involves sexuality, but it also seems to set concern for women's welfare against respect for freedom of expression, both values that feminists have good reasons for endorsing. Similarly, feminist opposition to militarism and other forms of violence seems to conflict with feminist goals of promoting women's economic and physical independence when these are expressed through desires for a career in the military or a determination to defend oneself physically. Such conflicts of principle may lead to apparently self-contradictory conclusions, such as the need to "fight against violence" or even "fight for peace."

Another significant reason that some issues have become especially controversial for contemporary feminists is that they involve challenges to institutions or practices, such as mothering, soldiering, or heterosexuality, in which many women, including some feminists, assert that they are willing participants. Unlike practices such as sexual harassment, rape, incest, and sexual discrimination in employment, which are universally condemned by feminists, many women, including feminists, do not necessarily perceive themselves as either victims or victimizers when they participate in some of the institutions and practices evaluated in this book. Those who regard themselves as having chosen freely to participate in these institutions and practices naturally become defensive when other feminists challenge that participation—and these feminists are often distinctly hostile to other feminists' suggestions that their choice to participate in these institutions and practices may have been less than fully informed or uncoerced. Issues of individual choice and responsibility are always morally and emotionally loaded because they touch the core of our conception of ourselves as free and responsible moral agents. They are also a notorious philosophical quagmire, involving such problematic notions as self-deception, unconscious motivation, foreseen but unintended consequences, coercive offers, and even "false consciousness." Unfortunately, feminists can sometimes find no way around this quagmire.

Policies and practices are also likely to become controversial among feminists when they affect different groups of women differently, thus triggering conflicts among various loyalties and priorities. Even issues such as rape that are problematic for all women typically affect some groups differently from others; for instance, women who cannot afford cars are especially vulnerable to rape by strangers. Many of the policies and practices explored in this book are particularly clear in their varying implications for different groups of women, and many raise issues of race or class, age or disability, as well as gender. For example, women hired to be so-called surrogate mothers are likely to be poor, whereas women who hire them are likely to be wealthy—or at least married to wealthy men. In a racist society, moreover, "surrogacy" also has a racial dimension. Women, invariably white, who can afford to hire so-called surrogate mothers are unlikely to employ women of color as "surrogates"—unless the situation is one of a so-called full surrogacy, where the woman is hired to gestate a previously fertilized ovum. In that case, we may well see the ghosts of African American slave women wetnursing the white babies of plantation owners.

Typically, therefore, the issues about which feminists disagree are highly charged emotionally as well as morally, and they are politically complex. Usually they cannot be reduced to simple "pro" and "con" positions because they have many more than two sides. These issues may involve conflicts of interest and loyalty among overlapping social groups, incompatibilities among important feminist values or principles, desires thought to be "unfeminist," or perceived needs to utilize political means that are in contradiction with socially desirable ends. What such issues all have in common is a capacity to generate moral dilemmas—or trilemmas or multilemmas—between courses of action that are all to some extent distasteful from a feminist point of view.

The experience of confronting such difficult choices, and the sense that any consequent action is likely to be open to some feminist objection, has led feminists to coin the phrase "living with contradictions." It is a phrase that simultaneously expresses the moral discomfort that feminists feel so frequently and our determination to carry on anyway with our lives. This book is intended both to illuminate the contradictions feminists face and suggest some means of reducing them.

## Addressing Feminist Contradictions

Since the late 1960s, academic philosophers have devoted unprecedented attention to practical moral and political concerns. Often they have described these concerns as issues in applied ethics because they have hoped to resolve them by appealing to—or applying—general moral or ethical principles articulating ideals such as freedom, justice, rights, or the general welfare. Typically, however, the hopes of these philosophers have remained unfulfilled. Although philosophers have sometimes made considerable progress in clarifying specific moral and political issues, this progress has rarely resulted from the simple application of general ethical principles.

One reason for this failure is that to cover a wide range of cases, ethical principles typically are formulated at a high level of abstraction and consequently leave much room for individual discretion—and therefore for disagreement—in determining how to apply them. For instance, even the simplest moral injunctions, such as "Don't kill," "Don't steal," and "Don't break promises," permit considerable latitude in deciding what counts as stealing or breaking promises and how far the scope of the prohibition against killing should extend. In addition, individual discretion is always required to determine which principle or principles are appropriate for a given situation and, in cases of conflict between them, which principles should take precedence over others. Is it morally justified, for instance, to steal or break a promise to save a life or even to take one life to save more?

Most philosophers now agree that practical moral and political issues cannot be resolved through the simple application of general moral principles. The assumption that what people ought to do in specific situations may somehow be deduced from independently validated ethical principles is regarded increasingly as mistaken, resting on a misleadingly positivist model of moral justification. Ethical principles are not accepted prior to or independently of people's intuitive sense of what they should do in particular situations; instead, such principles are derived from efforts to refine and systematize that sense. The consideration of particular cases thus plays an indispensable role in formulating moral principles; it is also a central part of the process by which people commit themselves to some principles rather than others. Thus, the relationship between general moral principles and specific moral decisions must be understood as one of mutual interdependence rather than one-way entailment.

Accepting this reconceptualization of the relation between general principles and specific decisions, most contemporary philosophers have abandoned the dream of finding some quick and foolproof decision procedure for the resolution of practical moral and political problems. Although they recognize the usefulness of general principles in drawing attention to the full moral implications of practical issues, thus suggesting considerations salient to their resolution, few philosophers continue to assume that some sufficiently creative and sophisticated formulation of a few key principles will magically untangle moral perplexities. Instead, they acknowledge that there are no moral shortcuts capable of bypassing detailed and careful reflection on specific situations from as many points of view as possible.

At the end of the 1960s, as the present wave of Western feminism was rising, many feminists were as optimistic as their philosophical contemporaries about the possibility of finding a relatively simple decision procedure for resolving social problems involving women. In 1970, for instance, New York Radical Women issued a set of principles that read in part as follows:

We take the woman's side in everything.
We ask not if something is "reformist," "radical," "revolutionary," or "moral."
We ask: is it good for women or bad for women?

This principle is attractively simple and has a wonderful rhetorical ring, though it also sounds outrageously partial. However, the preceding discussion of the relationship between general principles and specific issues should lead us to suspect that even for those prepared to adopt it, the principle of putting women's interests first does not provide a simple solution for feminists' moral and political questions.

One reason for the inadequacy of the principle is obvious: Women are not a homogeneous group. We represent a variety of nationalities, ethnicities, classes, and abilities and disabilities. We are single, married, divorced, widowed, mothers, childfree, bisexual, lesbian, heterosexual, and celibate. Some of us are madams, and some of us are maids; our interests sometimes coincide and sometimes conflict. Thus, what is good or bad for one group of women may not be good or bad for another.

New York Radical Women were not oblivious to this difficulty, and they responded to it by defining "the best interests of women as the best interests of the poorest, most insulted, most despised, most abused woman on earth." Even thus clarified, however, the principle is insufficient to resolve many moral and political problems since it is often far from evident just who this most abused woman is. Previous attempts to determine which women are "most oppressed" have been divisive and destructive for feminism. They are also in principle inconclusive because the ways in which women are subordinated vary qualitatively as well as quantitatively. Even within the contemporary United States, for instance, the subordination of a working-class Chicana lesbian is very different from that of an elderly white widow or an African American law professor. Although it would be foolish to deny that some women have more privileges than others, there are no uncontroversial criteria for ranking the oppressions suffered by different, and overlapping, groups of women.

Does this recognition of the limitations of the principle formulated by New York Radical Women mean that feminists have no guide at all through the moral and political thickets that confront us? Not necessarily. Even though this principle is no more capable than other, more orthodox moral or political principles of providing a mechanical decision procedure for resolving moral and political problems involving women, it does have certain strengths as well as limitations. Most notably, it expresses the sound moral intuition that in addressing moral and political problems, we must give the interests of more disadvantaged women special consideration. The principle cannot indicate any clear path through moral thickets, but it does point in the right general direction. When it is interpreted as giving special weight to the needs and interests of women with special disadvantages, New York Radical Women's principle turns out to be far more impartial than it appeared initially. Although it was deliberately and provocatively formulated to challenge dominant conceptions of impartiality by its expressed bias in favor of women, the principle's special concern for disadvantaged women means that when good faith efforts are made to apply it to specific situations, the interests of most men usually will not be disregarded. This is because women who might reasonably be included among the poorest, most insulted, despised, and abused typically regard their interests as inseparable from those of their husbands, sons, fathers, and other males of their group—which is not to say that the women's interests are *identical* with the men's. Just as most "human" (and "class," "race," and "national") issues are simultaneously feminist, so most issues that are feminist in the sense of raising concerns about women's subordination are unlikely to be *exclusively* feminist. That is to say, their connection with women's subordination is usually not their only problematic aspect. For instance, concerns about the wages and working conditions of women migrant workers in agriculture clearly overlap with concerns about the wages and conditions of their male coworkers, illuminating the complex ways in which issues of male domination intersect with issues of race and class domination.

Because women's situations are so various and the forms of oppression we suffer are usually multiple, most feminist issues are inextricably involved with questions of economic justice and racial or other kinds of bias. Thus, committing ourselves to ending the subordination of insulted, despised, and abused women requires us also to challenge various injustices that affect men, though in somewhat different ways. To put the most abused women first is not, in the end, to disregard the ways in which many men are abused.

Recognizing that the subordination of women is inextricably interconnected with issues of economic justice, racial bias, environmental damage, and individual freedom demonstrates not only that feminism is central to most other issues of contemporary social concern. Nor does it mean only that these other issues are impossible to resolve without a wholehearted commitment to ending women's subordination. Such a recognition also teaches that this feminist commitment can never be single- or simple-minded. Our commitment to ending women's subordination inevitably leads us to confront complex, multidimensional problems that require us to balance a variety of values and to evaluate the claims and interests of a variety of groups or even species, including a variety of groups of women.

There is no magic formula for reaching fair and workable resolutions of these pressing and complicated problems. The best we can do is resolve to be as open and sensitive as we can to the diversity of interests and range of values involved. This in turn requires us to commit ourselves to seeking as many different perspectives as possible. If we are sincerely concerned with ending the subordination of *all* women, feminists cannot afford unquestioned assumptions, orthodoxies, or dogmatic commitments to positions alleged to be "politically correct." Instead, we must find ways of hearing the voices of women muted in the dominant culture, and we must respond to those voices by giving special attention and weight to the concerns they express. This book is intended as a contribution to that undertaking.

In a truly feminist world, we would not have to address many of the issues with which we find ourselves presently confronted. We would not have been socialized to prefer meat over grains or boys over girls, and we would not have learned to become aroused by sexual practices that perpetuate male dominance. We would not have to consider how to defend ourselves against violent assault, whether to abort a disabled or female fetus, or what to do about pornography that eroticizes the subordination of women. We would never feel compelled to choose between our gender identity and our ethnic or class identity. Feminists' long-term ideal is the creation of a world in which these and similar issues do not arise. In the short term, however, we must struggle to live as honorably, courageously, and cheerfully as we can with the contradictions inevitably generated by a painfully prefeminist world.

### References

New York Radical Women. "Principles." In *Sisterhood Is Powerful,* edited by Robin Morgan, 520. New York: Vintage Books, 1970.

# PART ONE

# EQUALITY

Because feminism is often defined as a commitment to social equality between men and women, equality immediately suggests itself as a natural standard for resolving controversies that arise within feminism. Unfortunately, equality's ability to fulfill this function is undermined by the fact that the concept of equality is itself a focus of feminist controversy.

Even outside the context of feminist concerns, the main traditions in nineteenth- and twentieth-century Western politics may be characterized by reference to competing conceptions of equality. Political conservatives, for instance, construe equality simply as equality before the law, a position known as formal equality. Political radicals, by contrast, advocate more substantive conceptions of equality according to which people's living standards should be roughly the same. Between these extremes lies the liberal conception of equality, which interprets the ideal in terms of equality of opportunity. These various conceptions of equality as well as the relations between them are in turn open to a variety of competing interpretations. Some would argue, for instance, that genuine equality of opportunity cannot be achieved in a society that includes gross inequalities in standards of living.

Western feminists have drawn on the nonfeminist tradition of thinking about equality in our reflections on sex equality. In the nineteenth century, feminists fought hard for the then radical goal of sex equality before the law, but in the twentieth century formal sex equality has come to be regarded by most feminists as inadequate for guaranteeing full social equality between men and women. In the twentieth century, liberal feminists, who advocate construing sex equality in terms of equality of opportunity, contend with socialist feminists, who argue that full equality between men and women requires the abolition of class inequalities.

Although Western feminists have inevitably drawn on nonfeminist thinking about equality, many have found that nonfeminist conceptions of equality are inadequate to comprehend the variety of ways in which male privilege over women is expressed. In consequence, some feminists have worked to develop new conceptions of equality that are more sensitive to feminist concerns; others have rejected equality itself as a characteristically masculine ideal.

The readings in this first part of the book offer a brief overview of the main issues at stake in the contemporary feminist debate over the meaning and even the desirability of sex equality. These selections have been chosen partly because they are compre-

13

hensive and partly because they include some distinctively feminist insights about the nature of equality.

The first article, "Sexual Difference and Sexual Equality," which I wrote in the mid-1980s, explains the unfortunate consequences that result from consistent policies of treating men and women either identically or differently. When women are treated identically to men, as some feminists have recommended, we are penalized for our differences because we are measured against a male norm. When we are treated differently from men, as recommended by other feminists, even the provision of so-called special benefits, rights, or protections may often have damaging consequences insofar as it reifies currently perceived sex differences, confirms stereotypes, obliterates differences between women, and reinforces the status quo. In opposing ways, therefore, both strategies seem doomed to perpetuate women's subordination.

To avoid these consequences, I argue that it is necessary to rethink prevailing understandings of the differences between men and women. Feminists must challenge both the assumption that sex differences are universal, given, and unchangeable and the assumption that men's lives constitute the norms according to which women's differences are counted as deficiencies.

My article suggests that recognizing current differences between the sexes as a consequence as well as a cause of male dominance encourages feminists to develop flexible policies designed to change as women and men succeed in changing themselves. Viewed over time, such flexibility could be construed as inconsistency—but new social circumstances require creativity in institutionalizing justice and equality. In the meantime, feminists must live with the contradictions resulting from divergent and sometimes incompatible strategies for gaining equality.

In conclusion, I assert that refusing to accept men's lives as the norm encourages us to envision alternatives to contemporary ways of organizing social life. There is, of course, no single blueprint for a feminist utopia; feminists have experimented and continue to experiment with a variety of alternatives. These alternatives could be construed as moving toward a more substantive or finer-grained conception of equality or even as moving beyond that ideal.

The most incisive recent contributions to the feminist equality debate have come from legal theorists, who are struggling to translate feminist moral and political insights into workable legal terms. In "Reconstructing Sexual Equality," Christine A. Littleton provides a more detailed analysis of the various strategies developed by feminist legal theorists, categorizing them as versions of either symmetrical or asymmetrical models. Whereas symmetrical models emphasize similarities between men and women and urge that both sexes be treated the same in law, asymmetrical models recommend the legal recognition of various differences between the sexes.

Littleton herself proposes a model of sex equality as "acceptance." This asymmetrical model accepts existing differences between the sexes and seeks to make them socially "costless." By this, Littleton means that the life decisions often made by women, such as taking up historically female occupations or accepting less demanding jobs so as to be able to fulfill family responsibilities, should not be more socially "expensive" than conventionally masculine life decisions. Implementing this proposal obviously would lead to the radical restructuring of social institutions, including rethinking the nature of work and how varying social contributions might be recognized and rewarded. Littleton refuses to predict the long-term outcome of reducing the costs of being a social woman—people's present imaginations, she says, are too constrained by the experience of growing up male or female in circumstances of male domination.

Catharine A. MacKinnon is certainly the best-known contemporary feminist legal theorist because she has authored or coauthored a number of highly publicized legal initiatives. The most innovative feature of her approach is to conceptualize various issues involving women's sexuality in terms of sex discrimination, a concept obviously dependent on the notion of sex equality. MacKinnon was successful in getting sexual harassment recognized in the United States as a form of sex discrimination, but her point of view has not so far prevailed in the United States with respect to pornography. In Canada, however, her arguments influenced the adoption in 1992 of legislation banning violent pornography.

In the present selection, "Toward Feminist Jurisprudence," MacKinnon provides a sweeping challenge to what she calls mainstream—that is, nonfeminist—legal conceptions of sex equality. These conceptions, she argues, have been incapable of comprehending women's experience of forms of inequality that are distinctively sexualized. These include incest, rape, domestic battery, prostitution, and pornography. Because contemporary sexuality is constructed so that male dominance and female subordination are sexually arousing for both men and women, the sexual abuse of women by men is perceived as natural, an expression of sex difference rather than of sex dominance or inequality. Even though inequality between men and women is institutionalized throughout daily life, male forms of power over women are embodied in law as individual rights. In particular, the sexual power of men is protected by rights to claim privacy or freedom of speech and to make mistakes about whether women consent to sexual relations.

MacKinnon advocates a feminist jurisprudence that assumes that men dominate women unless shown otherwise and that recognizes a variety of issues involving sexuality as issues of sex equality. These issues, in MacKinnon's view, include rape, abortion, pornography, prostitution, so-called surrogate motherhood, and gay and lesbian rights. Until these are recognized in the law as forms of sex inequality, she argues, law is not neutral between men and women but instead mystifies and legitimates male dominance.

In "Demarginalizing the Intersection of Race and Sex: A Black Feminist Critique of Antidiscrimination Doctrine, Feminist Theory, and Antiracist Politics," Kimberle Crenshaw examines a number of court rulings involving discrimination against Black women. Some of these rulings denied Black women the right to represent all women on the grounds that Black women's experience was different from white women's; others insisted that white women could represent all women on the assumption that the experience of Black and white women was similar in the relevant respects. In an interesting analogy to white feminist findings that women have been harmed sometimes by being treated identically to men and sometimes by being treated differently,

Crenshaw shows that Black women have been harmed sometimes by being treated identically to white women and sometimes by being treated differently.

Crenshaw asserts that Black women in the United States are multiply burdened, subject not only to discrimination on the grounds of *either* race or sex but also to discrimination on grounds of *both* race and sex simultaneously. She argues that attention to sex discrimination alone is insufficient to protect Black women, especially when sex discrimination is understood in terms of white experience. Such an understanding of sex discrimination takes race privilege as given and assumes that only minor adjustments are necessary in employment systems. It also means that antidiscrimination law is likely to help primarily those who are already relatively privileged and, by perpetuating existing privilege, to discourage employees from banding together to challenge broader inequities.

Feminist theory and politics, according to Crenshaw, have often been as racist as legal theory insofar as they have assumed white women's experience as paradigmatic. This assumption has marginalized or denied the experience of Black women, obscuring the ways in which their lives are shaped by distinctively racist forms of male dominance. Crenshaw offers the example of Black women's experience of rape as a weapon of *racial* terror.

Crenshaw's article demonstrates clearly that gender is not a simple or univocal concept. The social meanings of femininity incorporate norms of race, class, disability, and so on, with the result that women of different class and racial/ethnic identities may differ sharply in their senses of what it is to be a woman. Such differences complicate feminist evaluations of various social institutions and practices, but feminists cannot ignore them if our goal is to end the subordination of *all* women.

These four papers offer little more than an introduction to the contemporary feminist equality debate, but they demonstrate that the ideal of sex equality is itself so contested that it cannot provide a clear standard for resolving the practical dilemmas that feminists confront. For this reason, feminism is defined in this book, not as a commitment to sex equality, but as a commitment to ending women's subordination. The notion of subordination is less encumbered with theoretical baggage than the notion of equality and so is easier to use as a standard in evaluating various social practices. In addition, because the notion of subordination generates fewer assumptions than that of equality, it is perceived to leave more questions open for debate.

Feminist discussions of equality provide a clear illustration of what feminists mean when we speak of living with contradictions. If we demand to be treated identically to men, we may often deepen our subordination—but our subordination may also be reinforced when we are treated differently from men. We seem to be in a classic double bind: damned if we do and damned if we don't.

Despite these difficulties, feminist discussions of sex equality have been far from fruitless. Even though equality continues to be disputed among feminists, both as an ideal and a strategy, our debates nevertheless offer several distinctive contributions to prevailing understandings of equality. Of particular interest in the discussions included here are the challenge to the male norm, the attack on the gender bias implicit in the public/private distinction, and the recognition that generalizations about women are likely to obscure race and class privileges. Indeed, these insights illuminate a variety of moral issues. And other themes running through the equality debate, themes counterposing sameness and difference, masculinity and femininity, assimilation and transformation, emerge in feminist debates around many issues of moral practice.

# Sexual Difference
# and Sexual Equality

## Alison M. Jaggar

The persistence and intensity of the perennial interest in sexual difference is not sustained by simple curiosity. Instead, it derives from an urgent concern with issues of sexual justice. For almost two and a half millennia, ... men and later women have debated the nature, extent, and even existence of the differences between the sexes and reflected on their relevance for the just organization of society.

...

Equality is a contested ideal notoriously open to a variety of interpretations. In the first part of this paper, I outline two ways in which some contemporary feminists have construed equality in legal contexts, identifying some of the problems that accompany each construal. In the second, I argue that both these conceptions of sexual equality presuppose unacceptable interpretations of sexual difference, and I go on to sketch an approach to understanding sexual difference that is more adequate to recent feminist insights. I suggest that this alternative approach to sexual difference casts the initial construals of sexual equality in a new light, pointing to the need for rethinking and perhaps even moving beyond the traditional ideal of western feminism.

## Equality

### Sexual Equality as Blindness to Sexual Difference

Western feminists have not always been unanimous in demanding sexual equality. Even though this ideal inspired not only some of the earliest English feminists but also participants in the U.S. Seneca Falls Convention of 1848, most nineteenth-century feminists in the United States did not endorse such a radical demand, preferring instead to retain membership in women's separate sphere.[1] Despite the ideology of separate spheres, however, feminist challenges to such inequities in the legal system as women's inability to vote or to control their own property on marriage developed eventually into demands for identity of legal rights for men and women or, as it came to be called, equality before the law. By the end of the 1960s, mainstream feminists in the United States had come to believe that the legal system should be sex-blind, that it should not differentiate in any way between women and men. This belief was expressed in the struggle for an Equal Rights Amendment to the U.S. Constitution, an amendment that, had it passed, would have made any sex-specific law unconstitutional.

Nineteenth-century feminist demands for the suffrage and for property rights drew on a variety of arguments, sometimes claiming that women possessed distinctive ethical insight and nurturant capacities.[2] A persistent theme in the feminist argument, however, was insistence on women's capacity to reason, an insistence conditioned by the classical liberal assumption that the ability to reason was the only legitimate ground for the ascription of democratic rights. From the eighteenth century on, feminists have argued consistently that women's reasoning capacity is at least equal to men's (though not necessarily identical to it) and have attributed women's lesser intellectual attainments primarily to their inferior education.[3] Such arguments obviously tend to minimize the significance of the physiological differences between the sexes, since those differences are construed as irrelevant to the ascription of political rights. By the late 1960s and early 1970s, at the beginning of the most recent wave of western feminism, a conspicuously rationalist approach to women's equality was shared widely, though not universally, by English-speaking feminists, and arguments for so-called *androgyny* were common. The androgyny recommended typically was not physical, but mental and moral.[4]

Over the past two decades, ... however, it has become apparent that strict equality before the law may not always benefit women, at least not in the short term. Differences between the sexes have emerged as sufficiently significant to motivate some feminists as well as nonfeminists to recall the second part of the Aristotelian dictum: justice consists not only in treating like cases alike but also in treating different cases differently.

Contemporary feminists have identified a wide variety of differences between the sexes as relevant to sexual justice, though it should be noted that they are not always unanimous either about the list of differences or about the significance of its various items. What follow are only a few examples of differences between the sexes that many feminists claim it is unjust to ignore. Some of the differences seem almost inseparable from female biology, while others are linked more obviously with women's social circumstances.

The apparently biologically based differences between the sexes generally are connected with women's procreative capacity. The most evident and most frequently debated of such differences is women's ability to become pregnant and to give birth. In the now notorious case of *Gilbert v. General Electric* (1976), most feminists argued that a disability plan excluding disabilities related to pregnancy and childbirth discriminated against women, or treated women unequally, despite the indisputable fact that such a plan would fail "equally" to cover any man who became pregnant. A structurally similar example was a purportedly sex-blind ordinance forbidding firefighters to breast-feed between calls, an ordinance that of course applied "equally" to male and female firefighters.

...

In the domestic sphere ... some feminists recently have come to question whether justice is served best by treating men and women exactly alike. For example, no-fault divorce settlements dividing family property equally between husband and wife almost invariably leave wives in a far worse economic situation than they do husbands. In one study, for instance, ex-husbands' standard of living was found to have risen by 42 percent a year after divorce, whereas ex-wives' standard of living was reduced by 78 percent.[5] This huge discrepancy in the outcome of divorce results from a variety of factors, including the fact that women and men typically are differently situated in the job market, with women usually having much lower job qualifications and less work experience. Child custody is another aspect of family law in which feminists recently have questioned the justice of viewing men and women as indistinguishable. For example, some feminists have argued that the increasingly popular assignment of joint custody to mothers and fathers unfairly penalizes women because joint custody statutes increase the bargaining strength of men at divorce and thereby aggravate the dependence of women, threatening their economic rights, their ability to raise their children without interference, and their geographic mobility.[6]

... We live in a society divided deeply by gender, in which differences between the sexes, whatever their cause, are pronounced and inescapable. When these differences are ignored in the name of formal equality between the sexes, continuing substantive inequalities between women and men may be either obscured or rationalized and legitimated. At least in the present social context, sexual equality in procedure often may ensure rather than obliterate sexual *in*equality in outcome.

## Sexual Equality as Responsiveness to Sexual Difference

Within the last ten or fifteen years, increasing numbers of feminists have been challenging the assumption that sexual equality always requires sex-blindness. The growing public recognition that equality in areas other than gender relations is compatible with and may even require substantive differences in practical treatment adds plausibility to this challenge. For instance, equality in education ordinarily is taken to be compatible with, and even to require, the provision of different educational programs and bilingual or otherwise specially qualified teachers to serve the needs of children with varying abilities and disabilities. Similarly, there is increasing public willingness to provide special resources for people who are disabled or differently abled: readers for the blind, interpreters for the deaf, and adequate work space and access for those confined to wheelchairs.

Commitment to affirmative action in hiring probably constituted the first contemporary feminist challenge to the traditional sex-blind understanding of sexual equality. Affirmative action programs are generally uncontroversial among feminists because they are conceived as temporary expedients, as means rather than as ends. Typically such programs are defended as special protections for women (and other "suspect categories"), necessary in the short term in order to counter existing inequality of opportunity, but as something that should be abandoned once opportunities have been equalized. Rather than challenging the ideal of deinstitutionalizing sexual difference, therefore, affirmative action ultimately presupposes that ideal.

Most of the other proposals for achieving sexual equality through the recognition of sexual difference are considerably more controversial than affirmative action, even among feminists. One such proposal is that employers should be forbidden to terminate or to refuse a reasonable leave of absence to workers disabled by pregnancy or childbirth even though such leaves may not be available to workers who are disabled for other reasons. The *Miller-Wohl* and *California Federal* cases, for instance, sharply divided the feminist legal community.[7]

Even more controversial than special pregnancy and maternity leaves are proposals to loosen the standard criteria of legal responsibility for women in some circumstances. For instance, there have been moves to recognize so-called premenstrual syndrome, which by definition afflicts only women, as a periodically disabling condition during which women enjoy diminished legal responsibility.[8] Other feminist lawyers have proposed that there should be special criteria for identifying self-defense, criteria that go beyond immediate life-threatening danger, in the cases of women who kill their abusive husbands.[9]

...

It is easy to understand why most proposals for achieving sexual equality through the institutional recognition of sexual difference are controversial among feminists. The reason is that the supposed benefits of such recognition are bought only at a certain price to women. This price includes the danger that measures apparently designed for women's special protection may end up protecting them primarily from the benefits that men enjoy. This has happened frequently in the past. For instance, as one author remarks,

> The protective labor legislation that limited the hours that women could work, prohibited night work and barred them from certain dangerous occupations such as mining may have promoted their health and safety and guaranteed them more time with their families. But it also precluded them from certain occupations requiring overtime, barred them from others where the entry point was the night shift, and may have contributed to the downward pressure on women's wages by creating a surplus of women in the jobs they are permitted to hold.[10]

...

A further problem with treating women differently from men is that it reinforces sexual stereotypes. Among the most familiar and pervasive of prevailing stereotypes are the correlative assumptions that men by nature are sexual aggressors and that women's very presence is sexually arousing and constitutes a temptation to aggression. In recent years these assumptions have been the basis of court decisions excluding women from the job of prison guard in Alabama maximum security prisons and even from the job of chaplain in a male juvenile institution.[11] Such decisions have not only the direct consequence of "protecting" women from jobs that may be the best paid available to them (in the case of the prison guard) or to which they may even feel a religious calling (in the case of the chaplain); they also have far-reaching indirect consequences insofar as they perpetuate the dangerous and damaging stereotype that women by nature are the sexual prey of men. This cultural myth serves as an implicit legitimation for the prostitution, sexual harassment, and rape of women, because it implies that such activities are in some sense natural. Other legislation designed to draw attention to the need to protect women's sexuality, such as legislation defining the subjects in pornography paradigmatically as female, may well have similar consequences.

Legal recognition of women as a specially protected category may also encourage homogenization of "essentialism," the view that women are all alike. ... As the present wave of feminism has rolled on, middle-class white feminists have been forced to recognize that their definitions of women's nature and women's political priorities too often have been biased by factors like race, class, age, and physical ability. Legislation that separates women into a single category inevitably will define that category in a way that makes a certain subgroup of women into the paradigm for the whole sex. One group of women may be penalized by being forced to accept protection that another genuinely may need. One example is insurance plans that require all female employees to pay premiums for coverage of disabilities arising out of pregnancy and childbirth but which do not require the same contributions from male employees. Such a requirement forces lesbians, infertile women, and women who are not sexually active to underwrite the costs of heterosexual activity by some women—and, of course, by some men.[12]

When the risks involved in the sex-responsive approach to sexual equality become apparent, feminist theory arrives at an impasse. Both the sex-blind and the sex-responsive interpretations of equality seem to bear unacceptable threats to women's already vulnerable economic and social status. In the next section I suggest that each interpretation of sexual equality rests on a construal of sexual difference that is inadequate for feminism.

## Difference

The sex-blind interpretation of sexual equality rests on an assumption that existing differences between women have relatively little social significance. The obvious defect of this denial is that it ignores the extent to which sex and gender affect every aspect of everyone's life. People's work and play, dress and diet, income level and even speech patterns are regulated by social expectations regarding the appropriate appearance and behavior of sexed individuals, so that on all these dimensions people vary systematically, though not solely, according to sex. Prevailing norms of gender may be and often are challenged by certain individuals in certain areas, but for most people most of the time these norms are simply the given framework of daily life. Feminists cannot deal with sexual difference simply by closing their eyes to its social institutionalization and refusing to recognize existing social and political realities.

The sex-responsive conception of sexual equality by definition is sensitive to these realities, but there are others to which it is blind. These are the realities of the differences *between* women, differences of race, class, sexual preference, religion, age, ethnicity, marital status, physical ability, and so on. Increasingly, contemporary feminists are recognizing that there is no typical woman, no essence of womanhood that underlies these other characteristics—which often constitute additional vectors of domination. Any conception of sexual difference that ignores these features is inadequate for a feminism seeking to represent the interests of all women.[13]

There is an additional problem with the conception of sexual difference that underlies the sex-responsive conception of sexual equality. This problem emerges when sex-responsiveness is justified, as it invariably is, in terms of "protection" or "compensation," terms suggesting that women are damaged or disabled in comparison with men. Sometimes women's disabilities are seen as resulting from social causes, war wounds sustained by women as a result of life in a male-dominated society; sometimes women's disabilities are seen as presocial in origin, akin to female birth defects. In either case, however, the sex-responsive interpretation of sexual equality usually rests on a conception of sexual difference according to which women are inferior to men at least in some ways.

In what follows, I outline an approach to understanding sexual difference that is more adequate to insights that feminists recently have emphasized. I focus especially on two characteristics of this approach.

## A Dynamic Approach to Sexual Difference

In saying that a more deeply feminist understanding of sexual difference must be dynamic rather than static, I mean that it must reflect the continually expanding feminist awareness of the ways in which the history of women's subordination, especially as this intersects with the history of other subordinated groups, has shaped and continues to shape both existing differences between the sexes and the ways in which we perceive and evaluate those differences.

A more fully feminist understanding of sexual difference does not deny that deep differences may exist between the sexes, but it does not assume that these differences are presocial or biological givens, unambiguous causes of women's apparently universal inequality and subordination. Instead, feminists must be committed to exploring the ways in which not only women's cognitive and emotional capacities, but even our bodies and our physical abilities, have been marked by a history of inequality and domination. ... The differences we perceive between men and women may be results as much as causes of sexual inequality.[14]

...

[In addition] the context of social inequality is likely ... to condition the values assigned to perceived sexual differences, so that male attributes are interpreted as assets and female attributes as defects. Social inequality of the sexes may even force revision of the standards by which sexual difference is measured, if men do not measure up well by those standards. The early development of I.Q. tests provides a clear example of this: when females performed better than males on the tests, their superior performance was taken as an indicator of the tests' invalidity and the tests were revised until the males performed up to the female standard. One doubts that the tests would have been revised if females had performed worse than males.

...

## Valorizing Women's Differences

As a direct result of their awareness that social inequality has shaped not only perceptions of sexual difference and even difference itself but also the ways in which sexual difference has been valued, a number of feminists now are consciously reevaluating sexual difference. In addition to challenging biologically reductionist accounts of sexual difference, they have begun to look at difference in a more woman-centered way, not just as evidence of women's weakness but as a possible source of women's strength.

The most evident difference between the sexes is women's capacity to become pregnant and give birth. Existing sex-responsive conceptions of sexual equality typically have viewed this capacity as a disability for which women deserve social compensation. But more feminists now are emphasizing that the ability to give birth is a uniquely valuable potential. Some claim it is a potential that is valuable not only in itself but in its giving rise to characteristically feminine ways of approaching and dealing with the world, ways that may provide a basis for feminist reconstruction.

A wide variety of feminist arguments now purports to demonstrate that familiar western modes of conceptualizing reality in fact are distinctively masculine. Nancy Hartsock, for instance, argues that women's daily experience of transforming natural substances through activities like cooking, in addition to women's experiences in procreation (menstruation, coitus, pregnancy, childbirth, lactation), engender:

> opposition to dualisms of any sort, valuation of concrete, everyday life, sense of a variety of connectednesses and continuities both with other persons and with the natural world. If material life structures consciousness, women's relationally defined existence, bodily experience of boundary challenges, and activity of transforming both physical objects and human beings must be expected to result in a world view to which dichotomies are foreign.[15]

Feminine experience in Hartsock's view generates an ontology of relations and of continual process, an ontology she believes superior to an atomist metaphysics.

... Carol Gilligan's work on moral development recently has received widespread popular attention.[16] Gilligan is widely interpreted as claiming to have established that the moral development of women is significantly different from the moral development of men. On this interpretation, Gilligan claims to have discovered that women tend to construe moral dilemmas as breaches in relationships and seek to resolve those dilemmas in ways that will mend the holes in the relationship network. Supposedly, women are less likely than men to make or justify moral decisions by the application of abstract moral rules; instead they are more likely to act on their feelings of love and compassion for particular individuals. Gilligan's work has aroused a storm of controversy.[17] ... Some feminists, however, have taken Gilligan's identification of this supposedly feminine approach to morality to offer a basis for the development of an ethics that would be distinctively feminist and preferable or superior to the traditional western preoccupation with justice.[18]

When sexual difference comes to be understood in ways that are dynamic and woman-affirming rather than static and woman-devaluing, a new light is thrown on the ideal of sexual equality.

## A Different Feminism

A dynamic approach to understanding sexual difference helps to explain the inadequacy of both the sex-blind and the sex-responsive ways of construing sexual equality. Because it recognizes the reality of sexual difference, such an approach shows why a sex-blind procedure may be unjust if it makes sexual inequality in outcome more likely. Simultaneously, through its recognition both of differences between women and of the social genesis of many inter- and intrasex differences, it shows the dangers of self-fulfilling prophecy that lurk in the sex-responsive approach to sexual equality. A dynamic understanding of sexual difference demonstrates why feminism must rethink traditional interpretations of sexual equality. Contemporary feminist revalorizations of sexual difference indicate some directions in which this rethinking may proceed.

Equality has always been open to the charge (usually made by anti-egalitarians) that it involves a leveling down, a degradation of the exceptional to the ordinary, a reduction to the lowest common denominator. In the historical context of male dominance, the call for women to be equal with men may have appeared as a threat to some men, but certainly it was perceived by most feminists as a promise, the promise to grant them male privileges, to raise them to the level of men. The valorization of women's differences, however, makes the ideal of sexual equality suddenly far less attractive to feminists. Rather than appearing as the extension to women of the full human status enjoyed by men, sexual equality starts to look like an attempt to masculinize women and negate their special capacities.

...

Equality ... is a weapon that feminists seem forced to use, but some fear that it may turn against feminism. For some feminists, the language of equality is not women's "mother tongue"; instead, it is a language that some men developed at a particular point in European history, a language that western women have borrowed and sometimes put to good use. In its prevailing interpretations it is a language of impartiality and abstraction, a language of rational distance rather than of close connection. It presupposes scarcity and a preoccupation with getting one's fair share. It conjures up a rationalized and bureaucratic society of procedurally regulated competition, not an abundant, sensuous, and emotional world rich with human uniqueness and diversity.

...

... Feminists seem caught in the dilemma of simultaneously demanding and scorning equality with men.

My own view is that feminists should embrace both horns of this dilemma, abandoning neither our short-term determination to reform existing society nor our long-term desire to transform it. We should develop both the pragmatic and the utopian strands in our thinking, in the hope that each may strengthen the other.

On the one hand, feminists should continue to struggle for women to receive a fair share of the pie, carcinogenic though it ultimately may be.[19] They should use the rhetoric of equality in situations where women's interests clearly are being damaged by their being treated either differently from or identically with men. It seems likely that neither of the two prevailing interpretations of equality is best in all circumstances. Sometimes equality in outcome may be served best by sex-blindness, sometimes by sex-responsiveness—and sometimes by attention to factors additional to or other than sex. Because perceived sexual differences so often are the result of differences in treatment, it seems prudent to advocate only short-term rather than permanent protections for women. For example, affirmative action and special legal defenses for chronically abused women seem less dangerous to women's status than premenstrual exemptions from legal responsibility. Some questions that have been presented as issues of sexual equality, such as antipornography ordinances and moves to draft women, may be decided better by reference to considerations other than those of equality.

Throughout the battle for sexual equality, it is necessary to remain critical of the standards by which that equality is measured. In particular, feminists should be ready constantly to challenge norms that may be stated in gender-neutral language but that are established on the basis of male experience, and so likely to be biased in favor of men. One example of such a norm is the ordinance forbidding firefighters to breast-feed between calls; another is the minimum height requirement for airline pilots, a requirement based on the seemingly sex-blind concern that pilots be able to reach the instrument panel. Feminist challenges to such norms should mitigate at least to some extent the concern that sexual equality simply will "masculinize" women by assimilating them to male standards. The need to redesign the organization of both paid work and of domestic responsibility in order to avoid this kind of male bias must surely modify the extremes of gender polarization.

Simultaneously with insisting on sexual equality in a world presently racked by scarcity and injustice, feminists should develop their long-term visions of a world in which equality is less a goal than a background condition, a world in which justice is not "the first virtue of social institutions,"[20] but in which justice and equality are overshadowed by the goods of mutual care. But this must be care in a new sense, not the feminized, sentimentalized, privatized care with which we are familiar; not care as a nonrational or even irrational feeling; not care as self-sacrifice (Noddings' "motivational displacement"), nor care as contrasted with justice. Feminists need to develop a distinctive conception of care, one that draws on but transcends women's traditional practice. Feminist care must be responsive both to our common humanity and our inevitable particularity. Neither narrowly personal nor blandly impersonal, it can consist neither in the mechanical application of abstract rules nor in an uncritical surge of feeling, but must transcend both rationalism and romanticism.[21]

The development of such a conception of care is a practical and political as much as an intellectual project. It cannot take place in a world that is structured by domination, where the public sphere is separated sharply from the private, and where inequality is justified in terms of such familiar, gender-linked, western oppositions as culture/nature, mind/body, reason/emotion—dichotomies in which each of the first terms is associated with the masculine and considered superior to each of the second. Instead, experimentation with ways of transcending equality requires an enriched and in some ways protected environment, a consciously feminist community dedicated to discovering less rigid and less hierarchical ways of living and thinking. We need not fear that such an environment will be so sheltered as to produce a weakened, hothouse plant. Far from being sheltered from the cold winds of the larger world, alternative communities may be particularly vulnerable to them. It is stimulating but hardly comfortable to live daily with contradictions.

## Notes

1. Estelle Freedman, "Separatism as Strategy: Female Institution Building and American Feminism, 1870–1930," *Feminist Studies* (1979): 512–29.

2. Rosalind Rosenberg, *Beyond Separate Spheres: Intellectual Roots of Modern Feminism* (New Haven: Yale University Press, 1982).

3. Mary Wollstonecraft, *The Rights of Woman* (London: Dent, 1965); John Stuart Mill, *The Subjection of Women* (London: Dent, 1965).

4. Carolyn G. Heilbrun, *Toward a Recognition of Androgyny* (New York: Alfred A. Knopf, 1973).

5. Lenore J. Weitzman, *The Divorce Revolution* (New York: Free Press, 1985).

6. Katharine T. Bartlett and Carol B. Stack, "Joint Custody, Feminism, and the Dependency Dilemma," *Berkeley Women's Law Journal* (Winter 1986–87).

7. Linda J. Krieger, "Through a Glass Darkly: Paradigms of Equality and the Search for a Woman's Jurisprudence," *Hypatia* 2 (1987).

8. Hilary Allen, "At the Mercy of Her Hormones: Premenstrual Tension and the Law," *m/f* 9 (1984).

9. Cynthia Gillespie, *Justifiable Homicide: Battered Women's Self Defense and the Law* (Columbus: Ohio State University Press, 1989).

10. Wendy Williams, "The Equality Crisis: Some Reflections on Culture, Courts, and Feminism," *Women's Rights Law Reporter* 7 (1982): 196, n. 114.

11. Ibid., 188, n. 75.

12. Ynestra King, private conversation, 1985.

13. Elizabeth V. Spelman, *Inessential Woman: Problems of Exclusion in Feminist Thought* (Boston: Beacon, 1988).

14. Alison M. Jaggar, "Sex Inequality and Bias in Sex Differences Research," *Canadian Journal of Philosophy*, suppl. 13 (1987).

15. Nancy Hartsock, *Money, Sex and Power: Toward a Feminist Historical Materialism* (New York: Longman, 1983), 23.

16. Carol Gilligan, *In a Different Voice: Psychological Theory and Women's Development* (Cambridge: Harvard University Press, 1982).

17. Idem, "Reply," *SIGNS* 11 (1986).

18. See, for example, Sheila Mullett, "Only Connect: The Place of Self-Knowledge in Ethics," *Canadian Journal of Philosophy*, suppl. 13 (1987).

19. Ynestra King, "Postscript," in Adrienne Harris and Ynestra King, eds., *Rocking the Ship of State: Towards a Feminist Peace Politics* (Boulder, Colo.: Westview, 1989).

20. John Rawls, *A Theory of Justice* (Cambridge: Harvard University Press, 1971), 3.

21. Barbara Ehrenreich and Deirdre English, *For Her Own Good: 150 Years of the Experts' Advice to Women* (New York: Anchor, 1979).

# Reconstructing Sexual Equality

## Christine A. Littleton

### Development of Feminist Legal Theory

*Feminist Responses*

Feminist legal theory has been primarily reactive, responding to the development of legal racial equality theory. The form of response, however, has varied. One response has been to attempt to equate legal treatment of sex with that of race and deny that there are in fact any significant natural differences between women and men; in other words, to consider the two sexes symmetrically located with regard to *any* issue, norm, or rule.[1] This response, which I term the "symmetrical" approach, classifies asymmetries as illusions, "overboard generalizations," or temporary glitches that will disappear with a little behavior modification. A competing response rejects this analogy, accepting that women and men are or may be "different," and that women and men are often asymmetrically located in society. This response, which I term the "asymmetrical" approach, rejects the notion that all gender differences are likely to disappear, or even that they should.

1. **Symmetrical Models of Sexual Equality.** ... There are two models of the symmetrical vision—referred to here as "assimilation" and "androgyny." Assimilation, the model most often accepted by the courts, is based on the notion that women, given the chance, really are or could be just like men. Therefore, the argument runs, the law should require social institutions to treat women as they already treat men—requiring, for example, that the professions admit women to the extent they are "qualified," but also insisting that women who enter time-demanding professions such as the practice of law sacrifice relationships (especially with their children) to the same extent that male lawyers have been forced to do.

Androgyny, the second symmetrical model, also posits that women and men are, or at least could be, very much like each other, but argues that equality requires institutions to pick some golden mean between the two and treat both sexes as androgynous persons would be treated. However, given that all of our institutions, work habits, and pay scales were formulated without the benefit of substantial numbers of androgynous persons, androgynous symmetry is difficult to conceptualize, and might require very substantial restructuring of many public and private institutions. In order to be truly androgynous within a symmetrical framework, social institutions must find a single norm that works equally well for all gendered characteristics. Part of my discomfort with androgynous models is that they depend on "meeting in the middle," while I distrust the ability of any person, and especially any court, to value women enough to find the "middle." Moreover, the problems involved in determining such a norm for even one institution are staggering. At what height should a conveyor belt be set in order to satisfy a symmetrical androgynous ideal?

Symmetry appears to have great appeal for the legal system, and this is not surprising. The hornbook definition of equal protection is "that those who are similarly situated be similarly treated."[2] ... Symmetrical analysis also has great appeal for liberal men,[3] to whom it appears to offer a share in the feminist enterprise. If perceived difference between the sexes is only the result of overly rigid sex roles, the men's liberty is at stake too. Ending this form of sexual inequality could free men to express their "feminine" side, just as it frees women to express their "masculine" side.

**2. Asymmetrical Models of Sexual Equality.** Asymmetrical approaches to sexual equality take the position that difference should not be ignored or eradicated. Rather, they argue that any sexually equal society must somehow deal with difference, problematic as that may be. Asymmetrical approaches include "special rights," "accommodation," "acceptance," and "empowerment."

The special rights model affirms that women and men *are* different, and asserts that cultural differences, such as childrearing roles, are rooted in biological ones, such as reproduction. Therefore, it states, society must take account of these differences and ensure that women are not punished for them. This approach, sometimes referred to as a "bivalent" model,[4] is closest to the "special treatment" pole of the asymmetrical/symmetrical equality debate. Elizabeth Wolgast, a major proponent of special rights, argues that women cannot be men's "equals" because equality by definition requires sameness.[5] Instead of equality, she suggests seeking justice, claiming special rights for women based on their special needs.[6]

The second asymmetrical model, accommodation, agrees that differential treatment of biological differences (such as pregnancy, and perhaps breastfeeding) is necessary, but argues that cultural or hard-to-classify differences (such as career interests and skills) should be treated under an equal treatment or androgynous model. Examples of accommodation models include Sylvia Law's approach to issues of reproductive biology[7] and Herma Hill Kay's "episodic" approach to the condition of pregnancy.[8] These approaches could also be characterized as "symmetry, with concessions to asymmetry where necessary." The accommodationists limit the asymmetry in their models to biological differences because, like Williams, they fear a return to separate spheres ideology should asymmetrical theory go too far.

My own attempt to grapple with difference, which I call an "acceptance" model, is essentially asymmetrical. While not endorsing the notion that cultural differences between the sexes are biologically determined, it does recognize and attempt to deal with both biological and social differences. Acceptance does not view sex differences as problematic per se, but rather focuses on the ways in which differences are permitted to justify inequality. It asserts that eliminating the unequal consequences of sex differences is more important than debating whether such differences are "real," or even trying to eliminate them altogether.

Unlike the accommodationists, who would limit asymmetrical analysis to purely biological differences, my proposal also requires equal acceptance of cultural differences. The reasons for this are twofold. First, the distinction between biological and cultural, while useful analytically, is itself culturally based. Second, the inequality experienced by women is often presented as a necessary consequence of cultural rather than of biological difference. If, for instance, women do in fact "choose" to become nurses rather than real estate appraisers, it is not because of any biological imperative. Yet, regardless of the reasons for the choice, they certainly do not choose to be paid less. It is the *consequences* of gendered difference, and not its sources, that equal acceptance addresses.

...

The foregoing asymmetrical models, including my own, share the notion that, regardless of their differences, women and men must be treated as full members of society. Each model acknowledges that women may need treatment different than that accorded to men in order to effectuate their membership in important spheres of social life; all would allow at least some such claims, although on very different bases, and probably in very different circumstances.

A final asymmetrical approach, "empowerment," rejects difference altogether as a relevant subject of inquiry.[9] In its strongest form, empowerment claims that the subordination of women to men has itself constructed the sexes, and their differences. ... A somewhat weaker version of the claim is that we simply do not and cannot know whether there are any important differences between the sexes that have not been created by the dynamic of domination and subordination. In either event, the argument runs, we should forget about the question of differences and focus directly on subordination and domination. If a law, practice, or policy contributes to the subordination of women or their domination by men, it violates equality. If it empowers women or contributes to the breakdown of male domination, it enhances equality.

The reconceptualization of equality as antidomination, like the model of equality as acceptance, attempts to respond directly to the concrete and lived-out experience of women. Like other asymmetrical models, it allows different treatment of women and men when necessary to effectuate its overall goal of ending women's subordination. However, it differs substantially from the acceptance model in its rejection of the membership, belonging, and participatory aspects of equality.

**3. The Difference That Difference Makes.** Each of the several models of equality discussed above, if adopted, would have a quite different impact on the structure of society. If this society wholeheartedly embraced the symmetrical approach of assimilation—the point of view that "women are just like men"—little would need to be changed in our economic or political institutions except to get rid of lingering traces of irrational prejudice, such as an occasional employer's preference for male employees. In contrast, if society adopted the androgyny model, which views both women and men as bent out of shape by current sex roles and requires both to conform to an androgynous model, it would have to alter radically its methods of resource distribution. In the employment context, this might mean wholesale revamping of methods for determining the "best person for the job." Thus, while assimilation would merely require law firms to hire women who have managed to get the same credentials as the men they have traditionally hired, androgyny might insist that the firm hire only those persons with credentials that would be possessed by someone neither "socially male" nor "socially female."

If society adopted an asymmetrical approach such as the accommodation model, no radical restructuring would be necessary. Government would need only insist that women be given what they need to resemble men, such as time off to have babies and the freedom to return to work on the same rung of the ladder as their male counterparts. If, however, society adopted the model of equality as acceptance, which seeks to make difference costless, it might additionally insist that women and men who opt for socially female occupations, such as child-rearing, be compensated at a rate similar to those women and men who opt for socially male occupations, such as legal practice. Alternatively, such occupations might be restructured to make them equally accessible to those whose behavior is culturally coded "male" or "female."

...

The various models of equality arise out of common feminist goals and enterprises: trying to imagine what a sexually equal society would look like, given that none of us has ever seen one; and trying to figure out ways of getting there, given that the obstacles to sexual equality are so many and so strong.

The perception among feminist legal thinkers that the stakes in the symmetrical vs. asymmetrical debate are high is correct. Difference indeed makes a difference. Yet, the frantic nature of the debate about difference between the sexes makes the divergent views within feminist legal thought appear as a deadly danger rather than an exciting opportunity. The label "divisive" gets slapped on before the discussion even gets underway.

We need to recognize difference among women as diversity rather than division, and difference between women and men as opportunity rather than danger. Audre Lorde calls for the recognition of difference among women in terms that should apply to all human difference:

> As a tool of social control, women have been encouraged to recognize only one area of human difference as legitimate, those differences which exist between women and men. And we have learned to deal across those differences with the urgency of all oppressed subordinates. ... We have recognized and negotiated these differences, even when this recognition only continued the old dominant/subordinate mode of human relationship, where the oppressed must recognize the masters' difference in order to survive.
> *But our future survival is predicated upon our ability to relate within equality.*[10]

There must be choices beyond those of ignoring difference or accepting inequality. So long as difference itself is so expensive in the coin of equality, we approach the variety of human experience with blinders on. Perhaps if difference were not so costly, we, as feminists, could think about it more clearly. Perhaps if equality did not require uniformity, we, as women, could demand it less ambivalently.

## Equality as Acceptance

The model of equality as acceptance ... [insists] that equality can ... be applied *across* difference. It is not, however, a "leveling" proposal. Rather, equality as acceptance calls for equalization across only those differences that the culture has encoded as gendered complements. The theory of comparable worth provides one example of this, and the field of athletics yields another.

Most proponents of comparable worth have defined the claim along the following lines: jobs that call for equally valuable skills, effort, and responsibility should be paid equally, even though they occur in different combinations of predominantly female and predominantly male occupations. Thus, when an employer has defined two job classifications as gendered complements, the employer should pay the same to each. Equality as acceptance makes the broader claim that *all* behavioral forms that the culture (not just the employer) has encoded as "male" and "female" counterparts should be equally rewarded. Acceptance would thus support challenges to the overvaluation of "male" skills (and corresponding undervaluation of "female" ones) by employers, rather than limiting challenges to unequal application of an existing valuation or to the failure to make such a valuation.

In the sphere of athletics, equality as acceptance would support an argument that equal resources be allocated to male and female sports programs regardless of whether the sports themselves are "similar." In this way, women's equality in athletics would not depend on the ability of individual women to assimilate themselves to the particular sports activities traditionally engaged in by men.

Under the model of equality as acceptance, equality analysis does not end at the discovery of a "real" difference. Rather, it attempts to assess the "cultural meaning" of that difference, and to determine how to achieve equality despite it. This formulation ... [locates] difference in the relationship between women and men rather than in women alone, as accommodation arguably does. Acceptance would thus provide little support for the claim that traditionally male sports (such as football) should be modified so as to accommodate women (or vice versa). Equality as acceptance does not prescribe the superiority of socially female categories, nor even the superiority of androgynous categories. It does, however, affirm the equal validity of men's and women's lives.

Finally, equality is acceptance ... [acknowledges] that women and men frequently stand in asymmetrical positions to a particular social institution. It recognizes that women are frequently disadvantaged by facially neutral practices and insists that such asymmetries be reflected in resource allocation. To carry forward the athletics example, equality as acceptance would support an equal division of resources between male and female programs rather than dividing up the available sports budget per capita. Since women and men do not stand symmetrically to the social institution of athletics, per capita distribution would simply serve to perpetuate the asymmetry, diverting more resources to male programs, where the participation rate has traditionally been high, and away from female programs, where the participation rate has been depressed both by women's exclusion from certain sports and by the subordination of those activities women have developed for themselves.

It may be apparent from the preceding paragraphs that equal acceptance as a legal norm does not automatically produce one and only one "right answer" to difficult questions of equality. Instead, it provides support for new remedial strategies as well as a method of uncovering deeper layers of inequality.

## Acceptance, Not Accommodation

Asymmetrical equality theorists have usually been taken to mean that male institutions should take account of women's differences by accommodating those differences. "Reasonable accommodation" can be asked of a court (although the people usually being asked to be "reasonable" are those asking for accommodation), and if the choice truly is between accommodation and nothing, "half a loaf" *is* better than none.

...

The distinction between accommodation and acceptance may be illustrated by a rather commonplace example. I remember a feminist lawyer walking up to a podium to deliver a speech. The podium was high enough that she could not reach the microphone. While arrangements were being modified, she pointedly noted, "Built for a man!" Accommodation is a step platform brought for her to stand on. Acceptance is a podium whose height is adjustable.

...

---

### Notes

1. In the 1970's, the first wave of feminist litigators chose this approach, and this led to the rather counterintuitive use of male plaintiffs in most of the major constitutional sex discrimination cases of the 1970's. *See e.g.*, Califano v. Goldfarb, 430 U.S. 199 (1977); Weinberger v. Wiesenfeld, 420 U.S. 636 (1975); Kahn v. Shevin, 416 U.S. 351 (1974). For a sympathetic interpretation of this phenomenon, *see* Cole, *Strategies of Difference: Litigating for Women's Rights in a Man's World*, 2 J.L. & INEQUALITY 33, 53–92 (1984).

2. Tussman & tenBroek, *The Equal Protection of the Laws*, 37 CALIF. L. REV. 341, 344 (1949).

...

3. The least critical symmetrical approaches are found in the work of male legal theorists. Richard Wasserstrom, for example, envisions the sexually equal society as one in which biological sex is "no more significant than eye color," and in which asking whether a new baby is a boy or a girl is no more common than asking whether it has large or small feet. Wasserstrom, [*Racism, Sexism, and Preferential Treatment: An Approach to the Topics*, 24 UCLA L. REV. 581, 606 (1977)]. ...

4. *See* Scales, [*Towards a Feminist Jurisprudence*, 56 IND. L.J. 375, 430–34 (1981)]; *see also* E. WOLGAST, EQUALITY AND THE RIGHTS OF WOMEN 61–63 (1980).

5. E. WOLGAST, *supra* note 4, at 122. ...

6. ... *Id.* at 157. ...

7. Law, *Rethinking Sex and the Constitution*, 132 U. Pa. L. Rev. 955, 1007–13 (1984) (calling for equal treatment in all areas *except* reproduction, where an analysis based on an empowerment approach ... should be adopted).

8. Kay, *Equality and Difference: the Case of Pregnancy*. 1 Berkeley Women's L.J. 1, 27–37 (1985) (sex differences should be ignored, *except* during the time a female is actually pregnant).

9. This model has been articulated most fully by Catharine MacKinnon, and draws heavily on the work of radical feminist theorists such as Andrea Dworkin. *See* C. MacKinnon [Sexual Harassment of Working Women (1979)] (examining sexual harassment in context of male power structure); MacKinnon, *Feminism, Marxism, Method and the State: Toward Feminist Jurisprudence*, 8 Signs 635 (1983) (examining how traditional theories of "the state" perpetuate male power to exclude women's perspective) ... ; A. Dworkin, Our Blood 96–111 (1976); A. Dworkin, Pornography: Men Possessing Women 13–24 (1979). ...

10. A. Lorde, *Age, Race, Class and Sex: Women Redefining Difference*, in Sister Outsider, 114, 122 [1984] (emphasis added).

# *Toward Feminist Jurisprudence*

## Catharine A. MacKinnon

...

Sex equality in law has not been meaningfully defined for women, but has been defined and limited from the male point of view to correspond with the existing social reality of sex inequality. An alternative approach to this mainstream view threads through existing law. It is the reason sex equality law exists at all. In this approach, inequality is a matter not of sameness and difference, but of dominance and subordination. Inequality is about power, its definition, and its maldistribution. Inequality at root is grasped as a question of hierarchy, which—as power succeeds in constructing social perception and social reality—derivatively becomes categorical distinctions, differences. Where mainstream equality law is abstract, this approach is concrete; where mainstream equality law is falsely universal, this approach remains specific.[1] The goal is not to make legal categories that trace and trap the status quo, but to confront by law the inequalities in women's condition in order to change them.

This alternate approach centers on the most sex-differential abuses of women as a gender, abuses that sex equality law in its sameness/difference obsession cannot confront. It is based on the reality that feminism, beginning with consciousness raising, has most distinctively uncovered, a reality about which little systematic was known before 1970: the reality of sexual abuse. It combines women's sex-based destitution and enforced dependency and permanent relegation to disrespected and starvation-level work—the lived meaning of class for women—with the massive amount of sexual abuse of girls apparently endemic to the patriarchal family, the pervasive rape and attempted rape about which nothing is done, the systematic battery of women in homes, and prostitution—the fundamental condition of women—of which the pornography industry is an arm. Keeping the reality of gender in view makes it impossible to see gender as a difference, unless this subordinated condition of women is that difference. This reality has called for a new conception of the problem of sex inequality, hence a new legal conception of it, both doctrinally and jurisprudentially.

Experiences of sexual abuse have been virtually excluded from the mainstream doctrine of sex equality because they happen almost exclusively to women and because they are experienced as sex. Sexual abuse has not been seen to raise sex *equality* issues because these events happen specifically and almost exclusively to women as women. Sexuality is socially organized to require sex inequality for excitement and satisfaction. The least extreme expression of gender inequality, and the prerequisite for all of it, is dehumanization and objectification. The most extreme is violence. Because sexual objectification and sexual violence are almost uniquely done to women, they have been systematically treated as the sex difference, when they represent the socially situated subjection of women to men. The whole point of women's social relegation to inferiority as a gender is that this is not generally done to men. The systematic relegation of an entire people to a condition of inferiority is attributed to them, made a feature of theirs, and read out of equality demands and equality law, when it is termed a "difference." This condition is ignored entirely, with all the women who are determined by it, when only features women share with the privileged group are allowed to substantive equality claims.

It follows that seeing sex equality questions as matters of reasonable or unreasonable classification of relevant social characteristics expresses male dominance in law. If the shift in perspective from gender as difference to gender as dominance is followed, gender changes from a distinction that is ontological and presumptively valid to a detriment that is epistemological and presumptively suspect. The given becomes the contingent. In this light, liberalism, purporting to discover gender, has discovered male and female in the mirror of nature; the left has discovered masculine and feminine in the mirror of society. The approach from the standpoint of the subordination of women to men, by contrast, criticizes and claims the specific situation of women's enforced inferiority and devaluation, pointing a way out of the infinity of reflections in law-and-society's hall of mirrors where sex equality law remains otherwise trapped.

Equality understood substantively rather than abstractly, defined on women's own terms and in terms of women's concrete experience, is what women in society most need and most do not have. Equality is also what society holds that women have already, and therefore guarantees women by positive law. The law of equality, statutory and constitutional, therefore provides a peculiar jurisprudential opportunity, a crack in the wall between law and society. Law does not usually guarantee rights to things that do not exist. This may be why equality issues have occasioned so many jurisprudential disputes about what law is and what it can and should do. Every demand from women's point of view looks substantive, just as every demand from women's point of view requires change. Can women, demanding actual equality through law, be part of changing the state's relation to women and women's relation to men? The first step is to claim women's concrete reality. Women's inequality occurs in a context of unequal pay, allocation to disrespected work, demeaned physical characteristics, targeting for rape, domestic battery, sexual abuse as children, and systematic sexual harassment. Women are daily dehumanized, used in denigrating entertainment, denied reproductive control, and forced by the conditions of their lives into prostitution. These abuses occur in a legal context historically characterized by disenfranchisement, preclusion from property ownership, exclusion from public life, and lack of recognition of sex-specific injuries.[2] Sex inequality is thus a social and political institution.

The next step is to recognize that male forms of power over women are affirmatively embodied as individual rights in law. When men lose power, they feel they lose rights. Often they are not wrong. Examples include the defense of mistaken belief in consent in the rape law, which legally determines whether or not a rape occurred from the rapists' perspective; freedom of speech, which gives pimps right to torture, exploit, use, and sell women to men through pictures and words, and gives consumers rights to buy them; the law of privacy, which defines the home and sex as presumptively consensual and protects the use of pornography in the home; the law of child custody, which purports gender neutrality while applying a standard of adequacy of parenting based on male-controlled resources and male-defined norms, sometimes taking children away from women but more generally controlling women through the threat and fear of loss of their children. Real sex equality under law would qualify or eliminate these power of men, hence men's current "rights" to use, access, possess, and traffic women and children.

In this context, many issues appear as sex equality issues for the first time—sexual assault, for example. Rape is a sex-specific violation. Not only are the victims of rape overwhelmingly women, perpetrators overwhelmingly men, but also the rape of women by men is integral to the way inequality between the sexes occurs in life. Intimate violation with impunity is an ultimate index of social power. Rape both evidences and practices women's low status relative to men. Rape equates female with violable and female sexuality with forcible intrusion in a way that defines and stigmatizes the female sex as a gender. Threat of sexual assault is threat of punishment for being female. The state has laws against sexual assault but it does not enforce them. Like lynching at one time, rape is socially permitted, though formally illegal. Victims of sex crimes, mostly women and girls, are thus disadvantaged relative to perpetrators of sex crimes, largely men.

A systemic inequality between the sexes therefore exists in the social practice of sexual violence, subjection to which defines women's status, and victims of which are largely women, and in the operation of the state, which *de jure* outlaws sexual violence but de facto permits men to engage in it on a wide scale. Making sexual assault laws gender neutral does nothing to address this, nothing to alter the social equation of female with rapable, and may obscure the sex specificity of the problem. Rape should be defined as sex by compulsion, of which physical force is one form. Lack of consent is redundant and should not be a separate element of the crime.[3] Expanding this analysis would support as sex equality initiatives laws keeping women's sexual histories out of rape trials[4] and publication bans on victims' names and identities.[5] The defense of mistaken belief in consent—which measures whether a rape occurred from the standpoint of the (male) perpetrator—would violate women's sex equality rights by law because it takes the male point of view on sexual violence against women.[6] Similarly, the systematic failure of the state to enforce the rape law effectively or at all excludes women from equal access to justice, permitting women to be savaged on a mass scale, depriving them of equal protection and equal benefit of the laws.

...

The changes that a sex equality perspective provides as an interpretive lens include the law of sex equality itself. The intent requirement would be eliminated. The state action requirement would weaken. No distinction would be made between nondiscrimination and affirmative action. Burdens of proof would presuppose inequality rather than equality as a factual backdrop and would be more substantively sensitive to the particularities of sex inequality. Comparable worth would be required. Statistical proofs of disparity would be conclusive. The main question would be: does a practice participate in the subordination of women to men, or is it no part of it? Whether statutes are sex specific or gender neutral would not be as important as whether they work to end or reinforce male supremacy, whether they are concretely grounded in women's experience of subordination or not. Discrimination law would not be confined to employment, education, and accommodation. Civil remedies in women's hands would be emphasized. Gay and lesbian rights would be recognized as sex equality rights. Since sexuality largely defines gender, discrimination based on sexuality is discrimination based on gender. Other forms of social discrimination and exploitation by men against women, such as prostitution and surrogate motherhood, would become actionable.

The relation between life and law would also change. Law, in liberal jurisprudence, objectifies social life. The legal process reflects itself in its own image, makes be there what it puts there, while presenting itself as passive and neutral in the process. To undo this, it will be necessary to grasp the dignity of women without blinking at the indignity of women's condition, to envision the possibility of equality without minimizing the grip of inequality, to reject the fear that has become so much of women's sexuality and the corresponding denial that has become so much of women's politics, and to demand civil parity without pretending that the demand is neutral or that civil equality already exists. In this attempt, the idealism of liberalism and the materialism of the left have come to much the same for women. Liberal jurisprudence that the law should reflect nature or society and left jurisprudence that all law does or can do is reflect existing social relations are two guises of objectivist epistemology. If objectivity is the epistemological stance of which women's sexual objectification is the social process, its imposition the paradigm of power in the male form, then the state appears most relentless in imposing the male point of view when it comes closest to achieving its highest formal criterion of distanced aperspectivity. When it is most ruthlessly neutral, it is most male; when it is most sex blind, it is most blind to the sex of the standard being applied. When it most closely conforms to precedent, to "facts," to legislative intent, it most closely enforces socially male norms and most thoroughly precludes questioning their content as having a point of view at all.

Abstract rights authorize the male experience of the world. Substantive rights for women would not. Their authority would be the currently unthinkable: nondominant authority, the authority of excluded truth, the voice of silence. It would stand against both the liberal and left views of law. The liberal view that law is society's text, its rational mind, expresses the male view in the normative mode; the traditional left view that the state, and with it the law, is superstructural or ephiphenomenal, expresses it in the empirical mode. A feminist jurisprudence, stigmatized as particularized and protectionist in male eyes of both traditions, is accountable to women's concrete conditions and to changing them. Both the liberal and the left view rationalize male power by presuming that it does not exist, that equality between the sexes (room for marginal corrections conceded) is society's basic norm and fundamental description. Only feminist jurisprudence sees that male power does exist and sex equality does not, because only feminism grasps the extent to which antifeminism is misogyny and both are as normative as they are empirical. Masculinity then appears as a specific position, not just the way things are, its judgments and partialities revealed in process and procedure, adjudication and legislation.

Equality will require change, not reflection—a new jurisprudence, a new relation between life and law. Law that does not dominate life is as difficult to envision as a society in which men do not dominate women, and for the same reasons. To the extent feminist law embodies women's point of view, it will be said that its law is not neutral. But existing law is not neutral. It will be said that it undermines the legitimacy of the legal system. But the legitimacy of existing law is based on force at women's expense. Women have never consented to its rule—suggesting that system's legitimacy needs repair that women are in a position to provide. It will be said that feminist law is special pleading for a particular group and one cannot start that or where will it end. But existing law is already special pleading for a particular group, where it has ended. The question is not where it will stop, but whether it will start for any group but the dominant one. It will be said that feminist law canot win and will not work. But this is premature. Its possibilities cannot be assessed in the abstract but must engage the world. A feminist theory of the state has barely been imagined; systematically, it has never been tried.

---

## Notes

1. Examples are Loving v. Virginia, 388 U.S. 1 (1967); Brown v. Board of Education, 347 U.S. 483 (1954); some examples of the law against sexual harassment (e.g., Barnes v. Costle, 561 F. 2d 983 [D.C. Cir. 1977]; Vinson v. Taylor, 753 F. 2d 141 [D.C. Cir. 1985], aff'd. 477 U.S. 57 (1986); Priest v. Rotary, 98 F.R.D. 755 [D.Cal. 1983]), some athletics cases (e.g., Clark v. Arizona Inter-

scholastic Assn., 695 F. 2d 1126 [9th Cir. 1986]), some affirmative action cases (e.g., Johnson v. Transportation Agency, Santa Clara County, 480 U.S. 616 [1987]), and California Federal Savings and Loan Association v. Guerra, 492 U.S. 272 (1987).

2. This context was argued as the appropriate approach to equality in an intervention by the Women's Legal Education and Action Fund (LEAF) in Law Society of British Columbia v. Andrews (May 22, 1987) before the Supreme Court of Canada. This approach to equality in general, giving priority to concrete disadvantage and rejecting the "similarly situated" test, was adopted by the Supreme Court of Canada in that case (1989)—DLR (3d)—.

3. See Ill. Rev. Stat. 1985, ch. 38, par. 12–14; People v. Haywood, 515 N.E.2d 45 (Ill. App. 1987) (prosecution not required to prove nonconsent, since sexual penetration by force implicitly shows nonconsent); but cf. People v. Coleman, 520 N.E.2d 55 (Ill. App. 1987) (state must prove victim's lack of consent beyond reasonable doubt).

4. This is argued by LEAF in its intervention application with several groups in Seaboyer v. The Queen (12 July 1988) and Gayme v. The Queen (18 November 1988), both on appeal before the Supreme Court of Canada. The rulings below are The Queen v. Seaboyer and Gayme (1986) 50 C.R. (3d) 395 (Ont. C.A.).

5. LEAF and a coalition of rape crisis centers, groups opposing sexual assault of women and children, and feminist media made this argument in an intervention in The Queen v. Canadian Newspapers Co., Ltd. The Canadian statute was upheld by a unanimous court. (1988)— D.L.R. (3d)—.

6. This is argued by LEAF intervening in The Queen v. Gayme.

# *Demarginalizing the Intersection of Race and Sex: A Black Feminist Critique of Antidiscrimination Doctrine, Feminist Theory, and Antiracist Politics*

## Kimberle Crenshaw

One of the very few Black women's studies books is entitled *All the Women Are White, All the Blacks Are Men, But Some of Us Are Brave.*[1] I have chosen this title as a point of departure in my efforts to develop a Black feminist criticism because it sets forth a problematic consequence of the tendency to treat race and gender as mutually exclusive categories of experience and analysis.[2] ... I want to examine how this tendency is perpetuated by a single-axis framework that is dominant in anti-discrimination law and that is also reflected in feminist theory and antiracist politics.

I will center Black women in this analysis in order to contrast the multidimensionality of Black women's experience with the single-axis analysis that distorts these experiences. Not only will this juxtaposition reveal how Black women are theoretically erased, it will also illustrate how this framework imports its own theoretical limitations that undermine efforts to broaden feminist and antiracist analyses. With Black women as the starting point, it becomes more apparent how dominant conceptions of discrimination condition us to think about subordination as disadvantage occurring along a single categorical axis. I want to suggest further that this single-axis framework erases Black women in the conceptualization, identification and remediation of race and sex discrimination by limiting inquiry to the experiences of otherwise-privileged members of the group. In other words, in race indiscrimination cases, discrimination tends to be viewed in terms of sex- or class-privileged Blacks; in sex discrimination cases, the focus is on race- and class-privileged women.

This focus on the most privileged group members marginalizes those who are multiply-burdened and obscures claims that cannot be understood as resulting from discrete sources of discrimination. I suggest further that this focus on otherwise-privileged group members creates a distorted analysis of racism and sexism because the operative conceptions of race and sex become grounded in experiences that actually represent only a subset of a much more complex phenomenon.

After examining the doctrinal manifestations of this single-axis framework, I will discuss how it contributes to the marginalization of Black women in feminist theory and in antiracist politics. I argue that Black women are sometimes excluded from feminist theory and antiracist policy discourse because both are predicated on a discrete set of experiences that often does not accurately reflect the interaction of race and gender. These problems of exclusion cannot be solved simply by including Black women within an already established analytical structure. Because the intersectional experience is greater than the sum of racism and sexism, any analysis that does not take intersectionality into account cannot sufficiently address the particular manner in which Black women are subordinated. Thus, for feminist theory and antiracist policy discourse to embrace the experiences and concerns of Black women, the entire framework that has been used as a basis for translating "women's experience" or "the Black experience" into concrete policy demands must be rethought and recast.

As examples of theoretical and political developments that miss the mark with respect to Black women because of their failure to consider intersectionality, I will briefly discuss the feminist critique of rape and separate spheres ideology. ...

## The Antidiscrimination Framework

### A. The Experience of Intersectionality and the Doctrinal Response

One way to approach the problem of intersectionality is to examine how courts frame and interpret the stories of Black women plaintiffs. While I cannot claim to know the circumstances underlying the cases that I will discuss, I nevertheless believe that the way courts interpret claims made by Black women is itself part of Black women's experience and, consequently, a cursory review of cases involving Black female plaintiffs is quite revealing. To illustrate the difficulties inherent in judicial treatment of intersectionality, I will consider three Title VII[3] cases: *DeGraffenreid v General Motors*,[4] *Moore v Hughes Helicopters*[5] and *Payne v Travenol*.[6]

**1. DeGraffenreid v General Motors.** In *DeGraffenreid*, five Black women brought suit against General Motors, alleging that the employer's seniority system perpetuated the effects of past discrimination against Black women. Evidence adduced at trial revealed that General Motors simply did not hire Black women prior to 1964 and that all of the Black women hired after 1970 lost their jobs in a seniority-based layoff during a subsequent recession. The district court granted summary judgment for the defendant, rejecting the plaintiff's attempt to bring a suit not on behalf of Blacks or women, but specifically on behalf of Black women. The court stated:

> [P]laintiffs have failed to cite any decisions which have stated that Black women are a special class to be protected from discrimination. The Court's own research has failed to disclose such a decision. The plaintiffs are clearly entitled to a remedy if they have been discriminated against. However, they should not be allowed to combine statutory remedies to create a new 'super-remedy' which would give them relief beyond what the drafters of the relevant statutes intended. Thus, this lawsuit must be examined to see if it states a cause of action for race discrimination, sex discrimination, or alternatively either, but not a combination of both.[7]

Although General Motors did not hire Black women prior to 1964, the court noted that "General Motors has hired ... female employees for a number of years prior to the enactment of the Civil Rights Act of 1964."[8] Because General Motors did hire women—albeit *white women*—during the period that no Black women were hired, there was, in the court's view, no sex discrimination that the seniority system could conceivably have perpetuated.

After refusing to consider the plaintiffs' sex discrimination claim, the court dismissed the race discrimination complaint and recommended its consolidation with another case alleging race discrimination against the same employer.[9] The plaintiffs responded that such consolidation would defeat the purpose of their suit since theirs was not purely a race claim, but an action brought specifically on behalf of Black women alleging race *and* sex discrimination. ...

...

**2. Moore v Hughes Helicopters, Inc.** *Moore v Hughes Helicopters, Inc.*[10] presents a different way in which courts fail to understand or recognize Black women's claims. *Moore* is typical of a number of cases in which courts refused to certify Black females as class representatives in race *and* sex discrimination actions.[11] In *Moore*, the plaintiff alleged that the employer, Hughes Helicopter, practiced race and sex discrimination in promotions to upper-level craft positions and to supervisory jobs. Moore introduced statistical evidence establishing a significant disparity between men and women, and somewhat less of a disparity between Black and white men in supervisory jobs.[12]

Affirming the district court's refusal to certify Moore as the class representative in the sex discrimination complaint on behalf of all women at Hughes, the Ninth Circuit noted approvingly:

> ... Moore had never claimed before the EEOC that she was discriminated against as a female, *but only* as a Black female. ... [T]his raised serious doubts as to Moore's ability to adequately represent white female employees.[13]

The curious logic in *Moore* reveals not only the narrow scope of antidiscrimination doctrine and its failure to embrace intersectionality, but also the centrality of white female experiences in the conceptualization of gender discrimination. One inference that could be drawn from the court's statement that Moore's complaint did not entail a claim of discrimination "against females" is that discrimination against Black females is something less than discrimination against females. More than likely, however, the court meant to imply that Moore did not claim that *all* females were discriminated against *but only* Black females. But even thus recast, the court's rationale is problematic for Black women. The court rejected Moore's bid to represent all females apparently because her attempt to specify her race was seen as being at odds with the standard allegation that the employer simply discriminated "against females."

The court failed to see that the absence of a racial referent does not necessarily mean that the claim being made is a more inclusive one. A white woman claiming discrimination against females may be in no better position to represent all women than a Black woman who claims discrimination as a Black female and wants to represent all females. The court's preferred articulation of "against females" is not necessarily more inclusive—it just appears to be so because the racial contours of the claim are not specified.

The court's preference for "against females" rather than "against Black females" reveals the implicit grounding of white female experiences in the doctrinal conceptualization of sex discrimination. For white women, claiming sex discrimination is simply a statement that but for gender, they would not have been disadvantaged. For them there is no need to specify discrimination as *white* females because their race does not contribute to the disadvantage for which they seek redress. The view of discrimination that is derived from this grounding takes race privilege as a given. Discrimination against a white female is thus the standard sex discrimination claim; claims that diverge from this standard appear to present some sort of hybrid claim. More significantly, because Black females' claims are seen as hybrid, they sometimes cannot represent those who may have "pure" claims of sex discrimination. The effect of this approach is that even though a challenged policy or practice may clearly discriminate against all females, the fact that it has particularly harsh consequences for Black females places Black female plaintiffs at odds with white females.

...

**3. Payne v Travenol.** Black female plaintiffs have also encountered difficulty in their efforts to win certification as class representatives in some race discrimination actions. This problem typically arises in cases where statistics suggest significant disparities between Black and white workers and further disparities between Black men and Black women. Courts in some cases[14] have denied certification based on logic that mirrors the rationale in *Moore:* The sex disparities between Black men and Black women created such conflicting interests that Black women could not possibly represent Black men adequately. In one such case, *Payne v Travenol,*[15] two Black female plaintiffs alleging race discrimination brought a class action suit on behalf of all Black employees at a pharmaceutical plant.[16] The court refused, however, to allow the plaintiffs to represent Black males and granted the defendant's request to narrow the class to Black women only. Ultimately, the district court found that there had been extensive racial discrimination at the plant and awarded back pay and constructive seniority to the class of Black female employees. But, despite its finding of general race discrimination, the court refused to extend the remedy to Black men for fear that their conflicting interests would not be adequately addressed.[17]

...

In sum, several courts have proved unable to deal with intersectionality, although for contrasting reasons. In *DeGraffenreid,* the court refused to recognize the possibility of compound discrimination against Black women and analyzed their claim using the employment of white women as the historical base. As a consequence, the employment experiences of white women obscured the distinct discrimination that Black women experienced.

Conversely, in *Moore,* the court held that a Black woman could not use statistics reflecting the overall sex disparity in supervisory and upper-level labor jobs because she had not claimed discrimination as a women, but "only" as a Black woman. The court would not entertain the notion that discrimination experienced by Black women is indeed sex discrimination—provable through disparate impact statistics on women.

Finally, courts, such as the one in *Travenol,* have held that Black women cannot represent an entire class of Blacks due to presumed class conflicts in cases where sex additionally disadvantaged Black women. As a result, in the few cases where Black women are allowed to use overall statistics indicating racially disparate treatment Black men may not be able to share in the remedy.

Perhaps it appears to some that I have offered inconsistent criticisms of how Black women are treated in antidiscrimination law: I seem to be saying that in one case, Black women's claims were rejected and their experiences obscured because the court refused to acknowledge that the employment experience of Black women can be distinct from that of white women, while in other cases, the interests of Black women are harmed because Black women's claims were viewed as so distinct from the claims of either white women or Black men that the court denied to Black females representation of the larger class. It seems that I have to say that Black women are the same and harmed by being treated differently, or that they are different and harmed by being treated the same. But I cannot say both.

This apparent contradiction is but another manifestation of the conceptual limitations of the single-issue analyses that intersectionality challenges. The point is that Black women can experience discrimination in any number of ways and that the contradiction arises from our assumptions that their claims of exclusion must be unidirectional. Consider an analogy to traffic in an intersection, coming and going in all four directions. Discrimination, like traffic through an intersection, may flow in one direction, and it may flow in another. If an accident happens in an intersection, it can be caused by cars traveling from any number of directions and, sometimes, from all of them. Similarly, if a Black women is harmed because she is in the intersection, her injury could result from sex discrimination or race discrimination.

…

To bring this back to a non-metaphorical level, I am suggesting that Black women can experience discrimination in ways that are both similar to and different from those experienced by white women and Black men. Black women sometimes experience discrimination in ways similar to white women's experiences; sometimes they share very similar experiences with Black men. Yet often they experience double-discrimination—the combined effects of practices which discriminate on the basis of race, and on the basis of sex. And sometimes, they experience discrimination as Black women—not the sum of race and sex discrimination, but as Black women.

…

## B. The Significance of Doctrinal Treatment of Intersectionality

*DeGraffenreid, Moore* and *Travenol* are doctrinal manifestations of a common political and theoretical approach to discrimination which operates to marginalize Black women. Unable to grasp the importance of Black women's intersectional experiences, not only courts, but feminist and civil rights thinkers as well have treated Black women in ways that deny both the unique compoundedness of their situation and the centrality of their experiences to the larger classes of women and Blacks. Black women are regarded either as too much like women or Blacks and the compounded nature of their experience is absorbed into the collective experiences of either group or as too different, in which case Black women's Blackness or femaleness sometimes has placed their needs and perspectives at the margin of the feminist and Black liberationist agendas.

While it could be argued that this failure represents an absence of political will to include Black women, I believe that it reflects an uncritical and disturbing acceptance of dominant ways of thinking about discrimination. Consider first the definition of discrimination that seems to be operative in antidiscrimination law: Discrimination which is wrongful proceeds from the identification of a specific class or category; either a discriminator intentionally identifies this category, or a process is adopted which somehow disadvantages all members of this category.[18] According to the dominant view, a discriminator treats all people within a race or sex category similarly. Any significant experiential or statistical variation within this group suggests either that the group is not being discriminated against or that conflicting interests exist which defeat any attempts to bring a common claim. Consequently, one generally <u>cannot combine these categories</u>. Race and sex, moreover, become significant only when they operate to <u>explicitly *disadvantage* the</u> victims; because the <u>privileging of whiteness or maleness is implicit</u>, it is generally not perceived at all.

Underlying this conception of discrimination is a view that the wrong which antidiscrimination law addresses is the use of race or gender factors to interfere with decisions that would otherwise be fair or neutral. This process-based definition is not grounded in a bottom-up commitment to improve the substantive conditions for those who are victimized by the interplay of numerous factors. Instead, <u>the dominant message of antidiscrimination law is that it will regulate only the limited extent to which race or sex interferes with the process of determining outcomes</u>. This narrow objective is facilitated by the top-down strategy of using a singular "but for" analysis to ascertain the effects of race or sex. Because the scope of antidiscrimination law is so limited, sex and race discrimination have come to be defined in terms of the experiences of those who are privileged *but for* their racial or sexual characteristics. Put differently, the paradigm of sex discrimination tends to be based on the experiences of white women; the model of race discrimination tends to be based on the experiences of the most privileged Blacks. Notions of what constitutes race and sex discrimination are, as a result, narrowly tailored to embrace only a small set of circumstances, none of which include discrimination against Black women.

To the extent that this general description is accurate, the following analogy can be useful in describing how Black women are marginalized in the interface between antidiscrimination law and race and gender hierarchies: Imagine a basement which contains all people who are disadvantaged on the basis of race, sex, class, sexual preference, age and/or physical ability. These people are stacked—feet standing on shoulders—with those on the bottom being disadvantaged by the full array of factors, up to the very top, where the heads of all those disadvantaged by a singular factor brush up against the ceiling. Their ceiling is actually the floor above which only those who are *not* disadvantaged in any way reside. In efforts to correct some aspects of domination, those above the ceiling admit from the basement only those who can say that "but for" the ceiling, they too would be in the upper room. A hatch is developed through which those placed immediately below can crawl. Yet this hatch is generally available only to those who—due to the singularity of their burden and their otherwise privileged position relative to those below—are in the position to crawl through. Those who are multiply-burdened are generally left below unless they can somehow pull themselves into the groups that are permitted to squeeze through the hatch.

As this analogy translates for Black women, the problem is that they can receive protection only to the extent that their experiences are recognizably similar to those whose experiences tend to be reflected in antidiscrimination doctrine. If Black women cannot conclusively say that "but for" their race or "but for" their gender they would be treated differently, they are not invited to climb through the hatch but told to wait in the unprotected margin until they can be absorbed into the broader, protected categories of race and sex.

...

## Feminism and Black Women: "Ain't We Women?"

...

In 1851, Sojourner Truth declared "Ain't I a Woman?" and challenged the sexist imagery used by male critics to justify the disenfranchisement of women. The scene was a Women's Rights Conference in Akron, Ohio; white male hecklers, invoking stereotypical images of "womanhood," argued that women were too frail and delicate to take on the responsibilities of political activity. When Sojourner Truth rose to speak, many white women urged that she be silenced, fearing that she would divert attention from women's suffrage to emancipation. Truth, once permitted to speak, recounted the horrors of slavery, and its particular impact on Black women:

> Look at my arms! I have ploughed and planted and gathered into barns, and no man could head me—and ain't I a woman? I would work as much and eat as much as a man—when I could get it—and bear the lash as well! And ain't I a woman? I have born thirteen children, and seen most of 'em sold into slavery, and when I cried out with my mother's grief, none but Jesus heard me—and ain't I a woman?[19]

By using her own life to reveal the contradiction between the ideological myths of womanhood and the reality of Black women's experience, Truth's oratory provided a powerful rebuttal to the claim that women were categorically weaker than men. Yet Truth's personal challenge to the coherence of the cult of true womanhood was useful only to the extent that white women were willing to reject the racist attempts to rationalize the contradiction—that because Black women were something less than real women, their experiences had no bearing on true womanhood. Thus, this 19th-century Black feminist challenged not only patriarchy, but she also challenged white feminists wishing to embrace Black women's history to relinquish their vestedness in whiteness.

...

The value of feminist theory to Black women is diminished because it evolves from a white racial context that is seldom acknowledged. Not only are women of color in fact overlooked, but their exclusion is reinforced when *white* women speak for and as *women*. The authoritative universal voice—usually white male subjectivity masquerading as non-racial, non-gendered objectivity—is merely transferred to those who, but for gender, share many of the same cultural, economic and social characteristics. When feminist theory attempts to describe women's experiences through analyzing patriarchy, sexuality, or separate spheres ideology, it often overlooks the role of race. Feminists thus ignore how their own race functions to mitigate some aspects of sexism and, moreover, how it often privileges them over and contributes to the domination of other women.[20] Consequently, feminist theory remains *white*, and its potential to broaden and deepen its analysis by addressing non-privileged women remains unrealized.

...

Because ideological and descriptive definitions of patriarchy are usually premised upon white female experiences, feminists and others informed by feminist literature may make the mistake of assuming that since the role of Black women in the family and in other Black institutions does not always resemble the familiar manifestations of patriarchy in the white community, Black women are somehow exempt from patriarchal norms. For example, Black women have traditionally worked outside the home in numbers far exceeding the labor participation rate of white women.[21] An analysis of patriarchy that highlights the history of white women's exclusion from the workplace might permit the inference that Black women have not been burdened by this particular gender-based expectation. Yet the very fact that Black women must work conflicts with norms that women should not, often creating personal, emotional and relationship problems in Black women's lives. Thus, Black women are burdened not only because they often have to take on responsibilities that are not traditionally female but, moreover, their assumption of these roles is sometimes interpreted within the Black community as either Black women's failure to live up to such norms or as another manifestation of racism's scourge upon the Black community.[22] This is one of the many aspects of intersectionality that cannot be understood through an analysis of patriarchy rooted in white experience.

Another example of how theory emanating from a white context obscures the multidimensionality of Black women's lives is found in feminist discourse on rape. A central political issue on the feminist agenda has been the pervasive problem of rape. Part of the intellectual and political effort to mobilize around this issue has involved the development of a historical critique of the role that law has played in establishing the bounds of normative sexuality and in regulating female sexual behavior.[23] Early carnal knowledge statutes and rape laws are understood within this discourse to illustrate that the objective of rape statutes traditionally has not been to protect women from coercive intimacy but to protect and maintain a property-like interest in female chastity.[24] Although feminists quite rightly criticize these objectives, to characterize rape law as reflecting male control over female sexuality is for Black women an oversimplified account and an ultimately inadequate account.

Rape statutes generally do not reflect *male* control over *female* sexuality, but *white* male regulation of *white* female sexuality.[25] Historically, there has been absolutely no institutional effort to regulate Black female chastity.[26] Courts in some states had gone so far as to instruct juries that, unlike white women, Black women were not presumed to be chaste.[27] Also, while it was true that the attempt to regulate the sexuality of white women placed unchaste women outside the law's protection, racism restored a fallen white woman's chastity where the alleged assailant was a Black man.[28] No such restoration was available to Black women.

The singular focus on rape as a manifestation of male power over female sexuality tends to eclipse the use of rape as a weapon of racial terror.[29] When Black women were raped by white males, they were being raped not as women generally, but as Black women specifically: Their femaleness made them sexually vulnerable to racist domination, while their Blackness effectively denied them any protection. This white male power was reinforced by a judicial system in which the successful conviction of a white man for raping a Black woman was virtually unthinkable.

In sum, sexist expectations of chastity and racist assumptions of sexual promiscuity combined to create a distinct set of issues confronting Black women.[30] These issues have seldom been explored in feminist literature nor are they prominent in antiracist politics. The lynching of Black males, the institutional practice that was legitimized by the regulation of white women's sexuality, has hitorically and contemporaneously occupied the Black agenda on sexuality and violence. Consequently, Black women are caught between a Black community that, perhaps understandably, views with suspicion attempts to litigate questions of sexual violence, and a feminist community that reinforces those suspicions by focusing on white female sexuality.[31] The suspicion is compounded by the historical fact that the protection of white female sexuality was often the pretext for terrorizing the Black community. Even today some fear that antirape agendas may undermine antiracist objectives. This is the paradigmatic political and theoretical dilemma created by the intersection of race and gender: Black women are caught between ideological and political currents that combine first to create and then to bury Black women's experiences.

. . .

## Expanding Feminist Theory and Antiracist Politics by Embracing the Intersection

If any real efforts are to be made to free Black people of the constraints and conditions that characterize racial subordination, then theories and strategies purporting to reflect the Black community's needs must include an analysis of sexism and patriarchy. Similarly, feminism must include an analysis of race if it hopes to express the aspirations of non-white women. Neither Black liberationist politics nor feminist theory can ignore the intersectional experiences of those whom the movements claim as their respective constituents. In order to include Black women, both movements must distance themselves from earlier approaches in which experiences are relevant only when they are related to certain clearly identifiable causes (for example, the oppression of Blacks is significant when based on race, of women when based on gender). The praxis of both should be centered on the life chances and life situations of people who should be cared about without regard to the source of their difficulties.

I have stated earlier that the failure to embrace the complexities of compoundedness is not simply a matter of political will, but is also due to the influence of a way of thinking about discrimination which structures politics so that struggles are categorized as singular issues. Moreover, this structure imports a descriptive and normative view of society that reinforces the status quo.

It is somewhat ironic that those concerned with alleviating the ills of racism and sexism should adopt such a top-down approach to discrimination. If their efforts instead began with addressing the needs and problems of those who are most disadvantaged and with restructuring and remaking the world where necessary, then others who are singularly disadvantaged would also benefit. In addition, it seems that placing those who currently are marginalized in the center is the most effective way to resist efforts to compartmentalize experiences and undermine potential collective action.

It is not necessary to believe that a political consensus to focus on the lives of the most disadvantaged will happen tomorrow in order to recenter the discrimination discourse at the intersection. It is enough, for now, that such an effort would encourage us to look beneath the prevailing conceptions of discrimination and to challenge the complacency that accompanies belief in the effectiveness of this framework. By so doing, we may develop language which is critical of the dominant view and which provides some basis for unifying activity. The goal of this activity should be to facilitate the inclusion of marginalized groups for whom it can be said: "When they enter, we all enter."

---

## Notes

1. Gloria T. Hull, et al, eds (The Feminist Press, 1982).

2. The most common linguistic manifestation of this analytical dilemma is represented in the conventional usage of the term "Blacks and women." Although it may be true that some people mean to include Black women in either "Blacks" or "women," the context in which the term is used actually suggests that often Black women are not considered. See, for example, Elizabeth Spelman, *The Inessential Woman* 114–15 (Beacon Press, 1988) (discussing an article on Blacks and women in the military where "the racial identity of those identified as 'women' does not become explicit until reference is made to Black women, at which point it also becomes clear that the category of women excludes Black women"). It seems that if Black women were explicitly included, the preferred term would be either "Blacks and white women" or "Black men and all women."

3. Civil Rights Act of 1964, 42 USC & 2000e, et seq as amended (1982).

4. 413 F Supp 142 (E D Mo 1976).

5. 708 F2d 475 (9th Cir 1983).

6. 673 F2d 798 (5th Cir 1982).

7. *De Graffenreid*, 413 F Supp at 143.

8. Id at 144.

9. Id at 145. In *Mosley v General Motors*, 497 F Supp 583 (E D Mo 1980), plaintiffs, alleging broad-based racial discrimination at General Motors' St. Louis facility, prevailed in a portion of their Title VII claim. The seniority system challenged in *DeGraffenreid*, however, was not considered in *Mosley*.

10. 708 F2d 475.

11. See also *Moore v National Association of Securities Dealers*, 27 EPD (CCH) ¶ 32,238 (D DC 1981); but see *Edmondson v Simon*, 86 FRD 375 (N D Ill 1980) (where the court was unwilling to hold as a matter of law that no Black female could represent without conflict the interests of both Blacks and females).

12. 708 F2d at 479. Between January 1976 and June 1979, the three years in which Moore claimed that she was passed over the promotion, the percentage of white males occupying first-level supervisory positions ranged from 70.3 to 76.8%; Black males from 8.9 to 10.9%; white women from 1.8 to 3.3%; and Black females from 0 to 2.2%. The overall male/female ratio in the top five labor grades ranged from 100/0% in 1976 to 98/1.8% in 1979. The white/Black ratio was 85/3.3% in 1976 and 79.6/8% in 1979. The overall ratio of men to women in supervisory positions was 98.2 to 1.8% in 1976 to 93.4 to 6.6% in 1979; the Black to white ratio during the same time period was 78.6 to 8.9% and 73.6 to 13.1%.

For promotions to the top five labor grades, the percentages were worse. Between 1976 and 1979, the percentage of white males in these positions ranged from 85.3 to 77.9%; Black males 3.3 to 8%; white females from 0 to 1.4%, and Black females from 0 to 0%. Overall, in 1979, 98.2% of the highest level employees were male; 1.8% were female.

13. 708 F2d at 480 (emphasis added).

14. See *Strong v Arkansas Blue Cross & Blue Shield, Inc.*, 87 FRD 496 (E D Ark 1980); *Hammons v Folger Coffee Co.*, 87 FRD 600 (W D Mo 1980); *Edmondson v Simon*, 86 FRD 375 (N D Ill 1980); *Vuyanich v Republic National Bank of Dallas*, 82 FRD (N D Tex 1979); *Colston v Maryland Cup Corp.*, 26 Fed Rules Serv 940 (D Md 1978).

15. 416 F Supp 248 (N D Miss 1976).

16. The suit commenced on March 2, 1972, with the filing of a complaint by three employees seeking to represent a class of persons allegedly subjected to racial discrimination at the hands of the defendants. Subsequently, the plaintiffs amended the complaint to add an allegation of sex discrimination. Of the original named plaintiffs, one was a Black male and two were Black females. In the course of the three-year period between the filing of the complaint and the trial, the only named male plaintiff received permission of the court to withdraw for religious reasons. Id at 250.

17. As the dissent in *Travenol* pointed out, there was no reason to exclude Black males from the scope of the remedy *after* counsel had presented sufficient evidence to support a finding of discrimination against Black men. If the rationale for excluding Black males was the potential conflict between Black males and Black females, then "[i]n this case, to paraphrase an old adage, the proof of plaintiffs' ability to represent the interests of Black males was in the representation thereof." 673 F2d at 837–38.

18. In much of antidiscrimination doctrine, the presence of intent to discriminate distinguishes unlawful from lawful discrimination. See *Washington v Davis*, 426 US 229, 239–45 (1976) (proof of discriminatory purposes required to substantiate Equal Protection violation). Under Title VII, however, the Court has held that statistical data showing a disproportionate impact can suffice to support a finding of discrimination. See *Griggs*, 401 US at 432. Whether the distinction between the two analyses will survive is an open question. See *Wards Cove Packing Co., Inc. v Atonio*, 109 S Ct 2115, 2122–23 (1989) (plaintiffs must show more than mere disparity to support a prima facie case of disparate impact). For a discussion of the competing normative visions that underlie the intent and effects analyses, see Alan David Freeman, *Legitimizing Racial Discrimination Through Antidiscrimination Law: A Critical Review of Supreme Court Doctrine*, 62 Minn L Rev 1049 (1978).

19. Eleanor Flexner, *Century of Struggle: The Women's Rights Movement in the United States* 91 (Belknap Press of Harvard University Press, 1975). See also Bell Hooks, *Ain't I a Woman* 159–60 (South End Press, 1981).

20. For example, many white females were able to gain entry into previously all white male enclaves not through bringing about a fundamental reordering of male versus female work, but in large part by shifting their "female" responsibilities to poor and minority women.

21. See generally Jacqueline Jones, *Labor of Love, Labor of Sorrow: Black Women, Work, and the Family from Slavery to the Present* (Basic Books, 1985); Angela Davis, *Women, Race and Class* (Random House, 1981).

22. As Elizabeth Higginbotham noted, "women, who often fail to conform to 'appropriate' sex roles, have been pictured as, and made to feel, inadequate—even though as women, they possess traits recognized as positive when held by men in the wider society. Such women are stigmatized because their lack of adherence to expected gender roles is seen as a threat to the value system." Elizabeth Higginbotham, *Two Representative Issues in Contemporary Sociological Work on Black Women*, in Hull, et al, eds, *But Some of Us Are Brave* at 95 (cited in note 1).

23. See generally Susan Brownmiller, *Against Our Will* (Simon and Schuster, 1975); Susan Estrich, *Real Rape* (Harvard University Press, 1987).

24. See Brownmiller, *Against Our Will* at 17; see generally Estrich, *Real Rape*.

25. One of the central theoretical dilemmas of feminism that is largely obscured by universalizing the white female experience is that experiences that are described as a manifestation of male control over females can be instead a manifestation of dominant group control over all subordinates. The significance is that other nondominant men may not share in, participate in or connect with the behavior, beliefs or actions at issue, and may be victimized themselves by "male" power. In other contexts, however, "male authority" might include nonwhite men, particularly in private sphere contexts. Efforts to think more clearly about when Black women are dominated as *women* and when they are dominated as *Black women* are directly related to the question of when power is *male* and when it is *white male*.

26. See Note, *Rape, Racism and the Law,* 6 Harv Women's L J 103, 117–23 (1983) (discussing the historical and contemporary evidence suggesting that Black women are generally not thought to be chaste). See also Hooks, *Ain't I a Woman* at 54 (cited in note 19) (stating that stereotypical images of Black womanhood during slavery were based on the myth that "all black women were immoral and sexually loose"); Beverly Smith, *Black Women's Health: Notes for a Course,* in Hull et al, eds, *But Some of Us Are Brave* at 110 (cited in note 1) (noting that "… white men for centuries have justified their sexual abuse of Black women by claiming that we are licentious, always 'ready' for any sexual encounter").

27. The following statement is probably unusual only in its candor: "What has been said by some of our courts about an unchaste female being a comparatively rare exception is no doubt true where the population is composed largely of the Caucasian race, but we would blind ourselves to actual conditions if we adopted this rule where another race that is largely immoral constitutes an appreciable part of the population." *Dallas v State,* 76 Fla 358, 79 So 690 (1918), quoted in Note, 6 Harv Women's L J at 121 (cited in note 26).

Espousing precisely this view, one commentator stated in 1902: "I sometimes hear of a virtuous Negro woman but the idea is so absolutely inconceivable to me … I cannot imagine such a creature as a virtuous Negro woman." Id at 82. Such images persist in popular culture. See Paul Grein, *Taking Stock of the Latest Pop Record Surprises,* LA Times § 6 at 1 (July 7, 1988) (recalling the controversy in the late 70s over a Rolling Stones recording which included the line "Black girls just wanna get fucked all night")…

28. Because the way the legal system viewed chastity, Black women could not be victims of forcible rape. One commentator has noted that "[a]ccording to governing [stereotypes], chastity could not be possessed by Black women. Thus, Black women's rape charges were automatically discounted, and the issue of chastity was contested only in cases where the rape complainant was a white woman." Note, 6 Harv Women's L J at 126 (cited in note 26). Black women's claims of rape were not taken seriously regardless of the offender's race. A judge in 1912 said: "This court will never take the word of a nigger against the word of a white man [concerning rape]." Id at 120. On the other hand, lynching was considered an effective remedy for a Black man's rape of a white woman. Since rape of a white woman by a Black man was "a crime more horrible than death," the only way to assuage society's rage and to make the woman whole again was to brutally murder the Black man. Id at 125.

29. See *The Rape of Black Women as a Weapon of Terror,* in Gerda Lerner, ed, *Black Women in White America* 172–93 (Pantheon Books, 1972). See also Brownmiller, *Against Our Will* (cited in note 23). Even where Brownmiller acknowledges the use of rape as racial terrorism, she resists making a "special case" for Black women by offering evidence that white women were raped by the Klan as well. Id at 139. Whether or not one considers the racist rape of Black women a "special case," such experiences are probably different. In any case, Brownmiller's treatment of the issue raises serious questions about the ability to sustain an analysis of patriarchy without understanding its multiple intersections with racism.

30. Paula Giddings notes the combined effect of sexual and racial stereotypes: "Black women were seen having all of the inferior qualities of white women without any of their virtues." Giddings, *When and Where I Enter: The Impact of Black Women on Race and Sex in America* 82 (William Morrow and Co, Inc, 1st ed 1984).

31. Susan Brownmiller's treatment of the Emmett Till case illustrates why antirape politicization makes some African Americans uncomfortable. Despite Brownmiller's quite laudable efforts to discuss elsewhere the rape of Black women and the racism involved in much of the hysteria over the Black male threat, her analysis of the Till case places the sexuality of white women, rather than racial terrorism, at center stage. Brownmiller states: "Rarely has one single case exposed so clearly as Till's the underlying group-male antagonisms over access to women, for what began in Bryant's store should not be misconstrued as an innocent flirtation. ... In concrete terms, the accessibility of all white women was on review." Brownmiller, *Against Our Will* at 272 (cited in note 23). ...

# PART TWO

# WOMEN WORKING

Since the late 1960s, many of the most intense and even bitter debates concerning feminism have raged around issues of women and work. Much antifeminist sentiment has been fueled by the perception that contemporary Western feminists are concerned primarily with securing high-paying, high-prestige jobs in the marketplace and are scornful of the work traditionally performed by women in the home—work such as cooking, cleaning, gardening, and caring for children, the sick, and the old. Even though this perception of feminist priorities has been relentlessly promoted by the antifeminist media, it does, like most stereotypes, contain a kernel of truth. At the beginning of this wave of feminism, when it was taken for granted not only that marriage was the destiny of most women but also that married women should assume the primary responsibility for childrearing and housekeeping, relying for economic support on their breadwinning husbands, middle-class feminist leaders were preoccupied with challenging this gendered division of labor. Their arguments emphasized women's aptitude for political and professional leadership—debunking the "raging hormones" theory of female instability, for instance—and asserted the injustice of discriminating against women in any area of paid employment. Feminists did regularly note that men were capable of learning—or being trained to—domestic competence, but this was a subordinate theme. The tone of much, though not all, feminist writing in the late 1960s and early 1970s suggested that work in the home was menial and unrewarding.

Challenges to these assumptions quickly emerged both from outside and inside feminism. Women who had been compelled by economic circumstances to work outside as well as inside their homes—and who included disproportionate numbers of women of color—pointed out that the opportunity to stay at home could be a privilege as well as a trap. Meanwhile, other women who had devoted their lives to the care of their husbands, children, and homes expressed understandable resentment at suggestions that their sacrifices had been unchosen and their contributions unnecessary or insignificant. Feminists' perceived contempt for domestic work generated accusations that Western feminism measured individual fulfillment as well as social contribution in terms that were class biased, race biased, individualistic, masculine—or all of these at once.

Feminists in the 1970s responded to these accusations in several ways. Some began a revaluation of domestic work. Liberal feminists, for instance, began to extol the importance of individual choice, arguing that the options of working outside or inside the home or of arranging some mutually satisfactory combination should be available equally to women and men in heterosexual couples. Many Marxist feminists engaged in a rather esoteric debate about whether domestic work was "productive" in the technical Marxist sense of producing surplus value. Meanwhile, some radical feminists rediscovered the value of women's traditional work, and some socialist feminists argued in favor of pay for housework, though this strategy was always more popular in Europe than in North America since a much larger proportion of European women remained outside the paid labor force.

In addition to revaluing domestic work, feminists also developed a more critical attitude toward women's work outside the home. For instance, they began to explore the ways in which a gendered division of labor occurs not only between paid and unpaid work but also within paid employment. They were especially interested in examining divisions between conventionally "male" and "female" occupations and, on a more subtle level, the ways in which gender expectations assert themselves even within occupations. For instance, feminists explored the inexplicit but nevertheless unavoidable expectation that women in many paid occupations should, in addition to their official job descriptions, perform emotional and/or sexual labor such as caring for people's feelings and making men feel sexually powerful. Some radical feminists sought to develop opportunities for working in enterprises that undermined, rather than perpetuated, values associated with capitalism and male dominance.

With the arrival of the 1990s, the attention of many feminists has moved away from the issues that preoccupied us twenty or even ten years ago. This shift is partly due to changing economic circumstances, which allow the option of staying at home to fewer and fewer women. When more than half of all women with children younger than six work outside as well as inside the home, the question of whether mothers should engage in paid labor becomes moot. The shift in contemporary feminist concerns is also due to a changing cultural and political climate: few feminists are any longer inclined to force their theory into an orthodox Marxist framework, and many radical feminist enterprises have been forced by market realities to compromise some of their more idealistic principles. Within the United States, cutbacks in public spending have transformed the wages for housework debate into a debate over mothers' rights to welfare: should mothers on welfare be forced to work outside the home, and should their benefits be cut or terminated if they have more children while on welfare?

Finally, a number of issues around women and work are no longer alive because twenty-five years of feminist activism have resulted in some significant victories, at least in North America. Sex-segregated job advertisements have been outlawed, sex discrimination in hiring and pay scales is illegal, sexual harassment has been legally recognized as a form of sex discrimination, and the more blatant symbols of the sexualization of female workers have been eliminated, at least in some occupations. For instance, airlines have been forced to relax the stringent weight, age, and dress restrictions placed on female flight attendants.

None of this should be taken to suggest that most feminist concerns around women's work have now been resolved. The wage labor force remains sex segregated; the jobs available to most women are increasingly low paying, insecure, unrewarding, and often hazardous; the gendered wage gap persists; sexual harassment remains rampant; and typical career patterns and even the working day are still structured on the assumption that the normal worker has a wife at home to take care of his domestic needs and responsibilities. In consequence, many U.S. feminists today work actively on issues such as family leave policies, which are designed to protect the jobs of either men or women needing leave from their employment to care for an ailing family member.

Despite the urgency of these work-related problems, they are not explored in this book because most feminists agree not only on their importance but also on what should be done to remedy them. Within feminism, though not outside it, these are not particularly controversial issues. I have instead chosen issues more controversial among feminists for this part on women working.

## Affirmative Action and Comparable Worth

One of the issues addressed here is that of affirmative action—otherwise known as the issue of preferential treatment or even reverse discrimination. This issue has been around for a long time; indeed, the expression "affirmative action" was used originally in the context of President Lyndon Johnson's Executive Order 11246, which required that all institutions doing business with the federal government or receiving federal grants refrain from direct racial, sexual, or religious discrimination and also take "affirmative action to ensure that applicants are employed, and that employees are treated during their employment, without regard to their race, color, religion, sex, or national origin." Affirmative action is now used more generally to refer to any institutional policy designed to open up fields dominated by white, able-bodied males to individuals previously excluded from those fields.

Within the United States, affirmative action is usually taken to include advertising available positions in places where women of all races or ethnicities and male members of U.S. racial or ethnic minorities are likely to see them, together with public assurances that nonracist and nonsexist criteria will be used in evaluating candidates. In addition, affirmative action is sometimes interpreted as requiring that specific numbers of U.S. minorities or white women be hired within a definite time period to make the numbers appointed proportional to their numbers in the pool of applicants. However, affirmative action in the United States does not require or even permit specific populations to be hired according to rigid quotas, nor does it allow a less qualified white woman or member of a U.S. minority to be hired in preference to a white male. It does support hiring white women or members of U.S. racial or ethnic minorities on occasions where their qualifications are equal with those of the best-qualified white males.

Affirmative action has always been controversial because it is easily construed as a violation of precisely those principles of meritocratic justice to which feminists, among others, often appeal. Since the early 1970s, moreover, there has been a contraction in the number of manufacturing jobs available in many of the longer-industrialized nations, jobs held traditionally by white—and sometimes Black—men, and a corresponding expansion in the number of service and clerical jobs conventionally defined as female. Male unemployment, in consequence, has risen sharply, while female employment has increased. Many white men have been traumatized by unemployment, which they often experience as a threat to their masculinity, and they have sometimes responded by attacking affirmative action, charging that white women and members of U.S. racial and ethnic minorities are taking "their" jobs. Meanwhile, many younger women, often unknowing beneficiaries of earlier feminist activism, have not experienced the kinds of blatant discrimination suffered by their mothers. They believe that they are now stigmatized by affirmative action and argue that the time for these programs has passed.

Anyone engaged for many years in the debate over affirmative action experiences an overwhelming sense of déjà vu. Few new points are made, and the same arguments are constantly recycled. The two articles selected to represent conflicting feminist views on affirmative action date from the 1970s, but their arguments remain salient even today.

Affirmative action remains so controversial that feminists fighting for it may sometimes forget its limitations as a strategy for ending women's inferior position in the labor force. These limitations hinge on the inability of affirmative action to challenge the assumption that man is still the measure of all things. Catharine MacKinnon has forcefully expressed the limits of affirmative action as it is ordinarily understood by noting that "virtually every quality that distinguishes men from women is already affirmatively compensated in this society." Thus, affirmative action is able to help only women who have succeeded in constructing what MacKinnon calls "a biography that somewhat approximates the male norm, at least on paper." Such women, she notes, are actually those who have been damaged least by male dominance. In addition, affirmative action does nothing to challenge the persistent undervaluing of jobs held predominantly by women.

Comparable worth is a feminist strategy designed to address precisely this problem. Also known as pay equity, comparable worth means that jobs deemed to be of "equal value to the employer" should pay the same, regardless of their sex or race typing. The first wage comparability case before the courts was based on race. However, subsequent attempts to apply the U.S. Civil Rights Act of 1964 to nonidentical jobs have focused on wage differences originating from gender-based job segregation.

The first selection on this topic, a statement from the National Committee on Pay Equity, offers an overview of women's situation in the labor force and a brief statement of the social benefits thought likely to result from implementing pay equity. This statement is followed immediately by "An Argument Against Comparable Worth," an article opposing pay equity because it violates the principles of a market economy. June O'Neill, author of this article, argues that the existing pay differential between male and female workers is due less to discrimination against women than to such facts as (1) women tend to be less qualified than men, (2) women have chosen to put homemaking and child care before paid jobs, and (3) women choose jobs compatible with domestic responsibilities. She does acknowledge that some degree of employment discrimination against women exists but asserts that its exact contribution to the sex pay differential cannot be measured. O'Neill goes on to argue that disrupting the market determination of wages by introducing comparable worth would likely result in unemployment for many women workers, reinforcement of the sex segregation of the labor force, and diversion of attention from genuine discrimination against women. She concludes that comparable worth is likely to work against feminism's goal of ending women's inferior situation in the labor force.

In "Some Implications of Comparable Worth," Laurie Shrage defends comparable worth not only against proponents of the market, like O'Neill, but also against critics from the Left, who charge that the standards used for evaluating the relative worth of various jobs reflect an elitist bias and will not help those workers most in need, whose jobs are calculated to have the least worth. In response to O'Neill, who asserts that wages are currently determined by the operation of a free market in which discrimination plays a small, perhaps negligible, part, Schrage develops the concept of structural or institutional discrimination. In response to leftist critics, who complain that comparable worth fails to address issues of workers' needs while reinforcing elitist notions of which kinds of work are more valuable, Schrage notes that comparable worth does not endorse class-biased measures of the worth of a job but merely demands that accepted standards of reward not be applied in a racist or sexist way. Although comparable worth is not in itself revolutionary, it is likely to have some impact on the feminization of poverty, which perpetuates women's domestic subordination. In addition, it challenges the economic domination of the market and may encourage a revaluation of the worth of women's work in the home.

Part of the disagreement between those who endorse comparable worth and those who reject it stems from incompatible understandings of what counts as a free choice. Those who reject comparable worth emphasize the sense in which many women workers have chosen predominantly female occupations, whereas those who endorse comparable worth emphasize the constraints on these women's choices and the limited options available to them. Indeed, conventional notions of choice and consent are debated by feminists in many practical arenas, one of which is women's alleged choice to engage in sex work.

## Sex Work

The second issue discussed in this part is that of sex work, especially prostitution. Western feminists have been concerned about prostitution at least since the nineteenth century, and typically their concern has been to find ways of getting rid of it. Feminists are not alone in their disapproval of prostitution, of course, but feminist criticisms should be distinguished from conventional condemnations of this institution insofar as they link sex work directly with the subordination of women, whether as cause, consequence, or symbol.

Conventional North American and European criticisms of prostitution often rest on certain assumptions about sexual activity: that sex outside marriage is wrong or sinful or that sex should occur only in the context of love and affection, so that engaging in sexual activity for payment is degrading and alienating. Some nonfeminist criticisms of prostitution even assume that sex itself is dirty and disgusting, so that prostitution degrades both participants. Conventional opinion typically blames the prostitute for the existence of prostitution and often views her as sinful, degraded, and diseased. Although she is sometimes portrayed in romantic fiction as having a "heart of gold," the prostitute is regarded conventionally as unscrupulously exploiting men's "normal" sexual desires for her own gain, thus justifying the use of "whore" and "tart" as common epithets.

Feminists, by contrast, have usually perceived prostitutes as victims forced into prostitution through a variety of forms of social coercion, of which the most obvious is economic necessity. Asserting that prostitutes are motivated by economic need is not in itself distinctively feminist, of course, nor does it distinguish prostitution from many other kinds of work performed from economic motivation. The claim that women are economically forced into prostitution becomes feminist only when the supply of female prostitutes is seen as a consequence of gendered discrimination in employment, which limits women's opportunities for other kinds of work.

In addition to economic necessity, feminists identify a number of other gendered factors forcing women into prostitution or preventing them from leaving. For instance, feminists charge that female prostitutes are controlled—sometimes even enslaved— by male pimps and panderers, who exploit their sexuality. These critics add that many, if not most, female prostitutes are survivors of childhood sexual abuse, which has taught them sexual submission and encouraged them to believe that their only value lies in sexual service. These are not necessarily feminist arguments because exploitation, enslavement, and childhood sexual abuse may be suffered by males as well as females. They become feminist in the context of a social analysis that links the social construction of masculinity and femininity with norms of sexual dominance and subordination. According to these norms, supposedly internalized by both men and women, men are entitled to sexual access to and control of women. This cultural analysis helps explain why twice as many girls as boys are sexually abused and why the abusers are usually heterosexual men. Extending this analysis, some feminists argue that all girls, even those who have not been subjected to what is ordinarily defined as sexual abuse, have been "primed" for prostitution insofar as feminine socialization takes the form of sexualizing girls in this gender-specific way.

Given this analysis of contemporary sexuality, feminists have typically been unwilling to accept the lines conventionally drawn between "good" and "bad" women, madonnas and whores. They have pointed to the sexual element evident in many ostensibly nonsexual female occupations as well as in marriages where the wife depends on her husband for economic support. A common European and North American feminist attitude toward prostitutes has been "There but for the grace of the goddess go I," and feminists traditionally have been concerned with finding ways of "rescuing" or "rehabilitating" prostitutes.

Feminists justify their wish to "save" women from prostitution partly on the grounds that prostitution is a highly dangerous as well as conventionally disreputable occupation: Prostitutes are frequently beaten, raped, and murdered. Other occupations are dangerous, too, of course, but some feminists argue that the dangers encountered by prostitutes are distinctively gendered insofar as they are deliberate, rather than accidental, inspired directly by hatred of women.

Finally, many feminists oppose the institution of prostitution because it reinforces the subordination even of those women not directly involved in it. It confirms male-dominant conceptions of masculinity, femininity, and sexuality, according to which normal male sexuality is expressed as a physical drive to dominate women, while women exist primarily for male sexual enjoyment. In addition, the existence of prostitution operates as a threat to control all women's heterosexual activity: whereas a man's status often rises if he "has" many women, a woman who "is had" by a number of men becomes stigmatized as a whore.

Although feminists have historically condemned prostitution, recent years have seen prostitution or sex work revalidated on explicitly feminist grounds. Some prostitutes are now asserting their identity as feminists and arguing for the dignity of both their work and themselves as sex workers. They claim that prostitution is a better job than most other jobs available to women because it provides good pay for short hours and considerable control over the work environment. The prostitute decides what she will and will not do and with whom she will or will not do it. She gets paid for what other women give for free and has far more independence than a typical wife. The alleged advantages of this occupation lend credence to prostitutes' assertions that they have made a free decision to take it up.

Some prostitutes defend prostitution as a highly skilled occupation, sometimes a kind of entertainment or artistry in which the workers define what is erotic, express their own sexuality and creativity, and derive a sense of empowerment. On other occasions, they present prostitution as sex therapy in a nonjudgmental context, a valuable service that, far from being distinctively gendered, should also be available to women.

Rather than reinforcing conventional views about sexuality, some prostitutes assert that prostitution undermines narrow sexual values by validating extramarital sex, anonymous sex, recreational sex, and sexual novelty and variety. It challenges the male-dominant stereotype that women should have only one sexual partner, and rather than undermining the status and dignity of all women, prostitution confers benefits on nonprostitute women because, judged by conventional values, they look good by comparison.

Denying the traditional feminist assumption that prostitutes have been forced into their trade, some prostitutes now insist that they have chosen this occupation freely and challenge the "matronizing" attitude implicit in the traditional feminist desire to rescue or rehabilitate them. These prostitutes reject feminist assertions that they are controlled by male pimps; some prostitutes live with women, and if they do live with men, these men may be their lovers. They point out that laws against pimping in effect operate to isolate prostitutes socially and deprive them of intimate companions. They reject as similarly "maternalistic" feminist proposals to ban prostitution for the protection of the prostitutes. Other hazardous occupations are not banned, and even though it is true that prostitutes are often attacked, so are other women. Indeed, most battering occurs, some prostitutes assert, in the context of long-term relationships. Prostitutes argue that the violence they endure is mostly a result of the low status of their occupation and the legal restrictions on it, which they view as a form of sex discrimination. Women's rights to freedom of speech and movement should allow them to solicit and stand on street corners. After all, other businesses advertise, and women's solicitations are much less threatening than men's—which are ubiquitous.

Most of these arguments can be found in the selections on prostitution included in this book. The first one, "Prostitution," written by me in the late 1970s, offers an overview of three contrasting feminist attitudes toward prostitution: the liberal feminist, the Marxist feminist, and the radical feminist. My article does not include feminist defenses of sex work as highly skilled, creative, and socially valuable, claims that entered feminist discourse only in the 1980s.

The next two articles are both written by women engaged in sex work. In "A Most Useful Tool," Sunny Carter describes how working as a prostitute provided the time and money necessary to support her son, who had cystic fibrosis, and Debi Sundahl, a women's studies major while in college and a long-time feminist activist, narrates in "Stripper" how she moved from stripping for men to stripping for women. Both writers emphasize that their work is not only lucrative but also skilled, often therapeutic for the clients, and personally rewarding.

By contrast with this portrayal of prostitutes as talented women who are admirably independent of men, Evelina Giobbe argues, in "Confronting the Liberal Lies About Prostitution," that women are forced into prostitution by the whole structure of male-dominant society, with women of color being especially vulnerable to these pressures. She asserts that "prostitution isn't like anything else. Rather, everything else is like prostitution because it is the model for women's condition."

Carole Pateman develops this theme in "What's Wrong with Prostitution?" disputing the claim often made by both liberals and Marxists that prostitution is no better or worse than any other employment contract or the sale of any other service. Prostitution is different from all other jobs or services, Pateman argues, because nothing is an acceptable substitute for the body of a living woman. Unlike other economic transactions, the whole person is necessarily involved in prostitution because, though people's identities are not reducible to their bodies, neither are they entirely separable from them. Pateman asserts that contemporary masculine and feminine gender identities are constructed around the norms of sexual dominance and subordination and argues that it is therefore simplistic to regard prostitution as a simple economic transaction between two individuals who happen to be male and female. Instead, the existence of prostitution as an institution provides public confirmation of the construction of men as sexual masters and women, even or perhaps especially willing women, as the sexual subordinates or even sexual slaves of men. Prostitution thus harms all women, even those who are not involved in it directly.

In contrast with these principled feminist criticisms of prostitution, many prostitutes have asserted that the main problem with prostitution is not the nature of the work but rather the laws that interfere with prostitutes' practice of their trade. Rather than perceiving prostitution as expressing and reinforcing women's subordination, such prostitutes argue that it is the laws interfering with the practice of their trade that discriminate against them. Laws against advertising, for instance, force prostitutes onto the street, where laws against solicitation violate their freedom of expression without threatening men's freedom to harass women. Laws against brothels make it possible for landlords to blackmail prostitutes, and laws against pimping deprive them of domestic companionship. Labeling women as prostitutes deprives them of many civil rights; such women may lose custody of their children, be deported if they are immigrants, lose the chance of any other employment so that they are trapped in prostitution, and be refused entry to other countries either as tourists or immigrants. The final selection on prostitution, "International Committee for Prostitutes' Rights World Charter and World Whores' Congress Statements," by the International Committee for Prostitutes' Rights, therefore explores various remedies for such forms of legal discrimination against prostitutes. It discusses these remedies in the broader social context of women's, children's, and human rights.

Feminist reflections on prostitution raise a variety of difficult conceptual and ethical questions. Is the sale of sexual services morally different from the sale of other services? Is sexual objectification harmless in certain contexts? What is a free choice? How do we recognize self-deception? When do social constraints become coercive? Which decisions are private, and which are political? How is gender produced and reproduced through our daily activities? What is collaboration with the subordination of women, and what is resistance to it? How do we negotiate in a context of limited options and with institutions that may have simultaneously repressive and emancipatory aspects? How, in short, do we live with the contradictions of female sex work?

### References

Catharine A. MacKinnon. "Difference and Dominance." In *Discourses on Life and Law*, 36. Cambridge, Mass.: Harvard University Press, 1987.

# Section A:
## Affirmative Action and Comparable Worth

# *Reverse Discrimination as Unjustified*

## Lisa H. Newton

I have heard it argued that "simple justice" requires that we favor women and blacks in employment and educational opportunities, since women and blacks were "unjustly" excluded from such opportunities for so many years in the not so distant past. It is a strange argument, an example of a possible implication of a true proposition advanced to dispute the proposition itself, like an octopus absent-mindely slicing off his head with a stray tentacle. A fatal confusion underlies this argument, a confusion fundamentally relevant to our understanding of the notion of the rule of law.

Two senses of justice and equality are involved in this confusion. ... It is important for my argument that the moral ideal of equality be recognized as logically distinct from that condition (or virtue) of justice in the political sense. Justice in this sense exists *among* a citizenry, irrespective of the number of the populace included in that citizenry. Further, the moral ideal is parasitic upon the political virtue, for "equality" is unspecified—it means nothing until we are told in what respect that equality is to be realized. In a political context, *equality* is specified as "equal rights"—equal access to the public realm, public goods and offices, equal treatment under the law—in brief, the equality of citizenship. If citizenship is not a possibility, political equality is unintelligible. The ideal emerges as a generalization of the real condition and refers back to that condition for its content.

Now, if justice ... is equal treatment under law for all citizens, what is injustice? Clearly, injustice is the violation of that equality, discriminating for or against a group of citizens, favoring them with special immunities and privileges or depriving them of those guaranteed to the others. When the southern employer refuses to hire blacks in white-collar jobs, when Wall Street will hire women only as secretaries with new titles, when Mississippi high schools routinely flunk all black boys above ninth grade, we have examples of injustice, and we work to restore the equality of the public realm by ensuring that equal opportunity will be provided in such cases in the future. But of course, when the employers and the schools *favor* women and blacks, the same injustice is done. Just as the previous discrimination did, this reverse discrimination violates the public equality which defines citizenship and destroys the rule of law for the areas in which these favors are granted. To the extent that we adopt a program of discrimination, reverse or otherwise, justice in the political sense is destroyed, and none of us, specifically affected or not, is a citizen, a bearer of rights— we are all petitioners for favors. And to the same extent, the ideal of equality is undermined, for it has content only where justice obtains, and by destroying justice we render the ideal meaningless. It is, then, an ironic paradox, if not a contradiction in terms, to assert that the ideal of equality justifies the violation of justice; it is as if one should argue, with William Buckley, that an ideal of humanity can justify the destruction of the human race.

Logically, the conclusion is simple enough: all discrimination is wrong prima facie because it violates justice, and that goes for reverse discrimination, too. No violation of justice among the citizens may be justified (may overcome the prima facie objection) by appeal to the ideal of equality, for that ideal is logically dependent upon the notion of justice. Reverse discrimination, then, which attempts no other justification than an appeal to equality, is wrong. But let us try to make the conclusion more plausible by suggesting some of the implications of the suggested practice of reverse discrimination in employment and education. My argument will be that the problems raised there are insoluble, not only in practice but in principle.

We may argue, if we like, about what "discrimination" consists of. Do I discriminate against blacks if I admit none to my school when none of the black applicants are qualified by the tests I always give? How far must I go to root our cultural bias from my application forms and tests before I can say that I have not discriminated against those of different cultures? Can I assume that women are not strong enough to be roughnecks on my oil rigs, or must I test them individually? But this controversy, the most popular and well-argued aspect of the issue, is not as fatal as two others which cannot be avoided: if we are regarding the blacks as a "minority" victimized by discrimination, what is a "minority"? And for any group—blacks, women, whatever—that has been discriminated against, what amount of reverse discrimination wipes out the initial discrimination? Let us grant as true that women and blacks were discriminated against, even where laws forbade such discrimination, and grant for the sake of argument that a history of discrimination must be wiped out by reverse discrimination. What follows?

First, are there other groups which have been discriminated against? For they should have the same right of restitution. What about American Indians, Chicanos, Appalachian whites, Puerto Ricans, Jews, Cajuns, and Orientals? And if these are to be included, the principle according to which we specify a "minority" is simply the criterion of "ethnic (sub) group," and we're stuck with every hyphenated American in the lower-middle class clamoring for special privileges for *his* group—and with equal justification. For be it noted, when we run down the Harvard roster, we find not only a scarcity of blacks (in comparison with the proportion in the population) but an even more striking scarcity of those second-, third-, and fourth-generation ethnics who make up the loudest voice of Middle America. Shouldn't they demand *their* share? And eventually, the WASPs will have to form their own lobby, for they too are a minority. The point is simply this: there is no "majority" in America who will not mind giving up just a bit of their rights to make room for a favored minority. There are only other minorities, each of which is discriminated against by the favoring. The initial injustice is then repeated dozens of times, and if each minority is granted the same right of restitution as the others, an entire area of rule governance is dissolved into a pushing and shoving match between self-interested groups. Each works to catch the public eye and political popularity by whatever means of advertising and power politics lend themselves to the effort, to capitalize as much as possible on temporary popularity until the restless mob picks another group to feel sorry for. Hardly an edifying spectacle, and in the long run no one can benefit: the pie is no larger—it's just that instead of setting up and enforcing rules for getting a piece, we've turned the contest into a free-for-all, requiring much more effort for no larger a reward. It would be in the interests of all the participants to reestablish an objective rule to govern the process, carefully enforced and the same for all.

Second, supposing that we do manage to agree in general that women and blacks (and all the others) have some right of restitution, some right to a privileged place in the structure of opportunities for a while, how will we know when that while is up? How much privilege is enough? When will the guilt be gone, the price paid, the balance restored? What recompense is right for centuries of exclusion? What criterion tells us when we are done? Our experience with the civil-rights movement shows us that agreement on these terms cannot be presupposed: a process that appears to some to be going at a mad gallop into a black takeover appears to the rest of us to be at a standstill. Should a practice of reverse discrimination be adopted, we may safely predict that just as some of us begin to see "a satisfactory start toward righting the balance," others of us will see that we "have already gone too far in the other direction" and will suggest that the discrimination ought to be reversed again. And such disagreement is inevitable, for the point is that we could not *possibly* have any criteria for evaluating the kind of recompense we have in mind. The context presumed by any discussion of restitution is the context of rule of law. Law sets the rights of men and simultaneously sets the method for remedying the violation of those rights. You may exact suffering from others and/or damage payments for yourself if and only if the others have violated your rights; the suffering you have endured is not sufficient reason for them to suffer. And remedial rights exist only where there is law: primary human rights are useful guides to legislation but cannot stand as reasons for awarding remedies for injuries sustained. But then, the context presupposed by a discussion of restitution is the context of preexistent full citizenship. No remedial rights could exist for the excluded; neither in law nor in logic does there exist a right to *sue* for a standing to sue.

From these two considerations, then, the difficulties with reverse discrimination became evident. Restitution for a disadvantaged group whose rights under the law have been violated is possible by legal means, but restitution for a disadvantaged group whose grievance is that there was no law to protect them simply is not. First, outside of the area of justice defined by the law, no sense can be made of "the group's rights," for no law recognizes that group of the individuals in it, qua members, as bearers of rights (hence *any* group can constitute itself as a disadvantaged minority in some sense and demand similar restitution). Second, outside of the area of protection of law, no sense can be made of the violation of rights (hence the amount of the recompense cannot be decided by any objective criterion). For both reasons, the practice of reverse discrimination undermines the foundation of the very ideal in whose name it is advocated; it destroys justice, law, equality, and citizenship itself, and replaces them with power struggles and popularity contests.

---

# *Fairness, Meritocracy, and Reverse Discrimination*

## Hardy Jones

Is reverse discrimination ever justified? In recent years this question has received careful attention and the proposed answers are, predictably, quite varied. I will defend a "counterfactual meritocracy theory" for the justification of reverse discrimination. I argue that, subject to certain qualifications and under certain conditions, preferential treatment for members of certain groups is both permitted and required by justice. I assume that discrimination against females and blacks is unjust. The issue is whether employment discrimination against white males in favor of less qualified persons of another sex or color is ever morally justifiable. Another assumption is that employers can use objective standards for determining actual job qualifications—that they have access to, and can follow, nonsexist and nonracist criteria. This assumption may often fail in practice, but that should not affect the moral issue of concern here.

The position I advance differs from much of what is often urged in favor of reverse discrimination. There are several goals of this practice that, while worthy, are not sufficient to justify preferential treatment. ...

*To insure that discrimination against blacks and females does not continue. ...*
*To present a symbolic denunciation of the racist and sexist past. ...*
*To provide role models for victimized blacks and females. ...*

All of these appear to be eminently good reasons for instituting programs of reverse discrimination. None of them, however, carries us very far into the serious complexities of the issue; and, even taken collectively, they aren't strong enough to provide an adequate defense of preferential treatment. What is?

## 1

Reverse discrimination is an important way of compensating victims by preferring them over beneficiaries of injustice. It seems fair to give extra benefits to those who have been treated unjustly and thus to make an effort toward "evening the score." Those benefiting directly from preferential treatment may not have been discriminated against, but they have suffered from injustices done to their ancestors. The effects of such injustices may involve their having been deprived of the wealth, education, health, or employment essential to equal opportunity competition. The white males to be discriminated against may not be responsible for unfair treatment, but many have greatly benefited from it. So it seems not improper for them now to be deprived, for the sake of fair compensation, of further benefits (in the form of jobs) of past acts of unjust discrimination.[1]

It is important to consider how persons have come to have their actual qualifications for positions. Many better qualified white males would have been far less qualified had they not reaped the benefits of an unjust system favoring them at virtually every turn. And certain now-worse-qualified blacks and females would have been much better qualified if they and their ancestors had received fair, equal treatment from the start and all along the way. One meritocratic view holds that persons deserve jobs solely on the basis of present merit or ability—whatever their actual qualifications now happen to be. Here I reject this "meritocracy of present qualifications." What is also relevant is how applicants have obtained their qualifications and what these would have been if certain crucial features of their histories had been different.

The notion employed here is "counterfactual meritocracy." Persons are deserving, within the limits specified, of jobs on the basis of what their qualifications would have been if they had been neither victims nor beneficiaries of injustice. There are no insurmountable objections to the practice of a fair meritocracy.[2] What makes the usual meritocracy pernicious is that it allows past injustice to flow into the present by failing to factor out unjust causes of present job qualifications. Whatever its own defects, fair counterfactual meritocracy attempts to provide a certain sort of corrective. ...

It might seem that I am committed to the view that "the sins of the fathers be visited on the sons." Now I do not think that sons should be punished for their fathers' sins or even that they should be required to make restitution for them. It is *not* unreasonable, though, that sons sometimes be deprived of certain benefits that rather naturally derive from injustices done by their ancestors. Such deprivation is especially appropriate when they are competing for jobs with persons who have suffered from sins like those generating the benefits. Such benefits are not "due" them. They do not have a "right" to these good things even if they have themselves violated no one's rights. A son who has inherited stolen property should not be jailed for the theft; but he has no right to the goods and may reasonably be expected to give them up. It seems entirely appropriate that they be transferred to the daughter or son of the thief's deceased victim. The analogy with reverse discrimination is imperfect; but it illustrates a guiding intuition underlying the fair counterfactual meritocracy.

...

## 2

I wish to discuss certain standard objections to reverse discrimination. I will try to show that, subject to certain qualifications, the counterfactual meritocracy theory can withstand this critical scrutiny. And it is natural here to develop and refine the position by considering criticisms.

*Insufficient Knowledge?* A scheme based on the notion of counterfactual meritocracy appears to require more knowledge about particular cases than one is likely to obtain. If one does not know that the white male to be passed over, in favor of a lesser qualified black or female, has benefited from injustice in acquiring his qualifications, then one runs a risk of unfairly discriminating against him. There is a strong, and widely shared, intuition that "two wrongs do not make a right"—that we cannot rightly rectify old injustices by committing new ones. It is difficult to evaluate counterfactual claims about what a white male's qualifications would have been without the benefits of injustice or what a black person's qualification would have been without the liabilities of injustice. How can one tell? ... The smooth operation of a counterfactual meritocracy appears to require an ideal social observer who knows how everyone has been affected by injustice and how things would have been in a just world. Never having such a God's-eye view of human society, we seem destined to be too ignorant to implement a fair program of preferential treatment.

This is a powerful objection, but it can be shown to be not at all devastating. The risk of unfair treatment of white males can be sharply reduced by establishing minimal differentials between better and lesser (yet acceptable) qualifications. A black female would perhaps receive the job if she were slightly less qualified than a white male who happens to be the very best qualified. If the difference is now very small it seems reasonable to suppose that but for unfair, past discrimination the black female would be better. Only a superficial knowledge of racist and sexist injustice in our history is required to show that unfair treatment has been widespread and has touched the lives of almost everyone. Though lacking the knowledge of a godlike observer, we are not wholly ignorant of the effects of injustice. It is surely possible to increase our knowledge through interviews and other inquiries into the social backgrounds of job applicants. In many cases there will be sufficient information at least to be reasonably confident that preferential treatment is not unjust. In cases in which a small fraction of the needed knowledge is available, the job might standardly be given to the actually best qualified. A program of reverse discrimination need not be scrapped simply for lack of complete knowledge in all cases likely to arise.

It is also important to be realistic about the quality of available information bearing on present, actual qualifications. Experienced hiring officers have learned that it is quite difficult, and often impossible, to come to know the details of applicants' qualifications. It is not as though one ever has perfect knowledge of this and of how well a person who "looks good on paper (and in person)" will do once he starts the job. ...

It is useful to reflect on epistemically unavoidable risks in other areas of the social system. It is often difficult to get enough evidence to know whether a defendant is guilty or not guilty. The criminal trial system and the schedule of punishments present serious risks. Some innocent people will be found guilty and punished for crimes they did not commit; some guilty persons will be found not guilty and escape the punishment they deserve. Realistic about such pitfalls, we continue to support they system of indictments, trials, and punishments. We regard the risks of injustice as worth taking. If we are reasonable about this, then surely we are not unreasonable to implement a program of reverse discrimination with *its* attendant risks of unfair treatment. And an injustice of rejecting a deserving white male applicant seems far less serious than that of punishing an innocent person. With the latter we countenance a kind of tragedy. But with generally better opportunities now prevailing for white males, it does not seem tragic to unfairly prefer a female or a black.

...

... If persons are hired solely on the basis of present qualifications, then many counterfactually deserving but actually less qualifed females and blacks will be rejected. Not having a program for reverse discrimination runs a risk of more extensively victimizing persons already unfairly treated. This risk is more serious than that of unfairly preferring a black or a female to a white male who has not been badly victimized by injustice. It should be clear that I am not endorsing the weaker view that reverse discrimination is always unjust but sometimes overridden by other moral considerations. This part of the discussion can be summarized as follows. (1) Many cases of reverse discrimination will not be unjust and will be required by justice, because the counterfactual factors make the actually less qualified more deserving. (2) When the program of preferential hiring yields cases of injustice to white males, it is justified provided that not having it would involve even more, and more serious, injustices.

*Individuals or Groups?* There are problems in preferring persons because they are members of a group most of whose members are victims of injustice and in rejecting persons because they are members of a group most of whose members are beneficiaries of injustice. One difficulty is simply that not everyone deserving compensation will receive it. A preferential hiring scheme cannot accommodate all.[3] One must, I think, acknowledge that reverse discrimination is *only one* method for compensating *some* victimized persons for *some* of the wrongs from which they suffer. It is out of the question to expect it to rectify all injustice. ...

But there is a more troubling problem. The counterfactual meritocracy would presumably allow market criteria to determine which members of victimized groups get jobs. These persons must still compete among themselves for positions, and the best qualified will obtain them. One result is that those who have suffered most lose out to persons who have suffered less. The better qualified are the ones likely to have suffered less from previous injustices, and those more greatly victimized will be lesser qualified. So the less deserving receive compensation at the expense of those who deserve it more. Compensatory benefits are not distributed in fair proportion to the degree of injustice-engendered liabilities.[4]

"Best qualified" and "better qualified" here refer to actual qualifications of members of the disadvantaged groups. One first groups those who have suffered from acts of unjust treatment. One then ranks these persons in terms of their actual qualifications. The "market criteria" approach would favor the best qualified (from this group) being hired over the actually best qualified of the group of beneficiaries of injustice. But an alternative approach would, if feasible, be more desirable. First, one groups victims of injustice. Next, one ranks them on a scale of actual qualifications. The third step would be to rank them on a scale of "degrees of victimization." Lastly, one adds scores from the second and third steps. The person with the highest score would then be hired, provided that the difference between his actual qualifications and those of the best qualified (of the beneficiaries) is within an acceptable range. If the difference is too large, one could revert to the first approach and select the actually best qualified of the victims. If the difference is still too large, then one would not have any preferential treatment.

A more extreme but not obviously unreasonable alternative would be to select the worst victimized, provided that his actual merit is above a minimal level. The "degrees of injustice" considerations are also relevant here. Reliance on market competition for selection *within* victimized groups would seem less unjust than hiring the actually best qualified and compensating no one. As knowledge of victimization grows, one can gradually incorporate new information so as to award jobs in better proportion to counterfactual merit.

*Efficiency?* It is arguable that, even with adequate knowledge as to who deserves how much compensation, the program of reverse discrimination would be socially undesirable. A counterfactual meritocracy, comprehensively administered, could drastically reduce efficiency and productivity. To maintain these at high levels, jobs must be allocated according to actual merit rather than hypothetical "what would have been" qualifications. Everyone will suffer if many of the lesser qualified are preferred over best qualified applicants. And those who are already victims will probably suffer more than the rest. Poor or disadvantaged black students, for example, have a great need for the very best instructors in their schools.

…

… There are simple methods for minimizing the inefficiency of the scheme. One way is to establish a "threshold of minimal qualifications" variable from job to job. Anyone who is hired should have a degree of actual merit requisite for minimal competence. A person without training in music should not get a job as an opera singer even if it is injustice that has deprived him of the necessary background. Counterfactual merit, even in large amounts, is not a sufficient condition for being hired. No applicant could fall below the minimal standard and still be hired; no one could be hired if he were clearly unqualified. But the very best qualified might be rejected without unacceptable losses of efficiency. Another efficiency-conserving device is a "maximum differential of qualifications," again varying from job to job.

This could insure that a lesser qualified applicant would not be hired if he were too far less qualified than someone else. Ideally, the differential would be small enough to minimize inefficiency, yet large enough that some victimized persons are given preference.

*Unfairness to White Males?* A consequence of reverse discrimination is that white male applicants, new candidates for newly available positions, bear the major burden of compensation. They are the ones to suffer from this rectification of injustice. But why? Though most young white males have probably benefited from discrimination, they are surely not the only ones. Though some of them have perpetrated injustices against blacks and females, other persons are more largely responsible for unfair treatment. And though white males have tolerated injustices, so has virtually everyone else. Indeed, some victims have, perhaps unwittingly, tolerated injustices against themselves and others in cases in which they could have succeeded in preventing them. So why must white males be the ones to make the heavy sacrifices imposed by demands of compensatory justice? The costs of rectification appear to be unevenly shared among a large group of beneficiaries of injustice.[5]

Again, one must compare the degree of injustice caused by reverse discrimination with that rectified by it. Employment on the model of actual meritocracy brooks injustice by allowing the effects of past unfairness to penetrate into the future. The failure to give compensatory treatment is a failure to rectify injustices, but it also permits them to prevail and to remain infused in our society. All things considered, the amount of injustice tolerated without reverse discrimination may exceed that involved in making young white males bear the burden.

. . .

But there is another facet to the "white male objection." The case for reverse discrimination appears to rest not merely on blacks and females having suffered from injustice, but also on white males having benefited from it. But what if the latter is not the case? Suppose that even without a history of unfair discrimination, certain white males would have developed qualifications as good as or better than those they now have. Is preferential treatment justified under *these* conditions? I believe that it is, though perhaps the case for giving it is weaker. But why is there here any reason at all for preferring blacks or females with lesser qualifications? My answer is that there is surely a sense in which the white males have been benefited or advantaged *relative to the victimized*. Since the black females' qualifications are lesser than they would have been without injustice, it is injustice which now places the white males in a more favorable position (from the perspective of actual merit). Even if they have never before benefited from unfair treatment, to prefer them over all those who have suffered would allow them now to benefit from debilitating consequences of injustice to others. It is difficult to see why one should think they have a claim or right to such benefits.

So even if the qualifications of white males are invariant across factually unjust and counterfactually just worlds, it is not now unjust to reject them in favor of black females whose unjust world qualifications are somewhat lower. This is true even though the white males suffer so as to rectify injustices that they have neither caused nor exploited. Their suffering is not good, but it is not as bad as making blacks and females *continue* to suffer.

Still another dimension of the problem is that the white males to suffer are mostly young and thus new to the job market. Others who already have jobs have probably benefited more from injustice than new applicants for newly available positions. Older white males have in many cases had secure, satisfying, lucrative, and long careers. Their positions were acquired during times when there was not even the pretense of fair treatment and equal opportunity for blacks and females. And many well-entrenched individuals have been perpetrators, not mere beneficiaries, of injustice. They are much more "guilty" than the young who confront dismal job markets for the first time. It seems only fair that the former be required to share the burden of rectification.

What can be done about this problem? Realistically, probably not very much. But if the society were to choose to pursue compensation in a very thorough way, ways of doing so could be devised. One extreme and presently alarming strategy would be to subject all positions to "reconsideration" and proceed to "hire" again from scratch. Everyone—formerly secure veterans as well as hopeful new candidates—would have to apply.[6] Positions would be filled, within the constraints of knowledge and efficiency, in accordance with some combination of the criteria of actual merit and counterfactual desert. This proposal is interesting, but there is virtually no chance of its being even seriously considered.

...

*Self-respect?* If blacks and females know that they have been chosen over better qualified persons, they may suffer losses of self-respect. But if someone believes he deserves his job because of his merit, ability, and prospects for success, then he can have a strong feeling of dignity or self-worth. Furthermore, wouldn't reverse discrimination be counter-productive with regard to the purposes of being employed? One strong motivation for having a good position is surely enhancement of self-esteem. This aim may be frustrated if persons are not hired solely because they possess the best qualifications.[7]

The criticism can, I think, be met rather easily. First, there are considerations of self-respect that cut in a different direction. There is hardly much rational self-respect on the part of persons whose good qualifications derive heavily from discrimination against others. One cannot expect to enhance reasonable self-esteem by holding a job solely on the basis of actual merit. A useful way for white males to increase self-respect might be to resign and then compete under fair conditions. It would, of course, be unreasonable for individuals to do this unilaterally, but a social system aimed at maximizing self-esteem might try it. White males should suffer no serious losses (as regards respect) if they are rejected in favor of very well qualified persons who have been hurt by injustice. There would appear to be a stronger sense of self-esteem in foregoing benefits of injustice and in wishing not to profit from unfairness to others.[8]

Should a victimized lesser qualified person who has been hired lose self-respect? It is surely desirable that employees and prospective employees not be deceived about why they are hired, and it would not be right to tell them that the best qualified are chosen. (Being lied to is still another source of diminished self-respect.) Assuming they should know the truth, how should it be presented to them? I believe that persons given preferential treatment should be told that their lesser qualifications are seen as being due to injustice. If this is correct and if the main claims of this paper are sound, then those who are hired can have the appropriately secure feeling that, whatever detractors may insinuate, they are getting what they deserve.

## 3

The counterfactual meritocracy theory may be viewed as a natural extension of an intuitive notion of equal opportunity.[9] It compensates for the lack of actual equal opportunity by considering what things would have been like with it. So far as this is determinable, jobs are awarded in accordance with counterfactual merit. One treats persons now so that what they receive is more closely approximate to what they would have naturally obtained in a just world. Such treatment is one good way of lessening the harmful consequences of injustice, but it is not sufficient to assure justice in hiring and working. My view is compatible with the sort of Marxist perspective from which it is claimed that complete justice requires far more drastic alterations in work arrangements. Providing equal opportunity and rectifying violations of equal opportunity are not enough. Social conditions may be such that all workers are exploited and thus treated unjustly even if the hiring processes are untainted by unfair discrimination and invidious selection. The sources of injustice run far deeper than failure to accord equal treatment.[10]

I have not wished to deny or to de-emphasize any of this. My suggestions regarding counterfactual meritocracy as an extension of equal opportunity are proposals for making social systems less unjust. Hiring in accord with certain counterfactual qualifications provides some increases in justice—or at least curtails further injustices. In a perfectly just counterfactual meritocracy all employees may be exploited by work arrangements, but none are additionally wronged by unfair discrimination. Appropriately cynical, we may view the justice engendered by reverse discrimination as taking place within a wider institutional setting which is itself unjust.

---

### Notes

I am indebted to the referees for *Social Theory and Practice* for their criticisms and suggestions. Some ideas contained herein were much less thoroughly developed in my "On the Justifiability of Reverse Discrimination" in *Reverse Discrimination,* ed. Barry R. Gross (Buffalo: Prometheus Books, 1977), 348–57. A version of that paper was presented at the American Philosophical Association (Western Division) meeting in 1976. I am grateful to Gertrude Ezorsky and Virginia Held for comments on that occasion.

1. Here I am indebted to Louis Katzner, "Is the Favoring of Women and Blacks in Employment and Educational Opportunities Justified?" in *Philosophy of Law,* ed. Joel Feinberg and Hyman Gross (Encino: Dickinson, 1975), 291–96.

On compensation, see also Michael Bayles, "Compensatory Reverse Discrimination in Hiring," *Social Theory and Practice* 2 (Fall 1972): 301–12; James W. Nickel, "Preferential Policies in Hiring and Admissions: A Jurisprudential Approach," *Columbia Law Review* 75 (April 1975): 537–44; and George Sher, "Justifying Reverse Discrimination in Employment," *Philosophy and Public Affairs* 4 (Winter 1975): 160–67.

2. On meritocracy, see John Rawls, *A Theory of Justice* (Cambridge: Harvard University Press, 1971), 100–08.

For a view which questions the practice of "rewarding by desert," see Thomas Nagel, "Equal Treatment and Compensatory Discrimination," *Philosophy and Public Affairs* 2 (Summer 1973): 348–63.

3. Objections like this are offered by Robert Simon, "Preferential Hiring," *Philosophy and Public Affairs* 3 (Spring 1974): 314–17.

4. An excellent discussion of this problem is provided by Alan H. Goldman, "Reparation to Individuals or Groups?" *Analysis* 35 (April 1975): 168–70.

5. See Nickel, 545–49.

6. For an interesting discussion of similar, and alternative, proposals, see Virginia Held, "Reasonable Progress and Self-Respect," *The Monist* 57 (January 1973): 23–27.

7. Cf. Nickel, 553–55.

8. I am indebted here to Held, 21–27.

9. On equality and equal opportunity, see Ronald Dworkin, "The De Funis Case: The Right to Go to Law School," *The New York Review of Books* 23 (February 5, 1976): 29–33.

10. Joel Feinberg has noted interesting complications in the concept of justice. He has shown that acts of injustice are not confined to cases in which persons are unfairly treated in relation to and by comparison with others. See "Noncomparative Justice," *The Philosophical Review* 83 (July 1974): 297–338.

# *The Wage Gap: Myths and Facts*

## National Committee on Pay Equity

### 1. The United States Labor Force Is Occupationally Segregated by Race and Sex.

- In 1990, women constituted 45.4 percent of all workers in the civilian labor force (over 53 million women).[1]
- People of Color constituted 14.1 percent of all workers.[2]
- Labor force participation is almost equal among white women, Black women and women of Hispanic origin. In 1990, 57.8 percent (6.8 million) of Black women, 57.5 percent (47.9 million) of white women and 53.2 percent (3.6 million) of Hispanic women were in the paid labor force.[3]

- In 1990, women were:

    99.1 percent of all secretaries

    94.5 percent of all registered nurses

    97.0 percent of all child care workers

    89.0 percent of all telephone operators

    73.7 percent of all teachers (excluding colleges and universities)

    87.2 percent of all data entry keyers

  Women were only:

    9.5 percent of all dentists

    8.0 percent of all engineers

    20.8 percent of all lawyers and judges

    13.8 percent of all police and detectives

    8.5 percent of all precision, production, craft and repair workers

    19.3 percent of all physicians[4]

The U.S. Labor force is segregated by sex and race:

## *Occupations with the Highest Concentration by Race/Ethnicity/Sex*

| | |
|---|---|
| Black women: | Private household workers, cooks, housekeepers, welfare aides |
| Black men: | Stevedores, garbage collectors, longshore equipment operators, baggage porters |
| Hispanic women: | Graders and agricultural workers, housekeepers, electrical assemblers, sewing machine operators |
| Hispanic men: | Farm workers, farm supervisors, elevator operators, concrete finishers |
| Asian women: | Marine life workers, electrical assemblers, dressmakers, launderers |
| Asian men: | Physicians, engineers, professors, technicians, baggage porters, cooks, launderers, longshore equipment operators |
| Native American women: | Welfare aides, child care workers, teacher's aides, forestry (except logging) |
| Native American men: | Marine life workers, hunters, forestry (except logging), fishers |
| White women: | Dental hygienists, secretaries, dental assistants, occupational therapists[5] |

## 2. Economic Status.

- In (March) 1988, 59% of all women were either the sole supporter of their families or their husbands earned $15,000 or less per year.[6] (Source: *20 Facts*)

- Over 11.1 million women work full time in jobs which pay wages below the poverty line (in 1989 for a family of three the poverty line was $9,890 per year). They work in jobs such as day care, food counter, and many service jobs. Many more women than men are part of the working poor (125 percent of the poverty level) and work in jobs such as clerical, blue collar, and sales jobs.[7a]
- In 1987, married couple families with 2 children present had a median income of $36,807 while female headed households with 2 children present had a median income of only $11,257.[7b]

Women of color are in the lowest paid jobs.

Occupations and Average Salaries of Occupations with a High Percentage of Women of Color[8]

| Occupation | Annual Salary | Percentage of Women of Color* |
|---|---|---|
| Child care worker | $7,119 | 26.4 |
| Sewing machine operator | 7,568 | 29.6 |
| Maids and housemen | 7,945 | 35.5 |
| Nursing aides | 8,778 | 29.6 |
| Health aides | 9,489 | 19.5 |
| Food preparation workers | 7,132 | 18.9 |

*Women of color represented 7.59 percent of the United States workforce in the 1979 Census data.

The majority of women, just as the majority of men, work out of economic necessity to support their families. Women do not work for "pin money."

## 3. The Wage Gap Is One of the Major Causes of Economic Inequality in the United States Today.

- In 1989, all men, working year-round full-time, were paid a median salary of $27,430 per year.
- All women, working year-round full-time, were paid a median salary of $18,780 per year.
- Therefore, women were paid 68.5 cents compared to each dollar paid to men.

The breakdown by race shows the double burden that women of color face because of race and sex discrimination.

Year-Round Full-Time Earnings for 1989[9]

| Race/Sex | Earnings | Earnings as a Percentage of White Men's |
|---|---|---|
| White men | $28,541 | 100.0 |
| Black men | 20,426 | 71.5 |
| Hispanic men | 18,358 | 64.3 |
| White women | 18,922 | 66.2 |
| Black women | 17,389 | 60.9 |
| Hispanic women | 15,662 | 54.8 |

- In 1980 according to the United States Census Bureau, workers were paid the following average annual salaries based on race and sex.

| Race/Sex | 1980 Earnings | Earnings as a Percentage of White Men's |
|---|---|---|
| White men | $20,335 | 100.0 |
| Asian men | 20,148 | 99.1 |
| Native American men | 16,019 | 78.8 |
| Hispanic men | 14,935 | 73.4 |
| Black men | 14,372 | 70.7 |
| Asian women | 12,432 | 60.0 |
| White women | 11,213 | 55.1 |
| Black women | 10,429 | 51.3 |
| Native American women | 10,052 | 49.4 |
| Hispanic women | 9,725 | 47.8 |

## 4. The Wage Gap Has Fluctuated, But Has Not Disappeared in the Last Several Decades.

Comparison of Median Earnings of Year-Round Full-Time Workers, by Sex, Selected Years

| Year | Median Earnings Women | Men | Women's Earnings as a Percentage of Men's | Year | Median Earnings Women | Men | Women's Earnings as a Percentage of Men's |
|---|---|---|---|---|---|---|---|
| 1989 | $18,780 | $27,430 | 68.5 | 1972 | $5,903 | $10,202 | 57.9 |
| 1988 | 17,606 | 26,656 | 66.0 | 1971 | 5,593 | 9,399 | 59.5 |
| 1987 | 16,909 | 26,008 | 65.0 | 1970 | 5,323 | 8,966 | 59.4 |
| 1986 | 16,232 | 25,256 | 64.3 | 1969 | 4,977 | 8,227 | 60.5 |
| 1985 | 15,624 | 24,195 | 64.5 | 1966 | 3,973 | 6,848 | 58.0 |
| 1984 | 14,780 | 23,218 | 63.7 | 1965 | 3,823 | 6,375 | 60.0 |
| 1983 | 13,915 | 21,881 | 63.6 | 1964 | 3,690 | 6,195 | 59.6 |
| 1982 | 13,014 | 21,077 | 61.7 | 1963 | 3,561 | 5,978 | 59.6 |
| 1981 | 12,001 | 20,260 | 59.2 | 1962 | 3,446 | 5,974 | 59.5 |
| 1980 | 11,197 | 18,612 | 60.2 | 1961 | 3,351 | 5,644 | 59.4 |
| 1979 | 10,151 | 17,014 | 59.7 | 1960 | 3,293 | 5,317 | 60.8 |
| 1978 | 9,350 | 15,730 | 59.4 | 1959 | 3,193 | 5,209 | 61.3 |
| 1977 | 8,618 | 14,626 | 58.9 | 1958 | 3,102 | 4,927 | 63.0 |
| 1976 | 8,099 | 13,455 | 60.2 | 1957 | 3,008 | 4,713 | 63.8 |
| 1975 | 7,504 | 12,758 | 58.8 | 1956 | 2,827 | 4,466 | 63.3 |
| 1974 | 6,772 | 11,835 | 57.2 | 1955 | 2,719 | 4,252 | 63.9 |
| 1973 | 6,335 | 11,186 | 56.6 | 1946 | 1,710 | 2,588 | 66.1 |

## 5. The Cause of the Wage Gap Is Discrimination.

Differences in education, labor force experience, and commitment (years in the labor force) do not account for the entire wage gap.

- The National Academy of Sciences found in 1981 that usually less than a quarter (25 percent), and never more than half (50 percent), of the wage gap is due to differences in education, labor force experience, and commitment.

- According to the 1986 NAS study, entitled *Women's Work, Men's Work*, "each additional percentage point female in an occupation was associated with $42 less in median annual earnings."

- According to the 1987 NCPE study, in New York State, for every 5 to 6 percent increase in Black and Hispanic representation in a job there is a one salary grade decrease. (A one salary grade decrease amounts to a 5 percent salary decrease.)

- In 1985, both women and men had a median educational level of 12.8 years.

- In 1985, the United States Bureau of the Census reported that differences in education, labor force experience, and commitment account for only 14.6% of the wage gap between women and men.

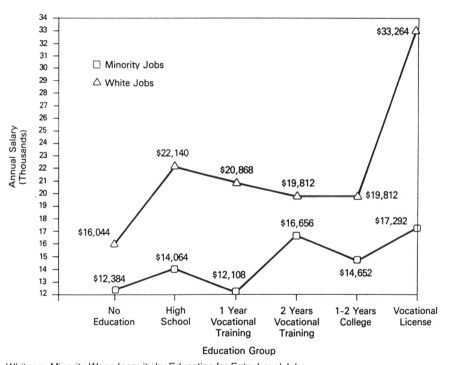

White vs. Minority Wage Inequity by Education for Entry Level Jobs

## 6. Employers Are Always Comparing Different Jobs in Order to Set Wages.

- Two-thirds (²/₃) of employees are paid according to a formal job evaluation system.

## 7. The Cost of Implementing Pay Equity.

- Achieving pay equity usually costs about 2 to 5 percent of an employer's pay roll budget.

For example, in the State of Minnesota, after conducting a job evaluation study, it was determined that there was a 20 percent gap between comparable male-dominated and female-dominated jobs. It cost the state 3.7 percent of the payroll budget to eliminate this inequity. The adjustments are being phased-in over a 4-year period.

## 8. Pay Equity Is Not a "Looney Tunes" Idea; It Is Being Addressed All Over the Country.

- All but 5 states (Alaska, Arkansas, Delaware, Georgia, and Idaho) have addressed the issue of pay equity.
- 22 states and Washington, D.C. have conducted or are conducting job evaluation studies to determine if their wage setting systems are discriminatory.
- 20 states have begun to make pay equity adjustments.
- 4 states (New York, New Jersey, Florida, and Wisconsin) and Washington, D.C. have addressed race in addition to sex discrimination.[10]

## 9. Everyone in Society Benefits from Pay Equity.

A. Men's wages will not be lowered. Employers cannot remedy discrimination by penalizing another group. Men who are working in predominantly female jobs will also be paid more if pay equity adjustments are made.

Everyone benefits from women being paid fairly. Whether it is your mother, sister, wife or daughter, wage discrimination hurts the entire family.

Men of color will benefit in additional ways to those listed for all men
  - elimination of race from the wage setting system.
  - more likely to be in undervalued women's occupations.

B. Employers benefit because the employees' productivity will increase if there is a sense of fairness in how wages are set.

C. Society benefits because if wage discrimination is eliminated, the need for government subsidies for food stamps, health care, etc., will not be necessary. In addition when workers whose wages were lowered by discrimination are paid fairly, their pensions will be greater upon retirement.

## Where We Get the Statistics

The U.S. Census Bureau collects wage data every 10 years. This data provides in-depth data for Blacks, whites, Hispanics, Asian Pacific Islanders and Native Americans.

The most recent salary data is from 1979. The United States Census Bureau also provides annual salary data for Blacks, whites, and Hispanics. They gather this information in March of the following year and release it in August. Therefore, the annual salary data for 1986 will not have been released until August of 1987.

The Bureau of Labor Statistics (BLS) provides quarterly reports each year on weekly salaries for Blacks, whites and Hispanics. They also provide an annual average of weekly wages.

The Women's Bureau releases "20 Facts on Working Women" on an annual basis.

The BLS and the Women's Bureau are part of the United States Department of Labor.

---

### Notes

1. *Employment and Earnings,* Bureau of Labor Statistics, Jan., 1991.

2. U.S. Census Bureau, represents Black, Asian, Native American, and some but not all persons of Hispanic origin.

3. Employment and Earnings, Black and white women; Women of Hispanic Origin in the Labor Force, Women's Bureau, Aug., 1989, Hispanic women.

4. *Employment and Earnings.*

5. *Pay Equity: An Issue of Race, Ethnicity and Sex,* by the NCPE, February, 1987.

6. *20 Facts.*

7a. U.S. Census Bureau, Current Population Series P-60 #168.

7b. Working Mothers and Their Children, Women's Bureau, Aug., 1989.

8. *Pay Equity: An Issue of Race, Ethnicity and Sex.*

9. U.S. Census Bureau, Current Population Series P-60 #154, most recent annual data available.

10. Pay Equity Activity in the Public Sector 1979–1989, by the NCPE, October, 1989.

# *An Argument Against Comparable Worth*

## June O'Neill

...

The traditional goal of feminists has been equal opportunity for women—the opportunity for women to gain access to the schools, training, and jobs they choose to enter, on the same basis as men. This goal, however, basically accepts the rules of the game as they operate in a market economy. In fact the thrust has been to improve the way the market functions by removing discriminatory barriers that restrict the free supply of workers to jobs. By contrast, the more recent policy of "comparable worth" would dispense with the rules of the game. In place of the goal of equality of opportunity it would substitute a demand for equality of results, and it would do this essentially through regulation and legislation. It proposes, therefore, a radical departure from the economic system we now have, and so should be scrutinized with the greatest care.

The topics I will cover in this paper and the main points I will make are as follows:

1. The concept of comparable worth rests on a misunderstanding of the role of wages and prices in the economy.

2. The premises on which a comparable worth policy is based reflect a misconception about the reasons why women and men are in different occupations and have different earnings. Both the occupational differences and the pay gap to a large extent are the result of differences in the roles of women and men in the family and the effects these role differences have on the accumulation of skills and other job choices that affect pay. Discrimination by employers may account for some of the occupational differences, but it does not, as comparable worth advocates claim, lower wages directly in women's occupations.

3. Comparable worth, if implemented, would lead to capricious wage differentials, resulting in unintended shortages and surpluses of woekrs in different occupations with accompanying unemployment. Moreover, it would encourage women to remain in traditional occupations.

4. Policies are available that can be better targeted than comparable worth on any existing discriminatory or other barriers. These policies include the equal employment and pay legislation now on the books.

## The Concept of Comparable Worth

By comparable worth I mean the view that employers should base compensation on the inherent value of a job rather than on strictly market considerations. It is not a new idea—since the time of St. Thomas Aquinas, the concept of the "just price," or payment for value, has had considerable appeal. Practical considerations, however, have won out over metaphysics. In a free market, wages and prices are not taken as judgments of the inherent value of the worker or the good itself, but reflect a balancing of what people are willing to pay for the services of these goods with how much it costs to supply them. Market prices are the efficient signals that balance supply and demand. Thus, in product markets we do not require that a pound of soybeans be more expensive than a pound of Belgian chocolates because it is more nutritious, or that the price of water be higher than that of diamonds because it is so much more important to our survival. If asked what the proper scale of prices should be for these products, most people—at least those who have taken Economics I—would give the sensible answer that there is no proper scale—it all depends on the tastes and needs of millions of consumers and the various conditions that determine the costs of production and the supplies of these products.

What is true of the product market is equally true of the labor market. There is simply no independent scientific way to determine what pay should be in a particular occupation without recourse to the market. Job skills have "costs of production" such as formal schooling and on-the-job training. Different jobs also have different amenities that may be more or less costly for the employer to provide—for example, part-time work, safe work, flexible hours, or a pleasant ambience. And individuals vary in their talents and tastes for acquiring skills and performing different tasks. The skills required change over time as the demand for products changes and as different techniques of production are introduced. And these changes may vary by geographic region. In a market system, these changing conditions are reflected in changing wage rates, which in turn provide workers with the incentive to acquire new skills or to migrate to different regions.

The wage pattern that is the net outcome of these forces need not conform to anyone's independent judgment based on preconceived notions of comparability or of relative desirability. The clergy, for example, earn about 30 percent less than brickmasons.[1] Yet the clergy are largely college graduates; the brickmasons are not. Both occupations are more than 95 percent male—so one cannot point to sex discrimination. Possibly the reason for the wage disparity lies in unusual union power of construction workers and is an example of market imperfections. But other explanations are possible too. The real compensation to the clergy, for example, may include housing and spiritual satisfaction as fringe benefits. On the other hand, the high risk of unemployment and exposure to hazards of brickmasons may be reflected in additional monetary payments. If enough people require premiums to become brickmasons and are willing to settle for nonmonetary rewards to work as clergy, and if the buyers of homes are willing to pay the higher costs of brickmasons, while churchgoers are satisfied with the number and quality of clergy who apply, the market solution may well be satisfactory.[2]

One can also think of examples of jobs that initially may seem quite comparable but that would not command the same wage, even in nondiscriminatory and competitive markets. The following example is based on a case that has been used before, but it illustrates the point so well it bears repeating.[3] Consider two jobs—one a Spanish-English translator and the other a French-English translator. Most job evaluators would probably conclude that these jobs are highly comparable and should be paid the same. After all, the skills required, the mental demands, the working conditions, and responsibility would seem to be nearly identical. But "nearly" is not equal, and the difference in language may in fact give rise to a legitimate pay differential. The demand for the two languages may differ—for example, if trade with Spanish-speaking countries is greater. But the supply of Spanish-English translators may also be greater. And this would vary by geographic area. It would be difficult to predict which job will require the higher wage and by how much in order to balance supply and demand.

TABLE 1   Female-Male Ratios of Median Usual Weekly Earnings of Full-Time Wage and Salary Workers, by Age, 1971–1983

*I. Unadjusted Ratios*

| Age | May 1971 | May 1973 | May 1974 | May 1975 | May 1976 | May 1977 | May 1978 | 2nd Quarter 1979 | Annual Average 1979 | 1982 | 1983 |
|---|---|---|---|---|---|---|---|---|---|---|---|
| 16–19 | .89 | .82 | .82 | .86 | .86 | .88 | .86 | .85 | .87 | .88 | .94 |
| 20–24 | .78 | .77 | .76 | .76 | .80 | .78 | .75 | .75 | .76 | .83 | .84 |
| 25–34 | .65 | .64 | .65 | .66 | .67 | .65 | .66 | .67 | .66 | .72 | .73 |
| 35–44 | .59 | .54 | .55 | .57 | .55 | .56 | .53 | .58 | .58 | .60 | .60 |
| 45–54 | .57 | .57 | .57 | .59 | .57 | .56 | .54 | .57 | .56 | .59 | .58 |
| 55–64 | .62 | .63 | .60 | .63 | .61 | .59 | .60 | .60 | .58 | .60 | .62 |
| Total, 16 years and over | .62 | .62 | .61 | .62 | .61 | .61 | .61 | .62 | .62 | .65 | .66 |

*II. Adjusted for Male-Female Differences in Full-Time Hours[1]*

| Age | May 1971 | May 1973 | May 1974 | May 1975 | May 1976 | May 1977 | May 1978 | 2nd Quarter 1979 | Annual Average 1979 | 1982 | 1983 |
|---|---|---|---|---|---|---|---|---|---|---|---|
| 16–19 | .94 | .86 | .87 | .90 | .90 | .92 | .91 | .90 | .92 | .91 | .96 |
| 20–24 | .85 | .83 | .82 | .82 | .86 | .84 | .80 | .81 | .82 | .88 | .89 |
| 25–34 | .73 | .72 | .72 | .73 | .74 | .72 | .73 | .74 | .73 | .79 | .80 |
| 35–44 | .66 | .61 | .61 | .63 | .61 | .62 | .59 | .64 | .64 | .66 | .66 |
| 45–54 | .62 | .62 | .62 | .63 | .62 | .61 | .59 | .63 | .61 | .64 | .63 |
| 55–64 | .67 | .69 | .65 | .67 | .67 | .65 | .65 | .66 | .64 | .65 | .67 |
| Total, 16 years and over | .68 | .68 | .67 | .68 | .68 | .67 | .67 | .68 | .68 | .71 | .72 |

[1]Female-male earnings ratios were adjusted for differences in hours worked by multiplying by age-specific male-female ratios of average hours worked per week (for nonagricultural workers on full-time schedules).

SOURCE: [Data from] Earnings by age and sex are from unpublished tabulations from the Current Population Survey provided by the Bureau of Labor Statistics, U.S. Department of Labor. Hours data are from U.S. Bureau of Labor Statistics, Employment and Earnings series, January issues, annual averages.

What the market does is to process the scarcity of talents, the talents of heterogeneous individuals and the demands of business and consumers in arriving at a wage. The net outcome would only coincidentally be the same as a comparable worth determination. There are simply too many factors interacting in highly complex ways for a study to find the market clearing wage.

## Why Abandon the Market?

The argument for abandoning market determination of wages and substituting "comparable worth," where wage decisions would be based on an independent assessment of the "value" of occupations, is based on the following premises: (1) the pay gap between women and men is due to discrimination and has failed to narrow over time; (2) this discrimination takes the form of occupational segregation, where women are relegated to low-paying jobs; and (3) pay in these female-dominated occupations is low simply because women hold them.

## The Pay Gap

In 1983 the pay gap, viewed as the ratio of women's to men's hourly pay, was about 72 percent overall (Table 1).[4] Among younger groups the ratio is higher (and the pay gap smaller)—a ratio of 89 percent for 20–24-year-olds and 80 percent for the age 25–34 years old. Among groups age 35 and over the ratio is about 65 percent.

What accounts for the pay gap? Clearly, not all differentials reflect the discrimination. Several minorities (Japanese and Jewish Americans, for example) have higher than average wages, and I do not believe anyone would ascribe these differences to favoritism towards these groups and discrimination against others.

A growing body of research has attempted to account for the pay gap, and the researchers have come to different conclusions. These studies, however, use different data sources, refer to different populations and control for many, but not always the same set of variables. Even the gross wage gap—the hourly earnings differential before adjusting for diverse characteristics—varies from study to study, ranging from 45 to 7 percent depending on the type of population considered. Studies based on national samples covering the full age range tend to show a gross wage gap of 35 to 40 percent. Studies based on more homogeneous groups, such as holders of advanced degrees or those in specific professions, have found considerably smaller gross wage gaps.

After adjusting for various characteristics, the wage gap narrows. Generally, the most important variables contributing to the adjustment are those that measure the total number of years of work experience, the years of tenure on current job, and the pattern or continuity of previous work experience.

Traditional home responsibilities of married women have been an obstacle to their full commitment to a career. Although women are now combining work and marriage to a much greater extent than in the past, older women in the labor foce today have typically spent many years out of the labor force raising their families. Data from the National Longitudinal Survey (NLS) indicate that in 1977 employed white women in their forties had worked only 61 percent of the years after leaving school, and employed black women had worked 68 percent of the years.[5] By contrast, men are usually in the labor force or the military on a continuing basis after leaving school.

In a recent study I examined the contribution of lifetime work experience and other variables using the NLS data for men and women aged 25 to 34. White women's hourly wage rate was found to be 66 percent of white men's—a wage gap of 34 percent. This wage gap narrowed to 12 percent after accounting for the effects of male-female differences in work experience, job tenure, and schooling, as well as differences in plant size and certain job characteristics, such as the years of training required to learn a skill, whether the occupation was hazardous, and whether the occupation had a high concentration of women.

The gross wage gap between black men and black women was 18 percent. The gross wage gap was smaller for blacks than for whites because job-related characteristics of black women and black men are closer than those of white women and white men. Black women have somewhat fewer years of work experience in their teens and early twenties than white women, which may be related to earlier childbearing. They are more likely to work continuously and full time later on, however, and thus accumulate more total work experience and longer tenure on their current jobs than white women. The adjustment for differences in the measured characteristics cited above narrowed the wage gap of black men and women to 9 percent.

Are the remaining, unaccounted-for differences a measure of discrimination in the labor market?

If all the productivity differences between women and men are not accurately identified and measured, labor market discrimination would be overestimated by the unexplained residual. Many variables were omitted from this analysis and from other studies because relevant data are not available. These include details on the quality and vocational orientation of education; on the extent of other work-related investments, such as job search; and on less tangible factors, such as motivation and effort. Differences in these factors could arise from the priority placed on earning an income versus fulfilling home responsibilities. If women, by tradition, assume the primary responsibility for homemaking and raising children, they may be reluctant to take jobs that demand an intense work commitment.

On the other hand, the unexplained residual may underestimate discrimination if some of the included variables, such as years of training to learn a job, or the sex typicality of occupations, partially reflect labor market discrimination. Some employers may deny women entry into lengthy training programs or be reluctant to hire them in traditionally male jobs. It is difficult with available data to distinguish this situation from one where women choose not to engage in training because of uncertainty about their long-run career plans or choose female occupations because they are more compatible with competing responsibilities at home.

## Occupational Segregation

Although occupational segregation clearly exists, it is in large part the result of many of the same factors that determine earnings: years of schooling, on-the-job training, and other human capital investments, as well as tastes for particular job characteristics. In a recently completed study, I found that women's early expectations about their future life's work—that is, whether they planned to be a homemaker or planned to work outside the home—are strongly related to the occupations they ultimately pursue.[6] Many women who initially planned to be homemakers, in fact, become labor force participants, but they were much more likely to pursue stereotyped female occupations than women who had formed their plans to work at younger ages. Early orientation influences early training and schooling decisions, and as a result women may be locked into or out of certain careers. Some women, however, by choice, maintain an ongoing dual career—combining work in the home with an outside job—and this leads to an accommodation in terms of the number of hours that women work and other conditions that influence occupational choice.

Women and men were also found to differ sharply in the environmental characteristics of their occupations. Women were less likely to be in jobs with a high incidence of outdoor work, noisy or hazardous work, or jobs requiring heavy lifting. These differences may reflect employer prejudice or the hostile attitudes of male coworkers, but they may also reflect cultural and physical differences.

In sum, a substantial amount of the differences in wages and in occupations by sex has been statistically linked to investments in work skills acquired in school or on the job. Varied interpretations of these results are possible, however. Thus, the precise amount that can be labeled as the result of choices made by women and their families rather than the result of discrimination by employers is not known.

...

## Are Women's Occupations Underpaid?

A major contention of comparable worth supporters is that pay in women's occupations is lower because employers systematically downgrade them. The argument differs from the idea that pay in women's occupations is depressed because of an oversupply of these occupations. An oversupply could arise either because large numbers of women entering the labor force choose these occupations (which is compatible with no discrimination) or because women are barred from some causing an oversupply in others (a discriminatory situation). Although comparable worth advocates have taken the view that overcrowding is caused by restrictive measures, they have lately come to believe that this explanation is not the whole cause of "low payment" in women's jobs.[7] The argument is made that employers can pay less to women's jobs regardless of supply considerations, simply reflecting prejudice against such jobs because they are held by women.

The ability of firms to wield such power is highly questionable. If a firm underpaid workers in women's occupations, in the sense that their wages were held below their real contributions to the firm's receipts, other firms would have a strong incentive to hire workers in these occupations away, bidding up the wages in these occupations. Thus, competition would appear to be a force curtailing employer power. This process could only be thwarted by collusion, an unrealistic prospect considering the hundreds of thousands of firms.

Killingsworth (1984) has suggested that the market for nurses may be an example of collusion by a centralized hospital industry that has conspired to hold wages down. Without more careful analysis of the hospital industry, it is difficult to verify whether this is a valid hypothesis. Basic facts about wages and supply in nursing, however, suggest that collusion either does not exist or is ineffective. Despite a perennial "shortage" of nurses that seems to have existed as far back as one can go, the number of nurses has increased dramatically, both absolutely and as a percentage of the population. In 1960 there were 282 registered nurses per 100,000 population. In 1980 there were 506 nurses per 100,000. This rate of increase is even more rapid than the increase in doctors over the past decade, and the supply of doctors has been rapidly increasing. Why did the increase occur? Were women forced into nursing because they were barred from other occupations? That does not seem to be the case in recent times. What has happened is that nursing, along with other medical professions, has experienced a large increase in demand since the middle 1960s when medicare and medicaid were introduced, and private health insurance increased. As a result, the pay of nurses increased more rapidly than in other fields. Between 1960 and 1978 the salary of registered nurses increased by 250 percent, while the pay of all men rose by 206 percent and the pay of all women rose by 193 percent. During the 1970s the rate of pay increase for nurses slowed, which is not surprising considering the increase in supply. And entry of women into nursing school has recently slowed, suggesting a self-correcting mechanism is at work.

Another way to attempt to evaluate the contention that lower pay in female-dominated occupations reflects discrimination is through statistical analysis of the determinants of earnings in occupations. In a recent study, I asked the question—after accounting for measurable differences in skill, do these predominantly female occupations still pay less? In an analysis of data on more than 300 occupations, I found that after adjusting for schooling, training, part-time work, and environmental conditions (but not actual years of work experience or job tenure, which were not available), the proportion female in an occupation was associated with lower pay in that occupation for both women and for men. But the effect was not large. For each 10 percentage point increase in the percent female in an occupation, the wage in the occupation went down by 1.5 percent. Again, however, one is left with a question mark. Are there other characteristics of occupations that women, on the average, may value more highly than men because of home responsibilities or differences in tastes and for which women, more so than men, are willing to accept a lower wage in exchange? Characteristics that come to mind might be a long summer vacation, such as teaching provides, or a steady 9 to 5 job close to home that certain office or shop jobs may provide. The true effect of sex on occupational differences or wage rates is, therefore, another unresolved issue. There are many good reasons why women would be in lower paying occupations than men, even in the absence of sex discrimination on the part of employers. That does not rule out the existence of discrimination, but it weakens the case for seeking an alternative to the market determination of occupational wage rates.

## Comparable Worth in Practice—
## The Washington State Example

What would happen if wages were set in accordance with comparable worth standards and independently of market forces? Any large-scale implementation of comparable worth would necessarily be based on job evaluations that assign points for various factors believed to be common to disparate jobs. For example, in the State of Washington, where a comparable worth study was commissioned, a job evaluation firm assisted a committee of 13 politically chosen individuals in rating the jobs used as benchmarks in setting pay in State employment. The committee's task was to assign points on the basis of knowledge and skills, mental demands, accountability, and working conditions. In the 1976 evaluation a registered nurse at level IV was assigned 573 points, the highest number of points of any job—280 points for knowledge and skills, 122 for mental demands, 160 for accountability, and 11 for working conditions. A computer systems analyst at the IV level received a total of only 426 points—212 points for knowledge and skills, 92 points for mental demands, 122 points for accountability, and no points for working conditions. In the market, however, computer systems analysts among the highest paid workers. National data for 1981 show that they earn 56 percent more than registered nurses. The Washington job evaluation similarly differs radically from the market in its assessment of the value of occupations throughout the job schedule. A clerical supervisor is rated equal to a chemist in knowledge and skills and mental demands, but higher than the chemist in accountability, thereby receiving more total points. Yet the market rewards chemists 41 percent higher pay. The evaluation assigns an electrician the same points for knowledge and skills and mental demands as a level I secretary and 5 points less for accountability. Auto mechanics are assigned lower points than the lowest level homemaker or practical nurse for accountability as well as for working conditions. Truckdrivers are ranked at the bottom, assigned lower points on knowledge and skills, mental demands, and accountability than the lowest ranked telephone operator or retail clerk. The market, however, pays truckdrivers 30 percent more than telephone operators, and the differential is wider for retail clerks.

Should the market pay according to the comparable worth scale? Or is the comparable worth scale faulty? In Washington State, AFSCME, the American Federation of State, County, and Municipal Employees, brought suit against the State on the grounds that failure to pay women according to the comparable worth scale constituted discrimination. Judge Jack E. Tanner agreed and ruled in favor of the union. The decision was based largely on the fact that the State had conducted the study. Whether or not the study was a reasonable standard for nondiscriminatory wage patterns was never an issue. The State, in fact, was disallowed from presenting a witness who would have critically evaluated the study.

What would happen if comparable worth were to be adopted as a pay-setting mechanism? Take the example of registered nurses and computer systems analysts. Nurses are 95 percent female. If a private firm employing both occupations were required to adopt the rankings from the Washington State comparable worth study, it would likely have to make a significant pay adjustment. It could either lower the salary of systems analysts below that of nurses or raise the pay of nurses above systems analysts. If it lowered the pay of systems analysts, it would likely find it impossible to retain or recruit them. The more popular remedy would be to raise the pay of nurses. If the firm did so, it would also be compelled to raise its prices. Most likely, demand for the firm's product would fall, and the firm would of necessity be required to cut back production. It would seek ways of lowering costs—for example, by reducing the number of registered nurses it employed, trying to substitute less skilled practical nurses and orderlies where possible. Some women would benefit—those who keep their jobs at the higher pay. But other women would lose—those nurses who become unemployed, as well as other workers who are affected by the cutback.

Of course, if the employer is a State government, the scenario may be somewhat different. The public sector does not face the rigors of competition to the same extent as a private firm. I suspect this is one reason why public sector employees seem to be in the forefront of the comparable worth movement. The public sector could not force workers to work for them if the remedy was to lower the wage in high-paying male jobs. But that is not usually what employee groups request. It can, however, pay the bill for the higher pay required to upgrade wages in female-dominated occupations by raising taxes. But in the long run, the State may have financing problems, since taxpayers may not be willing to foot the bill, and the result would be similar to that in the private firm—unemployment of government workers, particularly women in predominantly female occupations, as government services are curtailed.

## Concluding Remarks

Advocates of comparable worth see it as a way of raising women's economic status and, quite expectedly, tend to minimize costs. A typical comment is as follows (Center for Philosophy and Public Policy):

> Certainly, the costs incurred would vary widely depending on the scope of the approach chosen. But the economic costs of remedying overt discrimination should not prove staggering. Employers and business interests have a long history of protesting that fair treatment of workers will result in massive economic disruption. Similar claims were made preceding the abolishment of child labor and the establishment of the minimum wage, and none of the dire predictions came to pass.

Evidently the author is unaware of the numerous economic studies showing the disemployment effects of the minimum wage. However, what this statement fails to see is that comparable worth is in a bigger league than the child labor law or the minimum wage laws that have actually been implemented. It is far more radical. Instituting comparable worth by means of studies such as the one conducted in Washington State could be more like instituting a $15 an hour minimum wage or passing sweeping legislation like Prohibition. Moreover, the costs in terms of economic distortion would be much more profound than the dollars required to pay the bills. Curiously, this is recognized by one comparable worth proponent[8] who then suggests "that we give very serious consideration to the idea that firms that do raise pay for 'disadvantaged occupations' get special tax incentives for capital equipment that will raise the productivity of these workers. We can't expect firms to swallow these losses; that's crazy." Barrett is willing to go to these lengths because she thinks it might be a way to raise the incomes of poor women heading families on welfare. Long-term welfare recipients, however, are not the women holding the jobs covered by comparable worth schemes. The work participation of women in this situation is very low. Moreover, the lesson of studies of minimum wage effects has been that those who are most vulnerable to disemployment as a result of wage hikes that exceed national market rates are the disadvantaged—those with little education, poor training, and little work experience. Comparable worth would hurt, not help, these women. Subsidies to try to prevent these effects from occurring would be impractical to implement and prohibitively costly.

With all the difficulties that would ensue from implementing comparable worth, it is striking that it would not achieve many of the original goals of the women's movement such as the representation of women as electricians, physicists, managers, or plumbers. In fact, it would likely retard the substantial progress that has been made in the past decade. Younger women have dramatically shifted their school training and occupational choices. They have been undertaking additional training and schooling because the higher pay they can obtain from the investment makes it worthwhile. Raising the pay of clerical jobs, teaching, and nursing above the market rates would make it less rewarding to prepare for other occupations and simply lead to an oversupply to women's fields, making it still harder to find a stable solution to the problem of occupational segregation.

Another byproduct of comparable worth is that it diverts attention away from the real problems of discrimination that may arise. Such problems need not be confined to women in traditional jobs. Pay differences between men and women performing the same job in the same firm at the same level of seniority may no longer be an important source of discrimination. The form discrimination more likely takes is through behavior that denies women entry into on-the-job training or promotions on the same basis as men. The obvious solution is the direct one—namely, allowing or encouraging women whose rights are being denied to bring suit. Existing laws were intended to cover this very type of problem.

The pay-setting procedure in all levels of government employment is another area where remedies other than comparable worth would be more direct and effective. Governments usually do not have the flexibility to meet market demands. The need to adhere to rigid rules under considerable political pressure may result in paying wages that are too high in some occupations and too low in others. (By "too high" I mean that an ample supply of workers could be obtained at a lower wage.) This could occur if the private plants covered in a pay survey for a particular occupation are themselves paying above market—for example, as the result of a powerful union. Such a situation could lead to unnecessary pay differentials between certain occupations that are male dominated (which are more likely to be represented by such strong unions) and other male, mixed, and female occupations whose private sector wages are more competitive. Comparable worth is not the solution, however, since it does not address the problem. Pay-setting procedures can be improved by changing the nature of the pay surveys and by introducing market criteria—for example, by considering the length of the queue to enter different government jobs and the length of time vacancies stay open. Such changes may help women and also improve the efficiency of government.

Dramatic changes have occurred in women's college enrollment, in labor force participation, and in entrance into formerly male occupations, particularly in the professions. These changes are taking place because of fundamental changes in women's role in the economy and in the family—changes that themselves reflect a response to rising wage rates as well as changing social attitudes. Pay set according to comparable worth would distort wage signals, inducing inappropriate supply response and unemployment. If women have been discouraged by society or barred by employers from entering certain occupations, the appropriate response is to remove the barriers, not try to repeal supply and demand. Comparable worth is no shortcut to equality.

## Notes

1. These statistics are based on the median hourly earnings of workers in these occupations in 1981. Rytina, 1982.

2. If brickmasons' wages are artificially high because of union power, the market would be unstable. More workers would desire to be brickmasons than would be hired at the artificially high wage. Would comparable worth policy help the situations? Not likely. A comparable worth solution would likely require higher pay for clergy than for brickmasons because of the heavy weight placed on readily measured items like education. A wage for clergy that is too high would also be unstable. Only the removal of the union power or restrictions on unions would satisfactorily resolve the issue.

3. This example was originated by Sharon Smith and described in Killingsworth (1984), who notes it is cited in Gold (1983).

4. The commonly cited pay gap—where women are said to earn 59 cents out of every dollar earned by men—is based on a comparison of the annual earnings of women and men who work year round and are primarily full time. In 1982 this ratio was 62 percent. This figure is lower than the figure of 72 percent cited above because the annual earnings measure is not adjusted for differences in hours worked during the year, and men are more likely than women to work overtime or on second jobs.

5. O'Neill, 1984.

6. O'Neill, 1983.

7. Hartmann, 1984.

8. Barrett, 1984.

## References

Barrett, Nancy, 1984. "Poverty, Welfare and Comparable Worth," in Phyllis Schlafly, ed., *Equal Pay for Unequal Work, A Conference on Comparable Work.*

Hartmann, Heidi I. 1984. "The Case for Comparable Worth," in Phyllis Schlafly, ed., *Equal Pay for Unequal Work, A Conference on Comparable Work.*

Killingsworth, Mark. 1984. *Statement on Comparable Worth.* Testimony before the Joint Economic Committee, U.S. Congress, Apr. 10, 1984.

O'Neill, June. 1983. "The Determinants and Wage Effects of Occupational Segregation." Working Paper, The Urban Institute.

O'Neill, June. 1984. "Earnings Differentials: Empirical Evidence and Causes" in G. Schmid, ed., *Discrimination and Equalization in the Labor Market: Employment Policies for Women in Selected Countries.*

O'Neill, June. 1984. "The Trend in the Male–Female Wage Gap in the United States." *Journal of Labor Economics,* October.

Rytina, Nancy F. 1982. "Earnings of Men and Women: A Look at Specific Occupations." *Montly Labor Review,* April 1982.

# *Some Implications of Comparable Worth*

## Laurie Shrage

...

## 1. Introduction

The passage of the Equal Pay Act in 1963 established the principle of "equal pay for equal work" in the American legal system. Workers who perform identical work must be paid equivalent wages, regardless of a worker's sex or race. However, due to historic occupational segregation, the vast majority of men and women do not perform work that is essentially similar in content. Moreover, occupational categories in which the incumbents are predominantly women (nurse, clerical worker, nursery school teacher, and the like) provide, on average, lower wages than those awarded to jobs predominantly performed by men.

The persistent gap in wages between male and female dominated professions involving similar training, experience, and working conditions, indicates *prima facie* that wage differentials are affected by gender discrimination. For the past decade, feminist civil rights organizations have affirmed the existence of gender-based wage discrimination, and the need to compensate women more equitably for their work. The remedy they commonly advocate appeals to the principle of comparable worth: jobs which are dissimilar in content, but comparable in terms of their value to an employer, should be rewarded equally. While the idea of "equal pay for jobs of comparable worth" is widely accepted among feminists, it is established neither in the law nor in the academy.

...

Recently, comparable worth has attracted criticism not only from conservatives but from progressives as well. Critics on the left argue that comparable worth primarily serves the class interests of middle-class white women, and fails to address the needs of minorities, the poor, and working class people.[1] Because the principle of comparable worth ties compensation to job merit—rather than, for example, to employee need—its enforcement, these critics allege, will primarily benefit those in our society whose work carries high social status (in other words, white-collar, managerial and professional workers over blue-collar, skilled or unskilled manual laborers).

... Since comparable worth is motivated by a concern for equality, its proponents should be especially sensitive to the charge that their goals reflect some degree of middle-class elitisim. This paper will examine the theoretical assumptions behind the demand for comparable worth, in order to see if it can be maintained in light of the criticisms raised by progressive theorists.

## 2. The Theory of Comparable Worth and Its Justification

The demand for comparable worth contains five distinct components:

1. Work which is dissimilar in content, but which requires similar levels of training, experience, and responsibility, and is performed under similar conditions, is of comparable value to employers. Workers whose work is of comparable value should receive equal compensation from employers, regardless of race or sex.

2. The occurrence of systemic economic discrimination against women and minorities in our society can be inferred from a pervasive pattern of salary differentials—a pattern in which wages paid for work performed predominantly by women and minorities average approximately 60–75 percent of wages paid to white men for work of comparable value.

3. The job evaluation systems developed by business and management experts, and which have a long history of use by employers, are helpful for comparing jobs in terms of their value to an employer.

4. However, job evaluation techniques that are currently in use must be reexamined to eliminate sex and ethnic bias both in their form (for example, how job factors are weighted, which factors are chosen, how jobs are described, and so forth) and in their application (for example, whether women and minorities participate in administering them).[2]

5. Public and private employers must conduct their own bias-free job evaluation studies to determine the extent to which wage differentials in their institutions have been affected by race or gender, and must then make appropriate adjustments to their wage structure if inequities are found to exist.[3] If employers do not voluntarily undertake these actions, then such studies and adjustments should be brought about by union negotiations, or by state or federal law.

Parts (1), (4) and (5) summarize the prescriptive components of the demand for comparable worth: that adjustments to wages should be made in accordance with the principle of equal pay for work of comparable value, using the findings of gender and ethnic neutral job evaluation techniques. Parts (2) and (3) summarize the empirical presuppositions of comparable worth theory: that statistical data on existing wage differentials, together with the findings of unbiased job evaluation studies, strongly imply the existence of systemic race and sex discrimination in our society in the setting of compensation levels. Components (2) and (3) provide some justification for (1), (4) and (5) in that if discrimination against women and minorities in the form of wage suppression exists, and if we believe the wage structure should be equitable, it follows that some steps to remedy this situation should be taken. However, what does not follow from these claims is that the remedy morally and practically required is the one proposed in (1), (4) and (5). Hence, to justify the prescriptive components of the theory, additional considerations and principles which indicate their unique remedial potential must be brought forth. In this section I will explore and develop some of these considerations.

Economists report that "women who work full time all year earn about 60 percent of what full-time men earn."[4] Despite the entrance of women in past years into jobs traditionally held by men, and despite a dramatic increase in the number of women in the work force, the gap in earnings between women and men has remained constant, or has even slightly increased, since 1955. Conversely, workers in male-dominated occupations earn 30–50% more than those in integrated or female-dominated occupations, and "the more an occupation is dominated by women, the less it pays."[5]

Some of the differences in earnings between men and women can be explained by the amount of labor supplied, in other words, the number of hours worked. This is one example of a so-called "human capital" or "productivity-related job content" variable that economists and sociologists attempt to isolate and hold constant, in order to explain some portion of the wage gap. By identifying relevant variables, social scientists attempt to determine whether factors which are independent of employer bias (such as an employee's years of training, previous experience, or the level of responsibility a job demands) can account for salary differentials between male- and female-dominated occupations. While some portion of the earnings gap can be predicted by observing variation in "human capital" characteristics other than gender or race, even conservative critics find that these correlations leave a significant portion of the gap in wages (perhaps 60 percent) unexplained.[6]

Some social scientists maintain that the unpredicted portion of the wage gap merely reflects the degree of difficulty involved in measuring certain "human capital" variables. By contrast, other scholars claim that the "unexplained" portion fo the wage gap is predictable when wage differentials are correlated with human capital features, such as race and sex. However, such correlations imply the occurrence of sex and race discrimination in the evolution of the wage structure; thus, they raise controversial issues. Nevertheless, according to civil rights attorney Winn Newman, the occurrence of discrimination can be inferred from "a consistent pattern of underpayment of women's jobs ... in virtually every work place, public and private, in this country."[7] ...

The theories of liberal economists generally make little use of the notion of discrimination because discrimination—as liberals conceive of it—is difficult to observe and measure. For them "discrimination in hiring and promotion" refers to the extent to which individual employers make decisions based upon their own biases or prejudices against particular segments of the population. To determine the extent of this phenomenon, one must measure the number of intentionally discriminatory acts of individuals. Thus, even where all Jills earn less than all Jacks, let alone in a single instance, commonsense will not dictate that discriminatory acts by employers have necessarily occurred. It is at least theoretically possible that all Jills have engaged in intentional action which is causally responsible for this state of affairs. Indeed, some would argue that given that all Jills have been socialized in a similar fashion, it is more plausible to assume that they have acted in a common fashion than to assume that their employers have. To assume common intentional action on the part of employers is to postulate a conspiracy, which is not only unlikely, but the product of paranoid thinking.

Some explanations of social phenomena employ a conception of discrimination that differs from the liberal model. By "discrimination in hiring and promotion," some theorists are referring to implicit principles of social organization which have adverse consequences for certain social groups, but which are generally not recognized by individuals because they are subsumed or entailed by the accepted, unquestioned values of their society. ... Employers may promote and perpetuate discrimination of this sort even if their individual actions happen to be relatively free of personal bias or the intention to discriminate. Indeed, they perpetuate economic discrimination against women and minorities when their actions are merely consistent with dominant cultural beliefs and stereotypes. In short, one need not be aware of the principles which organize our social institutions in order to behave "normally," just as one need not be aware of the syntactical rules of one's native language in order to speak grammatically. Nevertheless, as social theorists, we can recognize the existence of rules which structure our social interaction, and which reproduce a social hierarchy that places women and minorities in the weakest economic positions. Because this type of discrimination focuses on structural features of cultural systems or institutions, it is variously referred to as "structural," "systemic" or "institutional" discrimination."[8]

Given the statistical data on earnings, few would dispute that discrimination against women and minorities, as our second model defines it, exists in our society. What remains at issue, however, is how to reorganize our society in order to achieve a more equitable wage structure. In other words, even if components (2) and (3) are valid, do they justify the prescriptive claims in (1), (4) and (5)?

Comparable worth proponents are skeptical of the proposition that free market competition will in its course bring about an equitable wage structure. ...

...

Proponents of comparable worth also doubt that the current level of regulation on the market is high enough to bring about an equitable wage structure. In other words, they believe the achievement of equal pay for substantively equal work, ... [is] not sufficient to correct historical wage suppression. Women and minorities who work in occupations which have been traditionally dominated by their sex or race will continue to feel the effect of past discrimination on their wages: their wages are and will remain lower than they would be if these jobs were, or had been, performed predominantly by white men.[9] … Therefore, policies which raise the wages of traditionally undervalued occupations are necessary, both to compensate equitably those unaffected by new opportunities for mobility into jobs traditionally held by white males, and to attract white males into occupations from which they have been historically absent.

Since progressive political theorists doubt the therapeutic effects of the forces of supply and demand, they should be sympathetic to the demand for regulations that are designed to correct existing inequities. Moreover, since discrimination against certain economic classes in society and the underpayment of labor similarly reflect implicit structures of discrimination, theorists on the left should have little difficulty recognizing systemic economic discrimination based on race and sex. Despite these areas of compatibility between radical political philosophy and comparable worth theory, some radical theorists argue that comparable worth wrongly implies that once the market is corrected for sex and race discrimination and other imperfections through regulation, the wage structure in our society will be fair. Comparable worth theorists assume, according to these critics, that all white males in our society (including working class men), are equitably compensated for their work, and once women and minorities receive equal rates of compensation for comparable work, their wages too will be equitable. In other words, the doctrine uncritically assumes that wide differentials in pay are fair as long as they are correlated with features other than race or gender. For this reason they charge the doctrine of comparable worth with legitimating an elitist system of compensation, and with overlooking the injustices of our society's class system.[10]

In the following sections, I will try to respond to the serious issues raised by leftist critics of comparable worth. … I am … concerned with showing which principles of fair distribution actually underlie the demand for comparable worth, rather than arguing for the ultimate acceptability of any specific principle. In particular, I will argue that proponents of comparable worth need not, as radicals have claimed, embrace liberal, meritocratic principles of justice. I will argue this by showing, first, that comparable worth proponents are not committed to the view that the wages white men generally receive for their labor are fair. At most, they assume that the rate of compensation white males receive is, on average, less exploitative than the rate received by women and minority workers. Second, I will show that in making judgments regarding the relative worth of different job categories, comparable worth proponents are not endorsing meritocratic compensation, but are merely urging consistent application of accepted standards of reward. These defenses will be developed in the next two sections.

## 3. Equality and Worth

The theory of comparable worth is based on the fundamental assumption that the wages workers receive should not reflect their race or sex. Such attributes are irrelevant to the value of the work performed, and thus, to equitable rates of compensation.[11] In other words, the theory presupposes a fundamental equality of ability, talent and intelligence between persons of different gender and color. One consequence of the assumption of equality is the desire to have compensation levels set with consistency and impartiality. This means that whatever standards are employed to establish pay rates, they should be applied without regard to an employee's gender or race.

The theory's use of the concept of "worth" may be misleading. The crucial assumption underlying the theory's claims about worth is *not* that wages should be proportionate to worth, but that the labor of women and minorities is of equal worth to the labor of white men. If salary levels among white males were roughly equivalent—in other words, if large disparities in pay did not exist—then comparable worth would entail comparable salary levels and differentials for women and minorities. Moreover, it is consistent with the doctrine of comparable worth to acknowledge that some white male workers are compensated unfairly under the present system. At most, comparable worth assumes, as I have already stated, that the wages white male workers receive are, on average, less exploitative than the wages received by women and minorities.

   ...

## 4. Does Comparable Worth Reflect Class Bias?

Comparable worth advocates often emphasize statistics which show that women with college degrees, on average, earn less than men without high school diplomas; for example, childcare workers are often paid less than janitors, and librarians are often paid less than truck drivers. These comparisons suggest that proponents place a high value on credentials gained through formal education. ... Comparable worth proponents are not arguing for awarding higher value to credentials gained through formal education. They are merely in favor of rewarding these credentials impartially, without regard to the sex or race of the person who has earned them. If women with formal credentials are earning less than men without them, and men without formal credentials are earning significantly less than men with them, then women are being compensated at a lower rate than men for work dependent upon such achievements. Comparable worth proponents are in favor of women receiving an equal rate of return on their achievements, and do not necessarily favor a higher rate of compensation for formal credentials relative to other qualifications, *per se*. Thus, the criticism that the comparable worth movement is guilty of a credentialing bias shows a fundamental misunderstanding of its aims.

   ...

Comparable worth supporters focus on factors such as education to illustrate dramatically that women receive a lower rate of return on comparable credentials. Donald Treiman, Heidi Hartmann, and Patricia Roos estimate that "about 40 percent of the earnings gap between male- and female-dominated occupations can be attributed to differences in job characteristics and 60 percent to differences in the rate of return of these characteristics."[12] ... Because of this situation, comparable worth supporters are demanding equal rates of return for comparable skills and qualifications, regardless of the sex or race of the employees.

Unfortunately, in stressing comparisons between formally educated female workers and formally uneducated male workers, comparable worth proponents may have made themselves vulnerable to the misunderstanding that their demands are anti-blue-collar. Such comparisons are useful, however, to counter the objection that women, on average, are paid less than men only because the average woman's level of education or job training is lower than the average man's. It is indeed the case that the average woman's "human capital investment" is lower. But this discrepancy does not account for the entire wage gap. If it did, then we would expect to see women compensated at a level equal to their comparably educated male cohorts. But this does not generally happen. In short, the human capital theory simply cannot "explain such facts as why a woman with a college degree made on average only as much as a man with an eighth grade education," which is the point of these comparisons.[13]

...

The presumption that comparable worth is a middle-class reform has also led to the charge that it is anti-minority. Blue-collar jobs are disproportionately filled by minority men and women, and hence, if comparable worth contained an anti-working-class bias, it would adversely affect minority workers. Yet, as I have argued, comparable worth is neither anti-blue-collar nor pro-white-collar. Moreover, comparable worth pertains as much to wage discrimination based on race as it does to discrimination based on gender. ...

Leftist intellectuals are in an awkward position when they tell women and minorities who have struggled to obtain their credentials that their expectation of comparable compensation and social privileges is anti-working class. Denigrating the worth of these credentials when women and minorities achieve them reflects not a pro-working class position, but one that is anti-women and anti-minority. While comparable worth advocates do not claim that formal credentials outweigh all other factors, they do assume that these credentials have positive value, in other words, that they reflect worthwhile achievements. To argue against comparable worth on these grounds is like arguing against busing because the practice assumes that black children ought to have an equal opportunity to attain a formal education. Since this assumption grants positive value to having such an education, it is also open to the charge of elitism. Because the aim of these movements is the elimination of discrimination based on sex or race in the distribution of social goods, to criticize these movements by denigrating the achievements they aim to reward fairly, or facilitate access to, is to reject reform out of an unrealistic desire for revolution. The result, of course, is not revolution, but continuation of the *status quo*.

## 5. The Potential Impact of Comparable Worth

...

Comparable worth could have more extensive impact on our society than its opponents will allow. According to Roslyn Feldberg:

> While conservatives have fought hard against comparable worth, radicals have been re-
> luctant to fight for it. In part I think that reluctance stems from seeing the narrow pres-
> entations in comparable worth litigation as the natural limits of the concept ... By taking
> seriously the value of women's work and their right to equitable wages, comparable
> worth not only can increase women's earnings but can also set the stage for ending their
> economic dependency ... Its theoretical and political impact will reach far beyond the
> liberal framework in which it was conceived and force a rethinking of assumptions un-
> derlying gender hierarchy and the dominance of the market.[14]

We have seen that comparable worth challenges both gender and racial bias in wage differentials, and the ability of market mechanisms to correct this bias. Nevertheless, Feldberg is correct to point out that the principle of comparable worth has been narrowly applied. For example, due to the kinds of complaints that have been litigated, comparable worth supporters have generally confined themselves to urging equal pay for comparable jobs within the conventional wage-labor market. However, there is no need to limit the demand for equal pay to this range of work. The doctrine of comparable worth has implications for work falling outside the system of monetary exchange (work which is therefore often invisible as "work"), such as the job of homemaking. If we assume that the relative value of a job can be assessed—its value relative to other types of jobs—then we can estimate the relative value of housework, in monetary terms, by comparing it to jobs performed for wages outside the home. Comparisons of this sort can be used to support the demand for pay for housework equal to that of comparably valued work, and thus to support the general demand for "wages for housework."

The confinement of women to unpaid labor in the home contributes substantially to women's economic and social subordination. In return for her full-time house-work, the "housewife" receives neigher social status nor economic independence. To achieve greater economic independence for women, feminist reformers argue for the unrestricted right of women to enter the paid labor force. In addition, some feminists assert the need for "wages for housework," that is, for granting a woman a legally protected right to some portion of her spouse's (or the biological father's) income, or for awarding a mother a state-subsidized income. These latter reformers argue that the work women perform in the home contributes to, among other things, the reproduction and maintenance of society's labor force. It is, therefore, socially necessary and valuable work, for which women should be compensated in monetary terms. Moreover, in order for a woman to both raise a family and perform work that grants her an income, the work of raising a family must become recognized as socially valuable work: it must become paid work.[15] In other words, the unrestricted right to enter the paid labor force is not sufficient to guarantee women both economic independence and the freedom to be mothers and wives.

The theory of comparable worth lends additional support to the case for wages for housework. For example, the following chart shows that many common tasks of a homemaker are comparable to work performed in other occupations.[16] In the leftmost column of the chart, the work of a homemaker is compared to that of a nursemaid, a dietitian, a maintenance "man," chauffeur, and so forth. Although the

| Job | Hours per week | Rate per hour | Value per week |
|---|---|---|---|
| Nursemaid | 44.5 | $2.00 | $89.00 |
| Dietitian | 1.2 | 4.50 | 5.40 |
| Food buyer | 3.3 | 3.50 | 11.55 |
| Cook | 13.1 | 3.25 | 42.58 |
| Dishwasher | 6.2 | 2.00 | 12.40 |
| Housekeeper | 17.5 | 3.25 | 56.88 |
| Laundress | 5.9 | 2.50 | 14.75 |
| Seamstress | 1.3 | 3.25 | 4.22 |
| Practical Nurse | .6 | 3.75 | 2.25 |
| Maintenance man | 1.7 | 3.00 | 5.10 |
| Gardener | 2.3 | 3.00 | 6.90 |
| Chauffeur | 2.0 | 3.25 | 6.50 |
| Total: $257.53 or $13,391.56 a year (1972) | | | |

rate per hour in the middle section of the chart reflects the "going rate" and not necessarily an equitable rate of compensation for these jobs, the composite comparison offers us a rough way to reach an estimate of the social and monetary value of an average homemaker's work. (This chart is based on 1972 statistics, and thus the rates should be adjusted upward to account for inflation.) If we assume that the underpayment of labor in all cases constitutes economic exploitation, then the failure to provide homemakers with monetary compensation (or its equivalent in terms of property, support or pension rights) is exploitative.

… By encouraging comparisons which force a reevaluation of traditionally devalued categories of work, the theory of comparable worth will make its greatest impact. If work performed inside the home were treated as comparable to work performed outside, then states which do not recognize a homemaker's right to some portion of her spouse's financial assets might be forced to changed their laws.

## 6. Conclusion

This paper tries to demonstrate how the concept of systemic discrimination can be used to acquire a better understanding of the statistical data on wage differentials and, consequently, of the way in which inequitable distributions of income are to be redressed. By introducing this concept, we can give greater credibility to claims of discrimination—claims for which there is little evidence in terms of the liberal model. I have argued that claims of discrimination can be sustained, not by observing individual acts or intentions, but by observing a pattern of wage disparities that signifies the existence of rules which implicitly organize our social institutions and which adversely affect specific portions of our population. In saying these rules are implicit, I mean that they are not usually recognized explicitly by members of our society. Nevertheless we can, and indeed must, recognize them in constructing our social policies. The prescriptions of comparable worth theory constitute social policy proposals which recognize and aim to redress implicit structures of discrimination.

In sum, the concept of systemic discrimination provides a powerful theoretical tool for challenging our economic system and for motivating institutional, judicial or legislative reform.[17]

...

---

## Notes

1. Drew Christie, "Comparable Worth and Distributive Justice," a paper presented on April 25, 1985 in Chicago to a meeting of the Radical Philosophy Association held in conjunction with the American Philosophical Association Western Division meetings.
2. For a summary of how sex bias can enter job evaluation systems, see Helen Remick, "Major Issues in *a priori* Applications," in *Comparable Worth and Wage Discrimination,* Helen Remick, ed. (Philadelphia: Temple University Press, 1984), pp. 106–108.
3. Remick, p. 99.
4. Paula England, "Explanations of Job Segregation and the Sex Gap in Pay," in *Comparable Worth: Issue for the 80's,* Vol. 1, p. 54. ...
5. Andrea Beller, "Occupational Segregation and the Earnings Gap," in *Comparable Worth: Issue for the 80's* (Washington, D.C.: U.S. Commission on Civil Rights, 1984), Vol. 1, p. 23. According to Paula England, "each one percent female in an occupation was found to have a net depressing effect on annual earnings of $30 for males and $17 for females. This means that the difference between the median annual earnings of full-time workers in two occupations of equivalent value in their combinations of skill demands, but differing in that one is 90 percent female and one is 90 percent male, is $1,360 for women and $2,400 for men." Paula England, "Explanation of Job Segregation and the Sex Gap in Pay," pp. 61–62.
6. England, "Explanation of Job Segregation and the Sex Gap in Pay," p. 60.
7. Winn Newman, Statement to the U.S. Commission on Civil Rights at their Consultation on Comparable Worth, June 7, 1984, in *Comparable Worth: Issue for the 80's,* Vol. 2, p. 87.
8. The data on occupational segregation, like the data on wage differentials, attest to the existence of systemic race and sex discrimination in employment, and can be redressed by affirmative action in hiring and promotion, as well as by comparable worth.
9. See Ronnie Steinberg, "Identifying Wage Discrimination and Implementing Pay Equity Adjustments," in *Comparable Worth: Issue for the 80's,* Vol. 1, p. 99. ...
10. Christie, "Comparable Worth and Distributive Justice."
11. While our legal system recognizes that, in some cases, a person's gender or religion is inherent to the work performed (a "*bona fide* occupational qualification")—for example, being Jewish is inherent to being a cantor; being female is inherent to modeling women's clothes, acting a woman's part in a play, being a wetnurse or a private attendant, and so on—these characteristics should not be relevant to determining the salary levels for such work.
12. Donald Treiman, Heidi Hartmann, and Patricia Roos, "Assessing Pay Discrimination Using National Data," in *Comparable Worth and Wage Discrimination,* p. 147.
13. Ray Marshall and Beth Paulin, "The Employment and Earnings of Women: The Comparable Worth Debate," in *Comparable Worth: Issues for the 80's,* Vol. 1, p. 202. Nor can human capital theory explain why unskilled, male-dominated entry level jobs pay more than unskilled, female-dominated entry level jobs. Presumably the human capital investment in male and female unskilled labor is the same. Moreover, since the supply of unskilled workers of both sexes is higher than the number of jobs, the scarcity hypothesis does not explain this differential either.
14. Roslyn Feldberg, "Comparable Worth: Toward Theory and Practice in the United States," in *Signs* 10 (1984): 328.

15. According to Gisela Bock and Barbara Duden, our contemporary notion of "housework," and the association of this type of work with women, arose in the 17th and 18th centuries with the transition from a pre-capitalist, pre-industrial economy to an industrial capitalist one. They argue that in the transition to modern production, the need for the efficient (and cheap) reproduction and maintenance of the worker forced the basic family unit structure to homogenize across class and ethnic groups. The family structure which evolved to suit the needs of capitalist production was one that linked the relatively modern chores of homemaking and childrearing to the wife's economic role. See Gisela Bock and Barbara Duden, "Labor of Love—Love as Labor: On the Genesis of Housework in Capitalism," in *From Feminism to Liberation*, Edith Hoshino Altbach, ed. (Cambridge, Mass.: Schenkman Publishing Company, Inc., 1980), pp. 153–92.

16. This chart is taken from Ann Crittenden Scott, "The Value of Housework," in *Feminist Frameworks*, A. Jaggar and P. Rothenberg, eds. (New York: McGraw Hill, 1984), p. 315.

17. I am grateful to Sandra Bartky, Elizabeth Segal, Daniel Segal, and the *STP* editors for their helpful comments and suggestions on earlier drafts of this paper. I am also grateful to the Radical Philosophy Association for their session on comparable worth where these ideas were first presented. Finally, I am indebted to Norman Segal, of Mudge, Rose, Guthrie, Alexander, and Ferdon, for his assistance in examining the judicial history of comparable worth.

# *Prostitution*

## Alison M. Jaggar

...

... A philosophical theory of prostitution ... should state exactly what prostitution is, should tell us what, if anything, is wrong with it and should help us determine what, if anything, should be done about it. In this paper, ... I compare the relative merits of three attempts to provide such a theory and identify the philosophical basis on which a comprehensive theory of prostitution must rest. Thus I view my paper as a prolegomenon to a theory of prostitution.

The three approaches to prostitution that I shall discuss are the liberal, the classical Marxist, and the radical feminist approaches. ... Each begins from the paradigm case of the prostitute as a woman selling her sexual services, but each picks out very different features as essential to that situation. Thus, a comparison of these theories of prostitution illustrates an important general point about the appropriate philosophical methodology for approaching not only the issue of prostitution but also a number of other normative social issues.

### I. Liberalism

The standard liberal position on prostitution is that it should be decriminalized. ...

...

[But] ... agreement on the decriminalization of prostitution does not mean that liberals share a common view about its moral status. Liberal feminists have always seen prostitution as degrading to women and conclude that it should receive no encouragement even though it should be decriminalized. This attitude is implicit in the report of the NOW Task Force on prostitution which supports

> full prosecution of any acts of coercion to any person, public agency or group to influence women to become prostitutes.[1]

Others, however, claim to see nothing wrong with prostitution. Some prostitutes view themselves as entrepreneurs, choosing to go into business for themselves rather than to work for someone else.[2] One prostitute remarked that the work was really not tiring, that it was often less humiliating than dating.[3] The prostitute may see herself as the boss because she can say "No" to the deal;[4] as someone, therefore, who is less exploited than exploiting. Thus it may be argued that decriminalization will finally allow "the oldest profession" to take its place among the other professions so that prostitutes will be respected as offering a skilled service.

These liberal reflections on the moral status of prostitution, however, are generally taken as mere side comments. The central liberal line of argument is to stress the need for decriminalization by appeal to classical liberal ideals. Thus, liberal arguments emphasize the importance of equality before the law and of individual rights. They attempt to minimize government interference in the lives of individuals and they assume that there is a "private" sphere of human existence. ... Prostitution, they believe, falls obviously within that sphere.

The usual liberal recommendation on prostitution, then, is that it should be treated as an ordinary business transaction, the sale of a service; in this case, of a sexual service. Because the prostitute engages in it out of economic motivation, liberals view prostitution as quite different from a sexual act committed by physical force or under threat of force; they view prostitution as quite different, for instance, from rape. Instead, they see it as a contract like other contracts, entered into by each individual for her or his own benefit, each striking the best bargain that she or he is able. The state has exactly the same interest in the prostitution contract as in all other contracts and may therefore regulate certain aspects by law. For instance, the law may concern itself with such matters as hygiene, control of disease, minimum standards of service and of working conditions, misleading advertising, payment of taxes and social security, etc. It should also ensure equal opportunity by redrawing the legal definition of prostitution so that an individual of either sex may be a prostitute. In these sorts of ways, the state would fulfill its traditional liberal function of ensuring fair trading practices. It should assure consumers of "a clean lay at a fair price."[5]

At first sight, the liberal approach to prostitution seems refreshingly straightforward and uncomplicated. As so often happens, however, this appearance is deceptive. One problem concerns the normative assumption that prostitution is a contract whose legitimacy is equal to that of other business contracts.[6] Although liberals view the paradigmatic social relation as contractual, they do not believe that all contracts are legitimate. Mill, for instance, denied the legitimacy of contracts by which individuals permanently abdicated or alienated their freedom to decide on future courses of action, and on this ground he argued that the state should not enforce either lifelong marriage contracts or contracts where an individual sold her- or himself into slavery.[7] ... The early liberal conviction that the primary purpose of the state was to uphold the sanctity of contracts has been weakened in contemporary times and liberals now also expect the state

> to provide against those contracts being made which, from the helplessness of one of the parties to them, instead of being a security for freedom, become an instrument of disguised oppression.[8]

These restrictions on legitimate contracts might be strong enough to exclude prostitution. It may well be that prostitution constitutes the sort of selling of oneself that a liberal would refuse to countenance. And it is surely not implausible to consider many prostitution contracts as instruments of not very well disguised oppression. Those liberals, therefore, are being too hasty who simply assume the legitimacy of prostitution contracts. In order to establish that prostitution is simply an ordinary business contract, they need a clear theory of what kinds of contracts are legitimate. … And they need a clear analysis of prostitution together with a normative theory of sexuality.

Liberal writers have not devoted much attention to the latter question at least. Since they ordinarily assume that sexual relations fall within the "private" realm and hence are outside the sphere of legal regulation, the development of a normative theory of sexuality has not seemed important for their political philosophy.[9] Their main contribution to the analysis of prostitution has been to insist that a prostitute may be either male or female. Thus, liberals would rewrite laws regarding prostitution in gender-neutral language and would also, presumably, wish to revise the first part of the definition of "prostitution" in *Webster's New Twentieth Century Dictionary* which currently reads:

> *prostitute, n.* 1, a woman who engages in promiscuous sexual intercourse for pay; whore; harlot.

Here, liberals would presumably substitute "person" for "woman" and would construe "sexual intercourse" broadly enough to cover sexual encounters between individuals of either sex. Such an interpretation would also allow so-called massage parlors within the definition of "prostitution." This liberal revision of the concept of prostitution may seem at first sight to be in line with common usage, with common sense and with common justice. As we shall see, however, there are other accounts of prostitution which draw the boundaries quite differently.

A final problem with the liberal position on prostitution concerns its assumption that the prostitute enters into the transaction voluntarily. It has often been pointed out in other contexts that the liberal concept of coercion is very weak. It may well turn out that the sorts of economic considerations that impel some persons into prostitution do indeed constitute a sort of coercion and that the prostitution contract may therefore be invalidated on those grounds. This is one of the objections made by the Marxist theory of prostitution, to which I now turn.

## II. Marxism

The Marxist approach to prostitution is considerably wider-ranging than the liberal approach, both because it attempts to understand prostitution in its social context and because it construes prostitution much more broadly. For instance, Marxists view prostitution as including not only the sale of an individual's sexual services; they see it also as the exchange of all those tangible and intangible services that a married woman provides to her husband in return for economic support. Sometimes they believe that prostitution may cover even the exchange of the services that a man provides when he marries a rich woman.

Whether or not marriage is a form of prostitution is determined, for the Marxist, by the economic class of the marriage partners. It is only where property is involved that marriage degenerates into prostitution; where no property is involved, for instance among the proletariat, marriage is based solely on mutual inclination. ...

In describing bourgeois marriage as a form of prostitution, Marx and Engels assume not only that men as well as women may prostitute themselves; they assume also that what is sold may not be restricted to sexual services. From this, it is but a short step to describing the sale of a number of other services as types of prostitution. Indeed, in the *Economic and Philosophical Manuscripts,* Marx asserts that all wage labor is a form of prostitution. He writes, "Prostitution (in the ordinary sense) is only a *specific* expression of the *general* prostitution of the *labourer.*"[10]

Someone might object that this usage of Marx's is merely metaphorical, that he is simply utilising the pejorative connotations of "prostitution" in order to condemn wage labor. But the following entry in *Webster's New Twentieth Century Dictionary* supports the claim that Marx's broader usage is not metaphorical:

> *prostitute, n.* 2. a person, as a writer, artist, etc., who sells his services for low or unworthy purposes.

If *Webster's* too is mistaken, and if there is indeed a philosophically significant distinction to be made between the woman who sells sexual services and the individual who sells services of any kind, then that distinction must be given a philosophical rationale.

Does the Marxist corpus contain such a rationale or does it, on the other hand, provide a reason for assimilating wage labor to prostitution? I think that it contains traces of both but that the tendency to assimilate prostitution to wage labor is probably stronger. Some of Engels's objections to prostitution in the narrower sense seem to depend on two specific normative beliefs about sexuality, that sex should be linked with love and that "sexual love is by its nature exclusive."[11] It is because of the latter belief that he worries, since he views both monogamy and prostitution as results of the same state of affairs (namely, male ownership of the means of production), whether "prostitution [can] disappear without dragging monogamy with it into the abyss?"[12] He is anxious to make monogamy, or at any rate sexual fidelity, "a reality—also for men."[13] Similarly, he wants to make the "paper"[14] description of bourgeois marriage into a reality by turning an economic transaction into a free agreement based on mutual sex-love. ... Unfortunately, the theory of sexuality on which these objections to prostitution are based is left undeveloped. We are given no reason to believe that Engels's notion of "modern individual sex-love," which he describes as "the greatest moral advance we owe to [monogamy],"[15] is in fact anything more than a romantic Victorian prejudice.

Even if our intuitions about sexual relations do not agree with Engels's, however, I do not think that we are necessarily thrown back to the liberal view about prostitution. Instead I believe that it is possible to draw from the Marxist corpus another, more searching, more plausible, and more specifically Marxist critique of prostitution. This critique, however, is very similar to the critique of wage labor and thus leads us in the direction of assimilating female prostitution to the wage labor of either sex.

...

... Both the bourgeois wife and the wage laborer ... can be seen as "instruments of production," the latter of commodities, the former of babies. Prostitutes in the narrower, more conventional sense cannot be viewed in this way, of course. They perform a service rather than create a product.[16] Nevertheless, Marx presents prostitution as a paradigm case of the sort of alienated relationships that are created by capitalism, where money substitutes for concrete human characteristics. He writes that, under capitalism,

> What I am and can do is, therefore, not at all determined by my individuality. I am ugly, but I can buy the most beautiful woman for myself. Consequently, I am not ugly, for the effect of ugliness, its power to repel, is annulled by money.[17]

Just as the capacity to labor becomes a commodity under capitalism, so does sexuality, especially the sexuality of women. Thus prostitutes, like wage laborers, have an essential human capacity alienated. Like wage laborers, they become dehumanized and their value as persons is measured by their market price. And like wage laborers, they are compelled to work by economic pressure; prostitution, if not marriage, may well be the best option available to them.

...

Given this critique, it is hardly surprising to find in *The Communist Manifesto* the explicit statement that it is necessary to abolish "prostitution both public and private."[18] But Marx and Engels certainly do not suggest that this end may be achieved by legal prohibition. Since all forms of prostitution result from inequality of wealth, such inequality must be eliminated. And in our time this means that capitalism must be abolished. For it is capitalism that gives men control over the means of production, thus forcing women to sell their bodies and allowing men to maintain a sexual double standard in marriage. And of course it is capitalism, by definition, that maintains the wage system and so forces the majority of the population to prostitute themselves by selling whatever capacities to labor that they may possess. Thus Marxists believe that the elimination of prostitution demands a full communist revolution. Until then, in one way or another, "capital screws us all."

...

## III. Radical Feminism

For contemporary radical feminists, prostitution is the archetypal relationship of women to men. Karen Lindsey sums it up this way:

> We have long held that all women sell themselves: that the only available roles of a woman—wife, secretary, girlfriend—all demand the selling of herself to one or more men.[19]

Even a century ago, some feminists saw marriage as a form of prostitution. … Contemporary radical feminists have extended this insight and now perceive most social interaction between women and men as some form of prostitution.[20] Thus, they believe that almost every man/woman encounter has sexual overtones and typically is designed to reinforce the sexual dominance of men. Correspondingly, men reward this sexual service in a variety of ways: the payment may range from a very tangible dinner to the intangible but nonetheless essential provision of male approval and patronage. Paradoxically, radical feminists argue, some women are even forced to prostitute themselves by selling their celibacy. They may retain their alimony or their social security payments only by remaining "chaste."[21]

This radical feminist view contrasts both with liberalism and with Marxism in its insistence that prostitutes must be defined as women. It differs from liberalism in its broad construal of what constitutes sexual services and from Marxism in its refusal to assimilate prostitution to other types of wage labor. It sees the social function of prostitution primarily as a means neither for sexual enjoyment nor for profit. Instead, radical feminists see prostitution as an institution to assert the dominance and power of men over women.

With respect to prostitution in the narrow conventional sense, radical feminists admit that it may indeed satisfy the physical desires of men, but they see this as being only a subsidiary function. Primarily, they believe,

> Prostitution exists to meet the desire of men to degrade women. Studies made by men reveal that very few even pretend they frequent prostitutes primarily for sexual gratification. Young boys admit they go to achieve a sense of male camaraderie and freedom. They usually go in groups and gossip about it at length afterward in a way that is good for their egos. Other men have expressed the prime motive as the desire to reaffirm the basic 'filth' of all women; or to clearly separate 'good' from 'bad' women in their minds, or for the opportunity to treat another person completely according to personal whim.[22]

In addition, conventional prostitution is seen as a way of controlling other women who are not culturally defined as prostitutes.

> The existence of a category of women defined by this function of sex object, plus the fact that every woman must guard against 'slipping' into this category or being assigned to it (and the absence of a comparable group of men), is sufficient to understanding prostitution as oppressive to all women. By the ubiquitous 'threat' of being treated like a 'common prostitute' we are kept in our places and our freedom is further contracted.[23]

Thus,

> The [prostitution] laws are fundamental to the male protection racket—to maintaining most women as private rather than public property.[24]

… The radical feminist denies the liberal contention that conventional prostitution is a victimless crime. The victims are all women, but particularly the prostitutes themselves, outcast, degraded and exploited by all the men who, directly or indirectly, enjoy the benefits of prostitution.[25] …

[But] unlike religious reforms of the past, feminists do not base opposition to prostitution on anti-sex values. Just as with marriage, our opposition is to the economics of the situation. Sex is a fine thing when it is the free choice of the individuals involved—free of economic coercion. No one should be dependent on selling herself for support; all love should be free love.[26]

So it is the economic coercion underlying prostitution, which requires that a woman's sexuality can be expressed only in a manner pleasing to men, that provides the basic feminist objection to prostitution. This economic coercion means that ultimately the moral status of prostitution is identical with that of rape. Like rape, prostitution perpetuates the oppression of women by encouraging the view that women are mere sexual objects, hence reinforcing male dominance and female inferiority.

Needless to say, radical feminists want to eliminate prostitution in all its forms. For this, they see two preconditions. One is that the male demand for prostitutes should be eliminated. This requires a total transformation of men's attitudes towards women and it also requires the abandonment of such conventional myths about male sexuality as that men have a much stronger biological appetite for sex than women. When masculinity is no longer so inseparably tied to heterosexual performance, feminists hypothesize that men will no longer demand prostitutes.

Recognition that the demand for prostitutes is not a biological inevitability is a comparatively recent insight in our culture. But feminists have always recognized that the *supply* of prostitutes is a function of women's inferior social status. Over fifty years ago, Emma Goldman remarked:

Nowhere is woman treated according to the merit of her work but rather as a sex. It is therefore almost inevitable that she should pay for her right to exist, to keep a position in whatever line, with sex favors. Thus it is merely a question of degree whether she sells herself to one man, in or out of marriage, or to many men. Whether our reformers admit it or not, the economic and social inferiority of woman is responsible for prostitution.[27]

Radical feminists believe, therefore, that the eradication of prostitution requires the abolition of the male monopoly of economic power together with an abandonment of the view that women are primarily sexual objects. So long as these two interdependent conditions exist, almost any significant transaction between a woman and a man must be a form of prostitution. … Until they are [abolished], radical feminists believe that, contrary to what conventional morality may indicate, women are confronted by a choice which is morally indistinguishable: it is the choice between "sucking cock and kissing ass."[28]

To many people and especially to many men, the radical feminist account of prostitution seems startling and offensive. A number of objections to it spring immediately to mind. In order to try to make the radical feminist account more plausible, I shall outline some of these objections and probable radical feminist answers to them.

One common objection to the radical feminist view of prostitution argues that it is preposterous to suppose that, when a man brings gifts to a woman he loves or takes her out to dinner, he is treating her as a prostitute. Such gestures are intended and should be received simply as tokens of affection. The radical feminist answer to this objection is that individuals' intentions do not necessarily indicate the true nature of what is going on. Both man and woman might be outraged at the description of their candlelit dinner as prostitution, but the radical feminist argues this outrage is due simply to the participants' failure or refusal to perceive the social context in which their dinner date occurs. This context is deeply sexist: the chances are that the man has more economic power than the woman; and it is certain that much of woman's social status depends on her attractiveness as defined by men. ...

But "almost inevitable" is not inevitable. It may be true that many more dinner dates are forms of prostitution than would appear at first sight. But surely it is not logically necessary that a man is prostituting a woman when he takes her out to dinner. What about the occasions when she pays for herself? Or even when she pays for him? Surely it is logically possible for a woman to treat a man as a prostitute? Some men even define themselves as prostitutes.

Here again the radical feminists point to the social context. They point out that ... given the different social status of women and men in our society, it is always true that, in sexual encounters between women and men, a man "has" and a woman "is had." And [if] a man "has" another man, he is depriving him of his masculine status. Young dependent males in prison are even referred to as "women."

In arguing that prostitution is paradigmatically a relation of women to men, radical feminists are remembering the sexism that has structured our history and that continues to pervade every aspect of contemporary life. They are remembering that women appear to have been defined always as "sexual objects" and that the "traffic in women" appears to have been the earliest form of exchange.[29] They are remembering that people's personal identity is grounded on their gender-identity so firmly that, while they may "pass" for black or white or be upwardly or downwardly mobile from their class, any attempt to change their gender is met inevitably with extreme anxiety, confusion and even hostility. They are remembering that a defining feature of gender is the way in which sexuality is expressed so that homosexuals, for instance, are commonly viewed as failing to be appropriately masculine or feminine. And finally, radical feminists are remembering that not only is gender in general tied up inextricably with sexuality but also that femininity in particular is defined in large part by the ability to be attractive sexually to men. Most women have internalized the need to be "attractive" in this way and even those who have not done so usually cannot afford to be indifferent to men's opinions. Whether housewife or wage-earner, therefore, and whether or not she allows genital contact, a woman must sell her sexuality. And since, unlike a man, she is defined largely in sexual terms, when she sells her sexuality she sells herself.

## IV. Towards a Philosophical Theory of Prostitution

Although these arguments may not establish conclusively the correctness of the radical feminist approach to prostitution, they do make it much more plausible. And the questions raised by radical feminism help to determine what is required for a philosophical account of prostitution that is adequate.

First of all, an adequate account of prostitution requires a philosophical theory of sexuality. Such a theory must be in part conceptual, in part normative. It must help us to draw the conceptual boundaries of sexual activity, enabling us to answer both how non-genital activity can still be sexual and even how genital activity may not be sexual. Given our ordinary ways of thinking, this latter suggestion may sound paradoxical but it is becoming a commonplace for feminists to define rape as a form of physical assault rather than as a form of sexual expression. Similarly, some feminists are now insisting that prostitution raises no issues of *sexual* privacy: "Prostitution is a professional or economic option, unrelated to sexual/emotional needs."[30] And we have seen other feminists deny that the main purpose of prostitution is sexual, even for men. Not only must the needed philosophical theory of sexuality help us to identify just what sexual activity is; it must also help us to make the conceptual connections and distinctions between forms of sexual expression on the one hand and gender and personal identity on the other hand. It must clarify the relationship, if any, between sexual expression and love. And it must compare the human capacity for sexual activity to the human capacity to labor. Thus it must tell us, for instance, whether there is anything especially degrading about the sale of sexual services.

An adequate account of prostitution also rests, obviously, on a philosophical account of coercion. In particular, we need to know whether economic inducements are coercive and, if so, in what circumstances. Only from this philosophical basis can we work out the conceptual relationships between prostitution, rape and "free enterprise."

In addition to these conceptual and normative presuppositions, a useful account of prostitution also requires an investigation of the way in which the institution functions in contemporary society. We need to know why women engage in prostitution and why men do so. We need to understand the relationship between "the traffic in women" and other forms of exchange in our society; in other words, we need to understand the political economy of prostitution. Without such knowledge, our account of prostitution will remain at a very high level of abstraction; [and] we will not be able to understand the specific phenomenon of prostitution in contemporary society. ...

    ...

... Is there a single correct analysis of prostitution on which we must agree before we can construct a normative moral and political theory about it? And is such a correct analysis to be found by looking up dictionary definitions or paying closer attention to ordinary usage?

I do not think so. I think that the issue of prostitution presents a clear example of the futility of that conventional wisdom which recommends that we begin by defining our terms. For the divergence in the competing definitions of prostitution does not result from failing to consult the dictionary or from paying insufficient attention to ordinary usage. It results from normative disagreements on what constitutes freedom, on the moral status of certain activities and, ultimately, on a certain view of what it means to be human. Thus, the disagreement on what constitutes prostitution is merely a surface manifestation of a disagreement over the fundamental categories to be used in describing social activities and over what are the important features of social life which need to be picked out. The inability of moral theorists to agree on what constitutes prostitution is an instance of the interdependence of principles and intuitions, of theory and data, even of fact and value. …

---

### Notes

© 1980 by Alison M. Jaggar. A draft of this paper was read to the Society for Women in Philosophy at the Pacific Division meetings of the American Philosophical Association in March 1976, and also to the Canadian Philosophical Association in June 1970. The commentators were Christine Pierce, Susan Sherwin, and Winnie Villeneuve; to all of them I am indebted for their helpful suggestions. I am also grateful to the following people who were kind enough to send me written comments: Sara Ann Ketchum, Sara Ruddick, Michael Fox, Alan Soble, and Rollin Workman. Penelope Smith helped me with resources.

1. NOW Resolution 141, passed at the sixth national conference of the National Organization for Women in Washington, D.C., in February, 1973.

2. Kate Millett, "Prostitution: A Quartet for Female Voices," in Vivian Gornick and Barbara K. Moran, eds., *Woman in Sexist Society* (New York: Basic Books, 1971) p. 52. It should be noted, however, that the woman who makes this claim also condemns prostitution as "slavery, psychologically."

3. *Ibid.*, p. 59.

4. *Ibid.*, p. 48.

5. Susan Brownmiller, "Speaking Out on Prostitution," in Anne Koedt and Shulamith Firestone, eds., *Notes From the Third Year* (New York: Notes From the Second Year, Inc., 1971), p. 38.

6. I owe this, together with a number of other important points, to Professor Christine Pierce who commented on an earlier draft of this paper when it was read to the Pacific Division of the American Philosophical Association in March, 1976.

7. John Stuart Mill, *On Liberty,* reprinted in *The Utilitarians* (New York: Anchor Books, 1973), p. 583.

8. T. H. Green, *Liberal Legislation and Freedom of Contract* III, p. 388, quoted in D. J. Manning, *Liberalism* (New York: St. Martin's Press, 1976), p. 20.

9. Robert Solomon identifies liberal views on sexuality as a "mythology [which] appears to stand upon a tripod of mutually supporting platitudes: (1) and foremost, that the essential aim (and even the sole aim) of sex is enjoyment; (2) that sexual activity is and ought to be essentially private activity, and (3) that any sexual activity is as valid as any other." R. Solomon, "Sexual Paradigms," in Alan Soble, ed., *Philosophy of Sex: Contemporary Readings* (Totowa, N.J.: Littlefield Adams, 1980), pp. 89–99; p. 92.

10. Karl Marx, *The Economic and Philosophical Manuscripts of 1844,* edited with an introduction by Dirk J. Struik (New York: International Publishers, 1964), p. 133, footnote.

11. Frederick Engels, *The Origin of the Family, Private and the State* (New York: International Publishers, 1942), p. 42. I do not know how far Marx shared this belief, but it is certainly echoed in Lenin's rejection of "the glass-of-water" theory of sex in communist society. "To be sure, thirst has to be quenched. But would a normal person normally lie down in the gutter and drink from a puddle? Or even from a glass whose edge has been greased by many lips?" V. I. Lenin, *the Emancipation of Women* (New York: International Publishers, 1934), p. 106.

12. Engels, *op. cit.,* p. 67.

13. *Ibid.*

14. *Ibid.*, p. 72.

15. *Ibid.*, p. 61.

16. Professor Sara Ketchum pointed this out to me in a letter which discussed prostitution and Marxist theory in a very illuminating and helpful way.

17. Marx, *op. cit.*, p. 167.

18. Karl Marx and Frederick Engels, "Manifesto of the Communist Party," reprinted in *Selected Works of Marx and Engels* (Moscow and New York: New World Paperbacks, 1968), p. 51.

19. Karen Lindsey, "Prostitution and the Law," *The Second Wave* 1, No. 4 (1972), p. 6.

20. … "Wifehood is slavery with a measure of status and security; prostitution is a bit of freedom coupled with the stigma of outcast." Barbara Mehrhof and Pamela Kearon, "Prostitution," *Notes from the Third Year, op. cit.*, p. 72.

21. Mary Lathan, "Selling Celibacy," *Women: A Journal of Liberation* 3, No. 1 (1972), pp. 24–25.

22. Mehrhof and Kearon, *op. cit.*, p. 72. A similar claim is made by one of the prostitutes interviewed by Kate Millett: "There's a special indignity in prostitution, as if sex were dirty and men can only enjoy it with someone low. It involves a type of contempt, a kind of disdain, and a kind of triumph over another human being." Kate Millett, *op. cit.*, p. 54.

23. Mehrhof and Kearon, *op. cit.*, p. 74.

24. Jackie MacMillan, "Prostitution as Sexual Politics," *Quest: A Feminist Quarterly* IV, No. 1 (Summer 1977), p. 43.

25. The men who profit from prostitution, according to the radical feminist, are not merely the customer and the pimp, but also the policemen, the prostitution lawyer, the judge, organized crime and ultimately, because of the "class significance" of prostitution, every man in this society.

26. Linda Thurston, "Prostitution and the Law," *The Second Wave* 1, No. 4 (1972), p. 8.

27. Emma Goldman, *The Traffic in Women* (New York: Times Change Press, 1970), p. 20.

28. Cathy Nossa, "Prostitution: Who's Hustling Women?," *Women: A Journal of Liberation* 3, No. 1 (1972), p. 29.

29. Gayle Rubin, "The Traffic in Women," in Ranya Reiter, ed., *Towards An Anthropology of Women* (New York: Monthly Review Press, 1975), pp. 157–210.

30. Jackie MacMillan, *op. cit.*, p. 47.

# *A Most Useful Tool*

## Sunny Carter

For five days my infant son lay in an oxygen tent flushed with fever. He was not responding to antibiotics. His pneumonia seemed determined to not go away. A nurse hurried briskly into our room carrying yet another tray holding several syringes. She squirted them into Brennan's tiny mouth one by one. Too weak to resist, he swallowed the medicines, his baby face wrinkling at the bad taste. Then he turned his little head wearily and vomited the stuff back up, the pinkish mixture puddling on the white hospital sheet.

The nurse clicked her tongue in exasperation. "Now look what you've done. We'll have to take these all over again." Brennan began to cry. I pulled back the plastic tent and picked him up, rocking him against my breast.

"No, goddammit, just leave him alone." Exhausted from worry and very little sleep, I began to cry, too. "Why can't you just leave him alone?"

She stared at me with cold indignity and turned on her heel to leave the room. Dr. Dannon stood in the doorway. "Never mind the oral medicines," he said. "We're starting him on IV's. That will be all."

She hurried past him, leaving us alone.

"You look worn out," he said.

"Yeah. So do you," I replied, seeing his drawn, kind face.

"I have some bad news. Brennan has cystic fibrosis."

I was a medical technician. I remembered vaguely studying the various genetic illnesses of children. Cystic fibrosis. Cystic fibrosis. "My God," I said, the knowledge dawning. "That's fatal."

He nodded, sorrow in his eyes. "He won't die now. Now that we know what's going on, he'll respond to the IV drugs. The average life expectancy is twelve years. Some live longer. I'm sorry."

I held my baby against me, numb with fear and exhaustion. I couldn't believe it. My son was going to die.

...

Cystic fibrosis is a disease which primarily affects the lungs and the digestive system. Pneumonia occurs frequently. CF children produce [a] copious amount of thick, sticky mucus which clogs the tiny airways in the lungs, creating a perfect breeding ground for invading bacteria.

"This is a very expensive disease," Dr. Dannon said. "During the years when he's relatively well, the average cost per child per year is ten thousand dollars. Can you come up with that kind of money?"

My yearly salary in 1976 was nine thousand dollars. Now I would need another ten thousand each year to keep my son alive. How in God's name was I going to get that money?

"Sure I can," I replied.

*       *       *

Brennan was released from the hospital a week later. I learned to do the chest percussion treatments he would need three times daily for the rest of his life. Every day I turned him head down on my lap and literally pounded the mucus loose so that he could cough it up and out of his lungs. How could I go back to work and still be there to give him treatments? How could I be at work during the times when he would be hospitalized? And how the hell was I going to come up with ten thousand extra dollars a year?

While Brennan slept, my mind raced. I could sell drugs. No, that wouldn't work. Drug dealers get arrested, then who would take care of my boy? I could rob banks or 7-11 stores. No, they get busted sooner or later, too. Well, I thought, I could learn to be a hooker. Even if they get busted, they usually just pay a fine. Hmmmm. Yeah, that was it. I'd learn to hook.

   ...

So, after a phone call and a meeting ... I became one. ...

I went shopping for what I imagined to be proper "hooker clothes": a long, flowing dressing gown, garter belts and stockings, ridiculously high heels. I practiced walking the length of my apartment until I felt confident that I could wear the damn things without falling down. I felt I had to call attention to my only good feature— my legs. The rest of me was twenty pounds overweight, I had no waist at all, my breasts were big, but droopy. My face was passing, but nothing to write home about. Still, nobody had ever kicked me out of bed, so, as I waited for my very first client, a fellow named Harold, I walked back and forth to make sure I had the shoes down pat, smoked one cigarette after another and made several trips to the john to check my make-up and hair.

The apartment was spotlessly clean, fresh sheets on my bed. I lit the candles I had bought, figuring the less he could see, the better off we both would be. ...

   ...

*The doorbell.*

My God, he was here. ... Where were my shoes? Oh, Jesus, there, in the middle of the floor, get them on, quick ... the doorbell again, Jesus, don't wake the baby up, that's all I need, "Just a minute! I'm coming ..."

I draw a breath, pulled my face into a smile. I opened the door.

There stood Harold Wong. All five feet three inches of him. All one-hundred-twenty-pounds of him. At five-feet-nine, not to mention four more inches of high heels, I towered over him as we stood in the doorway. I had a good thirty-five pounds on him. Stricken suddenly with the ludicrous picture we made, I began to laugh. Harold's face broke into a broad smile.

"Ah! So glad to see you so happy! And so big! I love big blonde woman!"

It was over before I knew it.

Twenty minutes had passed from the time he walked in until the moment he left, bowing and thanking me for a lovely time.

I sat on my bed, holding the hundred-dollar bill. He had actually *tipped* me. It was that easy. He had literally come and gone, and I was one hundred dollars richer in just twenty minutes.

I went into the bathroom and looked and looked at my reflection. I didn't look different, just happier. And I felt ... well ... *just fine.* No pangs of guilt, no remorse, no shame. What I felt was smug, joyous elation. By God, I was on to something here *and I knew it.*

Over the next few weeks I saw many ... clients. Brennan was very well, and the future looked rosy enough to use some of the incredible money that was stacking up to move to a better, more centrally located apartment. I found a place that actually had a nursery right on the block. I could schedule several appointments in the afternoon and drop my son off at the nursery, come home and deal with my clients, then pick him up by dinner time.

I loved it. I made a solemn vow that I would save half of every dollar I earned toward the day Brennan would need to be hospitalized again. I also started a hobby—some people collect stamps, some model airplanes. I began to collect fifty- and one-hundred dollar bills. Every time someone gave me a bill, into an envelope it would go. In no time my "hobby" had mounted to four thousand dollars.

One afternoon my mother came to visit. There was no way to hide the fact that I no longer worked in a doctor's office, so I figured I might as well let her in on my new-found occupation. I handed her the envelope. She looked inside, amazed, then horror spread across her face.

"My God, honey, there's more than four thousand dollars in here! You didn't steal this, or do something …"

"Mom, I guess you could say I've become something of a, well, professional mistress to a couple of very well off, very nice people … It's really not too bad, and I don't want you to worry or …"

"How long have you been doing this?"

"A couple of months."

She began to re-count the money, her eyes wide.

"A couple of *months?*"

"Yeah."

"My God, I wish I had thought of doing this when *I* was your age." That's my mom.

As the months rolled on, I started to advertise in a local newspaper, in the personals column. Every week my post office box was stuffed with mail. Many of the letters went directly into my trash basket; those poorly-written with bad spelling on lined paper didn't have a chance. But a well-written letter on good linen paper, or better yet, typed with a company letterhead, got my immediate response.

I screened new clients by insisting that they give me their work phone number. Sometime in the next few days, I called that number and asked for Mr. Jones, or whoever. If the secretary connected me, I knew I had the man's real name and place of employment, so I felt fairly sure he was neither a knife-wielding psycho or a cop.

…

Once a psychologist called me. He was treating a young man who had a particular fetish. He couldn't maintain an erection unless he was wearing women's panties. And they had to be pink, no less.

The first time I saw "Pinky," we had sex while he wore his panties. The second time, I had him pull them down to his knees. The third time, I had him leave them around one knee, and *imagine* he was actually wearing them. Finally he was able to have sex with the panties lying on the bed beside me, where he could see and touch them.

Then, one day I put the panties under my pillow. He had to imagine them, see them in his mind. Within a short time, he was able to just think about his lovely panties to achieve an erection and orgasm. He still had his fetish, but at least he didn't have to be embarrassed by the presence of his little lacy drawers.

By and large, my clients became my friends. I refused to deal with men who held me in low regard, those who wanted my services, yet still looked down on hookers. I didn't need them. There seemed to be an endless supply of very nice men whose company I enjoyed, men who enriched my life (as well as my pocketbook) in many ways.

Prostitution, in itself, is neither good nor bad. Each woman brings to it what she will. How else can a woman without the years of education necessary to become a doctor or lawyer still earn the kind of money a lawyer or doctor earns? In fewer hours? How else could I have had so much time to spend with my son, when time was so precious?

My earnings enabled us to travel, gave him an opportunity to see more than would have otherwise been possible. By the time my son was seven, he had flown in an airplane more than many people do in a lifetime. We lived in New York for a year, where he saw dinosaurs and whales at the Natural History museum. We lived on an island in the U.S. Virgin Islands for several years, where he learned to snorkel the incredible coral reef, seeing the splendor of the underwater world. He collected hundreds of hermit crabs and built them an intricate home in an aquarium which he called Crab Condo. He learned to strip the outer edge of coconut fronds away, leaving only the long, fibrous center which he tied into a slip knot, the perfect way to sneak up on a fat lizard, slip the loose knot around its neck and with a flick of his wrist, capture it. Together we caught whole jars full of lizards, picked a favorite, then let them go from the center of a huge chalk-drawn circle, cheering for our favorite as the lizards raced away.

I provided as full a life for my son as I could, and money was the key. Prostitution provided that money, and, even more importantly, it gave me the spare time I wouldn't have had with any nine-to-five "real" job. It provided the best private schooling, the chance to travel, the best medical care.

On October the first, 1985, my son died. He would have been ten years old that December.

Now I am "retired," I became involved with a Prostitution and AIDS study funded by the government, interviewing prostitutes and drawing blood samples anonymously to see what percentage of prostitutes in my home city are infected with the AIDS virus. The experience led to my expanded interest in AIDS, and now I work with AIDS patients in many capacities.

Prostitution served me very well, indeed. It was a most useful tool.

I have no regrets, no shame, no remorse. Indeed, I look back on my prostitution experience with a sense of pride and accomplishment. I did it, I'm glad I did it, and I applaud those who do it now.

Here's to the Ladies of the Night—Carry on! Save your money, make wise investments, and above all else—*love yourself.*

# *Stripper*

## Debi Sundahl

For the last five years, I have been working full-time as an erotic performer in San Francisco. I love being a stripper. I consider the theater where I work to be a model of what all sexual entertainment theaters should be. Because of the money I make, the wonderful women I work with, and the standards of quality at the theater, I have come to enjoy the art of burlesque and have passed that knowledge on to others.

Before moving to San Francisco and becoming a stripper, I was a student at the University of Minnesota with a double major in Women's Studies and History. I was active in both feminist and Marxist politics. Also, I worked as an advocate at the Harriet Tubman Shelter for Battered Women in Minneapolis, and for two years I worked with Women Against Violence Against Women (WAVAW), where I helped organize Minnesota's annual Take Back the Night March. At that time, feminism most actively focused on issues of violence against women. Many times, I presented an educational slide show which focused on degrading and/or violent images of women in the media. The show, initially produced by Women Against Pornography in Los Angeles, dealt mainly with rape, battering and incest, making only occasional anti-pornography references.

It was through feminism, and through my involvement with WAVAW, that I came out as a lesbian and met my lover, with whom I am still living. Coming out was the beginning of exploring my sexuality and sex in general. The first time I slept with a woman, I had physical feelings I did not know my body could have. It was an awakening, and I did not want to stop there. I wanted to explore all the taboo areas of sex.

I was well aware, through feminism, of the theory of oppression, and the lies, secrets, and silences that oppressed groups live with. It was obvious to me that sex workers were an oppressed group, suffering from stereotypes and social oppression, much the same as lesbians. Having just come out as a lesbian, I was not afraid to enter yet another unknown territory, and so, when I arrived in San Francisco, I answered an ad in the *San Francisco Chronicle*: "Dancers Wanted. Must be over 18. Part-time job for students and homemakers." Here was an indication that sex workers were not who society at large thought they were.

My suspicions proved true. The owners of the Lusty Lady Theater were involved in founding the Venusian Church in Seattle as well as the Institute for the Advanced

Study of Human Sexuality in San Francisco. They were decidedly interested in the positive expression of human sexuality. The institute provided the education. The church expressed that education in an entertainment form the public could enjoy. The Church staged erotic performances and masturbation fantasies in a sensual place where people could feel comfortable. The managers of the Lusty Lady Theater, mostly women, kept a clean theater, paid their performers well, and were very supportive of both the dancers' and the clientele's expressing their sexuality. Alcohol and drugs were not permitted in the theater, the management was well organized, and I liked the other dancers, who were primarily young college students or struggling artists.

The hardest part of the job was dealing with my feminist principles concerning the objectification of women. Dancing nude is the epitome of woman as sex object. As the weeks passed, I found I liked being a sex object, because the context was appropriate. I resent being treated as a sex object on the street or at the office. But as an erotic dancer, that is my purpose. I perform to turn you on, and if I fail, I feel I've done a poor job. Women who work in the sex industry are not responsible for, nor do they in any way perpetuate, the sexual oppression of women. In fact, to any enlightened observer, our very existence provides a distinction and a choice as to when a woman should be treated like a sex object and when she should not be. At the theater, yes; on the street, no. Having the distinction so obviously played out at work, I felt more personal power on the street. I was far less inclined to put up with harassment than I was before, even when I had taken self-defense training. Therefore, I did not feel exploited personally, either outside of my job or in it. I was no more the personal intimate sexual partner of the men for whom I performed than an actress is the character she portrays in a film or play. When people ask me, as they often do, "How does your lover deal with your being a stripper?" I respond by saying I'm a stripper not because I'm looking for other lovers but because it's my job. For the first time I felt I could express my sexuality in a safe environment. I was in control. Understanding that it was perfectly okay for a woman to be a sex object in the appropriate context, and distinguishing what those contexts *were* allowed me to get on with the business of learning and enjoying my craft.

After I had worked at the Lusty Lady's peep show for two years, I was ready to move on. Fortunately, I lived in a city that has one of the best erotic entertainment theaters in the world. At the Mitchell Brothers' O'Farrell Street Theater, I was introduced to the art of burlesque in its traditional form. Burlesque has a long history and plays an important sexual role in society. A true art form, it has had its great artists and changes in style and form over the years. It is an insulting misconception about burlesque that anyone in a drunken, uninhibited state can strip. It takes practice and talent to be able to pull off an entertaining and truly erotic performance. To create good art, an artist must have a sophisticated and sensitive knowledge of her subject. Of the many strippers I have known, the best were those who had explored and were accepting their sexuality. The pool of knowledge and emotions from which these women drew their creativity was sophisticated and deep. They liked themselves sexually and they held their profession in high regard.

The Mitchell Brothers' theater has a large stage and a superb lighting and sound system, and a beautiful, comfortable theater indicated the owners' respect for sexual entertainment. It was a big step for me to go from a small peep show, with its private booths, to a full-blown theater environment. My wages tripled, and so did my self-respect as an erotic dancer. The first time I saw the show, I cried because it was so beautiful, and because it is so difficult to *find* this beauty. Here was erotic entertainment as it should be, and it was here that I became committed to a career in the sex industry.

Of the crew of sixty performers (some of the best strippers in the country), half were, and still are, lesbians. We lamented the fact that very few women would come to the theater to watch us perform. The sex industry, and the institutions of the sex industry—the theaters, bookstores, and publications—have all been created by men, for men, and are the last great boys' club left totally untouched by feminism. It is a rare stripper who is not a feminist, and so we decided it was time to demand equal access to sexual entertainment.

I started the first women-only strip show at a lesbian bar in San Francisco in July 1984. The weekly shows were an instant success. The dancers loved performing for the all-female audiences because they had more freedom of expression. They were not limited to ultra-feminine acts only; they could be butch, they could dress in masculine attire. They adored the audience feedback, which was enthusiastic, verbal, and supportive. Judging by the response and by the crowds, women were (and are) hungry for sexual entertainment and enthralled by the fact that, for the first time in modern history, they could have sexual entertainment to call their own. ...

... During this time, and in this spirit, I published the first issue of *On Our Backs,* a lesbian sexual entertainment magazine. I also began to make adult or X-rated videos for lesbians under the name of Fatale, which is from the name I had chosen for myself as a stripper, Fanny Fatale.

I am aware that I have been fortunate to have had a positive experience as an erotic dancer. It is because of this experience that I am strongly in favor of sexual entertainment. But stripping is traditional women's work as much as waitressing, teaching and secretarial work is. Consequently, it suffers from the same low pay. Considering the high demand for erotic performers and the low supply, and the fact that the service they provide is a rare commodity, most erotic performers are vastly underpaid. The working conditions, overall, are also poor; many theaters are run on a quasi-legitimate financial basis, and are not clean or safe. Often, the basic tools necessary for the job—like adequate sound and light systems, ample dressing room space, and equipment (like washers, dryers, and irons) to care for costumes—are not provided. Even though most dancers work more than forty hours a week, no vacation or overtime pay is provided, nor are there any health benefits. Many dancers fear becoming ill because missing one day of work will put their jobs in jeopardy.

...

The sex industry suffers from sexist attitudes as much as any other area. Women have traditionally been bottom-level workers while men have held management and ownership positions. Only in the past few years have women begun to hold positions of power in the sex industry. The ramifications of women controlling the means of production of erotic entertainment materials will be revolutionary. The fact that women have had virtually no erotica created by them, for them is intrinsically tied to the sexist attitude that a woman's role in society is to be housewife/mother/sexual servant. ...

The future looks promising and challenging. Women are opening vibrator stores, publishing erotic materials for other women, making adult videos with women in mind, and producing erotic entertainment. These women remember the early days of sixties feminism, when the right to control your body meant the right to be sexual as well. ... Women are demanding the right to explore their sexual identity, defining the many possible ways of being sexual, and encouraging tolerance for *all* sexual expression.

I for one am tired of being the moral guardian of male sexuality and of suffering ostracism and condemnation if I choose to be sexually active or sexually autonomous. Sex education and the ability to communicate about all aspects of sex is essential to fostering social respect for sex workers as well as respect for personal sexual choice and expression. Like many oppressed minorities, we have suffered under the assumption that we must be protected from ourselves. The quasi-illegal and illegal nature of our work robs us of the power to define and control the conditions under which we are employed. We know better than anyone what is healthy and what is not healthy about our work.

These last five years, I have lived a rewarding and rich life as a stripper. Like most artists, I feel I have something special to say and something of interest to offer them. I see a bright and lively future for those on the progressive edge of sexual entertainment, and feel fortunate to be numbered among its outspoken participants. I know how good it can be, and am committed to sharing with others the wonderful realities of my job and the potential for the industry in general.

---

# *Confronting the Liberal Lies About Prostitution*

## Evelina Giobbe

WHISPER[1] is a national organization of women who have survived the sex industry. Our purpose is to expose the conditions that make women and children vulnerable to commercial sexual exploitation and trap them in systems of prostitution, to expose and invalidate cultural myths about women used in prostitution and pornography, and to end trafficking in women and children. We define systems of prostitution as any industry in which women's or children's bodies are bought, sold, or traded for sexual use and abuse. These systems include pornography, live sex shows, peep shows, international sexual slavery, and prostitution as it is commonly defined.[2] All these industries are merely different commercial vehicles through which men traffic in women and children.

We chose the acronym WHISPER because women in systems of prostitution whisper among themselves about the coercion, degradation, sexual abuse and battery upon which the sex industry is founded, while myths about prostitution are shouted out in pornography and the mainstream media, and by self-appointed "experts." This mythology, which hides the abusive nature of prostitution, is illustrated by the ideology of the sexual liberals which erroneously claims that prostitution is a career choice; that prostitution epitomizes women's sexual liberation; that prostitutes set the sexual and economic conditions of their interactions with customers; that pimp/prostitute relationships are mutually beneficial social or business arrangements that women enter into freely; and that being a prostitute or a pimp is an acceptable, traditional occupation in communities of color.

...

The central flaw in the sexual liberals' analysis is that it ignores survivors of prostitution who have testified repeatedly that they did not experience prostitution as a career (WHISPER, 1988). Survivors have described the act of prostitution as "disgusting," "abusive," and "like rape," and explained that they learned to cope with it by disassociating themselves from their bodies or by using drugs and alcohol to numb physical and emotion pain (WHISPER, 1988). It would be more accurate to describe the act of prostitution as intrusive, unwanted, and often overtly violent sex that women endure. Further, the analysis doesn't consider the social function of prostitution: to extend to all men the right of unconditional sexual access to women and girls in addition to those privileges enjoyed by husbands and fathers within the institution of marriage. These dynamics are clearly understood by women used in systems of prostitution, as illustrated by the remarks of a survivor who made the connections between the physical and emotional abuse to which she was subjected in her family and her marriages, and her subsequent recruitment into prostitution by a pimp: "I basically just thought that women were put on this earth for men's sexual pleasure in exchange for a roof over your head and food in your stomach" (WHISPER, 1988).

Some sexual liberals justify prostitution as the altruistic creation of women of color. "Prostitution is no alien thing to Black women," write Carmen and Moody. "In every southern city in the 1920's and '30s the red light district was on the other side of the tracks in the Black ghetto [where] young white boys 'discovered their manhood' with the help of a 'two-dollar whore' ... Prostitutes ... were integrating blacks and whites long before there was a civil rights movement" (1985: pp. 184–185). Astonishingly, Carmen and Moody consider the buying and selling of women of color by white men and their sons to be the vanguard of desegregation.

White-male supremacy intensifies oppressive conditions that make women of color particularly vulnerable to recruitment or coercion into prostitution. By limiting educational and career opportunities and fostering dependence on an inadequate and punitive welfare system, racism creates economic vulnerability. …

> As a Black coming up in Indiana in the steel mill industry up there, they hired men. All the men got jobs in the mills there; very few women. You really had to be very cute or know someone, and so there wasn't jobs in the field, there wasn't jobs in offices for you, unless you knew someone or something; but there were lots of jobs for you in strip joints, dancing, or even down at some of the restaurants and bars outside of the steel mills for when the guys came in. (WHISPER, 1988)

Racist stereotypes of women of color in pornography and racist policies that zone pornographic bookstores, peep shows, topless bars, and prostitution into poor black and ethnic neighborhoods, create an environment in which women of color are particularly vulnerable. …

By not providing effective intervention programs to women of color who are trapped in abusive relationships—including prostitution—in their own communities, racist policies send out a message to these women that they are not deserving of help. …

…

Racist law enforcement policies disproportionately target women of color for harassment, arrest, imprisonment and fines (Bernard Cohen, cited in Nancy Erbe, 1984). Such actions create a revolving door through which women are shunted from the streets to the courts to the jails and back onto the streets again to raise money to pay these penalties. Selective application of laws prohibiting prostitution creates a kind of de facto regulation in which a tax is levied primarily against women of color by white men who design, maintain, control and benefit from the system of abuse in which the women are trapped.

Lastly, institutional racism puts women of color in a double bind by forcing them to go to white-dominated agencies to seek relief and redress for their injuries. If they speak out about the abuses they sustained in their own communities, they risk isolation, the possibility that their complaint will be used to fuel racist stereotypes and the probability that they will not receive effective advocacy. If they remain silent, they are left with limited resources with which to find an effective solution. Thus, racism holds women of color hostage to familial loyalties and community ties. …

The role of racism in the recruitment of women into systems of prostitution and as an impediment to their escape is complex and multifaceted. This is a problem that survivors have begun to investigate with women of color in the larger feminist community. This discourse must begin with an understanding of the social realities under which women of color are forced to live in a white-male supremacist culture and the acknowledgment that any strategies for change must come from women of color, particularly those who have survived commercial sexual exploitation. Without this kind of leadership, racist and misogynist analyses of prostitution in communities of color—like those put forth by Carmen and Moody—will continue to facilitate and maintain the traffic in women and children of color.

...

In an attempt to turn straw into gold, the sexual liberals spin an argument in support of prostitution based on false assumptions and outright lies. They claim that prostitution is a manifestation of both women's sexual freedom and gender equality. They claim that women freely choose prostitution as a career alternative. They claim that women control both sexual and financial interactions between themselves and their customers. They claim pimps are small-business managers who can and should be made accountable to their employees through labor negotiations.

There are approximately one million adult prostitutes in the United States. ... Many are women of color. ... Many have dependent children. The average age of entry into prostitution is fourteen. ... Others were "traditional wives" who escaped from or were abandoned by abusive husbands and forced into prostitution in order to support themselves and their children. Additionally, there are approximately one million children used in the sex industry in this country (D. Boyer, 1984). Although estimates vary due to the covert nature of child prostitution, we know that without effective intervention most of these children will grow up to be adult prostitutes.

Women in prostitution have few resources. Most have not completed high school.[3] Few have had any job experience outside of the sex industry.[4] Most have been victims of childhood sexual abuse, incest, rape, and/or battery prior to their entry into prostitution. WHISPER has pointed out that the function of the institution of prostitution is to allow males unconditional sexual access to women and children limited solely by their ability to pay for this privilege. A preliminary analysis of data collected by the WHISPER Oral History Project has isolated culturally supported tactics of power and control which facilitate the recruitment or coercion of women and children into prostitution and effectively impede their escape. These tactics include child sexual abuse, rape, battery, educational deprivation, job discrimination, poverty, racism, classism, sexism, heterosexism, and unequal enforcement of the law. These same tactics are used by individual men to keep women trapped in abusive relationships outside of prostitution.[5]

Ninety percent of the women who participated in the WHISPER Oral History Project reported having been subjected to an inordinate amount of physical and sexual abuse during childhood: ninety percent had been battered in their families; seventy-four percent had been sexually abused between the ages of 3 and 14.[6] Of this group, fifty-seven percent had been repeatedly abused over a period of one to five years; forty-three percent had been victimized by two or three perpetrators; ninety-three percent had been abused by a family member.[7] Additionally, fifty percent of this group had also been molested by a non-family member (see, for example, Mimi Silbert, 1982).

Once in prostitution, these women and girls were further victimized by both pimps and customers. Seventy-nine percent of the women interviewed had been beaten by their pimps. All the women interviewed thus far had been harassed, assaulted, raped, kidnaped, and/or forced to turn tricks by a pimp or a gang of pimps. That some of the women had pimps at the time of the assault did not dissuade other pimps from preying on them. Seventy-four percent reported assaults by customers;

of these, seventy-nine percent reported beatings by a customer, and fifty percent re-ported rapes. Seventy-one percent of these women were victims of multiple cus-tomer assaults. (These findings are consistent with Mimi Silbert, 1982; Diana Gray, 1973.) The conditions these women were subjected to in prostitution replicated the abuse they had sustained at the hands of their fathers and husbands.

...

... Prostitution is taught in the home, socially validated by a sexual libertarian ide-ology, and enforced by both church and state. That is to say the male hierarchies of both the conservative right and the liberal left collude to teach and keep women in prostitution: the right by demanding that women be socially and sexually subordi-nate to one man in marriage, and the left by demanding that women be socially and sexually subordinate to all men in prostitution and pornography. Their common goal is to maintain their power to own and control women in both the private and public spheres.

Prostitution isn't like anything else. Rather, everything else is like prostitution be-cause it is the model for women's condition. The line between wife and prostitute—madonna and whore—has become increasingly blurred, beginning in the 1960s when women's attempts to free themselves of the double standard was frustrated by the liberal left's adoption and promotion of the "Playboy Philosophy." This resulted in the replacement of the double standard by a single male standard in which sexual liberation became synonymous with male sexual objectification of and uncondi-tional sexual access to women. With the invasion of the home by pornographic cable programs and video cassettes, the "good wife" has become equated with the "good whore," as more and more women are pressured into emulating the scenarios of por-nography. In this context, the wife is pressured, seduced, and/or forced into the role of the prostitute while her husband adopts the role of the "john." Contests promoted by pornographers, like *Hustler's* "Beaver Hunt"[8] and pornographic computer bulle-tin boards like *High Society's* "Sex-Tex,"[9] have resulted in a proliferation of home-made pornography. In this situation the wife is compelled to assume the role of "porn queen" when her husband adopts the role of the pornographer. The growth of "swingers' magazines" and "wife-swapping clubs" have allowed men to assume si-multaneously the role of john and pimp, paying for the use of another man's partner by making his wife available in exchange. The last barrier separating the roles of wife and prostitute is smashed when men engineer sexual encounters with prostitutes which include their wives. One prostitution survivor describes the dynamics of such an experience:

> A lot of men enjoyed bringing me in as a third party with their wives. Usually what would end up happening is we'd watch some pornographic film, say, and then he'd say, "All right, I want you to do that to my wife." Now, in these instances, I felt the wife was the victim, and that I was there to hurt the wife. I felt there was a real power play there, where the man was obviously saying to the wife, "If you don't do this, I'm going to leave you." I mean there were great overtones of manipulation and coercion. (WHISPER, 1988)

In each of these ways the prostitute symbolizes the value of women in society. She is paradigmatic of women's social, sexual, and economic subordination in that her status is the basic unit by which all women's value is measured and to which all women can be reduced. The treatment that a man pays to inflict on the most despised women—prostitutes—sets the standard by which he may treat the women under his control—his wife and his daughters.

The role of prostitute is taught to girls in the home through paternal sexual abuse. The fact that an estimated seventy-five percent of women in the sex industry were sexually abused as children suggests that the ramifications of incest and sexual assault in childhood contribute to the recruitment of women and children into prostitution.[10] ...

The role of prostitute is taught to women individually and as a class through the social sanctioning of commercial sexual exploitation of women by pornographers, which maintains our second-class status yet is touted by sexual liberals as women's sexual liberation. Preliminary data collected by the WHISPER Oral History Project refute the sexual liberals' argument that pornography is harmless fantasy or sexually liberating entertainment, suggesting instead that pornography is an important factor in the seasoning of women and girls into prostitution. Fifty-two percent of the women interviewed revealed that pornography played a significant role in teaching them what was expected of them as prostitutes. Thirty percent reported that their pimps regularly exposed them to pornographic material in order to indoctrinate them into an acceptance of the practices depicted. ...

This situation is compounded by the use of pornography by johns. Eighty percent of survivors reported that their customers showed them pornography to illustrate the kinds of sexual activities in which they wanted to engage, including sadomasochism, bondage, anal intercourse, urination and defecation, and the shaving of pubic hair to give an illusion of prepubescence. ...

...

Prostitution is *not* a "career choice":

> I look at my life and when I came into this world, you know as a child, I expected to be fed, clothed, sheltered and to be treated with respect and kindness as any human being would so desire. ... I don't think I came into this world with the desire to be a prostitute. I think that that was something that was put on me by the dynamics of society. Something that was taught me. (WHISPER, 1988)

Prostitution is *not* a "victimless crime":

> Prostitution is violence against women ... it's the worst form of violence against women because you get abused by the johns, you get abused by the pimps, you get abused by the police. Society in general turns their back on you. (WHISPER, 1988)

Prostitution is a crime committed against women by men in its most traditional form. It is nothing less than the commercialization of the sexual abuse and inequality that women suffer in the traditional family and can be nothing more.

> The laws are made by men and men desire to keep women in prostitution because they desire to control them, so the thing that would change prostitution is not legalizing it, but by putting an end to it and stopping it, and I don't believe that men want to do that. I think women are going to have to do that. (WHISPER, 1988)

Dismantling the institution of prostitution is the most formidable task facing contemporary feminism.

---

## Notes

1. Women Hurt In Systems of Prostitution Engaged in Revolt, Lake Street Station, Box 8719, Minneapolis, Minnesota 55408.

2. Streetwalkers, "Call Girl" or "Escort" Services, brothels, saunas, massage parlors, etc.

3. Mary Magdalene Project, Reseda, California (1985); Operation De Novo, Minneapolis; WHISPER Oral History Project (1988).

4. Council for Prostitution Alternatives, Portland, Oregon; Genesis House, Chicago; WHISPER, Minneapolis; PRIDE, Minneapolis.

5. The WHISPER Oral History Project is an ongoing research project designed to document common experiences of women used in prostitution. Respondents participated in a single 2–3 hour oral interview which was subsequently transcribed for data analysis. Preliminary findings are based on 19 interviews with women ranging from ages 19–37.

6. Of these, 36 percent were rape victims.

7. 50 percent were abused by a natural, step-, or foster father.

8. *Hustler* offers payment to readers who submit the best "beaver shots" (pornographic photographs) of wives or girlfriends.

9. "Sex-Tex" is a computer service of *High Society* Magazine which provides an unregulated market through which pornographic material can be distributed.

10. The Mary Magdalene Project in Reseda, California, reports 80 percent of the women they've worked with were sexually abused as children; Genesis House in Chicago reports 94 percent were abused as children (in The First National Workshop For Those Working With Female Prostitutes, Wayzata, Minnesota, October 16–18, 1985).

## References

Boyer, D. (1984, January). A cultural construction of a negative sex role: The female prostitutes.

Carmen, Arlene and Moody, Howard. (1985). *Working women: The subterranean world of street prostitution.* New York: Harper and Row.

Erbe, Nancy. (1984). Prostitution: Victims of men's exploitation and abuse. *Law and Inequality,* 2:609.

Gray, Diana. (1973). Turning-out: A study of teenage prostitutes. *Urban Life and Culture.*

Silbert, Mimi. (1982, November). *Sexual assault of prostitutes.* Phase I, Final Report. San Francisco: National Center for the Prevention and Control of Rape, National Institute for Mental Health.

WHISPER. (1988). *Prostitution: A matter of violence against women.* Video. Minneapolis: WHISPER.

# *What's Wrong with Prostitution?*

## Carole Pateman

… Prostitution is an integral part of patriarchal capitalism. Wives are no longer put up for public auction (although in Australia, the United States and Britain they can be bought by mail-order from the Philippines), but men can buy sexual access to women's bodies in the capitalist market. Patriarchal right is explicitly embodied in 'freedom of contract'.

Prostitutes are readily available at all levels of the market for any man who can afford one and they are frequently provided as part of business, political and diplomatic transactions. Yet the public character of prostitution is less obvious than it might be. Like other forms of capitalist enterprise, prostitution is seen as private enterprise, and the contract between client and prostitute is seen as a private arrangement between a buyer and a seller. Moreover, prostitution is shrouded in secrecy despite the scale of the industry. … One estimate is that $40 million per day is spent on prostitution in the United States.[1] The secrecy exists in part because, where the act of prostitution is not itself illegal, associated activities such as soliciting often are. The criminal character of much of the business of prostitution is not, however, the only reason for secrecy. Not all men wish it generally to be known that they buy this commodity. To be discovered consorting with prostitutes can, for example, still be the downfall of politicians. The empirical evidence also indicates that three-quarters of the clients of prostitutes are married men. …

…

A radical change has now taken place in arguments about prostitution. Prostitution is unequivocally defended by [contractarian advocates of the free market]. … Many recent feminist discussions have argued that prostitution is merely a job of work and the prostitute is a worker, like any other wage labourer. Prostitutes should, therefore, have trade union rights, and feminists often put foward proposals for workers' control of the industry. To argue in this fashion is not necessarily to defend prostitution—one can argue for trade union rights while calling for the abolition of capitalist wage labour—but, in the absence of argument to the contrary, the implicit suggestion in many feminist discussions is that, if the prostitute is merely one worker among others, the appropriate conclusion must be that there is nothing wrong with prostitution. At the very least, the argument implies that there is nothing wrong with prostitution that is not also wrong with other forms of work.

...

Defenders of prostitution admit that some reforms are necessary in the industry as it exists at present in order for a properly free market in sexual services to operate. Nevertheless, they insist that 'sound prostitution' is possible (the phrase is Lars Ericcson's).[2] The idea of sound prostitution illustrates the dramatic shift that has taken place in arguments over prostitution. The new, contractarian defence is a universal argument. Prostitution is defended as a trade fit for anyone to enter. Freedom of contract and equality of opportunity require that the prostitution contract should be open to everyone and that any individual should be able to buy or sell services in the market. Anyone who needs a sexual service should have access to the market, whether male or female, young or old, black or white, ugly or beautiful, deformed or handicapped. Prostitution will then come into its own as a form of therapy—'the role of a prostitute as a kind of therapist is a natural one'[3]—or as a form of social work or nursing (taking care 'of the intimate hygiene of disabled patients').[4] No one will be left out because of inappropriate attitudes to sex. The female hunchback as well as the male hunchback will be able to find a seller of services.[5]

A universal defence of prostitution entails that a prostitute can be of either sex. Women should have the same opportunity as men to buy sexual services in the market. 'The prostitute' is conventionally pictured as a woman, and, in fact, the majority of prostitutes are women. However, for contractarians, this is a merely contingent fact about prostitution; if sound prostitution were established, status, or the sexually ascriptive determination of the two parties (the man as a buyer and the woman as a seller of services), will give way to contract, to a relation between two 'individuals'. A moment's contemplation of the story of the sexual contract suggests that there is a major difficulty in any attempt to universalize prostitution. Reports occasionally appear that, in large cities like Sydney, a few male heterosexual prostitutes operate (the older figure of the gigolo belongs in a very different context), but they are still rare. Male homosexual prostitutes, on the other hand, are not uncommon, and, from the standpoint of contract, they are no different from female prostitutes. The story of the sexual contract reveals that there is good reason why 'the prostitute' is a female figure.

...

Any discussion of prostitution is replete with difficulties. Although contractarians now deny any political significance to the fact that (most) prostitutes are women, one major difficulty is that, in other discussions, prostitution is invariably seen as a problem about the prostitute, as a problem about *women*. The perception of prostitution as a problem about women is so deep-seated that any criticism of prostitution is likely to provoke the accusation that contemporary contractarians bring against feminists, that criticism of prostitution shows contempt for prostitutes. To argue that there is something wrong with prostitution does not necessarily imply any adverse judgement on the women who engage in the work. When socialists criticize capitalism and the employment contract they do not do so because they are contemptuous of workers, but because they are the workers' champions. Nevertheless, appeals to the idea of false consciousness, popular a few years ago, suggested that the problem about capitalism was a problem about workers. To reduce the question of capitalism to deficiencies in workers' consciousness diverts attention from the capitalist, the other participant in the employment contract. Similarly, the patriarchal assumption that prostitution is a problem about women ensures that the other participant in the prostitution contract escapes scrutiny. ... Prostitution [is rather] a problem about *men*. The problem of prostitution then becomes encapsulated in the question why men demand that women's bodies are sold as commodities in the capitalist market. The [short answer is that] prostitution is part of the exercise of the law of male sex-right, one of the ways in which men are ensured access to women's bodies.

...

[A claim often made in defense of prostitution is that it] is a universal feature of human society. [This] relies not only on the cliché of 'the oldest profession' but also on the widely held assumption that prostitution originates in men's natural sexual urge. There is a universal, natural (masculine) impulse that, it is assumed, requires, and will always require, the outlet provided by prostitution. Now that arguments that extra-marital sex is immoral have lost their social force, defenders of prostitution often present prostitution as one example of 'sex without love', as an example of the satisfaction of natural appetites.[6] The argument, however, is a *non sequitur*. Defenders of sex without love and advocates of what once was called free love, always supposed that the relationship was based on mutual sexual attraction between a man and woman and involved mutual physical satisfaction. Free love and prostitution are poles apart. Prostitution is the use of a woman's body by a man for his own satisfaction. There is no desire or satisfaction on the part of the prostitute. Prostitution is not mutual, pleasurable exchange of the use of bodies, but the unilateral use of a woman's body by a man in exchange for money. That the institution of prostitution can be presented as a natural extension of a human impulse, and that 'sex without love' can be equated with the sale of women's bodies in the capitalist market, is possible only because an important question is begged: why do men demand that satisfaction of a natural appetite must take the form of public access to women's bodies in the capitalist market in exchange for money?

In arguments that prostitution is merely one expression of a natural appetite, the comparison is invariably made between prostitution and the provision of food. To claim that 'we all need food, so food should be available to us. ... And since our sexual desires are just as basic, natural, and compelling as our appetite for food, this also holds for them', is neither an argument for prostitution nor for any form of sexual relations.[7] Without a minimum of food (or water, or shelter) people die, but to my knowledge no one has ever died for want of an outlet for their sexual appetites. There is also one fundamental difference between the human need for food and the need for sex. Sustenance is sometimes unavailable but everyone has the means to satisfy sexual appetites to hand. There is no natural necessity to engage in sexual *relations* to assuage sexual pangs. Of course, there may be cultural inhibition against use of this means, but what counts as food is also culturally variable. In no society does the form of food production and consumption, or the form of relations between the sexes, follow directly, without cultural mediation, from the natural fact that all humans feel hunger and sexual impulses. The consequences of sexual inhibitions and prohibitions are likely to be less disastrous than prohibitions on what counts as food.

…

… Part of the construction of what it means to be a man, part of the contemporary expression of masculine sexuality[, is that the] satisfaction of men's natural sexual urges must be achieved through access to a woman, even if her body is not directly used sexually. Whether or not any man is able and willing to find release in other ways, he can exhibit his masculinity by contracting for use of a woman's body. The prostitution contract is [an] example of an actual 'original' sexual contract. The exemplary display of masculinity is to engage in 'the sex act'. (Hence, sale of men's bodies for homosexual use does not have the same social meaning.) The institution of prostitution ensures that men can buy 'the sex act' and so exercise their patriarchal right. The activities that, above all else, can appropriately be called prostitution are 'the sex act', and associated activities such as 'hand relief' and oral sex (fellatio), for which there is now a very large demand.[8] Some of the most prevalent confusions in discussions of prostitution might be avoided if other activities were seen as part of the wider sex industry. The market includes a vigorous demand for 'bondage and discipline' or fantasy slave contracts. The mass commercial replication of the most potent relations and symbols of domination is a testament to the power and genius of contract, which proclaims that a contract of subordination is (sexual) freedom.

…

… Marxist critics of prostitution take their lead from Marx's statement that 'prostitution is only a *specific* expression of the *general* prostitution of the *laborer*.' … [But to] see prostitutes as epitomizing exploitation under capitalism, and to represent the worker by the figure of the prostitute, is not without irony. 'The worker' is masculine—yet his degradation is symbolized by a female emblem, and patriarchal capitalism is pictured as a system of universal prostitution. The fact that the prostitute seems to be such an obvious symbol of the degradation of wage labour, raises the suspicion that what she sells is not quite the same as the labour power contracted out by other workers. …

…

The capitalist has no intrinsic interest in the body and self of the worker, or, at least, not the same kind of interest as the man who enters into the prostitution contract. … The employer can and often does replace the worker with machines or, in the 1980s, robots and other computerized machines. … In contrast to employers, the men who enter into the prostitution contract have only one interest; the prostitute and her body. A market exists for substitutes for women's bodies in the form of inflatable dolls, but, unlike the machines that replace the worker, the dolls are advertised as 'lifelike'. The dolls are a literal substitute for women, not a functional substitute like the machine installed instead of the worker. Even a plastic substitute for a woman can give a man the sensation of being a patriarchal master. In prostitution, the body of the woman, and sexual access to that body, is the subject of the contract.

To have bodies for sale in the market, as bodies, looks very like slavery. To symbolize wage slavery by the figure of the prostitute rather than that of the masculine worker is thus not entirely inappropriate. But prostitution differs from wage slavery. No form of labour power can be separated from the body, but only through the prostitution contract does the buyer obtain unilateral right of direct sexual use of a woman's body.

...

... In modern patriarchy, sale of women's bodies in the capitalist market involves sale of a self in a different manner, and in a more profound sense, than [for example] sale of the body of a male baseball player or sale of ... the labour (body) of a wage slave. The ... patriarchal construction of the difference between masculinity and femininity is the political difference between freedom and subjection, and ... sexual mastery is the major means through which men affirm their manhood. When a man enters into the prostitution contract he is not interested in sexually indifferent, disembodied services; he contracts to buy sexual use of a *woman* for a given period. Why else are men willing to enter the market and pay for 'hand relief'? Of course, men can also affirm their masculinity in other ways, but, in relations between the sexes, unequivocal affirmation is obtained by engaging in 'the sex act'. Womanhood, too, is confirmed in sexual activity, and when a prostitute contracts out use of her body she is thus selling *herself* in a very real sense. Women's selves are involved in prostitution in a different manner from the involvement of the self in other occupations. Workers of all kinds may be more or less 'bound up in their work', but the integral connection between sexuality and sense of the self means that, for self-protection, a prostitute must distance herself from her sexual use.

Women engaged in the trade have developed a variety of distancing strategies, or a professional approach, in dealing with their clients. Such distancing creates a problem for men, a problem that can be seen as another variant on the contradiction of mastery and slavery. The prostitution contract enables men to constitute themselves as civil masters for a time, and, like other masters, they wish to obtain acknowledgment of their status. Eileen McLeod talked to clients as well as prostitutes in Birmingham and, noting that her findings are in keeping with similar investigations in Britain and the United States, she states that 'nearly all the men I interviewed complained about the emotional coldness and mercenary approach of many prostitutes they had had contact with.'[9] A master requires a service, but he also requires that the service is delivered by a person, a self, not merely a piece of (disembodied) property. John Stuart Mill remarked of the subordination of wives that, 'their masters require something more from them than actual service. Men do not want solely the obedience of women, they want their sentiments. All men, except the most brutish, desire to have, not a forced slave but a willing one, not a slave merely, but a favourite.'[10]

An employer or a husband can more easily obtain faithful service and acknowledgment of his mastery than a man who enters into the prostitution contract. The ... employment and marriage contracts create long-term relationships of subordination. The prostitution contract is of short duration and the client is not concerned with daily problems of the extraction of labour power. The prostitution contract is, one might say, a contract of specific performance, rather than open-ended like the employment contract and, in some of its aspects, the marriage contract. There are also other differences between the employment and prostitution contracts. For example, the prostitute is always at a singular disadvantage in the 'exchange'. The client makes direct use of the prostitute's body and there are no 'objective' criteria through which to judge whether the service has been satisfactorily performed. Trade unions bargain over pay and conditions for workers, and the products of their labours are 'quality controlled'. Prostitutes, in contrast, can always be refused payment by men who claim (and who can gainsay their subjective assessment?) that their demands have not been met.

The character of the employment contract also provides scope for mastery to be recognized in numerous subtle ways as well as in an open, direct fashion. ... The brief duration of the prostitution contract gives less room for subtlety; but, then, perhaps it is not so necessary. There need be no such ambiguities in relations between men and women, least of all when a man has bought a woman's body for his use as if it were like any other commodity. In such a context, 'the sex act' itself provides acknowledgment of patriarchal right. When women's bodies are on sale as commodities in the capitalist market, ... men gain public acknowledgment as women's sexual masters—that is what is wrong with prostitution.

...

---

## Notes

1. Cited in *San Francisco Examiner* (3 February 1985).

2. The term is used by L. Ericcson, 'Charges Against Prostitution: An Attempt at a Philosophical Assessment', *Ethics*, 90 (1980), pp. 335–66.

3. D.A.J. Richards, *Sex, Drugs, Death, and the Law: An Essay on Human Rights and Decriminalization,* (Totowa, NJ, Rowman and Littlefield, 1982), p. 115; also p. 108.

4. Ericcson, 'Charges Against Prostitution', p. 342.

5. The example comes from M. McIntosh, 'Who Needs Prostitutes? The Ideology of Male Sexual Needs', in *Women, Sexuality and Social Control,* ed. C. Smart and B. Smart (London, Routledge and Kegan Paul, 1978), p. 54.

6. For this use of the phrase, see, e.g., J. R. Richards, *The Sceptical Feminist: A Philosophical Enquiry* (Harmondsworth, Penguin Books, 1980), p. 244.

7. Ericcson, 'Charges Against Prostitution', p. 341. Compare D. A. J. Richards, *Sex, Drugs, Death, and the Law,* p. 49.

8. In the 1930s in the United States, only 10 per cent of customers demanded oral sex; by the 1960s nearly 90 per cent did so, either instead of or in addition to intercourse (figures cited by R. Rosen, *The Lost Sisterhood: Prostitution in America, 1900–1918* [Baltimore and London, The Johns Hopkins University Press, 1982], p. 97). Could it be conjectured that men's current widespread demand to buy women's bodies to penetrate their mouths is connected to the revitalization of the feminist movement and women's demand to speak?

9. E. McLeod, *Women Working: Prostitution Now* (London and Canberra, Croom Helm, 1982), p. 84.

10. J. S. Mill, 'The Subjection of Women', in *Essays on Sex Equality,* ed. A. S. Rossi (Chicago and London, University of Chicago Press, 1970), p. 141.

# International Committee for Prostitutes' Rights World Charter and World Whores' Congress Statements

## International Committee for Prostitutes' Rights

## WORLD CHARTER

### Laws

Decriminalize all aspects of adult prostitution resulting from individual decision.

Decriminalize prostitution and regulate third parties according to standard business codes. It must be noted that existing standard business codes allow abuse of prostitutes. Therefore special clauses must be included to prevent the abuse and stigmatization of prostitutes (self-employed and others).

Enforce criminal laws against fraud, coercion, violence, child sexual abuse, child labor, rape, racism everywhere and across national boundaries, whether or not in the context of prostitution.

Eradicate laws that can be interpreted to deny freedom of association, or freedom to travel, to prostitutes within and between countries. Prostitutes have rights to a private life.

### Human Rights

Guarantee prostitutes all human rights and civil liberties, including the freedom of speech, travel, immigration, work, marriage, and motherhood and the right to unemployment insurance, health insurance and housing.

Grant asylum to anyone denied human rights on the basis of a "crime of status," be it prostitution or homosexuality.

### Working Conditions

There should be no law which implies systematic zoning of prostitution. Prostitutes should have the freedom to choose their place of work and residence. It is essential that prostitutes can provide their services under the conditions that are absolutely determined by themselves and no one else.

There should be a committee to insure the protection of the rights of the prostitutes and to whom prostitutes can address their complaints. This committee must be comprised of prostitutes and other professionals like lawyers and supporters.

There should be no law discriminating against prostitutes associating and working collectively in order to acquire a high degree of personal security.

## Health

All women and men should be educated to periodical health screening for sexually transmitted diseases. Since health checks have historically been used to control and stigmatize prostitutes, and since adult prostitutes are generally even more aware of sexual health than others, mandatory checks for prostitutes are unacceptable unless they are mandatory for all sexually active people.

## Services

Employment, counseling, legal, and housing services for runaway children should be funded in order to prevent child prostitution and to promote child well-being and opportunity.

Prostitutes must have the same social benefits as all other citizens according to the different regulations in different countries.

Shelters and services for working prostitutes and re-training programs for prostitutes wishing to leave the life should be funded.

## Taxes

No special taxes should be levied on prostitutes or prostitute businesses.

Prostitutes should pay regular taxes on the same basis as other independent contractors and employees, and should receive the same benefits.

## Public Opinion

Support educational programs to change social attitudes which stigmatize and discriminate against prostitutes and ex-prostitutes of any race, gender or nationality.

Develop educational programs which help the public to understand that the customer plays a crucial role in the prostitution phenomenon, this role being generally ignored. The customer, like the prostitute, should not, however, be criminalized or condemned on a moral basis.

We are in solidarity with all workers in the sex industry.

## Organization

Organizations of prostitutes and ex-prostitutes should be supported to further implementation of the above charter.

# DRAFT STATEMENTS FROM THE
# 2ND WORLD WHORES' CONGRESS (1986)

## Prostitution and Feminism

The International Committee for Prostitutes' Rights (ICPR) realizes that up until now the women's movement in most countries has not, or has only marginally, included prostitutes as spokeswomen and theorists. Historically, women's movements (like socialist and community movements) have opposed the institution of prostitution while claiming to support prostitute women. However, prostitutes reject support that requires them to leave prostitution; they object to being treated as symbols of oppression and demand recognition as workers. Due to feminist hesitation or refusal to accept prostitution as legitimate work and to accept prostitutes as working women, the majority of prostitutes have not identified as feminists; nonetheless, many prostitutes identify with feminist values such as independence, financial autonomy, sexual self-determination, personal strength, and female bonding.

During the last decade, some feminists have begun to re-evaluate the traditional anti-prostitution stance of their movement in light of the actual experiences, opinions, and needs of prostitute women. The ICPR can be considered a feminist organization in that it is committed to giving voice and respect to all women, including the most invisible, isolated, degraded, and/or idealized. The development of prostitution analyses and strategies within women's movements which link the condition of prostitutes to the condition of women in general and which do justice to the integrity of prostitute women is therefore an important goal of the committee.

### Financial Autonomy

Financial autonomy is basic to female survival, self-determination, self-respect, and self-development. Unlike men, women are often scorned and/or pitied for making life choices primarily in the interest of earning money. True financial independence includes the means to earn money (or the position to have authority over money) and the freedom to spend it as one needs or desires. Such means are rarely available to women even with compromise and struggle. ... The financial initiative of prostitutes is stigmatized and/or criminalized as a warning to women in general against such sexually explicit strategies for financial independence. Nonetheless, "being sexually attractive" and "catching a good man" are traditional female strategies for survival, strategies which may provide financial sustenance but rarely financial independence. ... *The ICPR affirms the right of women to financial initiative and financial gain, including the right to commercialize sexual service or sexual illusion (such as erotic media), and to save and spend their earnings according to their own needs and priorities.*

## Occupational Choice

The lack of educational and employment opportunities for women throughout the world has been well documented. Occupational choice for women (especially for women of color and working-class women), and also for men oppressed by class and race prejudice, is usually a choice between different subordinate positions. Once employed, women are often stigmatized and harassed. Furthermore, they are commonly paid according to their gender rather than their worth. Female access to jobs traditionally reserved for men, and adequate pay and respect to women in jobs traditionally reserved for women are necessary conditions of true occupational choice. Those conditions entail an elimination of the sexual division of labor. Prostitution is a traditional female occupation. Some prostitutes report job satisfaction, others job repulsion; some consciously chose prostitution as the best alternative open to them; others rolled into prostitution through male force or deceit. Many prostitutes abhor the conditions and social stigma attached to their work, but not the work itself. *The ICPR affirms the right of women to the full range of education and employment alternatives and to due respect and compensation in every occupation, including prostitution.*

## Alliance Between Women

Women have been divided into social categories on the basis of their sexual labor and/or sexual identity. Within the sex industry, the prostitute is the most explicitly oppressed by legal and social controls. Pornography models, strip-tease dancers, sexual maseuses, and prostitutes euphemistically called escorts or sexual surrogates often avoid association with prostitution labels and workers in an effort to elevate their status. ... Efforts to distance oneself from explicit sex work reinforce prejudice against prostitutes and reinforce sexual shame among women. Outside the sex industry, women are likewise divided by status, history, identity, and appearance. Non-prostitutes are frequently pressured to deliver sexual services in the form of sex, smiles, dress or affection; those services are rarely compensated with pay and may even diminish female status. ... *The ICPR calls for alliance between all women within and outside the sex industry and especially affirms the dignity of street prostitutes and of women stigmatized for their color, class, ethnic difference, history of abuse, marital or motherhood status, sexual preference, disability, or weight. The ICPR is in solidarity with homosexual male, transvestite and transsexual prostitutes.*

## Sexual Self-Determination

The right to sexual self-determination includes women's right to set the terms of their own sexuality, including the choice of partner(s), behaviors, and outcomes (such as pregnancy, pleasure, or financial gain). Sexual self-determination includes the right to refuse sex and to initiate sex as well as the right to use birth control (including abortion), the right to have lesbian sex, the right to have sex across lines of color or class, the right to engage in sado-masochistic sex, and the right to offer sex for money. … Necessarily, no one is entitled to act out a sexual desire that includes another party unless that party agrees under conditions of total free will. The feminist task is to nurture self-determination both by increasing women's sexual consciousness and courage and also by demanding conditions of safety and choice. *The ICPR affirms the right of all women to determine their own sexual behavior, including commercial exchange, without stigmatization or punishment.*

### Healthy Childhood Development

Children are independent upon adults for survival, love, and development. Pressure upon children, either with kindness or force, to work for money or to have sex for adult satisfaction, is a violation of rights to childhood development. Often the child who is abused at home runs away but can find no subsistence other than prostitution, which perpetuates the violation of childhood integrity. Some research suggests that a higher percentage of prostitutes were victims of childhood abuse than of non-prostitutes. Research also suggests that fifty percent of prostitutes were not abused and that twenty-five percent of non-prostitutes were abused. … A victim deserves no stigmatization either in childhood or adulthood. *The ICPR affirms the right of children to shelter, education, medical or psychological or legal services, safety, and sexual self-determination. Allocation of government funds to guarantee the above rights should be a priority, in every country.*

### Integrity of All Women

Violence against women and girls has been a major feminist preoccupation for the past decade. Specifically, rape, sexual harassment at work, battering, and denial of motherhood rights have been targeted as focal areas for concern, research, and activism. Within the context of prostitution, women are sometimes raped or sexually harassed by the police, by their clients, by their managers, and by strangers who know them to be whores. Prostitute women, like non-prostitute women, consider rape to be any sexual act forced upon them. The fact that prostitutes are available for sexual negotiation does not mean that they are available for sexual harassment or rape. *The ICPR demands that the prostitute be given the same protection from rape and the same legal recourse and social support following rape that should be the right of any woman or man.*

Battering of prostitutes, like battering of non-prostitutes, reflects the subordination of women to men in personal relationships. Laws against such violence are often discriminately and/or arbitrarily enforced. Boyfriends and husbands of prostitutes, in addition to anyone else assumed to profit from prostitution earnings (such as family and roommates), are often fined or imprisoned in various countries on charges of "pimping" regardless of whether they commit a violent offense or not. Boyfriends and husbands of non-prostitute women are rarely punished for battering, even when the woman clearly presses charges against them. *The ICPR affirms the right of all women to relational choice and to recourse against violence within any personal or work setting.*

Women known to be prostitutes or sex workers, like women known to be lesbians, are regularly denied custody of their children in many countries. The assumption that prostitute women or lesbian women are less responsible, loving, or deserving than other women is a denial of human rights and human dignity. The laws and attitudes which punish sexually stigmatized women function to punish their children as well by stigmatizing them and by denying them their mothers. *The ICPR considers the denial of custodial rights to prostitutes and lesbians to be a violation of the social and psychological integrity of women.*

...

## Migration of Women Through Prostitution ("Trafficking")

Trafficking of women and children, an international issue among both feminists and non-feminists, usually refers to the transport of women and children from one country to another for purposes of prostitution under conditions of force or deceit. The ICPR has a clear stand against child prostitution under any circumstances. In the case of adult prostitution, it must be acknowledged that prostitution both within and across national borders can be an individual decision to which an adult woman has a right. ... Women who choose to migrate as prostitutes ... should enjoy the same rights as other immigrants. For many women, female migration through prostitution is an escape from an economically and socially impossible situation in one country to hopes for a better situation in another. ... Given the increased internationalization of industry, including prostitution, the rights and specific needs of foreign women workers must be given special attention in all countries.

*The ICPR objects to policies which give women the status of children and which assume migration through prostitution among women to be always the result of force or deceit. Migrant women, also those who work as prostitutes, deserve both worker rights and worker protections. Women who are transported under conditions of deceit or force should be granted choice of refuge status or return to their country of origin.*

## A Movement for All-Women's Rights

It is essential that feminist struggle include the rights of all women. Prostitutes (especially those also oppressed by racism and classism) are perhaps the most silenced and violated of all women; the inclusion of their rights and their own words in feminist platforms for change is necessary. *The ICPR urges existing feminist groups to invite whore-identified women into their leading ranks and to integrate a prostitution consciousness in their analyses and strategies.*

...

## Prostitution and Human Rights

The European Convention on Human Rights was drafted within the Council of Europe in 1950 and came into force in 1953. All twenty-one of the member States have ratified it. Those States include: Austria, Belgium, Cyprus, Denmark, France, Federal Republic of Germany, Greece, Iceland, Ireland, Italy, Liechtenstein, Luxembourg,

Malta, the Netherlands, Norway, Portugal, Spain, Sweden, Switzerland, Turkey, and the United Kingdom. A published summary of the Convention is reprinted at the end of this statement.

The International Committee for Prostitutes' Rights (ICPR) demands that prostitutes, ex-prostitutes, and all women regardless of their work, color, class, sexuality, history of abuse, or marital status be granted the same human rights as every other citizen. At present, prostitutes are officially and/or unofficially denied rights both by States within the Council of Europe and by States outside of it. No State in the world is held accountable by any international body for those infractions. To the contrary, denial of human rights to prostitutes is publicly justified as a protection of women, public order, health, morality, and the reputation of dominant persons or nations. Those arguments deny prostitutes the status of ordinary persons and blame them for disorder and/or disease and for male exploitation of and violence against women. Criminalization or state regulation of prostitution does not protect anyone, least of all prostitutes. Prostitutes are systematically robbed of liberty, security, fair administration of justice, respect for private and family life, freedom of expression, and freedom of association. In addition, they suffer from inhuman and degrading treatment and punishment and from discrimination in employment and housing. Prostitutes are effectively excluded from the Human Rights Convention.

The World Charter of Prostitutes' Rights which was adopted by the ICPR in 1985 demands that prostitution be redefined as legitimate work and that prostitutes be redefined as legitimate citizens. Any other stance functions to deny human status to a class of women (and to men who sexually service other men).

The European Parliament recently took a step toward decriminalizing prostitution and prostitute workers by adopting a resolution on violence against women which includes the following clauses (see Hedy d'Ancona resolution, June session of Parliament, 1986):

"In view of the existence of prostitution the European Parliament calls on the national authorities in the Member States to take the necessary legal steps:

(a) to decriminalize the exercise of this profession,

(b) to guarantee prostitutes the rights enjoyed by other citizens,

(c) to protect the independence, health and safety of all those exercising this profession ...

(d) to reinforce measures which may be taken against those responsible for duress or violence to prostitutes ...

(e) to support prostitutes' self-help groups and to require police and judicial authorities to provide better protection for prostitutes who wish to lodge complaints ..."

Concrete implementation of those steps requires specifications of the violations in each State. One goal of the Second World Whores' Congress is for prostitutes from countries represented within the Council of Europe and outside of it to specify those violations. The summarized list stated here will be elaborated at the congress.

## Violations of the Human Rights of Prostitutes

**1. The right to life.** Murder of prostitutes is a common occurrence throughout the world. And, those murders are commonly considered less offensive than other murders, as evidenced by the fact that prostitute murderers are often not sought, found, or prosecuted.

**2. The right to liberty and security of person.** The physical safety of prostitutes is threatened by the criminal sphere in which they are forced to work.

The physical liberty of prostitutes is restricted by state and city regulations which prohibit their presence in certain districts or at certain times. For example, a woman standing on the street "looking as if she is a prostitute" can be fined for passive solicitation in France even if she is not negotiating a sexual transaction. Or, a prostitute in Toronto, Canada can be given a curfew (21:00) by the court if she hasn't paid three or four solicitation tickets; if she disobeys the order, she can be sentenced to six months in prison for disobeying a court order.

The right to liberty and security of persons is totally denied to women who are deceitfully or forcefully made to practice prostitution. In particular, the common transport of third world women to the West under false pretenses denies both liberty and security to women. The right *not* to work as a prostitute is as essential as the right to work if one so decides. Sexist and racist denial of both rights is widespread.

Prostitutes usually do not enjoy the same police protection of their liberty and security as other citizens. Due to the criminalization of their profession, they risk fines or arrests so they avoid calling upon police for protection. Police are frequently known to grant immunity from criminal action in exchange for information and/or sex, i.e. rape by the state as the cost for liberty.

Forced medical testing which denies choice of one's own doctor and medical facility denies liberty to prostitutes. Denial of worker's compensation prevents prostitutes from liberty and health security in case of illness.

Forced or pressured registration with the police stigmatizes prostitutes and frequently violates their privacy and liberty to change professions if they so choose. Prostitutes are denied job mobility by requirements for letters of good conduct which are granted only to those who can prove that they have not engaged in commercial sex for at least three years (for example, in Switzerland).

**3. The right to fair administration of justice.** Application of laws and regulations against prostitution is usually arbitrary, discriminatory, corrupt, and hypocritical. In Paris, for example, street prostitutes are given an average of three tickets per week for passive or active solicitation; at the same time, they are heavily taxed for their prostitution earnings.

Prostitutes who are raped or physically battered are unlikely to succeed in bringing charges against the rapist or batterer. The prostitute is considered fair game for abuse even by state and judiciary authorities.

Foreign women who were deceitfully or forcefully transported for purposes of prostitution rarely succeed in bringing charges against the violating party.

Male law enforcement officials, like other men, are frequently customers and/or violators of prostitute women. Police, for example, in the United States, Canada, and Great Britain, regularly entrap women by posing as customers and arresting them as soon as they mention a price for sex. Even if the prostitute is careful not to mention a price (many have learned to expect police deceit), she may be convicted because a police officer's word carries more credit than a whore's word in court.

Prostitution laws are discriminately enforced against women, especially third world and poor women, and against third world male associates of those women.

**4. Respect for private and family life, home and correspondence.** Laws which criminalize those who profit from the earnings of prostitutes are frequently used against the family of prostitutes, for example in the United States and France. Such "anti-pimping" laws violate a prostitute's right to a private life by putting all of her personal associates, be they lovers or children or parents or roommates, under (even more) risk of arrest than exloiters and physical violators.

Confiscation of personal letters or literary work of prostitutes, for example in the United States, is a clear denial of respect for home and correspondence, not to mention a denial of freedom of expression.

**5. Freedom of expression and to hold opinions.** The word of prostitutes is generally assumed to be invalid in public, for example as evidence in court. The opinions of prostitutes are rarely given a hearing, even in relation to their own lives.

In private, prostitutes are often used as police informants and as counselors to male customers. In public, be it on the street or in court, their testimony and opinion are silenced.

**6. Freedom of peaceful assembly and association, including the right to join a trade union.** Prostitutes are prevented from working together for purposes of safety, cooperation, and/or commercial advantage by specific statutes which criminalize "keeping a house" or other necessarily cooperative work forms.

Until prostitutes are recognized as legitimate workers, rather than as outlaws or vagrants or bad girls, they cannot officially form trade unions.

**7. The right to marry and found a family.** Both the right to marry and the right not to marry are frequently denied to women, in particular to the prostitute woman. Marriage is impossible if husbands thereby become outlaws, i.e. pimps. The denial of rights and legitimacy to unmarried women, on the other hand, can force women to marry against their will. A prostitute may also be denied the privilege of motherhood when the courts declare her unfit on the basis of her profession.

**8. The right to peaceful enjoyment of possessions.** The possessions of prostitutes and their associates are confiscated on the ground that they were obtained with "illegal" money; they are also confiscated when a prostitute cannot pay the fines levied against her for the practice of her profession.

**9. The right to leave a country including one's own.** Prostitutes are denied the right to travel across national borders by signs or cuts on their passports (or identity cards) which indicate their profession. Also, police records registered on computers at certain borders will prevent prostitutes from leaving or entering the country.

**10. Prohibition of torture and inhuman or degrading treatment and punishment.** The above mentioned violations indicate inhuman treatment. Degradation of prostitutes is the norm both among official bodies, such as governmental and judiciary institutions, and among community bodies, such as neighborhood committees and social service agencies.

Forced prostitution should be recognized as a case of torture.

**11. Prohibition of slavery, servitude and forced labour.** Servitude exists both in cases of forced prostitution and in cases of voluntary prostitution under forced conditions. State regulated brothels such as found in Hamburg (Germany) and Nevada (United States) allow no choice in clientele, no right to refusal, no right to a fair share of the earnings, forced isolation, and forced overwork. Most brothels in the Netherlands force unhealthy practices such as no condoms (or less earnings for condom sex) and/or forced alcohol consumption.

Juvenile prostitution is a case of forced labour but the managers, be they managers of pornography or prostitution, are rarely prosecuted whereas the children are often stigmatized and punished.

**12. Prohibition of discrimination in the enjoyment of rights and freedoms guaranteed by the Convention.** Prostitutes are discriminated against in the enjoyment of every right and freedom. Prostitutes of color, foreign prostitutes, street prostitutes, drug addicted prostitutes, and juvenile prostitutes suffer extra and often extreme discrimination.

**13. Prohibition of the collective expulsion of aliens.** Expulsion of foreign women who entered the country under conditions of deceit or force and who often await persecution in their native country is a violation of human rights.

# PART THREE

# MARKETING  FEMININITY

This part extends the discussion of several themes raised in the previous one. In particular, it examines the cultural construction of women as objects of masculine sexual desire and explores the complex interconnections among women's subordination, our sexualization, and the making of profits. These connections are explored through a focus on two issues: the representation of women in the context of pornography, art, and popular culture and the presentation of women in the context of fashion and beauty. One question of particular concern is whether these social institutions, which at first sight may seem merely to reflect and reinforce women's subordination, may nevertheless provide opportunities for feminist resistance.

## Representing Women: Pornography, Art, and Popular Culture

During the 1980s, Western feminists were bitterly divided by the issue of pornography. While some argued that pornography was necessarily predicated on the subordination of women, others extolled the liberatory aspects of portraying women enjoying sex outside marriage, sometimes with a number of partners and in contexts suggesting little interest in procreation. Since pornography is clearly a form of sex work, at least for the models and actors involved, some of the feminist pornography debate revolves around the same questions as the feminist prostitution debate: Is providing sex for money intrinsically more degrading than providing any other service? How do we distinguish free from unfree choices? What is the cultural meaning of sex between men and women? But because pornography involves not only sexual performances but also representations of sexuality and sexual performances, it also raises additional questions about the interpretation of words and images, the relation between speech and action, and the nature of freedom of expression. The selections that follow explore these questions by discussing Western representations of women in the context of pornography and of popular and high culture.

Explicit depictions and descriptions of sexual acts and organs seem to have always existed, and we may surmise that in earlier societies these depictions fulfilled a variety of functions including but not limited to inducing sexual arousal. Only in contemporary Western industrial societies, however, has a wide variety of sexually explicit materials become easily available to virtually everyone, a development resulting, at least in part, from the technological possibilities of cheap mass production and distribution—and consequent opportunities for making a profit. Some people speculate that other reasons for the recent increase in the availability of sexually explicit material include a weakening of the link between sex and procreation in the industrialized nations, as a result of both the increasing availability of contraception and decreasing infant mortality, and consequent new attitudes toward sexual activity as entertainment and recreation. In addition, some feminists have wondered whether representations of women as sexually available may provide a way for men to deal emotionally with the growing sexual independence of real women, which itself results from the related phenomena of lower fertility rates and increasing female labor force participation.

Nonfeminist objections to pornography typically have been based on opposition to sexually explicit material, often called "indecent" or "obscene," which is said to appeal to "prurient" interests. In the twentieth century, explicit sexual material has often been tolerated only if "redeemed" by literary, artistic, political, or scientific merit sufficient to outweigh the harm supposedly inherent in its sexually arousing nature. Once judged redeemed by its contribution to some nonsexual value, sexually explicit material is described, not as pornography, but as educational or political material, art, or literature. In conservative conceptualizations, therefore, the term *pornography* clearly has a derogatory connotation insofar as by definition it lacks any value other than its power of sexual arousal.

Conservative criticisms of pornography often fail to make clear exactly why stimulating sexual arousal should be considered socially harmful, but it may be because the arousal occurs through imagining sexual engagement in situations not socially legitimated. Sexually explicit material interests people in sexual interactions with individuals other than their marriage partners, perhaps with people of their own sex or with groups of people, and in sexual practices that are in no way intended for procreation. Thus for many conservatives, the harm of pornography may be its subversion of established sexual norms.

Although some feminists may agree with such conservative critiques of pornography, these critiques are obviously not feminist because they fail to explore possible connections between pornography and the subordination of women. Indeed, it is not easy to demonstrate that encouraging an interest in nonprocreative and/or nonmarital sexual activity necessarily contributes to this subordination; on the contrary, many Western feminists regard established or conventional sexual norms as themselves reflecting and/or reinforcing women's subordination. Distinctively feminist opposition to pornography cannot therefore be based on the simple fact that pornography promotes sexual arousal. Instead, such opposition must be based on claims that pornography reflects and reinforces the subordination of women. Some feminists go further and claim that pornography is itself a practice of subordination.

Feminists opposed to pornography argue that women are coerced into pornographic modeling and acting in much the same way that they are coerced into prostitution; the story of Linda Marciano, aka Linda Lovelace, the actress in the celebrated pornographic film *Deep Throat,* is often used in illustration of this claim. To the extent that pornographic actors are forced to perform sexual acts, feminists have noted that their work is indistinguishable from prostitution; indeed, a connection with prostitution is evident even in the etymology of "pornography," which derives from two Greek words meaning "representation of prostitutes." Inside the pornography industry, feminists argue, women are controlled, even enslaved, by men in much the same way as prostitutes; pimps get rich through the sexual exploitation of women, and pornographers get even richer because pornography is a multibillion-dollar industry much larger than the legitimate publishing business.

Many feminists go on to argue that even women who are entirely outside the pornography industry, who may never even have encountered pornographic material, nevertheless are harmed by the existence of pornography. Feminists who make these claims define pornography, not in the nongendered terms of sexual explicitness, but in overtly gendered terms as the eroticization of women's subordination for men's sexual pleasure. By teaching that women's subordination is sexually gratifying, pornography is thought to encourage male sexual violence toward women. This gendered understanding of pornography, which presents men as the paradigmatic users of pornography and women as its paradigmatic subjects, is not simply an empirical claim disconfirmable by a few counterexamples. On the contrary, this understanding reinterprets apparent counterexamples by asserting that, if a woman enjoys pornography, she is behaving in a culturally masculine way and that, if a male subject is portrayed as a sexual subordinate, he is being feminized.

In the first selection on this topic, "Why Pornography Matters to Feminists," Andrea Dworkin provides a succinct and forceful expression of this feminist view, which is elaborated by Helen E. Longino in the following selection. In "Pornography, Oppression, and Freedom: A Closer Look," Longino offers a comprehensive and carefully reasoned argument that defines pornography as endorsing sexual degradation or abuse—typically, though not invariably, of women or children; she thus distinguishes pornography from both sexually explicit material and material that portrays sexual degradation or abuse without endorsing it. Longino goes on to argue that pornography encourages crimes of violence against women, disseminates the lie that women enjoy being sexually degraded, and encourages women's subordination by promoting the view that women are less than human. She believes that pornography should not be protected by appeal either to privacy or freedom of expression—protected, in the United States, by the First Amendment to the Constitution. Although the individual production or enjoyment of pornography may be guaranteed by the right to privacy, Longino believes that this right does not protect the public distribution of defamatory material. Nor does she think such distribution is protected by the right to free expression of ideas since the right to freedom of expression is instrumental and limited, rather than intrinsic and absolute, justified only insofar as it guarantees individual independence and equality. Because Longino regards pornography as undermining respect for women, she asserts that it should be viewed as an abuse rather than a legitimate use of freedom of expression.

Although this uncompromisingly antipornography position is frequently regarded as feminist orthodoxy, in fact it is questioned by many other feminists who challenge both the preceding definitions of pornography and claims that pornography is invariably harmful to women. These feminists also suggest that the legal remedies for pornography proposed by other feminists may actually be worse than the disease.

In "Feminism, Moralism, and Pornography," Ellen Willis challenges the distinction some feminists make between erotica and pornography, asserting that the distinction is viewed better as a difference of taste and class than as a difference in meaning and message. Even though Willis acknowledges that some pornography is offensive, she argues that representations of sexuality can arouse people only if they appeal to responses learned in circumstances of male domination. The circumstances do not yet exist for ideal or postrevolutionary sexualities to come into being; in the meantime, condemning representations of contemporary heterosexuality as pornographic serves only to make women who enjoy such representations ashamed of their own sexuality. Willis asserts that, even though much pornography glorifies male supremacy, it still expresses a radical impulse insofar as it challenges sexual repression and hypocrisy. In conclusion, she argues that pornography should be protected under the First Amendment since it is indeed a form of political speech—something antipornographers themselves concede—and she expresses concern that any legislation restricting pornography will be interpreted in a male-dominant society as permitting the suppression of various forms of sexual dissidence, including feminism and homosexuality.

Willis's argument is developed by Lisa Duggan, Nan D. Hunter, and Carole S. Vance in "False Promises: Feminist Antipornography Legislation." They forcefully oppose controlling pornography through legislation, whether this be traditional obscenity law or feminist-inspired legislation conceptualizing pornography as a practice of discrimination against women. They argue that the legislation of this type that has been proposed not only utilizes vague definitions of pornography that incorporate traditional sexist assumptions about male and female sexuality; it also rests on dubious assumptions about the harmfulness of pornography to women. In opposition to feminist antipornographers, Duggan, Hunter, and Vance argue, first, that the sexual images in question do not cause more harm to women than other aspects of misogynist culture; second, that sexually explicit speech, even in male-dominated society, serves positive social functions for women; and third, that the passage and enforcement of antipornography laws are more likely to impede than advance feminist goals.

Tracey A. Gardner's article, "Racism in Pornography and the Women's Movement," argues that pornography is especially harmful to Black women because it presents them in ways that draw on racist sexual stereotypes. Gardner notes that many Black as well as white men enjoy pornography, even though it also exploits Black men's sexuality in specifically racist ways. Despite this, Black women are usually able to communicate their concerns to Black men, and they will not join with white women in ending pornography until white women have dealt with their own racism.

In "Confessions of a Feminist Porno Star," Nina Hartley, a well-known star of both heterosexual and lesbian pornographic videos, defends her work in feminist terms.

Not only does she find the job enjoyable, but she also denies that it contributes to the sexual degradation or subordination of women. On the contrary, she presents herself as a sex reformer whose films portray women enjoying a wide variety of sexual activities.

Most of the feminist debates on pornography have focused on heterosexual pornography, which they portray as consisting in predominantly female figures being sexually exploited for the pleasure or heterosexual men. By contrast, Cindy Patton's article, "The Cum Shot: Takes on Lesbian and Gay Sexuality," addresses the issues in the context of gay, especially lesbian, pornography. She describes the confict between the feminist antipornography lesbians, who regard most pornography as sexual exploitation, and the feminist sex radicals, who extol the liberatory potential of pornography. Like Ellen Willis, Patton suggests that at least some of this disagreement concerns opposing evaluations of contrasting production styles: some women like glossy productions in which "artsy" erotic performances occur in tasteful settings; others regard such productions as romanticizing sex while commodifying women. The latter prefer more realistic and "raunchy" pornography, which seems more "natural" and which, in its amateurish qualities, suggests that the sex portrayed is illicit and therefore more exciting. Patton concludes that lesbian pornography is an ongoing exploration of female-centered sex. Its potential for transforming our sexual ideas and practices is created by the specific historical context of those who make and enjoy it.

The last two articles in this section explore some of the ways in which themes that many feminists have asserted to be characteristically pornographic are also evident in both popular and high culture. Ann Barr Snitow's examination of Harlequin romances, "Mass Market Romance: Pornography for Women Is Different," reveals how these novels, produced specifically for women readers, eroticize both traditional masculine and feminine roles by counterposing the danger and aggression represented by male sexuality against female sexual anxiety and passivity. John Berger's discussion of the European tradition of nude oil painting, "Ways of Seeing," argues that these paintings, produced by male artists for male patrons, characteristically portray their female subjects as sexual objects available for the pleasure of the male viewer. Berger asserts that the relatively few European oil paintings of naked women that portray their subjects as well-loved individuals, rather than as objectified abstractions, are so exceptional that they should not be seen as part of the nude tradition. Snitow and Berger define both pulp romances and a central tradition of European high culture in terms identical to those in which many feminists define pornography—namely, as depending for their appeal on the eroticization of male dominance and female subordination.

Feminist discussion has revealed that pornography, like most other institutions in contemporary North America, reflects a variety of deep social divisions. These not only include divisions of gender and sexuality, categories that now seem indispensable in discussing pornography, though it is worth remembering that their relevance went largely unrecognized until revealed by feminists; they also include divisions of race, class, age, physical ability, and sexual preference. Some feminists argue that pornography reinforces these invidious distinctions and that the law should be used to curtail it. Feminists who dispute this conclusion typically do not deny that some pornography is implicated in the subordination of women, just as feminists who are pro-choice on abortion do not deny that the availability of this procedure makes it possible for some women to be forced into "choosing" it. Instead, the feminists who are pro-choice on pornography tend to argue that the meanings of pornography are ambiguous and contestable, so that pornography often includes themes—such as interracial, lesbian, autoerotic, or group sex—that may subvert as well as reinforce invidious social stereotypes and divisions. They oppose the imposition of legal constraints on pornography in part on the grounds that pornography no more reinforces the sexual subordination of women than do many other forms of Western culture; moreover, they fear that once the state has authority to move against any form of sexually explicit material, it may use this authority to suppress portrayals of any unorthodox, including feminist, sexual activity. Their fear may be well founded. The first material challenged under a 1992 Canadian law prohibiting sexually explicit material that subordinated or degraded women was indeed gay pornography seized from a lesbian/gay bookstore.

## Presenting Women: Fashion and Beauty

In 1968, a group of feminists picketing the Miss America pageant in Atlantic City brought along a "Freedom Trash Can" into which they threw a number of things associated with what they called the sexual objectification of women. The discarded objects included makeup, curlers, girdles, and bras. Many young men of the time were demonstrating their opposition to the Indochina war by burning their draft cards, and in an effort to draw a parallel between the antiwar protests and the protest against women's sexual objectification, one reporter covering the event described the women as burning their bras. From this time on, feminists were regularly portrayed in the mainstream media as bra burners, a characterization simultaneously suggesting that feminists were irrationally preoccupied with trivial issues and diverting attention away from the many other issues that feminists of the time addressed.

Like most stereotypes, the image of feminists as bra burners contained a germ of truth. For although no feminists are recorded as having actually burned their bras and relatively few even threw them away, feminists have continued to be concerned with the ways in which conventional standards of feminine attractiveness both reflect and reinforce women's subordination. Although the cultural standards of feminine beauty are often derided as a "personal" issue, a distraction from "real" social problems, most feminists argue that these standards have far-reaching social ramifications. The questions surrounding women's appearance offer a prime example of how the personal may be political—not to mention economic.

When feminists in the late 1960s and early 1970s complained of sexual objectification, they were often challenged, by women as well as men, to explain exactly what was wrong with being a sex object. Many women said they enjoyed being perceived in sexual terms, and some men said that they only wished more women would see them that way. As the title of her article indicates, Linda Lemoncheck tackles head-on the question "What's Wrong with Being a Sex Object?" She analyzes the concept of sexual objectification via a careful discussion of the various contexts in which it is or is not appropriate to treat women as objects of sexual desire. She distinguishes treating women as sexually attractive from treating them as sex objects: women can be regarded as sexually attractive but still be treated as moral equals, whereas sexual objectification involves subjugation, subordination, and the intimidation produced by psychological control. Lemoncheck's conclusion is that women are dehumanized by being treated as sex objects.

In the following article (an interview by Wendy Chapkis), "Bibo" complains that feminist opposition to fashion and makeup is simplistic and puritanical, possibly revealing feminists' own lack of self-esteem. Bibo's attitude is shared by Janet Radcliffe Richards, who challenges what she takes to be the reasoning behind many feminists' perceived resistance to making themselves sexually attractive to men. In "The Unadorned Feminist," Richards argues that being beautiful and being sexually attractive are legitimate goals for women, and she criticizes the idea of beauty as "natural."

Andrea Dworkin's description of Chinese footbinding, in "Gynocide: Chinese Footbinding," confirms that what is conventionally regarded as female beauty is often far from natural. Dworkin insists that feminist concerns about fashion and beauty are not primarily that evaluating women in terms of their appearance is unfair or objectifying. The main issue, for Dworkin, is that standards of beauty define women's relationship to their own bodies and to that extent define women's physical freedom. The processes of female beautification were agonizing for Chinese women; even for contemporary Western women such processes are frequently painful. Mother/daughter relationships are poisoned by mothers pushing their daughters to conform to conventional standards of feminine beauty, whatever the pain in doing so. At the same time, Dworkin argues, daughters' early experience of pain teaches them to be masochistic, subservient, and materialistic while diverting them from intellectual or creative achievements. Dworkin's article suggests that in contexts of male domination, the beautification of women is necessarily a practice of subordination.

Even though girls' early beautification practices may be encouraged or even enforced by their mothers, standards of feminine beauty are quickly internalized so that older girls and women of all ages learn to police their own bodies. This is especially evident with respect to the contemporary Western cult of slenderness, addressed in the next two articles. Both describe how, in order to be slender, women will go to desperate lengths that endanger their health and sometimes even their lives. In "Do Something About Your Weight," Carol Schmidt describes two "elective" surgeries on her digestive system, each of which had disastrous consequences. She complains that even feminists often fail to recognize her obesity as a disability, or different ability, and perceive it instead as a character flaw. Naomi Wolf's article, "Hunger," discusses what Wolf calls the weight-loss cult, explaining how it has generated an epidemic of eating disorders among young women. Wolf analyzes this cult in political terms, suggesting that the loss of self-esteem it induces in women is not an unfortunate by-product of the cult but rather its real purpose. She argues that the weight-loss cult is a reaction by "the dominant culture" against twentieth-century Western feminist advances, a means of controlling women by undermining our sense of self-worth.

In "Skin Deep," Wendy Chapkis explores further the cultural meanings that may attach to women's appearance; sometimes women's appearance may symbolize the Good Life of Western consumer societies and sometimes resistance to Western values. Chapkis asserts that men's political and economic interests are pursued on the terrain of women's bodies. Her concerns are illustrated in the following article, an interview by Chapkis of "Marieme," an Algerian woman who explains the changing meanings of the veil in an Islamic society. Whereas at one time it was an anticolonial symbol, now it may express a strong religious commitment or even a commitment to the exclusion of women from public life.

Roberta Galler's "The Myth of the Perfect Body" offers a feminist perspective on physical disability. She notes how feminists' reactions against the conventional romanticization of feminine fragility and vulnerability have generated alternative ideals of physical strength and independence that may be oppressive to women who sometimes need help. Although disabled and aging women need help more frequently than other people, every woman needs it at some points in her life. Feminists must challenge prevailing perceptions of disabled and aging women as stigmatized, asexual, or even less than human. No one's body is perfect, and feminists must learn to accept ourselves and each other with our limitations and weaknesses as well as our strengths.

The last two articles in this section address possible means by which women may resist oppressive standards of feminine beauty. Kathryn Pauly Morgan's article, "Women and the Knife: Cosmetic Surgery and the Colonization of Women's Bodies," reveals the increasing social pressures on women to "choose" cosmetic surgery and discusses how we may resist these pressures. Morgan identifies three paradoxes of choice confronting women who undergo cosmetic surgery. First, these women's apparently self-creating choices reveal a deep conformity to conventional norms of beauty and compulsory heterosexuality. Second, their expressed intention of liberating and caring for themselves is deployed through capitulation to dominant norms of male supremacy, class bias, racism, anti-Semitism, ageism, and ableism. Third, the normalization of technological interventions stigmatizes those reluctant to submit to such treatments and puts coercive pressure on them to do so. Morgan suggests that feminists might resist the normalization of technologically achieved ideals of beauty either by making themselves conventionally ugly or by drawing attention to the cultural commodification of women's bodies through offering grotesque "body contours" for sale.

The final article in this section, Alice Walker's "Beauty: When the Other Dancer Is the Self," describes how the author finally came to accept her eye, permanently damaged in childhood. Walker's piece raises many issues for feminists; especially interesting in the present context is her story of how losing her eye affected her confidence and behavior throughout her childhood—not because the eye no longer functioned as an organ of sight, but because she regarded it as ugly. Although Walker's story provides an inspiring account of one individual's successful resistance to conventional norms of feminine beauty, it is doubtful that all or even most women presently have the emotional or economic resources to follow her example.

Like other issues already considered, the contemporary Western institutions of feminine beauty and fashion raise deep and complex questions for feminism. How can we distinguish autonomy from exploitation, reason from rationalization, choice from manipulation or coercion? How can we avoid both puritanism and commodification? How can we negotiate the multiple and often contradictory meanings attached to women's appearance? How can we reclaim our bodies, our beauty, and our sexuality while resisting discriminatory norms that valorize whiteness, youth, wealth, and physical ability? These questions cannot be avoided: No matter what personal appearance we present, it will inevitably carry some cultural significance. Somehow we must learn to live with the contradictions of feminine fashion and beauty.

# *Why Pornography Matters to Feminists*

## Andrea Dworkin

...

Pornography is an essential issue because pornography says that women want to be hurt, forced, and abused; pornography says women want to be raped, battered, kidnapped, maimed; pornography says women want to be humiliated, shamed, defamed; pornography says that women say No but mean Yes—Yes to violence, Yes to pain.

Also: pornography says that women are things; pornography says that being used as things fulfills the erotic nature of women; pornography says that women are the things men use.

Also: in pornography women are used as things; in pornography force is used against women; in pornography women are used.

Also: pornography says that women are sluts, cunts; pornography says that pornographers define women; pornography says that men define women; pornography says that women are what men want women to be.

Also: pornography shows women as body parts, as genitals, as vaginal slits, as nipples, as buttocks, as lips, as open wounds, as pieces.

Also: pornography uses real women.

Also: pornography is an industry that buys and sells women.

Also: pornography sets the standard for female sexuality, for female sexual values, for girls growing up, for boys growing up, and increasingly for advertising, films, video, visual arts, fine art and literature, music with words.

Also: the acceptance of pornography means the decline of feminist ethics and an abandonment of feminist politics; the acceptance of pornography means feminists abandon women.

Also: pornography reinforces the Right's hold on women by making the environment outside the home more dangerous, more threatening; pornography reinforces the husband's hold on the wife by making the domestic environment more dangerous, more threatening.

Also: pornography turns women into objects and commodities; pornography perpetuates the object status of women; pornography perpetuates the self-defeating divisions among women by perpetuating the object status of women; pornography perpetuates the low self-esteem of women by perpetuating the object status of women; pornography perpetuates the distrust of women for women by perpetuating the object status of women; pornography perpetuates the demeaning and degrading of female intelligence and creativity by perpetuating the object status of women.

Also: pornography is violence against the women used in pornography and pornography encourages and promotes violence against women as a class; pornography dehumanizes the women used in pornography and pornography contributes to and promotes the dehumanization of all women; pornography exploits the women used in pornography and accelerates and promotes the sexual and economic exploitation of women as a class.

Also: pornography is made by men who sanction, use, celebrate, and promote violence against women.

Also: pornography exploits children of both sexes, especially girls, and encourages violence against children, and does violence to children.

Also: pornography uses racism and anti-Semitism to promote sexual arousal; pornography promotes racial hatred by promoting racial degradation as "sexy"; pornography romanticizes the concentration camp and the plantation, the Nazi and the slaveholder; pornography exploits demeaning racial stereotypes to promote sexual arousal; pornography celebrates racist sexual obsessions.

Also: pornography numbs the conscience, makes one increasingly callous to cruelty, to the infliction of pain, to violence against persons, to the humiliation or degradation of persons, to the abuse of women and children.

Also: pornography gives us no future; pornography robs us of hope as well as dignity; pornography further lessens our human value in the society at large and our human potential in fact; pornography forbids sexual self-determination to women and to children; pornography uses us up and throws us away; pornography annihilates our chance for freedom.

# Pornography, Oppression, and Freedom: A Closer Look

## Helen E. Longino

...

## What Is Pornography?

I define pornography as *verbal or pictorial explicit representations of sexual behavior that,* in the words of the Commission on Obscenity and Pornography, *have as a distinguishing characteristic "the degrading and demeaning portrayal of the role and status of the human female ... as a mere sexual object to be exploited and manipulated sexually."* In pornographic books, magazines, and films, women are represented as passive and as slavishly dependent upon men. The role of female characters is limited to the provision of sexual services to men. To the extent that women's sexual pleasure is represented at all, it is subordinated to that of men and is never an end in itself as is the sexual pleasure of men. What pleases women is the use of their bodies to satisfy male desires. While the sexual objectification of women is common to all pornography, women are the recipients of even worse treatment in violent pornography, in which women characters are killed, tortured, gang-raped, mutilated, bound, and otherwise abused, as a means of providing sexual stimulation or pleasure to the male characters. It is this development which has attracted the attention of feminists and been the stimulus to an analysis of pornography in general.[1]

Not all sexually explicit material is pornography, nor is all material which contains representations of sexual abuse and degradation pornography.

A representation of a sexual encounter between adult persons which is characterized by mutual respect is, once we have disentangled sexuality and morality, not morally objectionable. Such a representation would be one in which the desires and experiences of each participant were regarded by the other participants as having a validity and a subjective importance equal to those of the individual's own desire and experiences. In such an encounter, each participant acknowledges the other participant's basic human dignity and personhood. Similarly, a representation of a nude human body (in whole or in part) in such a manner that the person shown maintains self-respect—e.g., is not portrayed in a degrading position—would not be morally objectionable. … While some erotic materials are beyond the standards of modesty held by some individuals, they are not for this reason immoral.

A representation of a sexual encounter which is not characterized by mutual respect, in which at least one of the parties is treated in a manner beneath her or his dignity as a human being, is no longer simple erotica. That a representation is of degrading behavior does not in itself, however, make it pornographic. Whether or not it is pornographic is a function of contextual features. Books and films may contain descriptions or representations of a rape in order to explore the consequences of such an assault upon its victim. What is being shown is abusive or degrading behavior which attempts to deny the humanity and dignity of the person assaulted, yet the context surrounding the representation, through its exploration of the consequences of the act, acknowledges and reaffirms her dignity. Such books and films, far from being pornographic, are (or can be) highly moral, and fall into the category of moral realism.

What makes a work a work of pornography, then, is not simply its representation of degrading and abusive sexual encounters, but its implicit, if not explicit, approval and recommendation of sexual behavior that is immoral, i.e., that physically or psychologically violates the personhood of one of the participants. Pornography, then, is verbal or pictorial material which represents or describes sexual behavior that is degrading or abusive to one or more of the participants *in such a way as to endorse the degradation.* The participants so treated in virtually all heterosexual pornography are women or children, so heterosexual pornography is, as a matter of fact, material which endorses sexual behavior that is degrading and/or abusive to women and children. As I use the term "sexual behavior," this includes sexual encounters between persons, behavior which produces sexual stimulation or pleasure for one of the participants, and behavior which is preparatory to or invites sexual activity. Behavior that is degrading or abusive includes physical harm or abuse, and physical or psychological coercion. In addition, behavior which ignores or devalues the real interests, desires, and experiences of one or more participants in any way is degrading. Finally, that a person has chosen or consented to be harmed, abused, or subjected to coercion does not alter the degrading character of such behavior.

Pornography communicates its endorsement of the behavior it represents by various features of the pornographic context: the degradation of the female characters is represented as providing pleasure to the participant males and, even worse, to the participant females, and there is no suggestion that this sort of treatment of others is inappropriate to their status as human beings. These two features are together sufficient to constitute endorsement of the represented behavior. The contextual features which make material pornographic are intrinsic to the material. In addition to these, extrinsic features, such as the purpose for which the material is presented—i.e., the sexual arousal/pleasure/satisfaction of its (mostly) male consumers—or an accompanying text, may reinforce or make explicit the endorsement. Representations which in and of themselves do not show or endorse degrading behavior may be put into a pornographic context by juxtaposition with others that are degrading, or by a text which invites or recommends degrading behavior toward the subject represented. In such a case the whole complex—the series of representations or representations with text—is pornographic.

...

## Pornography: Lies and Violence Against Women

What is wrong with pornography ... is its degrading and dehumanizing portrayal of women (and *not* its sexual content). Pornography, by its very nature, requires that women be subordinate to men and mere instruments for the fulfillment of male fantasies. To accomplish this, pornography must lie. Pornography lies when it says that our sexual life is or ought to be subordinate to the service of men, that our pleasure consists in pleasing men and not ourselves, that we are depraved, that we are fit subjects for rape, bondage, torture, and murder. Pornography lies explicitly about women's sexuality, and through such lies fosters more lies about our humanity, our dignity, and our personhood.

Moreover, since nothing is alleged to justify the treatment of the female characters of pornography save their womanhood, pornography depicts all women as fit objects of violence by virtue of their sex alone. Because it is simply being female that, in the pornographic vision, justifies being violated, the lies of pornography are lies about all women. Each work of pornography is on its own libelous and defamatory, yet gains power through being reinforced by every other pornographic work. The sheer number of pornographic productions expands the moral issue to include not only assessing the morality or immorality of individual works, but also the meaning and force of the mass production of pornography.

The pornographic view of women is thoroughly entrenched in a booming portion of the publishing, film, and recording industries, reaching and affecting not only all who look to such sources for sexual stimulation, but also those of us who are forced into an awareness of it as we peruse magazines at newsstands and record albums in record stores, as we check the entertainment sections of city newspapers, or even as we approach a counter to pay for groceries. It is not necessary to spend a great deal of time reading or viewing pornographic material to absorb its male-centered definition of women. No longer confined within plain brown wrappers, it jumps out from billboards that proclaim "Live X-rated Girls!" or "Angels in Pain" or "Hot and Wild," and from magazine covers displaying a woman's genital area being spread open to the viewer by her own fingers. Thus, even men who do not frequent pornographic shops and movie houses are supported in the sexist objectification of women by their environment. Women, too, are crippled by internalizing as self-images those that are presented to us by pornographers. Isolated from one another and with no source of support for an alternative view of female sexuality, we may not always find the strength to resist a message that dominates the common cultural media.

The entrenchment of pornography in our culture also gives it a significance quite beyond its explicit sexual messages. To suggest, as pornography does, that the primary purpose of women is to provide sexual pleasure to men is to deny that women are independently human or have a status equal to that of men. It is, moreover, to deny our equality at one of the most intimate levels of human experience. This denial is especially powerful in a hierarchical, class society such as ours, in which individuals feel good about themselves by feeling superior to others. Men in our society have a vested interest in maintaining their belief in the inferiority of the female sex, so that no matter how oppressed and exploited by the society in which they live and work, they can feel that they are at least superior to someone or some category of individuals—a woman or women. Pornography, by presenting women as wanton, depraved, and made for the sexual use of men, caters directly to that interest.[2] The very intimate nature of sexuality which makes pornography so corrosive also protects it from explicit public discussion. The consequent lack of any explicit social disavowal of the pornographic image of women enables this image to continue fostering sexist attitudes even as the society publicly proclaims its (as yet timid) commitment to sexual equality.

In addition to finding a connection between the pornograhic view of women and the denial to us of our full human rights, women are beginning to connect the consumption of pornography with commiting rape and other acts of sexual violence against women. … A growing body of research is documenting (1) a correlation between exposure to representations of violence and the committing of violent acts generally, and (2) a correlation between exposure to pornographic materials and the committing of sexually abusive or violent acts against women.[3] While more study is needed to establish precisely what the causal relations are, clearly so-called hard-core pornography is not innocent.

From "snuff" films and miserable magazines in pornographic stores to *Hustler,* to phonograph album covers and advertisements, to *Vogue,* pornography has come to occupy its own niche in the communications and entertainment media and to acquire a quasi-institutional character (signaled by the use of diminutives such as "porn" or "porno" to refer to pornographic material, as though such familiar naming could take the hurt out). Its acceptance by the mass media, whatever the motivation, means a cultural endorsement of its message. As much as the materials themselves, the social tolerance of these degrading and distorted images of women in such quantities is harmful to us, since it indicates a general willingness to see women in ways incompatible with our fundamental human dignity and thus to justify treating us in those ways. The tolerance of pornographic representations of the rape, bondage, and torture of women helps to create and maintain a climate more tolerant of the actual physical abuse of women. The tendency on the part of the legal system to view the victim of a rape as responsible for the crime against her is but one manifestation of this.

In sum, pornography is injurious to women in at least three distinct ways:

1. Pornography, especially violent pornography, is implicated in the committing of crimes of violence against women.
2. Pornography is the vehicle for the dissemination of a deep and vicious lie about women. It is defamatory and libelous.

3. The diffusion of such a distorted view of women's nature in our society as it exists today supports sexist (i.e., male-centered) attitudes, and thus reinforces the oppression and exploitation of women.

Society's tolerance of pornography, especially pornography on the contemporary massive scale, reinforces each of these modes of injury: By not disavowing the lie, it supports the male-centered myth that women are inferior and subordinate creatures. Thus, it contributes to the maintenance of a climate tolerant of both psychological and physical violence against women.

## Pornography and the Law

*Congress shall make no law respecting the establishment of religion, or prohibiting the free exercise thereof; or abridging the freedom of speech, or of the press; or the right of the people peaceably to assemble, and to petition the Government for a redress of grievances.*

—**First Amendment, Bill of Rights**
**of the United States Constitution**

Pornography is clearly a threat to women. Each of the modes of injury cited above offers sufficient reason at least to consider proposals for the social and legal control of pornography. The almost universal response for progressives to such proposals is that constitutional guarantees of freedom of speech and privacy preclude recourse to law.[4] While I am concerned about the erosion of constitutional rights and also think for many reasons that great caution must be exercised before undertaking a legal campaign against pornography, I find objections to such a campaign that are based on appeals to the First Amendment or to a right to privacy ultimately unconvincing.

...

There are three ways of arguing that control of pornography is incompatible with adherence to constitutional rights. The first argument claims that regulating pornography involves an unjustifiable interference in the private lives of individuals. The second argument takes the First Amendment as a basic principle constitutive of our form of government, and claims that the production and distribution of pornographic material, as a form of speech, is an activity protected by that amendment. The third argument claims not that the pornographer's rights are violated, but that others' rights will be if controls against pornography are instituted.

The privacy argument is the easiest to dispose of. Since the open commerce in pornographic materials is an activity carried out in the public sphere, the publication and distribution of such materials, unlike their use by individuals, is not protected by rights to privacy. The distinction between the private consumption of pornographic material and the production and distribution of, or open commerce in, it is sometimes blurred by defenders of pornography. But I may entertain, in the privacy of my mind, defamatory opinions about another person, even though I may not broadcast them. So one might create without restraint—as long as no one were harmed in the course of preparing them—pornographic materials for one's personal use, but be restrained from reproducing and distributing them. In both cases what one is doing—in the privacy of one's mind or basement—may indeed be deplorable, but immune from legal proscription. Once the activity becomes public, however— i.e., once it involves others—it is no longer protected by the same rights that protect activities in the private sphere.

In considering the second argument (that control of pornography, private or public, is wrong in principle), it seems important to determine whether we consider the right to freedom of speech to be absolute and unqualified. If it is, then obviously all speech, including pornography, is entitled to protection. But the right is, in the first place, not an unqualified right: There are several kinds of speech not protected by the First Amendment, including the incitement to violence in volatile circumstances, the solicitation of crimes, perjury and misrepresentation, slander, libel, and false advertising. That there are forms of proscribed speech shows that we accept limitations on the right to freedom of speech if such speech, as do the forms listed, impinges on other rights. The manufacture and distribution of material which defames and threatens all members of a class by its recommendation of abusive and degrading behavior toward some members of that class simply in virtue of their membership in it seems a clear candidate for inclusion on the list. The right is therefore not an unqualified one.

Nor is it an absolute or fundamental right, underived from any other right: If it were there would not be the exceptions or limitations. The first ten amendments were added to the Constitution as a way of guaranteeing the "blessings of liberty" mentioned in its preamble, to protect citizens against the unreasonable usurpation of power by the state. The specific rights mentioned in the First Amendment—those of religion, speech, assembly, press, petition—reflect the recent experiences of the makers of the Constitution under colonial government as well as a sense of what was and is required generally to secure liberty.

. . .

This second argument against the suppression of pornographic material ... rests on a premise that must be rejected, namely, that the right to freedom of speech is a right to utter anything one wants. It thus fails to show that the production and distribution of such materials is an activity protected by the First Amendment. Furthermore, an examination of the issues involved leads to the conclusion that tolerance of this activity violates the rights of women to political independence.

The third argument (which expresses concern that curbs on pornography are the first step toward political censorship) runs into the same ambiguity that besets the arguments based on principle. These arguments generally have as an underlying assumption that the maximization of freedom is a worthy social goal. Control of pornography diminishes freedom—directly the freedom of pornographers, indirectly that of all of us. But ... what is meant by "freedom"? It cannot be that what is to be maximized is license—as the goal of a social group whose members probably have at least some incompatible interests, such a goal would be internally inconsistent. If, on the other hand, the maximization of political independence is the goal, then that is in no way enhanced by, and may be endangered by, the tolerance of pornography. ...

In summary, neither as a matter of principle nor in the interests of maximizing liberty can it be supposed that there is an intrinsic right to manufacture and distribute pornographic material.

The only other conceivable source of protection for pornography would be a general right to do what we please as long as the rights of others are respected. Since the production and distribution of pornography violates the rights of women—to respect and to freedom from defamation, among others—this protection is not available.

## Conclusion

...

Appeals for action against pornography are sometimes brushed aside with the claim that such action is a diversion from the primary task of feminists—the elimination of sexism and of sexual inequality. This approach focuses on the enjoyment rather than the manufacture of pornography, and sees it as merely a product of sexism which will disappear when the latter has been overcome and the sexes are socially and economically equal. Pornography cannot be separated from sexism in this way: Sexism is not just a set of attitudes regarding the inferiority of women but the behaviors and social and economic rules that manifest such attitudes. Both the manufacture and distribution of pornography and the enjoyment of it are instances of sexist behavior. The enjoyment of pornography on the part of individuals will presumably decline as such individuals begin to accord women their status as fully human. A cultural climate which tolerates the degrading representation of women is not a climate which facilitates the development of respect for women. Furthermore, the demand for pornography is stimulated not just by the sexism of individuals but by the pornography industry itself. Thus, both as a social phenomenon and in its effect on individuals, pornography, far from being a mere product, nourishes sexism. The campaign against it is an essential component of women's struggle for legal, economic, and social equality, one which requires the support of all feminists.[5]

### Notes

1. Among recent feminist discussions are Diana Russell, "Pornograhy: A Feminist Perspective" and Susan Griffin, "On Pornography," *Chrysalis,* Vol. I, No. 4, 1978; and Ann Garry, "Pornography and Respect for Women," *Social Theory and Practice,* Vol. 4, Spring 1978, pp. 395–421.

2. Pornography thus becomes another tool of capitalism. One feature of some contemporary pornography—the use of Black and Asian women in both still photographs and films—exploits the racism as well as the sexism of its white consumers. For a discussion of the interplay between racism and sexism under capitalism as it relates to violent crimes against

women, see Angela Y. Davis, "Rape, Racism, and the Capitalist Setting," *The Black Scholar*, Vol. 9, No. 7, April 1978.

3. Urie Bronfenbrenner, *Two Worlds of Childhood* (New York: Russell Sage Foundation, 1970); H. J. Eysenck and D.K.B. Nias, *Sex, Violence and the Media* (New York: St. Martin's Press, 1978); and Michael Goldstein, Harold Kant, and John Hartman, *Pornography and Sexual Deviance* (Berkeley: University of California Press, 1973). ...

4. Cf. Marshall Cohen, "The Case Against Censorship," *The Public Interest*, No. 22, Winter 1971, reprinted in John R. Burr and Milton Goldinger, *Philosophy and Contemporary Issues* (New York: Macmillan, 1976), and Justice William Brennan's dissenting opinion in *Paris Adult Theater I* v. *Slaton*, 431 U.S. 49.

5. Many women helped me to develop and crystallize the ideas presented in this paper. I would especially like to thank Michele Farrell, Laura Lederer, Pamela Miller, and Dianne Romain for their comments in conversation and on the first written draft. ...

# *Feminism, Moralism, and Pornography*

## Ellen Willis

...

When I first heard there was a group called Women Against Pornography, I twitched. Could I define myself as Against Pornography? Not really. In itself, pornography—which, my dictionary and I agree, means any image or description intended or used to arouse sexual desire—does not strike me as the proper object of a political crusade. As the most cursory observation suggests, there are many varieties of porn, some pernicious, some more or less benign. About the only generalization one can make is that pornography is the return of the repressed, of feelings and fantasies driven underground by a culture that atomizes sexuality, defining love as a noble affair of the heart and mind, lust as a base animal urge centered in unmentionable organs. Prurience—the state of mind I associate with pornography—implies a sense of sex as forbidden, secretive pleasure, isolated from any emotional or social context. I imagine that in utopia, porn would wither away along with the state, heroin, and Coca-Cola. At present, however, the sexual impulses that pornography appeals to are part of virtually everyone's psychology. For obvious political and cultural reasons nearly all porn is sexist in that it is the product of a male imagination and aimed at a male market; women are less likely to be consciously interested in pornography, or to indulge that interest, or to find porn that turns them on. But anyone who thinks women are simply indifferent to pornography has never watched a bunch of adolescent girls pass around a trashy novel. Over the years I've enjoyed various pieces of pornography—some of them of the sleazy Forty-second Street paperback sort—and so have most women I know. Fantasy, after all, is more flexible than reality, and women have learned, as a matter of survival, to be adept at shaping male fantasies to their own purposes. If feminists define pornography, per se, as the enemy, the result will be to make a lot of women ashamed of their sexual feelings and afraid to be honest about them. And the last thing women need is more sexual shame, guilt, and hypocrisy—this time served up as feminism.

So why ignore qualitative distinctions and in effect condemn all pornography as equally bad? WAP organizers answer—or finesse—this question by redefining pornography. They maintain that pornography is not really about sex but about violence against women. Or, in a more colorful formulation, "Pornography is the theory, rape is the practice." Part of the argument is that pornography causes violence; much is made of the fact that Charles Manson and David Berkowitz had porn collections. This is the sort of inverted logic that presumes marijuana to be dangerous because most heroin addicts started with it. It is men's hostility toward women—combined with their power to express that hostility and for the most part get away with it—that causes sexual violence. Pornography that gives sadistic fantasies concrete shape—and, in today's atmosphere, social legitimacy—may well encourage suggestible men to act them out. But if *Hustler* were to vanish from the shelves tomorrow, I doubt that rape or wife-beating statistics would decline.

Even more problematic is the idea that pornography depicts violence rather than sex. Since porn is by definition overtly sexual, while most of it is not overtly violent, this equation requires some fancy explaining. ... Robin Morgan and Gloria Steinem ... distinguish pornography from erotica. According to this argument, erotica (whose etymological root is "eros," or sexual love) expresses an integrated sexuality based on mutual affection and desire between equals; pornography (which comes from another Greek root—"porne," meaning prostitute) reflects a dehumanized sexuality based on male domination and exploitation of women. The distinction sounds promising, but it doesn't hold up. The accepted meaning of erotica is literature or pictures with sexual themes; it may or may not serve the essentially utilitarian function of pornography. Because it is less specific, less suggestive of actual sexual activity, "erotica" is regularly used as a euphemism for "classy porn." Pornography expressed in literary language or expensive photography and consumed by the upper middle class is "erotica"; the cheap stuff, which can't pretend to any purpose but getting people off, is smut. The erotica-versus-porn aproach evades the (embarrassing?) question of how porn is *used*. ... If pornography is to arouse, it must appeal to the feelings we have, not those that by some utopian standard we ought to have. Sex in this culture has been so deeply politicized that it is impossible to make clear-cut distinctions between "authentic" sexual impulses and those conditioned by patriarchy. Between, say, *Ulysses* at one end and *Snuff* at the other, erotica/pornography conveys all sorts of mixed messages that elicit complicated and private responses. In practice, attempts to sort out good erotica from bad porn inevitably come down to "What turns me on is erotica; what turns you on is pornographic."

It would clearer and more logical simply to acknowledge that some sexual images are offensive and some are not. ... As I've suggested, there is a social and psychic link between pornography and rape. In terms of patriarchal morality both are expressions of male lust, which is presumed to be innately vicious, and offenses to the putative sexual innocence of "good" women. But feminists supposedly begin with different assumptions—that men's confusion of sexual desire with predatory aggression reflects a sexist system, not male biology; that there are no good (chaste) or bad (lustful) women, just women who are, like men, sexual beings. From this standpoint, to lump pornography with rape is dangerously simplistic. Rape is a violent physical assault. Pornography can be a psychic assault, both in its content and in its public intrusions on our attention, but for women as for men it can also be a source of erotic pleasure. A woman who is raped is a victim; a woman who enjoys pornography (even if that means enjoying a rape fantasy) is in a sense a rebel, insisting on an aspect of her sexuality that has been defined as a male preserve. Insofar as pornography glorifies male supremacy and sexual alienation, it is deeply reactionary. But in rejecting sexual repression and hypocrisy—which have inflicted even more damage on women than on men—it expresses a radical impulse.

That this impulse still needs defending, even among feminists, is evident from the sexual attitudes that have surfaced in the anti-porn movement. In the movement's rhetoric pornography is a code word for vicious male lust. To the objection that some women get off on porn, the standard reply is that this only shows how thoroughly women have been brainwashed by male values. ... And the view of sex that most often emerges from talk about "erotica" is as sentimental and euphemistic as the word itself: lovemaking should be beautiful, romantic, soft, nice, and devoid of messiness, vulgarity, impulses to power, or indeed aggression of any sort. Above all, the emphasis should be on *relationships,* not (yuck) *organs.* This goody-goody concept of eroticism is not feminist but feminine. It is precisely sex as an aggressive, unladylike activity, an expression of violent and unpretty emotion, an exercise of erotic power, and a specifically genital experience that has been taboo for women. ...

... If all manifestations of patriarchal sexuality are violent, then opposition to violence cannot explain why pornography (rather than romantic novels) should be singled out as a target. Besides, such reductionism allows women no basis for distinguishing between consensual heterosexuality and rape. ... To attack pornography, and at the same time equate it with heterosexual sex, is implicitly to condemn not only women who like pornography, but women who sleep with men. This is familiar ground. The argument that straight women collaborate with the enemy has often been, among other things, a relatively polite way of saying that they consort with the beast. ...

... Susan Brownmiller and other WAP organizers claim not to advocate censorship and dismiss the civil liberties issue as a red herring dragged in by men who don't want to face the fact that pornography oppresses women. Yet at the same time, WAP endorses the Supreme Court's contention that obscenity is not protected speech, a doctrine I—and most civil libertarians—regard as a clear infringement of First Amendment rights. Brownmiller insists that the First Amendment was designed to protect political dissent, not expressions of woman-hating violence. But to make such a distinction is to defeat the amendment's purpose, since it implicitly cedes to the government the right to define "political." (Has there ever been a government willing to admit that its opponents are anything more than anti-social troublemakers?) Anyway, it makes no sense to oppose pornography on the grounds that it's sexist propaganda, then turn around and argue that it's not political. Nor will libertarians be reassured by WAP's statement that "We want to change the definition of obscenity so that it focuses on violence, not sex." Whatever their focus, obscenity laws deny the right of free expression to those who transgress official standards of propriety. ... The basic purpose of obscenity laws is and always has been to reinforce cultural taboos on sexuality and suppress feminism, homosexuality, and other forms of sexual dissidence. No pornographer has ever been punished for being a woman-hater, but not too long ago information about female sexuality, contraception, and abortion was assumed to be obscene. In a male supremacist society the only obscenity law that will not be used against women is no law at all.

As an alternative to an outright ban on pornography, Brownmiller and others have advocated restricting its display. There is a plausible case to be made for the idea that anti-woman images displayed so prominently that they are impossible to avoid are coercive, a form of active harassment that oversteps the bounds of free speech. But aside from the evasion involved in simply equating pornography with misogyny or sexual sadism, there are no legal or logical grounds for treating sexist material any differently from (for example) racist or anti-Semitic propaganda; an equitable law would have to prohibit any kind of public defamation. And the very thought of such a sweeping law has to make anyone with an imagination nervous. Could Catholics claim they were being harassed by nasty depictions of the pope? Could Russian refugees argue that the display of Communist literature was a form of psychological torture? Would pro-abortion material be taken off the shelves on the grounds that it defamed the unborn? I'd rather not find out.

   ...

# False Promises: Feminist Antipornography Legislation

## Lisa Duggan, Nan D. Hunter, and Carole S. Vance

...

... Antipornography laws have mixed roots of support. ... Though they are popular with the conservative constituencies that traditionally favor legal restrictions on sexual expression of all kinds, they were drafted and are endorsed by antipornography feminists who oppose traditional obscenity and censorship laws. The model law of this type ... was drawn up [but then vetoed by the Mayor] in the politically progressive city of Minneapolis by two radical feminists, author Andrea Dworkin and attorney Catharine MacKinnon. ... [A similar law was enacted in Indianapolis but then ruled unconstitutional by the Supreme Court in 1986. Thus, at this time, none of the versions of the proposed ordinance has ever become law.]

...

... How can this be happening? How can feminists be entrusting the patriarchal state with the task of legally distinguishing between permissible and impermissible sexual images? ... In fact this new development is not as surprising as it at first seems. ... Pornography has come to be seen as a central cause of women's oppression by a significant number of feminists. Some even argue that pornography is the root of virtually all forms of exploitation and discrimination against women. It is a short step from such a belief to the conviction that laws against pornography can end the inequality of the sexes. But this analysis takes feminists very close—indeed far too close—to measures that will ultimately support conservative, anti-sex, procensorship forces in American society, for it is with these forces that women have forged alliances in passing such legislation.

...

[Antipornography laws take] advantage of everyone's relative ignorance and anxious ambivalence about sex, distorting and oversimplifying what confronts us in building a sexual politic. For example, antipornography feminists draw on several feminist theories about the role of violent, aggressive or sexist representations. The first is relatively straightforward: that these images trigger men into action. The second suggests that violent images act more subtly, to socialize men to act in sexist or violent ways by making this behavior seem commonplace and more acceptable, if not expected. The third assumption is that violent, sexually explicit or even sexist images are offensive to women, assaulting their sensibilities and sense of self. Although we have all used metaphor to exhort women to action or illustrate a point, antipornography proponents have frequently used these conventions of speech as if they were literal statements of fact. But these metaphors have gotten out of hand, as Julie Abraham has noted, for they fail to recognize that the assult committed by a wife beater is quite different from the visual "assault" of a sexist ad on TV. The nature of that difference is still being clarified in a complex debate within feminism that must continue; [Dworkin and MacKinnon's proposal for a] law cuts off speculation, settling on a causal relationship between image and action that is starkly simple, if unpersuasive.

This metaphor also paves the way for reclassifying images that are merely sexist as also violent and aggressive. Thus, it is no accident that [legal] briefs supporting the legislation first invoke violent images and rapidly move to include sexist and sexually explicit images without noting that they are different. The equation is made more easy by the constant shifts back to examples of depictions of real violence, almost to draw attention away from the sexually explicit or sexist material that in fact would be affected by the laws.

Most important, what underlies this legislation and the success of its analysis in blurring and exceeding boundaries is an appeal to a very traditional view of sex: sex is degrading to women. By this logic, any illustrations or descriptions of explicit sexual acts that involve women are in themselves affronts to women's dignity. ... Embedded in this view are several other familiar themes: that sex is degrading to women, but not to men; that men are raving beasts; that sex is dangerous for women; that sexuality is male, not female; that women are victims, not sexual actors; that men inflict "it" on women; that penetration is submission; that heterosexual sexuality, rather than the institution of heterosexuality, is sexist.

These assumptions, in part intended, in part unintended, lead us back to the traditional target of obscenity law: sexually explicit material. What initially appeared novel, then, is really the reappearance of a traditional theme. It's ironic that a feminist position on pornography incorporates most of the myths about sexuality that feminism has struggled to displace.

...

... Three major problems should dissuade feminists from supporting this kind of law: first, the sexual images in question do not cause more harm than other aspects of misogynist culture; second, sexually explicit speech, even in male-dominated society, serves positive social functions for women; and third, the passage and enforcement of antipornography laws ... are more likely to impede, rather than advance, feminist goals.

... Proponents contend that pornography does cause violence because it conditions male sexual response to images of violence and thus provokes violence against women. The strongest research they offer is based on psychology experiments that employ films depicting a rape scene, toward the end of which the woman is shown to be enjoying the attack. ...

In addition, the argument that pornography itself plays a major role in the general oppression of women contradicts the evidence of history. It need hardly be said that pornography did not lead to the burning of witches or the English common law treatment of women as chattel property. If anything functioned then as the prime communication medium for woman-hating, it was probably religion. Nor can pornography be blamed for the enactment of laws from at least the eighteenth century that allowed a husband to rape or beat his wife with impunity. In any period, the causes of women's oppression have been many and complex, drawing on the fundamental social and economic structures of society. Ordinance proponents offer little evidence to explain how the mass production of pornography—a relatively recent phenomenon—could have become so potent a causative agent so quickly.

The silencing of women is another example of the harm attributed to pornography. Yet if this argument were correct, one would expect that as the social visibility of pornography has increased, the tendency to credit women's accounts of rape would have decreased. In fact, although the treatment of women complainants in rape cases is far from perfect, the last 15 years of work by the women's movement has resulted in marked improvements. In many places, the corroboration requirement has now been abolished; cross-examination of victims as to past sexual experiences has been prohibited; and a number of police forces have developed specially trained units and procedures to improve the handling of sexual assault cases. The presence of rape fantasies in pornography may in part reflect a blacklash against these women's movement advances, but to argue that most people routinely disbelieve women who file charges of rape belittles the real improvements made in social consciousness and law.

The third type of harm ... is a kind of libel: the maliciously false characterization of women as a group of sexual masochists. ...

To claim that all pornography ... is a lie is a false analogy. If truth is a defence to charges of libel, then surely depictions of consensual sex cannot be thought of as equivalent to a falsehood. For example, some women (and men) do enjoy being tied up or displaying themselves. The declaration by fiat that even sadomasochism is a "lie" about sexuality reflects an arrogance and moralism that feminists should combat, not engage in. When mutually desired sexual experiences are depicted, pornography is not "libelous."

Not only does pornography not cause the kind and degree of harm that can justify the restraint of speech, but its existence serves some social functions, which benefit women. Pornographic speech has many, often anomalous, characteristics. One is certainly that it magnifies the misogyny present in the culture and exaggerates the fantasy of male power. Another, however, is that the existence of pornography has served to flout conventional sexual mores, to ridicule sexual hypocrisy and to underscore the importance of sexual needs. Pornography carries many messages other than woman-hating: it advocates sexual adventure, sex outside of marriage, sex for no reason other than pleasure, casual sex, anonymous sex, group sex, voyeuristic sex, illegal sex, public sex. Some of these ideas appeal to women reading or seeing pornography, who may interpret some images as legitimating their own sense of sexual urgency or desire to be sexually aggressive. Women's experience of pornography is not as universally victimizing as the ordinance would have it.

... Antipornography laws, as restrictions on sexual speech, in many ways echo and expand upon the traditional legal analysis of sexually explicit speech under the rubric of obscenity. The U.S. Spreme Court has consistently ruled that sexual speech defined as "obscenity" does not belong in the system of public discourse, and is therefore an exception to the First Amendment and hence not entitled to protection under the free speech guarantee. (The definition of obscenity has shifted over the years and remains imprecise.) In 1957 the Supreme Court ruled that obscenity could be suppressed regardless of whether it presented an imminent threat of illegal activity. In the opinion of the Supreme Court, graphic sexual images do not communicate "real" ideas. These, it would seem, are only found in the traditionally defined public arena. Sexual themes can qualify as ideas if they use sexuality for argument's sake, but not if they speak in the words and images of "private" life—that is, if they graphically depict sex itself. At least theoretically, and insofar as the law functions as a pronouncement of moral judgment, sex is consigned to remain unexpressed and in the private realm.

The fallacies in this distinction are obvious. Under the U.S. Constitution, for example, it is acceptable to write "I am a sadomasochist" or even "Everyone should experiment with sadomasochism in order to increase sexual pleasure." But to write a graphic fantasy about sadomasochism that arouses and excites readers is not protected unless a court finds it to have serious literary, artistic or political value, despite the expressive nature of the content. Indeed, the fantasy depiction may communicate identity in a more compelling way than the "I am" statement. For sexual minorities, sexual acts can be self-identifying and affirming statements in a hostile world. Images of those acts should be protected for that reason, for they do have political content. Just as the personal can be political, so can the specifically and graphically sexual.

...

The consequences of enforcing such ... law[s], however, are much more likely to obstruct than advance feminist political goals. On the level of ideas, further narrowing of the public realm of sexual speech coincides all too well with the privatization of sexual, reproductive and family issues sought by the far right. ... Practically speaking, the ordinances could result in attempts to eliminate the images associated with homosexuality. Doubtless there are heterosexual women who believe that lesbianism is a "degrading" form of "subordination." Since the ordinances allow for suits against materials in which men appear "in place of women," far-right antipornography crusaders could use these laws to suppress gay male pornography. Imagine a Jerry Falwell-style conservative filing a complaint against a gay bookstore for selling sexually explicit materials showing men with other men in "degrading" or "submissive" or "objectified" postures—all in the name of protecting women.

And most ironically, while the ordinances would do nothing to improve the material conditions of most women's lives, their high visibility might well divert energy from the drive to enact other, less popular laws that would genuinely empower women—comparable worth legislation, for example, or affirmative action requirements or fairer property and support principles in divorce laws.

Other provisions of the ordinances concern coercive behavior: physical assault which is imitative of pornographic images, coercion into pornographic performance and forcing pornography on others. On close examination, however, even most of these provisions are problematic.

Existing law already penalizes physical assault, including when it is associated with pornography. Defenders of the [proposed legislation] often cite the example of models who have been raped or otherwise harmed while in the process of making pornographic images. But victims of this type of attack can already sue or prosecute those responsible. ... Indeed, the ordinances do not cover assault or other harm incurred while producing pornography, presumably because other laws already achieve that end.

The ordinances do penalize coercing, intimidating or fraudulently inducing anyone into performing for pornography. Although existing U.S. law already provides remedies for fraud or contracts of duress, this section of the [proposed] ordinance seeks to facilitate recovery of damages by, for example, pornography models who might otherwise encounter substantial prejudice against their claims. Supporters of this section have suggested that it is comparable to the Supreme Court's ban on child pornography. The analogy has been stretched to the point where the City of Indianapolis brief argued that women, like children, need "special protection." "Children are incapable of consenting to engage in pornographic conduct, even absent physical coercion and therefore require special protection," the brief stated. "By the same token, the physical and psychological well-being of women ought to be afforded comparable protection, for the coercive environment in which most pornographic models work vitiates any notion that they consent or 'choose' to perform in pornography."

The reality of women's lives is far more complicated. Women do not become pornography models because society is egalitarian and they exercise a "free choice," but [neither] do they "choose" this work because they have lost all power for deliberate, volitional behavior. Modeling or acting for pornography, like prostitution, can be a means of survival for those with limited options. For some women, at some points in their lives, it is a rational economic decision. Not every woman regrets having made it, although no woman should have to settle for it. The fight should be to expand the options and to insure job safety for women who do become porn models. By contrast, the impact of the [proposed] ordinance as a whole would be either to eliminate jobs or drive the pornography industry further underground.

One of the vaguest provisions in the ordinance prohibits "forcing" pornography on a person. "Forcing" is not defined in the law, and one is left to speculate whether it means forced to respond to pornography, forced to read it or forced to glance at it before turning away. Also unclear is whether the perpetrator must in fact have some superior power over the person being forced—that is, is there a meaningful threat that makes the concept of force real.

Again, widely varying situations are muddled and a consideration of context is absent. "Forcing" pornography on a person "in any public space" is treated identically to using it as a method of sexual harassment in the workplace. The scope of "forcing" could include walking past a newsstand or browsing in a bookstore that had pornography on display. The force involved in such a situation seems mild when compared, for example, to the incessant sexist advertising on television.

...

[Antipornography] laws, which would increase the state's regulation of sexual images, present many dangers for women. Although [they] draw much of their feminist support from women's anger at the market for images of sexual violence, they are aimed not at violence, but at sexual explicitness. ... Underlying virtually every section of ... proposed laws there is an assumption that sexuality is a realm of unremitting, unequaled victimization for women. Pornography appears as the monster that made this so. ... But this analysis is not the only feminist perspective on sexuality. Feminist theorists have also argued that the sexual terrain, however power-laden, is actively contested. Women are agents, and not merely victims, who make decisions and act on them, and who desire, seek out and enjoy sexuality.

---

## Acknowledgements

For stimulating discussion and political comradeship, thanks to FACT (Feminist Anti-Censorship Task Force), New York, and to members of the Scholar and the Feminist IX study group (Julie Abraham, Hannah Alderfer, Meryl Altman, Jan Boney, Frances Doughty, Kate Ellis, Faye Ginsburg, Diane Harriford, Beth Jaker, Barbara Kerr, Mary Clare Lennon, Marybeth Nelson, Ann Snitow, Paula Webster and Ellen Willis). Special thanks to Rayna Rapp and Janice Irvine for comments and criticisms, to Lawrence Krasnoff for graphics and to Ann Snitow for aid above and beyond the call of duty. We are grateful to Varda Burstyn for her helpful suggestions and patience. We remain responsible for the opinions expressed here.

# Racism in Pornography and the Women's Movement

## Tracey A. Gardner

...

*There is a group of women, all-white, marching outside a pornography shop, passing out leaflets, and talking about how men are exploiting and abusing women.*

*A Black woman, holding a little Black boy by the hand, averts her eyes, embarrassed and angry, when a white demonstrator tries to give her a leaflet and a speech.*

*The white woman turns back to her group and mumbles, "But doesn't she realize how we're being hurt? If she'd only look at what they're doing to Black women too."*

*   *   *

When I began writing this ... I said to myself, racism in pornography? So what? Because from my point of view, racism is everywhere, including the Women's Movement, and the only time I really need to say something special about it is when I *don't* see it—and the first time that happens, I'll tell you about it.

When I talk about pornography and racism, I want you to understand who I am, my feelings and experiences, and what it means for me to be talking to you. I want you to understand that when a person of color is used in pornography, it's not the physical appearance of that person which makes it racist. Rather, it's how pornography capitalizes on the underlying history and myths surrounding and oppressing people of color in this country which makes it racist.

...

What I'm going to tell you is not the "Truth," but rather a starting point from which we can begin discussing the issue. It must be understood that I am *a Black* woman. I cannot represent Hispanic, Asian, or Native American women. I cannot even represent Black women. I am only one Black woman, and you should be listening just as hard to what any other woman of color has to say.

...

What I'm going to do is talk about what I have direct experience of—being Black. I hope by opening up my history and feelings and showing their neglected complexity, you will realize how little you know about other races. It is this ignorance which prevents the unification of all women in the struggle to expose and end violence against women.

\*            \*            \*

...

I have not been able to find any indication that pornography existed in African society. This could be because there has not been enough investigation into African sexual practices. Or it could be because Africa was not technologically developed enough to produce pornography. (For pornography to become a common feature of a society, a technology is needed that can reproduce images and the written word on a mass scale.) Or it could be that because of the sex-role types particular to West African culture and how the African woman was valued (which is not to say that there were not always ways in which she was oppressed), pornography could not be a natural outgrowth of that culture.

When African people arrived in the New World, they were confronted by a drastic cultural shock. Their families were broken up, their native tongues outlawed, their customs and arts forbidden. Africans have the distinction of being the only race brought to this land of the free against their will.

The tremendous coping ability Africans showed in surviving slavery was later used by white men in the 1960's as justification for further injustices. Unsettled by the sixties riots, white men tried to explain away the current unrest among Blacks by claiming that the price Blacks had paid for surviving the "unfortunate" institution of slavery was that they had become an immoral and culturally deprived people.

Black folks are not deprived, we are denied. Our culture was not destroyed by slavery, it just went underground, and it is what we stand on. We have been forced to take on white cultural forms in order to survive, but the meaning we give to things is still our own.

Stereotypes are, in part, based on the realities of how people have had to adapt themselves in order to deal with oppression. Take the stereotypes of Black people and sex. There is definitely some reality to it. Black people *are* really sexy. But you have to put it in the context of our very rich and earthy heritage and our relationship to our land, which was quite different from puritanical Europe.

Writer James Weldon Johnson said,

> In the core of the heart of the American race problem the sex factor is rooted, rooted so deeply that it is not always recognized when it shows at the surface. Other factors are obvious and are the ones we dare to deal with; but regardless of how we deal with these, the race situation will continue to be acute as long as the sex factor persists.

American slavery relied on the denial of the humanity of Black folks, on the undermining of our sense of nationhood and family, and on the structuring of Black men and women into the American system of *white* male domination.

Much of this was achieved through the sexual exploitation, brutalization, and degradation of the enslaved people. Sexual and racial oppression in America are inseparable for both Black women and men. The raping of enslaved women and the castration of enslaved males were common practices.

White men, in their treatment of Black males, were motivated by two other myths of their own invention: (1) Black men are phallic symbols. Just the sight of an African's dark skin told you he had a monster penis. (2) Bigness connoted power, and the measure of masculinity was a man's power over other men and over women. The size of a penis was a significant factor in determining the latter. White men feared Black men as sexual rivals.

White people, men and women, came out of the puritanical European tradition, which alienated them from their bodies. They were simultaneously threatened and drawn to what they believed to be the uninhibited, guilt-free sexuality of Blacks. The unmentionable sexual feelings as well as the unacceptable acts of aggression of the white people were easily projected onto the enslaved Africans. Thus, many white men who feared that Black men would rape white women were daily raping Black women.

...

In the eighteenth and nineteenth centuries in the United States, it was common for white men to have two families, one white and one Black. If anything was regarded as wrong about having that second, not so hidden family, it was not that the white man economically and physically forced the Black woman's sexual services. No, what was wrong was that the offspring made for the pollution of white blood. The crime was to acknowledge that a white man could be in a "relationship" with a Black woman.

What were the societal positions available to Black women? To be the sexual object of the white enslaver was perhaps the best, most projected and rewarding position because the Black woman was then subjected to the abuse of only one man. Then there was being a house servant and mammy, taking care of the white woman's home and children, while she had no place she could call her own and her children had to look after themselves. She might be a breeder woman who had children every nine months, most of whom she'd never get to know. Finally, there was the position of field mule. If a field mule got pregnant, she was treated special—two weeks before she was due, there was no punishment if she did not finish her work. A Black woman could serve in all these positions in her lifetime.

What were white women doing? Some tried to intercede on behalf of the enslaved people. Most did not. They were oppressed by their own position as mute ornaments in society.

Sometimes white women would confuse who their real oppressors were, and they would be active accomplices in the victimization of the enslaved. Often white women would blame Black women for "tempting" their husbands. There are accounts of white women's vindictiveness and cruelty toward Black women. They would pull out their teeth; have them stripped, chained, and flogged until bleeding; drop hot sealing wax on their breasts; damage their sexual organs by various means.

At the same time the white man was exploiting the Black woman, he was obsessive about protecting the white woman from the Black man. White women were told that the Black man was unnatural and dangerous, having an ape's penis, which, if it were to penetrate her, would split her vagina and cause permanent damage. The Black man was held up as one more reason why the white woman needed the protection of the white man.

The white man projected his own savagery upon the Black man, and one myth he employed to this end was that of the Pathological Black Rapist of white women.

This is not to say that Black men did not rape white women. They were fed fantasies about white women, that they were a delicacy to be protected, while Black women were trash, thrown out too many times.

But most of the interracial rapes in this country were committed by white men. White men have always had the power: social, economic, political, military, and psychological. Black men had to be more realistic about living out their fantasies. They got killed for just looking. Social writers of that time affirmed the myth that rape was a crime committed exclusively by Black men, and they explained the "rampant raping" by Black men as being the result of the "talk of social equality," which just excited the "ignorant nigger" and made him uppity. And as late as 1944 a study of white people's opinions about Blacks showed that they thought that Black people desired—over and above political, economic, and social justice—sex with white people.

...

... It was thought that a Black man having a relationship with a white woman degraded the white woman. There were laws in almost every state against interracial sex and marriage, which were usually enforced only when the man in the relationship was of color, and it was not until 1967 that the Supreme Court declared these laws unconstitutional. Sixteen states still had these laws on the books at that time. Yet, when a white man had a relationship with a Black woman or took sexual services from her, she was elevated in the world. By the 1950's the image of the Black woman was still that of a slut who could take anything sexually.

The Black Liberation Movement is restoring the history and dignity of our people. But often it has remained trapped within the mores and attitudes of our white European male oppressors. Its efforts go toward proving that Black folks are *just as good* as whites, rather than showing that we are *different* and that it is not just slavery which affected the sex roles and relationships of Black men and women, but also who we were before slavery. Because of this misleading emphasis, the dominant motif of the Black Movement has been Black masculinity.

Black women are sometimes the target of the Black man's efforts to restore his sense of power, rather than the white man who has been the one out to destroy it. Sometimes when the Black man is with the Black woman, he is ashamed of how she has been treated, and how he has been powerless, and that they have always had to work together and protect each other. Some Black men, full of the white man's perspective and values, see the white woman or Blond Goddess as part of the American winning image.

Frantz Fanon said about white women,

By loving me she proves that I am worthy of white love. I am loved like a white man. I am a white man. I marry the culture, white beauty, white whiteness. When my restless hands caress those white breasts, they grasp white civilization and dignity and make them mine.

So how does a Black woman feel when her Black man leaves *Playboy* on the coffee table?

"It's a white folks' thing, and it's corrupting our men."

That is what several Black women I have talked to think. Pornography speaks to the relationship *white* men and women have always had with each other. Because they have been forced to live under the values of white people, the identity of Afro-Americans has been distorted and belittled to the point where pornography also speaks in part to our relationships.

The pornography I am reacting to is *soft-core* pornography, which objectifies but at least retains the woman's body in one piece. Most women in this country, white and Third World, are unaware of the nature of hard-core pornography and how widespread it is. I know that if any woman of color were to see some of the brutal and deadly hard-core pornography around, she would be outraged by it no matter what the color of the woman being exploited was.

But when you talk about soft-core pornography, it's difficult for a Black woman to identify totally with what white women feel about it. Soft-core pornography is an extension of mass advertising and the beauty market; it is the Beauty Queen revealed. Until recently the Beauty Queen was by definition white: fair complexion, straight hair, keen features, and round eyes. Soft-core pornography was the objectification of white purity, white beauty, and white innocence.

To little Black, Asian, or Hispanic girls, growing up with dark skin, kinky hair, African, Asian, or Latin features, everything around them—in storybooks and the media, in dolls in stores—announced that something was wrong with them. They could be whores but not beauty queens. There used to be a lot of Black women who used bleaching creams and stayed out of the sun, and there are still many who straighten their hair because they feel they have to, not because they want to. There also have been Asian women who have had eyelid operations. It is not so much that women of color are trying consciously to become white as that they are trying to look beautiful in a white-dominated society.

This has been changing somewhat. What is beautiful now also includes that which is unusual or exotic, such as women of color. We have started appearing in *Vogue* and in *Playboy*.

Black women were allowed in *Playboy* in the last ten years as a result of the sixties riots, which also won a few Black men the right to wear business suits and carry briefcases and have wives who stayed at home. So, Black women have been elevated from the status of whore to "Playmate." Now white boys can put them in *Playboy* without damaging the magazine's respectability too much (though after the first appearance of Black women in *Playboy*, there were some angry letters to the editor saying "get them niggers out").

Black men are exploited in pornography too. In 1978 *Hustler* magazine ran a full-page cartoon of a white man sitting on a raised chair and a Black shoeshine boy at his feet who is looking surprised as he is polishing the white man's gigantic penis.

I have noticed that while white men like Black women "looking baaad" in leather with whips, Black men like Black women in bondage, helpless and submissive. Check out the album covers of groups like the Ohio Players and New York City.

The Black man, like the white man, is buying pornography. He is beating, raping, and murdering all kinds of women. Black women are going to have to deal with him on this. But when we do, we must deal with the Black man as a Black man, not as a white man. In this country it is the *white* man who is producing pornography, and it is the *white* man who is profiting from it.

We need to hear from other races in this country, especially those, such as the Japanese, who have had their own highly developed tradition of violent pornography. We need to know how *all* women of *all* cultures are affected by violence within their communities and in the larger, white, male-dominated society.

Unification of all women in the struggle to end violence against women can happen only if women of color share their experiences, hurts, and confusions with white women. Before this can happen though, white women must understand that while sexism might be the ultimate oppression for many of them, it is only *one* of the ways in which women of color are oppressed. White women must recognize the ways in which they have bought into the oppression and stereotyping of communities of color.

...

# *Confessions of a Feminist Porno Star*

## Nina Hartley

"A feminist porno star?" Right, tell me another one, I can hear some feminists saying. I hear a chorus of disbelief, a lot like the two crows in the Disney movie "Dumbo"— "I thought I'd seen everything till I saw an elephant fly." On the surface, contradictions seem to abound. But one of the most basic tenets of feminism, a tenet with which I was inculcated by the age of ten, was the *right* to sexual free expression, without being told by society (or men) what was right, wrong, good, or bad. But why porno? Simple—I'm an exhibitionist with a cause: to make sexually graphic (hard core) erotica, and today's porno is the only game in town. But it's a game where there is a possibility of the players, over time, getting some of the rules changed.

As I examine my life, I uncover the myriad influences that led me to conclude that it was perfectly natural for me to choose a career in adult films. I find performing in sexually explicit material satisfying on a number of levels. First, it provides a physically and psychically safe environment for me to live out my exhibitionistic fantasies. Secondly, it provides a surprisingly flexible and supportive arena for me to grow in as a *performer*, both sexually and non-sexually. Thirdly, it provides me with erotic material that I like to watch for my own pleasure. Finally, the medium allows me to explore the theme of celebrating a positive female sexuality—a sexuality that has heretofore been denied us. In choosing my roles and characterizations carefully, I strive to show, always, women who thoroughly enjoy sex and are forceful, self-satisfying and guilt-free without also being neurotic, unhappy or somehow unfulfilled.

...

Once I passed puberty, two books in particular were very influential in the continuing development of my personal sexual philosophy: *Our Bodies, Ourselves,* and *The Happy Hooker.* The former taught me that women deserved to be happy sexually, that their bodies were wonderful and strong, and that all sexual fantasies were natural and okay as long as coercion was not involved. The latter book taught me that an intelligent, sexual woman could choose a job in the sex industry and not be a victim, but instead emerge even stronger and more self-confident, with a feeling, even, of self-actualization.

High school was uneventful—I became deeply involved in the excellent drama department at Berkeley High, exploring a long-standing interest in the theater arts. Contrary to a lot of adolescents' experiences with peer pressure in the realm of sex and drugs, I was lucky to have no pressure placed on me one way or another. ... Consequently, I had a more active fantasy life than sex life, and was very ripe when I lost my virginity at eighteen to a man with whom I had my first long term relationship. This, unfortunately, had more forgettable moments than memorable ones. The sex and intimacy were mediocre at best, and I realized that my libido was not to have a good future with this man. My present husband is just the opposite. He gave full support for my long-dormant lesbian side; for the past four years I have lived with him and his long term woman lover in a close-knit, loving, supportive and intellectually stimulating *menage-a-trois.*

I stripped once a week while getting my bachelor's degree in nursing, magna cum laude, enjoying it to the fullest and using the performance opportunity to develop the public side of my sexuality. I went into full time movie work immediately following graduation, having done a few movies while still in school.

I know there are people who wonder, "Is she naive or something? What kind of a cause is porno?" But let's face it, folks: while the sex drive may be innate, modes of sexual behavior are learned, and I don't see Nancy Reagan setting up any "Happy, Healthy, Sex Life" institutes in the near future. If the media can have an effect on people's behavior, and I believe it does, why is it assumed that sex movies must always reinforce the most negative imagery of women? That certainly isn't what I'm about. From my very first movie I have always refused to portray rape, coercion, pain-as-pleasure, woman-as-victim, domination, humiliation and other forms of nonconsensual sex.

I can look back on all of my performances and see that I have not contributed to any negative images or depictions of women; and the feedback I get from men and women of all ages supports my contention. I get a lot of satisfaction from my job— for me it is a job of choice. As feminists, we must all fight to change our society so that women who don't want to do gender-stereotyped jobs can be free to work, support their families decently, and fulfill their potential in whatever job they choose. This includes not feeling compelled to do sex work because other well-paying options are severely limited.

Each of us has some idea or action that we hate but that is still protected by the First Amendment. I consider myself a reformer, and as a reformer I need a broad interpretation of the First Amendment to make my point. As a feminist I have principles that won't allow me to take license with that precious right to free speech. There have always been, and to some degree will always be, extremists who see the First Amendment as their license to do or say whatever, and not as a right which has implied responsibilities. Of course the sexual entertainment medium is not exception to this. I say censure them, but do not censor me.

---

# The Cum Shot: Takes on Lesbian and Gay Sexuality

## Cindy Patton

Two camps of lesbians are on a collision course in the debates about representation of female sexuality (and, though not as often discussed, the representation of female orgasm). Lesbians active in the antipornography movement claim lesbian-feminist pornographers dabbling in the genre are "pimps for the pornography industry." In their critique, they also include gay male porn makers, who have a small industry, but a more direct and organic connection with their market and with gay politics, as well. The feminist sex radicals, meanwhile, produce porn and erotica in print and video, lecture at universities, hold forums to discuss the nuances of meaning in different production styles, and accuse the radical antiporn feminists of being in league with moral majoritarian antiporn, profamily antiabortionists. A third, much larger group of lesbians just want to see and get turned on by seeing lesbians having sex, and are bored by the intellectual hat tricks.

A recent traveling art show produced by feminist students at Bryn Mawr College, attempted to differentiate between erotica and porn. While the group could not agree on where—or whether—to draw the line, discussion about the show produced interesting results. Some women felt hurt or offended by documentary pictures showing women grimacing in sexual ecstasy. They said they preferred gentle smiling pictures, which were posed and artsy, because they felt these better represented their experience of sex. Lesbians disagree on whether the "authentic" representation of our sexuality is cinema verité, or carefully constructed scenes that are airbrushed or stylized. While pretending to be risqué, the latter style insists on shaved and bleached body hair and avoids any appearance of moisture that might remind the viewer of smells female and coital.

The feminist concern with objectification of women, with using bodies to sell products, has created a schism over how desire is contructed: is sex a natural extension of getting in tune with our true essence as women? Does its political dimension come in purging any remnants of what radical feminists call "hetero-reality"? Or is sex unnatural, perverse, and confrontational, political in its role as a daily subversion of patriarchal capitalism's demands for order? Does sexual expression have a natural narrative structure of a beginning, middle, and end, and clear boundaries between the erotic and the public or secular? Or is it fragmented, spilling out and around daily life, montage-like, erotic precisely because it brings into contact unexpected desires and strange objects?

Pornography retains qualities of both views of the real and the natural, occupying an uncomfortable position between documentary and art. Our cultural hang-ups about our bodies and the basic grittiness of sex are writ large: we want to see what we really look like, but we don't want it to be too messy. People who are just beginning to examine whether they like pornography—a by-product of the home video boom—are shocked by the rawness of most porn. They find oppressive the "Johnny Wad"–style films that use none-too-beautiful models under harsh lights. What they mean is that scrawny models who obviously aren't having a good time don't turn them on. They demand a more aesthetic porn, and are willing to pay for it.

The raw slime that once made porn seem exotic and illicit must now compete with a consumer culture that sells products with bodies, and demands taste above all. Newer gay and yuppy-aimed straight porn is much glitzier and presents sex in a broader context. Ferraris and ferns in real *House and Garden* condos replace dental chairs hauled into a flimsy set for a half-day shoot. Today's viewers equate cinematic style with the quality—even morality—of the sex. In fact, production values seem more important than the gender of the participants.

At a recent Lesbian and Gay Health Conference workshop on sex, it turned out that lesbians who liked raunchier lesbian porn also liked raunchy gay male porn. The lousy production values spelled "illicit," and that was exciting to these women. A number of gay men who did not like gay porn, said they enjoyed the lyrical lesbian porn film *Erotic in Nature* and conceded some interest in the new gay male safe sex film, *Inevitable Love.*

The ability of lesbians and gay men to identify with characters across sex lines—though perhaps not across gender *roles*—suggests that porn may work in a more complicated way than the porn-causes-(or at least reinforces)-violence-against-women argument indicates. Perhaps cinematic depictions of desire work on a more compelling level than desire constructed around gender. Or, perhaps desire has little to do directly with gender or what's natural, but rather is mediated by a person who intercedes between the desiring subject and artifacts (a penis, vagina, leg, lip, shoe, violin case) or narratives (fantasy, hazy orderings of events, spaces, places, or positions).

At bottom, pornography is a crude attempt to document the subjective experience of sex: in pornography, the viewer is seeking to validate his or her experience, and possibly develop a fantasy-based, material-oriented sexual practice (not a bad "safe sex" choice!). Lesbian porn and gay male non-cum-shot-centered porn are attempts to reassure ourselves against the cultural paradigm of cum worship that our sex is real, is hot. As viewers of the film, we can say, "Look, there we are in all our explicitness." As subjects of the film, we can assess "truth" by our sexual response (what Chris Berchall, writing in the now-defunct Canadian *Body Politic,* called "the wet test").

Gay male porn is attempting to network old codes to demonstrate the erotic power of safe sex, to find new images for the body-pleasure tie that binds the urban gay male community in the age of AIDS. Lesbian porn is trying out an initial visual vocabulary subject to debate, cathexis, and transformation as we begin articulating our experience and commenting on female-centered sex.

As we make our own pornography and narrative films about our lives, we are at once subject and viewer, potentially freed from the old codes that continue to equate sex with gender, sexual identity with sexual practice. We must pay attention to our real historical conditions—our oppression as well as our capacity for oppressing—and our vision of the future. Both the sleek style of the Hollywood that knows no queers and the crude pornography of our outlaw past have created the terms of the cinema we make today. It is our challenge to continually remake ourselves in our own image, not to settle for images of seduction that tell someone else's story.

# *Mass Market Romance: Pornography for Women Is Different*

## Ann Barr Snitow

…

Last year 109 million romantic novels were sold under an imprint you will not see in the *New York Times* best-seller lists or advertised in its *Book Review*. The publisher is Harlequin Enterprises, Ltd., a Canadian company, and its success, a growth of 400 percent since 1976, is typical of the boom in romantic fiction marketed for women.[1]

…

Are Harlequin romances pornography?

> She had never felt so helpless or so completely at the mercy of another human being … a being who could snap the slender column of her body with one squeeze of a steel-clad arm.
> No trace of tenderness softened the harsh pressure of his mouth on hers … there was only a savagely punishing intentness of purpose that cut off her breath until her senses reeled and her body sagged against the granite hardness of his. He released her wrists, seeming to know that they would hang helplessly at her sides, and his hand moved to the small of her back to exert a pressure that crushed her soft outlines to the unyielding dominance of his and left her in no doubt as to the force of his masculinity.[2]

In an unpublished talk,[3] critic Peter Parisi has hypothesized that Harlequin romances are essentially pornography for people ashamed to read pornography. In his view, sex is these novels' real *raison d'être*, while the romance and the promised marriage are primarily salves to the conscience of readers brought up to believe that sex without love and marriage is wrong. Like me, Parisi sees the books as having some active allure. They are not just escape; they also offer release, as he sees it, specifically sexual release.

This is part of the reason why Harlequins, so utterly denatured in most respects, can powerfully command such a large audience. I want to elaborate here on Parisi's definition of *how* the books are pornography and, finally, to modify his definition of what women are looking for in a sex book.

Parisi sees Harlequins as a sort of poor woman's D. H. Lawrence. The body of the heroine is alive and singing in every fiber; she is overrun by a sexuality that wells up inside her and that she cannot control. ("The warmth of his body close to hers was like a charge of electricity, a stunning masculine assault on her senses that she was powerless to do anything about."[4]) The issue of control arises because, in Parisi's view, the reader's qualms and are allayed when the novels invoke morals, then affirm a force, sexual feeling, strong enough to override those morals. He argues further that morals in a Harlequin are secular; what the heroine risks is a loss of social face, of reputation. The books uphold the values of their readers, who share this fear of breaking social codes, but behind these reassuringly familiar restraints they celebrate a wild, eager sexuality that flourishes and is finally affirmed in "marriage," which Parisi sees as mainly a code word for "fuck."

Parisi is right: *every* contact in a Harlequin romance is sexualized:

> Sara feared he was going to refuse the invitation and simply walk off. It seemed like an eternity before he inclined his head in a brief, abrupt acknowledgement of acceptance, then drew out her chair for her, his hard fingers brushing her arm for a second, and bringing an urgent flutter of reaction from her pulse.[5]

Those "hard fingers" are the penis; a glance is penetration; a voice can slide along the heroine's spine "like a sliver of ice." The heroine keeps struggling for control but is constantly swept away on a tide of feeling. Always, though, some intruder or some "nagging reminder" of the need to maintain appearances stops her. "His mouth parted her lips with bruising urgency and for a few delirious moments she yielded to her own wanton instincts." But the heroine insists on seeing these moments as out of character: She "had never thought herself capable of wantonness, but in Carlo's arms she seemed to have no inhibitions."[6] Parisi argues that the books' sexual formula allows both heroine and reader to feel wanton again and again while maintaining their sense of themselves as not that sort of women.

I agree with Parisi that the sexually charged atmosphere that bathes the Harlequin heroine is essentially pornographic (I use the word pornographic as neutrally as possible here, not as an automatic pejorative). But do Harlequins actually contain an affirmation of female sexuality? The heroine's condition of passive receptivity to male ego and male sexuality is exciting to readers, but this is not necessarily a free or deep expression of the female potential for sexual feeling. Parisi says the heroine is always trying to humanize the contact between herself and the apparently under-socialized hero, "trying to convert rape into love making." If this is so, then she is engaged on a social as well as a sexual odyssey. Indeed, in women, these two are often joined. Is the project of humanizing and domesticating male sexual feeling an erotic one? What is it about this situation that arouses the excitement of the anxiously vigilant heroine and of the readers who identify with her?

In the misogynistic culture in which we live, where violence toward women is a common motif, it is hard to say a neutral word about pornography either as a legitimate literary form or as a legitimate source of pleasure. Women are naturally overwhelmed by the woman-hating theme so that the more universal human expression sometimes contained by pornography tends to be obscured for them.

In recent debates, sex books that emphasize both male and female sexual feeling as a sensuality that can exist without violence are being called "erotica" to distinguish them from "pornography."[7] This distinction blurs more than it clarifies the complex mixture of elements that make up sexuality. Erotica is soft core, soft focus; it is gentler and tenderer sex than that depicted in pornography. Does this mean true sexuality is diffuse while only perverse sexuality is driven, power hungry, intense, and selfish? I cannot accept this particular dichotomy. It leaves out too much of what is infantile in sex—the reenactment of early feelings, the boundlessness and omnipotence of infant desire and its furious gusto. In pornography all things tend in one direction, a total immersion in one's own sense experience, for which one paradigm must certainly be infancy. For adults this totality, the total sexualization of everything, can only be a fantasy. But does the fact that it cannot be actually lived mean this fantasy must be discarded? It is a memory, a legitimate element in the human lexicon of feelings.

In pornography, the joys of passivity, of helpless abandon, of response without responsibility are all endlessly repeated, savored, minutely described. Again this is a fantasy often dismissed with the pejorative "masochistic" as if passivity were in no way a pleasant or a natural condition.

Yet another criticism of pornography is that it presents no recognizable, delineated *delineated* characters. In a culture where women are routinely objectified it is natural and progressive to see as threatening any literary form that calls dehumanization sexual. Once again, however, there is another way to analyze this aspect of pornography. Like a lot of far more respectable twentieth-century art, pornography is not about personality but about the explosion of the boundaries of the self. It is a fantasy of an extreme state in which all social constraints are overwhelmed by a flood of sexual energy. Think, for example, of all the pornography about servants fucking mistresses, old men fucking young girls, guardians fucking wards. Class, age, custom—all are deliciously sacrificed, dissolved by sex.

Though pornography's critics are right—pornography *is* exploitation—it is exploitation of *everything*. Promiscuity by definition is a breakdown of barriers. Pornography is not only a reflector of social power imbalances and sexual pathologies; it is also all those imbalances run riot, run to excess, sometimes explored *ad absurdum*, exploded. Misogyny is one content of pornography; another content is the universal infant desire for complete, immediate gratification, to rule the world out of the very core of passive helplessness.

In a less sexist society, there might be a pornography that is exciting, expressive, interesting, even, perhaps, significant as a form of social rebellion, all traits that, in a sexist society, are obscured by pornography's present role as escape valve for hostility toward women, or as metaphor for fiercely guarded power hierarchies. Instead, in a sexist society, we have two pornographies, one for men, one for women. They both have, hiding within them, those basic human expressions of abandon I have described. The pornography for men enacts this abandon on women as objects. How different is the pornography for women, in which sex is bathed in romance, diffused, always implied rather than enacted at all. This pornography is the Harlequin romance.

I described above the oddly narrowed down, denatured world presented in Harlequins. Looking at them as pornography obviously offers a number of alternative explanations for these same traits: the heroine's passivity becomes sexual receptivity and, though I complained earlier about her vapidity, in pornography no one need have a personality. ... [Harlequin heroines] have no particular qualities, but pornography by-passes this limitation and reaches straight down to the infant layer where we all imagine ourselves the center of everything by birthright and are sexual beings without shame or need for excuse.

Seeing Harlequins as pornography modifies one's criticism of their selectivity, their know-nothing narrowness. Insofar as they are essentially pornographic in intent, their characters have no past, no context; they live only in the eternal present of sexual feeling, the absorbing interest in the erotic sex object. Insofar as the books are written to elicit sexual excitation, they can be completely closed, repetitive circuits always returning to the moment of arousal when the hero's voice sends "a velvet finger"[8] along the spine of the heroine. In pornography, sex is the whole content; there need be no serious other.

Read this way, Harlequins are benign if banal sex books, but sex books for women have several special characteristics not included in the usual definitions of the genre pornography. In fact, a suggestive, sexual atmosphere is not so easy to establish for women as it is for men. A number of conditions must be right.

In *The Mermaid and the Minotaur*, an extraordinary study of the asymmetry of male and female relationships in all societies where children are primarily raised by women, Dorothy Dinnerstein discusses the reasons why women are so much more dependent than men on deep personal feeling as an ingredient, sometimes a precondition, for sex. Beyond the obvious reasons, the seriousness of sex for the partner who can get pregnant, the seriousness of sex for the partner who is economically and socially dependent on her lover, Dinnerstein adds another, psychological reason for women's tendency to emotionalize sex. She argues that the double standard (male sexual freedom, female loyalty to one sexual tie) comes from the asymmetry in the way the sexes are raised from infancy. Her argument is too complex to be entirely recapitulated here but her conclusion seems crucial to our understanding of the mixture of sexual excitement and anti-erotic restraint that characterizes sexual feeling in Harlequin romances:

> Anatomically, coitus offers a far less reliable guarantee of orgasm—or indeed of any intense direct local genital pleasure—to woman than to man. The first-hand coital pleasure of which she is capable more often requires conditions that must be purposefully sought out. Yet it is woman who has less liberty to conduct this kind of search ... societal and psychological constraints ... leave her less free than man to explore the erotic resources of a variety of partners, or even to affirm erotic impulse with any one partner. These constraints also make her less able to give way to simple physical delight without a sense of total self-surrender—a disability that further narrows her choice of partners,

and makes her still more afraid of disrupting her rapport with any one partner by acting to intensify the delight, that is, by asserting her own sexual wishes. ...

What the double standard hurts in women (to the extent that they genuinely, inwardly, bow to it) is the animal center of self-respect: the brute sense of bodily prerogative, of having a right to one's bodily feelings. ... Fromm made this point very clearly when he argued, in *Man for Himself,* that socially imposed shame about the body serves the function of keeping people submissive to societal authority by weakening in them some inner core of individual authority. ... On the whole ... the female burden of genital deprivation is carried meekly, invisibly. Sometimes it cripples real interest in sexual interaction, but often it does not: indeed, it can deepen a woman's need for the emotional rewards of carnal contact. What it most reliably cripples is human pride.[9]

This passage gives us the theoretical skeleton on which the titillations of the Harlequin formula are built. In fact, the Harlequin heroine cannot afford to be only a mass of responsive nerve endings. In order for her sexuality, and the sexuality of the novels' readers, to be released, a number of things must happen that have little to do directly with sex at all. Since she cannot seek out or instruct the man she wants, she must be in a state of constant passive readiness. Since only one man will do, she has the anxiety of deciding, "Is this *the* one?" Since an enormous amount of psychic energy is going to be mobilized in the direction of the man she loves, the man she sleeps with, she must feel sure of him. A one-night stand won't work; she is only just beginning to get her emotional generators going when he is already gone. And orgasm? It probably hasn't happened. She couldn't tell him she wanted it and couldn't tell him *how* she wanted it. If he is already gone, there is no way for her erotic feeling for him to take form, no way for her training of him as a satisfying lover to take place.

Hence the Harlequin heroine has a lot of things to worry about if she wants sexual satisfaction. Parisi has said that these worries are restraints there merely to be deliciously overridden, but they are so constant an accompaniment to the heroine's erotic feelings as to be, under present conditions, inseparable from them. She feels an urge toward deep emotion; she feels anxiety about the serious intentions of the hero; she role-plays constantly, presenting herself as a nurturant, passive, receptive figure; and all of this is part of sex to her. Certain social configurations feel safe and right and are real sexual cues for women. The romantic intensity of Harlequins—the waiting, fearing, speculating—are as much a part of their functioning as pornography for women as are the more overtly sexual scenes.

Nor is this just a neutral difference between men and women. In fact, as Dinnerstein suggests, the muting of spontaneous sexual feeling, the necessity that is socially forced on women of channeling their sexual desire, is in fact a great deprivation. In *The Mermaid and the Minotaur* Dinnerstein argues that men have a number of reasons, social and psychological, for discomfort when confronted by the romantic feeling and the demand for security that so often accompany female sexuality. For them growing up and being male both mean cutting off the passionate attachment and dependence on woman, on mother. Women, potential mother figures themselves, have less need to make this absolute break. Men also need to pull away from that inferior category, Woman. Women are stuck in it and naturally romanticize the powerful creatures they can only come close to through emotional and physical ties.

The Harlequin formula perfectly reproduces these differences, these tensions, between the sexes. It depicts a heroine struggling, against the hero's resistance, to get the right combination of elements together so that, for her, orgasmic sex can at last take place. The shape of the Harlequin sexual fantasy is designed to deal women the winning hand they cannot hold in life: a man who is romantically interesting—hence, distant, even frightening—while at the same time he is willing to capitulate to her needs just enough so that she can sleep with him not once but often. His intractability is exciting to her, a proof of his membership in a superior class of beings but, finally, he must relent to some extent if her breathless anticipation, the foreplay of romance, is to lead to orgasm.

Clearly, getting romantic tension, domestic security, and sexual excitement together in the same fantasy in the right proportions is a delicate balancing act. Harlequins lack excellence by any other measure, but they are masterly in this one respect. In fact, the Harlequin heroine is in a constant fever of anti-erotic anxiety, trying to control the flow of sexual passion between herself and the hero until her surrender can be on her own terms. If the heroine's task is "converting rape into love making," she must somehow teach the hero to take time, to pay attention, to feel, while herself remaining passive, undemanding, unthreatening. This is yet another delicate miracle of balance that Harlequin romances manage quite well. How do they do it?

The underlying structure of the sexual story goes something like this:

1. The man is hard (a walking phallus).
2. The woman likes his hardness.
3. But, at the outset, this hardness is *too hard*. The man has an ideology that is anti-romantic, anti-marriage. In other words, he will not stay around long enough for her to come, too.
4. Her final release of sexual feeling depends on his changing his mind, but *not too much*. He must become softer (safer, less likely to leave altogether) but not too soft. For good sex, he must be hard, but this hardness must be *at the service of the woman*.

The following passage from Anne Mather's *Born Out of Love* is an example:

His skin was smooth, more roughly textured than hers, but sleek and flexible beneath her palms, his warmth and maleness enveloping her and making her overwhelmingly aware that only the thin material of the culotte suit separated them. He held her face between his hands, and his hardening mouth was echoed throughout the length and breadth of his body. She felt herself yielding weakly beneath him, and his hand slid from her shoulder, across her throat to find the zipper at the front of her suit, impelling it steadily downward.

"No, Logan," she breathed, but he pulled the hands with which she might have resisted him around him, arching her body so that he could observe her reaction to the thrusting aggression of his with sensual satisfaction.

"No?" he probed with gentle mockery, his mouth seeking the pointed fullness of her breasts now exposed to his gaze. "Why not? It's what we both want, don't deny it." ...

Somehow Charlotte struggled up from the depth of a sexually induced lethargy. It wasn't easy, when her whole body threatened to betray her, but his words were too similar to the words he had used to her once before, and she remembered only too well what had happened next. …

She sat up quickly, her fingers fumbling with the zipper, conscious all the while of Logan lying beside her, and the potent attraction of his lean body. God, she thought unsteadily, what am I doing here? And then, more wildly: Why am I leaving him? *I want him!* But not on his terms, the still small voice of sanity reminded her, and she struggled to her feet.[10]

In these romantic love stories, sex on a woman's terms is romanticized sex. Romantic sexual fantasies are contradictory. They include both the desire to be blindly ravished, to melt, and the desire to be spiritually adored, saved from the humiliation of dependence and sexual passivity through the agency of a protective male who will somehow make reparation to the woman he loves for her powerlessness.

Harlequins reveal and pander to this impossible fantasy life. Female sexuality, a rare subject in all but the most recent writing, is not doomed to be what the Harlequins describe. Nevertheless, some of the barriers that hold back female sexual feeling are acknowledged and finally circumvented quite sympathetically in these novels. They are sex books for people who have plenty of good reasons for worrying about sex.

While there is something wonderful in the heroine's insistence that sex is more exciting and more momentous when it includes deep feeling, she is fighting a losing battle as long as she can define deep feeling only as a mystified romantic longing on the one hand, and as marriage on the other. In Harlequins the price for needing emotional intimacy is that she must passively wait, must anxiously calculate. Without spontaneity and aggression, a whole set of sexual possibilities is lost to her just as, without emotional depth, a whole set of sexual possibilities is lost to men.

Though one may dislike the circuitous form of sexual expression in Harlequin heroines, a strength of the books is that they insist that good sex for women requires an emotional and social context that can free them from constraint. If one dislikes the kind of social norms the heroine seeks as her sexual preconditions, it is still interesting to see sex treated not primarily as a physical event at all but as a social drama, as a carefully modulated set of psychological possibilities between people. This is a mirror image of much writing more commonly labeled pornography. In fact one cannot resist speculating that equality between the sexes as child rearers and workers might well bring personal feeling and abandoned physicality together in wonderful combinations undreamed of in either male or female pornography as we know it.

The ubiquity of the books indicates a central truth: romance is a primary category of the female imagination. The women's movement has left this fact of female consciousness largely untouched. While most serious women *novelists* treat romance with irony and cynicism, most women do not. Harlequins may well be closer to describing women's hopes for love than the work of fine women novelists. Harlequins eschew irony; they take love straight. Harlequins eschew realism; they are serious about fantasy and escape. In spite of all the audience manipulations inherent in the Harlequin formula, the connection between writer and reader is tonally seamless; Harlequins are respectful, tactful, friendly toward their audience. The letters that pour in to their publishers speak above all of involvement, warmth, human values. The world that can make Harlequin romances appear warm is indeed a cold, cold place.

---

## Notes

1. Harlequin is 50 percent owned by the conglomerate controlling the *Toronto Star*. If you add to the Harlequin sales figures (variously reported from between 60 million to 109 million for 1978) the figures for similar novels by Barbara Cartland and those contemporary romances published by Popular Library, Fawcett, Ballantine, Avon, Pinnacle, Dell, Jove, Bantam, Pocket Books, and Warner, it is clear that hundreds of thousands of women are reading books of the Harlequin type.

2. Elizabeth Graham, *Mason's Ridge* (Toronto: Harlequin Books, 1978), p. 63.

3. Delivered April 6, 1978, Livingston College, Rutgers University.

4. Rebecca Stratton, *The Sign of the Ram* (Toronto: Harlequin Books, 1977), p. 132.

5. Ibid., p. 112.

6. Ibid., pp. 99, 102, and 139.

7. Gloria Steinem, "Erotica and Pornography: A Clear and Present Difference," *MS* (November 1978), and other articles in this issue. An unpublished piece by Brigitte Frase, "From Pornography to Mind-Blowing" (MLA talk, 1978), strongly presents my own view that this debate is specious. See also Susan Sontag's "The Pornographic Imagination," in *Styles of Radical Will* (New York: Delta, 1978), and the Jean Paulhan preface to *Story of O,* "Happiness in Slavery" (New York: Grove Press, 1965).

8. Stratton, *The Sign of the Ram*, p. 115.

9. Dorothy Dinnerstein, *The Mermaid and the Minotaur: Sexual Arrangements and Human Malaise* (New York: Harper and Row, 1976), pp. 73–75.

10. Anne Mather, *Born Out of Love* (Toronto: Harlequin Books, 1977), pp. 70–72.

# *Ways of Seeing*

## John Berger

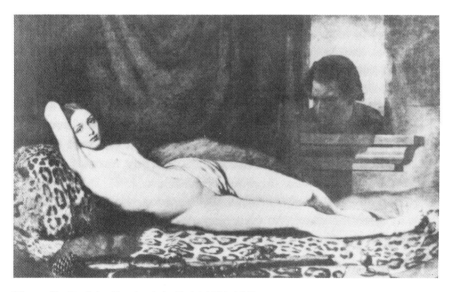

[**Figure 1**]	Reclining Bacchante by Trutat 1824–1848

According to usage and conventions which are at last being questioned but have by no means been overcome, the social presence of a woman is different in kind from that of a man. A man's presence is dependent upon the promise of power which he embodies. If the promise is large and credible his presence is striking. If it is small or incredible, he is found to have little presence. The promised power may be moral, physical, temperamental, economic, social, sexual—but its object is always exterior to the man. A man's presence suggests what he is capable of doing to you or for you. His presence may be fabricated, in the sense that he pretends to be capable of what he is not. But the pretence is always towards a power which he exercises on others.

By contrast, a woman's presence expresses her own attitude to herself, and defines what can and cannot be done to her. Her presence is manifest in her gestures, voice, opinions, expressions, clothes, chosen surroundings, taste—indeed there is nothing she can do which does not contribute to her presence. Presence for a woman is so intrinsic to her person that men tend to think of it as an almost physical emanation, a kind of heat or smell or aura.

To be born a woman has been to be born, within an allotted and confined space, into the keeping of men. The social presence of women has developed as a result of their ingenuity in living under such tutelage within such a limited space. But this has been at the cost of a woman's self being split into two. A woman must continually watch herself. She is almost continually accompanied by her own image of herself. Whilst she is walking across a room or whilst she is weeping at the death of her father, she can scarcely avoid envisaging herself walking or weeping. From earliest childhood she has been taught and persuaded to survey herself continually.

And so she comes to consider the *surveyor* and the *surveyed* within her as the two constituent yet always distinct elements of her identity as a woman.

She has to survey everything she is and everything she does because how she appears to others, and ultimately how she appears to men, is of crucial importance for what is normally thought of as the success of her life. Her own sense of being in herself is supplanted by a sense of being appreciated as herself by another.

Men survey women before treating them. Consequently how a woman appears to a man can determine how she will be treated. To acquire some control over this process, women must contain it and interiorize it. That part of a woman's self which is the surveyor treats the part which is the surveyed so as to demonstrate to others how her whole self would like to be treated. And this exemplary treatment of herself by herself constitutes her presence. Every woman's presence regulates what is and is not 'permissible' within her presence. Every one of her actions—whatever its direct purpose or motivation—is also read as an indication of how she would like to be treated. If a woman throws a glass on the floor, this is an example of how she treats her own emotion of anger and so of how she would wish it to be treated by others. If a man does the same, his action is only read as an expression of his anger. If a woman makes a good joke this is an example of how she treats the joker in herself and accordingly of how she as a joker-woman would like to be treated by others. Only a man can make a good joke for its own sake.

One might simplify this by saying: *men act* and *women appear*. Men look at women. Women watch themselves being looked at. This determines not only most relations between men and women but also the relation of women to themselves. The surveyor of woman in herself is male: the surveyed female. Thus she turns herself into an object—and most particularly an object of vision: a sight.

*       *       *

In one category of European oil painting women were the principal, ever-recurring subject. That category is the nude. In the nudes of European painting we can discover some of the criteria and conventions by which women have been seen and judged as sights.

The first nudes in the tradition depicted Adam and Eve. It is worth referring to the story as told in Genesis:

> And when the woman saw that the tree was good for food, and that it was a delight to the eyes, and that the tree was to be desired to make one wise, she took of the fruit thereof and did eat; and she gave also unto her husband with her, and he did eat.
>
> And the eyes of them both were opened, and they knew that they were naked; and they sewed fig-leaves together and made themselves aprons. ... And the Lord God called unto the man and said unto him, 'Where are thou?' And he said, 'I heard thy voice in the garden, and I was afraid, because I was naked, and I hid myself.' ...
>
> Unto the woman God said, 'I will greatly multiply thy sorrow and thy conception; in sorrow thou shalt bring forth children; and thy desire shall be to thy husband and he shall rule over thee.'

What is striking about this story? They became aware of being naked because, as a result of eating the apple, each saw the other differently. Nakedness was created in the mind of the beholder.

The second striking fact is that the woman is blamed and is punished by being made subservient to the man. In relation to the woman, the man becomes the agent of God.

...

When the tradition of painting became more secular, other themes also offered the opportunity of painting nudes. But in them all there remains the implication that the subject (a woman) is aware of being seen by a spectator.

She is not naked as she is.
She is naked as the spectator sees her.

Often—as with the favourite subject of Susannah and the Elders—this is the actual theme of the picture. We join the Elders to spy on Susannah taking her bath. She looks back at us looking at her. [Figure 2]

In another version of the subject by Tintoretto, Susannah is looking at herself in a mirror. Thus she joins the spectators of herself. [Figure 3]

The mirror was often used as a symbol of the vanity of woman. The moralizing, however, was mostly hypocritical. You painted a naked woman because you enjoyed looking at her, you put a mirror in her hand and you called the painting *Vanity,* thus morally condemning the woman whose nakedness you had depicted for your own pleasure. [Figure 4]

The real function of the mirror was otherwise. It was to make the woman connive in treating herself as, first and foremost, a sight.

...

It is worth noticing that in other non-European traditions—in Indian art, Persian art, African art, Pre-Columbian art—nakedness is never supine in this way. And if, in these traditions, the theme of a work is sexual attraction, it is likely to show active sexual love as between two people, the woman as active as the man, the actions of each absorbing the other. [Figure 5]

[**Figure 2**]  Susannah and the Elders by Tintoretto

[**Figure 3**]  Susannah and the Elders by Tintoretto 1518–1594

[**Figure 4**]   Vanity by Memling 1435–1494

[**Figure 5** (top to bottom)]   Rajasthan 18th century; Vishnu and Lakshmi 11th century; Mochica pottery

[**Figure 6**]

We can now begin to see the difference between nakedness and nudity in the European tradition. In his book on *The Nude* Kenneth Clark maintains that to be naked is simply to be without clothes, whereas the nude is a form of art. According to him, a nude is not the starting point of a painting, but a way of seeing which the painting achieves. To some degree, this is true—although the way of seeing 'a nude' is not necessarily confined to art: there are also nude photographs, nude poses, nude gestures. What is true is that the nude is always conventionalized—and the authority for its conventions derives from a certain tradition of art. [Figure 6]

What do these conventions mean? What does a nude signify? It is not sufficient to answer these questions merely in terms of the art-form, for it is quite clear that the nude also relates to lived sexuality.

To be naked is to be oneself.

To be nude is to be seen naked by others and yet not recognized for oneself. A naked body has to be seen as an object in order to become a nude. (The sight of it as an object stimulates the use of it as an object.) Nakedness reveals itself. Nudity is placed on display.

To be naked is to be without disguise.

To be on display is to have the surface of one's own skin, the hairs of one's own body, turned into a disguise which, in that situation, can never be discarded. The nude is condemned to never being naked. Nudity is a form of dress.

In the average European oil painting of the nude the principal protagonist is never painted. He is the spectator in front of the picture and he is presumed to be a man.

[**Figure 7**]    Bacchus, Ceres and Cupid by Von Aachen 1552–1615

Everything is addressed to him. Everything must appear to be the result of his being there. It is for him that the figures have assumed their nudity. But he, by definition, is a stranger—with his clothes still on.

...

It is true that sometimes a painting includes a male lover. [Figure 7]

But the woman's attention is very rarely directed towards him. Often she looks away from him or she looks out of the picture towards the one who considers himself her true lover—the spectator-owner.

There was a special category of private pornographic paintings (especially in the eighteenth century) in which couples making love make an appearance. But even in front of these it is clear that the spectator-owner will in fantasy oust the other man, or else identify with him. By contrast the image of the couple in non-European traditions provokes the notion of many couples making love. 'We all have a thousand hands, a thousand feet and will never go alone.'

[**Figure 8**]   Les Oréades by Bouguereau 1825–1905

Almost all post-Renaissance European sexual imagery is frontal—either literally or metaphorically—because the sexual protagonist is the spectator-owner looking at it.

The absurdity of this male flattery reached its peak in the public academic art of the nineteenth century. [Figure 8] Men of state, of business, discussed under paintings like this. When one of them felt he had been outwitted, he looked up for consolation. What he saw reminded him that he was a man.

*            *            *

There are a few exceptional nudes in the European tradition of oil painting to which very little of what has been said above applies. Indeed they are no longer nudes—

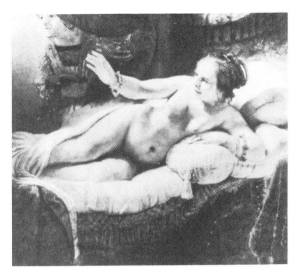

[**Figure 9**]   Danäe by Rembrandt 1606–1669

they break the norms of the art-form; they are paintings of loved women, more or less naked. Among the hundreds of thousands of nudes which make up the tradition there are perhaps a hundred of these exceptions. In each case the painter's personal vision of the particular women he is painting is so strong that it makes no allowance for the spectator. The painter's vision binds the woman to him so that they become as inseparable as couples in stone. The spectator can witness their relationship—but he can do no more: he is forced to recognize himself as the outsider he is. He cannot deceive himself into believing that she is naked for him. He cannot turn her into a nude. The way the painter has painted her includes her will and her intentions in the very structure of the image, in the very expression of her body and her face. [Figure 9]

. . .

The nude in European oil painting is usually presented as an admirable expression of the European humanist spirit. This spirit was inseparable from individualism. And without the development of a highly conscious individualism the exceptions to the tradition (extremely personal images of the naked), would never have been painted. Yet the tradition contained a contradiction which it could not itself resolve. A few individual artists intuitively recognized this and resolved the contradiction in their own terms, but their solutions could never enter the tradition's *cultural* terms.

The contradiction can be stated simply. On the one hand the individualism of the artist, the thinker, the patron, the owner: on the other hand, the person who is the object of their activities—the woman—treated as a thing or an abstraction. [Figure 10]

. . .

[**Figure 10**]    Man drawing reclining woman by Dürer 1471–1528

In the art-form of the European nude the painters and spectator-owners were usually men and the persons treated as objects, usually women. This unequal relationship is so deeply embedded in our culture that it still structures the consciousness of many women. They do to themselves what men do to them. They survey, like men, their own femininity.

...

\*        \*        \*

Today the attitudes and values which informed that tradition are expressed through other more widely diffused media—advertising, journalism, television.

But the essential way of seeing women, the essential use to which their images are put, has not changed. Women are depicted in a quite different way from men—not because the feminine is different from the masculine—but because the 'ideal' spectator is always assumed to be male and the image of the woman is designed to flatter him. If you have any doubt that this is so, make the following experiment. Choose ... an image of a traditional nude. Transform the woman into a man. Either in your mind's eye or by drawing on the reproduction. Then notice the violence which that transformation does. Not to the image, but to the assumptions of a likely viewer.

# What's Wrong with Being a Sex Object?

## Linda Lemoncheck

...

One of the challenges of a thorough analysis of sex objectification is the wide variety of opinion of what that actually is, variety both in the nature or form which the sex objectification takes and in the normative evaluations that persons make of it. For example, both the practice of raping a woman and the mental act of merely fantasizing about her sexual merits have each been called treating her as a sex object. And both the act of whistling at a woman standing on a street corner and whistling at a woman performing a striptease have been considered by different people to be inappropriate, permissible, or recommended. What appears clear from the outset is that treating a woman as a sex object can mean either conceiving of her as a sex object or acting toward her as a sex object—or both—and it is clear that any one case of sex objectification may be at once objectionable to some and enjoyable to others. Thus, any satisfactory characterization of sex objectification we offer should be broad enough to scope to account for such variety.

... We want to develop a characterization that can explain why some persons might complain about being treated as sex objects while others might not, as well as why someone might make the particular complaints she does and not other complaints instead. So, for example, we not only want a characterization that would account for the fact that some people find sex objectification demeaning and some do not, but one that shows why sex objectification might be construed as demeaning at all, as distinct from being viewed as uncharitable or spiteful or simply inconvenient.

...

Our first case is that of "the free spirit": Imagine a woman in her late teens walking home from school on a bright clear day. Since it is quite warm outside, she is barelegged, and dressed in a sleeveless cotton sundress and sandals. She walks by a construction site near her house at which three men are working. The minute they see her, one lets out a loud wolf-whistle, one taunts her with "Hey fox, give us a smile!" and the third simply stares in silence, thinking, "Now that's a nice piece of ass!"

Grinning broadly, they are full of the self-importance that accompanies seeing themselves as sexually confident initiators of the encounter and as dominators of the action. However the free spirit reacts, she will react to their intrusion and their attention. But the workers do not really expect the free spirit to smile for them on demand, much less stop to investigate their intentions further, although such an investigation would be fully welcomed; nor do they really care whether she takes their attentions as a compliment, although they wonder why so many women do not. In fact, their experience has led them to believe that women only pretend they do not want sex when they really do most of the time. If the women they meet really do not want it, the men contend, then they are just frigid or lesbians. Why, they wonder, would a woman wear a short dress unless she really wanted to show off a good pair of legs? Being coy, they assume, is just part of the feminine role women adopt in any personal encounter they have with men, so why not play the corresponding masculine aggressive role to get the ball rolling? To them, it seems to be the natural order of things.

The free spirit's reaction to the cat calls and comments from the workers is a combination of embarrassment, anger, and fear. She does not really know whether a smile is all they want (she knows that rapes have been initiated, indeed justified, on less); thus, she is afraid to tell them that she thinks what they do is rude and upsetting. She immediately looks down at her dress to be sure it has not fluttered too high above her knees in the wind. She blushes with a self-conscious sense of her own sexuality that she had not had until this moment: "I feel as if they could see right through my dress," she thought. Furthermore, she is angry with herself for not noticing the men soon enough to avoid walking past them; but she is even angrier that she should have to maintain that kind of awareness against men at all. To do so would certainly mean that the freedom and spontaneity which she enjoys in her life would all but disappear. With a sigh, she determines to reroute her walk home from school, even though this particular walk is the shortest and pleasantest, but, she feels helpless to alter her current situation. All she can think to do is to hurry away from the site, flustered and humiliated, while the men return to their work, laughing among themselves. But what she really wanted to do was to walk right up to the construction workers and reply, "Women are a lot more than sex objects, you know!"

Compare this case with the one of "the unhappy wife": A husband and wife, both lawyers, are readying themselves for bed after attending a cocktail party at the home of one of their friends. She is tired, but willing to chat about the events of the evening; he is drunk and wants nothing from her but sex. Not noticing her fatigue, the husband pulls his wife playfully but firmly onto their bed, and in a voice both whining and demanding, says, "C'mon, baby doll, *I* wanna screw." ... She is simply too exhausted to fend off his presumptions and unwelcome overtures. ... Sex, of all things, she thinks, as her husband lies asleep after the predictable two minutes, should be a shared experience, an intimate exchange of stimulation and satisfaction, not a truncated, one-sided activity. "I might as well put him to bed with a sexually stimulating machine, for all he might care, so long as he is satisfied sexually. Yet he is so attentive at parties. And just this evening, I overheard him bragging about the great defense I presented in court today. Why is it that I'm considered a person when I'm a party companion or a lawyer, but when it comes to sex, I'm nothing more than a feelingless object?"

And finally, note the case of "the assistant manager": The male president of a business firm notices both the sexual attractiveness and the intelligence of a certain female assistant manager working in his office. "Now that's the kind of woman that really turns me on," he muses, "one with a body and brains!" He is doubtful that a married, middle-aged executive is the sort of man to whom she might be sexually attracted, much less the sort with whom she would willingly have an affair. However, he is convinced that the lure of a good promotion can get him what he wants. In light of these facts, the president calls the assistant manager into his office one morning and suggests that he would be willing to promote her to manager of her division if she were to consent to have sex with him at an apartment he is renting near the office. "That's about the only way I know that women get ahead in business," he assures her. And moving closer, he adds, "Besides, sugar, why not mix a little business with pleasure?" The assistant manager, who has worked diligently at her job to qualify for promotion, turns away from him in disgust. ... "I don't know the guy and I don't want to," she thinks. "What right does he think he has, that he can use me to play with himself? He knows I'm bright, even an economic asset to the company. But that doesn't matter in the end. All I'm good for is sex, sex, sex. I suppose I'm expected to act like some appreciative pet and accept the juicy morsel offered to me. It's as if all this time we've been talking, he's been plotting how to get me in bed—how humiliating!" But she is torn: she deserves her promotion and does not want to resign. (It would only seem to prove his point that women couldn't get ahead without sex.) On the other hand, she cannot tolerate working around men who think of women as servants to their sexual whims. All she can manage to do is walk out the door, sobbing, "I'm sick and tired of men who think women are nothing but sex objects!"

The first thing to notice about the three cases above is that, even though they are all cases of women complaining about being treated as sex objects by men, the circumstances of their sex objectification are very different. For example, in the case of the free spirit, her objectifiers are strangers to her, acting in concert; in the cases of the unhappy wife and assistant manager, they know their objectifiers by name, and their objectifiers act alone. Indeed, the unhappy wife's objectifier is her own husband. Furthermore, the case of the unhappy wife suggests that sex objectification can occur in perfectly appropriate settings for sexual relations; the bedroom is as conducive to such treatment (if not more so) as the boardroom or construction site. Nor does the objectification necessarily involve the public recognition or discussion of a woman's more private body parts; the treatment of the unhappy wife is in the privacy of her own home, even though hers is the only case in which her body is physically exposed. Moreover, unlike the case of the free spirit, the cases of the unhappy wife and assistant manager suggest that no perceived threat of physical harm, much less actual assault, need play any role in the encounter. We can suppose that the wife knows her husband to be of a basically non-violent sort; and the assistant manager may not get promoted for refusing the president, but she does not expect to be assaulted for it.

This is not to suggest that the abruptness of a stranger, the inappropriateness of the context, or the threat of harm are not factors to be considered when assessing what is objectionable about any one case of sex objectification. It is simply to point out that such specific facts cannot appear in any characterization of sex objectification which would attempt to generalize over a variety of cases. In fact, our characterization of sex objectification must also account for the fact that there may be something about sex objectifying thoughts or attitudes as well as their practices that are a source for complaint. For while the husband and company president ultimately feel compelled to confront their sex objects with their demands, the silent, staring construction worker is happy to stand back and grin while his partners carry on. We could even imagine the free spirit walking by the one construction worker completely oblivious to his thoughts about her. Yet, if she were told about the nature of his thoughts after the fact, the free spirit's reaction would very probably take the form that she does not appreciate being thought about that way.

Then what sort of treatment is it that is common to each of the examples above that the women in those examples are complaining about? First, let us note what those who worry about sex objectification do *not* mean by that expression. Following Elizabeth Eames, we must make a distinction between woman as "sex thing" and woman as "object of sexual desire."[1] The term "object" is often used in the sense of "objective" or "something intended or aimed at" such as "objects of attention," "objects of affection," or "objects of effort and organization." When "sex object" is translated "sexual objective" or "aim of sexual desire" or even "someone to have sex with," it does not carry with it the necessary disapprobation that many women claim it has. It is quite plausible to suppose, for example, that the free spirit, the unhappy wife, and the assistant manager all enjoy sexual intercourse, but nevertheless dislike being treated as sex objects. ... It is only when women are regarded as inanimate objects, bodies, or animals, where their status as the moral equals of persons has been demeaned or degraded, that the expression "sex objectification" is correctly used. ...

Furthermore, it is equally misleading to think that what women object to when they complain about being treated as sex objects is that they are being treated as *nothing but* objects of sexual desire. The unhappy wife is considered by her husband to be, among other things, a successful lawyer, and the assistant manager is considered a valuable employee by her boss. Even the free spirit is probably regarded as a source of peer-esteem or a good laugh, as well as sexually attractive. Nevertheless, such women still complain about being treated as sex objects.

To mark out the context in which women are treated as objects of sexual desire appears to be much more helpful. The free spirit is treated as an object of sexual desire in a context where she should be treated as a passerby, but is not. The assistant manager is treated as an object of sexual desire in a context where she should be treated as a business associate. The problem then becomes one of specifying in which contexts persons are inappropriately treated as sexually desirable. However, while the context issue is necessary to understanding the moral offense in the above cases, the case of the unhappy wife shows us that it is not sufficient. For in her case, it is not true that she is being treated as an object of sexual desire in a context where she should be treated as something else. The context is, at least on the surface, appropriate; indeed, treating her as "something else," such as dwelling on her brilliant defense in court that day, might make sex less enjoyable for her than if her husband just treated her as sexy. What we need in our analysis of her case is not only a discussion of the context in which the sexual relations occur, but also the very nature of the relations themselves: the unhappy wife is not being treated as a sex partner in her sexual relations with her husband; she is being treated as a sex *object*.

Just as the complaints against sex objectification are not directed against "sex" *per se*, so too, the complaints against it should not be directed against "objectification" *per se*. There are several examples of circumstances in which persons regard themselves or other persons as things, bodies, parts of bodies, even animals, but which we would not regard as *prima facie* objectionable. Imagine the artist gazing fixedly at the human form he represents on canvas, or imagine the designer of children's clothes hemming a garment draped around the immobile figure of a six-year-old.[2] Imagine the surgeon operating on her patient or the photographer using a face in a crowd (instead of a lamppost or a tree) to focus his camera. Or suppose I shuffle behind a classmate during a ten-year high school reunion to avoid the necessity of conversing with the class gossip. Imagine the kindly uncle playing 'horsey' with his niece, or the anthropologist classifying the members of the species *Homo sapiens* as higher order mammals.

Why do the subjects of the above sorts of treatment fail to complain about their circumstances while the women in our three examples find so much to complain about? One is tempted to say that what distinguishes the former cases from the latter is that the women in our three examples are treated as objects, *but not as persons*,[3] while the artist's model, the surgical patient, the classmate, and so on are treated as objects *but also as persons*. ...

...

... There is nothing wrong with treating an X as a Y, a rock as paperweight, an uncle as a brother, Queen Elizabeth as the girl next door, or a person as an object, unless we also stipulate that X is being treated as a Y in ways it should be treated as an X, but is not being so treated. So, for example, it would be inappropriate to treat Queen Elizabeth as the girl next door, if we could show that being Queen Elizabeth carries with it certain rights and requests of us certain attitudes that are violated or rejected when she is treated as the girl next door. Similarly, then, it is not simply that the free spirit, unhappy wife, and assistant manager are being treated as objects and not as persons, or as persons some of whose desires are being disregarded; they are being treated as objects in ways they should be treated as persons, but are not. Furthermore, the situation in which this treatment occurs may itself be inappropriate for sexual encounters, making the moral evaluation of the treatment in such cases one of context as well as one of content.

...

… One way in which we can explain why the artist's model might not mind being treated "as an object" is that the model is being treated as if she were an object (a stationary mass, a figurine, a body) but also as a moral equal: she is a person with a body that is useful for creating figures in oil paintings, and who is both regarded as the bearer of the human rights to well-being and freedom equal to those of other persons and acted toward in a way which is not in violation of those rights.

In the ideal case, for example, she is neither coerced nor humiliated into standing erect or changing positions on demand. Moreover, she has full control over how much of her body she wants others to observe. She is not being exploited by being deceived about the payment she shall receive or about what is expected of her while on the job. We can suppose the artist is neither rude to her nor attempts to become too intimate in the face of any of the model's clear desires to the contrary. In fact, as far as we can tell, he may presume that she is only interested in business as usual. He does not try to subordinate her interests to his; we can imagine that she chooses to model out of her own personal preference, finding a great deal of personal satisfaction in helping an artist create a beautiful work of art.

On the other hand, the well-being and freedom of the three women in our examples of sex objectification have been severely diminished by their objectifiers. The free spirit feels embarrassed by the fact that her more "private" parts are now the subject of public discussion and a kind of disconcerting curiosity by persons she does not even know. She wonders how many men have been "checking her out" without her knowing it. Some anxiety, even some paranoia over the thought of such constant public scrutiny begins to set in. She is frightened by the thought that men have been known to rape women with no provocation. She finds the behavior of the workers a rude intrusion on her daily routine; in fact, she feels she can no longer walk freely and unselfconsciously down her own street in broad daylight. As far as she is concerned, her rights to privacy, freedom of movement and expression, and to at least civil behavior from the construction workers have been violated in this context.

The unhappy wife begins to wonder where the intimacy in her sexual relationship with her husband has gone. His insensitivity to her own feelings about sex makes her wonder whether he ever tries to look at sex from her point of view. In fact, if she had not overheard him bragging about her brilliant legal defense, she would wonder just what else she means to him besides a "quick lay." Because her husband refuses to think that her own sexual needs have any real bearing on her happiness at all, she begins to wonder herself just how important those needs really are. Thus, a certain degree of her own self-respect diminishes. She need not feel this way; the point is that it is easy for her to feel this way, given the dominating and controlling attitude of her husband.

The assistant manager fumes at the fact that her boss has exploited the power relationship that exists between them to try to convince her to go to bed with him. She feels unfairly used by him for an easy turn-on; she is disgusted by his self-display and feels that brain or no brain, she is ultimately a sexual tool for his own personal purposes, without really considering her purposes. The offer of sex in exchange for promotion intimidates her, since she feels she cannot refuse without leaving the company, yet she does not wish to submit. Thus, she feels a certain lack of freedom to pursue her own sex life (and career) in the way that she would otherwise wish. She also finds it presumptuous of her boss to think that she would be happy to "mix a little business with pleasure."

...

A central theme of our examples would seem to be the subjugation, subordination, intimidation or psychological domination of the sex object.[4] Such a theme is consistent with the claim that the sex objectifier treats the sex object as less than a moral equal, as one less deserving, not equally so, of the rights to well-being and freedom that he enjoys. Notice that the willingness to dominate the interests of another, to humiliate, threaten, or otherwise constrain the freedom of another seems to typify the attitude of men like the construction workers, husband, and company president. They all show an attitude that conceives of women as less than moral equals. The free spirit is considered to be "a nice piece of ass." The unhappy wife sees herself, through the eyes of her husband, as "a sexually stimulating machine." The assistant manager regards her position as one of "a sexual servant" or "an appreciative pet." They react strongly and negatively to the fact that they are treated as the sexual toys, tools, props, or pets of the men with whom they come in contact. But as the case of the artist's model suggests, being treated as an object, body, or animal is not the whole story. Nor is it necessary that the sex object react or even react negatively to her sex objectification. ... What is necessary to identify an incident as sex objectification is that the sex object be treated as an object, body, or animal but not also as the moral equal of persons. She is treated as if she lacked one or more of the distinctive human capacities upon which her rights to a certain level of well-being and freedom are based. She is treated as if she were the sort of creature who had no such rights or rights of a very limited sort. This is equivalent to saying that with respect to her rights to well-being and freedom, she is treated in the very way she would commonly be treated, if she were an animal, body, or object.

Given the thesis that the sex object is treated as less than a moral equal by her objectifier, we can explain the pervasive complaint that sex objectification degrades women or demeans women. The sex objective is a moral inferior or moral subordinate; she literally has been lowered in status not merely from that of person to object, but from that of moral equal to moral subordinate. She is treated as if she were the sort of being with more restricted rights, less of the rights, or none of the rights to well-being and freedom that other persons (in particular, her objectifiers) enjoy. Some or all of the sex object's feelings, desires, or interests are subordinated, subverted, and manipulated to satisfy the sex objectifier's own, in a *prima facie* inappropriate way. We shall call such degradation or subordination "dehumanization" to distinguish it from the simple "objectification" of the artist's model in our example. What this analysis suggests is that one can treat a woman as sexually attractive without treating her as a sex object, by treating her as a sexually attractive moral equal or person. This suggestion matches the intuition of at least some people that while a woman may be complimented for her sexy body, or regarded as an erotic bedmate, she need not automatically be construed as a sex object.[5] In short, a person is dehumanized when that person is treated as an animal, body, part of body, or object in ways she or he should be treated as a person, that is as a moral equal. The woman who is treated as a sex object is a woman dehumanized.

...

---

### Notes

1. Elizabeth Eames, "Sexism and Woman as Sex Object," *Journal of Thought* 11, No. 2 (April, 1976), p. 142.
2. *See* Norvin Richards, "Using People," *Mind* 87, No. 345 (January, 1978), p. 102. Richards uses the example of a designer and fashion model. However, since some women find modelling an instance of, or at least contributing to a climate of sex objectification, I have used a less controversial example.
3. *See* Eames, *op. cit.,* p. 141.
4. For a similar theme about the sexual relations between men and women, *see* Kathleen Barry, *Female Sexual Slavery* (Englewood Cliffs, New Jersey: Prentice-Hall, 1979); *also see* Michael Korda, *Male Chauvinism! How It Works* (New York: Ballentine Books, 1973).
5. For example, *see* Eames, *op. cit.,* p. 141 and Korda, *op. cit.,* p. 102. ...

# *Bibo*

## Interview by Wendy Chapkis

*"The movement's position on beauty was always radical, simplistic and puritanical to the core."*

My family was old style New Englanders. My mother, who was really beautiful, never wore make-up. That was not uncommon. Women who were educated, had gone to Smith, "proper" women, didn't wear make-up. Women who wore make-up were working class and prostitutes. Also, if "you didn't need it, you shouldn't wear it." And the funny thing was, whenever they did wear make-up, it looked like they had gobs on because all they ever wore was bright red lipstick. Later, when make-up styles changed, women wore a lot more make-up to look as if they weren't wearing any—to look Natural.

I had a lot of fights in the women's movement because I never stopped wearing it. Besides, I had heard all this already a thousand years ago. We don't need it so we shouldn't wear it. Proper (read now to be politically correct) women don't wear make-up. I knew this argument. I thought it was a stupid issue, and in the sense that I thought it an interesting one, it was never broached as anything but a simplistic problem.

The movement's position on beauty was always radical, simplistic and puritanical to the core. People who have lived beyond that period and are still interested in those issues are all left trying to resolve them into a kind of synthesis that has yet to happen.

I had a long friendship with a woman who was at the opposite end of the fashion spectrum from me. Because we worked and got along well together, we used to have these fights right up front. She wore the most extreme example of sneakers, dungarees and flannel shirts. If she was going to see the president, that was what she wore. She used to tease me about spending time thinking about what to wear, worrying about how I looked. I would say that she worried every bit as much as I did about the way she looked.

I get dressed and there is a certain theatricality to it. But then I forget it. Because to me, it's not identity, it's theater. What she wore was always part of her identity. It was really important to her. I was into masks. I would wear a miniskirt and play She Was a Lesbian Separatist Dresser. Which was more serious?

I now have a number of women who come into the shop from the alternative scene who want me to help them make themselves over to enter the job market. They don't have any sense of what is appropriate to pass without appearance being an issue. They don't have that bank of experience. And it is a skill.

Unless you have a whole lot of money, there is also a certain amount of talent involved in matching what you think you are inside with what you want to look like outside—and to whatever reality is playing into that, say your job. It demands skills a lot of women don't have. And a certain amount of time—without a lot of money, you can't shortcut it by buying style directly. Most important of all, it takes self-confidence.

I have outrageous self-doubts, but I have never not liked myself. I sometimes forget that there are just too many women who don't like themselves. Women who have internalized the hatred and misogyny of the culture. That is a basic and real problem: how can someone have fun doing something—dressing up—for which the basis of that pleasure—self-respect—isn't fully functioning?

# The Unadorned Feminist

## Janet Radcliffe Richards

...

### Sensual Pleasure

There can be no reasonable feminist principle which says that women ought not to want men, and if women want men they must be willing to be pleasing to them. If, therefore, the rejection of feminine adornment is to be seen as a refusal to please men (which it certainly often is) *and* an integral part of feminism, it must be seen as directed more specifically against particular types of pleasure. It must be directed against men who want women for the wrong reasons. These men are usually said to be the ones who want women as sex objects; the ones who want them for sex and nothing else.

It is probably worthwhile to note in passing a distinction which some feminists draw between women as sex objects (exemplified by the pictures of women in the girlie magazines) and beauty objects (like the ones on the cover of *Vogue*). It is difficult to draw a firm line between the two, since obviously beauty in women is attractive to men even when the beauty is not actually sexy in form, but there is a difference between them. Perhaps the essence of the feminist position can be caught by saying that the protest is against the male's demand that the female should be sensually pleasing to him in all respects, and his (presumed) lack of interest in very much else about her.

Anyway, feminists do complain that men have for far too long wanted women only for these superficial characteristics, and it seems that the feminist refusal to please men sensually may be a way of trying to separate the men who want women for the right reasons from the ones who (as our grandmothers would have said) want only one thing. And certainly it is easy to see why this feeling among women should lead to their determination not to adorn themselves. It is beyond all question true that if you refuse to be sexually pleasing you are not much use as a sex object, and if you are not beautiful you are unlikely to be loved for your beauty. If the aim of the deliberately unadorned feminist is to make sure that men who have the wrong attitude to women have no interest in her, she is likely to succeed.

That, however, does not conclude the matter. Although the method may be a very effective one for getting rid of the tares, it has the rather serious disadvantage of being likely to eliminate most of the wheat in the process as well. Certainly, it will get rid of the men who are interested in women only from the point of view of sensual pleasing, but it is bound to affect at the same time not only them, but also the ones with excellent senses of priority; the ones who value character, intelligence, kindness, sympathy, and all the rest far above mere sensual pleasing, but nevertheless would like that too if they could get it *as well* as all these other things. Caring about such matters is not the same thing as caring exclusively, or even mainly, about them. The best-judging man alive, confronted with two women identical in all matters of the soul but not equal in beauty, could hardly help choosing the beautiful one. Whatever anyone's set of priorities, *the pleasing in all respects must be preferable to the pleasing in only some,* and this means that any feminist who makes herself unattractive must deter not only the men who would have valued her *only* for her less important aspects, but many of the others too. Or if they did still choose her, they would be less well pleased with her than they would have been if she had been physically attractive as well. A man who would not change his woman for any other in the world might still know that she would please him even more if she looked like the centre fold from the latest *Playboy.*

If feminists make themselves deliberately unattractive, they are not only keeping off the men who would value their more important qualities too little, but are also lessening their chances of attaching men who care about such things *at all.* If they think that is a good thing to do, they must be prepared to argue that it is positively bad to care about whether people are sensually pleasing or not; that if you do not care at all about people's beauty you are morally superior to someone who does. Perhaps some people think that is true. If so, however, they must also think it morally bad to care about beauty at all, since beauty is the same sort of thing whether it is in paintings, sunsets or people, and *someone who does not care about beauty in people is someone who simply does not care about beauty.*

Now of course beauty is often of a low priority, and it is morally good to care relatively little about it when people are hungry, or unjustly treated, or unhappy in other ways. Most of us, however, would like people to have beauty as well as other things, because for most of them it is one of the delights of life; we complain when the government does not subsidize the arts, and get angry when people live in ugly environments. Some people do not care about art and environmental beauty, it is true, but that just means that they are aesthetically insensitive. It is not actually wicked to be aesthetically insensitive, but neither is it a virtue, any more than being tone deaf, or not feeling the cold, or having no interest in philosophy or football. People who do care about it are good when they sacrifice their pleasure in beauty for something more important, but only then. There is nothing whatever to be said for the puritanical idea that self-denial is good in itself. It is good only as a means to an end.

Much the same goes for the sensual enjoyment of sex. We may perhaps say that sex is a lower thing than the love of souls, but in order to blame men for caring about it at all in women it is necessary to argue that it is actually a *bad thing, positively* bad, rather than simply something which is less important than other things. But if sensual pleasure is a good thing, why not wear pretty clothes? Why not wear a provocative bra, especially if it is as comfortable as any other? To do so is simply to make yourself more pleasing, in more respects, and with very little effort. To refuse to do that may show that you are not interested in men who are interested in sex, but that is a personal preference, and nothing to do with feminist ideals. It can be no part of a serious feminism to argue that there is anything inherently wrong with the sensual enjoyment of sex.

Although it may be morally good to give up sensual pleasure to achieve some other end, there is nothing to be said for giving it up *unless* there is some other end to achieve. Women cannot reasonably regard it as morally reprehensible in men that they should care about what women look like, even though they may reasonably expect them to care more about other things. It is, however, amazing how much general confusion there is about this subject, and how ready the careless sentimental of all types (not only feminist) are to assure everyone that it doesn't matter if you are plain or deformed, because a really nice person won't care. A particularly striking example of this occurred in [a] … series of advice-giving broadcasts. … A woman was in extreme distress about relationships with men because she had just had a mastectomy, and the panel of experts, astoundingly, did tell her just that: nice men wouldn't mind. They even went on, in what sounded like a caricature of popular psychology, to assure her that what was really bothering her was her relationship with her mother when she had been a child.

This sort of thing is appalling. There cannot be a man in existence who would not, other things being equal, prefer a woman with two breasts to a woman with only one, and niceness has absolutely nothing to do with such preferences. The attitude of the advisors is one which only drives the unfortunate further into their misfortune, by making it impossible for them to find anyone to take their very real misery seriously. The only person on the panel who gave the woman any useful advice was the one layman, who made suggestions about how she could cope with the situation, minimize shock and embarrassment, and make men comfortable with her. This is just the sort of thing which is needed, and the sort of thing, incidentally, for which the despised women's magazines are invaluable. All the muddled distributors of moral reflections and cold comfort, feminist or otherwise, succeed in doing is to invite bitterness when people realize that according to these impossible standards there are very few 'nice' people around.

It is useless to argue that to foster this kind of attitude discriminates against ugly women. There is no question of fostering, merely of recognizing the inevitable. Of course it is unfair in some sense that some people are born more beautiful than others, just as it is unfair that some are cleverer than others, or have parents who brought them up to be pleasant rather than unpleasant, or are stronger or more agile than other people. Of course we should see what can be done to make things less unjust. However, it is not the solution to cosmic unfairnesses in the distribution of things to try to prove that they do not matter, or that they only seem to matter because of the evils of society. It is not an evil in society that beauty matters: other things being equal, it is impossible that it should not matter.

...

The simple fact is that for a woman to make herself physically or sexually unattractive is to deflect all sexual interest: it is to distance alike the good and bad among men; the ones who have sexual interests among others and the ones whose interest in women is all sexual. That, of course, may be what some of the women who do it want. If that is so, however, it must be regarded as a personal inclination of their own; it cannot be seen as a reasonable feminist policy. Most women want to attract men, and if they do they must (at the very least) not make themselves deliberately unattractive. It is no part of the moral corruption of men that they care about beauty in women, and it is no mark of the highest sexual relationship that it should have no sensual content. For the woman who wants to separate the sheep from the lecherous goats, there is, unfortunately, no alternative to the tedious process of hand-sorting. It may be fraught with attendant risks of mistake and calculated deception, but it has to be done; the feminist who tries to make a short cut by her refusal to be beautiful or feminine is left with nothing but the grim satisfaction of finding, after having measured men with an infinite yardstick, that they are all wanting.

## Packaging

Let us then take it that there is nothing at all to be said for being deliberately unattractive, unless you actually want to keep off everyone who might be interested at all in sensual pleasures, and move on to what is unquestionably another idea at the back of many minds: that it is bad that women should put any *effort* into making themselves attractive to men. As was mentioned before, this is clearly not the whole of the argument agaisnt 'woman garbage' because it does not account for deliberate efforts to look unattractive, and choosing one style of appearance rather than another within the constraints of a given amount of effort. Still it certainly is an issue in its own right, and for some feminists perhaps the main one. To dress up, or beautify, or aim to titillate men, is said to amount to *packaging*, which turns women into commodities, and is degrading.

There are a good many aspects to this issue, and it is made very difficult to deal with by the fact that its parts get entangled together and with parts of other separate issues. Still, they must be separated for the purpose of making them clear. A good starting point is the comment of one feminist speaking bitterly during a television broadcast about the effort women were expected to put into their appearance: 'They can't love you as you are, they must love you for what you have become.'

Forgetting the specific issue of beauty for the moment (it will reappear shortly), what about the general idea of being wanted for what you are, rather than what you have become? There are difficulties even about what this means (if it means anything), since what you have become *is* now what you are. However, it sounds as though what is implied is that you ought not to have to make any efforts to change yourself; whatever you are like, people ought to want you that way.

But what is the great advantage in remaining as you are? You might be something quite undesirable. ... In most matters, like education and manners and morals, people are all in favour of improvement. ... For some reason, however, there seems to be an idea that there is something very different about *natural beauty,* and this is a point at which feminists find themselves slipping into the company of surprising allies in the conservative world. Something needs to be said about that in particular, therefore, and the main thing which needs doing is to separate various questions. 'Natural beauty' hides a multitude of confusions, which tend to coalesce into a blur under the general heading.

First, perhaps relatively unimportant in feminism but still worth mentioning, there is the sentimental idea that people are all by nature equally beautiful 'in their own way,' and what we should be doing is getting people to recognize that, rather than encouraging everyone to try to conform to current tastes. This one can be dismissed straight away. By any possible standard it is quite straightforwardly *false* that everyone is equally beautiful. It makes no difference to argue that standards change and that there is some standard which could make anyone beautiful: even if that were true (which it almost certainly is not) it is irrelevant. Even if you would have been beautiful according to the taste of five hundred years ago it is not much consolation for being thought ugly now. It is no good to say that we ought to change our standards of beauty to incorporate everyone. No doubt we should aim for greater flexibility, but we cannot alter our standards to the extent of making everyone beautiful without getting rid of ideas of beauty altogether; there can be no standard of beauty if nothing would count as ugly. We cannot recommend that women should do nothing to improve themselves on the grounds that what they should really be doing is trying to make people accept that they are all beautiful just as they are.

The second idea about natural beauty is, roughly, that you can't possibly improve on nature, and therefore should leave well alone. That seems to put an unwarranted amount of faith in nature. Of course people *can* make themselves hideous with too much powder and paint, but that is not the point. That some people fail does not suggest that success is impossible in the nature of things. *Of course* there are things which people can do to make themselves more beautiful and otherwise attractive. It does not matter if beauty is in the eye of the beholder; you can always find out what the beholder likes. You can darken your lashes or pluck your brows or curl your hair, and if those things are thought beautiful, you can in doing them make yourself more beautiful.

And finally (for this purpose) there is the idea shared by feminists and, as I recall, one elderly nonconformist minister, that to attract by artificial beauty is to use false pretences. The idea of this one, presumably, is that a man is cheated if he thinks he has acquired a beautiful woman, and finds too late that when she takes off her false hair and eyelashes and nails, and removes the paint and corsets and padded bra, she is not what she seemed. If that is the idea of false pretences, of course, it does not apply to various beautifying procedures like plastic surgery, careful hair cutting and perming, slimming and the like, since those all have lasting effects. Any objection to that sort of thing must be another confusion about the 'natural' person being the real thing, and the unreal thing being a deception. But what about the less permanent cosmetic devices? Are men entitled to feel cheated by such artificial beauty in women? These days, of course, it hardly applies, since they usually have plenty of time to find out before being inveigled by these illusions into marriage. But anyway, a man who gets a woman who knows how to make herself *look* well, even though nature has made little of her, is obviously better off than a man who gets one who is beautiful neither by nature nor by contrivance; beauty is not a matter of what you *are*, it is a matter of what you *look* like. The idea that beauty is truth, however deeply entrenched in the romantic mind, is just nonsense. And to consider the matter again from the point of view of cheating, it might plausibly be argued that the man who gets a woman with the artistic skill to improve herself is actually doing better than one whose partner is beautiful only by nature: skill in making oneself beautiful has the advantage over natural beauty that it does not turn grey, or wrinkle, or sag, or spread.

Ideas of natural beauty, however they are defined and defended, cannot show that women ought to be satisfied with their looks as they are. …

…

# *Gynocide:*
# *Chinese Footbinding*

## Andrea Dworkin

### Instructions Before Reading …

1. Find a piece of cloth 10 feet long and 2 inches wide
2. Find a pair of children's shoes
3. Bend all toes except the big one under and into the sole of the foot. Wrap the cloth around these toes and then around the heel. Bring the heel and toes as close together as possible. Wrap the full length of the cloth as tightly as possible
4. Squeeze foot into children's shoes
5. Walk
6. Imagine that you are 5 years old
7. Imagine being like this for the rest of your life

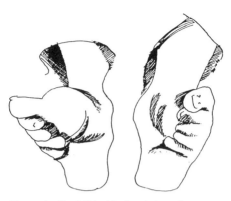

**Figure 1**   Feet: 3 to 4 Inches in Length

The origins of Chinese footbinding, as of Chinese thought in general, belong to that amorphous entity called antiquity. The 10th century marks the beginning of the physical, intellectual, and spiritual dehumanization of women in China through the institution of footbinding. That institution itself, the implicit belief in its necessity and beauty, and the rigor with which it was practiced lasted another 10 centuries. There were sporadic attempts at emancipating the foot—some artists, intellectuals, and women in positions of power were the proverbial drop in the bucket. Those attempts, modest as they were, were doomed to failure: footbinding was a political institution which reflected and perpetuated the sociological and psychological inferiority of women; footbinding cemented women to a certain sphere, with a certain function—women were sexual objects and breeders. Footbinding was mass attitude, mass culture—it was the key reality in a way of life lived by real women—10 centuries times that many millions of them.

...

... An elderly Chinese woman, as late as 1934, remembered vividly her childhood experience:

> Born into an old-fashioned family in P'ing-hsi, I was inflicted with the pain of footbinding when I was seven years old. I was an active child who liked to jump about, but from then on my free and optimistic nature vanished. Elder Sister endured the process from six to eight years of age [this means that it took Elder Sister two years to attain the 3-inch foot]. It was in the first lunar month of my seventh year that my ears were pierced and fitted with gold earrings. I was told that a girl had to suffer twice, through ear piercing and footbinding. Binding started in the second lunar month; mother consulted references in order to select an auspicious day for it. I wept and hid in a neighbor's home, but Mother found me, scolded me, and dragged me home. She shut the bedroom door, boiled water, and from a box withdrew binding, shoes, knife, needle and thread. I begged for a one-day postponement, but Mother refused: "Today is a lucky day," she said. "If bound today, your feet will never hurt; if bound tomorrow they will." She washed and placed alum on my feet and cut the toenails. She then bent my toes toward the plantar with a binding cloth ten feet long and two inches wide, doing the right foot and then the left. She finished binding and ordered me to walk, but when I did the pain proved unbearable.

That night, Mother wouldn't let me remove the shoes. My feet felt on fire and I couldn't sleep; Mother struck me for crying. On the following days, I tried to hide but was forced to walk on my feet. Mother hit me on my hands and feet for resisting. Beatings and curses were my lot for covertly loosening the wrappings. The feet were washed and rebound after three or four days, with alum added. After several months, all toes but the big one were pressed against the inner surface. Whenever I ate fish or freshly killed meat, my feet would swell, and the pus would drip. Mother criticized me for placing pressure on the heel in walking, saying that my feet would never assume a pretty shape. Mother would remove the bindings and wipe the blood and pus which dripped from my feet. She told me that only with the removal of the flesh could my feet become slender. If I mistakenly punctured a sore, the blood gushed like a stream. My somewhat fleshy big toes were bound with small pieces of cloth and forced upwards, to assume a new-moon shape.

Every two weeks, I changed to new shoes. Each new pair was one- to two-tenths of an inch smaller than the previous one. The shoes were unyielding, and it took pressure to get into them. Though I wanted to sit passively by the K'ang, Mother forced me to move around. After changing more than ten pairs of shoes, my feet were reduced to a little over four inches. I had been in binding for a month when my younger sister started; when no one was around, we would weep together. In summer, my feet smelled offensively because of pus and blood; in winter, my feet felt cold because of lack of circulation and hurt if they got too near the K'ang and were struck by warm air currents. Four of the toes were curled in like so many dead caterpillars; no outsider would ever have believed that they belonged to a human being. It took two years to achieve the three-inch model. My toenails pressed against the flesh like thin paper. The heavily creased plantar couldn't be scratched when it itched or soothed when it ached. My shanks were thin, my feet became humped, ugly, and odiferous; how I envied the natural-footed![1]

Bound feet were crippled and excruciatingly painful. The woman was actually "walking" on the outside of toes which had been bent under into the sole of the foot. The heel and instep of the foot resembled the sole and heel of a high-heeled boot. Hard callouses formed; toenails grew into the skin; the feet were pus-filled and bloody; circulation was virtually stopped. The footbound woman hobbled along, leaning on a cane, against a wall, against a servant. To keep her balance she took very short steps. She was actually falling with every step and catching herself with the next. Walking required tremendous exertion.

Footbinding also distorted the natural lines of the female body. It caused the thighs and buttocks, which were always in a state of tension, to become somewhat swollen (which men called "voluptuous"). A curious belief developed among Chinese men that footbinding produced a most useful alteration of the vagina. A Chinese diplomat explained:

The smaller the woman's foot, the more wondrous become the folds of the vagina. (There was the saying: the smaller the feet, the more intense the sex urge.) Therefore marriages in Ta-t'ung (where binding is most effective) often take place earlier than elsewhere. Women in other districts can produce these folds artificially, but the only way is by footbinding, which concentrates development in this one place. There consequently develop layer after layer (of folds within the vagina); those who have personally experienced this (in sexual intercourse) feel a supernatural exaltation. So the system of footbinding was not really oppressive.[2]

Medical authorities confirm that physiologically footbinding had no effect whatsoever on the vagina, although it did distort the direction of the pelvis. The belief in the wondrous folds of the vagina of footbound women was pure mass delusion, a projection of lust onto the feet, buttocks, and vagina of the crippled female. Needless to say, the diplomat's rationale for finding footbinding "not really oppressive" confused his "supernatural exaltation" with her misery and mutilation.

...

One asks the same questions again and again, over a period of years, in the course of a lifetime. The questions have to do with people and what they do—the how and the why of it. How could the Germans have murdered 6,000,000 Jews, used their skins for lampshades, taken the gold out of their teeth? How could white people have bought and sold black people, hanged them and castrated them? How could "Americans" have slaughtered the Indian nations, stolen the land, spread famine and disease? How could the Indochina genocide continue, day after day, year after year? How is it possible? Why does it happen?

As a woman, one is forced to ask another series of hard questions: Why, everywhere, the oppression of women throughout recorded history? How could the Inquisitors torture and burn women as witches? How could men idealize the bound feet of crippled women? How and why?

The bound foot existed for 1,000 years. In what terms, using what measure, could one calculate the enormity of the crime, the dimensions of the transgression, the *amount* of cruelty and pain inherent in that 1,000-year herstory? In what terms, using what vocabulary, could one penetrate to the meaning, to the reality, of that 1,000-year herstory?

Here one race did not war with another to acquire food, or land, or civil power; one nation did not fight with another in the interest of survival, real or imagined; one group of people in a fever pitch of hysteria did not destroy another. None of the traditional explanations or justifications for brutality between or among peoples applies to this situation. On the contrary, here one sex mutilated (enslaved) the other in the interest of the *art* of sex, male-female *harmony,* role-definition, beauty.

Consider the magnitude of the crime.

Millions of women, over a period of 1,000 years, were brutally crippled, mutilated, in the name of erotica.

Millions of human beings, over a period of 1,000 years, were brutally crippled, mutilated, in the name of beauty.

Millions of men, over a period of 1,000 years, reveled in love-making devoted to the worship of the bound foot.

Millions of men, over a period of 1,000 years, worshiped and adored the bound foot.

Millions of mothers, over a period of 1,000 years, brutally crippled and mutilated their daughters for the sake of a secure marriage.

Millions of mothers, over a period of 1,000 years, brutally crippled and mutilated their daughters in the name of beauty.

But this thousand-year period is only the tip of an awesome, fearful iceberg: an extreme and visible expression of romantic attitudes, processes, and values organically rooted in all cultures, then and now. It demonstrates that man's love for woman, his sexual adoration of her, his human definition of her, his delight and pleasure in her, require her negation: physical crippling and psychological lobotomy. That is the very nature of romantic love, which is the love based on polar role definitions, manifest in herstory as well as in fiction—he glories in her agony, he adores her deformity, he annihilates her freedom, he will have her as sex object, even if he must destroy the bones in her feet to do it. Brutality, sadism, and oppression emerge as the substantive core of the romantic ethos. That ethos is the warp and woof of culture was we know it.

Women should be beautiful. All repositories of cultural wisdom from King Solomon to King Hefner agree: women should be beautiful. It is the reverence for female beauty which informs the romantic ethos, gives it its energy and justification. Beauty is transformed into that golden ideal, Beauty—rapturous and abstract. Women must be beautiful and Woman is Beauty.

Notions of beauty always incorporate the whole of a given societal structure, are crystallizations of its values. A society with a well-defined aristocracy will have aristocratic standards of beauty. In Western "democracy" notions of beauty are "democratic": even if a woman is not born beautiful, she can make herself *attractive.*

The argument is not simply that some women are not beautiful, therefore it is not fair to judge women on the basis of physical beauty; or that men are not judged on that basis, therefore women also should not be judged on that basis; or that men should look for character in women; or that our standards of beauty are too parochial in and of themselves; or even that judging women according to their conformity to a standard of beauty serves to make them into products, chattels, differing from the farmer's favorite cow only in terms of literal form. The issue at stake is different, and crucial. Standards of beauty describe in precise terms the relationship that an individual will have to her own body. They prescribe her mobility, spontaneity, posture, gait, the uses to which she can put her body. *They define precisely the dimensions of her physical freedom.* And, of course, the relationship between physical freedom and psychological development, intellectual possibility, and creative potential is an umbilical one.

In our culture, not one part of a woman's body is left untouched, unaltered. No feature or extremity is spared the art, or pain, of improvement. Hair is dyed, lacquered, straightened, permanented; eyebrows are plucked, penciled, dyed; eyes are lined, mascaraed, shadowed; lashes are curled, or false—from head to toe, every feature of a woman's face, every section of her body, is subject to modification, alteration. This alteration is an ongoing, repetitive process. It is vital to the economy, the major substance of male–female role differentiation, the most immediate physical and psychological reality of being a woman. From the age of 11 or 12 until she dies, a woman will spend a large part of her time, money, and energy on binding, plucking, painting, and deodorizing herself. It is commonly and wrongly said that male transvestites through the use of makeup and costuming caricature the women they would

218

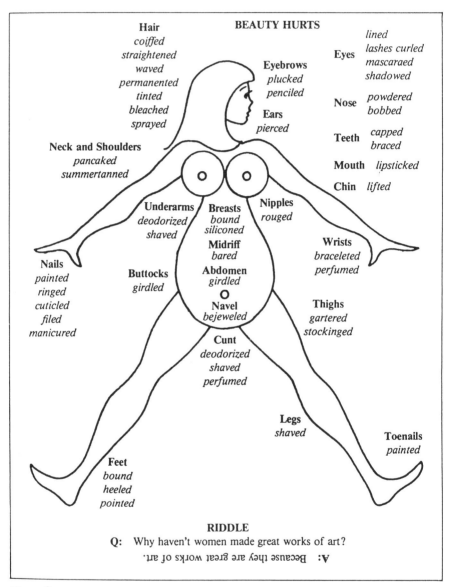

**BEAUTY HURTS**

**Hair**
*coiffed*
*straightened*
*waved*
*permanented*
*tinted*
*bleached*
*sprayed*

**Eyebrows**
*plucked*
*penciled*

**Ears**
*pierced*

**Eyes**
*lined*
*lashes curled*
*mascaraed*
*shadowed*

**Nose**
*powdered*
*bobbed*

**Teeth**
*capped*
*braced*

**Mouth** *lipsticked*

**Chin** *lifted*

**Neck and Shoulders**
*pancaked*
*summertanned*

**Underarms**
*deodorized*
*shaved*

**Breasts**
*bound*
*siliconed*

**Nipples**
*rouged*

**Midriff**
*bared*

**Wrists**
*braceleted*
*perfumed*

**Nails**
*painted*
*ringed*
*cuticled*
*filed*
*manicured*

**Buttocks**
*girdled*

**Abdomen**
*girdled*

**Navel**
*bejeweled*

**Thighs**
*gartered*
*stockinged*

**Cunt**
*deodorized*
*shaved*
*perfumed*

**Legs**
*shaved*

**Toenails**
*painted*

**Feet**
*bound*
*heeled*
*pointed*

**RIDDLE**
Q:  Why haven't women made great works of art?
A:  Because they are great works of art.

Figure 2

become, but any real knowledge of the romantic ethos makes clear that these men have penetrated to the core experience of being a woman, a romanticized construct.

The technology of beauty, and the message it carries, is handed down from mother to daughter. Mother teaches daughter to apply lipstick, to shave under her arms, to bind her breasts, to wear a girdle and high-heeled shoes. Mother teaches daughter concomitantly her role, her appropriate behavior, her place. Mother teaches daughter, necessarily, the psychology which defines womanhood: a woman must be beautiful, in order to please the amorphous and amorous Him. What we have called the romantic ethos operates as vividly in 20th-century America and Europe as it did in 10th-century China.

This cultural transfer of technology, role, and psychology virtually affects the emotive relationship between mother and daughter. It contributes substantially to the ambivalent love-hate dynamics of that relationship. What must the Chinese daughter/child have felt toward the mother who bound her feet? What does any daughter/child feel toward the mother who forces her to do painful things to her own body? The mother takes on the role of enforcer: she uses seduction, command, all manner of force to coerce the daughter to conform to the demands of the culture. It is because this role becomes her dominant role in the mother–daughter relationship that tensions and difficulties between mothers and daughters are so often unresolvable. The daughter who rejects the cultural norms enforced by the mother is forced to a basic rejection of her own mother, a recognition of the hatred and resentment she felt toward that mother, an alienation from mother and society so extreme that her own womanhood is denied by both. The daughter who internalizes those values and endorses those same processes is bound to repeat the teaching she was taught—her anger and resentment remain subterranean, channeled against her own female offspring as well as her mother.

Pain is an essential part of the grooming process, and that is not accidental. Plucking the eyebrows, shaving under the arms, wearing a girdle, learning to walk in high-heeled shoes, having one's nose fixed, straightening or curling one's hair—these things *hurt*. The pain, of course, teaches an important lesson: no price is too great, no process too repulsive, no operation too painful for the woman who would be beautiful. *The tolerance of pain and the romanticization of that tolerance begins here,* in preadolescence, in socialization, and serves to prepare women for lives of childbearing, self-abnegation, and husband-pleasing. The adolescent experience of the "pain of being a woman" casts the feminine psyche into a masochistic mold and forces the adolescent to conform to a self-image which bases itself on mutilation of the body, pain happily suffered, and restricted physical mobility. It creates the masochistic personalities generally found in adult women: subservient, materialistic (since all value is placed on the body and its ornamentation), intellectually restricted, creatively impoverished. It forces women to be a sex of lesser accomplishment, weaker, as underdeveloped as any backward nation. Indeed, the effects of that prescribed relationship between women and their bodies are so extreme, so deep, so extensive, that scarcely any area of human possibility is left untouched by it.

Men, of course, like a woman who "takes care of herself." The male response to the woman who is made up and bound is a learned fetish, societal in its dimensions. One need only refer to the male idealization of the bound foot and say that the same dynamic is operating here. Romance based on role differentiation, superiority based on a culturally determined and rigidly enforced inferiority, shame and guilt and fear of women and sex itself: all necessitate the perpetuation of these oppressive grooming imperatives.

The meaning of this analysis of the romantic ethos surely is clear. A first step in the process of liberation (women from their oppression, men from the unfreedom of their fetishism) is the radical redefining of the relationship between women and their bodies. The body must be freed, liberated, quite literally: from paint and girdles and all varieties of crap. Women must stop mutilating their bodies and start living in them. Perhaps the notion of beauty which will then organically emerge will be truly democratic and demonstrate a respect for human life in its infinite, and most honorable, variety.

---

### Notes

1. Howard S. Levy, *Chinese footbinding: The history of a curious erotic custom* (New York: W. Rawls, 1966), p. 39. …

2. Ibid., p. 141.

# *"Do Something About Your Weight"*

## Carol Schmidt

"You have such a pretty face—why don't you do something about your weight?" "Don't you know the medical consequences of obesity? Do something about your weight," or "We can't hire you until you do something about your weight." The usual criticisms fat women hear imply that it is *possible* to "do something about your weight." I tried. Everything known to medical science: intestinal bypass and stomach stapling and total fasting and pills and shots and hypnosis and diet candies and 15 stints at Weight Watchers and almost as many at Overeaters Anonymous … No one ever told me to "do something" about my green eyes or brown hair or 5′8″ frame, only about the 300 pounds, give or take 100 pounds at any one time, on that frame.

Only the fat liberation movement accepts the idea that obese people don't have much of a choice—except at some stage to finally accept that we will never be thin, and urge people to stop lining the wallets of the diet industry anymore. The side effects of attempting to lose weight by almost every method can be worse than the "problem," which is mainly in the eyes of the beholder anyway. If there were no discrimination against fat people, almost all my problems would be solved—except for the remaining consequences of the "choices" I've made in my life-long struggle to be thin. I've always lost—not weight, but other valuables, mainly my health.

…

In 1975 I was married and living in Los Angeles with a "hippie" style hubby who worked part-time in a tropical fish store that dealt drugs on the side, and I was trapped in a job at a medical journal publishing house where I could hide out in a back office and interview doctors by phone for my articles. At this point I decided to once and for all "do something about my weight." That something was intestinal bypass surgery, and I was not one of the 1–6% who die outright on the operating table in this surgery, though that was a chance I was willing to take. I was that miserable. More than anything it was the economic discrimination—I was stuck in that back office making $1000 a month less than I deserved for the rest of my life unless I did "something." Who knew the consequences? Who was told all the consequences? But as I said, I wouldn't have cared—but I did have a choice—I had been able to get a job, and had medical insurance. A lot of fat women have absolutely no chances at employment and cannot be covered by medical insurance. I've had to make a lot of decisions about my life based around how I could still hold on to health insurance; I am sure I would be doing better self-employed as a writer, or at least would be happier, but in this age of massive health costs and due to my past health record, I am tied to my insurance plan. This is a common thread in the lives of differently abled women.

After the intestinal bypass surgery, I wanted to die—from the hemorrhoids. Who would have thought that undigested food racing through only 14 inches of small intestine, in big chunks with pure stomach acid, would rip through the bowels and explode in diarrhea that tore open the blood vessels? I spent three weeks almost nonstop on the toilet crying. My husband went out and had an affair.

Then it was wonderful—I became a spokesperson for the joys of intestinal bypass! I lost 165 pounds, and all was well—until the odor started.

Apparently a lot of bypass patients develop infections in the bypassed 22 feet of small intestine, which is just lying there, waiting in case it must someday be reconnected (today almost all bypass patients have been reconnected and almost no one still does the surgery). The diarrhea had always smelled, but now there was something else. A terrible odor, that came out of my mouth and every pore and drove people away. I couldn't go to the bathroom at work—I had to drive home for every bout of diarrhea. No one came into my office—my editors worked with me by phone. I didn't even know that I had the odor until finally my therapist told me, and worked with me on a plan to attack the problem. My doctor didn't believe the problem existed, in his nicely aerated, air conditioned office—and the odor would come and go, to make it worse. I never knew if I smelled or not. I took a friend to the theatre and had to sit on the steps by the door, because the people around me were gagging and leaving the theatre, and my friend couldn't drive home with me with all the car windows wide open.

After hundreds of remedies, I discovered that one medication, flagyl, stopped the odor—but then it was implicated in breast cancer, and no one was supposed to take more than one or two doses a year. I had been on it for months. I transferred to tetracycline, raising to higher and higher doses, until I was taking 3000 milligrams a day. This was a good period in my life, despite working my schedule around the timing for the tetracycline, which I could only take when I had not eaten or had any milk for many hours, nor planned any food intake.

My husband couldn't take the changes, or my newly awakened sexuality, or the fact that now I was clearly superior to him in many arenas. He moved out. I got a divorce and did a complete changearound and obtained my present job, when I was "down" to 185 lbs, the thinnest I had ever been since age 14.

Then a new lover told me I smelled, and I realized the tetracycline no longer worked. Nothing new worked. No doctor in the country knew what to do about this medical complication of intestinal bypass, which was cropping up in patient after patient. I made an appointment to have the bypass reversed and stomach stapling substituted.

Stomach stapling was the new wonder operation, for those of us who finally decided to "do something about our weight." There are several approaches, with slightly different names, but they all involved the principle of either stapling most of the stomach shut so that only a tiny amount of food can be eaten at one time, or wrapping the stomach or both. I had both. Somewhere during the operation my stomach perforated. This is the same as a bullet wound inside the stomach—gallons of unclean food particles mixed with stomach acids shot through my abdomen. This caused peritonitis.

I almost died. The doctor told my lover and sister I had an 80% chance of dying in the second surgery to repair the perforated stomach, and then I might not make it through the infections to follow. I did.

I don't even want to think about the month in the hospital, the weeks in intensive care, unable to talk because of the tube down my throat, my friends and loved ones trying not to show how scared they were. An attorney came in and had me sign some legal papers in case I died; I didn't have a will (I do now, and recommend them to all women, no matter how healthy).

...

All of my life has a quite different perspective today. The health problems did not end once I healed from that operation—I developed a massive hernia that made me look ten months pregnant, a huge disfigurement. No surgeon wanted to operate, because my insides were a mass of adhesions and scar tissues, but I finally found one who would. I have been ordered not to gain a single pound because the hernia repair (which involved putting in an 18-inch-square piece of strong mesh under the skin to keep in the intestines) could rip open. I am again trying to "do something about my weight."

I do not lack discipline—I work hard, I've accomplished a lot in my life, especially considering my background and my fat. I don't even have to justify to anyone why I do not fit the stereotype of fat women—it's the stereotype which is wrong. And too many feminists and our supposed political allies hold the stereotype just as strongly as those we know do not understand. I go out to dinner with a radical feminist who happens to be thin and I see she is watching every bite I eat and mentally counting calories for me—and it is not my paranoia which makes me think this. I have checked it out with some people, and they shamefacedly admit it—if they don't take the opportunity to tell me *I* should be doing it.

There are no real choices for obese people, and other differently abled people, at least not the range of choices that many others have. We do the best we can with what we've got, considering what we can and cannot do, and stretch the boundaries at all times, attempting to distinguish the real limitations from those which we or others impose on us. Sometimes it is an entirely different ballpark from the game being played by those who tell *us* to "do something" about a problem that makes *them* uncomfortable.

---

# *Hunger*

## Naomi Wolf

...

The weight-loss cult recruits women from an early age, and eating diseases are the cult's bequest. Anorexia and bulimia are female maladies: From 90 to 95 percent of anorexics and bulimics are women. America, which has the greatest number of women who have made it into the male sphere, also leads the world with female anorexia. Women's magazines report that there are up to a million American anorexics, but the American Anorexia and Bulimia Association states that anorexia and bulimia strike a million American women *every year;* 30,000, it reports, also become emetic abusers.

...

… Of ten young American women in college, two will be anorexic and six will be bulimic; only two will be well. The norm, then, for young, middle-class American women, is to be a sufferer from some form of the eating disease.

The disease is a deadly one. Brumberg reports that 5 to 15 percent of hospitalized anorexics die in treatment, giving the disease one of the highest fatality rates for a mental illness. … Forty to 50 percent of anorexics never recover completely, a worse rate of recovery from starvation than the 66 percent recovery rate for famine victims hospitalized in the war-torn Netherlands in 1944–45.

The medical effects of anorexia include hypothermia, edema, hypotension, brady-cardia (impaired heartbeat), lanugo (growth of body hair), infertility, and death. The medical effects of bulimia include dehydration, electrolyte imbalance, epileptic sei-zure, abnormal heart rhythm, and death. When the two are combined, they can re-sult in tooth erosion, hiatal hernia, abraded esophagus, kidney failure, osteoporosis, and death. Medical literature is starting to report that babies and children underfed by weight-conscious mothers are suffering from stunted growth, delayed puberty, and failure to thrive.

It is spreading to other industrialized nations: The United Kingdom now has 3.5 million anorexics or bulimics (95 percent of them female), with 6,000 new cases yearly. Another study of adolescent British girls alone shows that 1 percent are now anorexic. According to the women's press, at least 50 percent of British women suffer from disordered eating. Hilde Bruch states that in the last generation, larger patient groups have been reported in publications in Russia, Australia, Sweden, and Italy as well as Great Britain and the United States. Sweden's rate is now 1 to 2 percent of teenage girls, with the same percentage of women over sixteen being bulimic. The rate for the Netherlands is 1 to 2 percent; of Italian teenagers also, 1 percent suffer from anorexia or bulimia (95 percent of them female), a rise of 400 percent in ten years. That is just the beginning for Western Europe and Japan, since the figures re-semble numbers for the United States ten years ago, and since the rate is rising, as it did in America, exponentially. The anorexic patient herself is *thinner* now than were previous generations of patients. Anorexia followed the familiar beauty myth pattern of movement: It began as a middle-class disease in the United States and has spread eastward as well as down the social ladder.

Some women's magazines report that 60 percent of American women have serious trouble eating. The majority of middle-class women in the United States, it appears, suffer a version of anorexia or bulimia; but if anorexia is defined as a compulsive fear of and fixation upon food, perhaps most Western women can be called, twenty years into the backlash, mental anorexics.

What happened? Why now? … Until seventy-five years ago in the male artistic tra-dition of the West, women's natural amplitude was their beauty; representations of the female nude reveled in women's lush fertility. Various distributions of sexual fat were emphasized according to fashion—big, ripe bellies from the fifteenth to the sev-enteenth centuries, plump faces and shoulders in the early nineteenth, progressively generous dimpled buttocks and thighs until the twentieth—but never, until women's emancipation entered law, this absolute negation of the female state that fashion historian Ann Hollander in *Seeing Through Clothes* characterizes, from the point of view of any age but our own, as "the look of sickness, the look of poverty, and the look of nervous exhaustion."

Dieting and thinness began to be female preoccupations when Western women received the vote around 1920; between 1918 and 1925, "the rapidity with which the new, linear form replaced the more curvaceous one is startling." In the regressive 1950s, women's natural fullness could be briefly enjoyed once more because their minds were occupied in domestic seclusion. But when women came en masse into male spheres, that pleasure had to be overridden by an urgent social expedient that would make women's bodies into the prisons that their homes no longer were.

A generation ago, the average model weighed 8 percent less than the average American woman, whereas today she weighs 23 percent less. Twiggy appeared in the pages of *Vogue* in 1965, simultaneous with the advent of the Pill, to cancel out its most radical implications. Like many beauty-myth symbols, she was double-edged, suggesting to women the freedom from the constraint of reproduction of earlier generations (since female fat is categorically understood by the subconscious as fertile sexuality), while reassuring men with her suggestion of female weakness, asexuality, and hunger. Her thinness, now commonplace, was shocking at the time; even *Vogue* introduced the model with anxiety: " 'Twiggy' is called Twiggy because she looks as though a strong gale would snap her in two and dash her to the ground ... Twiggy is of such a meagre constitution that other models stare at her. Her legs look as though she has not had enough milk as a baby and her face has that expression one feels Londoners wore in the blitz." The fashion writer's language is revealing: Undernurtured, subject to being overpowered by a strong wind, her expression the daze of the besieged, what better symbol to reassure an establishment faced with women who were soon to march tens of thousands strong down Fifth Avenue?

In the twenty years after the start of the second wave of the women's movement, the weight of Miss Americas plummeted, and the average weight of Playboy Playmates dropped from 11 percent below the national average in 1970 to 17 percent below it in eight years. Model Aimee Liu in her autobiography claims that many models are anorexic; she herself continued to model as an anorexic. Of dancers, 38 percent show anorexic behavior. The average model, dancer, or actress is thinner than 95 percent of the female population. ...

As a result, a 1985 survey says, 90 percent of respondents think they weigh too much. On any day, 25 percent of women are on diets, with 50 percent finishing, breaking, or starting one. This self-hatred was generated rapidly, coinciding with the women's movement: Between 1966 and 1969, two studies showed, the number of high school girls who thought they were too fat had risen from 50 to 80 percent. Though heiresses to the gains of the women's movement, their daughters are, in terms of this distress, no better off: In a recent study of high school girls, 53 percent were unhappy with their bodies by age thirteen; by age eighteen and over, 78 percent were dissatisfied. The hunger cult has won a major victory against women's fight for equality if the evidence of the 1984 *Glamour* survey of thirty-three thousand women is representative: 75 percent of those aged eighteen to thirty-five believed they were fat, while only 25 percent were medically overweight (the same percentage as men); 45 percent of the *underweight* women thought they were too fat. But more heart-breaking in terms of the way in which the myth is running to ground hopes for women's advancement and gratification, the *Glamour* respondents chose losing ten to fifteen pounds above success in work or in love as their most desired goal.

...

... If our culture's fixation on female fatness or thinness were about sex, it would be a private issue between a woman and her lover; if it were about health, between a woman and herself. Public debate would be far more hysterically focused on male fat than on female, since more men (40 percent) are medically overweight than women (32 percent) and too much fat is far more dangerous for men than for women. In fact, "there is very little evidence to support the claim that fatness causes poor health among women. ... The results of recent studies have suggested that women may in fact live longer and be generally healthier if they weigh ten to fifteen percent *above* the life-insurance figures *and* they refrain from dieting," asserts *Radiance;* when poor health is correlated to fatness in women, it is due to chronic dieting and the emotional stress of self-hatred. The National Institutes of Health studies that linked obesity to heart disease and stroke were based on male subjects; when a study of females was finally published in 1990, it showed that weight made only a fraction of the difference for women that it made for men. ...

But female fat is the subject of public passion, and women feel guilty about female fat, because we implicitly recognize that under the myth, women's bodies are not our own but society's, and that thinness is not a private aesthetic, but hunger a social concession exacted by the community. A cultural fixation on female thinness is not an obsession about female beauty but an obsession about female obedience. Women's dieting has become what Yale psychologist Judith Rodin calls a "normative obsession," a never-ending passion play given international coverage out of all proportion to the health risks associated with obesity, and using emotive language that does not figure even in discussions of alcohol or tobacco abuse. The nations seize with compulsive attention on this melodrama because women and men understand that it is not about cholesterol or heart rate or the disruption of a line of tailoring, but about how much social freedom women are going to get away with or concede. The media's convulsive analysis of the endless saga of female fat and the battle to vanquish it are actually bulletins of the sex war: what women are gaining or losing in it, and how fast.

...

... Women do not eat or starve only in a succession of private relationships, but within a public social order that has a material vested interest in their troubles with eating. Individual men don't "spin out fashionable images" ... ; multinational corporations do that. The many theories about women's food crises have stressed private psychology *to the neglect of* public policy, looking at women's shapes to see how they express a conflict about their society rather than looking at how their society makes use of a manufactured conflict with women's shapes. Many other theories have focused on women's reaction to the thin ideal, but have not asserted that the thin ideal is *proactive,* a preemptive strike.

We need to reexamine all the terms again, then, in the light of a public agenda. What, first, is food? Certainly, within the context of the intimate family, food is love, and memory, and language. But in the public realm, food is status and honor.

Food is the primal symbol of social worth. Whom a society values, it feeds well. The piled plate, the choicest cut, say: We think you're worth this much of the tribe's resources. Samoan women, who are held in high esteem, exaggerate how much they eat on feast days. Publicly apportioning food is about determining power relations, and sharing it is about cementing social equality: When men break bread together, or toast the queen, or slaughter for one another the fatted calf, they've become equals and then allies. The word *companion* comes from the Latin for "with" and "bread"—those who break bread together.

But under the beauty myth, now that all women's eating is a public issue, our portions testify to and reinforce our sense of social inferiority. If women cannot eat the same food as men, we cannot experience equal status in the community. As long as women are asked to bring a self-denying mentality to the communal table, it will never be round, men and women seated together; but the same traditional hierarchical dais, with a folding table for women at the foot.

In the current epidemic of rich Western women who cannot "choose" to eat, we see the continuation of an older, poorer tradition of women's relation to food. Modern Western female dieting descends from a long history. Women have always had to eat differently from men: less and worse. In Hellenistic Rome, reports classicist Sarah B. Pomeroy, boys were rationed sixteen measures of meal to twelve measures allotted to girls. In medieval France, according to historian John Boswell, women received two thirds of the grain allocated to men. Throughout history, when there is only so much to eat, women get little, or none: A common explanation among anthropologists for female infanticide is that food shortage provokes it. According to UN publications, where hunger goes, women meet it first: In Bangladesh and Botswana, female infants die more frequently than male, and girls are more often malnourished, because they are given smaller portions. In Turkey, India, Pakistan, North Africa, and the Middle East, men get the lion's share of what food there is, regardless of women's caloric needs. "It is not the caloric value of work which is represented in the patterns of food consumption" of men in relation to women in North Africa, "nor is it a question of physiological needs. ... Rather these patterns tend to guarantee priority rights to the 'important' members of society, that is, adult men." In Morocco, if women are guests, "they will swear they have eaten already" or that they are not hungry. "Small girls soon learn to offer their share to visitors, to refuse meat and deny hunger." A North African woman described by anthropologist Vanessa Mahler assured her fellow diners that "she preferred bones to meat." Men, however, Mahler reports, "are supposed to be exempt from facing scarcity which is shared out among women and children."

"Third World countries provide examples of undernourished female and well-nourished male children, where what food there is goes to the boys of the family," a

UN report testifies. Two thirds of women in Asia, half of all women in Africa, and a sixth of Latin American women are anemic—through lack of food. Fifty percent more Nepali women than men go blind from lack of food. Cross-culturally, men receive hot meals, more protein, and the first helpings of a dish, while women eat the cooling leftovers, often having to use deceit and cunning to get enough to eat. "Moreover, what food they do receive is consistently less nutritious."

This pattern is not restricted to the Third World: Most Western women alive today can recall versions of it at their mothers' or grandmothers' table: British miners' wives eating the grease-soaked bread left over after their husbands had eaten the meat; Italian and Jewish wives taking the part of the bird no one else would want.

These patterns of behavior are standard in the affluent West today, perpetuated by the culture of female caloric self-deprivation. A generation ago, the justification for this traditional apportioning shifted: Women still went without, ate leftovers, hoarded food, used deceit to get it—but blamed themselves. Our mothers still exiled themselves from the family circle that was eating cake with silver cutlery off Wedgwood china, and we would come upon them in the kitchen, furtively devouring the remains. The traditional pattern was cloaked in modern shame, but otherwise changed little. Weight control became its rationale once natural inferiority went out of fashion.

The affluent West is merely carrying on this traditional apportioning. Researchers found that parents in the United States urged boys to eat, regardless of their weight, while they did so with daughters only if they were relatively thin. In a sample of babies of both sexes, 99 percent of the boys were breast-fed, but only 66 percent of the girls, who were given 50 percent less time to feed. "Thus," writes Susie Orbach, "daughters are often fed less well, less attentively and less sensitively than they need." Women do not feel entitled to enough food because they have been taught to go with less than they need since birth, in a tradition passed down through an endless line of mothers; the public role of "honored guest" is new to us, and the culture is telling us through the ideology of caloric restriction that we are not welcome finally to occupy it.

...

Now, if female fat is sexuality and reproductive power; if food is honor; if dieting is semistarvation; if women have to lose 23 percent of their body weight ... and chronic psychological disruption sets in at a body weight loss of 25 percent; if semistarvation is physically and psychologically debilitating, and female strength, sexuality, and self-respect pose the threats explored earlier against the vested interests of society; if women's journalism is sponsored by a $33-billion industry whose capital is made out of the political fear of women; then we can understand ... the thin "ideal" ... [it] is beautiful as a political solution.

...

The ideology of semistarvation undoes feminism; what happens to women's bodies happens to our minds. If women's bodies are and have always been wrong whereas men's are right, then women are wrong and men are right. Where feminism taught women to put a higher value on ourselves, hunger teaches us how to erode our self-esteem. If a woman can be made to say, "I hate my fat thighs," it is a way she has been made to hate femaleness. The more financially independent, in control of events, educated and sexually autonomous women become in the world, the more impoverished, out of control, foolish, and sexually insecure we are asked to feel in our bodies.

…

---

### References

Bruch, Hilde; Danita Czyzewski; and Melanie A. Suhr, eds. *Conversations with Anorexics*. New York: Basic Books, 1988.
Brumberg, Joan Jacobs. *Fasting Girls: The Emergence of Anorexia Nervosa as a Modern Disease.* Cambridge, Mass.: Harvard University Press, 1988.
Hollander, Ann. *Seeing Through Clothes*. New York: Penguin, 1988.
Orbach, Susie. *Fat Is a Feminist Issue.* London: Hamlyn, 1979.
_____. *Hunger Strike: The Anorexic's Struggle as a Metaphor for our Age.* London: Faber and Faber, 1986 (especially pp. 74–95).
Pomeroy, Sarah B. *Goddesses, Whores, Wives and Slaves: Women in Classical Antiquity.* New York: Schocken Books, 1975.

# *Skin Deep*

## Wendy Chapkis

"Mirror, mirror on the wall, who is the fairest of them all?" As children we accept that "the fairest" is the same sort of measure as the fastest, the tallest or the richest. Later, in the growing sophistication of adulthood, we determine that the most beautiful is more like the bravest, the most popular or the most powerful. It becomes a judgement about which one might have an *opinion* but remains a quality that ultimately can be established by an independent and attentive authority. "Ladies and Gentlemen, the judges have reached a decision. The new Miss World is. …"

Adults thus continue to pose the question "who is the fairest" as though it were meaningful, even when the category of "them all" includes women of diverse races and nationalities. Indeed female beauty is becoming an increasingly standardized quality throughout the world. A standard so strikingly white, Western and wealthy it is tempting to conclude there must be a conscious conspiracy afoot.

But in fact no hidden plot is needed to explain the pervasiveness of this image. The fantasy of the Good Life populated by Beautiful People wearing The Look has seized the imagination of much of the world. This Western model of beauty represents a mandate for a way of life for women throughout the world regardless of how unrelated to each of our ethnic or economic possibilities it is. We invest a great deal in the fantasy, perhaps all the more, the further we are from being able to attain it. This international fantasy becomes the basis of our myths of eroticism, success and adventure.

It is "Charlie's Angels" (women on a 1970s U.S. TV show) who appear to have a good time in the world, not women who are fat or small or dark-skinned. As the center of a world economic system, the U.S. owns the biggest share of the global culture machine. By entering that world in imagination, each woman aims to be whiter, more Western, more upper class. This goes beyond simple manipulation.

While the Hearst Corporation is trying to maximize profits on a global scale, that does not fully explain *Cosmopolitan's* popularity in seventeen languages around the world. The Cosmo package seems to offer everything: sexuality, success, independence and beauty. It is powerful and compelling. A woman working all day making microchips who buys lipstick or cigarettes is buying some tiny sense of dignity and self-esteem along with the glamour.

…

A "consumer-driven" view of marketing means focusing on that segment of any society likely to purchase a given product. For many products, in particular luxury items, the potential market in large parts of the world remains extremely limited. It is certainly true that members of these national elites often more closely resemble their counterparts in other countries than they do their own less affluent compatriots.

In turn, the upper class serves as the model of success and glamour for the rest of the nation. All the pieces of the picture begin to fit neatly together, confirming that there is but one vision of beauty. The woman on the imported American television program resembles the woman in the Clairol ad resembles the wife of the Prime Minister or industrial magnate who dresses in the latest French fashion as faithfully reported in the local version of *Cosmopolitan*.

…

Naturally, this trend toward global cultural homogenization has not gone unchallenged. Indigenous culture remains a powerful alternative to the white Western model of success and beauty. In some countries, traditional images are officially promoted as a response to the flood of imported Western culture. In other countries, local culture acts subversively as the bearer of otherwise illegal messages of political, economic and cultural resistance.

Following the Sandinista victory over the Somoza dictatorship in Nicaragua, sexist advertising was banned. If a woman now appears in an advertisement, there must be a reason other than providing a sexual come-on to the potential buyer. While *Vanidades* and *Cosmopolitan,* with their transnational advertising, can still be purchased in Managua, the local billboards do not offer images of the wealthy white glamour girl.

Another, although very different reaction to Western sexualized imagery of women, is evidenced in the Islamic countries of North Africa and the Middle East. A dramatic symbol of religious, national and patriarchal culture, the veil, is increasingly being adopted by women in these countries. The use of the veil to reclaim (and in some cases to re-invent) indigenous culture is clearly problematic but hardly inexplicable. Shortly before the overthrow of the Shah in Iran, the most popular women's magazine in that country was *Zan-e Ruz* (*Women of Today*) with a circulation of over 100,000. The periodical was filled with love stories starring blonde, blue-eyed heroines lifted directly from Western magazines. Of the 35 percent of the periodical taken up with ads, much focused on beauty and cosmetic products again often featuring blonde models. One researcher observed "the great stress on physical appearance in a situation of acute sexual repression is … somehow ironic."[1] More than ironic, the resulting tensions may have helped encourage both the Islamic revival and the subsequent return to the veil.

Significantly, while the veil may be an important and visible symbol of resistance to Western culture and values, it is worn by women only. Women throughout the world tend to be designated as culture bearers and given the burdensome responsibility of preserving traditional values and aesthetics. In recent studies in several African countries, researchers discovered that women were seen both as repositories of traditional culture and those most likely to succumb to Western influences. Women in Uganda, for example, were seen as:

> … scapegoats not only for male confusion and conflict over what the contemporary roles of women should be, but for the dilemmas produced by adjusting to rapid social change. Where men have given up traditional customs and restraints on dress, but feel traitors to their own culture, they yearn for the security and compensation of at least knowing that women are loyal to it.[2]

In much the same way, women in Zambia have been held responsible "when the state of morality was chaotic …" and when cultural traditions became "contaminated by Western influence." Unfortunately, women of the Third World single-handedly can no more turn back Western cultural domination than they can be held responsible for its powerful and enduring influence. And while women certainly *are* at the forefront of many forms of resistance including the cultural, "tradition" may not be the only element women will choose to draw on in creating a culture that speaks of and to their lives.

…

---

### Notes

1. Obbo, Christine, *African Women: their struggle for economic independence*, Zed Press, London 1980.

2. Glazer Shuste, Ilse, *New Women of Lusaka*, Mayfield, Palo Alto, California, 1979, cited in Gallagher, *Unequal Opportunities: the case of women and the media*, UNESCO, 1981, p. 59.

# *Marieme*

## Interview by Wendy Chapkis

*"Women are just the make-up for our societies in change"*

The issue of the veil in Algeria is a lot more complicated than you might think. Most Algerians are Berbers, and though women are supposed to have something covering their hair, in Berber culture there is no such thing as a veil. Still, if you go to the big cities these days everybody seems to be wearing one. Islamic fundamentalists have recently been responsible for the pressure on women to take up the veil, but the veil is more than a religious symbol. It has historical, political and class significance as well. For instance, when a man is promoted and moves his family from the village to the city, the woman tends to take up the veil as a symbol of city life and of her husband's success. When she returns to her village for a visit, she wears the veil to show her friends that she has moved up on the class ladder.

It has also been used as a symbol of cultural resistance to French colonialism. Before the start of the Algerian fight for independence from France in 1954, the veil was only worn in the cities and not at all in the countryside. Yet the image of the Algerian woman as seen through the French colonialist's eyes was of a woman who had to be freed from the veil.

In May 1958, after Algerie Française supporters in the army brought De Gaulle to power, peasant women were brought to Algiers to demonstrate support for what the French called fraternalization. These women were asked to publicly unveil and burn their veils as a symbol of their emancipation through Western culture. The idea was to show the French colonizer liberating Algerian women from our backward traditions.

So of course many young women of my generation—the generation of the liberation struggle—adopted the veil for the first time during the fight for independence. There was a whole ideology attached to it articulated by Frantz Fanon. I now find it all very painful. I mean, he really managed to mystify the veil for a lot of us.

Certainly the French used the veil as a symbol, but it was an extremely simplistic response for us to react by reclaiming the veil as our own. I think it made it more

possible to tame the demands of women in favor of other priorities—national liberation, class struggle, tradition.

During the period of colonialism when we were faced with tremendous violence
and violation, the most urgent task was to put an end to it. Many different political
groups joined together in a common front, but each kept enough autonomy to be
able to pursue its own political objectives within the front—except for women. We
weren't well enough organized before hand so it was far too easy to confuse us with
talk of priorities and involve us in blind support of traditions for the sake of a supposedly classless and genderless nation. Women came to bear the burden of keeping
up traditions and guarding the national identity. Finally, it became part of a whole
process of pushing women back to the most repressive kinds of traditions.

You always have to look at the idea of tradition in terms of power. What is handed
down to women as traditional is rarely in our favor. I don't mean that there aren't aspects of our indigenous culture that we will want to draw from, but even then, it
should never be seen as a fixed and sacred thing. Just show me a time when tradition
was "pure" and a-historical. Culture is not fixed in the past, unchanging and unchangeable. Tradition is constantly evolving.

So, in talking about the veil, you have to first recognize its complicated and ambiguous history. At one time, ten years ago or so, the veil did provide young Algerian
women with the opportunity to do more in the world. If they came from very traditional families, wearing a veil was the only way to be allowed to leave the house and
attend secondary school. It was good to be able to send girls to school and to the university, even at that cost.

But there is a price to be paid. And now the veil is clearly less and less progressive.
So why should we defend it simply because it has some complicated relationship to
tradition? Most of those people currently pushing for the veil in Algeria are religious
fundamentalists. They certainly don't see the veil as a means to increase the options
for women in the world. No, it is just part of the Islamic tradition.

Those in power are always very selective about the aspects of indigenous culture
they wish to preserve as traditional. At the same time that the state argues that it
wishes to use tradition to maintain a national identity, it is frantically pursuing modernization through industry and development. Those changes are considered acceptable; everyone agrees that our economy must modernize.

What is not accepted is that the outside image should change. And that image is
supposed to be synonymous with identity. But for me, that is only make-up. And
women are to be the make-up while men get to live in the real world.

In the summer of 1970, the first and only Pan-African Cultural Festival took place
in Algiers. It included a symposium on African culture. The delegate from Ghana
made a speech in which he attacked the idea of "negritude." He noted that while African elites were seeking Western industrial development and economic links to the
West, they wanted the lower classes to be in charge of preserving indigenous culture.
He said something to the effect of: you want them to be the niggers while you yourselves try to be Westerners. It was an historic event, the first public critique of negri-

tude. I remember being delighted because I thought this can be applied word for word to the situation of women.

We are just the make-up for our societies in change. Whether the state has socialist pretentions, as in Algeria, or is a monarchy like Morocco or is openly Westernized like Tunisia, women are in charge of preserving tradition. And the result is continued subservience.

The women I know who have adopted the veil in recent years are most often true believers in Islam. They are very honest people who fall into the arms of the fundamentalists without understanding that they are falling into the arms of the extreme right. The fundamentalists have money—a tremendous amount of money—and an international organization behind them. And they're important because they are the only ones dealing with the real needs of the people. The left doesn't, nor does the government.

The fundamentalists are the ones who provide basic cereals, who create mosques in every building, who distribute clothing. And the clothes they provide are, naturally, Islamic. For women they are in the Iranian fashion covering the entire body with something like the chador. They can encourage the use of the veil simply by giving clothing away or providing it at a very low cost.

In Algeria we don't have a huge media industry with glossy advertisements. The message of how a woman should look passes through political institutions not through the media. These channels are difficult to locate and describe. It might be an article in the paper, or a speech by an official, on what the Algerian woman should be. And of course it comes through everyday repression telling you what a woman should not be.

When women began wearing mini's (and that was not what you would call a mini; it was a knee length dress) we were beaten in the streets by young, very violent fundamentalists. This also happened when women tried to adopt the maxi fashion. Because fashion of any kind is seen as a way of focusing attention on a woman and that is exactly what is not to be done.

# *The Myth of the Perfect Body*

## Roberta Galler

A woman was experiencing severe abdominal pain. She was rushed to the emergency room and examined, then taken to the operating room, where an appendectomy was performed. After surgery, doctors concluded that her appendix was fine but that she had VD. It never occurred to them that this woman had a sexual life at all, because she was in a wheelchair.

> I saw a woman who had cerebral palsy at a neuro-muscular clinic. She was covered with bruises. After talking with her, it became clear that she was a battered wife. I brought her case to the attention of the medical director and social worker, both progressive practitioners who are knowledgeable about resources for battered women. They said, "But he supports her. Who else will take care of her? And besides, if she complains, the court might take custody of her children."

As a feminist and psychotherapist I am politically and professionally interested in the impact of body image on a woman's self-esteem and sense of sexuality. However, it is as a woman with a disability that I am personally involved with these issues. I had polio when I was 10 years old, and now with arthritis and some new aches and pains I feel in a rather exaggerated fashion the effects of aging, a progressive disability we all share to some degree.

Although I've been disabled since childhood, until the past few years I didn't know anyone else with a disability and in fact *avoided* knowing anyone with a disability. I had many of the same fears and anxieties which many of you who are currently able-bodied might feel about close association with anyone with a disability. I had not opted for, but in fact rebelled against the prescribed role of dependence expected of women growing up when I did and which is still expected of disabled women. I became the "exceptional" woman, the "super-crip," noted for her independence. I refused to let my identity be shaped by my disability. I wanted to be known for *who* I am and not just by what I physically cannot do.

Although I was not particularly conscious of it at the time, I was additionally burdened with extensive conflicts about dependency and feelings of shame over my own imperfections and realistic limitations. So much of my image and definition of myself had been rooted in a denial of the impact of my disability. Unfortunately, my values and emphasis on independence involved an assumption that any form of help implied dependence and was therefore humiliating.

As the aging process accelerated the impact of my disability, it became more difficult to be stoic or heroic or ignore my increased need for help at times. This personal crisis coincided in time with the growing national political organization of disabled persons who were asserting their rights, demanding changes in public consciousness and social policy, and working to remove environmental and attitudinal barriers to the potential viability of their lives.[1]

Disabled women also began a dialogue within the feminist community. ... Through mutual support and self-disclosure, [we] began to explore our feelings and to shed the shame and humiliation associated with needing help. We began to understand that to need help did not imply helplessness nor was it the opposite of independence. This increased appreciation of mutual interdependence as part of the human condition caused us to reexamine the feminist idea of autonomy versus dependence.

Feminists have long attacked the media image of "the Body Beautiful" as oppressive, exploitative, and objectifying. Even in our attempts to create alternatives, however, we develop standards which oppress some of us. The feminist ideal of autonomy does not take into account the realistic needs for help that disabled, aging—and, in fact, most—women have. The image of the physically strong "superwoman" is also out of reach for most of us.

As we began to develop disability consciousness, we recognized significant parallels to feminist consciousness. For example, it is clear that just as society creates an ideal of beauty which is oppressive for us all, it creates an ideal model of the physically perfect person who is not beset with weakness, loss, or pain. It is toward these distorted ideals of perfection in form and function that we all strive and with which we identify.

The disabled (and aging) woman poses a symbolic threat by reminding us how tenuous that model, "the myth of the perfect body," really is, and we might want to run from this thought. The disabled woman's body may not meet the standard of "perfection" in either image, form, or function. On the one hand, disabled women share the social stereotype of women in general as being weak and passive, and in fact are depicted as the epitome of the incompetent female. On the other hand, disabled women are not viewed as women at all, but portrayed as helpless, dependent children in need of protection. She is not seen as the sexy, but the sexless object, asexual, neutered, unbeautiful and unable to find a lover. This stigmatized view of the disabled woman reflects a perception of assumed inadequacy on the part of the non-disabled.

For instance, disabled women are often advised by professionals not to bear children, and are (within race and class groupings) more likely to be threatened by or be victims of involuntary sterilization. Concerns for reproductive freedom and child custody, as well as rape and domestic violence often exclude the disabled woman by assuming her to be an asexual creature. The perception that a disabled woman couldn't possibly get a man to care for or take care of her underlies the instances where professionals have urged disabled women who have been victims of brutal battery to stay with abusive males. Members of the helping professions often assume that no other men would want them.

Disability is often associated with sin, stigma and a kind of "untouchability." Anxiety, as well as a sense of vulnerability and dread, may cause others to respond to the "imperfections" of a disabled woman's body with terror, avoidance, pity and/or guilt.
…

…

These discomforts may evoke a wish that disabled women remain invisible and that their sexuality be a hidden secret. However, disabled (and aging) women are coming out; we are beginning to examine our issues publicly, forcing other women to address not only the issues of disability but to reexamine their attitudes toward their own limitations and lack of perfection, toward oppressive myths, standards, and social conditions which affect us all. …

In more direct and personal terms, to be a feminist with disability consciousness, or to be a friend or lover of a woman with a disability, you need to be aware of and include the limitations that disability places on her and on you. You must honor the reality of her oppression in the able-bodied world. You must join with her in the fight against external constraints and social injustice in the fields of employment, housing, and transportation accessibility. Feminist events should be accessible, and feminist issues expanded to include the specific concerns of disabled women.[2]

…

Even in the changing political climate of women challenging traditional options, if a disabled woman should decide to opt for a nontraditional or independent lifestyle, such as single motherhood, a professional career, or lesbianism, she is often not regarded as having made a choice but it perceived as not having a choice. For disabled women, "lifestyle, sexual preference and personal decisions are viewed as consequences of the disability rather than as choices."[3]

By emphasizing the external restraints, social stereotypes and perceptions of others, I do not mean to minimize the significance of the internal world of the disabled woman or her own sense of self-esteem and personal worth. Parallel to women's feelings about their fatness, … disabled women also often have a tendency to blame themselves, or imagine that if only they were different, better, and perfect, they would be good enough to do the impossible. Sometimes, like fat, disability can stand for everything a disabled woman feels to be bad about herself and is the focus of low self-esteem, embodying feelings of being damaged, inadequate, unworthy, and unlovable.

As women, we all know that constantly running into external barriers reduces a sense of self-worth. The expectations of others become part of the self-concept and self-expectation. This may perpetuate psychological sense of invisibility, self-estrangement, powerlessness, worthlessness, and lack of sexual entitlement among disabled women.

Society's standards of beauty and acceptability are embedded in our initial interactions with parents, caretakers, and health practitioners as they look at, comment about, and handle our bodies. In this way, external standards become internal realities. Too frequently our own bodies become our enemies. This is as true for nondisabled as it is for disabled women. If we are to be capable of seeing a disabled woman as a person instead of her disability, we must confront these feelings in ourselves. It is not easy to face our own limitations honestly, but to the extent that we are able to accept and make peace with the loss, pain, and vulnerability associated with our own lack of perfection, the freer we will be of myths which oppress us and with which we may oppress others.

Perhaps it is time for us all to "come out" and express our feelings about our bodily "defects." Together as women, all with imperfections, limitations, vulnerabilities, strengths and weaknesses, desires, fears and passions, we need to accept and embrace the human condition and move in the direction of being able to live and love in our imperfect bodies.

## Notes

1. Disabled women bear the disproportionate economic, social, and psychological burden of what it means to be disabled. Data and an excellent discussion of disabled women's extensive oppression (as compared to non-disabled women and disabled men) are provided in Michelle Fine and Adrienne Asch, "Disabled Women: Sexism without the Pedestal," *Journal of Sociology and Social Welfare,* July 1981. Their studies reveal that disabled women are more likely than disabled men to be without work: between 65 percent and 76 percent of disabled women are unemployed. Disabled women also earn substantially less than disabled men. For vocationally-rehabilitated men and women, the mean annual incomes are $4188 and $2744, respectively.

Disabled women generally receive inadequate training for personal and professional self-sufficiency and suffer the brunt of labor-force discrimination. Disabled men are more likely than women to be referred to vocational schools or on-the-job training and are somewhat more likely to be college-educated. As a result, women are less likely to find a job post-disability. Those women who do are more likely to absorb a cut in pay than disabled men and are more likely to live in families with incomes at or below the poverty level.

Disabled women are less likely to be married: they marry later and are more likely to be divorced. A greater percentage of female heads of households than male heads of households are disabled. There is a general social neglect of the sexual and reproductive roles of disabled women, because public opinion assumes disabled women to be inappropriate as mothers or sexual beings. ...

...

2. [One] workshop utilized experiential exercises to sensitize participants to disability issues.

*Exercise 1*: As the workshop participants entered the room, they were asked to fill out blank index cards listing what they did and didn't like about their bodies. Throughout the workshop, someone was writing these bodily characteristics on the blackboard in front of the room so that everyone faced a list of what they and other women either liked or did not like about their bodies.

*Exercise 2*: After a moment of relaxation and deep breathing, the participants were asked to close their eyes and imagine themselves in bodies with disabilities other than their own. For example, imagine that you are 50 pounds heavier, or 25 years older. Imagine that you have a mobility disability; perhaps you walk with a cane or crutches, or use a wheelchair. Imagine that you have difficulty or are unable to move or use your hands and arms. Perhaps you have a speech impediment causing difficulties in communication. Perhaps you have involuntary muscular spasms, gestures, or facial expressions. Imagine that you have a sensory impairment and are unable to see or hear, or do so only with difficulty. Or perhaps you have a hidden disability or illness like a heart condition, or have had a mastectomy, or must wear a catheter or ostomy bag. These body images are more or less uncomfortable to imagine having. Choose the image you are able to entertain.

Once they assumed their imaginary bodies, a series of questions guided the participants through a variety of situations. For example, "Now that you are in that body, when you woke up this morning and were preparing to come to this conference, what kind of clothes would you choose to wear? How does that differ from what you are actually wearing?" "How did you get out of your house? How did you come to the conference? What kind of transporation were you able to use in your imaginary body?" "How might you feel when you come into this room full of strangers?" "What if you were invited to a party after the conference? Could you go? How would you feel at the party?" "What if you visited or had to return to your family with these changes in your body? How would they react to you?" "What if you were invited to the beach by friends and you had to choose a new bathing suit? Could you go to the beach? Could you let your body show?" "Suppose you met someone you were attracted to, and he/she wanted to sleep with you. How would you respond in your imaginary body?" "Imagine yourself in the bedroom. How would you feel about undressing in front of them? Now imagine yourself in bed. How would you relate to them sexually?"

3. Adrienne Asch and Michelle Fine, "Disabled Women: Sexism without the Pedestal," op. cit.

# Women and the Knife: Cosmetic Surgery and the Colonization of Women's Bodies

## Kathryn Pauly Morgan

...

## Introduction

Consider the following passages:

> If you want to wear a Maidenform Viking Queen bra like Madonna, be warned: A body like this doesn't just happen. ... Madonna's kind of fitness training takes time. The rock star *whose muscled body was recently on tour* spends a minimum of three hours a day working out. ("Madonna Passionate About Fitness" 1990; italics added)

> A lot of the contestants [in the Miss America Pageant] do not owe their beauty to their Maker but to their Re-Maker. Miss Florida's nose came courtesy of her surgeon. So did Miss Alaska's. And Miss Oregon's breasts came from the manufacturers of silicone. (Goodman 1989)

> Jacobs [a plastic surgeon in Manhattan] constantly answers the call for cleavage. "Women need it for their holiday ball gowns." ("Cosmetic Surgery For the Holidays" 1985)

> We hadn't seen or heard from each other for 28 years. ... Then he suggested it would be nice if we could meet. I was very nervous about it. How much had I changed? I wanted a facelift, tummy tuck and liposuction, all in one week. (A woman, age forty-nine, being interviewed for an article on "older couples" falling in love; "Falling in Love Again" 1990)

> "It's hard to say why one person will have cosmetic surgery done and another won't consider it, but generally I think people who go for surgery are more aggressive, they are the doers of the world. It's like makeup. You see some women who might be greatly improved by wearing make-up, but they're, I don't know, granola-heads or something, and they just refuse." (Dr. Ronald Levine, director of plastic surgery education at the University of Toronto and vice-chairman of the plastic surgery section of the Ontario Medical Association; "The Quest to Be a Perfect 10" 1990)

> Another comparable limitation [of the women's liberation movement] is a tendency
> to reject certain good things only in order to punish men. ... There is no reason why a
> women's liberation activist should not try to look pretty and attractive. (Markovic 1976)

Now look at the needles and at the knives [Figure 1]. Look at them carefully. Look at them for a long time. *Imagine them cutting into your skin.* Imagine that you have been given [cosmetic] surgery as a gift from your loved one who read a persuasive and engaging press release from Drs. John and Jim Williams that ends by saying "The next morning the limo will chauffeur your loved one back home again, with a gift of beauty that will last a lifetime" (Williams, 1990). Imagine the beauty that you have been promised. ...

...We need a feminist analysis to understand why actual, live women are reduced and reduce themselves to "potential women" and choose to participate in anatomizing and fetishizing their bodies as they buy "contoured bodies," "restored youth," and "permanent beauty." In the face of a growing market and demand for surgical interventions in women's bodies that can and do result in infection, bleeding, embolisms, pulmonary edema, facial nerve injury, unfavorable scar formation, skin loss, blindness, crippling, and death, our silence becomes a culpable one. ...

... Not only is elective cosmetic surgery moving out of the domain of the sleazy, the suspicious, the secretively deviant, or the pathologically narcissistic, *it is becoming the norm.* This shift is leading to a preditable inversion of the domains of the deviant and the pathological, so that women who contemplate *not using* cosmetic surgery will increasingly be stigmatized and seen as deviant. ...

... Cosmetic surgery entails the ultimate envelopment of the lived temporal *reality* of the human subject by technologically created appearances that are then regarded as "the real." Youthful appearance triumphs over aged reality.

## I. "Just the Facts in America, Ma'am"

As of 1990, the most frequently performed kind of cosmetic surgery is liposuction, which involves sucking fat cells out from underneath our skin with a vacuum device. This is viewed as the most suitable procedure for removing specific bulges around the hips, thighs, belly, buttocks, or chin. It is most appropriately done on thin people who want to get rid of certain bulges, and surgeons guarantee that even if there is weight gain, the bulges won't reappear since the fat cells have been permanently removed. At least twelve deaths are known to have resulted from complications such as hemorrhages and embolisms. "All we know is there was a complication and that complication was death," said the partner of Toni Sullivan, age forty-three ("hardworking mother of two teenage children" says the press; "Woman, 43, Dies After Cosmetic Surgery" 1989). Cost: $1,000–$7,500.

The second most frequently performed kind of cosmetic surgery is breast augmentation, which involves an implant, usually of silicone. Often the silicone implant hardens over time and must be removed surgically. Over one million women in the United States are known to have had breast augmentation surgery. Two recent stud-

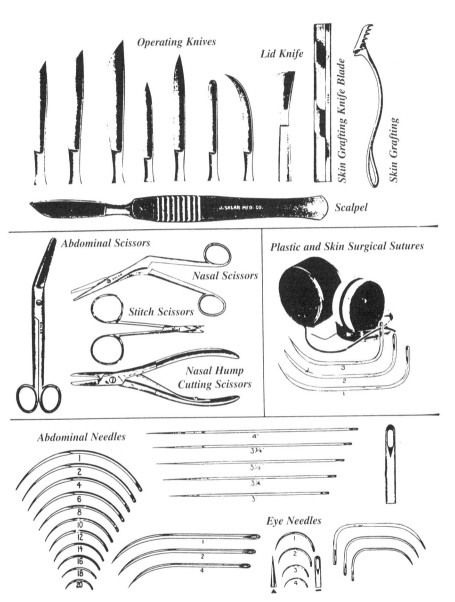

[**Figure 1**]   Originally published in Gina Luria and Virginia Tiger, *Every Woman* (Random House, 1974).

ies have shown that breast implants block X-rays and cast a shadow on surrounding tissue, making mammograms difficult to interpret, and that there appears to be a much higher incidence of cancerous lumps in "augmented women" ("Implants Hide Tumors in Breasts, Study Says" 1988). Cost: $1,500–$3,000.

"Facelift" is a kind of umbrella term that covers several sorts of procedures. In a recent Toronto case, Dale Curtis "dediced to get a facelift for her fortieth birthday. ... Bederman used liposuction on the jowls and neck, removed the skin and fat from her upper and lower lids and tightened up the muscles in the neck and cheeks. ... 'She was supposed to get a forehead lift but she chickened out,' Bederman says" ("Changing Faces" 1989). Clients are now being advised to begin their facelifts in their early forties and are also told that they will need subsequent facelifts every five to fifteen years. Cost: $2,500–$10,500.

"Nips" and "tucks" are cute, camouflaging labels used to refer to surgical reduction performed on any of the following areas of the body: hips, buttocks, thighs, belly, and breasts. They involve cutting out wedges of skin and fat and sewing up the two sides. These are major surgical procedures that cannot be performed in out-patient clinics because of the need for anaesthesia and the severity of possible post-operative complications. Hence, they require access to costly operating rooms and services in hospitals or clinics. Cost: $3,000–$7,000.

The number of "rhinoplasties" or nose jobs, has risen by 34 percent since 1981. Some clients are coming in for second and third nose jobs. Nose jobs involve either the inserting of a piece of bone taken from elsewhere in the body or the whittling down of the nose. Various styles of noses go in and out of fashion, and various cosmetic surgeons describe the noses they create in terms of their own surnames, such as "the Diamond nose" or "the Goldman nose" ("Cosmetic Surgery for the Holidays" 1985). Cost: $2,000–$3,000.

More recent types of cosmetic surgery, such as the use of skin-expanders and suction lipectomy, involve inserting tools, probes, and balloons *under* the skin either for purposes of expansion or reduction (Hirshson 1987).

Lest one think that women (who represent between 60 and 70 percent of all cosmetic surgery patients) choose only one of these procedures, heed the words of Dr. Michael Jon Bederman of the Centre for Cosmetic Surgery in Toronto:

> We see working girls, dental technicians, middle-class women who are unhappy with their looks or are aging prematurely. And we see executives—both male and female. ... Where before someone would have a tummy tuck and not have anything else done for a year, frequently we will do liposuction and tummy tuck and then the next day a facelift, upper and lower lids, rhinoplasty *and other things*. The recovery time is the same whether a person has one procedure or *the works*, generally about two weeks ("Changing Faces" 1989; italics added)

In principle, there is no area of the body that is not accessible to the interventions and metamorphoses performed by cosmetic surgeons intent on creating twentieth century versions of "femina perfecta."

## II. From Artifice to Artifact:
## The Creation of Robo Woman?

...

[Today, what] is designated "the natural" functions primarily as a frontier rather than as a barrier. While genetics, human sexuality, reproductive outcome, and death were previously regarded as open to variation primarily in evolutionary terms, they are now seen by biotechnologists as domains of creation and control. Cosmetic surgeons claim a role here too. For them, human bodies are the locus of challenge. As one plastic surgeon remarks:

> Patients sometimes misunderstand the nature of cosmetic surgery. It's not a shortcut for diet or exercise. *It's a way to override the genetic code.* ("Retouching Nature's Way," 1990; italics added)

... [Practices of coercion and domination are often camouflaged by practical rhetoric and supporting theories that appear to be benevolent, therapeutic, and voluntaristic. Previously, for example, colonizing was often done in the name of bringing "civilization" through culture and morals to "primitive, barbaric people," but contemporary colonizers mask their exploitation of "raw materials and human labor" in the name of "development."]

The beauty culture is coming to be dominated by a variety of experts, and consumers of youth and beauty are likely to find themselves dependent not only on cosmetic surgeons but on anaesthetics, nurses, aestheticians, nail technicians, manicurists, dietitians, hairstylists, cosmetologists, masseuses, aroma therapists, trainers, pedicurists, electrolysists, pharmacologists, and dermatologists. All these experts provide services that can be bought; all these experts are perceived as administering and transforming the human body into an increasingly artificial and ever more perfect object. ...

... For virtually all women as women, success is defined in terms of interlocking patterns of compulsion: compulsory attractiveness, compulsory motherhood, and compulsory heterosexuality, patterns that determine the legitimate limits of attraction and motherhood.[1] Rather than aspiring to self-determined and woman-centered ideals of health or integrity, women's attractiveness is defined as attractive-to-men; women's eroticism is defined as either nonexistent, pathological, or peripheral when it is not directed to phallic goals; and motherhood is defined in terms of legally sanctioned and constrained reproductive service to particular men and to institutions such as the nation, the race, the owner, and the class—institutions that are, more often than not, male-dominated. Biotechnology is now making beauty, fertility, the appearance of heterosexuality through surgery, and the appearance of youthfulness accessible to virtually all women who can afford that technology—and growing numbers of women are making other sacrifices in their lives in order to buy access to the technical expertise.

In Western industrialized societies, women have also become increasingly social-ized into an acceptance of technical knives. We know about knives that can heal: the knife that saves the life of a baby in distress, the knife that cuts out the cancerous growths in our breasts, the knife that straightens our spines, the knife that liberates our arthritic fingers so that we may once again gesture, once again touch, once again hold. But we also know about other knives: the knife that cuts off our toes so that our feet will fit into elegant shoes, the knife that cuts out ribs to fit our bodies into cor-sets, the knife that slices through our labia in episiotomies and other forms of genital mutilation, the knife that cuts into our abdomens to remove our ovaries to cure our "deviant tendencies" (Barker-Benfield 1976), the knife that removes our breasts in prophylactic or unnecessary radical mastectomies, the knife that cuts out our "use-less bag" (the womb) if we're the wrong color and poor or if we've "outlived our fer-tility," the knife that makes the "bikini cut" across our pregnant bellies to facilitate the cesarean section that will allow the obstetrician to go on holiday. We know these knives well.

And now we are coming to know the knives and needles of the cosmetic surgeons—the knives that promise to sculpt our bodies, to restore our youth, to cre-ate beauty out of what was ugly and ordinary. What kind of knives are these? Magic knives. Magic knives in a patriarchal context. Magic knives in a Eurocentric context. Magic knives in a white supremacist context. What do they mean? I am afraid of these knives.

## III. Listening to the Women

In order to give a feminist reading of any ethical situation we must listen to the wom-en's won reasons for their actions (Sherwin, 1984–85 and 1989). It is only once we have listened to the voices of women who have elected to undergo cosmetic surgery that we can try to assess the extent to which the conditions for genuine choice have been met and look at the consequences of these choices for the position of women. Here are some of those voices:

> *Voice 1* (*a woman looking forward to attending a prestigious charity ball*): "There will be a lot of new faces at the Brazilian Ball" ("Changing Faces" 1989). [Class/status symbol]
>
> *Voice 2*: "You can keep yourself trim. … But you have no control over the way you wrin-kle, or the fat on your hips, or the skin of your lower abdomen. If you are *hereditarily predestined* to stretch out or wrinkle in your face, you will. If you parents had puffy eyelids and saggy jowls, you're going to have puffy eyelids and saggy jowls" ("Changing Faces" 1989). [Regaining a sense of control; liberation from parents; transcending he-reditary predestination]
>
> *Voice 3*: "Now we want a nose that makes a statement, with tip definition and a strong bridge line" ("Changing Faces," 1989). [Domination; strength]
>
> *Voice 4*: "I decided to get a facelift for my fortieth birthday after ten years of living and working in the tropics had taken its toll" ("Changing Faces" 1989). [Gift to the self; erasure of a decade of hard work and exposure]
>
> *Voice 5*: "I've gotten my breasts augmented. I can use it as a tax write-off" ("Changing Faces" 1989). [Professional advancement; economic benefits]

*Voice 6*: "I'm a teacher and kids let schoolteachers know how we look and they aren't nice about it. A teacher who looks like an old bat or has a big nose will get a nickname" ("Retouching Nature's Way: Is Cosmetic Surgery Worth It?" 1990). [Avoidance of cruelty; avoidance of ageist bias]

*Voice 7*: "I'll admit to a boob job." (Susan Akin, Miss America of 1986 quoted in Goodman, 1989). [Prestige; status; competitive accomplishments in beauty contest]

*Voice 8*: (*forty-five year old grandmother and proprietor of a business*): "In my business, the customers expect you to look as good as they do" (Hirschson 1987). [Business asset; economic gain; possible denial of grandmother status]

*Voice 9*: "People in business see something like this as showing an overall aggressiveness and go-forwardness. *The trend is to, you know, be all that you can be*" ("Cosmetic Surgery for the Holidays" 1985). [Success; personal fulfillment]

*Voice 10* (*paraphrase*): "I do it to fight holiday depression" ("Cosmetic Surgery for the Holidays" 1985). [Emotional control; happiness]

*Voice 11*: "I came to see Dr. X for the holiday season. I have important business parties, and the man I'm trying to get to marry me is coming in from Paris" ("Cosmetic Surgery for the Holidays" 1985). [Economic gain; heterosexual affiliation"]

Women have traditionally regarded (and been taught to regard) their bodies, particularly if they are young, beautiful, and fertile, *as a locus of power* to be enhanced through artifice and, now, through artifact. In 1792, in *A Vindication of the Rights of Women,* Mary Wollstonecraft remarked: "Taught from infancy that beauty is woman's scepter, the mind shapes itself to the body and roaming round its gilt cage, only seeks to adorn its prison." How ironic that the mother of the creator of *Frankenstein* should be the source of that quote. We need to ask ourselves whether today, involved as we are in the modern inversion of "our bodies shaping themselves to our minds," we are creating a new species of woman-monster with new artifactual bodies that function as prisons or whether cosmetic surgery for women does represent a potentially liberating field of choice.

When Snow White's stepmother asks the mirror "Who is fairest of all?" she is not asking simply an empirical question. In wanting to continue to be "the fairest of all," she is striving, in a clearly competitive context, for a prize, for a position, for power. The affirmation of her beauty brings with it privileged heterosexual affiliation, privileged access to forms of power unavailable to the plain, the ugly, the aged, and the barren.

The Voices are seductive—they speak the language of gaining access to transcendence, achievement, liberation, and power. And they speak to a kind of reality. First, electing to undergo the surgery necessary to create youth and beauty artificially not only appears to but often actually does give a woman a sense of identity that, to some extent, she has chosen herself. Second, it offers her the potential to raise her status both socially and economically by increasing her opportunities for heterosexual affiliation (especially with white men). Third, by committing herself to the pursuit of beauty, a woman integrates her life with a consistent set of values and choices that bring her wide-spread approval and a resulting sense of increased self-esteem. Fourth, the pursuit of beauty often gives a woman access to a range of individuals who administer to her body in a caring way, an experience often sadly lacking in the day-to-day lives of many women. As a result, a woman's pursuit of beauty through transformation is often associated with lived experiences of self-creation, self-fulfillment, self-transcendence, and being cared for. The power of these experiences must not be underestimated.

While I acknowledge that these choices can confer a kind of integrity on a woman's life, I also believe that they are likely to embroil her in a set of interrelated contradictions. I refer to these as "Paradoxes of Choice."

## IV. Three Paradoxes of Choice

In exploring these paradoxes, I appropriate Foucault's analysis of the diffusion of power in order to understand forms of power that are potentially more personally invasive than are more obvious, publicly identifiable aspects of power. In the chapter, "Docile Bodies" in *Discipline and Punish,* Foucault (1979, 136–37) highlights three features of what he calls disciplinary power:

1. The *scale* of the control. In disciplinary power the body is treated individually and in a coercive way because the body itself is the *active* and hence apparently free body that is being controlled through movements, gestures, attitudes, and degrees of rapidity.

2. The *object* of the control, which involves meticulous control over the efficiency of movements and forces.

3. The *modality* of the control, which involves constant, uninterrupted coercion.

Foucault argues that the outcome of disciplinary power is the docile body, a body "that may be subjected, used, transformed, and improved" (Foucault 1979, 136). Foucault is discussing this model of power in the context of prisons and armies, but we can adapt the central insights of this notion to see how women's bodies are entering "a machinery of power that explores it, breaks it down, and rearranges it" through a recognizably political metamorphosis of embodiment (Foucault 1979, 138).[2] What is important about this notion in relation to cosmetic surgery is the extent to which it makes it possible to speak about the diffusion of power throughout Western industrialized cultures that are increasingly committed to a technological beauty imperative. It also makes it possible to refer to a set of experts—cosmetic surgeons—whose explicit power mandate is to explore, break down, and rearrange women's bodies.

*Paradox One: The Choice of Conformity—*
*Understanding the Number 10*

While the technology of cosmetic surgery could clearly be used to create and celebrate idiosyncrasy, eccentricity, and uniqueness, it is obvious that this is not how it is presently being used. Cosmetic surgeons report that legions of women appear in their offices demanding "Bo Derek" breasts ("Cosmetic Surgery for the Holidays" 1985). Jewish women demand reductions of their noses so as to be able to "pass" as one of their Aryan sisters who form the dominant ethnic group (Lakoff and Scherr, 1984). Adolescent Asian girls who bring in pictures of Elizabeth Taylor and of Japanese movie actresses (whose faces have already been reconstructed) demand the "Westernizing" of their own eyes and the creation of higher noses in hopes of better job and marital prospects ("New Bodies for Sale" 1985). Black women buy toxic bleaching agents in hopes of attaining lighter skin. What is being created in all of these instances is not simply beautiful bodies and faces but white, Western, Anglo-Saxon bodies in a racist, anti-Semitic context.

More often than not, what appear at first glance to be instances of choice turn out to be instances of conformity. The women who undergo cosmetic surgery in order to compete in various beauty pageants are clearly choosing to conform. So is the woman who wanted to undergo a facelift, tummy tuck, and liposuction all in one week, in order to win heterosexual approval *from a man she had not seen in twenty-eight years* and whose individual preferences she could not possibly know. In some ways, it does not matter who the particular judges are. Actual men—brothers, fathers, male lovers, male beauty "experts"—and hypothetical men live in the aesthetic imaginations of women. Whether they are male employers, prospective male spouses, male judges in the beauty pageants, or male-identified women, these modern day Parises are generic and live sometimes ghostly but powerful lives in the reflective awareness of women (Berger, 1972). A woman's makeup, dress, gestures, voice, degree of cleanliness, degree of muscularity, odors, degree of hirsuteness, vocabulary, hands, feet, skin, hair, and vulva can all be evaluated, regulated, and disciplined in the light of the hypothetical often-white male viewer and the male viewer present in the assessing gaze of other women (Haug, 1987). Men's appreciation and approval of achieved femininity becomes all the more invasive when it resides in the incisions, stitches, staples, and scar tissue of women's bodies as women choose to conform. And … women's public conformity to the norms of beauty often signals a deeper conformity to the norms of compulsory heterosexuality along with an awareness of the violence that can result from violating those norms. Hence the first paradox: that what looks like an optimal situation of reflection, deliberation, and self-creating choice often signals conformity at a deeper level.

## Paradox Two: Liberation into Colonization

As argued above, a woman's desire to create a permanently beautiful and youthful appearance that is not vulnerable to the threats of externally applied cosmetic artifice or to the aging process of the body must be understood as a deeply significant existential project. It deliberately involves the exploitation and transformation of the most intimately experienced domain of immanence, the body, in the name of transcendence: transcendence of hereditary predestination, of lived time, of one's given "limitations." What I see as particularly alarming in this project is that what comes to have primary significance is not the real given existing woman but her body viewed as a "primitive entity" that is seen only as potential, as a kind of raw material to be exploited in terms of appearance, eroticism, nurturance, and fertility as defined by the colonizing culture.[3]

But for whom is this exploitation and transformation taking place? Who exercises the power here? Sometimes the power is explicit. It is exercised by brothers, fathers,

male lovers, male engineering students who taunt and harass their female counterparts, and by male cosmetic surgeons who offer "free advice" in social gatherings to
women whose "deformities" and "severe problems" can all be cured through their
healing needles and knives. And the colonizing power is transmitted through and by
those women whose own bodies and disciplinary practices demonstrate the efficacy
of "taking care of herself" in these culturally defined feminine ways. Sometimes,
however, the power may be so diffused as to dominate the consciousness of a given
woman with no other subject needing to be present. ...

...

In electing to undergo cosmetic surgery, women appear to be protesting against
the constraints of the "given" in their embodied lives and seeking liberation from
those constraints. But I believe they are in danger of retreating and becoming more
vulnerable, at that very level of embodiment, to those colonizing forms of power that
may have motivated the protest in the first place. Moreover, in seeking independence, they can become even more dependent on male assessment and on the services of all those experts they initially bought to render them independent.

Here we see a second paradox bound up with choice: that the rhetoric is that of
liberation and care, of "making the most of yourself," but the reality is often the
transformation of oneself as a woman for the eye, the hand, and the approval of the
Other—the lover, the taunting students, the customers, the employers, the social
peers. And the Other is almsot always affected by the dominant culture, which is
male-supremacist, racist, ageist, heterosexist, anti-Semitic, ableist and class-biased.[4]

## Paradox Three: Coerced Voluntariness
## and the Technological Imperative

Where is the coercion? At first glance, women who choose to undergo cosmetic surgery often seem to represent a paradigm case of the rational chooser. Drawn increasingly from wider and wider economic groups, these women clearly make a choice,
often at significant economic cost to the rest of their life, to pay the large sums of
money demanded by cosmetic surgeons (since American health insurance plans do
not cover this elective cosmetic surgery).

Furthermore, they are often highly critical consumers of these services, demanding extensive consultation, information regarding the risks and benefits of various
surgical procedures, and professional guarantees of expertise. Generally they are relatively young and in good health. Thus, in some important sense, they epitomize relatively invulnerable free agents making a decision under virtually optimal conditions.

Moreover, on the surface, women who undergo cosmetic surgery choose a set of
procedures that are, by definition, "elective." This term is used, quite straightforwardly, to distinguish cosmetic surgery from surgical intervention for reconstructive
or health-related reasons (e.g., following massive burns, cancer-related forms of mutilation, etc.). The term also appears to distinguish cosmetic surgery from apparently
involuntary and more pathologically transforming forms of intervention in the bodies of young girls in the form of, for example, foot-binding or extensive genital muti-

lation.[5] But I believe that this does not exhaust the meaning of the term "elective" and that the term performs a seductive role in facilitating the ideological camouflage of the *absence of choice.* Similarly, I believe that the word "cosmetic" serves an ideological function in hiding the fact that the changes are *noncosmetic:* they involve lengthy periods of pain, are permanent, and result in irreversibly alienating metamorphoses such as the appearance of youth on an aging body.

... There are two important ideological, choice-diminishing dynamics at work that affect women's choices in the area of ... cosmetic surgery. The first of these is the *pressure to achieve perfection through technology.* The second ... is the *double-pathologizing of women's bodies.* The history of Western science and Western medical practice is not altogether a positive one for women. As voluminous documentation has shown, cell biologists, endocrinologists, anatomists, sociobiologists, gynecologists, obstetricians, psychiatrists, surgeons, and other scientists have assumed, hypothesized, or "demonstrated" that women's bodies are generally inferior, deformed, imperfect, and/or infantile. ...

[Now, women are being pressured to see plainness or being ugly as a form of pathology. Consequently, there is strong pressure] to be beautiful in relation to the allegedly voluntary nature of "electing" to undergo cosmetic surgery. It is clear that pressure to use this technology is on the increase. Cosmetic surgeons report on the wide range of clients who buy their services, pitch their advertising to a large audience through the use of the media, and encourage women to think, metaphorically, in terms of the seemingly trivial "nips" and "tucks" that will transform their lives. As cosmetic surgery becomes increasingly normal-ized through the concept of the female "make-over" that is translated into columns and articles in the print media or made into nationwide television shows directed at female viewers, as the "success stories" are invited on to talk shows along with their "makers," and as surgically transformed women win the Miss America pageants, women who refuse to submit to the knives and to the needles, to the anaesthetics and the bandages, will come to be seen as deviant in one way or another. Women who refuse to use these technologies are already becoming stigmatized as "unliberated," "not caring about their appearance" (a sign of disturbed gender identity and low self-esteem according to various health-care professionals), as "refusing to be all that they could be" or as "granola-heads."

And as more and more success comes to those who do "care about themselves" in this technological fashion, more coercive dimensions enter the scene. In the past, only those women who were perceived to be *naturally* beautiful (or rendered beautiful through relatively conservative superficial artifice) had access to forms of power and economic social mobility closed off to women regarded as plain or ugly or old. But now womanly beauty is becoming technologically achievable, a commodity for which each and every woman can, in principle, sacrifice if she is to survive and succeed in the world, particularly in industrialized Western countries. Now technology is making obligatory the appearance of youth and the reality of "beauty" for every woman who can afford it. Natural destiny is being supplanted by technologically grounded coercion, and the coercion is camouflaged by the language of choice, fulfillment, and liberation.

Similarly, we find the dynamic of the double-pathologizing of the normal and of the ordinary at work here. In the technical and popular literature on cosmetic surgery, what have previously been described as *normal* variations of female bodily shapes or described in the relatively innocuous language of "problem areas," are increasingly being described as "deformities," "ugly protrusions," "inadequate breasts," and "unsightly concentrations of fat cells"—a litany of descriptions designed to intensify feelings of disgust, shame, and relief at the possibility of recourse for these "deformities." Cosmetic surgery promises virtually all women the creation of beautiful, youthful-appearing bodies. As a consequence, more and more women will be labled "ugly" and "old" in relation to this more select population of surgically created beautiful faces and bodies that have been contoured and augmented, lifted and tucked into a state of achieved feminine excellence. I suspect that the naturally "given," so to speak, will increasingly come to be seen as the technologically "primitive"; the "ordinary" will come to be perceived and evaluated as the "ugly." Here, then, is the *third paradox:* that the technological beauty imperative and the pathological inversion of the normal are coercing more and more women to "choose" cosmetic surgery.

## V. Are There Any Politically Correct Feminist Responses to Cosmetic Surgery?

Attempting to answer this question is rather like venturing forth into political quicksand. Nevertheless, I will discuss two very different sorts of responses that strike me as having certain plausibility: the response of refusal and the response of appropriation.[6] I regard both of these as utopian in nature.

### The Response of Refusal

In her witty and subversive parable, *The Life and Loves of a She-Devil*, Fay Weldon puts the following thoughts into the mind of the cosmetic surgeon whose services have been bought by the protagonist, "Miss Hunter," for her own plans for revenge:

> He was her Pygmalion, but she would not depend upon him, or admire him, or be grateful. He was accustomed to being loved by the women of his own construction. A soft sigh of adoration would follow him down the corridors as he paced them, visiting here, blessing there, promising a future, regretting a past: cushioning his footfall, and his image of himself. But no soft breathings came from Miss Hunter. [He adds, ominously,] … he would bring her to it. (Weldon 1983, 215–216)

But Miss Hunter continues to refuse, and so will many feminist women. The response of refusal can be recognizably feminist at both an individual and a collective level. It results from understanding the nature of the risks involved—those having to do with the surgical procedures and those related to a potential loss of embodied personal integrity in a patriarchal context. And it results from understanding the conceptual shifts involved in the political technologizing of women's bodies and contextualizing them so that their oppressive consequences are evident precisely as they open up more "choices" to women. "Understanding" and "contextualizing" here mean seeing clearly the ideological biases that frame the material and cultural world in which cosmetic surgeons practice, a world that contains racist, anti-Semitic, eugenicist, and ageist dimensions of oppression, forms of oppression to which current practices in cosmetic surgery often contribute.

The response of refusal also speaks to the collective power of women as consumers to affect market conditions. If refusal is practiced on a large scale, cosmetic surgeons who are busy producing new faces for the "holiday season" and new bellies for the "winter trips to the Caribbean" will find few buyers of their services. Cosmetic surgeons who consider themselves body designers and regard women's skin as a kind of magical fabric to be draped, cut, layered, and designer-labeled, may have to forgo the esthetician's ambitions that occasion the remark that "the sculpting of human flesh can never be an exact art" (Silver 1989). They may, instead, (re)turn their expertise to the victims in the intensive care burn unit and to the crippled limbs and joints of arthritic women. This might well have the consequence of (re)converting those surgeons into healers.

Although it may be relatively easy for some individual women to refuse cosmetic surgery even when they have access to the means, one deep, morally significant facet of the response of refusal is to try to understand and to care about individual women who do choose to undergo cosmetic surgery. It may well be that one explanation for why a woman is willing to subject herself to surgical procedures, anaesthetics, postoperative drugs, predicted and lengthy pain, and possible "side-effects" that might include her own death is that her access to other forms of power and empowerment are or appear to be so limited that cosmetic surgery is the primary domain in which she can experience some semblance of self-determination. ... Choosing an artificial and technologically-designed creation of youthful beauty may not only be necessary to an individual woman's material, economic, and social survival. It may also be the way that she is able to choose, to elect a kind of subjective transcendence against a backdrop of constraint, limitation, and immanence. ...

As a feminist response, individual and collective refusal may not be easy. As Bartky, I, and others have tried to argue, it is crucial to understand the central role that socially sanctioned and socially constructed femininity plays in a male supremacist, heterosexist society. And it is essential not to underestimate the gender-constituting and identity-confirming role that femininity plays in bringing woman-as-subject into existence while simultaneously creating her as patriarchally defined object (Bartky 1988; Morgan 1986). In these circumstances, refusal may be akin to a kind of death, to a kind of renunciation of the only kind of life-conferring choices and competencies to which a woman may have access. And, under those circumstances, it may not be possible for her to register her resistance in the form of refusal. The best one can hope for is a heightened sense of the nature of the multiple double-binds and compromises that permeate the lives of virtually all women and are accentuated by the cosmetic surgery culture. As a final comment, it is worth remarking that although the response of refusal has a kind of purity to recommend it, it is unlikely to have much impact in the current ideological and cultural climate. ...

## The Response of Appropriation

... Rather than viewing the womanly/technologized body as a site of political refusal, the response of appropriation views it as the site for feminist action through transformation, appropriation, parody, and protest. This response grows out of that historical and often radical feminist tradition that regards deliberate mimicry, alternative valorization, hyperbolic appropriation, street theater, counterguerrilla tactics, destabilization, and redeployment as legitimate feminist politics. Here I am proposing a version of what Judith Butler regards as "Femininity Politics" and what she calls "Gender Performatives." ...

...

Rather than agreeing that participation in cosmetic surgery and its ruling ideology will necessarily result in further colonization and victimization of women, this feminist strategy advocates appropriating the expertise and technology for feminist ends. One advantage of the response of appropriation is that it does not recommend involvement in forms of technology that clearly have disabling and dire outcomes for the deeper feminist project of engaging "in the historical, political, and theoretical process of constituting ourselves as subjects as well as objects of history" (Hartsock 1990, 170).[7] Women who are increasingly immobilized bodily through physical weakness, passivity, withdrawal, and domestic sequestration in situations of hysteria, agoraphobia, and anorexia cannot possibly engage in radical gender performatives of an active public sort or in other acts by which the feminist subject is robustly constituted. In contrast, healthy women who have a feminist understanding of cosmetic surgery are in a situation to deploy cosmetic surgery in the name of its feminist potential for parody and protest.

... As Butler correctly observes, parody "by itself is not subversive" (139) since it always runs the risk of becoming "domesticated and recirculated as instruments of cultural hegemony." She then goes on to ask, in relation to gender identity and sexuality, what words or peformances would

> compel a reconsideration of the *place* and stability of the masculine and the feminine? And what kind of gender performance will enact and reveal the performativity of gender itself in a way that destabilizes the naturalized categories of identity and desire? (Butler 1990, 139)

We might, in parallel fashion, ask what sorts of performances would sufficiently destabilize the norms of femininity, what sorts of performances will sufficiently expose the truth of the slogan "Beauty is always made, not born." In response I suggest two performance-oriented forms of revolt.

The first form of revolt involves revalorizing the domain of the "ugly" and all that is associated with it. Although one might argue that the notion of the "ugly" is parasitic on that of "beauty," this is not entirely true since the ugly is also contrasted with the plain and the ordinary, so that we are not even at the outset constrained by binary oppositions. The ugly, even in a beauty-oriented culture, has always held its own fascination, its own particular kind of splendor. Feminists can use that and explore it in ways that might be integrated with a revalorization of being old, thus simultaneously attacking the ageist dimension of the reigning ideology. Rather than being the "culturally enmired subjects" of Butler's analysis, women might constitute themselves as culturally liberated subjects through public participation in Ms. Ugly Canada/America/Universe/Cosmos pageants *and use the technology of cosmetic surgery to do so.*

Contemplating this form of revolt as a kind of imaginary model of political action is one thing; actually altering our bodies is another matter altogether. And the reader may well share the sentiments of one reviewer of this paper who asked: "Having oneself surgically mutilated in order to prove a point? Isn't this going too far?" I don't know the answer to that question. If we cringe from contemplating this alternative, this may, in fact, testify (so to speak) to the hold that the beauty imperative has on our imagination and our bodies. If we recoil from *this* lived alteration of the contours of our bodies and regard it as "mutilation," then so, too, ought we to shirk from contemplation of the cosmetic surgeons who de-skin and alter the contours of women's bodies so that we become more and more like athletic or emaciated (depending on what's in vogue) mannequins with large breasts in the shop windows of modern patriarchal culture. In what sense are these not equivalent mutilations?

What this feminist performative would require would be not only genuine celebration of but *actual* participation in the fleshly mutations needed to produce what the culture constitutes as "ugly" so as to destabilize the "beautiful" and expose its technologically and culturally constitutive origin and its political consequences. Bleaching one's hair white and applying wrinkle-inducing "wrinkle creams," having one's face and breasts surgically pulled down (rather than lifted), and having wrinkles sewn and carved into one's skin might also be seen as destabilizing actions with respect to aging. And analogous actions might be taken to undermine the "lighter is better" aspect of racist norms of feminine appearance as they affect women of color.

A second performative form of revolt could involve exploring the commodification aspect of cosmetic surgery. One might, for example, envision a set of "Beautiful Body Boutique" franchises, responsive to the particular "needs" of a given community. Here one could advertise and sell a whole range of bodily contours; a variety of metric containers of freeze-dried fat cells for fat implantation and transplant; "body configuration" software for computers; sewing kits of needles, knives, and painkillers; and "skin-Velcro" that could be matched to fit and drape the consumer's body; variously-sized sets of magnetically attachable breasts complete with discrete nipple pumps; and other inflation devices carefully modulated according to bodily aroma and state of arousal. Parallel to the current marketing strategies for cosmetic breast surgeries, commercial protest booths, complete with "before and after" surgical make-over displays for penises, entitled "The Penis You Were Always Meant to Have" could be set up at various medical conventions and health fairs; demonstrations could take place outside the clinics, hotels, and spas of particularly eminent cosmetic surgeons—the possibilities here are endless. Again, if this ghoulish array offends, angers, or shocks the reader, this may well be an indication of the extent to which the ideology of compulsory beauty has anesthetized our sensibility in the reverse direction, resulting in the domesticating of the procedures and products of the cosmetic surgery industry.

In appropriating these forms of revolt, women might well accomplish the following: acquire expertise (either in fact or in symbolic form) of cosmetic surgery to challenge the coercive norms of youth and beauty, undermine the power dynamic built into the dependence on surgical experts who define themselves as aestheticians of women's bodies, demonstrate the radical maleability of the cultural commodification of women's bodies, and make publicly explicit the political role that technology can play in the construction of the feminine in women's flesh.

## Conclusion

I have characterized both these feminist forms of response as utopian in nature. What I mean by "utopian" is that these responses are unlikely to occur on a large scale even though they may have a kind of ideal desirability. In any culture that defines femininity in terms of submission to men, that makes the achievement of femininity (however culturally specific) in appearance, gesture, movement, voice, bodily contours, aspirations, values, and political behavior obligatory of any woman who will be allowed to be loved or hired or promoted or elected or simply allowed to live, and in any culture that increasingly requires women to purchase femininity through submission to cosmetic surgeons and their magic knives, refusal and revolt exact a high price. I live in such a culture.

---

### Notes

Many thanks to the members of the Canadian Society for Women in Philosophy for their critical feedback, especially my commentator, Karen Weisbaum, who pointed out how strongly visualist the cosmetic surgery culture is. I am particularly grateful to Sarah Lucia Hoagland, keynote speaker at the 1990 C-SWIP conference, who remarked at my session, "I think this is all wrong." Her comment sent me back to the text to rethink it in a serious way. ...

1. I say "virtually all women" because there is now a nascent literature on the subject of fat oppression and body image as it affects lesbians. For a perceptive article on this subject, see Dworkin (1989). I am, of course, not suggesting that compulsory heterosexuality and obligatory maternity affect all women equally. Clearly women who are regarded as "deviant" in some respect or other—because they are lesbian or women with disabilities or "too old" or poor or of the "wrong race"—are under enormous pressure from the dominant culture *not* to bear children, but this, too, is an aspect of patriarchal pronatalism.

2. I view this as a recognizably *political* metamorphosis because forensic cosmetic surgeons and social archaeologists will be needed to determine the actual age and earlier appearance of women in cases where identification is called for on the basis of existing carnal data. See Griffin's (1978) poignant description in "The Anatomy Lesson" for a reconstruction of the life and circumstances of a dead mother from just such carnal evidence. As we more and more pro-

foundly artifactualize our own bodies, we become more sophisticated archaeological repositories and records that both signify and symbolize our culture.

3. I intend to use "given" here in a relative and political sense. I don't believe that the notion that biology is somehow "given" and culture is just "added on" is a tenable one. I believe that we are intimately and inextricably encultured and embodied, so that a reductionist move in either direction is doomed to failure. For a persuasive analysis of this thesis, see Lowe (1982) and Haraway (1978, 1989). For a variety of political analyses of the "given" as primitive, see Marge Piercy's poem "Right to Life" (1980), Morgan (1989), and Murphy (1984).

4. The extent to which ableist bias is at work in this area was brought home to me by two quotations cited by a woman with a disability. She discusses two guests on a television show. One was "a poised, intelligent young women who'd been rejected as a contestant for the Miss Toronto title. She is a paraplegic. The organizers' excuse for disqualifying her: 'We couldn't fit the choreography around you.' Another guest was a former executive of the Miss Universe contest. He declared, 'Her participation in a beauty contest would be like having a blind man compete in a shooting match'" (Matthews 1985).

5. It is important here to guard against facile and ethnocentric assumptions about beauty rituals and mutilation. See Lakoff and Scherr (1984) for an analysis of the relativity of these labels and for important insights about the fact that use of the term "mutilation" almost always signals a distancing from and reinforcement of a sense of cultural superiority in the speaker who uses it to denounce what other cultures do in contrast to "our culture."

6. One possible feminist response (that, thankfully, appears to go in *and* out of vogue) is that of feminist fascism, which insists on a certain particular and quite narrow range of embodiment and appearance as the only range that is politically correct for a feminist. Often feminist fascism sanctions the use of informal but very powerful feminist "embodiment police," who feel entitled to identify and denounce various deviations from this normative range. I find this feminist political stance incompatible with any movement I would regard as liberatory for women and here I admit that I side with feminist liberals who say that "the presumption must be on the side of freedom" (Warren, 1985) and see that as the lesser of two evils.

7. In recommending various forms of appropriation of the practices and dominant ideology surrounding cosmetic surgery, I think it important to distinguish this set of disciplinary practices from those forms of simultaneous Retreat-and-Protest that Susan Bordo (1989, 20) so insightfully discusses in "The Body and the Reproduction of Femininity": hysteria, agoraphobia, and anorexia. What cosmetic surgery shares with these gestures is what Bordo remarks upon, namely, the fact that they may be "viewed as a surface on which conventional constructions of femininity are exposed starkly to view, through their inscription in extreme or hyperliteral form." What is different, I suggest, is that although submitting to the procedures of cosmetic surgery involves pain, risks, undesirable side effects, and living with a heightened form of patriarchal anxiety, it is also fairly clear that, most of the time, the pain and risks are relatively short-term. Furthermore, the outcome often appears to be one that generally enhances women's confidence, confers a sense of well-being, contributes to a greater comfortableness in the public domain, and affirms the individual woman as self-determining and risk-taking individual. All these outcomes are significantly different from what Bordo describes as the "languages of horrible suffering" (Bordo 1989, 20) expressed by women experiencing hysteria, agoraphobia, and anorexia.

## References

Barker-Benfield, G. J. 1976. *The horros of the half-known life*. New York: Harper and Row.
Bartky, Sandra Lee. 1988. Foucault, femininity, and the modernization of patriarchal power. In *Femininity and Foucault: Reflections of resistance*. Irene Diamond and Lee Quinby, eds. Boston: Northeastern University Press.

Berger, John. 1972. *Ways of seeing*. New York: Penguin Books.

Bordo, Susan R. 1989. The body and the reproduction of femininity: A feminist appropriation of Foucault. In *Gender/body/knowledge: Feminist reconstructions of being and knowing*. Alison Jagger and Susan Bordo, eds. New Brunswick, NJ: Rutgers University Press.

Brown, Beverley and Parveen Adams. 1979. The feminine body and feminist politics. *M/F* 3: 35–50.

Butler, Judith. 1990. *Gender trouble: Feminism and the subversion of identity*. New York: Routledge.

Changing Faces. 1989. *Toronto Star*. May 25.

Cosmetic surgery for the holidays. 1985. *Sheboygan Press*. New York Times News Service.

Falling in love again. 1990. *Toronto Star*. July 23.

Foucault, Michel. 1979. *Discipline and punish: The birth of the prison*. Alan Sheridan, trans. New York: Pantheon.

Goodman, Ellen. 1989. A plastic pageant. *Boston Globe*. September 19.

Hartsock, Nancy. 1990. Foucault on power: A theory for women? In *Feminism/postmodernism*. Linda Nicholson, ed. New York: Routledge.

Haug, Frigga, ed. 1987. *Female sexualization: A collective work of memory*. Erica Carter, trans. London: Verso.

Hirshson, Paul. 1987. New wrinkles in plastic surgery: An update on the search for perfection. *Boston Globe Sunday Magazine*. May 24.

Implants hide tumors in breasts, study says. 1988. *Toronto Star*. July 29. Summarized from article in *Journal of the American Medical Association*, July 8, 1988.

Lakoff, Robin Tolmach, and Raquel Scherr. 1984. *Face value: The politics of beauty*. Boston: Routledge and Kegan Paul.

Madonna passionate about fitness. 1990. *Toronto Star*. August 16.

Markovic, Mihailo. 1976. Women's liberation and human emancipation. In *Women and philosophy: Toward a theory of liberation*. Carol Gould and Marx Wartofsky, eds. New York: Capricorn Books.

Matthews, Gwyneth Ferguson. 1985. Mirror, mirror: Self-image and disabled women. *Women and disability: Resources for feminist research* 14(1): 47–50.

Morgan, Kathryn Pauly. 1986. Romantic love, altruism and self-respect: An analysis of Simone De Beauvoir. *Hypatia* 1 (1): 117–148.

New bodies for sale. 1985. *Newsweek*. May 27.

The quest to be a perfect 10. 1990. *Toronto Star*. February 1.

Retouching nature's way: Is cosmetic surgery worth it? 1990. *Toronto Star*. February 1.

Sherwin, Susan. 1984–85. A feminist approach to ethics. *Dalhousie Review*. 64(4): 704–713.

_____. 1989. Feminist and medical ethics: Two different approaches to contextual ethics. *Hypatia* 4(2): 57–72.

Silver, Harold. 1989. Liposuction isn't for everybody. *Toronto Star*. October 20.

Warren, Virginia. 1989. Feminist directions in medical ethics. *Hypatia* 4(2): 73–87.

Weldon, Fay. 1983. *The life and loves of a she-devil*. London: Coronet Books; New York: Pantheon Books.

Williams, John, M.D., and Jim Williams. 1990. Say it with liposuction. From a press release; reported in *Harper's* (August).

Woman, 43, dies after cosmetic surgery. 1989. *Toronto Star*. July 7.

# Beauty: *When the Other Dancer Is the Self*

## Alice Walker

It is a bright summer day in 1947. My father, a fat, funny man with beautiful eyes and a subversive wit, is trying to decide which of his eight children he will take with him to the county fair. My mother, of course, will not go. She is knocked out from getting us ready: I hold my neck stiff against the pressure of her knuckles as she hastily completes the braiding and then beribboning of my hair.

My father is the driver for the rich old white lady up the road. Her name is Miss May. She owns all the land for miles around, as well as the house in which we live. All I remember about her is that she once offered to pay my mother 75 cents for cleaning her house, raking up piles of her magnolia leaves, and washing her family's clothes, and that my mother—she of no money, eight children, and a chronic earache—refused it. But I do not think of this in 1947. I am two-and-a-half years old. I want to go everywhere my daddy goes. I am excited at the prospect of riding in a car. Someone has told me fairs are fun. That there is room in the car for only three of us doesn't faze me at all. Whirling happily in my starchy frock, showing off my biscuit polished patent leather shoes and lavender socks, tossing my head in a way that makes my ribbons bound, I stand, hands on hips, before my father. "Take me, Daddy," I say with assurance, "I'm the prettiest!"

...

It is Easter Sunday, 1950. I am dressed in a green, flocked, scalloped-hem dress (handmade by my adoring sister Ruth) that has its own smooth satin petticoat and tiny hot-pink roses tucked into each scallop. My shoes, new T-strap patent leather, again highly biscuit polished. I am six years old and have learned one of the longest Easter speeches to be heard in church that day, totally unlike the speech I said when I was two: "Easter lilies/pure and white/blossom in/the morning light." When I rise to give my speech I do so on a great wave of love and pride and expectation. People in the church stop rustling their new crinolines. They seem to hold their breath. I can tell they admire my dress, but it is my spirit, bordering on sassiness (womanishness), they secretly applaud.

...

*It was great fun being cute. But then, one day, it ended.*

*       *       *

I am eight years old and a tomboy. I have a cowboy hat, cowboy boots, checkered shirt and pants, all red. My playmates are my brothers, two and four years older than me. Their colors are black and green, the only difference in the way we are dressed. On Saturday nights we all go to the picture show, even my mother; Westerns are her favorite movies. Back home, "on the ranch," we pretend we are Tom Mix, Hopalong Cassidy, Lash LaRue (we've even named one of our dogs Lash LaRue); we chase each other for hours rustling cattle, being outlaws, delivering damsels from distress. Then my parents decide to buy my brothers guns. These are not "real" guns. They shoot "BBs," copper pellets my brothers say will kill birds. Because I am a girl, I do not get a gun. Instantly I am relegated to the position of Indian. Now there appears a great distance between us. They shoot and shoot at everything with their new guns. I try to keep up with my bow and arrows.

One day while I am standing on top of our makeshift "garage"—pieces of tin nailed across some poles—holding my bow and arrow and looking out toward the fields, I feel an incredible blow in my right eye. I look down just in time to see my brother lower his gun.

...

I am in shock. First there is intense fever, which my father tries to break using lily leaves bound around my head. Then there are chills: my mother tries to get me to eat soup. ... A week after the "accident" they take me to see a doctor. "Why did you wait so long to come?" he asks, looking into my eye and shaking his head. "Eyes are sympathetic," he says. "If one is blind, the other will likely become blind too."

This comment of the doctor's terrifies me. But it is really how I look that bothers me most. Where the BB pellet struck there is a glob of whitish scar tissue, a hideous cataract, on my eye. Now when I stare at people—a favorite pastime, up to now—they will stare back. Not at the "cute" little girl, but at her scar. For six years I do not stare at anyone because I do not raise my head.

*       *       *

Years later, in the throes of a mid-life crisis, I ask my mother and sister whether I changed after the "accident." "No," they say, puzzled. "What do you mean?"
*What do I mean?*

*       *       *

...

"You did not change," they say.
*Did I imagine the anguish of never looking up?*

*       *       *

I am twelve. When relatives come to visit I hide in my room. My cousin Brenda, just my age, whose father works in the post office and whose mother is a nurse, comes to find me. "Hello," she says. And then she asks, looking at my recent school picture which I did not want taken, and on which the "glob" as I think of it is clearly visible, "You still can't see out of that eye?"

"No," I say, and flop back on the bed over my book.

That night, as I do almost every night, I abuse my eye. I rant and rave at it, in front of the mirror. I plead with it to clear up before morning. I tell it I hate and despise it. I do not pray for sight. I pray for beauty.

"You did not change," they say.

*     *     *

I am fourteen and baby-sitting for my brother Bill who lives in Boston. He is my favorite brother and there is a strong bond between us. Understanding my feelings of shame and ugliness, he and his wife take me to a local hospital where the "glob" is removed by a doctor named O. Henry. There is still a small bluish crater where the scar tissue was, but the ugly white stuff is gone. Almost immediately I become a different person from the girl who does not raise her head. Or so I think. Now that I've raised my head, I win the boyfriend of my dreams. Now that I've raised my head, I have plenty of friends. Now that I've raised my head, classwork comes from my lips as faultlessly as Easter speeches did, and I leave high school as valedictorian, most popular student and *queen,* hardly believing my luck. Ironically, the girl who was voted most beautiful in our class (and was) was later shot twice through the chest by a male companion, using a "real" gun, while she was pregnant. But that's another story in itself. Or, is it?

"You did not change," they say.

*     *     *

It is now thirty years since the "accident." A gorgeous woman and famous journalist comes to visit and to interview me. She is going to write a cover story for her magazine that focuses on my last book. "Decide how you want to look on the cover," she says. "Glamorous, or whatever."

Never mind "glamorous," it is the "whatever" that I hear. Suddenly all I can think of is whether I will get enough sleep the night before the photography session: if I don't my eye will be tired and wander, as blind eyes will.

At night in bed with my lover I think up reasons why I should not appear on the cover of a magazine. "My meanest critics will say I've sold out," I say. "My family will now realize I write scandalous books." "But what's the real reason you don't want to do this?" he asks.

"Because in all probability," I say in a rush, "my eye won't be straight."

"It will be straight enough," he says. Then, "Besides I thought you'd made your peace with that."

And I suddenly realize that I have.

*     *     *

*I remember:*

I am talking to my brother Jimmy, asking if he remembers anything unusual about the day I was shot. He does not know I consider that day the last time my father, with his sweet home remedy of cool lily leaves, "chose" me, and that I suffered rage inside because of this. "Well," he says, "all I remember is standing by the side of the highway with Daddy, trying to flag down a car. A white man stopped, but when Daddy said he needed somebody to take his little girl to the doctor, he drove off."

*     *     *

*I remember:*

I am thirty-three years old. And in the desert for the first time. I fall totally in love with it. I am so overwhelmed by its beauty, I confront for the first time, consciously, the meaning of the doctor's words year ago: "Eyes are sympathetic. If one is blind, the other will likely become blind too." I realize I have dashed about the world madly, looking at this, looking at that, storing up images against the fading of the light. *But I might have missed seeing the desert!* The shock of that possibility—and gratitude for more than twenty-five years of sight—sends me literally to my knees. ...

*     *     *

*But mostly, I remember this:*

I am twenty-seven, and my baby daughter is almost three. Since her birth I have worried over her discovery that her mother's eyes are different from other people's. Will she be embarrassed? I wonder. What will she say? Every day she watches a television program called "Big Blue Marble." It begins with a picture of the earth as it appears from the moon. It is bluish, a little battered-looking but full of light, with whitish clouds swirling around it. Every time I see it I weep with love, as if it is a picture of Grandma's house. One day when I am putting Rebecca down for her nap, she suddenly focuses on my eye. Something inside me cringes, gets ready to try to protect myself. All children are cruel about physical differences, I know from experience, and that they don't always mean to be is another matter. I assume Rebecca will be the same.

But no-o-o-o. She studies my face intently as we stand, her inside and me outside her crib. She even holds my face maternally between her dimpled little hands. Then, looking every bit as serious and lawyerlike as her father, she says, as if it may just possibly have slipped my attention: "Mommy, there's a *world* in your eye." (As in, "Don't be alarmed, or do anything crazy.") And then, gently, but with great interest: "Mommy, where did you *get* that world in your eye?"

For the most part, the pain left then. (So what if my brothers grew up to buy even more powerful pellet guns for their sons. And to carry real guns themselves. So what if a young "Morehouse man" once nearly fell off the steps of Trevor Arnett Library because he thought my eyes were blue.) Crying and laughing I ran to the bathroom, while Rebecca mumbled and sang herself off to sleep. Yes indeed, I realized, looking into the mirror. There *was* a world in my eye. And I saw that it was possible to love it: that in fact, for all it had taught me, of shame and anger and inner vision, I *did* love it. Even to see it drifting out of orbit in boredom, or rolling up out of fatigue, not to mention floating back at attention in excitement (bearing witness, a friend has called it), deeply suitable to my personality, and even characteristic of me.

That night I dream I am dancing to Stevie Wonder's song "Always." As I dance, whirling and joyous, happier than I've ever been in my life, another bright-faced dancer joins me. We dance and kiss each other and hold each other through the night. The other dancer has obviously come through all right, as I have done. She is beautiful, whole and free. And she is also me.

# PART FOUR

# WOMEN´S FERTILITY—

# INDIVIDUAL CHOICES AND

# SOCIAL CONSTRAINTS

Why is fertility often regarded as primarily a women's issue? After all, both men and women are involved in producing children, and in Western Europe and North America, fathers as well as mothers are held legally responsible for the economic support of their children. Part of the answer may lie in human biology: pregnancy, childbirth, and lactation make far more demands on women's bodies than insemination does on men's. Beyond this, however, is the contemporary social organization of childrearing, which distributes responsibility for children's welfare unequally between fathers and mothers. Even though women's entry into the labor market has required many Western European and North American fathers to become increasingly involved in caring for their children, most women and men continue to assume that child care is primarily women's work; similarly, men's responsibility to provide economic support for their children often remains legally unenforced.

Fertility becomes a feminist as well as a women's issue when the disparity between men's and women's involvement in procreation is conceptualized as manifesting and/or reinforcing women's subordination. This part of the book considers a variety of feminist arguments exploring the connections between women's subordination and men's control over women's fertility. This control is evident in many ways: in the inability of many women to refuse sexual access to men, in a male-dominated legal system that denies abortion services to many women, and in male control of contraceptive and procreative technology. This part looks at a variety of feminist opinions on how women might achieve control over our own fertility and how we might exercise this control in ways that do not reinforce our own subordination.

## Abortion

Commitment to a legal right to abortion is sometimes taken as synonymous with feminism: on the one hand, women who advocate abortion choice are often characterized as feminist—with its popular connotations of "uppity," selfish, and indifferent to children; on the other hand, many opponents of abortion rights believe that their opposition makes it impossible for them to be accepted as feminist. But there is no necessary connection between feminism and the commitment to abortion rights: some people advocate abortion rights on grounds quite unrelated to feminism, whereas some feminists believe that the availability of abortion reflects and/or reinforces women's subordination.

Although many advocates of abortion rights are not feminist and although it is possible to be simultaneously feminist and opposed to the availability of abortion, it is undeniable that most feminists in contemporary Western Europe and North America support women's right to choose. The readings in this section therefore address only briefly the dispute between feminists who favor a legal right to abortion and those who oppose it. Instead, most of the readings explore various differences between pro-choice feminists: differences in conceptions of what abortion choice means, differences in how that choice may be justified, and differences in how it may be exercised.

Since the early 1970s, the availability of abortion has increased across most of Western Europe and North America. One exception is the United States, where there has been extreme public controversy and even street fighting over the issue of abortion. In 1973, in the historic case of *Roe* v. *Wade,* the U.S. Supreme Court appealed to an alleged right to privacy to justify removing most restrictions on the right to abortion in the first trimester. The decision allowed states to regulate abortion in the second trimester on the grounds of their interest in the health of the woman and to restrict and even prohibit abortion in the third trimester on the grounds of their interest in the life of a viable fetus.

Ever since the passage of *Roe* v. *Wade,* groups that oppose the availability of abortion have been working to limit its scope, and they have achieved considerable, though still limited, success. In a series of decisions passed since 1973, the U.S. Supreme Court has, on the one hand, struck down various restrictive abortion laws, such as residency requirements, the need to obtain the approval of two physicians and/or hospital committees, the need for a married woman to obtain her husband's consent, and the "informed consent" requirement that a woman seeking abortion should be told that a fetus is a "human life" and that abortion is a major surgical procedure. On the other hand, the Court has ruled that Medicaid funds may not be used for abortion even where the mother's life is at risk and that states may require a pregnant minor to notify both parents of her wish to have an abortion—regardless of whether either parent has custody or has even lived with the girl—and then impose a waiting period after parental notification. "Squeal rules," as many pro-choice activists call parental notification requirements, are held to be compatible with a 1976 Court ruling asserting minors' right to privacy because they mandate that a "judicial bypass" be available to girls seeking abortion. A judicial bypass allows a pregnant minor to seek a court hearing in which a judge determines if she is "mature" and if abortion is in her best interests.

From a feminist perspective, there are several noteworthy features of the current U.S. legal situation regarding abortion. First, *Roe* v. *Wade* makes abortion increasingly difficult to obtain as the pregnancy progresses—thus raising insuperable obstacles for those unfortunate and usually desperate women seeking third-trimester abortions, women who are likely to be very young, uneducated, poor, mentally disabled, abused, or abandoned by their male partners. Second, justifying abortion in terms of the right to privacy is problematic for feminists in several ways. As privacy was conceptualized in the *Roe* decision, it included not only a woman's right to be free from unwarranted intrusion into her reproductive decisionmaking but also a right to privacy in doctor-patient relations. Thus, it provided a basis for involving doctors as well as pregnant women in making abortion decisions, and this medical involvement increases as pregnancy progresses. Justifying the right to abortion in terms of a gender-neutral right to privacy also obscured the gendered aspects of abortion, diverting attention away from issues such as women's reproductive health and women's sexual and reproductive freedom. For instance, justifying abortion in terms of privacy prohibited states from banning abortion but failed to require that abortion be made available as part of women's health care. In general, many feminists who believe that the personal is political are uncomfortable with the common liberal—and U.S. Supreme Court—view that abortion is justified as a matter of personal privacy.

Many pro-choice advocates of the 1960s sought the repeal of all laws regulating abortion and were disappointed by the restrictions on abortion included in *Roe* v. *Wade.* During the 1970s and 1980s, however, intense attacks on the provisions of *Roe* caused most pro-choice advocates to weaken their proposals: mainstream groups now generally accept that women's right to abortion should be unrestricted only up to the twenty-fourth week of pregnancy and are willing to renounce women's right to third-trimester abortions. The idea that abortion should be completely unrestricted has virtually disappeared from public discourse.

The readings in this section begin with a rare contemporary demand for abortion law repeal. In "Deregulating Abortion," Ninia Baehr explains the difference between regulation and repeal by comparison with the differing legal status of alcohol and orange juice: alcohol is regulated, and its consumption is thus controlled by the government; orange juice is not specifically regulated, though its safety is guaranteed by non-orange-juice-specific Food and Drug Administration requirements. Baehr wants abortion to be entirely unregulated by the government except insofar as abortion procedures fall under general health care regulations.

In striking contrast to Baehr's radical pro-choice position, Anne M. Maloney asserts in "Women and Children First?" not only that the need for abortion is often a symptom of women's subordination but also that "abortion further victimizes women by giving society an 'easy out,' a cheap fix for deep, real problems, problems that abortion exacerbates rather than solves." Although Maloney's first claim is not unusual among feminists, it is highly unusual among opponents of abortion, who typically stress the importance of women's being sexually "responsible." Maloney's second claim, however, is highly unusual among feminists, despite her obvious feminist concerns. Like some revolutionaries, she fears that reforms that alleviate difficulties in people's daily lives may reduce the pressure for radical social change.

Catharine A. MacKinnon shares Maloney's perception that the need for abortion often expresses women's lack of both sexual and economic independence, and, also like Maloney, MacKinnon notices that the availability of abortion facilitates women's heterosexual availability to men. In "Abortion: On Public and Private," MacKinnon insists, unlike Maloney, that women must have abortion choice available to them but also argues that feminists should not defend this right on the grounds of some supposedly gender-neutral right to privacy. Historically, the right to privacy has functioned to legitimate men's domination over women; abortion must be reconceptualized as an issue of sex equality and abortion rights justified as one means of reducing men's control over women's sexuality. The following articles all defend abortion rights in terms other than privacy.

In the next article, "Abortion and a Woman's Right to Decide," written in 1973, I distinguish the question of when abortion is morally justifiable from the question of who should be legally empowered to make that decision. I argue that, if systems of social organization assign mothers the primary responsibility for guaranteeing children's welfare, those systems should make rights correlative with responsibilities and give women the sole legal authority to decide whether to terminate their pregnancies. Unlike appeals to privacy, this rationale for abortion choice is distinctively feminist because it justifies women's right to abortion in terms of their subordinate social position.

Among the most powerless and vulnerable groups of women in the United States are those younger than eighteen, who are, of course, legal minors. Laws mandating that these young women cannot receive abortions without the consent of their parents or guardians are widely accepted, and in 1992 the U.S. Supreme Court ruled that such laws were constitutional so long as a judicial bypass was available. In "Parental Consent Laws: Are They a 'Reasonable Compromise'?" Mike Males discusses the impact of these restrictions on pregnant teenagers. He finds that these laws disproportionately punish girls who are already poor and abused; rather than promoting family closeness, they disrupt families and may even provide an occasion for further violence against young women already victimized. Males notes the paradox involved in holding that girls too immature for abortion may be forced to become mothers.

In "Choosing Ourselves: Black Women and Abortion," Beverly Smith asserts that the meanings of abortion for women of color, especially Black women, are different from the meanings of abortion for white women. For one thing, large segments of the Black church are longtime fundamentalists and are opposed to abortion on principle; for another, Black people have a historical fear of genocide, a fear reinforced in recent years by their experience of forced sterilization and acquired immune deficiency syndrome. Desite these legitimate reasons for Black concern about abortion, Smith defends Black women's right to choose as an expression of love for Black women and of the value placed on the quality of their lives—sometimes simply on their own rights to life.

Kathryn Kolbert's "A Reproductive Rights Agenda for the 1990s" follows Beverly Smith in arguing that women's so-called right to choose should not be construed merely as a legal right to choose among existing social alternatives. Such a construction is inadequate because the available options are structured in ways that themselves are coercive. Kolbert shows how a genuine right to choose requires ending the subordination of women in all areas of life.

Public attitudes in Western Europe and North America affect abortion opportunities not only for European and North American women but also for women in the Third World because health care in the Third World is often partially funded by so-called development aid, which may come with antiabortion strings attached. Jodi L. Jacobson outlines the astronomical toll that the lack of legal abortion services imposes on Third World women, their children, and their entire societies in "The Global Politics of Abortion." Not only does the unavailability of legal abortion result in an extremely high rate of maternal mortality, causing perhaps one-fifth to one-half of all maternal deaths worldwide, but scarce health care resources are also drained by the need to provide care for women suffering from the complications of illegal abortion. Jacobson links the struggle for abortion with "the broader struggles of women to gain equality in all facets of life, from family and domestic issues to parity in the workplace" and suggests that much of the opposition to abortion rights may come from individuals or groups that feel threatened by those changes. Even though women and their existing children have the most immediately to gain from the availability of safe and legal abortion, Jacobson concludes that entire societies and ultimately the world as a whole will benefit from making abortion freely and safely available. (In Part VII of this volume, Jacobson's claim is developed by Ronnie Zoe Hawkins, who discusses the environmental consequences of denying abortions to women who wish for them.)

The next two articles in this section move away from the political issue of women's legal rights to abortion and instead address various moral questions concerning the justifiability of abortion. Helen B. Holmes and Betty B. Hoskins argue forcefully in "Prenatal and Preconception Sex Choice Technologies: A Path to Femicide?" that aborting a fetus because it is the "wrong" sex is always a sexist act. Holmes and Hoskins's argument against sex selective abortion recalls Kathryn Pauly Morgan's paradoxes of choice: Like the decision to undergo cosmetic surgery, women's "choice" to abort a female (or male) fetus is paradoxical or contradictory because, though at first sight the choice seems to increase women's control, on a deeper level it reveals conformity to the gender stereotypes that rationalize male dominance.

Deborah Kaplan also explores the implications of selective abortion, in this case the abortion of fetuses labeled "defective." In "Disability Rights Perspectives on Reproductive Technologies and Public Policy," Kaplan complains that prenatal screening undertaken to discover and abort disabled fetuses both rests on and reinforces "old" assumptions about disability. Central to these assumptions is that disability is a hopeless tragedy for both the individual and her family. Historically, this view has licensed extreme discrimination against disabled people, including forced incarceration and/or sterilization. By contrast, the "new" perspective recognizes that what constitutes a defect or disability is in part a reflection of social decisions about how to respond to difference; this perspective prohibits discrimination against disabled people. Disability activists, operating on this new understanding of disability, are changing the social contexts in which disabled women may bear children and in which pregnant women decide whether to abort fetuses that may be disabled. Kaplan concludes that disabled women need to be involved in debating how procreative rights may be reconciled with disability rights.

The last article in this section pulls together a number of themes evident in the preceding articles. In "Abortion Through a Feminist Ethics Lens," Susan Sherwin explains the differences between feminist and nonfeminist approaches to abortion, emphasizing that feminist discussions consider abortion in the broader context of women's lives. Many of the themes that Sherwin identifies, especially in ways in which women's choices are shaped by a variety of social, economic, and technological factors, are further developed in the readings in the next section, which explore some of the relations between procreative technology and procreative freedom.

## Procreative Technology and Procreative Freedom

"*Choice* and *information* have served as the cornerstones of the women's health and the reproductive rights movements." With these words, Barbara Katz Rothman begins the first selection on the topic of procreative technology and procreative freedom. These readings explore a variety of perspectives on the complex interrelationship between new procreative technologies and women's control over our fertility. Does the availability of these technologies enlarge or limit our choices, or does it simply change our options? Whose choices are we talking about anyway? Are the implications of various procreative technologies different for different groups of women, such as women of color, lesbians, or disabled women? How far is the availability of the various technologies themselves influenced by women's needs and interests—and, if so, by the needs and interests of which groups of women?

Choice or consent is usually understood in terms of three conditions: the rationality of the chooser, the absence of coercion, and the availability of all relevant information. But how is the presence or absence of these conditions to be determined in the context of procreative technology? When is a woman fully rational? (Can she be said to be rational when in labor, for instance, or immediately after giving birth?) When is she free from coercion, including economic or ideological coercion? And when is she fully informed about sophisticated and experimental technologies, often with undetermined health consequences and unknown chances of success? The following essays discuss these questions with a special emphasis on their connections with women's subordinate social status.

In "The Meanings of Choice in Reproductive Technology," Barbara Katz Rothman describes how the availability of various reproductive technologies not only opens some new choices for women but, through the provision of more medical information, may also provide a rationale for depriving women of choices previously available to them, such as the choice to decline a cesarean section. In addition, the availability of new technologies may close off previously existing options: In a parallel with the cosmetic surgery situation, technological intervention in procreation becomes increasingly difficult to refuse as it becomes the norm. Rothman writes, "It seems that, in gaining the choice to control the quality of our children, we may be losing the choice *not* to control the quality, the choice of simply accepting them as they are."

Rothman concludes her essay with some general reflections on the nature of individual choice. She notes that choices are always shaped by the options made socially available, so that people whose choices fit into those social options, who want what society wants them to want, are likely to experience themselves as free social agents. People who do not want what society wants them to want, however, may experience their choices as extremely limited, even coercive. (We may take as an example the experience of vegetarians seeking a restaurant meal; until recently a salad was often all that was available.) For women to truly control our own fertility, we must be able to restructure the social options available to us in accordance with feminist ideals.

Among the oldest procreative technologies are various methods of preventing conception. In addition to coitus interruptus and taboos on intercourse during various periods, women in the ancient world employed a variety of magical potions, vaginal pessaries, and cervical plugs. Traditional methods of preventing conception are technologically simple and inexpensive; many are quite effective, and most are relatively safe to use. Since the 1960s, however, massive investments in highly sophisticated technological research have been undertaken in attempts to discover techniques of contraception that will more sharply reduce women's fertility. In "Reproductive Rights and Wrongs," Betsy Hartmann identifies some of the conflicting interests involved in providing contraceptive technology. Women in both developed and developing nations have an urgent need for contraception that is reliable, available, and safe, but their male partners sometimes seek to control them by limiting their access to contraception. Even despite this overwhelming desire for contraception, relatively few women want techniques that are irreversible, especially women in developing nations whose economic insecurity forces them to rely on children as what Hartmann calls "their basic form of risk insurance." By contrast with these user interests, the companies producing contraceptives are motivated primarily by the desire to make a profit, while the U.S. government, which funds much contraceptive research as well as many family planning programs, is concerned with controlling "Third World" populations both at home and abroad.

The contraceptive technology that becomes available as well as the means of its delivery is influenced less by the concerns of its women users than by the interests of more powerful actors: governments, pharmaceutical companies, and male nonusers who refuse to take responsibility for controlling their own fertility. In consequence, contemporary contraceptive research focuses on women's, rather than men's, procreative capacities; emphasizes systematic and surgical methods as opposed to safer and more easily reversible barrier methods; and reveals callous disregard for women's health, especially the health of poor women in the Third World. Hartmann's discussion makes evident that women's control of our own fertility requires far more than individual access to existing contraceptive technologies, important as such access may be. In addition, available contraceptive options must reflect women's interests in methods that are reliable and safe, reversible, and controlled by the user.

In "Subtle Forms of Sterilization Abuse: A Reproductive Rights Analysis," Adele Clark identifies a variety of ways in which poor women are manipulated into "consenting" to sterilizations they later regret. Using the foregoing analysis of consent, we may say that sometimes sterilization is pressed on women when they are not "rational," for instance, when they are very young or on a delivery table; sometimes it is urged on them when they are less than fully informed about its implications or about alternative methods of contraception; and sometimes they are "coerced" by the absence of social supports for childbearing. Clark believes that the pressures on poor women to accept sterilization reflect "a patterned institutional discrimination on the basis of population control of poor people and people of color, that is, class, race and welfare related." She concludes with recommendations for reducing blatant and subtle sterilization abuse and enhancing women's and men's exercise of their reproductive rights.

The central insight of Clark's paper is that expressed consent is not necessarily "true" consent; it may have been manipulated in various ways. This insight is utilized by Gena Corea in "'Informed Consent': The Myth of Voluntarism," in which she discusses in vitro fertilization (IVF). Corea asserts that women's consent to this treatment is illusory, despite the desperate eagerness for it they often express. Not only are women who undertake IVF invariably uninformed about its experimental nature, its associated pain and health risks, and its low success rate, but they are brainwashed by "patriarchy" in believing that they are not real women unless they bear children for men. Corea argues that coercion may be emotional as well as physical, and she complains that focusing narrowly on individual choice disregards the role-defined context in which such choices are made.

Corea's descriptions of IVF portray it as causing extreme physical and psychological suffering to women and as undermining their agency and dignity. In this connection, she cites Janice Raymond's characterization of IVF as reducing women "to ultimately reproductive creatures, to medically manipulable Matter." Corea's disapproval of high-tech interventions in procreation is shared by Irene Diamond, who suggests, in "Babies, Heroic Experts, and a Poisoned Earth," that the new technologies supposedly facilitating fertility and "normal" babies for women in fact "pose profound threats to the dignity and well-being of human life itself." In addition, the technologies may be seen as a "male counterattack" by the "technodocs" on some primary goals of the feminist health care movement, which aims, among other things, to demystify and depathologize birth and regain women's control over it.

Diamond describes her own ambivalent attitude toward procreative technology, an ambivalence mirrored within feminism itself. On the one hand, feminists, as daughters of the Enlightenment, have often rejected custom and acceptance of natural contingency in favor of controlling the social and physical world through rationality, objectivity, and science; on the other hand, as frequent victims of what men have constructed as rationality, objectivity, and science, feminists have been profoundly critical of these Enlightenment ideals. A middle-aged woman who had recently undergone two miscarriages and the death of a fetus and who was uncertain about her ability to cope with a child with special needs, Diamond initially succumbed to the need for technological reassurance about her fetus, but after a certain point she refused further testing. She asserts that the search for a technological "fix" to infertility obscures the likelihood that infertility may itself result from previous technological "advances." Rather than depending on "heroic experts" to save us from the dangers of a poisoned earth, feminists need to find ways of ensuring the well-being of the earth's ecosystems.

Christine Overall's discussion of IVF, "Access to In Vitro Fertilization: Costs, Care, and Consent," indirectly addresses Diamond's suspicion of procreative technology and directly addresses two other feminist claims. Although Overall shares Diamond's concern about the health hazards of IVF, Overall clearly does not regard procreative technology as objectionable in principle. Instead, she identifies a number of measures that she believes capable of minimizing IVF's dangers to women and children and of recognizing and fostering women's dignity and self-determination. These measures include truly informed choice and consent, equal and fair access, adequate record-keeping, follow-up, and research, and appropriate support systems for all participants.

Overall responds to Corea's denial that women ever truly consent to IVF by acknowledging that women's felt need to bear children may be socially conditioned. Nevertheless, Overall challenges the presumption implicit in some feminists' claims to know the origins and significance of infertile women's desire for children better than the women themselves. How can such feminists be sure that their own desires are any less conditioned or more autonomous? In any case, desires that are socially constructed—and what desires are not?—may still be painful, urgent, and deserving of response.

Finally, Overall questions the frequent feminist claim that full procreative freedom requires that every method of technologically assisted procreation be made freely available to all who wish to take advantage of it. Overall distinguishes the right *not* to reproduce, which mandates access to contraception and abortion, from the right *to* reproduce, which, she says, can be interpreted either weakly or strongly, negatively or positively. While she defends the negative right to reproduce—that is, the right to be free from unwarranted interference in procreation—she is dubious about the positive right, which would entitle people to receive all necessary assistance to procreate. One problem with this, Overall suggests, is that it might infringe on other women's right *not* to reproduce. At the same time, Overall is uncomfortable with treating IVF as a privilege available only to those who can pay for it or who meet conventional criteria of suitability for motherhood. The feminist approach to IVF with which she concludes provides an alternative to treating IVF as a right or to banning it entirely.

Overall quotes Mary Anne Warren as saying, "Freedom is not an all or nothing affair. We can rarely be completely free of unjust or inappropriate social and economic pressures, but we can sometimes make sound and appropriate decisions, in the light of our own circumstances." This is the individual aspect of procreative freedom. The social aspect involves working together to eliminate what Warren calls unjust social and economic pressures and to restructure the procreative options available to women according to feminist ideals of caring and bringing an end to women's subordination.

# Deregulating Abortion

## Ninia Baehr

...

... What I want is *free* abortions for all women who choose them. I want abortions to be available from lay practitioners as well as from doctors. I want an abortion to be accessible to every woman who wants one, no matter how small her town is, how young she is, or how many months pregnant she is. I want positive, supportive policies in federal, state, and local budgets and in Department of Health rules and regulations. I want the repeal of all abortion laws. And this, of course, is only the beginning.

These days, many of us wear buttons that say "Keep Abortion Safe and Legal." Because our radical history has been hidden from us, most of us who are under 35 do not realize that the legality we seek to defend was in fact a compromise of the original demand for repeal. If you repeal something from the law, you take it out of the law entirely. If you legalize something, you grant control to the state. For example, alcohol is legal in this country, but the government doesn't trust each person to regulate her own relationship with alcohol. It tells her how old she must be to drink it, when and where she may buy it—and it changes the laws about alcohol as it sees fit. This is not true of, say, orange juice. The criminal code does not mention orange juice. The government lets us drink it when, where, and how we want to. The FDA still checks to make sure that the orange juice is safe. The government will even help us pay for our orange juice if we receive food stamps. Other than playing this supportive role, the government is silent on the matter of orange juice. Repeal activists wanted the orange juice situation, not the liquor situation, when it came to abortion. They knew that as long as the government maintained a voice in each woman's abortion decision, it would use that power to chip away at women's right to abortion. Clearly, their predictions have come true with a vengeance.

...

# Women and Children First?

## Anne M. Maloney

Women, as I tell the students in my feminist philosophy class, should be on the same list as the spotted owl. We are an endangered species. To be a woman in the United States today is to be the potential victim of battering and rape. Pornography eroticizes our victimization and screams it from every newsstand. The majority of families living below the poverty level are headed by women. Women are used as medical guinea pigs, subjected time after time to untested drugs and procedures. Witness DES, the IUD, the early form of the pill—now acknowledged to be a hormone bomb—and silicone breast implants. When abortions are performed for sex selection purposes—and they are performed for that reason—it is female fetuses that are killed.

Women are 51 percent of the U.S. population. We are beaten, raped, starved, experimented on, and killed because of our gender. I'm not even going into the rest of the world, where women are routinely sterilized, have their clitorises excised, and are killed as infants in a ritual called "giving the baby a bath" because their lives just aren't valuable enough.

Is abortion any solution to these brute facts of a woman's life? Indeed not. Abortion further victimizes women by giving society an "easy out," a cheap fix for deep, real problems, problems that abortion exacerbates rather than solves. Were you raped? Well, it isn't a safe world for women. But here, it's okay; have an abortion. Are you the victim of incest? Too bad. Men are powerful, aren't they? But hey, it's okay; have an abortion. Too many kids? Are you in poverty? Trying to finish school or hang on to your job? Being pregnant won't do. Don't expect society to change or help you. But hey, it's okay; have an abortion. This, ironically, is called "choice." In reality, abortion is no choice at all.

Let me give you an example from the front lines of our "pro-choice society." At a well-known East Coast women's university, a female Ph.D. candidate became pregnant in the fifth year of a five-year program. She petitioned for an extension so that she could have the baby and finish her doctoral dissertation in the following year. Similar extensions had been granted in the past to students with unexpected illnesses or personal crises. This student's request, however, was denied. The dean of graduate studies commented, after denying her request, that women who want their Ph.D.s shouldn't have children. This summa cum laude college graduate, fluent in three languages, is presently in a very tenuous job situation.

This is not an isolated or bizarre case. … According to Helen Norton of the Women's Legal Defense Fund, pregnant women, or women returning after maternity leave, are often made to give up responsibilities, denied pregnancy leave or granted leave with no guarantees, offered lesser jobs, denied promotion and pay raises, stripped of seniority, and cut off from meetings and information. This discrimination ranges from the blatant to the highly subtle; one female professional, after having given birth to her second child, was told by her boss, "I certainly hope you're finished." The boss in question prides himself on being pro-choice.

This kind of victimization's insidious and subtle nature makes it no less real. It is the echo of a society that tells a woman she has the "right" to surgically or chemically alter her own body so that she can operate in a world shaped and defined by men, so that she can *be* like men, have the freedom to walk away from sexual responsibility as easily as men do. What this so-called freedom of choice actually boils down to is "You have no choice." Don't expect the world to value your power to have and nurture children. Don't expect any societal support if you give birth. But don't worry; be happy! After all, you have freedom of choice: It's a pro-choice world!

When pro-choice rhetoricians claim that abortion decisions are never taken lightly but are usually anguished, they speak the truth, but with forked tongues. Surveys by pro-choice writers of women who had had abortions reveal that the vast majority did not want to abort, but when they turned to those they counted on for support in this difficult time, they were met instead with unbearable pressure. Boyfriends threaten to abandon girlfriends, husbands to divorce wives, leaving them to cope with raising children. Parents of unwed teens, more concerned with family shame, threaten to kick girls out. Career opportunities are shut off, and jobs are endangered. Those "friends" who don't want to be bothered drop out of sight. Nominally "pro-life" administrations cut back funding to the few remaining institutions that offer viable options for women. And family planning counselors, whose job it is to bring business to the clinic, slam the final nail into the coffin: "What choice do you have?"

As long as abortion remains the solution offered, there is no need, no incentive, no reason to change.

Some people argue that, if abortion is not legal, women will be desperate enough to resort to knitting needles and coat hangers. The solution these pro-choice people offer is *not* to address the cause of such desperation, *not* to root out and destroy the viruses inherent in a society that forces women to such measures. Oh, no. To the woman so beaten down by society's callousness that she resorts to killing her own offspring, they offer not food or a job or education or help. They offer her a cleaner knife to abort with, the so-called safe legal abortion.

…

Feminists for Life stands for a different vision, a society where women are valued and where their power to give and nurture life is valued. As long as abortion exists as a cheap and easy solution, this society will remain a dream. Abortion *exists* because it's a man's world. If men got pregnant, they would demand health care, living wages, family leaves, child care. They would demand that society value their ability to give and sustain life. But abortion? Having one's body forcibly violated, being told that the price of success is such constant violation? Forget it. Men would never stand for it. It's time for women to stop standing for it, too.

...

---

# *Abortion:*
# *On Public and Private*

## Catharine A. MacKinnon

*In a society where women entered sexual intercourse willingly, where adequate contraception was a genuine social priority, there would be no "abortion issue" ... Abortion is violence ... It is the offspring, and will continue to be the accuser of a more pervasive and prevalent violence, the violence of rapism.*

— **Adrienne Rich,** *Of Woman Born*

Most women who seek abortions became pregnant while having sexual intercourse with men. Most did not mean or wish to conceive. In women's experience, sexuality and reproduction are inseparable from each other and from gender. The abortion debate, by contrast, has centered on separating control over sexuality from control over reproduction, and on separating both from gender. Liberals have supported the availability of the abortion choice as if the woman just happened on the fetus,[1] usually on the implicit view that reproductive control is essential to sexual freedom and economic independence. The political right imagines that the intercourse that precedes conception is usually voluntary, only to urge abstinence, as if sex were up to women. At the same time, the right defends male authority, specifically including a wife's duty to submit to sex. Continuing this logic, many opponents of state funding of abortions would permit funding of abortions when pregnancy results from rape or incest.[2] They make exceptions for those special occasions on which they presume women did not control sex. Abortion's proponents and opponents share a tacit assumption that women significantly control sex.

Feminist investigations suggest otherwise. Sexual intercourse, still the most common cause of pregnancy, cannot simply be presumed coequally determined. Women feel compelled to preserve the appearance—which, acted upon, becomes the reality—of male direction of sexual expression, as if it were male initiative itself that women want, as if it were that which women find arousing. Men enforce this. It is much of what men want in a woman, what pornography eroticizes and prostitutes provide. Rape—that is, intercourse with force that is recognized as force—is adjudicated not according to the power or force that the man wields, but according to indices of intimacy between the parties. The more intimate one is with one's accused rapist, the less likely a court is to find that what happened was rape. Often indices of intimacy include intercourse itself. If "no" can be taken as "yes," how free can "yes" be?

...

In 1973 the Supreme Court found that a statute that made criminal all abortions except those to save the life of the mother violated the constitutional right to privacy.[3] The privacy right had been previously created as a constitutional principle in a case that decriminalized the prescription and use of contraceptives.[4] In other words, courts use the privacy rubric to connect contraception with abortion through privacy in the same way that feminism does through sexuality. In *Roe*, the right to privacy was found "broad enough to encompass a woman's decision whether or not to terminate her pregnancy." In 1981 three justices observed in a dissent: "In the abortion context, we have held that the right to privacy shields the woman from undue state intrusion in and external scrutiny of her very personal choice."[5]

In 1981 the Supreme Court decided that this right to privacy did not mean that federal Medicaid programs had to cover medically necessary abortions. Privacy, the Court had said, was guaranteed for "a woman's decision whether or not to terminate her pregnancy." The government was then permitted to support one decision and not another: to find continuing conceptions and not to fund discontinuing them. Asserting that decisional privacy was nevertheless constitutionally intact, the Court stated that "although the government may not place obstacles in the path of a woman's exercise of her freedom of choice, it need not remove those not of its own creation."[6] It is apparently a very short step from that in which the government has a duty *not* to intervene, to that in which it has *no* duty to intervene. ...

Regarded as the outer edge of the limitations on government, the idea of privacy embodies a tension between precluding public exposure or governmental intrusion on the one hand, and autonomy in the sense of protecting personal self-action on the other. This is a tension, not just two facets of one right. The liberal state resolves this tension by identifying the threshold of the state at its permissible extent of penetration into a domain that is considered free by definition: the private sphere. By this move the state secures "an inviolable personality" by ensuring "autonomy of control over the intimacies of personal identity."[7] The state does this by centering its self-restraint on body and home, especially bedroom. By staying out of marriage and the family—essentially meaning sexuality, that is, heterosexuality—from contraception through pornography to the abortion decision, the law of privacy proposes to guarantee individual bodily integrity, personal exercise of moral intelligence, and freedom of intimacy.[8] But have women's rights to access to those values been guaranteed? The law of privacy instead translates traditional liberal values into the rhetoric of individual rights as a means of subordinating those rights to specific social imperatives.[9] In particular, the logic of the grant of the abortion right is consummated in the funding decision, enforcing male supremacy with capitalism, translating the ideology of the private sphere into the individual woman's legal right to privacy as a means of subordinating women's collective needs to the imperatives of male supremacy.

Here, as in other areas of law, the way the male point of view constructs a social event or legal need will be the way that social event or legal need is framed by state policy. To the extent possession is the point of sex, illegal rape will be sex with a woman who is not yours unless the act makes her yours. If part of the thrill of pornography involves eroticizing the putatively prohibited, illegal pornography—obscenity—will be prohibited enough to keep pornography desirable without ever making it truly illegitimate or unavailable. If, from the male standpoint, male is the implicit definition of human, maleness will be the implicit standard by which sex equality is measured in discrimination law. In parallel terms, reproduction is sexual. Men control sexuality. The state supports the interest of men as a group. So why was abortion legalized? Why were women given even that much control? It is not an accusation of bad faith to answer that the interests of men as a social group converge with the definition of justice embodied in law through the male point of view. The abortion right frames the ways men arrange among themselves to control the reproductive consequences of intercourse. The availability of abortion enhances the availability of intercourse.

. . .

. . . The struggle of reproductive freedom has never included a woman's right to refuse sex. In the concept of sexual liberation which has undergirded the politics of choice, sexual equality has been a struggle for women to have sex with men on the same terms as men: "without consequences." Meaning, no children. In this sense the abortion right has been sought as freedom from the unequal reproductive consequences of sexual expression, with sexuality centered on heterosexual genital intercourse. It has been as if biological organisms, rather than social relations, reproduced the species. But if one's concern is not how more people can get more sex, but who defines sexuality—both pleasure and violation—and therefore who defines women, the abortion right is situated within a very different problematic: the social and political inequality of the sexes. This repositioning of the issue requires reformulating the problem of sexuality from the repression of drives by civilization to the oppression of women by men.

Even before *Roe v. Wade*, arguments for abortion under the rubric of feminism have rested upon the right to control one's own body, gender neutral. This argument has been appealing for the same reasons it is inadequate: socially, women's bodies have not been theirs; women have not controlled their meanings and destinies. Feminists have tried to assert that control without risking pursuit of the idea that something more than women's bodies might be at stake, something closer to a net of relations in which women are gendered and unequal.[10] Some feminists have noticed that women's right to decide has become merged with an overwhelmingly male professional's right not to have his judgment second-guessed by the government.[11] But whatever their underlying politics, most abortion advocates, at least since 1971, have argued in rigidly and rigorously gender-neutral terms.

...

Abortion promises women sex with men on the same terms on which men have sex with women. So long as women do not control access to their sexuality, this facilitates women's heterosexual availability. In other words, under conditions of gender inequality, sexual liberation in this sense does not so much free women sexually as it frees male sexual aggression. The availability of abortion removes the one real consequence men could not easily ignore, the one remaining legitimated reason that women have had for refusing sex besides the headache. As Andrea Dworkin puts it, analyzing male ideology on abortion: "Getting laid was at stake."[12]

Privacy doctrine is an ideal vehicle for this process. The liberal ideal of the private holds that, so long as the public does not interfere, autonomous individuals interact freely and equally. Privacy is the ultimate value of the negative state. Conceptually, this private is hermetic. It means that which is inaccessible to, unaccountable to, unconstructed by, anything beyond itself. By definition, it is not part of or conditioned by anything systematic outside it. It is personal, intimate, autonomous, particular, individual, the original source and final outpost of the self, gender neutral. It is defined by everything that feminism reveals women have never been allowed to be or to have, and by everything that women have been equated with and defined in terms of men's ability to have. To complain in public of inequality within the private contradicts the liberal definition of the private. In the liberal view, no act of the state contributes to shaping its internal alignments or distributing its internal forces, so no act of the state should participate in changing it. Its inviolability by the state, framed as an individual right, presupposes that the private is not already an arm of the state. In this scheme, intimacy is implicitly thought to guarantee symmetry of power. Injuries arise through violation of the private sphere, not within and by and because of it.

In private, consent tends to be presumed. Showing coercion is supposed to avoid this presumption. But the problem is getting anything private to be perceived as coercive. This is an epistemic problem of major dimensions and explains why privacy doctrine is most at home at home, the place women experience the most force, in the family, and why it centers on sex. Why a person would "allow" force in private (the "why doesn't she leave" question raised to battered women) is a question given its insult by the social meaning of the private as a sphere of choice. For women the measure of the intimacy has been the measure of the oppression. This is why feminism has had to explode the private. This is why feminism has seen the personal as the political. The private is public for those for whom the personal is political. In this sense, for women there is no private, either normatively or empirically. Feminism confronts the fact that women have no privacy to lose or to guarantee. Women are not inviolable. Women's sexuality is not only violable, it is—hence, women are—seen in and as their violation. To confront the fact that women have no privacy is to confront the intimate degradation of women as the public order. The doctrinal choice of privacy in the abortion context thus reaffirms and reinforces what the feminist critique of sexuality criticizes: the public/private split. The political and ideological meaning of privacy as a legal doctrine is continuous with the concrete consequences of the public/private split for the lives of women. In this light, the abortion funding ruling appears consistent with the larger meaning of the original granting of the abortion right.

...

Women were granted the abortion right as a private privilege, not as a public right. Women got control over reproduction which is controlled by "a man or The Man,"[13] an individual man or the doctors or the government. Abortion was not so much decriminalized as it was legalized. In *Roe v. Wade,* the government set the stage for the conditions under which women got this right. Most of the control that women won out of legalization has gone directly into the hands of men—husbands, doctors, or fathers—and what remains in women's hands is now subject to attempted reclamation through regulation.[14] This, surely, must be what is meant by reform.

...

To fail to recognize the meaning of the private in the ideology and reality of women's subordination by seeking protection behind a right to that privacy is to cut women off from collective verification and state support in the same act. When women are segregated in private, separated from each other one at a time, a right to that privacy isolates women at once from each other and from public recourse. This right to privacy is a right of men "to be let alone"[15] to oppress women one at a time. It embodies and reflects the private sphere's existing definition of womanhood. This instance of liberalism—applied to women as if they were persons, gender neutral—reinforces the division between public and private which is not gender neutral. It is an ideological division that lies about women's shared experience and mystifies the unity among the spheres of women's violation. It polices the division between public and private, a very material division that keeps the private beyond public redress and depoliticizes women's subjection within it. Privacy law keeps some men out of the bedrooms of other men.

---

### Notes

1. See, e.g., D. H. Regan, "Rewriting Roe v. Wade," 77 *Michigan Law Review* 1569 (1979), in which the Good Samaritan happens upon the fetus.

2. As of 1973, ten states that had made abortion a crime had exceptions for rape and incest; at least three had exceptions for rape only. Many of these exceptions were based on Model Penal Code 230.3 (Proposed Official Draft 1962), quoted in Doe v. Bolton, 410 U.S. 179, 205–207, App. B (1973). References to states with incest and rape exceptions can be found in Roe v.

Wade, 410 U.S. 113 n. 37 (1973). Some versions of the Hyde Amendment, which prohibits use of public money to fund abortions, have contained exceptions for cases of rape or incest. All require immediate reporting of the incident.

3. Roe v. Wade, 410 U.S. 113 (1973).

4. Griswold v. Connecticut, 381 U.S. 479 (1965).

5. H. L. v. Matheson, 450 U.S. 398, 435 (1981) (Marshall, J., dissenting).

6. Roe v. Wade, 410 U.S. 113, 153 (1973) ("a woman's decision whether or not to terminate her pregnancy"); Harris v. McRae, 448 U.S. 297 (1980) (referring to Maher v. Roe, 432 U.S. 464, 474 [1976], on no state responsibility to remove non-state-controlled obstacles).

7. T. Gerety, "Redefining Privacy," 12 *Harvard Civil Rights—Civil Liberties Law Review* 233, 236 (1977).

8. Kenneth I. Karst, "The Freedom of Intimate Association," 89 *Yale Law Journal* 624 (1980); "Developments—The Family," 93 *Harvard Law Review* 1157 (1980); Doe v. Commonwealth Att'y, 403 F. Supp. 1199 (E.D. Va. 1975) *aff'd without opinion,* 425 U.S. 901 (1976); but cf. People v. Onofre, 51 N.Y. 2d 476 (1980), *cert. denied,* 451 U.S. 987 (1981). The issue was finally decided, for the time, in Bowers v. Hardwick, 478 U.S. 186 (1986) (statute criminalizing consensual sodomy does not violate right to privacy).

9. Tom Grey, "Eros, Civilization, and the Burger Court," 43 *Law and Contemporary Problems* 83 (1980), was helpful to me in developing this analysis.

10. See Adrienne Rich, *Of Woman Born: Motherhood as Experience and Institution* (New York: Norton, 1976), chap. 3: "The child that I carry for nine months can be defined *neither* as me or as not-me" (p. 64).

11. Kristen Booth Glen, "Abortion in the Courts: A Lay Woman's Historical Guide to the New Disaster Area," *Feminist Studies* 4 (February 1978): 1.

12. Andrea Dworkin, *Right Wing Women* (New York: Perigee, 1983). ...

13. Johnnie Tillmon, "Welfare Is a Woman's Issue," *Liberation News Service,* February 26, 1972; reprinted in Rosalyn Baxandall, Linda Gordon, and Susan Reverby, eds., *America's Working Women: A Documentary History, 1600 to the Present* (New York: Random House, 1976), pp. 355–358.

14. See. H. L. v. Matheson, 450 U.S. 398 (1981); Bellotti v. Baird, 443 U.S. 622 (1979); but see Planned Parenthood of Central Missouri v. Danforth, 428 U.S. 52 (1976). Most attempts to regulate the right out of existence have been defeated; City of Akron v. Akron Reproductive Health Center, 462 U.S. 416 (1983). More recently, see Reproductive Health Service v. Webster, 851 F. 2d 1071 (8th Cir. 1988), *U.S. app. pndg.*

15. S. Warren and L. Brandeis, "The Right to Privacy," 4 *Harvard Law Review* 205 (1980). But note that the right of privacy under some state constitutions has been held to include funding for abortions: Committee to Defend Reproductive Rights v. Meyers, 29 Cal. 3d 252 (1981); Moe v. Secretary of Admin. and Finance, 417 N.E. 2d 387 (Mass. 1981).

# Abortion and a Woman's Right to Decide

## Alison M. Jaggar

...

In what follows I shall attempt to provide a moral justification for the claim that each woman should have the sole legal right to decide whether or not, in her own case, an abortion should be performed. ... I shall support my claim that each woman should have a legal right to abortion by appeal to an underlying moral right. The moral right to abortion for which I argue, however, is not a universal or absolute one enjoyed by all women, regardless of their social situation. Rather, it is a right whose existence depends on certain contingent features of the social situation in which women find themselves. Within our society, I shall argue, conditions are such that most women have a moral right to abortion, and, consequently, this right should be guaranteed by law. However, it is possible to describe other societies in which women do not have the sole moral right to decide on abortion, and indeed even within our own society there may be some women who do not have that right. ...

My argument for the conclusion that each woman should legally be guaranteed the right to decide whether or not she should abort attempts to bypass a number of difficult problems that are usually thought to complicate the issue. For example, I do not appeal to the unclear and dubious "right to one's own body." I skirt the general question of population control. I make no presuppositions about the moral status of unborn human beings other than to assume they do not have a right to life so absolute that the question of abortion may never be raised; that is, I assume it to be false that there are *no* circumstances that could conceivably justify abortion, but I do not commit myself to any stand on exactly what circumstances might do so. Finally, I avoid the general question of the purposes and limits of state authority. Instead I attempt to short-circuit all these difficulties and to resolve the issue of whether each woman should have a legal right to make her own decision about abortion by appeal to two relatively uncontroversial principles. Thus, if my argument works, it should be acceptable to people of most shades of political opinion and to anyone who will admit that abortion might occasionally be justified. ...

*         *         *

...

\*     \*     \*

There are two principles that I see as the key to determining whether or not each woman has the right to decide if she should terminate her pregnancy. The first principle is that the right to life, when it is claimed for a human being, means the right to a full human life and to whatever means are necessary to achieve this. Unfortunately I am not able to spell out precisely the necessary conditions for a full human life. This is a perennial subject of philosophical debate. To some extent, although not entirely, those conditions may be dependent on the level of development of the society in which the right to life is claimed. But certainly they go beyond the requirements for mere physiological survival to the less tangible requirements for full development as a human being, however those requirements should be construed. To be born, then, is only one of the necessary conditions for a full human life; the others presumably include nutritious food, breathable air, warm human companionship, and so on. If anyone has a right to life, she or he must be entitled to all of these.

The second principle to which I shall appeal is the principle that decisions should be made by those, and only by those, who are importantly affected by them. This principle provides the fundamental justification for democracy and is accepted by most shades of political opinion. Ideological differences arise not because of disagreement on the principle but because of disagreement on how to instatiate it.

How do these two principles apply to the issue of each woman's right to decide whether or not she should abort? The first principle suggests that if an individual or an organization does not make a genuine attempt to guarantee all of a child's needs, both before and after its birth, it cannot be viewed as the protector of that child's right to life. The protector of the child's right to life is that individual or organization that attempts to fulfill *all* the conditions necessary to the child's achieving a full human life. If an individual or organization knowingly and willfully neglects some of those necessary conditions, then there is no reason to grant it any special status as the child's protector. Hence, such an individual or organization has no special moral authority that would justify its insistence on just one of the many conditions necessary to a full human life, in circumstances where this would place the burden of fulfilling all the other conditions squarely on the shoulders of some other individual or organization. In particular, it cannot appeal to its special status as defender of the unborn's right to life in order to prohibit abortion, for it has no such special status.

The second principle entails that the decision about abortion should be made by all those whose lives are to be importantly affected by that decision. Which persons are included in that class is determined partly by certain features inherent in the situation (necessarily the lives of the woman and of the unborn are importantly affected), but it is also determined partly by the social context in which the question of abortion arises. For example, in a situation of very short food supply the whole community into which the child is to be born will be affected by the birth in a way in which it would not be affected if food were plentiful.

The two principles together entail that in our society each woman has the right to choose whether or not she should terminate her pregnancy. This conclusion follows from the application of the two principles to certain contingent features of our social organization. These features include the inadequate prenatal and postnatal health care provided by the state, the fact that the main responsibility for raising a child is laid on its biological mother, and the small proportion of the natural resources devoted to welfare.

*     *     *

To explain this, let us look … at the main candidates for a share in making the decision about abortion. Some of those who are eligible on the basis of having their lives affected by the decision are nevertheless unable in principle to participate in making it. They include the unborn child in question and future unborn generations. The world community at large, which is eligible on the same grounds, is also excluded from a share in making the decision—this time because of practical difficulties. This leaves the potential mother, the potential father, the medical staff who are asked to perform the abortion, and the state.

… The father's main claim to being able to decide whether or not his unborn child should be aborted [is] based on the fact that his life would be affected by the birth of a child. He has a legal obligation to contribute to the child's economic support, and if he happens to be married to the mother, it is conventionally understood that he will take at least a small part in raising the child; if he lives in the same house, he can hardly avoid some contact with it. In fact, however, the father has considerable choice as to how far his life is affected by the birth of his child. He may not live in the same house, and even if he does, present conventions about parenthood indicate that he will take a much smaller part in raising the child than will the mother, perhaps almost no part at all. Again, the father's obligation to provide economic support for the child may not be legally enforced. Finally, he does not have to go through the inconveniences, and even dangers, of pregnancy and childbirth. It is true that many fathers choose voluntarily to share as much as possible in the birth and raising of their children. But the fact remains that the choice is open to the father in a way in which it is not open to the mother. Biology, law, and social conditioning work together to ensure that most women's lives are totally changed as the result of the birth of a child, while men can choose how much they wish to be involved. It is for this reason that the potential mother, rather than the potential father, should have the ultimate responsibility for deciding whether or not an abortion should be performed, although this obviously does not exclude the mother from consulting the father if she wishes. If conventions regarding the degree of parental responsibility assumed by the mother and by the father were to change, or if the law prescribing paternal child support were to be enforced more rigorously, then perhaps we might require that the father share with the mother in making the decision (he could never take over the decision completely, of course, because it is not his body that is involved). But in the present social situation the right of a woman to decide if she should abort is not limited by any right of the father.

Still less should a woman's right to decide be limited by the claims of medical personnel. Their role is to present the medical information that she requests, not to determine the moral weight to be given to that information. They are not concerned in the long-term consequences of the abortion decision except insofar as they are members of the society into which the child will be born. This is not to say that even if the medical practitioners genuinely believe that abortion is morally wrong, they should still be compelled to perform it. But neither should they be able to prevent it. In practice, if there is a difficulty in finding the medical staff prepared to perform abortions, it is an indication that medical practitioners should be drawn from a broader spectrum of the population. Specifically, they should include more women. Generally, people are not slow in recognizing their rights, and if each woman has a right to choose whether or not she should abort, then female medical staff are unlikely to have moral qualms about helping her to exercise that right.

Let us now turn to the more difficult question of the claims of the state to participate in abortion decisions. ... The claim of the state rests on two grounds: the fact that the rest of the community is affected by the birth of new members and the alleged obligation of the state to protect the rights of even its unborn citizens. If our social situation were different, either of these arguments might be strong enough to justify the state's claim. But, as things are now, neither can outweigh the right of each woman to decide.

Certainly this right is not outweighed by the effects of the birth of new members on the rest of the community. While every woman's life is enormously affected by the birth of her child, the effect of new births on the rest of our society is small. Our food supply is ample ... and only a very small proportion of our resources is spent on welfare. The birth of more children still has a negligible effect on the lives of everyone except the mother. The father and the siblings may be in some degree exceptions to this, but their involvement is usually minor compared to that of the mother, who has to carry, give birth to, and raise the child. Therefore, the principle that only those who are affected importantly by a decision should share in making it indicates that, in our society, the potential mother rather than the state has the right to decide whether or not she should seek an abortion.

What about the alleged obligation of the state to protect the rights of the unborn? Feminists often try to answer this question by denying that the unborn has any rights. However, I think that this argument for state control of abortion can be answered without having to commit oneself to any stand on the difficult question of the moral status of the unborn or, indeed, to any position on the general justification of abortion. I have already argued that the rights of the unborn child cannot be separated from its rights after it is born; birth is just one necessary condition of an individual's exercising his or her right to life. But an individual's right to life is not fulfilled once she or he is born. She or he then acquires immediately a whole set of complex requirements in order to exercise her or his right to life. In our society the responsibility for fulfilling those needs falls primarily on the mother. The state does indeed provide schooling and a minimal degree of physical care for those children whose mothers are unable to support them. Such children do not usually starve or freeze to death. But, as is shown by the horrifying statistics on "battered" unwanted babies and the stunted physical and emotional development of children in state institutions, the state is far from guaranteeing the fulfillment of all their basic needs. Moreover, the offspring of a poor mother who keeps her children suffer in every way from their mother's poverty: they are malnourished, subject to disease, and perhaps aware that their very existence contributes to her poverty. For our society lays on each woman the bulk of the responsibility for protecting the right to life of her children. The state abandons most of this responsibility by refusing to guarantee for each child the necessary conditions of a full human life. Thus, since in our society the mother and not the state is the primary protector of the child's right to life, it is the pregnant woman and not the state who should decide whether or not, in her own case, abortion is justified.

...

To say that each woman in our society has the moral right to decide whether or not she should terminate her pregnancy is not to say that abortion is always justified. It implies nothing about what justifies abortion. Quite possibly, in deciding whether to abort or to bear the child, a woman will make the wrong decision. But the right to decide is hers.

Her right to decide is not derived from some obscure right to her own body; nor is it part of her right to privacy. It is a contingent right rather than absolute one, resulting from women's situation in our society. In this society each woman is primarily responsible for her own support, for the medical expenses she will incur during pregnancy and childbirth, and for providing her child with both its material and emotional needs. Because of this situation, women's lives are enormously affected by the birth of their children, whereas the community as a whole is affected only slightly. Moreover, because of this situation, each woman finds that she, rather than the state, is the primary protector of her child's right to life. Given these facts, and given the principle that those and only those who are significantly affected by a decision should share in making it, it seems plain that in this society each woman has the sole moral right to determine whether or not, in her case, abortion is justified.

\*     \*     \*

That each woman has this moral right is the basis of my claim that our legal system should guarantee to every woman the political right to decide whether or not to terminate her pregnancy. In making this claim, however, I am aware of possible problems: What should be done about very young women? What should be done about those women who are members of minority-group cultures where it is accepted that the family as a whole takes on the responsibility for fulfilling the needs of a child? And even, what should be done about women who are so rich that once a child is born, its existence may not affect their lives in any significant way? Surely circumstances like these would make us hesitate to claim that every woman in our society has the moral right to decide whether to terminate her pregnancy?

... I would argue that such cases are so few that they should not be allowed to limit the general conclusion that each woman in our society should be guaranteed the legal right to decide whether or not she should have her own pregnancy terminated. ...

The right-to-decide issue … shows why freedom and equality cannot be guaranteed simply through the establishment of political rights. As many poor women have pointed out, to grant a woman the legal right to decide whether or not she should seek an abortion does not guarantee that, in a more than trivial sense, a woman has both options open to her. If present social conditions remain unchanged, then the choice remains a merely formal rather than real choice. A real choice about abortion requires that a woman should be able to opt to have her child, as well as to abort it. This means that the full right to life of the child must be guaranteed, either by community aid to the mother who wishes to raise it herself, or by the provision of alternative arrangements that do not put the child who is not raised by its own mother at any significant disadvantage. Conversely, abortions must be made so cheap and convenient that any woman may be able to obtain one without hardship.

The latter condition is not difficult to achieve; indeed, for a number of reasons quite unconnected with women's liberation, it may well be on the way. But the former condition, while it is easy enough to state, would require social changes far-reaching enough to be accurately termed a revolution. Among other things it would require cheap or free medical care for all mothers and children, and probably, if children raised by their mothers are not to have an advantage over the others, the abandonment of the official ideology that sees the nuclear family as the ideal or normal living arrangement. In short, it would require that the community take over the responsibility for the physical and emotional welfare of all mothers and children. Therefore if a woman's right to decide whether or not she should abort is to be translated in practice into a genuine choice, uncoerced by economic stringency, it presupposes fundamental change in our most basic social institutions.

Now arises an apparent paradox. The moral right to decide for which I have been arguing is a right only for women in societies relevantly similar to this one. The existence of that right is contingent on the conditions obtaining in our society. But if these are radically altered, for example by the expenditure of a much greater proportion of our resources on welfare, then a woman's moral right to decide might be restricted. If the whole community were to assume responsibility for the welfare of mothers and children, then the application to the changed social conditions of the two principles that I used in defending the woman's right to decice would surely result in the conclusion that the community as a whole should have a share in judging whether or not a particular abortion should be performed. For the impact of new children on the whole community would be much greater, whereas the impact on the life of the mother would be considerably lessened, and might be reduced to the solely biological. Moreover, the mother's legal and conventional responsibility to protect her child's right to life would be no greater than that of any other member of the community. Of course, to say that the community as a whole should decide about abortions does not mean that the pregnant woman should not have a strong voice in making the decision: she is not just an ordinary member of the community in this matter, for it is still she who must bear and carry the child. Her wishes must therefore be accorded special weight. But she no longer would have the sole right or responsibility, depending on how one views it, for making the decision about whether or not to abort. The paradox, then, is that the attempt to guarantee the conditions in which each woman's right to decide about abortion would become a real option results in the achievement of conditions in which she no longer has that right.

The resolution of this paradox lies in the recognition that the establishment of political rights is inadequate as an ultimate social ideal. As such rights cannot guarantee justice, neither can they guarantee real freedom or equality. Unless our society is fundamentally changed, only a few women will be able to make a choice that is not determined by their economic situation. Hence, except for those fortunate few, the legal freedom to decide whether or not to abort will not result in genuine freedom of choice. And hence women's rights will not really be equal.

The abortion issue shows clearly why, in our search for justice, freedom, and equality, it may well be more fruitful to change our emphasis from the establishment of individual rights to the fulfillment of human needs. …

…

# Parental Consent Laws: Are They a "Reasonable Compromise"?

## Mike Males

Laws requiring parental consent before a girl under age 18 can obtain an abortion have won endorsement by the U.S. Supreme Court, the U.S. Senate, all three presidential candidates, 20 state legislatures and 80 percent of the American public—and are even seen by many pro-abortion choice adults as a "reasonable compromise."

Yet reaffirmation of parental consent laws is by far the most disturbing and intrusive element of the Supreme Court's June 30 [1992] ruling allowing new curbs on abortion, one that demonstrates the mechanism by which abortion rights can be summarily removed from vulnerable populations.

Parental consent laws authorize an outside party—a parent, or a judge if the girl goes to court to obtain an abortion without telling her parents—to force a teenage girl to bear a child against her will. Once another person can decide when a female must bear a child, the 1973 *Roe vs. Wade* decision guaranteeing access to abortion is abrogated. It becomes simply a matter of how many barriers can be raised to deny abortion to the only women who stand to lose the right in any case—the young and the poor.

Parental consent is already the most popular restriction enacted by states and Congress. In upholding such laws, justices again swept aside monumental realities regarding abortion patterns among teenagers, the family conditions of girls who cannot inform their parents, and the miserable experiences of states with such laws.

The court's ruling embodies diametrically opposing views of family life. In striking down spousal notice laws, justices recognized America's epidemic of domestic abuse and the plight of wives who cannot reveal abortion plans to their husbands for fear of violence and alienation. In upholding parental notice and consent, justices painted an idyllic portrait of loving family concern, ignoring that these same violent, disowning husbands can also be violent, disowning fathers.

Thus seven wealthy justices, averaging well over age 60, ignored the day-to-day realities of millions of girls such as L.V., a 16-year-old Montanan with abusive, alcoholic, estranged parents; impoverished, a prior victim of incest, pregnant by a 24-year-old man she planned to marry in an effort to escape harsh conditions but who had left town.

Montana has no parental consent law. Had such law been in effect, L.V. would have risked violent abuse by her parents when told of her pregnancy. The local judge, an anti-abortion fundamentalist, almost certainly would have refused any petition for her to obtain an abortion without parental consent. Thus her choices: self-abort, obtain an illegal abortion, have the child or leave school on a weekday to drive hours to seek an amenable judge.

The gasoline industry has been the chief beneficiary of parental consent laws. After Massachusetts passed such a law in 1981, Brandeis University researchers found 1,000 Massachusetts girls traveling to nearby states for abortions every year. Minnesota's similar law drove hundreds of girls to clinics in Fargo, N.D., and Wisconsin.

Parental consent laws highlight the cruelty of anti-abortion regulation; the rich and mobile retain the ability to go to other states or countries; the young and the poor are forced into untenable positions. The effect of such laws is to demand a useless, stressful judicial runaround for girls already facing difficult situations.

## Poverty, Rape, Abuse

Supporters of parental consent laws ignore the grim conditions of millions of youth. Six million children do not live with parents, according to the Casey Foundation. Four million children and adolescents were added to poverty rolls during the '80s. Three million children are physically abused, sexually abused or neglected every year. The National Women's Study indicates 500,000 to 1 million children and adolescents were raped in 1990; offender profiles show 90 percent of all rapists are adults. A recent Washington study shows two-thirds of all pregnant teenagers were sexually abused during childhood or adolescence, many by parents.

Impoverished, abused girls are by far the most likely to become pregnant. Having ignored worsening childhood poverty, abuse and health care which contribute to adolescent pregnancy and abortion, politicians now back harsh restrictive substitutes for genuine initiatives to help the young.

Surveys of Montana abortion clinics show that three-fourths of all minor girls voluntarily choose to include a parent in abortion decisions. Those who do not (nearly all of whom involve another trusted adult—an aunt, older sister, family friend) are overwhelmingly from homes where parents are violent or rigidly judgmental. Parental consent laws function to further traumatize that population of girls already subjected to childhood's worst abuses.

Parental involvement laws do not promote parental involvement. In Massachusetts and Minnesota, 40 to 45 percent of all girls (many after judge-shopping) obtain abortions without parental notice, a level higher than in Montana (24 percent), which has no law. "The law has, more than anything, disrupted and harmed families" and "can provoke violence," U.S. District Judge Donald Alsop wrote in a compelling opinion ignored by the Supreme Court.

In briefs filed in Judge Alsop's court reviewing parental consent and notification laws, Minnesota and Massachusetts judges recounted harassed, terrified, angry girls forced to reveal intimate details of their lives in intimidating court proceedings. "They find it a very nerve-racking experience," wrote one judge; another described "incredible amounts of stress" shown in "tone of voice, tenor of voice, shaking, wringing of hands," even physical illness. Judges, some personally opposed to abortion, unanimously agreed parental consent laws are useless and punitive.

While the Supreme Court upheld parental and judicial "rights" to decide that a minor girl must have a baby, there is no mandate that parents or the court pay her pregnancy expenses and the 18-year, $200,000 cost of raising a child she did not want to have—one an adult woman would have been allowed to abort. Bizarrely, a judge who finds a girl to immature for an abortion may force her to be a mother.

## Adult-Teen Sex

There is, further, no requirement that the male partner in "teenage" abortions face similar sanctions. The reason: It is *adult men,* not teenage boys, who cause or collaborate in the vast majority of all "teenage" pregnancies and abortions, including the 5 percent of all "teen" pregnancies that result from rape. Vital and health statistics records indicate 90 percent of all pregnancies among girls under age 18 are caused by adult men over age 18, and more than half by men over age 20. The "adult-teen" pregnancy and abortion reality is one lawmakers and justices refuse to face.

Thus the only ones left to punish are young girls. And yet, minor girls are hardly the cause of the prevalence of abortion that anti-abortion forces find so offensive. Only one out of 10 abortions is performed on a girl under age 18; less than 2 percent of all abortions in the country involve a pregnancy caused by a couple in which *both* partners are under age 18. The young, like the poor, are targeted for oppressive restrictions because they can't fight back.

Punishment appears, in the end, both the motive and result of parental consent laws. In a ... *Dateline* NBC report, the legislative sponsor of Ohio's parental notification law equated a pregnant teenage girl with a criminal who commits theft or vandalism. The laws' chief effects are delay, fear, stress, expense, hazard, forced motherhood and—now that the Supreme Court has invited states to experiment with harsher restrictions against teenagers and other vulnerable women—a return to dangerous illicit and self-induced measures.

---

# Choosing Ourselves: Black Women and Abortion

## Beverly Smith

...

... I want to talk about ... what it was like before abortion was legal, because I think there may be some people ... who don't have a clue about that. ... So I want to return to the days of yesteryear for a moment because I think that's where the passion comes from for many of us.

This story is about my first day at college. I had a roommate who was another Black woman. And I remember, here we were, nervous and anxious out of our minds. We went down to the basement to look for our trunks, and my new roommate, whom I had just met hours before, started throwing up. She claimed that she was nervous and later told me that she wasn't going to be able to finish out the year. I couldn't quite figure it out. Let me assure you, in 1965 I was quite an innocent. So I don't know how this popped into my mind but I said, the girl is pregnant. A few weeks later, she stayed out all night in violation of the rules that we had at that time. Then she came back and said she would be finishing out the year. So I believe she had an illegal abortion. This was in Chicago. I could have lost a roommate.

Now, of course, she never, ever told me what was going on. She never said that she was pregnant, she never said that she'd had an abortion. One of the most telling things she said—and this gets to the shame of all of this, both as a woman and as a Black woman—was, "You can take the girl out of the ghetto, but you can't take the ghetto out of the girl." That was a pretty intense way to start college, and we never, ever talked about it. When I was thinking of this story, I was thinking about the horrible secrecy that surrounded abortion at that time and how bad that is for the self-esteem and well-being of women.

Related to that secrecy and women's self-esteem is the fact that the reproductive rights movement has never been successful in putting forth certain arguments. Namely, we have never been willing to say clearly that we support abortion because being able to control our reproduction directly affects the quality of our lives, and, in some instances, affects whether we have any lives at all. I'm talking, of course, about death from illegal abortion. There are lots of reasons why we've never asserted this argument. One is that it goes directly against our sexist role conditioning. It's very hard for women to say that when the deal goes down, we choose ourselves. This may mean choosing not to have a baby.

When I wrote that phrase—choosing ourselves, rather than choosing to have a baby—it gave me some insight into the question of why there's been such strong lesbian involvement in the reproductive rights movement. I think it may be because this struggle has to do with giving our love to women. I think so many lesbians work on abortion because we deeply value women's lives, all women's lives, and know in our guts and in our hearts that women need access to abortion in order to have any kind of life at all.

...

... I would like to talk about some of the issues around Black women in the struggle for abortion. This is problematic, although there certainly have been many of us who have been involved. One thing I feel is that the feminist connection to abortion sometimes turns Black women off, particularly because feminism is so closely associated with white women. That's the immediate image.

Somewhat connected with that is religious fundamentalism. Because as I often say, you people haven't seen fundamentalism—all those TV evangelists to the contrary—until you have seen Black people be fundamentalists. That's not the only tradition of the Black church, at all, but some of us have been fundamentalists since the 19th century and "born again"; I heard that phrase long before it was picked up by the media. I think religious fundamentalism is something we have to grapple with because when you're talking about people who are still very involved in the church, abortion is a very difficult issue to raise.

Now we get to the fear of genocide. Last year I finally came to the conclusion that genocide is a real possibility. Now, of course, there has been a genocidal way of life in this country since we got here as slaves, but there's something about doing AIDS work and my sense that Black people's numbers are actually going to go down in the next decade or so that make me think about genocide in a whole different way. But Black people have always feared genocide, particularly around contraception and abortion.

I have always said that what's genocidal is not being able to control what happens to you. And as people have mentioned, forced sterilization is something that still goes on. The fact that sterilization is paid for or can be paid for through public funding, whereas abortion cannot, is itself a type of force—it's not even so subtle a force. There have been other even more blatant instances. I think with the specter of AIDS what we have to look at is Black women. Black women are 50 percent of the cases of women with AIDS, perhaps more at this point, closely followed by Latinas. When you're talking about women and AIDS, think women of color. Whenever you hear women and AIDS, think women of color. That should be your first image, because that gets lost. I have seen it get lost repeatedly on the part of people who are making policy for us.

We have to be very concerned about women of color being forced to be sterilized or have abortions because they are at high risk for AIDS or because they are HIV positive. And every woman, even a woman who is HIV positive, has the right to make the decision about whether she is going to have children or not.

Here are a couple of things in conclusion. One is that when we're talking about involving Black women in this movement or any movement, we have to look at where abortion and other health concerns fall in the priorities of Black women, particularly poor Black women. It takes space in your life and control of your life to be able to think about working on preserving a right which you might want to exercise in the future. Do you see how speculative that is? You know, maybe in the future or maybe my daughter... You see, that's not immediate and what people living on the edge are dealing with are immediate concerns. When obtaining food and shelter are your most pressing needs, fighting for abortion or doing political work around any issue is unlikely.

Health in general is not high up on the priority list of communities of color at this point. Because you can't really think about going to the doctor, let alone all the stuff that has been mashed on us in the last decade or so around wellness, if food and shelter are literally your priorities.

...

# A Reproductive Rights Agenda for the 1990s

## Kathryn Kolbert

### Introduction

Women's ability to control whether, when, with whom, and under what conditions they will have children—in short, women's power to control their fertility—is essential if women are to participate fully and equally in society. Only with the freedom to control their fertility are women free to learn and grow, to better themselves, to establish a home and family, to follow their dreams, or to express themselves and contribute as mothers, workers, artists, activists, scientists, or in whatever roles they choose.

To make truly voluntary decisions about their sexuality, childbearing, or parenting, women and men need access to sex education and counseling and affordable, comprehensive health care for themselves and their children. Women also need protection from unnecessary or invasive medical procedures and sterilization abuse, from family violence, and from hazardous workplace conditions.

Unless parents are able to ensure that adequate food, clothing, and shelter and quality child care and education are available for their children, their reproductive choices are limited. A fair and equitable welfare system and jobs that pay a living wage are critical to this effort.

When we think of how many women and families are now denied some or all of these rights because their income is too low or the color of their skin is too dark; because they live in rural communities, have physical disabilities, or have relationships with others of the same sex; or because they are uninformed, fearful, or stigmatized, we realize that the policy agenda for a pro-choice society is a very long one.

In a society based on gender equality, one that accepts the personhood of women by valuing their ability to be parents, to undertake meaningful work outside the home, and to have proud aspirations for their lives—one that encourages men similarly to combine work and nurturing roles—the bearing and rearing of children would not so often amount to a confining loss of opportunities for women. Such a society would foster the conditions that make true reproductive choice possible. Such a society would maximize reproductive choices and life options for all women and their families.

## 1. Freedom and Legal Rights to Make Voluntary Decisions

Our law and social institutions must enable women to make voluntary, thoughtful, and deliberate choices about their own sexuality, childbearing, and parenting and must respect the decisions that women make for themselves and their families.

All persons must have the legal right to make voluntary and informed decisions. Our legal system cannot be used to deprive women of equal access to a full range of reproductive options. Nor can it be used to coerce women's reproductive behavior or choices, regardless of age, ancestry, creed, disability, economic status, marital status, national origin, parental status, race, sex, or sexual orientation.

## 2. Comprehensive, Quality, and Affordable Health Care and Human Services

### A. A Full Range of Reproductive Options

Women must have access to existing methods of safe, quality birth control, and medical research must develop better, safer methods. Men as well as women must assume responsibility for birth control, and technologies must be developed that will enable them to do so.

Women who find themselves pregnant must have access to quality counseling to determine their reproductive choices. If they choose to terminate their pregnancies, they must have access to safe and affordable abortion services at or near their homes or jobs.

Women who choose to carry a pregnancy to term must have access to quality prenatal care, genetic screening and counseling, childbirth and postpartum care, and pediatric care for their children.

Pregnant women, especially poor women and women in Black, Hispanic, and Native American communities who are experiencing a crisis of drug and alcohol abuse, must be provided reproductive health and maternity services in an environment that is supportive and free of stigma. They msut be fully informed of the risks to themselves and their infants in a way that is caring and nonpunitive and that helps them to deal with additional problems of poverty, poor housing, and male violence.

All women must have access to confidential and quality care for sexually transmitted diseases. Women who are HIV positive or at risk for AIDS who are or may become pregnant have the same right to noncoercive counseling and choice as women with other disabilities or possible fetal impairments. AIDS testing, like prenatal diagnosis, should be offered on an anonymous or confidential and voluntary basis and within a program of counseling and education that respects all persons' rights to express their sexuality.

## B. Comprehensive Care

Because reproductive choice includes the ability to care for as well as bear children, comprehensive health care and human services must be available to all families. Whether offered through the Medicaid program, private insurance, or a national health plan, the services must be physically accessible—to disabled and rural women, to those dependent on public transportation, to those who work nights—and must be affordable to all.

## C. Safe and Quality Care

Health and human services including all reproductive health services should focus on health, wellness, and the prevention of problems, as well as on the cure and amelioration of problems, and should be provided in a culturally supportive manner, in an environment that is free from violence, deception, and fraud. Women should define their own needs and be enabled through the use of these services to make positive changes in their lives.

Medical practitioners must not adopt unnecessary or invasive practices that endanger women's lives or health and must not use their power or authority to coerce reproductive decisions. For example, procedures such as sterilization, hysterectomy, amniocentesis, ultrasound, Caesarean section, or electronic fetal monitoring should be used only when medically appropriate. To prevent further medical abuse, the crisis in malpractice and liability insurance which has forced medical practitioners to adopt unnecessary or invasive practices in order to protect against legal liability must be addressed without leaving women unprotected.

## D. Informed Consent and Informed Refusal

Principles of informed consent and informed refusal must be an intrinsic part of the decision making process and must be backed up by supportive counseling. Only when women have full knowledge about the ramifications of accepting or rejecting a particular health option, including explanations of medical procedures and their risks and benefits in understandable terms in the women's own language, can decisions be voluntary. At the same time, women must have the option of refusing particular types of information—e.g., the sex of the child after amniocentesis. In addition, informed consent must not become a pretext for harassment or discouragement of a particular reproductive choice, such as abortion or sterilization.

## 3. Sexuality, Reproductive, and Life Skill Education

Women, particularly teenage women, often become pregnant because they lack essential knowledge about sex, pregnancy, and contraception. Persons of all ages must have sufficient information about their sexuality and reproductive health to make intelligent decisions about sexuality, childbearing, and parenting. Information about how their bodies work, varied forms of sexuality, contraceptives, and sexually transmitted diseases must be provided to all persons at accessible locations, in a manner that is understandable and age-appropriate. Men as well as women must be taught that they have equal responsibility to be well informed about and to participate fully in choices related to sexual behavior, reproduction, and parenting.

As society grows increasingly concerned about the transmission of AIDS, women and men should be fully informed about the risks and pathology of AIDS and the necessity of using condoms or other "safe sex" practices. Public education campaigns to prevent AIDS should be administered in a context that respects all persons' needs to express their sexuality, both inside and outside the traditional framework of marriage and heterosexuality.

But education about sexuality and reproduction is only a part of the solution. Women, especially young women, often choose to become mothers because they have no realistic possibilities of advancement in society. Our educational system must provide women with the opportunity to set ambitious goals for their future, and the background to make these goals a reality, enabling women to choose motherhood when it is the best choice for them.

## 4. Freedom to Express One's Sexuality, and to Adopt Varied Family Arrangements or Lifestyles

If women and men are coerced or socialized into heterosexual relationships, or if childbearing or childrearing is permissible only within heterosexual relationships, then people's ability to make intimate decisions about reproduction, as well as about sexuality and parenting, is constrained. Society must not discriminate against, stigmatize, or penalize persons on the basis of their sexuality or sexual preference. Moreover, varied forms of sexual expression including heterosexuality, bisexuality, and homosexuality must be accepted as normal human responses, with positive meaning and value.

Women must be as free to say no to sexuality, childbearing, and parenting as they are to choose these options. Women must be free to express their sexuality in whatever noncoercive forms they choose, without recriminations, without effect on their value in our society or their self-esteem, and without fear of becoming pregnant if they do not wish to be so.

Varied forms of family and living arrangements must be acceptable choices. When women choose to parent outside of marriage, or to live collectively or intergenerationally, these choices must be respected. The legal barriers to and social stigma of unwed parenthood, inter-racial childbearing, or lesbian motherhood must be eliminated if true reproductive choice for all women is to be an option. Moreover, since pressure to have children is often brought about because there are few other acceptable adult-child relationships, we must encourage alternative forms of adult-child interaction.

## 5. Economic Equity and Reproduction

In order that all persons have equal opportunity to become parents, they must have the means to do so. The economic barriers to alternative forms of reproduction, such as the cost of adoption, donor insemination, in vitro fertilization, or embryo transfer must be lessened for low-income women through fee reduction or subsidies.

If we want a society in which children are truly an option, women must have the economic means to raise their children—to provide adequate food, clothing, and shelter and quality child care and education. We must work to eliminate the feminization of poverty that today so limits women's reproductive options and work to create jobs and a welfare system that afford dignity to all. Without an economy and social services that support women, women are unable to support their children and families; responsible parenting is possible only in a society that provides the necessary resources for parents.

Public policies must be enacted that will ease the burdens of working parents, caught between responsibilities of job and home. In addition to quality, affordable child care services, a reproductive rights agenda requires gender-neutral pregnancy and child care leave provisions and flexible work schedules available without penalty to fathers as well as mothers. To make these provisions available to all working parents and not just the most privileged, leave time must be paid. Corporate and governmental employers should be encouraged to initiate internal education programs, similar to those currently underway regarding sexual harassment, to change employee attitudes about male and same-sex partner participation in prenatal and child care tasks.

## 6. Freedom from Violence

Because fear of violence by a spouse or partner and fear of sexual assault limit everyone's ability to make intimate decisions, all persons must be free to choose whether, when, and with whom they have sex and have children, and to raise their children without fear of sexual assault, abuse, violence, or harassment in their homes, on the streets, or at their jobs.

## 7. Freedom from Reproductive Hazards

All persons must be free from reproductive hazards within the environment, in their homes, and at their workplaces. Rather than attempting to repair the effects of reproductive hazards by treating infertility or disease or by banning fertile women from hazardous worksites (and consequently from higher paying jobs), we must eliminate the hazards.

## 8. Family Law and Services

In order to enable all persons to freely form the arrangements in which they parent, they must be able to establish and terminate these arrangements without economic and social penalty. Fair and equitable divorce, child support, and child custody laws must be available and enforceable by women whose marriage or other family arrangements have dissolved or proven inadequate. In the event of the death or disability of both of a child's parents, governmental and community resources must provide for the well-being of the child. In the event of child abuse or neglect, governmental and community resources must provide necessary medical, social, and legal services to keep families together.

## 9. Political Participation

All persons must have the full right to express their views and, through organized, collective, and nonviolent action, to work actively for positive, systematic changes that will guarantee reproductive choice. Women must have the opportunity to be involved at all levels of the political process and within all political parties and be encouraged to take positions of leadership.

# The Global Politics of Abortion

## Jodi L. Jacobson

### The Invisible Plague

10:30 am, September 5, 1988: Ten women were lying, sitting and leaning on nine beds in three rooms ... five others were sprawled on the concrete floors of the hallway connecting these rooms. A few more were lying or seated on the floor outside the entrance to the Gynecology Admissions Ward. ... Although the temperature was warm, the dark, concrete environment and the condition of the women required blankets or covers. ... There were none. ... Many of these women came to the hospital for medical treatment of complications of incomplete, induced abortion. ... Most wait 12 hours for treatment from a physician. ... The nurses are often alone with women who are aborting on the floors or on their way to the single toilet at the end of the long hall. "All we can do is clean it up." Each day three out of ten illegally induced abortion patients complete their abortions on the concrete floor with no medical care. Nurses are not permitted to give medications or analgesics without a doctor's prescription.

According to the nurse-in-charge, the "average" woman ends up overnight on the floor. She receives no food or water because of the anticipated curettage procedure (surgical scraping of the uterus). [Consequently,] many women are dehydrated ... increasing the need for intravenous fluids once treatment begins. ... Many ... are in need of transfusions by the time they are taken into the operating room. Some refuse because of fear of HIV infection. Most who need blood, usually do not receive any because of shortages.[1]

This scene, a snapshot of what occurs daily on the wards of University Teaching Hospital in Lusaka, Zambia, where abortion is technically legal, might aptly describe conditions in any number of large-city hospitals in countries where illegal or clandestine abortion is widespread. Though it might not be apparent, the women described here are lucky; they are among the minuscule percentage of women who have even a chance of receiving health care after their lives or health have been threatened by complications in illegal abortion. Millions of others do not.

Throughout the Third World, the lifetime risk of maternal death is between 80 and 600 times higher than it is in industrial countries. Each year, according to WHO, at least a half-million women worldwide die from pregnancy-related causes. Of these, WHO attributes the loss of roughly 200,000 women's lives annually to illegal abortion, most of which are performed by unskilled attendants under unsanitary conditions or are self-inflicted with hangers, knitting needles, toxic herbal teas, and the like. In terms of sheer numbers, more than half the abortion-related deaths worldwide occur in South and Southeast Asia, followed by sub-Saharan Africa, and then Latin America and the Caribbean.[2]

...

Evaluation of trends within individual countries imply that maternal deaths could be far higher than is commonly believed. One study in India, for example, estimated that a half-million women die annually in that country alone due to complications of illegal abortion. And for every woman who dies, 30–40 more suffer serious, often lifelong health problems—among them hemorrhaging, infection, abdominal or intestinal perforations, kidney failure, and permanent infertility—that affect their ability to provide for themselves and for any children they already have.[3]

...

Perhaps the most distressing fact about abortion-related deaths and illnesses is that the vast majority of complications that lead to these outcomes are totally preventable. What consigns so many women around the world to death or physical impairment is not a deficiency in technology, but a deficiency in the value placed on women's lives. Technologically simple, inexpensive, easy-to-use tools for safe early abortion are well known, and widely used in some countries. But social intransigence, religious intolerance, economic self-interest, and political apathy all narrow the options for millions of women. Society's message to these women is, in effect, "carry this unwanted pregnancy or risk your life to end it."

Because of the social stigma of abortion, the dispersion of medical technologies for safe procedures is held back even while progress is made on other forms of health care. According to Julie DeClerque of the International Projects Assistance Services (IPAS), "data on infant mortality and hospital admissions for abortion complications in Santiago, Chile over a 20-year period show that while infant mortality dropped by over half, hospitalization from abortion complications increased by over 60 percent."[4]

Equally disturbing is the resounding silence on the part of international bodies concerned with health and development—the World Bank, the World Health Organization, the U.S. Agency for International Development, to name a few—about the human and economic costs of illegal abortion. Abortion-related deaths and illness are to them an invisible plague.

WHO studies in various settings indicate that the share of maternal deaths caused by induced abortion ranges from 7 percent to more than 50 percent. On average, between 20 and 25 percent of maternal mortality is attributable to illegal or clandestine abortion. In Latin America, complications of illegal abortion are thought to be the main cause of death in women between the ages of 15 and 39.[5]

The number of abortion deaths is a direct reflection of access to safe services. Thus it is not difficult to understand the high rates of abortion-related maternal mortality in Ceausescu's Romania. (See Table 1.) Wherever illegal abortions are widespread—

TABLE 1  Share of Maternal Deaths Due to Illegal or Clandestine Abortions, Selected Countries, Mid-Eighties (percent)

| Country | Share |
|---|---|
| Romania | 86 |
| Ethiopia | 54 |
| Chile | 36 |
| Argentina | 35 |
| Jamaica | 33 |
| Costa Rica | 30 |
| Colombia | 29 |
| Soviet Union | 29 |
| Zimbabwe | 28 |
| Nigeria | 25 |
| Tanzania | 21 |
| Sri Lanka | 13 |

SOURCE: Based on Erica Royston and Sue Armstrong, eds., *Preventing Maternal Deaths* (Geneva: World Health Organization, 1989); Erica Royston, "Estimating the Number of Abortion Deaths," Seminar on Abortion Research Methodology, Population Council, New York, December 12–13, 1989.

as they are in countries as disparate as Ethiopia, Argentina, and the Soviet Union—women's lives are at risk.

Abortion-related deaths are estimated to reach 1,000 per 100,000 illegal abortions in some parts of Africa, as opposed to less than 1 death per 100,000 legal procedures in the United States. Hospital admissions in African cities, virtually the only available indicator of abortion trends, are rising in tandem with reliance on abortion as a method of birth control Khama Rogo, a medical doctor and faculty member at the University of Nairobi, indicates that admissions of women suffering from complications of illegal abortions have risen 600–800 percent at Nairobi's Kenyatta National Hospital over the past decade. He estimates that in 1990 more than 74,000 African women may die following an illegal abortion.[6]

...

The problem is not limited to developing countries. It exists wherever access to safe abortion is blocked. Because doctors and other providers of abortion in the Soviet Union rely heavily on outdated techniques, the number of complications due to both legal (within the government system) and "illegal" abortions is high.

...

From one-fifth to half of all maternal deaths worldwide could be prevented by providing access to safe abortion services. No international effort to accomplish this is on the horizon, but in a few countries individual groups are working to furnish the technical means and training to deal more efficiently, at least, with complications. IPAS, for one, has been working in sub-Saharan Africa to train clinicians in safe use of the manual vacuum aspiration technique. Use of this in the treatment of incomplete abortions has reduced the time needed to treat women suffering from poorly executed operations, and lowered their risk of hemorrhage and infection. ...

Each roadblock to safe abortion raises the social costs of illegal procedures several-fold. Illegal abortions drain health resources. Complications from them require treatments that are in short supply. A study of 617 women suffering abortion complications who were admitted to 10 hospitals in Zaire found that 95 percent required antibiotics, 62 percent anesthetics, and 17 percent transfusions. Oftentimes, hospital supplies in Africa are so scarce that women must go to the local pharmacy and provide their own antibiotics—or not receive treatment. …

In a study of the effects on the health system in Latin America, demographer Judith Fortney concluded that illegal abortions require, on average, "2 or 3 days in the hospital, 15 or 20 minutes in the operating room, antibiotics, anaesthesia, and quite often a blood transfusion. In many hospitals, each of these resources is relatively scarce and their use for abortion patients may mean that other patients are deprived." When multiplied by the share of illegal abortions worldwide resulting in complications, the enormity of the problem becomes obvious. The costs could be reduced greatly if safe, legal abortions were accessible to all.[7]

…

Restricting access to safe abortion services increases the financial burdens on low-income women and their families. Procuring a clandestine abortion can be expensive, but for those women who suffer complications, the costs are higher still. In Thailand's rural Chayapoom province, women suffering complications of illegal abortion severe enough to require hospitalization lost an average of 12 days of time from their normal activities; those whose complications did not require a hospital stay still lost 6 days.[8]

A recent accounting by the Alan Guttmacher Institute of U.S. national and state expenditures on contraceptive counseling and supplies hints at the broader social costs of unwanted births. The research group estimated that every dollar spent to provide contraceptive services to women who might otherwise find it difficult or impossible to obtain them without help saved $4.40. In 1987, a total of $412 million was spent by federal and state governments for family planning. The study's authors calculated that without this funding about 1.2 million more unintended pregnancies would have occurred nationwide, leading to 509,000 mistimed or unwanted births and 516,000 abortions. Averting these unwanted pregnancies saved $1.8 billion that would otherwise have been spent on medical and nutritional services and on welfare payments.[9]

Children themselves are the other victims of restricted access. Studies indicate that the children born from an unwanted pregnancy are less likely to survive childhood and more likely than others their age to exhibit social and psychological problems. According to another study in rural Thailand, children wanted by one or neither parents were twice as likely to die before their first birthday as children wanted by both parents, even when accounting for other factors influencing child survival. Sociologist Ruth Dixon-Mueller suggests it "is possible that the widely noted higher mortality risks of infants born 'too early, too late, too many, or too close,' represent in some degree the disguised effects of the pregnancy having been unwanted."[10]

In *Born Unwanted: Developmental Effects of Denied Abortion,* Henry David assessed the psychological and social development of children in Czechoslovakia who
were born to women denied abortions for that particular pregnancy. As opposed to
children of planned and wanted pregnancies, these children had higher rates of behavioral and social adjustment problems and poorer performance in school.[11]

In the Third World, the lack of any kind of social support for the poor leaves
women who carry unwanted pregnancies to term few options. Among them is the
outright abandonment of children, which is increasing in developing and other
countries. ...

...

## The Power of Abortion Rights

What ... is the abortion debate really about? In the words of abortion rights activist
and medical doctor Warren Hern, it is a struggle over "who runs our society ... self-
determination ... individual choice, personal freedom and responsibility." This is
particularly and painfully true for women. The struggle for abortion rights cannot
be separated from the broader struggles of women to gain equality in all facets of life,
from family and domestic issues to parity in the workplace.[12]

In *Births and Power: Social Change and the Politics of Reproduction,* anthropologist
W. Penn Handwerker observes that while individual births are important to particular families or communities, on the whole births are "significant within societies ...
insofar as they cement or change power relationships." In societies where women's
access to resources is limited, childbearing is often their most secure investment activity. By proving her fertility, a woman may gain and keep a husband; by bearing
many children, she simultaneously expands her family's economic power and guarantees economic support in retirement. In sum, fertility is one path to power.[13]

But as economies evolve, so do families. Educational attainment becomes the criteria for advancement, and children become more expensive to raise. New opportunities for employment and new sources of empowerment open up for women.
Changes in property rights and family laws favoring greater access to resources for
women usually hasten this transition. Inevitably, women seek ways to limit their fertility, in part through contraception or abortion.

Increased competition for employment and income as well as changes in the
structure of the work force alter the power relationships among various groups, an
evolution that is well under way in the United States and throughout Western Europe. As roles change, tensions arise between the sexes, in much the same way as they
develop between racial and ethnic groups competing in similar circumstances. But
conflicts over the roles of men and women in society are complicated by religious
and social proscriptions against expressions of sexuality outside its role in procreation.

Individuals or groups that feel threatened by these changes may and often do attempt to retain the status quo. This pits them directly against women who, in weighing childbearing against other opportunities, seek to exercise control over when and

TABLE 2  Legal Abortions by Weeks of Gestation, Selected Countries, Most Recent Year (percent distribution)

| Country | 8 Weeks or Less | 9–12 Weeks | 13–16 Weeks | 17 Weeks or More |
|---|---|---|---|---|
| Canada | 33 | 55 | 8 | 3 |
| Denmark | 41 | 57 | 1 | 1 |
| Japan | 52 | 41 | 3 | 3 |
| Sweden | 41 | 55 | 3 | 1 |
| United States | 51 | 40 | 5 | 4 |

NOTE: Distributions do not add to 100 due to rounding.
SOURCE: Stanley K. Henshaw, "Induced Abortion: A World Review, 1990," *Family Planning Perspectives,* March/April 1990.

if to become a parent. As Handwerker notes, "The issue is not whether abortion is 'right' or 'wrong.' What is 'right' or 'wrong' varies with resource access ... and power relations. ... Abortion may improve or optimize resource access. ... Thus, the issue is choice. The conflict ... is intense because the issue is whether one group can deny to another the fundamental right to seek a better life."[14]

...

Each year, millions of individual women around the world of all cultural, religious, economic, and educational backgrounds come to the conclusion that, for whatever personal reason or constellation of causes, they cannot carry a pregnancy to term. Where abortion services are safe and affordable, by far the largest share of women terminate their pregnancies within the first trimester. (See Table 2.) Where those services are scarce or too expensive, they may delay until later stages.

What a growing collection of social science studies from around the world makes clear, however, is that each woman weighs the decision in the context of her own sense of fairness, ability to care for a child, and personal circumstances and needs. Yet opponents of abortion rights seek to impose on all women their vision that a fertilized egg and a just-born child each have equal rights in the world.

...

In developing countries, the issue of "choice" is often not so much about a "better" life as it is about the fundamental right to life itself. In societies where cultural constraints on women are strong and they remain economically and politically subservient to men, reproduction is simply one among many aspects of their lives in which women lack self-determination.

From childhood well into their reproductive years the power of individual women—to determine at what stage they become sexually active, whom they are bonded to, when sex will take place, or when and how to bear children—is low, if it exists at all. Women may be forced into unwanted sexual contact and unwanted pregnancies through violent attack, sexual coercion, or the more socially acceptable arranged and often forced marriage. Once wed, the decision on the timing and number of births is more often the prerogative of a woman's husband and family members than her own. Even where the means to prevent pregnancy are available to women in the Third World (and this is relatively rare), lack of spousal support often leads to high rates of contraceptive failure.

Equally reprehensible is the subjugation of women's desires to those of state-enforced pronatalism. Nicolae Ceausescu is only one among many heads of state who ... relegated women to reproduction in the interest of "national security." As demographer Judith Bruce states quite plainly, for women who by no choice of their own face unwanted pregnancy, "abortion is the final exit from a series of enforced conditions." For a large share of the millions of women whose only option is illegal abortion, that final exit is death.[15]

## From Crime to Common Sense

The impact of unwanted pregnancy embraces but extends beyond the individual to encompass broader objectives, including the struggle for women to become equal partners in society and efforts to improve health among women and children. Less well recognized but equally important is the role that abortion, whether legal or illegal, plays in the transition from high to low fertility.

An international consensus among a diverse body of policymakers already exists on the adverse effects of rapid population growth on economic performance, the environment, family welfare, health, and political stability. For reasons of politics many of these same leaders shy away from or ignore the role played by abortion in slowing birth rates. Yet as public health researchers Stephen Mumford and Elton Kessel note, "no nation wanting to reduce its growth to less than 1 percent can expect to do so without the widespread use of abortion." Policymakers who call for slower population growth while remaining silent on the issue of access to safe abortion are willing to achieve this goal at a high price in women's lives.[16]

The tremendous social gains to be reaped from eliminating illegal abortions cannot be ignored. First among them is a reduction in abortion-related maternal mortality of at least 25 percent and in related illnesses of far more. Reductions in illegal abortions and unwanted pregnancies would save billions in social and health care costs, freeing these resources for other uses.

Only by increasing access to family planning information and supplies, offering couples a wider and safer array of contraceptives, and improving the delivery of comprehensive reproductive health care services can the number of abortions be reduced. Some countries have already chosen this commonsense approach. Italy, for example, now requires local and regional health authorities to promote contraceptive services and other measures to reduce the demand for abortion, while Czech law aims to prevent abortion through sex education in schools and health facilities and through the provision of free contraceptives and associated care. Some countries now require postabortion contraceptive counseling and education; some mandate programs for men as well.[17]

...

The steps needed to make these gains universal are plain. Decriminalization and clarification of laws governing abortion would secure the rights of couples around the world to plan the size and spacing of their families safely. Policies that put abortion into the context of public health and family planning would immediately reduce the incidence of illegal operations. Removal of the administrative, financial, and geographic roadblocks to access not only to safe abortions but to family planning services in general would reduce overall abortion rates and further improve public health.

While the way is evident, the will is lacking. The missing ingredient is political commitment. Natural allies—representatives of groups concerned with women's rights, environmental degradation, family planning, health, and population growth—have failed to mount a concerted effort to dispel abortion myths. And despite the overwhelming evidence of the high human and social costs incurred by restrictive laws, abortion politics remains dominated by narrowly drawn priorities that reflect only one set of beliefs and attitudes. Respect for both ethical diversity and factual accuracy is a precondition for a truly "public" policy on the question of abortion.

Reforming restrictive laws may stir opposition. Failing to do so exacts an emotional and economic toll on society—and sentences countless women around the world to an early grave.

## Notes

1. Mary Ann Castle et al., "Observations on Abortion in Africa," *Studies in Family Planning,* July/August 1990.

2. Julie DeClerque, "Unsafe Abortion Practices in Subsaharan Africa and Latin America: A Call to Policymakers," presentation at Panel on Culture, Public Policy, and Reproductive Health, Association for Women in Development Conference, Washington, D.C., November 17–19, 1989; ... Erica Royston and Sue Armstrong, eds., *Preventing Maternal Deaths* (Geneva: World Health Organization [WHO] 1989). Stanley K. Henshaw, "Induced Abortion: A World Review, 1990," *Family Planning Perspectives,* March/April 1990.

3. Estimates on abortion deaths in India from Sudesh Bahl Dhall and Philip D. Harvey, "Characteristics of First Trimester Abortion Patients at an Urban Indian Clinic," *Studies in Family Planning,* March/April 1984; data on numbers of women whose health is impaired as a result of illegal abortion from DeClerque, "Unsafe Abortion Practices."

4. DeClerque, "Unsafe Abortion Practices."

5. Fred T. Sai and Janet Nassim, "The Need for a Reproductive Health Approach," *International Journal of Gynecology and Obstetrics,* Supplement 3, 1989; Royston and Armstrong, *Preventing Maternal Deaths;* Tomas Frejka and Lucille Atkin, "The Role of Induced Abortion in the Fertility Transition of Latin America," prepared for IUSSP/CELADE/CENEP Seminar on the Fertility Transition, Buenos Aires, Argentina, April 3, 1990.

6. Khama Rogo, "Induced Abortion in Africa" (unpublished draft), prepared for Population Association of America Annual Meeting, Toronto, Canada, May 2–3, 1990.

7. Judith A. Fortney, "The Use of Hospital Resources to Treat Incomplete Abortions: Examples from Latin America," *Public Health Reports,* November/December 1981.

8. Tongplaew Narkavonnakit and Tony Bennett, "Health Consequences of Induced Abortion in Rural Northeast Thailand," *Studies in Family Planning,* February 1981.

9. Jacqueline Darroch Forrest and Susheela Singh, "Public Sector Savings Resulting from Expenditures for Contraceptive Services," *Family Planning Perspectives,* January/February 1990.

ɔn-Mueller, "Abortion Policy and Women's Health in Developing Countries," *ɟournal of Health Sciences,* 20, no. 2, 1990; "Deaths from Abortion," in Erica Sue Armstrong, eds., *Preventing Maternal Deaths* (Geneva: World Health Orga- HO], 1989).

ïy P. David et al., *Born Unwanted: Developmental Effects of Denied Abortion* (New York: ⌐ɪ inger Publishing Company, 1988).

12. Warren Hern, "The Politics of Choice: Abortion as Insurrection," in W. Penn Handwerker, ed., *Births and Power: Social Change and the Politics of Reproduction* (Boulder, Colo.: Westview Press, 1990).

13. W. Penn Handwerker, "Politics and Reproduction: A Window on Social Change," in Handwerker, *Births and Power.*

14. Ibid.

15. Judith Bruce, Senior Associate, Programs Division, The Population Council, New York, private communication, April 4, 1990.

16. Stephen D. Mumford and Elton Kessel, "Is Wide Availability of Abortion Essential to National Population Growth Control Programs? Experiences of 116 Countries," *American Journal of Obstetrics and Gynecology,* July 15, 1984.

17. Rebecca J. Cook, "Abortion Laws and Policies," *International Journal of Gynecology and Obstetrics,* Supplement 3, 1989; National Abortion Rights Action League, "Post-*Webster* Anti-Choice Legislative Activity," Washington, D.C., memorandum, March 29, 1990.

# Prenatal and Preconception Sex Choice Technologies: A Path to Femicide?

## Helen B. Holmes and Betty B. Hoskins

...

Why are so many medical scientists in so many laboratories around the world working on so many different ways to select or detect sex of the unborn? Let us suggest at least six motivations. First there is always the challenge in understanding any of nature's mysteries. Something can be known that no human beings ever knew before! Men are especially interested in solving and appropriating the mysteries that belong to women.

Second, since knowledge is said to be power, that power can be wielded. Western humankind seems to assume that nature is poorly designed and must be 'improved' by technology, that natural processes can and must be controlled.

Third is the western love affair with technology, the compulsion to make devices to control nature.

Fourth is the wish to specify the sex of one's children, a modern and an ancient wish. The difference is that now science and technology might 'grant' that wish. If we think family-planning is a good thing, why not sex-planning? Is not this reproductive freedom?

The fifth reason commonly appears in the medical literature. When a mother carries the gene for a debilitating sex-linked disease, a sex-choice technology could prevent the production of children of the sex at risk, usually male; these children would be spared a life of suffering. (Selecting against a male in such a case, however, is not the same as choosing *for* a girl.)

The sixth reason we need to examine carefully. Sex selection [for male children] has been proposed as a means to control the population explosion. ... Clare Booth Luce ... has stated:

> The determining factor in the growth of all animal populations is ... the birth rate of female offspring. Only women have babies. And only girl babies grow up to be women. ... In the overpopulated countries, the preference for males amounts to an obsession. ... A pill ... which ... would assure the birth of a son would come as man-ah! [sic] from Heaven. (Luce 1978: pp. C–1)

## Sex Preferences and Imbalances

Luce is accurate about the preference for males. Son preference is a reality in both developed and developing nations. In many religions sons have specific ceremonial roles. In India and in parts of Europe the dowry that must be provided with each daughter upon marriage places a burden on families. In many countries over the globe, a woman's status and her treatment by those around her are determined by the number of sons she has produced. The need to bear a son in order to have worth as a person causes us to devalue ourselves. And in most countries we find also the desire that the *firstborn* be male. ... Roberta Steinbacher has said:

> When we add to the well-documented literature on son preference the findings on firstborns and firstborn male preference, the information is devastating to women. ... That firstborns have distinct advantages over later borns has been well-documented for years. ... The *de facto* second class status of women in the world would be confirmed *in fact, by choice*. (Steinbacher 1983).

...

What would social relations be like if sex choice were freely available? Several conjectures and flights of the imagination have been published. [Even John Postgate (who advocates male sex selection for population control) is pessimistic:]

> All sorts of taboos would be expected and it is probable that a form of *purdah* would become necessary. Women's right to work ... would probably be forgotten transiently. ...

Some might treat their women as queen ants, others as rewards for the most outstanding (or most determined) males. (Postgate 1973: p. 16)

Guttentag and Secord ... have studied several *actual* modern and historical populations with sex ratio imbalances. They observed that most societies with a preponderance of males have the following characteristics:

> bride-price and bride-service, great importance attached to virginity, emphasis on the sanctity of the family ... proscription against adultery ... marriage at an early age, and ... women ... regarded as inferior to men ... [in] reasoned judgment, scholarship and political affairs. (Guttentag and Secord 1983: p. 79)

In some such societies women are treated as possessions to be bought and sold. Paradoxically, certain countries where women are the minority so devalue the gender that they contribute further to the scarcity of females by female infanticide, girl child neglect, and bride murders.

## A Feminist Analysis

The real heart of the problem is that sex choice technologies would nurture patriarchy. All current forms of government are patriarchal: they foster competitiveness and have hierarchies of power and privilege; 'masculine' traits, such as aggressiveness, are rewarded. 'Feminine' qualities, such as compassion and co-operation, are disparaged. The earth, seen as feminine, is exploited. (The term 'patriarchal' does not necessarily mean 'male'; there are patriarchal women, and non-patriarchal men.) We believe that this patriarchal attitude towards the living and non-living earth, the weak, the poor, the 'others', is at the root of all the problems that are threatening the very existence of human life on this planet: poverty, pollution, nuclear war, and, yes, overpopulation.

*If* we were to use sex choice technologies and use them to select for males, we would nourish and confirm this omnipresent bias for the 'masculine.' And the mushrooming patriarchy could well lead to the end of human existence.

And why choose? Tabitha Powledge has said:

> [To] choose the sexes of our children ... is one of the most stupendously sexist acts in which it is possible to engage. It is the original sexist sin ... [Both pre- and post-conception technologies] make the most basic judgment about the worth of a human being rest first and foremost on its sex. (Powledge 1981: p. 196)

Even if people were to choose girls instead of boys, they would be emphasizing patriarchal values of rank-ordering and judgementalism. Many troubles result from needless dualisms and unnecessary choices. Hoskins (1983) concludes: 'In the case of sex preselection, a reasonable stance would be *not* to choose a girl or boy, but to welcome each *child*.'

But, what about reproductive freedom? This question poses a real dilemma to the feminist. If we should advocate restrictions of research into sex choice technologies, or if we should advocate regulations against the use of such technologies, we then can be understood as suggesting to policy makers that governments ought to regulate human reproduction. Hard-won reproductive freedoms would then be jeopardized. Thus, while standing in strong opposition to these technologies, we cannot urge laws against them (Powledge 1981).

And what about the severe population problem in the world? Some say that a bit of sexist prejudice is a less grave evil than the death by starvation of large numbers of people. However, to propose sex selection for population control is to be racist and classist as well as sexist. Advocates express no interest in having the rich white minority sacrifice any of its affluence for the benefit of the poor majority. Always it is the Third World or the poor who should have fewer, or only male, children. ...

The faulty ethic of such population control is that the end is used to justify the means. The end is that *Homo sapiens* must be kept going, no matter how horrible a creature 'he' becomes in planning for 'his' survival.

As a matter of fact, positive, morally good policies have been shown to lead to population reduction. Data on factors influencing the birthrate clearly demonstrate that increases in income levels, health care, employment opportunities, education, and the status of women all contribute to decreasing population growth. ...

## Conclusion

Sex selection can be touted as a 'choice' for women. However, so many of the choices that women face remain within the patriarchal framework. It is hard to choose out of that framework, and hard to raise a son or a daughter less stereotypically. There may be short-term benefits in a desired family configuration, but the long-term consequences are grim if patriarchal thinking is reinforced at the moment of conceiving a new human being.

In sum, then, our first purpose is to alert women about the widespread, international, clinical interest in developing sex choice technologies.

Our second purpose is to show women that sex choice can be another way of oppressing women. Under the guise of choice we may indeed exacerbate our own oppression.

Our third purpose is to emphasize that developers of such technologies may have racist and classist (as well as sexist) motivations, whether or not obscured by their professed concern about runaway population growth.

---

### References

Guttentag, Marcia, and Secord, Paul F., *Too Many Women? The Sex Ratio Question* (Beverly Hills: Sage Publications 1983).

Hoskins, Betty B., and Helen Bequaert Holmes. 'When not to choose: A case study'. *Journal of Medical Humanities and Bioethics* 6(1) (1985), 28–37.

Luce, Clare Booth, 'Next: Pills to make most babies male', *Washington Star* (19 July 1978), C–1, C–4.

:, John, 'Bat's chance in hell', *New Scientist*, 58 (841) (1973), pp. 12–16.
₁ᵤwⁱⁱᵉᵈge, Tabitha, 'Unnatural selection: On choosing children's sex', in Holmes, Helen B., Hoskins, Betty B., and Gross, M. (eds.), *The Custom-Made Child? Women-Centered Perspectives* (Clifton, NJ: The Humana Press 1981), pp. 193–9.
Steinbacher, Roberta, 'Sex preselection: From here to fraternity', in Gould, Carol (ed.), *Beyond Domination: New Perspectives on Women and Philosophy* (Totowa, NJ: Rowman and Allenheld 1983).

### For Further Reading

Holmes, Helen Bequaert. 'Sex preselection: Eugenics for everyone'? *Biomedical Ethics Reviews—1985*, 39–71.
Vines, Gail. 'The hidden cost of sex selection.' *New Scientist* 1 May 1993:12–13.
Warren, Mary Anne. *Gendercide: The implications of sex selection* (Totowa, NJ: Rowman & Allenheld, 1985).
Wertz, Dorothy C., and John C. Fletcher. 'Sex selection through prenatal diagnosis: A feminist critique.' In *Feminist perspectives in medical ethics*, ed. Helen Bequaert Holmes and Laura M. Purdy, pp. 240–253 (Bloomington: Indiana University Press, 1992).

# Disability Rights Perspectives on Reproductive Technologies and Public Policy

## Deborah Kaplan

My comments are founded in a social movement that promotes radical changes in the way we as a culture think about disability and disabled people. It is often referred to as the disability rights movement. Its major leaders are disabled themselves, and we are engaged in very broad social reform.

…

### Disability and Prenatal Screening

In the context of prenatal screening, the implicit and explicit perceptions about disability and disabled people are worth examining. Literature and promotional materials focus on the benefits to prospective parents of knowing that they will have a "normal, healthy" baby. Implicit is that a child with a disability is neither normal nor healthy. Words such as "defective" and "deformed" abound. At a recent conference in San Francisco of a national organization of abortion providers, a physician referred to disabled newborns as "gorks."

Needless to say, the disability rights movement does not seek to perpetuate such a perception or definition of disability. It points to the environment, rather than the individual, as the source of the problem. A person who uses a wheelchair is not "hopelessly confined" in a wheelchair-accessible building. A deaf person is not isolated from the outside world by his or her deafness so much as by the unavailability of sign language interpreters, telecommunication devices for the deaf (TDDs), and closed (or open) captioning on television. Disabled people are unemployed in larger numbers proportionately than any other group not for lack of talent or skills, but because of employer fears and lack of appropriate educational opportunities. The disability alone does not determine a person's ability to function or succeed. It is possible for an environment and society to support and accommodate people with disabilities, and to recognize that it is "normal" for a certain percentage of the population to be disabled.

## Social Policy Towards Disability

Our society's social policies towards disability and disabled people reflect a national schizophrenia; we cannot seem to make up our minds what we want to do. Historically, the old line has been that disability is inherently tragic, and that disabled people are a burden on their families and society. Large-scale institutions were created as a response to this perception. Disabled people did not hold any unique legal rights, and indeed, had fewer rights than others. "Ugly" laws were enacted, prohibiting disabled people from being seen in public. Many disabled people were forcibly incarcerated and/or sterilized. Disabled children were not entitled to a public education. ...

The new policies are represented by state and federal statutes prohibiting discrimination based on disability, and stipulating that disabled people are entitled to equality of opportunity and should be accommodated by social service systems, schools, and employers in order to participate fully in society. ...

In enacting ... new laws, ... Congress was specific about its perceptions and intent:

> The Congress finds that ... it is essential ... to assure that all individuals with handicaps are able to live their lives independently and with dignity, and that the complete integration of all individuals with handicaps into normal community living, working and service patterns be held as the final objective. White House Conference on Handicapped Individuals Act, 29 U.S.C. Section 701n.

Also typical of the new social policy is the decision of the California Supreme Court in *In re Marriage of Carney* 598 P.2d 36 (1979), a custody dispute in which the mother contested the father's custody of their two sons based on his disability, quadriplegia:

> ... it is erroneous to presume that a parent in a wheelchair cannot share to a meaningful degree in the physical activities of his child, should both desire it. On the one hand,

modern technology has made the handicapped increasingly mobile, as demonstrated by William's purchase of a van and his plans to drive it by means of hand controls …

At the same time the physically handicapped have made the public more aware of the many unnecessary obstacles to their participation in community life. Among the evidence of the public's change in attitude is a growing body of legislation intended to reduce or eliminate the physical impediments to that participation …

Both the state and federal governments now pursue the commendable goal of total integration of handicapped persons into the mainstream of society … No less important to this policy is the integration of the handicapped into the responsibilities and satisfactions of family life, cornerstone of our social system. *Id.* at 43–45.

Much of our society's thinking about prenatal screening is based on the old line and the stereotypes about disability that accompany it. It should be recognized that these issues invite a quick, emotional, gut-level response. In this case, such a response evokes our cultural aversion to disability, and our fears of becoming disabled or of having a disabled child. The often irrational thinking that accompanies these fears leads people to ignore the facts: that there are many severe disabilities that cannot be predicted through prenatal screening and that prenatal screening cannot predict the severity of the disability. In fact, many of the genetic conditions that are now included in prenatal screening are never severe. The inability to distinguish between anencephaly and mild spina bifida, for instance, results in a tendency to paint the picture with a very broad brush of hopelessness and tragedy. In spite of much evidence in the world around us that living with a moderate or mild disability is not necessarily tragic or burdensome, prenatal screening may require people to behave as though all disabilities are by their nature terrible.

Prenatal screening encourages people to overlook the social policy that is based on the fact that disability can be managed through technology, early intervention programs for very young disabled children, social support systems, and social change. The availability of prenatal screening influences social policy because, up until the present, the literature and materials of its proponents have unabashedly reinforced and strengthened negative attitudes towards disability and disabled people. It has also created the public misperception that soon we will be able to prevent almost all disabilities, no matter how realistic that myth may be. As a result, women and couples who go through prenatal screening may become less accepting of disabilities and disabled people. As prenatal screening becomes more widespread and available for younger women, the potential social impact should not be ignored.

## Reconciling Disability Rights and Reproductive Rights

How can we talk about or take advantage of prenatal screening without further stigmatizing disabled people? Can we? The point of this discussion is not to make a statement about prenatal screening itself, but rather to focus on the way that we talk about and promote it from the perspective of disability rights and the reproductive rights of disabled people. The relative lack of involvement of disabled people in this discussion to date is particularly startling when one considers that prenatal screening involves our perceptions of disability and disabled people in a central way. More broadly, disabled women are a significant group with a stake in specific and unique reproductive rights issues. One way to start making positive changes is to bring more disabled women and disabled people into the public policy debate.

The key to change, however, lies in attempting to reconcile the way we define and perceive reproductive rights issues with the new public policies that recognize and promote the civil rights of disabled people. It should be possible to talk about prenatal screening without assuming that disability is tragic, painful, and burdensome at all times for all people. Those who are involved in this field as theorists, practitioners, or consumers could, with few exceptions, stand to become better acquainted with existing services for disabled people and with the reality of having a disability. How this might be accomplished could be the subject of a conference in itself. It will not be accomplished without involving and becoming involved with disabled people at a much more intimate level than the current relationship of occasional contact, if any. Part of the process of change will of necessity involve enhancing the value given to disabled people and their lives.

...

## Conclusion

No one can seriously dispute that the world is an inequitable place for disabled people. For those disabled people and their supporters who are actively engaged in challenging and reforming those inequities, the issues involved in the debate over reproductive rights policy are directly relevant. Disabled women are engaged in personal and social struggles over their own sexual freedom and reproductive choices. ...

... The reproductive rights community needs to recognize that consideration of disability issues is central, not peripheral, to the discussion. Disabled women should be present to speak of their own experiences. Disabled theorists and activists should be engaged in the debate. The infusion of these new voices and perspectives will deepen the analysis, and make it more real and vital.

# Abortion Through a Feminist
# Ethics Lens

## Susan Sherwin

Abortion has long been a central issue in the arena of applied ethics, but, the distinctive analysis of feminist ethics is generally overlooked in most philosophic discussions. Authors and readers commonly presume a familiarity with the feminist position and equate it with liberal defences of women's right to choose abortion, but, in fact, feminist ethics yields a different analysis of the moral questions surrounding abortion than that usually offered by the more familiar liberal defenders of abortion rights. Most feminists can agree with some of the conclusions that arise from certain non-feminist arguments on abortion, but they often disagree about the way the issues are formulated and the sorts of reasons that are invoked in the mainstream literature.

Among the many differences found between feminist and non-feminist arguments about abortion, is the fact that most non-feminist discussions of abortion consider the questions of the moral or legal permissibility of abortion in isolation from other questions, ignoring (and thereby obscuring) relevant connections to other social practices that oppress women. They are generally grounded in masculinist conceptions of freedom (e.g., privacy, individual choice, individuals' property rights in their own bodies) that do not meet the needs, interests, and intuitions of many of the women concerned. In contrast, feminists seek to couch their arguments in moral concepts that support their general campaign of overcoming injustice in all its dimensions, including those inherent in moral theory itself.[1] There is even disagreement about how best to understand the moral question at issue: non-feminist arguments focus exclusively on the morality and/or legality of performing abortions, whereas feminists insist that other questions, including ones about accessibility and delivery of abortion services must also be addressed.

Although feminists welcome the support of non-feminists in pursuing policies that will grant women control over abortion decisions, they generally envision very different sorts of policies for this purpose than those considered by non-feminist sympathizers. ... Here, I propose one conception of the shape such an analysis should take.

# Women and Abortion

The most obvious difference between feminist and non-feminist approaches to abortion can be seen in the relative attention each gives to the interests and experiences of women in its analysis. Feminists consider it self-evident that the pregnant woman is a subject of principal concern in abortion decisions. In most non-feminist accounts, however, not only is she not perceived as central, she is rendered virtually invisible. Non-feminist theorists, whether they support or oppose women's right to choose abortion, focus almost all their attention on the moral status of the developing embryo or the fetus.

In pursuing a distinctively feminist ethics, it is appropriate to begin with a look at the role of abortion in women's lives. Clearly, the need for abortion can be very intense; women have pursued abortions under appalling and dangerous conditions, across widely diverse cultures and historical periods. No one denies that if abortion is not made legal, safe, and accessible, women will seek out illegal and life-threatening abortions to terminate pregnancies they cannot accept. Anti-abortion activists seem willing to accept this price, but feminists judge the inevitable loss of women's lives associated with restrictive abortion policies to be a matter of fundamental concern.

Although anti-abortion campaigners imagine that women often make frivolous and irresponsible decisions about abortion, feminists recognize that women have abortions for a wide variety of reasons. ...

...

Whatever the reason, most feminists believe that a pregnant woman is in the best position to judge whether abortion is the appropriate response to her circumstances. Since she is usually the only one able to weigh all the relevant factors, most feminists reject attempts to offer any general abstract rules for determining when abortion is morally justified. Women's personal deliberations about abortion include contextually defined considerations reflecting her commitment to the needs and interests of everyone concerned—including herself, the fetus she carries, other members of her household, etc. Because there is no single formula available for balancing these complex factors through all possible cases, it is vital that feminists insist on protecting each woman's right to come to her own conclusions. Abortion decisions are, by their very nature, dependent on specific features of each woman's experience; theoretically dispassionate philosophers and other moralists should not expect to set the agenda for these considerations in any universal way. Women must be acknowledged as full moral agents with the responsibility for making moral decisions about their own pregnancies.[2] Although I think that it is possible for a woman to make a mistake in her moral judgment on this matter (i.e., it is possible that a woman may come to believe that she was wrong about her decision to continue or terminate a pregnancy), the intimate nature of this sort of decision makes it unlikely that anyone else is in a position to arrive at a more reliable conclusion; it is, therefore, improper to grant others the authority to interfere in women's decisions to seek abortions.

Feminist analysis regards the effects of unwanted pregnancies on the lives of women individually and collectively as a central element in the moral evaluation of abortion. Even without patriarchy, bearing a child would be a very important event in a woman's life. It involves significant physical, emotional, social, and (usually) economic changes for her. The ability to exert control over the incidence, timing, and frequency of childbearing is often tied to her ability to control most other things she values. Since we live in a patriarchal society, it is especially important to ensure that women have the authority to control their own reproduction.[3] Despite the diversity of opinion among feminists on most other matters, virtually all feminists seem to agree that women must gain full control over their own reproductive lives if they are to free themselves from male dominance.[4] Many perceive the commitment of the political right wing to opposing abortion as part of a general strategy to reassert patriarchal control over women in the face of significant feminist influence (Petchesky 1980, p. 112).

Women's freedom to choose abortion is also linked with their ability to control their own sexuality. Women's subordinate status often prevents them from refusing men sexual access to their bodies. If women cannot end the unwanted pregnancies that result from male sexual dominance, their sexual vulnerability to particular men can increase, because caring for an(other) infant involves greater financial needs and reduced economic opportunities for women.[5] As a result, pregnancy often forces women to become dependent on men. Since a woman's dependence on a man is assumed to entail that she will remain sexually loyal to him, restriction of abortion serves to channel women's sexuality and further perpetuates the cycle of oppression.

In contrast to most non-feminist accounts, feminist analyses of abortion direct attention to the question of how women get pregnant. Those who reject abortion seem to believe that women can avoid unwanted pregnancies by avoiding sexual intercourse. Such views show little appreciation for the power of sexual politics in a culture that oppresses women. Existing patterns of sexual dominance mean that women often have little control over their sexual lives. They may be subject to rape by strangers, or by their husbands, boyfriends, colleagues, employers, customers, fathers, brothers, uncles, and dates. Often, the sexual coercion is not even recognized as such by the participants, but is the price of continued "good will"—popularity, economic survival, peace, or simple acceptance. Few women have not found themselves in circumstances where they do not feel free to refuse a man's demands for intercourse, either because he is holding a gun to her head or because he threatens to be emotionally hurt if she refuses (or both). Women are socialized to be compliant and accommodating, sensitive to the feelings of others, and frightened of physical power; men are socialized to take advantage of every opportunity to engage in sexual intercourse and to use sex to express dominance and power. Under such circumstances, it is difficult to argue that women could simply "choose" to avoid heterosexual activity if they wish to avoid pregnancy. Catherine MacKinnon neatly sums it up: "the logic by which women are supposed to consent to sex [is]: preclude the alternatives, then call the remaining option 'her choice' " (MacKinnon 1989, p. 192).

...

From a feminist perspective, a central moral feature of pregnancy is that it takes place in *women's bodies* and has profound effects on *women's* lives. Gender-neutral accounts of pregnancy are not available; pregnancy is explicitly a condition associated with the female body.[6] Because the need for abortion is experienced only by women, policies about abortion affect women uniquely. Thus, it is important to consider how proposed policies on abortion fit into general patterns of oppression for women. Unlike non-feminist accounts, feminist ethics demands that the effects on the oppression of women be a principal consideration when evaluating abortion policies.

## The Fetus

In contrast, most non-feminist analysts believe that the moral acceptability of abortion turns on the question of the moral status of the fetus. Even those who support women's right to choose abortion tend to accept the central premise of the anti-abortion proponents that abortion can only be tolerated if it can be proved that the fetus is lacking some criterion of full personhood.[7] Opponents of abortion have structured the debate so that it is necessary to define the status of the fetus as either valued the same as other humans (and hence entitled not to be killed) or as lacking in all value. Rather than challenging the logic of this formulation, many defenders of abortion have concentrated on showing that the fetus is indeed without significant value (Tooley 1972, Warren 1973); others, such as Wayne Sumner (1981), offer a more subtle account that reflects the gradual development of fetuses whereby there is some specific criterion that determines the degree of protection to be afforded them which is lacking in the early stages of pregnancy but present in the later stages. Thus, the debate often rages between abortion opponents who describe the fetus as an "innocent," vulnerable, morally important, separate being whose life is threatened and who must be protected at all costs, and abortion supporters who try to establish some sort of deficiency inherent to fetuses which removes them from the scope of the moral community.

The woman on whom the fetus depends for survival is considered as secondary (if she is considered at all) in these debates. The actual experiences and responsibilities of real women are not perceived as morally relevant (unless they, too, can be proved innocent by establishing that their pregnancies are a result of rape or incest). It is a common assumption of both defenders and opponents of women's right to choose abortion that many women will be irresponsible in their choices. The important question, though, is whether fetuses have the sort of status that justifies interfering in women's choices at all. In some contexts, women's role in gestation is literally reduced to that of "fetal containers"; the individual women disappear or are perceived simply as mechanical life-support systems.[8]

...

Within anti-abortion arguments, fetuses are identified as individuals; in our culture which views the (abstract) individual as sacred, fetuses *qua* individuals should be honoured and preserved. Extraordinary claims are made to try to establish the individuality and moral agency of fetuses. At the same time, the women who carry these fetal individuals are viewed as passive hosts whose only significant role is to re-frain from aborting or harming their fetuses. Since it is widely believed that the woman does not actually have to *do* anything to protect the life of the fetus, preg-nancy is often considered (abstractly) to be a tolerable burden to protect the life of an individual so like us.[9]

Medicine has played its part in supporting these sorts of attitudes. Fetal medicine is a rapidly expanding specialty, and it is commonplace in professional medical jour-nals to find references to pregnant women as "fetal environments." Fetal surgeons now have at their disposal a repertory of sophisticated technology that can save the lives of dangerously ill fetuses; in light of such heroic successes, it is perhaps under-standable that women have disappeared from their view. These specialists see fetuses as their patients, not the women who nurture them. Doctors perceive themselves as the *active* agents in saving fetal lives and, hence, believe that they are the ones in di-rect relationship with the fetuses they treat.

Perhaps even more distressing than the tendency to ignore the woman's agency al-together and view her as a purely passive participant in the medically controlled events of pregnancy and childbirth is the growing practice of viewing women as gen-uine threats to the well-being of the fetus. Increasingly, women are viewed as irre-sponsible or hostile towards their fetuses, and the relationship between them is char-acterized as adversarial (Overall 1987, p. 60). Concern for the well-being of the fetus is taken as licence for doctors to intervene to ensure that women comply with medi-cal "advice." Courts are called upon to enforce the doctors' orders when moral pres-sure alone proves inadequate, and women are being coerced into undergoing un-wanted Caesarean deliveries and technologically monitored hospital births. Some states have begun to imprison women for endangering their fetuses through drug abuse and other socially unacceptable behaviours. An Australian state recently intro-duced a bill that makes women liable to criminal prosecution "if they are found to have smoked during pregnancy, eaten unhealthful foods, or taken any other action which can be shown to have adversely affected the development of the fetus" (Warren 1989, p. 60).

In other words, physicians have joined with anti-abortionist activists in fostering a cultural acceptance of the view that fetuses are distinct individuals, who are physi-cally, ontologically, and socially separate from the women whose bodies they inhabit, and who have their own distinct interests. In this picture, pregnant women are either ignored altogether or are viewed as deficient in some crucial respect and hence sub-ject to coercion for the sake of their fetuses. In the former case, the interests of the women concerned are assumed to be identical with those of the fetus; in the latter, the women's interests are irrelevant because they are preceived as immoral, unim-portant, or unnatural. Focus on the fetus as an independent entity has led to pre-sumptions which deny pregnant women their roles as active, independent, moral agents with a primary interest in what becomes of the fetuses they carry. Emphasis on the fetus's status has led to an assumed licence to interfere with women's repro-ductive freedom.

## A Feminist View of the Fetus

Because the public debate has been set up as a competition between the rights of women and those of fetuses, feminists have often felt pushed to reject claims of fetal value in order to protect women's claims. Yet, as Addelson (1987) has argued, viewing abortion in this way "tears [it] out of the context of women's lives" (p. 107). There are other accounts of fetal value that are more plausible and less oppressive to women.

On a feminist account, fetal development is examined in the context in which it occurs, within women's bodies rather than in the imagined isolation implicit in many theoretical accounts. Fetuses develop in specific pregnancies which occur in the lives of particular women. They are not individuals housed in generic female wombs, nor are they full persons at risk only because they are small and subject to the whims of women. Their very existence is relational, developing as they do within particular women's bodies, and their principal relationship is to the women who carry them.

On this view, fetuses are morally significant, but their status is relational rather than absolute. Unlike other human beings, fetuses do not have any independent existence; their existence is uniquely tied to the support of a specific other. Most non-feminist commentators have ignored the relational dimension of fetal development and have presumed that the moral status of fetuses could be resolved solely in terms of abstract metaphysical criteria of personhood. They imagine that there is some set of properties (such as genetic heritage, moral agency, self-consciousness, language use, or self-determination) which will entitle all who possess them to be granted the moral status of persons (Warren 1973, Tooley 1972). They seek some particular feature by which we can neatly divide the world into the dichotomy of moral persons (who are to be valued and protected) and others (who are not entitled to the same group privileges); it follows that it is a merely empirical question whether or not fetuses possess the relevant properties.

But this vision misinterprets what is involved in personhood and what it is that is especially valued about persons. Personhood is a social category, not an isolated state. Persons are members of a community; they develop as concrete, discrete, and specific individuals. To be a morally significant category, personhood must involve personality as well as biological integrity.[10] It is not sufficient to consider persons simply as Kantian atoms of rationality; persons are all embodied, conscious beings with particular social histories. Annette Baier (1985) has developed a concept of persons as "second persons" which helps explain the sort of social dimension that seems fundamental to any moral notion of personhood:

> A person, perhaps, is best seen as one who was long enough dependent upon other persons to acquire the essential arts of personhood. Persons essentially are *second* persons, who grow up with other persons. ... The fact that a person has a life *history,* and that a people collectively have a history depends upon the humbler fact that each person has a childhood in which a cultural heritage is transmitted, ready for adolescent rejection and adult discriminating selection and contribution. Persons come after and before other persons. (P. 84–85; her emphasis.)

Persons, in other words, are members of a social community which shapes and values them, and personhood is a relational concept that must be defined in terms of interactions and relationships with others.

A fetus is a unique sort of being in that it cannot form relationships freely with others, nor can others readily form relationships with it. A fetus has a primary and particularly intimate relationship with the woman in whose womb it develops; any other relationship it may have is indirect, and must be mediated through the pregnant woman. The relationship that exists between a woman and her fetus is clearly asymmetrical, since she is the only party to the relationship who is capable of making a decision about whether the interaction should continue and since the fetus is wholly dependent on the woman who sustains it while she is quite capable of surviving without it.

However much some might prefer it to be otherwise, no one else can do anything to support or harm a fetus without doing something to the woman who nurtures it. Because of this inexorable biological reality, she bears a unique responsibility and privilege in determining her fetus's place in the social scheme of things. Clearly, many pregnancies occur to women who place very high value on the lives of the particular fetuses they carry, and choose to see their pregnancies through to term despite the possible risks and costs involved; hence, it would be wrong of anyone to force such a woman to terminate her pregnancy under these circumstances. Other women, or some of these same women at other times, value other things more highly (e.g., their freedom, their health, or previous responsibilities which conflict with those generated by the pregnancies), and choose not to continue their pregnancies. The value that women ascribe to individual fetuses varies dramatically from case to case, and may well change over the course of any particular pregnancy. There is no absolute value that attaches to fetuses apart from their relational status determined in the context of their particular development.

...

## Feminist Politics and Abortion

Feminist ethics directs us to look at abortion in the context of other issues of power and not to limit discussion to the standard questions about its moral and legal acceptability. Because coerced pregnancy has repercussions for women's oppressed status generally, it is important to ensure that abortion not only be made legal but that adequate services be made accessible to all women who seek them. This means that within Canada, where medically approved abortion is technically recognized as legal (at least for the moment), we must protest the fact that it is not made available to many of the women who have the greatest need for abortions: vast geographical areas offer no abortion services at all, but unless the women of those regions can afford to travel to urban clinics, they have no meaningful right to abortion. Because women depend on access to abortion in their pursuit of social equality, it is a matter of moral as well as political responsibility that provincial health plans should cover the cost of transport and service in the abortion facilities women choose. Ethical study of abortion involves understanding and critiquing the economic, age, and social barriers that currently restrict access to medically acceptable abortion services.[11]

Moreover, it is also important that abortion services be provided in an atmosphere that fosters women's health and well-being; hence, the care offered should be in a context that is supportive of the choices women make. Abortions should be seen as part of women's overall reproductive health and could be inclined within centres that deal with all matters of reproductive health in an open, patient-centered manner where effective counselling is offered for a wide range of reproductive decisions.[12] Providers need to recognize that abortion is a legitimate option so that services will be delivered with respect and concern for the physical, psychological, and emotional effects on a patient. All too frequently, hospital-based abortions are provided by practitioners who are uneasy about their role and treat the women involved with hostility and resentment. Increasingly, many anti-abortion activists have personalized their attacks and focussed their attention on harassing the women who enter and leave abortion clinics. Surely requiring a woman to pass a gauntlet of hostile protestors on her way to and from an abortion is not conducive to effective health care. Ethical exploration of abortion raises questions about how women are treated when they seek abortions,[13] achieving legal permission for women to dispose of their fetuses if they are determined enough to manage the struggle should not be accepted as the sole moral consideration.

...

Feminists support abortion on demand because they know that women must have control over their reproduction. For the same reason, they actively oppose forced abortion and coerced sterilization, practices that are sometimes inflicted on the most powerless women, especially those in the Third World. Feminist ethics demands that access to voluntary, safe, effective birth control be part of any abortion discussion, so that women have access to other means of avoiding pregnancy.[14]

Feminist analysis addresses the context as well as the practice of abortion decisions. Thus, feminists also object to the conditions which lead women to abort wanted fetuses because there are not adequate financial and social supports available to care for a child. Because feminist accounts value fetuses that are wanted by the women who carry them, they oppose practices which force women to abort because of poverty or intimidation. Yet, the sorts of social changes necessary if we are to free women from having abortions out of economic necessity are vast; they include changes not only in legal and health-care policy, but also in housing, child care, employment, etc. (Petchesky 1980, p. 112). Nonetheless, feminist ethics defines reproductive freedom as the condition under which women are able to make truly voluntary choices about their reproductive lives, and these many dimensions are implicit in the ideal.

Clearly, feminists are not "pro-abortion," for they are concerned to ensure the safety of each pregnancy to the greatest degree possible; wanted fetuses should not be harmed or lost. Therefore, adequate pre- and postnatal care and nutrition are also important elements of any feminist position on reproductive freedom. Where anti-abortionists direct their energies to trying to prevent women from obtaining abortions, feminists seek to protect the health of wanted fetuses. They recognize that far more could be done to protect and care for fetuses if the state directed its resources at supporting women who continue their pregnancies, rather than draining away resources in order to police women who find that they must interrupt their pregnancies. Caring for the women who carry fetuses is not only a more legitimate policy than is regulating them; it is probably also more effective at ensuring the health and well-being of more fetuses.

Feminist ethics also explores how abortion policies fit within the politics of sexual domination. Most feminists are sensitive to the fact that many men support women's right to abortion out of the belief that women will be more willing sexual partners if they believe that they can readily terminate an unwanted pregnancy. Some men coerce their partners into obtaining abortions the women may not want.[15] Feminists understand that many women oppose abortion for this very reason, being unwilling to support a practice that increases women's sexual vulnerability (Luker 1984, p. 209–15). Thus, it is important that feminists develop a coherent analysis of reproductive freedom that includes sexual freedom (as women choose to define it). That requires an analysis of sexual freedom that includes women's right to refuse sex; such a right can only be assured if women have equal power to men and are not subject to domination by virtue of their sex.[16]

In sum, then, feminist ethics demands that moral discussions of abortion be more broadly defined than they have been in most philosophic discussions. Only by reflecting on the meaning of ethical pronouncements on actual women's lives and the connections between judgments on abortion and the conditions of domination and subordination can we come to an adequate understanding of the moral status of abortion in our society. As Rosalind Petchesky (1980) argues, feminist discussion of abortion "must be moved beyond the framework of a 'woman's right to choose' and connected to a much broader revolutionary movement that addresses all of the conditions of women's liberation" (p. 113).

---

## Notes

Earlier versions of this paper were read to the Department of Philosophy, Dalhousie University and to the Canadian Society for Women in Philosophy in Kingston. I am very grateful for the comments received from colleagues in both forums; particular thanks go to Lorraine Code, David Braybrooke, Richmond Campbell, Sandra Taylor, Terry Tomkow and Kadri Vihvelin for their patience and advice.

1. For some idea of the ways in which traditional moral theory oppresses women, see Morgan (1987) and Hoagland (1988).

2. Critics continue to want to structure the debate around the *possibility* of women making frivolous abortion decisions and hence want feminists to agree to setting boundaries on acceptable grounds for choosing abortion. Feminists ought to resist this injunction, though. There is no practical way of drawing a line fairly in the abstract; cases that may appear "frivolous" at a distance, often turn out to be substantive when the details are revealed, i.e., frivolity is in the eyes of the beholder. There is no evidence to suggest that women actually make the sorts of choices worried critics hypothesize about: e.g., a woman eight months pregnant who

chooses to abort because she wants to take a trip or gets in "a tiff" with her partner. These sorts of fantasies, on which demands to distinguish between legitimate and illegitimate personal reasons for choosing abortion chiefly rest, reflect on offensive conception of women as irresponsible; they ought not to be perpetuated. Women, seeking moral guidance in their own deliberations about choosing abortion, do not find such hypothetical discussions of much use.

3. In her monumental historical analysis of the early roots of Western patriarchy, Gerda Lerner (1986) determined that patriarchy began in the period from 3100 to 600 B.C. when men appropriated women's sexual and reproductive capacity; the earliest states entrenched patriarchy by institutionalizing the sexual and procreative subordination of women to men.

4. There are some women who claim to be feminists against choice in abortion. See, for instance, Callahan (1987), [and Anne Maloney in this volume], though few spell out their full feminist program. For reasons I develop in this paper, I do not think this is a consistent position.

5. There is a lot the state could do to ameliorate this condition. If it provided women with adequate financial support, removed the inequities in the labour market, and provided affordable and reliable childcare, pregnancy need not so often lead to a woman's dependence on a particular man. The fact that it does not do so is evidence of the state's complicity in maintaining women's subordinate position with respect to men.

6. See Zillah Eisenstein (1988) for a comprehensive theory of the role of the pregnant body as the central element in the cultural subordination of women.

7. Thomson (1971) is a notable exception to this trend.

8. This seems reminiscent of Aristotle's view of women as "flower pots" where men implant the seed with all the important genetic information and the movement necessary for development and women's job is that of passive gestation, like the flower pot. For exploration of the flower pot picture of pregnancy, see Whitbeck (1973) and Lange (1983).

9. The definition of pregnancy as a purely passive activity reaches its ghoulish conclusion in the increasing acceptability of sustaining brain-dead women on life support systems to continue their functions as incubators until the fetus can be safely delivered. For a discussion of this new trend, see Murphy (1989).

10. This apt phrasing is taken from Petchesky (1984), p. 342.

11. Some feminists suggest we seek recognition of the legitimacy of non-medical abortion services. This would reduce costs and increase access dramatically, with no apparent increase in risk, provided that services were offered by trained, responsible practitioners concerned with the well-being of their clients. It would also allow the possibility of increasing women's control over abortion. See, for example, McDonnell (1984), chap. 8.

12. For a useful model of such a centre, see Van Wagner and Lee (1989).

13. See CARAL/Halifax (1990) for women's stories about their experiences with hospitals and free-standing abortion clinics.

14. Therefore, the Soviet model, where women have access to multiple abortions but where there is no other birth control available, must also be opposed.

15. See CARAL/Halifax (1990), p. 20–21, for examples of this sort of abuse.

16. It also requires that discussions of reproductive and sexual freedom not be confined to "the language of control and sexuality characteristic of a technology of sex" (Diamond and Quinby 1988, p. 197), for such languge is alienating and constrains women's experiences of their own sexuality.

## References

Addelson, Kathryn Pyne. 1987. "Moral Passages." In *Women and Moral Theory*. Edited by Eva Feder Kittay and Diana T. Meyers. Totowa, NJ: Rowman & Littlefield.

Baier, Annette. 1985. *Postures of the Mind: Essays on Mind and Morals*. Minneapolis: University of Minnesota Press.

Callahan, Sidney. 1987. "A Pro-life Feminist Makes Her Case." *Utne Reader* (March/April): 104–14.

CARAL/Halifax. 1990. *Telling Our Stories: Abortion Stories from Nova Scotia*. Halifax: CARAL/Halifax (Canadian Abortion Rights Action League).

Diamond, Irene, and Lee Quinby. 1988. "American Feminism and the Language of Control." In *Feminism & Foucault: Reflections on Resistance*. Edited by Irene Diamond and Lee Quinby. Boston: Northeastern University Press.

Eisenstein, Zillah R. 1988. *The Female Body and the Law*. Berkeley: University of California Press.

Hoagland, Sara Lucia. 1988. *Lesbian Ethics: Toward New Value*. Palo Alto, CA: Institute of Lesbian Studies.

Lange, Lynda. 1983. "Woman is Not a Rational Animal: On Aristotle's Biology of Reproduction." In *Discovering Reality: Feminist Perspectives on Epistemology, Metaphysics, Methodology, and Philosophy of Science*. Edited by Sandra Harding and Merill B. Hintickka. Dordrecht, Holland: D. Reidel.

Lerner, Gerda. 1986. *The Creation of Patriarchy*. New York: Oxford.

Luker, Kristin. 1984. *Abortion and the Politics of Motherhood*. Berkeley: University of California Press.

MacKinnon, Catherine. 1989. *Toward a Feminist Theory of the State*. Cambridge, MA: Harvard University Press.

McDonnell, Kathleen. 1984. *Not an Easy Choice: A Feminist Re-examines Abortion*. Toronto: The Women's Press.

Morgan, Kathryn Pauly. 1987. "Women and Moral Madness." In *Science, Morality and Feminist Theory*. Edited by Marsha Hanen and Kai Nielsen. *Canadian Journal of Philosophy*, Supplementary Volume 13: 201–26.

Murphy, Julien S. 1989. "Should Pregnancies Be Sustained in Brain-dead Women?: A Philosophical Discussion of Postmortem Pregnancy." In *Healing Technology: Feminist Perspectives*. Edited by Kathryn Srother Ratcliff et al. Ann Arbor: The University of Michigan Press.

Overall, Christine. 1987. *Ethics and Human Reproduction: A Feminist Analysis*. Winchester, MA: Allen & Unwin.

Petchesky, Rosalind Pollack. 1980. "Reproductive Freedom: Beyond 'A Woman's Right to Choose.' " In *Women: Sex and Sexuality*. Edited by Catharine R. Stimpson and Ethel Spector Person. Chicago: University of Chicago Press.

Sumner, L. W. 1981. *Abortion and Moral Theory*. Princeton: Princeton University Press.

Thomson, Judith Jarvis. 1971. "A Defense of Abortion." *Philosophy and Public Affairs*, 1: 47–66.

Tooley, Michael. 1972. "Abortion and Infanticide." *Philosophy and Public Affairs*, 2, 1 (Fall): 37–65.

Van Wagner, Vicki, and Bob Lee. 1989. "Principles into Practice: An Activist Vision of Feminist Reproductive Health Care." In *The Future of Human Reproduction*. Edited by Christine Overall. Toronto: The Women's Press.

Warren, Mary Anne. 1973. "On the Moral and Legal Status of Abortion." *The Monist*, 57: 43–61.

_____. 1989. "The Moral Significance of Birth." *Hypatia*, 4, 2 (Summer): 46–65.

Whitbeck, Carolyn. 1973. "Theories of Sex Difference." *The Philosophical Forum*, 5, 1–2 (Fall/Winter 1973–74): 54–80.

# The Meanings of Choice
# in Reproductive Technology

## Barbara Katz Rothman

...

*Choice* and *information* have served as the cornerstones of the women's health and the reproductive rights movements. We are, above all, pro-choice. We support the rights of the individual woman to choose, to choose pregnancy or abortion, to choose alternative medical treatments or none at all. And choice, we claim, rests firmly on information: to choose treatment for breast cancer, for example, requires information on the full range of medical treatments, their side effects, and their probability of success.

This emphasis on choice and information all sounded very logical at the time, sounded like women were going to get more and more control as first their access to information and then their choices expanded.

I'm beginning to have second thoughts.

Technology is also about information, and about choice. More information on how things work seems to give us more choices, new and better ways of doing things. That is true of the technology of transportation, which brings us cars and jets, and of the technology of reproduction, which brings us the Pill, amniocentesis and fetal monitors.

But while technology opens up some choices, it closes down others. The new choice is often greeted with such fanfare that the silent closing of the door on the old choice goes unheeded. For example, is there any meaningful way one could now choose horses over cars as a means of transportation? The new choice of a 'horseless carriage' eventually left us 'no choice' but to live with the pollution and dangers (as well as the conveniences and speed, of course) of a car-based transportation system.

Reproductive technology is heralded for its choice-giving capacity. For those who can afford it, the enormous growth of information about reproduction does make choice newly possible: the pregnant can choose whether or not to continue the pregnancy, can even learn more about the fetus and then choose whether or not to continue; the infertile can choose new ways of attempting pregnancy; birthing women can choose alternative ways of managing their labors and births. Choices abound. I want to look a bit at the negative side, though, look to see what, if any, choices are being lost to us, going the way of the horse.

Fetal monitoring is a good place to start. Fetal monitors, belts to go around the pregnant belly and electrodes to screw into the fetal head during labor, are a piece of reproductive technology whose sole stated purpose is to bring more information, to enable more and better choices. By knowing more about the condition of the fetus during labor, more informed choice was to be possible for the management of the labor. But some strange things happened. We didn't really get all that much more information than we had before—good nursing care always provided considerable information about the fetus. It certainly did *look* like more information though, with those long strips of print-out. But more importantly, the information came in a new context. Instead of having to approach the woman, to rest your head near her belly, to smell her skin, to feel her breathing, you could now read the information on the fetus from across the room, from down the hall. While still one being on the bed, medical personnel came to see the woman and fetus as separate, as *two different patients*. And indeed more choices could be made: the fetal heart rate indicates mild distress—should the mother be sectioned?

When a woman *chooses* to have a cesarean section because she is *informed* that the fetal monitor indicates some distress, is she gaining or losing control? In part, the answer is going to depend on the accuracy of the information. If medical practitioners are overly quick to read fetal distress, as they have been, then the loss of control is clear. The woman is having major surgery, with all of its attendant risks to her health and life, making herself sick, weak and dependent as she enters motherhood. But if the information is correct, and the fetus, her baby, is at risk and the section could ensure its greater health, then she is gaining control over her motherhood, as she makes this short-term sacrifice for the long-term health of her child.

What happens when the woman and her medical practitioners disagree, disagree either about the accuracy of the information, or about the choice which should be made based on the information? What if a pregnant woman does not want to make this sacrifice? Has all this new information expanded her choices? It seems not: medicine is once again turning to the state, as it has so many times in the past, to put medical choice ahead of women's choices. In several bedside Juvenile Court hearings, with a lawyer appointed to represent the unborn fetus, another representing the pregnant woman, and yet others representing the hospital, women have lost the right to choose, and have been ordered to submit to cesarean sections, the fetus within them claimed by the state as a 'dependent and neglected child'. (Hubbard, 1982)

Thus information may expand the opportunity for choices, but it certainly does not guarantee whose choices will be honored.

...

We thought that information would give us power. What we perhaps overlooked is that it is *power* which gives one control over both information and choice.

...

The choice of contraception simultaneously closed down some of the choices for large families. North American society is geared to small families, if indeed to any children at all. Everything from car and apartment sizes the picture book ideal of families encourages limiting fertility. Without the provision of good medical care, day care, decent housing, children are a luxury item, fine if you can afford them. So it is a choice all right that contraception gave us, and a choice we may very well experience as being under our control, but it may be a somewhat forced choice. In its extreme, legislation has been repeatedly introduced to punish 'welfare mothers' by cutting off payments if they have more children. Sterilization abuse is the flip side of the abortion battle: the same sorry record. ...

So there may be choice brought to us by information and technology, the choices we get when we learn how to use contraception and back-up abortion for fertility control, but the choices may very well be heavily weighted for, or against, us.

Both the medical monitoring and management of labor, and the use of contraception and abortion, are very well-established aspects of reproductive technologies; it is just the specifics which keep changing, as newer techniques, machinery and chemicals get introduced. The next level of reproductive technology I want to address combines fetal monitoring with fertility control to produce something new: 'quality control,' control not just of the number of children we bear, but of the 'quality' or condition of those children.

Amniocentesis and sonography are the technologies which provide the information to make this new set of reproductive choices possible. Sonography, the use of sound waves, allows the visualization of the fetus in utero, and the detection of gross anatomical deformities. Amniocentesis is the withdrawal of a small amount of the amniotic fluid which surrounds the fetus. When done between the sixteenth and twentieth weeks of pregnancy, the fetal cells in the fluid can be cultured and examined. Other tests can also be performed on the fluid. These techniques allow the diagnosis of many (under a hundred at this writing, but increasing all the time) genetic diseases and syndromes. Test results are available by the twenty-fourth week, the legal limit on abortion in the United States. If the fetus is found to have a terminal illness (like Tay Sachs disease which invariably kills in eary childhood), a severely incapacitating condition (a syndrome which leads to such profound retardation that the child would be unable to learn to walk or to talk), a moderately disabling condition (say, wheelchair-bound or unable to walk without assistance), or a socially undesirable condition (if, for example, the fetus is found to be of the 'wrong' sex, such as a third or fourth daughter), a woman can use this information to choose an abortion.

The opening up of choices and control with this technology is astounding. There is, of course, still no guarantee of a perfect baby—and even a perfect baby can be made terribly imperfect in accident or illness after birth—but one no longer need fear Down syndrome, spina bifida or a host of other diseases and unwanted conditions. This of course begs the basic question of what makes any particular condition either disabling or undesirable. Why Down syndrome, why daughters, why wheelchair-bound? But information is available, and information makes choice possible. And it is the woman's choice. There may be pressure, subtle or powerful, from genetic counselors, doctors, family members, but it is still the woman who chooses to abort or not to abort. Or is it?

When we have this information, when we make these choices for our children, are we not then accepting responsibility for their condition, responsibility without any genuine control? If we choose not to abort a 'defenctive' fetus, and the agonized adolescent it becomes hurls at us, as adolescents so often have, 'I didn't ask to be born!' whatever are we going to say now? Will our children be able to sue us for wrongful life, as they have successfully sued their doctors? The doctors failed to provide the information which would have given the mothers the choice of abortion. What of the mother who, given the information, chooses not to abort? Can she be held responsible for her child's condition, denied state services, insurance payments, even charged with child abuse?

And if we do choose to abort, is that truly a choice? What of the woman living in the fourth floor, walk-up apartment in a city designed without access for the disabled—is her 'choice' to abort a fetus with spina bifida an exercise in free will? What of the woman with few economic or family resources who chooses to abort a fetus with Down syndrome because she is fully and truly informed about the state services which will be available to her child after her own death?

It seems that, in gaining the choice to control the quality of our children, we may be losing the choice *not* to control the quality, the choice of simply accepting them as they are.

...

There are ... genetic conditions ... about which we might be better off not knowing. XYY, the genetic condition which some studies suggested may be linked to criminal behavior, is an example. The studies have been largely discredited, but my research shows there are women currently aborting XYY fetuses because, as one potential father said, 'It's hard enough to raise a normal kid. If he throws the blocks across the room will I think he's doing it because he's two, or because he's XYY?'

What will happen as we get even more information, if we can begin to predict not just retardation, but which fetuses are likely to become children of borderline ability; not just Tay Sachs, but which fetuses are likely to develop juvenile diabetes? All this information may be giving us choice, but is it coming any closer to giving us control?

And finally, briefly, what of the great expansion in the treatment of infertility, and its choices? ... All of the technology still leaves many couples, about a third or more of those treated for infertility, without a pregnancy. At what point is it simply not their fault, out of their control, inevitable, inexorable fate? At what point can they get on with their lives? If there is always one more doctor to try, one more treatment around, then the social role of infertility will always be seen in some sense as chosen: they chose to give up. Did taking away the sense of inevitability of their infertility and substituting the 'choice' of giving up truly increase their choice and their control?

There are those who are successful with the new technology, those for whom the drugs and surgery are a success. Surely they have now experienced the choice of parenthood, and so their choices have expanded and they have gained control over their lives. Indeed they have, just as contraception and abortion provide us with the very real and very true experience of controlling our fertility. Choices open and choices close. For those whose choices meet the social expectations, for those who want what the society wants them to want, the experience of choice is very real.

Perhaps what we should realize is that human beings living in society have precious little choice ever. There may really be no such thing as individual choice in a social structure, not in any absolute way. The social structure creates needs—the needs for women to be mothers, the needs for small families, the needs for 'perfect' children—and creates the technology which enables people to make the needed choices. The question is not whether choices are constructed but *how* they are constructed. Society, in its ultimate meaning, may be nothing more and nothing less than the structuring of choices.

The question then for feminism is not only to address the individual level of 'a woman's right to choose' but also to examine the social level, where her choices are structured. Yes, we will have to continue to fight the good fight for information and for choice, the rights of the individual woman to choose contraception, abortion, amniocentesis, pregnancy by in vitro fertilization, pregnancy by donor insemination, labors with and labors without electronic fetal monitoring, to have no children or to have one child or to have many children. We must not get caught into discussions of which reproductive technologies are 'politically correct,' which empower and which enslave women. They ALL empower and they ALL enslave, they all can be used by, for, or against us. We will have to lift our eyes from the choices of the individual woman, and focus on the control of the social system which structures her choices, which rewards some choices and punishes others, which distributes the rewards and punishments for reproductive choices along class and race lines.

There will never be 'free' choice, unstructured reproductive choice. But the structure in which choices are made should, and I believe ultimately can, be made fair, ethical, moral. Individual rights to information and to choice are an absolute necessity for such a system, but are not alone sufficient to ensure an ethics of reproduction.

The next step in the politics of reproductive control is the politics of social control.

### References

Hubbard, Ruth. 1982. 'Some Legal and Policy Implications of Recent Advances in Prenatal Diagnosis and Fetal Therapy.' *Women's Rights Law Reporter,* Spring, 7 (3): 201–18.

# *Reproductive Rights and Wrongs*

## Betsy Hartmann

…

… Today what should be a woman's birthright—the right to decide when to have a child and to practice safe birth control—is denied millions of women around the world. Pitted against them are a number of obstacles: economic discrimination, subordination within the family, religious and cultural restrictions, the nature of health care systems, and the distortion of family planning programs to serve the end of population control. Women's biology need not be her destiny, but today her reproductive fate is largely shaped by forces beyond her control.

### Women in Underdevelopment

In many Third World countries the economic subordination of women is directly linked to high birth rates, since it both increases their need for children and impedes their access to birth control. It is the result of a long history of exploitation, which in many cases was intensified by colonialism.

…

… The processes of migration and urbanization encouraged by colonialism disrupted traditional patterns of life, including social mechanisms to space births. In many areas of sub-Saharan Africa, for example, an interval of up to four years between births was achieved through a taboo on intercourse during lactation, reinforced by the practice of polygamy. "Long before the influx of Western ideas, the understanding of the importance of child spacing to maternal and infant health was widespread in these cultures," concludes a study of traditional birth control methods in Zaire.[1] Meanwhile, the "Western ideas" of the colonialists were strongly pronatalist, encouraging many births and discouraging birth control. Contraception and abortion were generally proscribed by law, and missionaries actively campaigned against abstinence and polygamy.[2]

…

… Today in many areas of the Third World, the traditional family is breaking down, and there are a growing number of female-headed households. According to one study of seventy-four Third World countries, one in five households is headed by a woman. Although many of these women work outside the home, it is usually in low-paying occupations. Their short-term independence then counts for precious little in the way of long-term security. They must rely on children as their basic form of risk insurance.[3]

In some cases, in fact, women want children, but not husbands. In Kenya's Central Province journalist Paula Park found that many young mothers preferred being single, since men drank too much liquor and spent too much money, undermining a woman's ability to care for her family.[4]

If women's powerlessness increases their need for children, then steps toward their empowerment could presumably have the opposite effect. This appears to be true in the case of literacy. The educational level of women is the single most consistent predictor of fertility and contraceptive use, even more important than income level.[5]

...

Although poverty and patriarchy serve as inducements to high fertility, it does not necessarily follow that women want to bear as many children as is biologically possible—eight, ten, even more. Many women would like to practice birth control, to space their pregnancies or to end them altogether once their need for children is met. What then is standing in their way?

## Barriers to Reproductive Control

...

Why women want to space or limit births is not difficult to fathom. The physical hardship of repeated pregnancies can exact a terrible toll on a woman's health. Between the ages of fifteen and forty-five, a woman in rural Bangladesh can now expect to have an average of eight pregnancies and to spend nearly seventeen years either pregnant or breast-feeding. This would be hard for any woman, but for already undernourished women the difficulty is greatly magnified. An estimated two thirds of all pregnant women in the Third World are anemic.[6]

Childbirth literally kills hundreds of thousands of poor women every year. Maternal mortality rates in excess of 500 per 100,000 live births are not uncommon in many Third World countries, compared to 5 to 30 in the industrialized world.

Put another way, the complications of pregnancy account for between 10 and 30 percent of *all* deaths of women of reproductive age in areas of Asia, Africa, and Latin America, but less than 2 percent in the United States and Europe.[7] The risk is greater for women under twenty or over thirty-four, and for women who have borne three or more children and suffer from the nutritional maternal depletion syndrome. Many women do not have access even to rudimentary medical care during childbirth, much less sophisticated emergency equipment, so that even minor problems can lead to death.

For desperately poor women, having many children can be a heavy economic and emotional burden. A Mexican woman told Perdita Huston: "If I am going to have more children, who is going to feed them? When my children are crying, is it God who comes to comfort them?"[8]

...

Male dominance is one of the strongest obstacles. In most cultures wives must have their husband's consent before they can decide to limit their fertility. And many men are reluctant to agree: They fear the possibility of their wife's infidelity or the loss of their control over her. ... Not surprisingly, in households where men and women share power more equally, acceptance of family planning is much higher. Including men in discussions with family planning workers also seems to make a difference. But more often than not, family planning programs are geared exclusively toward women, ignoring the basic reality of male dominance.

Male control of the medical profession also discourages many women from visiting family planning clinics. As a Mexican anthropologist explains:

> A woman is supposed to be the property of one man: her husband. If she goes to a clinic another man, the doctor, is going to see and touch her. Her husband won't let her go ... and she, too, is reluctant. This is a great barrier to the acceptance of family planning in Mexico.[9]

In many Muslim cultures the problem is intensified by the practice of female seclusion. If no men other than a woman's husband and close male relations are allowed to see her, much less touch her, how likely is it that she will be able to consult a male doctor about family planning?

...

Many governments also follow pronatalist policies in the belief that an expanding population is vital to national development, prestige, and security. ... In Latin America the Catholic Church has prevented many governments from establishing national family planning programs. ... Left-wing movements in Latin America have also tended to oppose family planning, failing to distinguish between population control interventions from abroad and women's real need for birth control. However, this opposition is beginning to fade under the influence of feminism.

...

It would be mistaken to view th[e] lack of reproductive control as simply a Third World women's problem. ...

...

... In the United States, teenagers' lack of access to contraception is reflected in record pregnancy rates. Out of every 1,000 teenagers aged fifteen to nineteen, 96 become pregnant, more than double the rate of Canada, England, and France.[10] Yet conservatives continue to fight sex education in the schools and the provision of contraceptives to minors without parental consent.

...

... In the Soviet Union, ... abortion is the primary means of birth control, not by choice but because other forms of contraception are virtually unavailable. According to one Soviet feminist:

> The scarcity of contraceptives is due to the Soviet Union's not considering women's needs an industrial priority; furthermore, the government wants (white [that is, the dominant Russian ethnic group]) Russians to have more children, because of its racist

concern about the greater growth of the ethnic populations in the other Soviet republics.[11] …

…

## Shaping Contraceptive Technology

…

… The contraceptive revolution of the second half of this century has been influenced more by the pursuit of population control, prestige, and profit than by people's need for safe birth control. Millions of dollars have flowed into the development, production, and promotion of technically sophisticated contraceptives such as the pill and injectables, despite their health risks, while the improvement of safer and simpler barrier methods has been virtually neglected.

The misdirection of contraceptive technology begins in the research phase and culminates in its use as a destructive and even deadly weapon in the war on population. It is mainly women who bear the cost, many paying dearly with their health and lives.

### The Search Behind the Research

…

… [In] the late 1960s … the Ford Foundation, the Rockefeller Foundation, and the Population Council increased their funding for contraceptive research and urged the United States government to do the same. Much of the early impetus came from India, scene of the first government-sponsored family planning program, backed strongly by Ford. U.S. officials blamed the program's poor results on the lack of a "technological breakthrough." One U.S. Agency for International Development (AID) official went so far as to call for a crash program to develop birth control technology akin to the "intensive and coordinated research and development effort which solved the problem of controlled nuclear explosion."[12]

By the late 1960s, the United States government, through AID and the National Institutes of Health, had become a major funder of contraceptive research. During the next decade, it overtook the pharmaceutical industry in terms of investment in the field. By 1983 the United States government provided 59 percent of the $167 million in total worldwide expenditures in basic reproductive research, contraceptive research and development, and the evaluation of the long-term safety of existing contraceptive methods. U.S. pharmaceutical industries contributed another 21 percent and United States foundations another 4 percent, for a total United States contribution of almost 85 percent.[13]

Both United States government and foundation funds for contraceptive research and development are now channeled to six major institutions:

- the Center for Population Research of the U.S. National Institute of Child Health and Human Development.
- the International Fertility Research Program of Family Health International, based in North Carolina.

- the Program for Applied Research on Fertility Regulation (PARFR) at Northwestern University.
- the Population Council's International Committee for Contraceptive Research.
- the World Health Organization's (WHO) Special Program of Research, Development and Research Training in Human Development.
- the Program for the Introduction and Adaptation of Contraceptive Technology (PIACT), based in Seattle, Washington.[14]

...

... Contraceptives are highly profitable items. The United States retail contraceptive market alone is estimated to be almost $1 billion a year; worldwide sales may be over twice this figure. Moreover, oral and injectable contraceptives are among the most lucrative of *all* pharmaceuticals.[15]

A ... compelling reason for the public sector's domination of contraceptive research lies in the close relationship between the companies and the population establishment.

## Common Interests

In the contraceptive field, as well as in many other scientific endeavors, there is not necessarily a dichotomy between government and private research. In the United States legal provisions allow private firms to incorporate government-sponsored contraceptive research into their own product development activities, and in some cases public agencies will finance trials of drugs developed by private industry. The companies thus directly benefit from public research funds, and a number of them are strong supporters of the population lobby in Congress.[16] Public research institutions on the other hand need the companies to manufacture the contraceptives since they do not have an industrial capacity.

The common interest between the companies and the population establishment runs much deeper, however. As health researcher Cary LaCheen points out in a recent study, both are interested in maximizing the volume of contraceptives distributed worldwide and in reaching new consumers or acceptors in the Third World.

Population control programs represent an important market for a number of pharmaceutical companies. AID, for example, has spent an average of $15 million annually on birth control pills since the mid-1970s. From 1972 to 1979 most of this money went to one company alone, the Syntex Corporation, accounting in some years for 25 to 30 percent of Syntex's total oral contraceptive sales. Similarly, between 1982 and 1984, AID bought all of its $6.7 million worth of IUDs from Finishing Enterprises. According to an industry source, Ansell Industries, which produces condoms, would probably go out of business without AID contracts.

Although not all companies rely so heavily on AID sales, the contraceptives they provide to population programs reach untapped markets where the companies would like to expand. Population agencies, in fact, play a vital role in advertising, promoting, and distributing industry products in the Third World.

...

In order to maintain the profitable alliance between themselves and the population establishment, industry officials not only lobby Congress on the need for population appropriations, but give donations to population control organizations. According to LaCheen, the Syntex Corporation, for example, gives several thousands of dollars each year to the Population Crisis Committee.[17] Interlocking directorates further cement the alliance.

...

In a number of ways, then, the interests of the contraceptive industry and the population establishment converge. Many would argue that there is nothing intrinsically wrong with such a convergence, if the end result is that new and better contraceptives are developed and distributed widely around the globe. Before accepting such an argument, however, it is important to look at how these institutions have helped to bias the direction of contraceptive technology.

## Contraceptive Biases

There are three basic biases in contemporary contraceptive research. First, research has focused overwhelmingly on the female reproductive system. In 1978, for example, 78 percent of public sector expenditures for the development of new contraceptives was for female methods, as opposed to only 7 percent for males.[18]

This is not only because women are the chief targets of population control programs but, according to Forrest Greenslade of the Population Council, "because of sexism." From top to bottom, men dominate the contraceptive research field, and many of them hold the view that reproduction is basically a woman's concern. As R. J. Ericsson, an early pioneer in male reproductive research, complained:

> Male contraceptive research has a dismal past. It is almost an illegitimate specialty within reproductive biology. For the most part, the brightest workers avoid it and those who do work in the area are looked on as rather strange fellows.[19]

This is slowly beginning to change. In the 1980–1983 period, for example, male methods accounted for 12 percent of total contraceptive research and development expenditures.[20] However, even though organizations such as the Population Council are now devoting more resources to male reproductive research, people in the field say it will take at least fifteen to twenty years to catch up in building a knowledge base from which to develop male contraceptives.

A second persistent bias is toward systemic and surgical forms of birth control, as opposed to safer barrier methods. Thus hormonal, immunological, and surgical methods received almost 70 percent of total public expenditures for the development of new contraceptives in 1978, while barrier methods such as the diaphragm and condom received only 2.2 percent.[21]

Today, due to consumer and feminist pressure, resources devoted to barrier methods are slowly increasing, both in the public and private sector. ... From 1980 to 1983 they averaged almost 5 percent of contraceptive research and development expenditures. The overwhelming emphasis is on *female* barrier methods, however—the male condom has been almost totally neglected.

Female hormonal methods in particular have received a disproportionate share of research funds, accounting for nearly 30 percent of contraceptive research and development expenditures from 1980 to 1983.[22] They continue to appeal to many members of the population establishment who are still searching for a "miracle" contraceptive that will solve the world's population problem. Their preference, as we shall see, is for long-acting methods that require little initiative by the user and minimal interaction between the user and provider, reducing both the risk of accidental pregnancy and the need for counseling and support services.

The pharmaceutical industry has concentrated on hormonal methods not only because they are highly profitable, much more profitable than a diaphragm, which can be used for a year or more, but because public research funds have flowed in this direction. For their part, medical researchers are drawn to sophisticated systemic methods, incorporating the latest in biomedical science, since these are more likely to win recognition, prestige, and lucrative contracts.

A third bias, linked to the previous two, is a greater concern for contraceptive efficacy than safety.

## Safety First—or Last?

From 1965 onward less than 10 percent of total expenditures on reproductive research and contraceptive development has been devoted to safety.[23] This relative disregard for safety is the single most important factor underlying contraceptive abuse.

Safety expenditures also remain concentrated in the industrialized countries, which have more financial resources and trained personnel to test and investigate new contraceptives and where the media and consumer and women's groups play a key role in keeping up public pressure for regulation. In the United States, the Food and Drug Administration (FDA) is the government's main watchdog agency over the pharmaceutical industry. Since many Third World (and other) governments depend heavily on FDA rulings to formulate their own guidelines, its influence extends far beyond United States borders.

...

... Compared to the absence of regulatory procedures in many Third World and even some European countries, the FDA provides an important measure of protection against potentially harmful contraceptives. Theoretically, this protection was extended overseas by a law that prohibited United States pharmaceutical manufacturers from exporting drugs not approved for sale in the United States. However, the companies got around this restriction by using foreign subsidiaries to manufacture and export unapproved drugs.

There has also been considerable pressure on Congress to change existing legislation so that United States firms can export new drugs even if not yet approved for use within the United States, if the drugs meet certain minimal safety standards and the specifications of the importing country. In late 1986 Congress passed legislation

that would allow such exports to twenty-one countries, mainly in Western Europe.
…

The eagerness of contraceptive manufacturers to circumvent United States regulations reflects a basic economic calculation: In contrast to the industrialized countries where near zero population growth has led to a saturation of the contraceptive market, the Third World presents a large, expanding market. Companies today are also shifting their initial research efforts abroad where drug regulations are not so rigid.[24]

In fact, in the contraceptive research business, the Third World has long been an important laboratory for human testing. From 1980 to 1983, at least one fifth of contraceptive research and development and safety evaluation projects were located in developing countries, with India, China, Chile, Mexico, and Brazil the major locations.[25] Not only can companies and research institutions get around Western guidelines by initiating or shifting their drug trials to the Third World, but Third World subjects are usually the prime target group for the new contraceptives.
…

Even those contraceptives approved in the West are often marketed in the Third World according to much looser standards. The printed list of side effects and precautions required to accompany each drug is often much more comprehensive in the United States than it is in Latin America, for example.
…

Many contraceptives are delivered to medical personnel in the Third World without any printed information on side effects. In Zimbabwe, a doctor reports that the packets of pills women receive do not even list the ingredients![26]

These practices imply a double standard: safety regulations for the West, but not for the Third World. Many members of the population establishment justify this double standard in terms of relative risks. They measure the risk of death from a given contraceptive against a woman's risk of dying in pregnancy or childbirth. In the Third World, where maternal mortality rates of over 500 per 100,000 live births are common in poor rural areas, contraceptive risks appear much lower than in the United States or Great Britain, for example, where the maternal mortality rate is roughly 10 per 100,000 live births.

This reasoning led the journal *Population Reports* to claim: "With all methods, family planning in developing countries is much safer than childbearing."[27] Indeed, this is the most common argument leveled against critics of indiscriminate contraceptive use in the Third World. But just how valid is the comparison between maternal mortality and contraceptive risk?

A close look at the logic reveals a number of very serious flaws:

1. The use of high rates of maternal mortality to justify higher contraceptive risk in effect *penalizes the poor for their poverty.* High maternal mortality rates result from inadequate nutrition, poor health care, and other effects of poverty. Addressing these problems first would not only alter the risk equation, but would establish a better foundation on which to build decent family planning services.

2. How can risk be precisely defined when the *long-term* risks of many contraceptives, such as the pill and injectables, will not be known for at least another one or

two decades? Moreover, if a particular contraceptive increases the risk of cancer, a woman's life may be shortened, but the contraceptive will not be seen as the cause of death.

3. The measure of contraceptive risk is generally based on data from industrialized countries. *Third World women may actually be at greater risk from certain contraceptives* owing to their lower body weights, lack of sanitary facilities, poor medical care, etc. Moreover, they are rarely adequately screened before or followed up after contraceptive use.

4. *Why should the measure of risk center solely on women,* when there are male contraceptive methods such as the condom and vasectomy? As Judith Bruce and S. Bruce Schearer of the Population Council point out: "No attempt has been made to take into account the fact that whereas the health risks of *childbearing* are unavoidably sex-specific, the health risks of *contraception* can be assumed by either partner."[28]

5. *Many contraceptives have other harmful effects,* aside from death, which can have a profound impact on a woman's life. For example, contraceptives like the IUD that carry the risk of impairing future fertility may be totally unacceptable to women, in spite of the risks they face from an unwanted pregnancy.

6. *Mortality risks in childbirth and mortality risks from a contraceptive do not necessarily belong in the same equation.* A woman may willingly assume the immediate risk of childbirth, while she may feel quite differently about the longer-term risk of death from the adverse effects of a contraceptive. Instead, the risk of a particular contraceptive should also be measured in comparison to other contraceptives, not only to giving birth. In health terms, barrier contraceptives, for example, are much safer than hormonal methods, even if they may be less effective in preventing pregnancy (a matter of dispute). Many women use contraceptives to *space* their pregnancies, not to end them altogether. An unplanned pregnancy resulting from the use of a barrier method might appear far more favorable to them than risking their lives on the pill.[29]

The acceptability of contraceptive risk is a personal decision as well as a scientific one. Many women are prepared to take health risks to prevent pregnancy, but each woman has a right to know all the risks and to make the decision for herself. Yet today, contraceptive manufacturers and population control programs are making that decision for millions of women.

. . .

. . . Judith Bruce and S. Bruce Schearer have pointed out the irony that the risks of modern contraception have given rise to a new public health problem in industrialized countries such as the United States: Although maternal mortality dropped by 75 percent between 1955 and 1975 in the United States, today about half that mortality is due to the adverse effects of new contraceptive technology, a cause that did not exist in 1955.[30]

. . .

Today the forces shaping contraceptive technology—the population establishment, the pharmaceutical companies, and the scientific community—are far removed from the individual woman or man who uses birth control. As a result, the technology does not respond so much to individual needs as it does to the biases of its creators. ...

---

## Notes

1. Ronald S. Waife, M.S.P.H., *Traditional Methods of Birth Control in Zaire*, Pathpapers No. 4 (the Pathfinder Fund, December 1978), p. 4.
2. See Lars Bondestam and Staffan Bergström, *Poverty and Population Control* (London: Academic Press, 1980), pp. 43–44; William Murdoch, *The Poverty of Nations* (Baltimore: Johns Hopkins, 1980), p. 28, and Barbara Rogers, *The Domestication of Women: Discrimination in Developing Societies* (New York: Tavistock Publishers, 1981), p. 111.
3. Study finding from Debbie Taylor, "Women: An Analysis," in *Women: A World Report* (London: Methuen Ltd., 1985), p. 12. This is an excellent source for up-to-date material on women, and it has lively chapters on women in different countries written by women journalists and novelists. ...
4. Personal interview with Paula Park.
5. See Taylor, "Women: An Analysis," p. 71; Murdoch, *The Poverty of Nations*, p. 41; and *World Development Report 1984* (Oxford: Oxford University Press, 1984), pp. 109–10.
6. Bangladesh statistics from Zafrullah Chowdhury, "A Double Oppression in Bangladesh," in Patricia W. Blair, ed., *Health Needs of the World's Poor Women* (Equity Policy, 1981), p. 5. Anemia statistic from Taylor, "Women: An Analysis," p. 43.
7. World Health Organization, Division of Family Health, *Health and the Status of Women* (Geneva: 1980), and "Healthier Mothers and Children Through Family Planning," *Population Reports*, Series J, No. 27 (May–June 1984), p. J661.
8. Perdita Huston, *Message from the Village* (New York: Epoch B Foundation, 1978), p. 131.
9. Huston, *Message from the Village*, p. 109.
10. Rate from W. J. Weatherby, "The Future New York Offers the World," *Guardian*, 27 March 1985.
11. Tatyana Mamonova, "The USSR: It's Time We Began with Ourselves," in Robin Morgan, ed., *Sisterhood Is Global: The International Women's Movement Anthology* (New York: Anchor Press/Doubleday, 1984), pp. 684–85.
12. Frances Gulick, "The Indian Family Planning Program: The Need for New Contraceptives," staff memorandum, USAID/India, April 1968, quoted in Phyllis Tilson Piotrow, *World Population Crisis: The United States Response* (New York: Praeger, 1973), p. 174. ...
13. Linda E. Atkinson, Richard Lincoln and Jacqueline D. Forrest, "Worldwide Trends in Funding for Contraceptive Research and Evaluation," *Family Planning Perspectives*, vol. 17, no. 5 (September/October 1985), Table 7, p. 204.
14. Ibid. See also Office of Technology Assessment, *World Population and Fertility Planning Technologies, The Next 20 Years* (Washington, D.C.: U.S. Government Printing Office, 1982), pp. 107–11; *Population Reports*, Series J, No. 26 (January–February 1983).
15. No exact figures on size of the market are available. ... On profitability of oral and injectable contraceptives, see Marjorie Sun, "Depo-Provera Debate Revs up at FDA," *Science*, vol. 217, no. 4558 (30 July 1982), p. 429; and OTA, *World Population and Fertility Planning Technologies*, p. 116.
16. See OTA, *World Population and Fertility Planning Technologies*, for description of how public and private sectors interact. See Cary LaCheen, "Population Control and the Contraceptive Industry," in Kathleen McDonnell, ed., *Adverse Effects: Women and the Pharmaceutical Industry* (Penang, Malaysia: International Organization of Consumers Unions, 1986), for examples of how industry officials lobby for more population research.

17. LaCheen, "Population Control," p. 116.

18. See Atkinson, et al., "Worldwide Trends in Funding."

19. Domination of contraceptive field by men from Judy Norsigian, "Redirecting Contraceptive Research," *Science for the People*, January/February 1979. Quote from Bruce Stokes, *Men and Family Planning*, Worldwatch Paper 41 (Washington, D.C.: Worldwatch Institute, December 1980), p. 24.

20. Atkinson et al., "Worldwide Trends in Funding."

21. See Table "Percentage Distribution of Public Sector Expenditures for Development of New Contraceptive Methods, 1978," in OTA, *World Population and Fertility Planning Technologies*, p. 110.

22. Atkinson et al., "Worldwide Trends in Funding," Table 3, p. 198.

23. Ibid., and OTA, *World Population and Fertility Planning Technologies*, p. 109.

24. John W. Egan, Harlow N. Higinbotham, and J. Fred Weston, *Economics of the Pharmaceutical Industry* (New York: Praeger Publishers, 1982), p. 105.

25. Atkinson et al., "Worldwide Trends in Funding."

26. Personal communication, 1984.

27. *Population Reports*, Series J, No. 27 (May–June 1984), p. J658.

28. See Judith Bruce and S. Bruce Schearer, *Contraceptives and Common Sense: Conventional Methods Reconsidered* (New York: Population Council, 1979), p. 51. This earlier work is sadly out of print.

29. Judith Bruce and S. Bruce Schearer, "Contraceptives and Developing Countries: The Role of Barrier Methods," paper read at the International Symposium, Research on the Regulation of Human Fertility, Needs of Developing Countries, and Priorities for the Future, Stockholm, February 1983, p. 416. This paper, available from the Population Council, is an informative examination of the present neglect and future potential of barrier methods. Also see Helen B. Holmes, "Reproductive Technologies: The Birth of a Woman-Centered Analysis," in H. B. Holmes, B. B. Haskins, and M. Gross, eds., *Birth Control and Controlling Birth: Women-Centered Perspectives* (Clifton, N.J.: Humana Press, 1980).

30. Bruce and Schearer, "Contraceptives and Developing Countries," p. 410.

# Subtle Forms of
# Sterilization Abuse:
# A Reproductive Rights Analysis

## Adele Clarke

...

In 1977, women workers in the lead pigment department of an American Cyanamid plant in West Virginia were given the 'choice' of being sterilized or moving to lower-paying jobs. Laws against sterilization abuse did not protect these women—after all, they were 'free' to remain fertile! All that would involve was leaving their current jobs—at $225 per week plus overtime—and transfering to jobs as janitors—at $175 per week maximum. Five of these women 'chose' to be sterilized. Several have regretted their decisions (Mereson, 1982: Stellman and Henifin, 1982).

...

*Sterilization abuse,* the coerced or unconsenting sterilization of women and men, occurs in both blatant and subtle forms. *Blatant* abuse includes forced sterilization against a person's will, sterilization without telling the person they will be sterilized, and (in the US) sterilization without the patient's informed consent to the procedure.

*Subtle* sterilization abuses include situations in which a woman or man *legally consents* to sterilization, but the *social conditions* in which they do so are abusive—the conditions of their lives constrain their capacity to exercise genuine reproductive choice and autonomy. While blatant abuses continue to occur in the US (though seemingly less frequently), subtle abuses appear to be much more common today.

This paper presents a reproductive rights analysis of subtle sterilization abuse. ... In the feminist tradition, the ideas presented here grew collectively.[1] ... In all our discussions of reproductive rights, there has been a characteristic tension between the personal and the political. How can we relate our personal reproductive experiences to larger social policy issues? It is through our joint attempts to address such contradictions that we have come to understand subtle sterilization abuse and what genuine reproductive freedom might be.

## Reproductive Rights Perspectives

The central argument of reproductive rights is that reproductive issues must be viewed in their specific social, historical and institutional contexts. Further, reproduction is a *fundamental human right:* neither the state nor the actions of others should deny any person autonomy over their reproductive processes.[2]

Reproductive freedom is prerequisite for any kind of liberation for women. The right to decide whether and when to bear a child is fundamental to a woman's control of her own body, her sexuality, her life choices. Involuntary motherhood precludes self-determination. This is why abortion, the final line of defense against an unwanted pregnancy, is the bottom-line requirement of the reproductive rights movement.[3]

Reproductive freedom, as Petchesky (1980: 665) has ably noted, is irreducibly social and individual at the same time because reproductive itself 'operates at the core of social life, as well as within and upon women's bodies.' Reproductive rights work, then, must address issues such as sterilization abuse at *both* social and individual levels of action to enhance women's and men's reproductive autonomy.

…

## From Blatant to Subtle Sterilization Abuse

Patterned *blatant* sterilization abuse began in the US in the late nineteenth century (Bajema, 1976; Haller, 1963). It continued quite actively under the authority of state eugenics (better people through better breeding) laws until about 1960, focused on the unconsenting and/or coerced sterilizations of the (usually incarcerated) mentally retarded, physically disabled and mentally ill, often immigrants (Fox, 1978; Robitscher, 1973).

During the 1950s and 1960s in the South, a new form of blatant sterilization abuse emerged: numerous cases of Black women and girls sterilized without their knowledge and/or consent came to the attention of civil rights workers. There were also several fresh state proposals for compulsory sterilization (mostly for illegitimacy). Both of these issues were taken up by the national press in 1964, when the Student Nonviolent Coordinating Committee also published a pamphlet 'Genocide in Mississippi' on these and similar issues (Paul, 1968). Sterilizations became so common in the South that they are known as 'Mississippi appendectomies' (Rodriguez-Trias, 1982: 150).

Blatant sterilization abuse became a core focus of the reproductive rights movement in the early 1970s as the result of several especially horrifying cases, including the Relf sisters (two young Black girls sterilized without their knowledge in Alabama), Norma Jean Seren (a Native American woman sterilized without her knowledge for 'socioeconomic reasons' in Pennsylvania), the patterned sterilization abuse of Native American women by the US Indian Health Service, and the series of abuses in Los Angeles of Mexican American women known as the Madrigal case (Ad Hoc Women's Studies Committee, 1978; National Lawyers' Guild, 1979; NWHN, 1981; Women Against Sterilization Abuse, 1977). Extensive abuses were also reported in

Puerto Rico and of Puerto Rican women on the mainland US (e.g., Rodriguez-Trias, 1982).

In response to these cases, reported extensively by the media, reproductive rights and civil rights activists organized and pushed for the enactment of *regulations* to protect women and men against such abuses through more rigorous required informed consent procedures for the surgeries. Today in the US, federal regulations cover all federally funded (Medicaid) sterilizations. Additionally, New York City and the state of California both have similar regulations which cover 'private pay' (third party/insurance and personal pay) patients.

Reproductive rights activists gradually began to understand that blatant abuses are really the tip of a much larger iceberg of sterilization abuse. Most abuse is likely to be *subtle and privatized,* taking place in physicians' offices, hospitals and even at home where women and men 'choose' sterilization as a means of contraception under constraining circumstances with inadequate and erroneous information about it and its consequences.

## Forms of Subtle Sterilization Abuse

Ten major situations in which the majority of subtle sterilization abuses occur have been identified by reproductive rights activists.

### *1. Lack of Abortion Options*

… Providing high quality, accessible abortion services has not been given adequate social policy priority in this country. In some whole states and many rural counties there are no abortion facilities or providers (NARAL, 1980). Moreover, since the 1977 Hyde Amendment, federal Medicaid coverage of almost all poor women's abortions has ceased.

But what does access to abortion mean in terms of an individual's 'choice' of contraception? Some data are available. In Illinois, newspapers reported that 'the poor are turning to sterilization as the ultimate means of birth control as a result of restrictions on government-funded abortions'; in that state in 1980, when Medicaid abortions were no longer easily available, the number of sterilizations rose to 6,219 compared to 3,625 in 1979 (UPI, 1981: A10). Crucially, when the federal government reimburses states for abortions, only 50 per cent of the actual costs of the abortion are covered. In sharp contrast, 90 per cent of sterilization costs are reimbursed, making sterilization more immediately cost-effective for the state.

Obviously, reproductive rights or even individual choice are meaningless when abortion and other birth control access is limited. Abortion is our last line of defense against an unwanted pregnancy; if it is unavailable, *all* our contraceptive options *except* sterilization are much less attractive.

### *2. Unnecessary Hysterectomy*

Hysterectomy is the most common major surgery in the US; if present rates continue, 50 per cent of all women in the US will have had this surgery by the time they are sixty-five years old (Scully, 1980: 141). …

The potential for subtle sterilization abuse through medically unnecessary hysterectomy is tremendous. Too many physicians are paternalistic, classist, racist and/or sexist and assume they should be the ultimate arbiters of women's fertility, especially that of poor women and women of color. This is a classic example of professionals exercising their autonomy over and against that of patients. For example, the highest rates of hysterectomy and tubal ligation in the US are in the South (Center for Disease Control, 1980; 1981), likely in part to reflect racism in reproductive care.

Some physicians have urged 'hysterectomy especially for those who usually fail to comply with medical and contraceptive management' (Roach et al., 1972). This is a common euphemism for poor women, women of color, and women for whom English is a second language who are often derogated as incompetent in the medical literature on sterilization (Arnold, 1978: 15).

...

[Also,] it has historically been common medical practice to hysterectomize mentally retarded girls and women to prevent childbearing (Bass, 1967) and to eliminate menstruation which is claimed to be 'unhygienic.'

### 3. Economic Constraints upon Reproductive Choice

There are two basic issues here. First, some workplaces abusively require women to be sterile or sterilized in order to qualify for employment. (To my knowledge, there have been no such requirements for men.) The classic case is the American Cyanamid Company's requirement described earlier. Stellman and Henifin (1982) have documented many similar cases in other industries. ...

...

Second, economic constraints are also manifest in our personal lives in high unemployment, deindustrialization and profound economic and social insecurity. Despite the absence of so-called 'medically effective' methods of contraception (the Pill, IUD, sterilization), birth rates dropped drastically during the Great Depression of the 1930s (Gordon, 1976; Petchesky, 1981). Over the past few years, how many women and men have 'chosen' sterilization because they 'can't afford' a child, another child or the costs of hospital delivery (which often must be paid in advance by those lacking medical insurance)? How many might be able to 'afford' the child but not the childcare necessary for them to continue working?

...

### 4. Lack of Knowledge of the Permanence of Sterilization

Many people do not fully understand that the surgery of sterilization is in almost all instances permanent and irreversible. In one study, some 39 percent of all the women interviewed did not know sterilization was permanent; among Black women—45 per cent, Hispanics—59 per cent, and whites—24 per cent. (Carlson and Vickers, 1982: 35). Of the previously sterilized women surveyed, 40 per cent thought they could become pregnant again (ibid.: 22).

...

… The lack of knowledge of permanence of sterilization trivializes the meaning and value of women's and men's reproductive capacities. This certainly serves the interests of population control perspectives. Further, when providers do not provide full and complete information to patients, they enhance their own control over the patient at the patients' expense. This has the flavor of the exercise of patriarchal professional authority—whether it is over women or men. …

## 5. Lack of Knowledge or Access to Other Means of Contraception

If sterilization is the only available contraceptive option, there is no choice. Lack of *knowledge* of and real access to alternative methods and their risks and benefits leads to subtle sterilization abuse. Carlson and Vickers's (1982) study of over 600 New York City women found no significant differences by race, income, religion or education with respect to the number of methods *heard of.* However, significant differences were found in *usage:* wealthier, better educated women had used more methods than poorer women; Black and Hispanic women had used fewer methods than white women and discussed fewer methods with their providers (ibid.: 20–2).

…

## 6. Simultaneous Sterilization and Childbirth or Abortion

Historically, blatant sterilization abuse often occurred in conjunction with childbirth, as in the Madrigal case (CARASA, 1979), and in conjunction with abortion, as 'package deals' in which women were offered 'free' abortions unavailable elsewhere if they allowed simultaneous sterilization (National Lawyers' Guild, 1979). As one doctor said, 'Unless we get those tubes tied before they go home (from abortion or childbirth), some of them will change their minds by the time they come back to the clinic' (Rodriguez-Trias, 1982: 152). In both instances, women were unnecessarily pushed to consider sterilization in situations of urgency and emotional stress.

Because of such abuses, reproductive rights advocates pushed to include in the regulations both a prohibition against obtaining consent during childbirth or abortion and a 'waiting period' between the time of *consent* to sterilization and the actual surgery. US federal regulations require a thirty-day wait. …

The one-month waiting period, while still engendering some regret, seems to be the best compromise between fair access to sterilization and prevention of regret. Thus pregnant women could decide during their pregnancies—but *not* on the delivery table—and women who had decided to be sterilized and then discovered an unwanted pregnancy could have simultaneous surgeries if desired.[4]

The issue of a waiting period essentially pits regulatory *protection of all women* against *individual convenience and preference.* It particularly demonstrates the differences between reproductive rights and individual choice supporters who have historically opposed regulations which constrained full freedom of choice. For example, in 1977, the California chapter of the National Organization of Women (NOW) testified against having any 'private pay' sterilization regulations in that state because they would constrain ease of access to sterilization.

NOW has historically reflected the opinions of middle-class women (Fee, 1975). Such women had themselves been victims of yet another kind of sterilization abuse—they were denied access to sterilization as a means of contraception unless and until they fulfilled the '120 rule.' This was an unofficial rule of thumb of the American College of Obstetricians and Gynecologists until about 1970, under which a woman's age multiplied by the number of children she had must equal 120 or more for her to obtain a sterilization for contraception (National Lawyers' Guild, 1979: 25). Obviously, the 120 rule is a classic example of 'doctor knows best' paternalism in action, this time against the reproductive autonomy of middle-class women.

The protection of women through regulations is complex and often difficult to formulate while respecting the diverse needs and desires of *all* women. Reproductive rights activists advocate guving primary consideration to the protection of the most vulnerable—the poor, the disabled, and people of color—who have historically suffered the most abuses.

### 7. Iatrogenic (medically-caused) Sterility or Infertility

Sterility (inability to conceive) or infertility (difficulty in conceiving) caused by medical treatment or its lack is epidemic. The National Center for Health Statistics' estimates for the US find only 56 percent of married women of childbearing age fertile; 18 percent sterilized for contraception, 10 percent for other reasons, and 16 percent unable to conceive for unknown reasons (United Press, 1983: 2). (These figures do not account for infertility among nonmarried women—heterosexual and lesbian—who might be desirous of bearing children.) In this study, possible causes of growing infertility rates include:

- increased rates of *socially transmitted diseases* (STDs), such as gonorrhea and syphilis, infections which can cause a build up of scar tissue leading to infertility, especially if inadequately or un-treated;
- the 600 percent increase in women using *IUDs* which increase risk of Pelvic Inflammatory Disease (PID), another infection leading to the build up of scar tissue and possible infertility (ibid.; Population Information Program, 1983).

Other possible sources include:

- inappropriate overuse of *cone biopsies and hysterectomies* for the medical diagnosis and treatment of cervical dysplasia (Clarke and Reaves, 1982);
- use of *Depo-Provera*, an injectable contraceptive, which has a wide range of severe side effects for many women, often including sterility (Hatcher et al., 1982; Rakusen, 1981);
- *inadequate treatment* of STDs and PID. …

### 8. Disproportionate Sterilization of Welfare Women

Reproductive rights activists long suspected that women on welfare were more likely to be sterilized than their non-welfare counterparts. For example, 97 percent of physicians in one study favored the sterilization of welfare mothers who had born 'illegitimate' children (Silver, 1972). Recent research in the US (Shapiro et al., 1982: 20), using data on over 18,000 women from the US Survey of Family Growth, found that women on welfare with three or more children were, in fact, 67 percent more likely to be sterilized than non-welfare women with the same numbers of children. The researchers concluded, 'something occurs in the process of delivering publicly-assisted family planning health care that channels services in the direction of more permanent services,' such as sterilizations, which are 'immediately cost effective' (ibid.: 21).

A parallel situation exists among Native Americans, who generally receive care from the welfare-like US Indian Health Services (IHS). Blatant sterilization abuses were found in the IHS in 1976, including inadequate record-keeping, lack of counseling for informed consent, and thirty-six clear violations in 3001 cases (including several sterilizations of women under twenty-one years old) (Women Against Sterilization Abuse, 1977: 2–3). Lee Brightman, President of United Native Americans, estimates that of the US Native population of about 800,000, as many as 42 percent of the women of childbearing age and 10 percent of the men have been sterilized (*Akwesasne Notes*, 1977a, 1977b …).

The disproportionate sterilization rates among welfare and IHS women reflect, I believe, a patterned institutional discrimination on the basis of population control of poor people and people of color, that is, class, race and welfare related.[5]

## 9. Ideologies of 'Appropriate' Family Size and Structure

…

Different racial and ethnic groups hold varying ideologies regarding favored family size, structure, what is known as 'legitimacy' and what is called 'the family' (e.g. see Davis, 1981; Mora and del Castillo, 1980; Stack, 1974). It is around the issue of 'proper' family size that population control groups (such as Zero Population Growth) have been most influential. In sharp contrast, reproductive rights groups have questioned this small nuclear family as the 'ideal' for all, especially as it ignores cultural as well as health differences.

Both reproductive rights and individual choice perspectives emphasize the autonomy of women in determining the number and timing of children they choose to bear. Especially challenging to us as feminists is how to simultaneously support women who genuinely choose to have children and even many children, while also supporting women who genuinely choose to have more. This issue of supporting a diversity of childbearing options must be extended to supporting a diversity of appropriate family structures as well.

## 10. Lack of Counseling to Prevent Regret of Sterilization

In a recent review of the literature on post-surgical regret, Chico [1984] notes that worldwide estimates of the number of sterilizations during the 1980s are as high as 180 million procedures. Even if regret *rates* are relatively low, say 5 per cent, by 1990 there would be in absolute numbers 9 *million* more women in the world who regretted their sterility. Moreover, estimates of *actual* rates of regret range from 1.5 percent to 43 percent (ibid.). This is, then, a problem of considerable magnitude.

Some proportion, perhaps even the majority of post-surgical regret, could be prevented through counseling focused on factors associated with such regret. Such factors include *age* at the time of surgery as younger women are more likely to regret (Carlson and Vickers, 1982; cf. Chico, forthcoming). Many people regret their sterilizations upon *remarriage* after the surgery, due to the desire to 'start a new family' (see Chico, forthcoming). Other factors, discussed earlier, are *poor contraceptive information* both on the permanence of sterilization and on alternative birth control, *shorter length of waiting period* between the decision to be sterilized and the actual surgery, and *sterilization simultaneous with childbirth or abortion*. Since Black and Hispanic women and poor women have reported higher rates of regret (Carlson and Vickers, 1982), counseling to prevent regret should especially address their reproductive needs and goals.

These factors associated with regret demonstrate the intensely *social* nature of the decision to become sterilized for contraceptive reasons.

## Conclusions

While contraceptive technologies have enhanced *control* over reproduction, economic and social *supports* for childbearing and rearing have become issues at the core of highly controversial policy debates around reproduction. The technologies of reproductive control do *not* intrinsically or necessarily bring about a social world which supports genuine reproductive freedom.

Understanding both increasing rates of contraceptive sterilization and its blatant and subtle abuse requires careful analysis. It should be clear that in each specific situation described, participants may or may not be conscious of the perspectives influencing their decision-making. One goal of the reproductive rights agenda is, in fact, to help women and men to become more fully aware of reproductive issues and related medical information.

Specific activities to enhance women's and men's exercise of their reproductive rights and to reduce blatant and subtle sterilization abuse do emerge from this analysis. They include, but are far from limited to:

- encouraging second and even third opinions regarding hysterectomies of women of childbearing age, with rigorous informed consent procedures and printed information (in various languages) regarding alternative treatments (as has just been required regarding breast surgeries in California);

- working toward legal, accessible, safe and affordable abortion services in the community;

- working against sterility as a job requirement or preference for *either* sex, against genetic screening for employment and for safe workplaces for all;

- working toward the separation of sterilization from both abortion and childbirth;

- enhancing women's and men's knowledge of all forms of contraception;
- pushing for more contraceptive research on methods which can be controlled by the user, including more low technology contraceptive options for both women and men;
- implementation of 'private pay' sterilization regulations in the currently unprotected forty-nine states;
- improved monitoring and enforcement of the existing federal, state and city sterilization regulations;
- educational outreach toward broader understanding of the permanence of sterilization;
- countering population control/overpopulation perspectives with those of reproductive rights, including enhanced legitimacy of families of various sizes and structures;
- fighting for improved perinatal care and nutrition, especially for poor women and women of color, to reduce infant and maternal mortality and morbidity;
- targeted support to welfare women and men and welfare rights organizations since this population appears most vulnerable to both blatant and subtle abuses;
- particular outreach to providers of medical care to promote their protection of fertility in all areas of treatment, and to pressure them to improve reproductive counseling, especially around sterilization, toward the prevention of regret.

Because of its permanence, contraceptive sterilization highlights problems which pervade reproductive health care. The concept of subtle sterilization abuse helps to extend our understanding of the interrelation of reproductive issues. This fundamental interrelation of social, medical, personal and political issues is at the core of the reproductive rights perspective. It must continue to inform us in our struggle toward reproductive freedom for all.

---

## Notes

1. I would like to express thanks to Sheryl Ruzek and Virginia Olesen of the Women's Health Program at UC, San Francisco for support of this research. Also the quality of the assistance of my writing group—Kathy Charmaz, Gail Hornstein, Marilyn Little, and S. Leigh Star—never ceases to amaze. To Ruth Mahaney, Alice Wolfson, Sioban Harlow and Gail Kaufman, appreciation for initial direction and ongoing comradeship. And to my sterilization group—Linda Okahara, Helen Wood, Valeria Purnell, Sandy Goldstein, Holly Finke and Anne Finger—this reflects all our work.

2. In *Skinner* v. *Oklahoma* in 1942, Supreme Court Justice Douglas said, 'The power to sterilize ... may have subtle, far-reaching and devastating effects. In evil or reckless hands it can cause races or types which are inimical to the dominant group to wither and disappear.' (Kittrie, 1971: 297)

3. For information on the reproductive rights perspective, see e.g. CARASA, 1979; CDRR, 1983; Petchesky, 1980; R2N2, 1983. To compare individual choice abortion views, see e.g. Fee, 1975; NARAL, 1980.

4. Some physicians argue for separating sterilization from both abortion and childbirth on medical grounds due to higher rates of thromboembolic complications (due to pregnancy, IUDs or the Pill) (Kimball et al., 1978; Hafetz, 1980). Others cite increased risks of infection and hemorrhage (Hernandez et al., 1977) and reduced efficacy rates (Poma, 1980).

5. This pattern holds in terms of birth control as well: in one study, 43 per cent of the women on welfare said their doctors had *not* told them of any risks associated with their birth control methods, compared to only 5 per cent of the women not on welfare (Carlson and Vickers, 1982: 21–2).

## References

Ad Hoc Women's Studies Committee Against Sterilization Abuse. 1978. *Workbook on Sterilization.* Available from Women's Studies, Sarah Lawrence College, Bronxville, New York 10708.

*Akwesasne Notes.* 1977a. 'Sterilization Blasted: GAO Investigation Reveals Indians Used as Guinea Pigs.' January: 1.

*Akwesasne Notes.* 1977b. 'Killing Our Future: Sterilization and Experiments.' Early Spring: 1, 4–5.

Arnold, Charles B. 1978. 'Public Health Aspects of Contraceptive Sterilization.' In Newman, S. H. and Z. E. Klein, eds. *Behavioral-Social Aspects of Contraceptive Sterilization.* Lexington Press, Lexington, MA.

Bajema, Carl, ed. 1976. *Eugenics Then and Now.* Benchmark Papers in Genetics/5. Dowden, Hutchinson & Ross, Stroudsburg, PA.

Bass, Medora. 1967. 'Attitudes of Parents of Retarded Children Toward Voluntary Sterilization.' *Eugenics Quarterly,* 14: 45–53.

Carlson, Jody and George Vickers. 1982. 'Voluntary Sterilization and Informed Consent: Are Guidelines Needed?' Manuscript available from UMCNews, 475 Riverside Dr., NY, NY 10115.

Center for Disease Control. 1980. *Surgical Sterilization Surveillance: Hysterectomy in Women Aged 15–44, From 1970–1975.* September.

Center for Disease Control. 1981. *Surgical Sterilization Surveillance: Tubal Sterilization, 1976–1978.* March.

Chico, Nan. [1984.] 'Sterilization Regrets: Who Seeks Reversals?' *Mobius.*

Clarke, Adele and Martina Reaves. 1982. 'Cervical Dysplasia: The Ambiguous "Condition."' *Second Opinion,* newsletter of the Coalition for the Medical Rights of Women, September: 1–2.

CARASA (Committee for Abortion Rights and Against Sterilization Abuse). 1979. *Women Under Attack: Abortion, Sterilization and Reproductive Freedom.* Available from CARASA, 17 Murray St., NY, NY 10007 ($2.50).

CDRR (Committee to Defend Reproductive Rights). 1983. 'Fighting for Private Pay Sterilization Regulations.' *CDRR NEWS,* March.

Davis, Angela, 1981. *Women, Race and Class.* Random House, New York.

Fee, Elizabeth. 1975/1982. 'Women and Health Care: A Comparison of Theories.' In Fee, Elizabeth, ed. *Women and Health: The Politics of Sex in Medicine.* Baywood, Farmingdale, NY.

Fox, Richard W. 1978. *So Far Disordered in Mind: Insanity in California, 1870–1930.* UC Press, Berkeley.

Gordon, Linda. 1976. *Woman's Body, Woman's Right: A Social History of Birth Control in America.* Penguin, New York.

Hafetz, G. 1980. *Human Reproduction.* Harper & Row, Hagerstown, MD.

Haller, Mark. 1963. *Eugenics: Hereditarian Attitudes in American Thought.* Rutgers University Press, New Brunswick, NJ.

Hatcher, R. A. et al. 1982. *Contraceptive Technology, 1982–1983.* Irvington, New York.

Hernandez, Ingrid et al. 1977. 'Postabortal Laparoscopic Tubal Sterilization: Results in Comparison to Interval Procedures.' *Obstetrics and Gynecology,* 50 (3): 356–8.

Kimball, Ann Marie et al. 1978. 'Deaths Caused by Pulmonary Thromboembolism After Legally Induced Abortion.' *American Journal of Obstetrics and Gynecology,* vol. 132: 169–74.

Kittrie, Nicholas N. 1971. *The Right to be Different: Deviance and Enforced Therapy.* Johns Hopkins University Press, Baltimore.

Mereson, Amy. 1982. 'The New "Fetal" Protectionism: Women workers are sterilized or lose their jobs.' *Civil Liberties,* July: 6–7.

Mora, Magdalena and Adelaida R. del Castillo, eds. 1980. *Mexican Women in the United States: Struggles Past and Present.* Occasional Paper no. 2, Chicano Studies Research Center Publications, UC, Los Angeles.

NARAL (National Abortion Rights Action League). 1980. Status of State Funding for Abortions.' *NARAL Newsletter,* 12(8): 5. Available from NARAL, 825 15th St NW, Washington, DC 20005.

National Lawyer's Guild, New York City Anti-Sexism Committee. 1979. *Reproductive Freedom: Speakers Handbook on Abortion Rights and Sterilization Abuse.* Available from NLG, 853 Broadway, 17th Floor, NY, NY 10003.

NWHN (National Women's Health Network). 1981. *Sterilization Abuse: What it is and how it can be controlled.* Available from NWHN, 224 7th St. SE, Washington, DC 20003.

Paul, Julius. 1968. "The Return of Punitive Sterilization Proposals: Current Attacks on Illegitimacy and the AFDC Program.' *Law and Society Review,* 3(1): 77–106.

Petchesky, Rosalind P. 1980. 'Reproductive Freedom: Beyond "A Woman's Right to Choose."' *Signs,* 5(4): 661–85.

Petchesky, Rosalind P. 1981. '"Reproductive Choice" in the Contemporary United States: A Social Analysis of Female Sterilization.' In Michaelson, Karen L., ed. *And the Poor Get Children: Radical Perspectives on Population Dynamics.* Monthly Review Press, New York.

Poma, Pedro. 1980. 'Why Women Seek Reversal of Sterilization.' *Journal of the National Medical Association,* 72(1): 41–8.

Population Information Program, Johns Hopkins University. 1983b. 'Infertility and Sexually Transmitted Disease: A Public Health Challenge.' *Population Reports,* Series L(4), July.

Rakusen, Jill. 1981. 'Depo-Provera: the extent of the problem—A case study in the politics of birth control.' In Roberts, Helen, ed. *Women, Health and Reproduction.* Routledge & Kegan Paul, London.

R2N2 (Reproductive Rights National Network). 1983. *Newsletter.* Available from R2N2, 17 Murray St, NY, NY 10007.

Roach, C. J. et al. 1972. 'Vaginal Hysterectomy for Sterilization.' *American Journal of Obstetrics and Gynecology,* 114.

Robitscher, Jonas, ed. 1973. *Eugenic Sterilization.* Charles C. Thomas, Springfield, Il.

Rodriguez-Trias, Helen. 1982. 'Sterilization Abuse.' In Hubbard, Ruth, Mary Sue Henifin, and Barbara Fried, eds. *Biological Woman—The Convenient Myth.* Schenkman, Cambridge, MA.

Scully, Diane. 1980. *Men Who Control Women's Health: The Miseducation of Obstetrician Gynecologists.* Houghton-Mifflin, New York.

Shapiro, Thomas, William Fisher and Augusto Diana. 1982. 'Family Planning and Female Sterilization.' Paper presented at the Annual Meetings of the American Sociological Association, San Francisco.

Silver, Morton A. 1972. 'Birth Control and the Private Physician.' *Family Planning Perspectives,* IV(2): 42–6.

ı74. *All Our Kin: Strategies for Survival in a Black Community.* Harper & Row,

.ne M. and Mary Sue Henifin. 1982. 'No Fertile Women Need Apply: Employ-
    .rimination and Reproductive Hazards in the Workplace.' In Hubbard, Ruth,
    .e Henifin and Barbara Fried, eds. *Biological Woman—The Convenient Myth.*
    .nan, Cambridge, MA.
United ı ress. 1983. 'Infertility Rate of U.S. Women Rises: Increase in Diseases Cited.' *San Fran-
    cisco Chronicle,* February 10: 2.
UPI, 1981. 'With Lid on Abortions, Women in Illinois Turning to Sterilizations.' *San Francisco
    Chronicle,* October 4: A10.
Women Against Sterilization Abuse. 1977. 'Summary of General Accounting Office Report on
    the Permanent Sterilization of Native American Women.' Unpublished manuscript.

# *"Informed Consent":*
# *The Myth of Voluntarism*

## Gena Corea

In vitro fertilization is a therapy developed by compassionate doctors to help humankind, according to the media presentation of it. There are no villains here, only
kind doctors helping desperate patients. Pharmacrats present the compelling desire
of women to bear children as a desire before which nothing must stand in the way.[1]
To help women, doctors simply remove a few eggs from their ovaries, fertilize the
eggs in a glass petri dish with the husbands' sperm, and return the fertilized eggs to
the women's wombs.

I argue ... that the situation is less benevolent than the pharmacracy portrays it.
Men are experimenting on women in ways more damaging to women than anyone
has publicly acknowledged. It may sound simple to just take a few eggs from a woman's ovary, fertilize them, and return them to her uterus, but in fact the manipulations of the woman's body and spirit involved in this procedure are extreme.

There are strong indications that women who were among the first IVF experimental subjects, including Lesley Brown, did not fully understand the experimental
nature of the programs in which they were enrolled. While it now appears that
women are clamoring for IVF, that, far from being coerced into participating in
these experiments, they are crushed when doctors deny them entry, in fact the
women *are* being coerced, but the coercion, which is emotional rather than physical,
has been rendered invisible.

...

[IV pioneer Dr. Robert Edwards wrote] ... that he and [his partner] Steptoe agreed on a certain point: That the hopes of the female "patients [sic] must not be raised unjustifiably and that they fully understood the situation—the opportunities and dangers and how they would be involved" (Edwards and Steptoe, 1980).

But Lesley Brown, mother of the world's first test-tube baby, did not understand. One of Brown's nurses wrote: "It was explained to the patient that oocyte recovery and in vitro fertilization was her only chance of pregnancy. She was thoroughly briefed in the implications of the experimental techniques so that she understood what she was involved in" (Harris, 1978).

So "thoroughly briefed" was Lesley Brown that until just before the birth of Louise, she assumed hundreds of test-tube babies had already been born. Describing the first meeting she and her husband John had with Patrick Steptoe, she wrote: "I don't remember Mr. Steptoe saying his method of producing babies had ever worked, and I certainly didn't ask. I just imagined that hundreds of children had already been born through being conceived outside their mothers' wombs. Having a baby was all that mattered. It didn't seem strange that I had never read about anyone who had had a child in that way before. I could understand their mothers wanting to keep quiet afterwards about how their children had been started off. It just didn't occur to me that it would almost be a miracle if it worked with me."
...

At some point during the experiments, Steptoe did tell Brown that the in vitro fertilization method had never worked before, but not in such a way that she took in that fact. ...
...

Lesley did not understand until very late in her pregnancy that human in vitro fertilization and embryo transfer had never been successfully done. Neither did her husband. Soon after Louise Brown's birth, the *Daily Telegraph* reported: "The proud new father was overjoyed with his new daughter—but not too happy about being the first test-tube dad. 'I didn't know we were to be the first test-tube parents—I wish we weren't,' said Mr. Brown" (Murche, 1978).
...

A woman who was in an Australian IVF program for four years and who underwent four operations without a successful pregnancy, told a radio interviewer: "I really didn't realize three years ago that it was at such a beginning stage." ...

Even if the women involved had fully understood that IVF was in the earliest stages of human experimentation and had knowingly consented to participate in the programs, we cannot say that they acted freely. The appearance of voluntarism is deceptive, for the control over women begins long before they can voice a "free choice."[2]

The patriarchy filters through all its institutions the propaganda that women are nothing unless they bear a man's children. This message comes at women from every direction: From philosophers like Arthur Schopenhauer, who argued in 1851 that "women exist, on the whole, solely for the propagation of the species" (Hays, 1964, p. 209). From psychiatrists like Dr. Bernard Rubin, who asserted that "Women have a psychobiological drive organization directed toward bearing children" (Rubin, 1965). From priests like Pope Paul VI, who declared in 1972 that true women's liberation does not lie in "formalistic or materialistic equality with the other sex, but in the recognition of that specific things in the feminine personality—the vocation of a woman to become a mother" (quoted in Daly, 1973, p. 3). Century after century, the message seeped deeply into woman: If she cannot produce children, she is not a real woman, for producing children is the function that defines woman.

Because patriarchy has for centuries so organized society that childbearing became the main purpose of women's lives and, frequently, the only way a woman could survive and gain any status, barrenness was the greatest shame a woman could know, the greatest curse she could suffer.

The association of womanhood with childbearing remains a deeply engrained one. Not surprisingly, one study has found the psychological impact of infertility to be far greater on women than on men. In the study by Dr. William R. Keye, Jr., nearly one third of the women said they felt bad about their bodies and saw themselves as less feminine because of infertility. Only 10 percent of the men reported a negative body image (*Ob/Gyn News*, 1982, Jan. 15, p. 6).

In 1977, Barbara Eck Menning, who is infertile, wrote that the words "infertile woman" seemed mutually exclusive to her: "I could be infertile or a woman but not both."

The propaganda Menning was subjected to—that women are nothing unless they bear children, that if they are infertile, they lose their most basic identity as women—has a coercive power. It conditions a woman's choices as well as her *motivations* to choose. Her most heartfelt desire, the pregnancy for which she so desperately yearns, has been—to varying degrees—conditioned.

Emotional coercion can be every bit as powerful as physical coercion. The law has always recognized that coercion need not involve physical force, as psychiatrist Willard Gaylin points out (Gaylin, 1974). "Economic loss, social ostracism, ridicule are all recognized by law in varying contexts as coercive forces because in a social animal the need for approval and acceptance will almost always be equated with its very survival," Gaylin wrote. To the unconscious, he continued, death can be seen as isolation, loss of love, rejection from the family group, or social humiliation.

Barren women risk all these symbolic equivalents of death.

When pharmacrats, and in some cases, husbands, speak to the unconscious of infertile women, playing on a fear of barrenness, which may signify to the women abandonment, loss of love, and nothingness, they are exercising what Gaylin calls an alternative kind of coercion.[3] Coercion through the manipulation of the unconscious can operate without the person's knowledge that she is being coerced, without her resentment, and with the appearance of her consent, Gaylin observed. ...

...

Sandra James, a 30-year-old New York woman who had undergone surgery and hormonal treatments to cure her infertility, said she used to sit in her rocking chair and cry and cry. "I felt like half a woman, not a whole woman. Sometimes I wanted to die." For a while, she tried to keep her infertility secret from her man, because she was afraid he might abandon her (Kleiman, 1979).

A 33-year-old Brooklyn woman saw more than twenty doctors and was hospitalized six times in an attempt to overcome her infertility. She suffered severe depression. *The New York Times* reported: "Her husband has no children, and said that, although he has not put pressure on her, she felt an instinctive need to give him a child" (3/19/79). ...

"You'll have to find yourself a proper woman," Lesley Brown repeatedly told her husband John when, month after month, she failed to become pregnant. "I've nothing to give our marriage now that I can't have a child." John wrote: "She [Lesley] was my wife, and I wanted her to have my baby." Steptoe recalled his first meeting with Lesley and John: "She felt she was letting John down by not having a baby. Their marriage had nearly broken apart. She had even tried to persuade her husband to divorce her so that he might marry someone else who could give him a child" (Brown, 1979; Edwards and Steptoe, 1980).

So women like Brown, women "desperate" for children, "besieged" hospitals, begging physicians to experiment on their bodies. Men claimed that women demanded in vitro fertilization "services" and in doing so obscured the social reality. Given patriarchy's proscription that women must produce children for their mates, free choice is conditioned. We can say of in vitro fertilization what Raymond says of transsexual surgery: that "the concept of volunteerism has taken hold, and the coercion of a role-defined environment is not recognized as an influential factor" (Raymond, 1979, p. 135).

Physicians launching IVF programs are themselves acting out of their belief about a woman's nature and her biologically determined social role. Their work on external fertilization is designed to enable barren women to fulfill their biological destiny (Rose and Hanner, 1976, p. 216). Edwards wrote that his primary preoccupation during the 1970s was "to study human embryology and allow women, who were seemingly condemned forever to a life of infertility, to bear their own children fathered by their husbands" (Edwards and Steptoe, 1980, p. 86).

...

The anguish an infertile woman suffers is most real. But the pharmacracy encourages us to focus our sympathy for that woman in such a away as to increase its control over her. Feminists have a different vision of where to focus our sympathy. As Raymond has pointed out, we ask *why* she suffers and we propose ways of dealing with that pain that confront the total situation, the situation of women under patriarchy. Through feminism, we have come to see the suffering of infertile women largely (but not wholly) in political and social terms. That is, we see it as the imposition on women of a definition of ourselves that leaves us, if we are not mothers, nonentities. In view of the deep-rooted source of her suffering and fear, we do not believe that encouraging an infertile woman to hand over her body to the pharmacracy for manipulation and experimentation is a truly sensitive response to her plight.

"When tolerance serves mainly to protect the fabric by which a sexist society is held together, then it neutralizes values," Raymond writes. "It is important to help break the concreteness of oppression ... by stretching minds to think about solutions that only *appear* to be sensitive and sympathetic."

Raymond also encourages us to ask at what costs to ourselves we are channeled into reproducing. With IVF therapy, she points out, women are reduced to ultimately reproductive creatures, to medically manipulatable Matter. Those enrolled in these programs have already undergone, as infertile women, many medical tests, exploratory procedures and treatments that are debilitating and destructive to them, she writes.

...

These are a few of the "unattractive" procedures the more "willing" women subject themselves to:

• Endometrial biopsy. The doctor scrapes the lining of the uterus with a sharp tool and examines the tissue specimen under a microscope to determine if the woman is ovulating properly. This can be extremely painful. Katie Berry underwent the procedure. "Mrs. Berry said she received no warning of the pain, nor any means to alleviate it," *The New York Times Magazine* reported (Kleiman, 1979). The biopsy in itself may impair fertility.

• Tubal insufflation. The doctor fills a woman's oviducts with pressurized carbon dioxide to determine if the tubes are open. This is painful.

• The doctor injects a dye into the uterus and X rays the organ to see if it is structurally impaired. This exam is excruciating.

• The same test can be conducted on the oviducts. Sheila Ballantyne describes it in *Norma Jean the Termite Queen:* "The dye is being injected into Norma Jean's tubes. She has been instructed to hold her breath until the technician has taken the picture. ... Her whole abdomen is filled with searing acid. She can't hold her breath. The picture is ruined. Now we'll have to do it again. She hears herself screaming, 'If it feels like this, I don't want children!' 'Just do it right this time; we can't afford to mess this one up.' Oh agony beyond imagining" (Ballantyne, 1975, p. 33).

• Treatment of hormonal "deficiencies" with various drugs.

• "Blowing out" the tubes of some women every one or two months to maintain an opening. The doctor forces pressurized liquid through the tubes. "When I have the therapy, I put a towel over my head and cry," said one woman (quoted in: Raymond, AAAS, 1979).

• Surgery, including: laparoscopy; procedures to remove endometrial tissue or adhesions; reconstructive surgery on the oviducts. Anthea Polson, mother of the world's fifth test-tube baby, underwent ten operations in vain *before* she entered an IVF program.

Barbara Eck Menning, director of *Resolve* and a proponent of IVF, recalls the four years "filled with medical and surgical mayhem" of her struggle with infertility:

There was a year of testing on me—biopsies, dyerotubogram, postcoitals; as well as repeated tests of my husband. We had a programmed sex life keyed to a basal temperature chart. At the end of that year an acute abdominal episode, improperly handled, cost me the ovary and tube cn the right side. After recovery from surgery, on to a new doctor—more tests, more programmed sex life—everything was just fine, 'relax.' Relaxing did no good. On to a new doctor. Discovery of a cyst on the left ovary—resection by surgery. Six months later, success. Pregnancy—followed by miscarriage at 13 weeks. On to another doctor—an activist. 'We'll have you pregnant again in no time!" Emergency admission to the hospital after an acute reaction to the fertility pills he prescribed. My cycles ceased. The best effort of men and their medicine could not coax another cycle forth. At 31 I experienced menopause due to the surgical and medical assault on my ovaries (Menning, 1981).

Menning quotes another woman who went through an infertility work-up:

There is no inner recess of me left unexplored, unprobed, unmolested. It occurs to me when I have sex that what used to be beautiful and very private is now degraded and terribly public. I bring my charts to the doctor like a child bringing home a report card. Tell me, did I do well? Did I ovulate? Did I have sex at all the right times as you instructed me? (Menning, 1980).

...

When, using many sources, I pieced together a picture of what women endure in IVF programs, their suffering overwhelmed me. Yet that suffering is never mentioned in the ethical literature on in vitro fertilization. It is the embryo, and later the fetus, ethicists worry about. The federal Ethics Advisory Board, in its report on IVF, stated: "The most frequently articulated argument against federal funding of in vitro fertilization was based on the moral status of the fertilized egg and embryo. Proponents of this argument believed that human life should be respected from the moment of fertilization" (DHEW, 1979).

The debate on IVF has been a debate among men, and embryos and fetuses—seen as a man's sperm personified—appear to be real to these men in a way women are not. The Ethics Advisory Board itself was composed of thirteen men and only two women. In his comprehensive review of the ethical literature on IVF for this Board, Dr. LeRoy Walters cites the views of twenty-nine persons and every one of them is male. Walters lists, in descending order of prevalence in the literature, the ethical issues involved in human research with IVF. Risks of the research to the embryo top the list. Risks to the woman—referred to as "the oocyte donor"—is number eight on a list of twelve.

Risks are not even the only threat IVF poses to a woman's well-being. The innumerable manipulations of her body, and the suffering they cause her, also threaten her well-being. Yet this issue is absent from the ethical and medical literature on IVF. It is an issue about which writer Julie Melrose has thought a great deal, though not specifically in the context of in vitro fertilization. Through her own experiences as a medical and surgical patient, Melrose came to focus on studying medical ethics issues, particularly in women's health care. In an interview, Melrose stated:

There is a discrepancy between the way the doctor defines a surgical procedure and the way the person experiences it. Doctors have a tendency to look at surgical procedures in a technical and mechanical way. If they see a way that they can manipulate the body to accomplish what they want without posing an extremely high risk, they define that procedure as a piece of cake. From their position as mechanics, it *is* a piece of cake, that is, an easy procedure for them to perform.

My feeling is that the human body has an integrity of its own and that it cannot be violated, even in a way that the doctor may see as minor, without there being physical and emotional consequences for the person on whom the surgery is performed.

Women often believe doctors when they say something is a piece of cake and believe that they shouldn't make a big deal about it but then, during and after the procedure, they often feel that it *was* a big deal and it did not feel like a piece of cake to *them*. Their immediate, and often lingering, response to the procedure in fact has depth and has strong emotions connected with it and may have changed them in significant ways.

What chance do the women who endure all the procedures involved in IVF have of becoming pregnant? ...

...

Of the thousands of women hoping to get a baby through the 200-odd IVF programs across the globe, the vast majority have been disappointed. The cycle of hopes raised (she's accepted into the program) and dashed (doctor could not get an egg), raised (got an egg) and dashed (egg was abnormal), raised (got a normal egg) and dashed (embryo did not implant), raised (embryo implanted) and dashed (miscarried) harms women in ways pharmacrats have not acknowledged.

Every fresh failure generates the same grief symptoms experienced by a couple that loses a baby through sudden infant death or stillbirth, cautions Valerie Edge, R.N., project coordinator of the IVF program at Baylor College of Medicine, Houston (COG, 1984).

Nancy was one of the "lucky" women who had a successful embryo transfer after her first laparoscopy in an Australian program. She was pregnant. Part of her cheered, while another part cautioned that the chances of success were small. "It was this incredible turmoil that I was in," she explained. After about a month, she lost the pregnancy.

"I wasn't really surprised when I lost it. Some other people who I've talked to in the program feel devastated. I didn't. I just felt real sad. I felt grief-ridden for a while, but I didn't think about giving up."

After her second laparoscopy, while she, still sore, was recovering from surgery, the doctor told her the eggs they had just harvested had been abnormal. "When I went in [that] second time and my egg didn't even fertilize, that was harder than the first time because I thought, 'Well, I've lost a pregnancy, but next time they're going to get it.'"

There were six more "next times"—seven operations in all—and they still had not "gotten it" by the time Nancy was interviewed in 1981.

When eggs are retrieved, when pregnancies take and hold, doctors consider those pregnancies high risk. They monitor them through a variety of invasive means including ultrasound and amniocentesis. Ultrasound allows the doctor to visualize the baby in the uterus. (One reporter, describing this, wrote that IVF mother Anthea Polson had "a womb with a view.") Risks of amniocentesis include hemorrhage, perforation of viscera and infection. In one study, about 20 percent of women undergoing the procedure reported cramps and discomfort lasting from a few hours to a few days (Golbus, 1974).

According to her husband John, Lesley Brown was nervous about the amniocentesis. After a first unsuccessful attempt to do it, she telephoned John. She was sobbing: "Mr. Steptoe tried to do the amniocentesis today, but he couldn't manage it," she said. "I was too worked up. Now I'm getting pains in my tummy. I'm sure I'm going to lose the baby." Lesley knew there was a slight risk that the amniocentesis might cause a miscarriage and this upset her (Brown, 1979, pp. 118–119). (In fact in 1980, one woman in an Australian IVF program did miscarry her test-tube baby at 20 weeks following amniocentesis [DM, 4/30/80].)

In a final manipulation of a woman's body in the IVF programs, doctors delivering test-tube babies often do so by cesarean section, subjecting the woman to the risks of major abdominal surgery. Steptoe performed a cesarean on Lesley Brown because she developed toxemia, a life-threatening condition characterized by swelling of hands and face, excess weight gain, protein in urine and elevated blood pressure. Brown developed toxemia three weeks before the operation and she spent those and several preceding weeks in the hospital. While ob/gyns generally maintain that the cause of the condition is unknown, evidence from a number of demonstration projects targeted at preventing toxemia indicates that it may be a disease of malnutrition.[4] If it is, Brown's toxemia could have been hospital-induced, for she had been eating hospital fare.

In his book, Steptoe describes the various needles, tubes and knives introduced into Lesley Brown's body and the manipulations performed on her organs during the cesarean: shot of atropine injected to dry up excess respiratory secretions; rubber tube passed into trachea; heart monitoring equipment applied to chest; separating bladder and womb; pushing Lesley's stomach until the baby's shoulders appeared in the wound in her abdomen, etc. After delivering the baby, Steptoe lifted the womb out of the body to demonstrate to the cameras that Lesley had no oviducts and so could not have conceived naturally. The baby was examined, weighed and handed to Steptoe. He recalls:

"A jubilant Bob and Jean joined me, and I passed Louise, as she was to be named, to Bob. It was his brain, skill and perseverance and Jean's hard-working devotion which had led to this wonderful moment of achievement. We stood briefly together for the cameras to preserve the moment and then returned Louise to her cot and her guardian nurse" (Edwards and Steptoe, 1980, p. 165).

During their triumph, Lesley lay unconscious on the table.

. . .

After the ordeals infertile women endure, are those who do finally bear a baby happy? Not always. Consider the woman who wrote to the newsletter of Resolve, an organization that counsels the infertile: "Since I had longed for a baby so desperately, I felt as though I could neither permit myself any negative feelings nor be less than the perfect mother." But the baby was colicky "for three horrid months, a period of time during which I never slept more than three hours or so at a time." One day a neighbor, having heard of her infertility history, said to her, "You must be so-o-o happy!" The new mother burst into tears and sobbed: "I hate the little bitch and the whole damn motherhood scene." The startled neighbor confided that she had hated her colicky baby too. The mother continued: "In truth, I was a victim of my successful pursuit of fertility. As I have finally discovered, at one time or another most mothers dislike their kids and wish for something besides motherhood. … I am finally getting to the point where I can enjoy the baby for what she is, not for the hoped-for fulfillment of all the fantasies that infertile people are prey to" (*Resolve Newsletter,* Dec. 1977; April, 1979).

Neither of these formerly infertile women were in IVF programs. Lesley Brown, of course, was. "It really shocked me once when I shouted at the baby because she kept crying," she wrote of Louise. "It wasn't a question of not loving her. It just seemed as if I didn't deserve her if I behaved like that. There were so many childless women who would have made better mothers, if they'd been given the same chance" (Brown, 1979, p. 187).

## Notes

1. For example, the Health Systems Agency report recommending approval of the Norfolk IVF clinic stated: "Thus, inasmuch as this program does not exist elsewhere in this country, disapproval of the project may constitute denial of a fundamental right to individuals desiring the procedure, and may, thus be legally indefensible." Why does the patriarchy give serious attention to this "right" of women—the right to submit to experimentation in an attempt to reproduce—and not to other rights such as those of equal protection under the law and equal pay for equal work? Why is its interest in women's rights so selective?

2. Dr. Janice Raymond, medical ethicist, has made this clear (Raymond, 1979). In my discussion of free choice, I am applying to IVF the analysis of informed consent Raymond presents in her important book, *The Transsexual Empire.*

3. I am applying Gaylin's insights to the situation barren women face. He does not write of this situation in his article.

4. Dr. Tom Brewer, an obstetrician who directed a prenatal nutrition program among the poor in Costra County, California, for twelve years, and Gail Brewer, author and childbirth educator, present the evidence for toxemia as a disease of malnutrition in their book, *What Every Pregnant Woman Should Know.* They explain: When a pregnant woman's diet is deficient, the liver, lacking vital nutrients, begins to malfunction. It cuts down on the synthesis of albumin, a protein critical for maintaining blood volume. When albumin synthesis drops, the water which should be in the blood circulation leaks into the tissue, causing swelling. With the mother's blood volume so low, the placenta fails to get enough blood and the nutrients the blood carries. Malnourished, it malfunctions. The fetus does not gain the necessary weight. Placental insufficiency, the Brewers maintain, is caused by the reduction in blood volume. If too little blood reaches it, the placenta may deteriorate, breaking off from the uterine wall in a catastrophe called placenta abruptio.

## Bibliography

Ballantyne, Sheila. 1975. *Norma Jean the Termite Queen.* Doubleday & Co. Garden City, New York.

Brewer, Gail Sforza with Tom Brewer. 1977. *What Every Pregnant Woman Should Know.* Random House. New York.

Brown, Lesley and John, with Sue Freeman. 1979. *Our Miracle Called Louise, a Parents' Story.* Paddington Press Ltd. New York and London.

COG. 1984, Jan. Referring your patient for in vitro fertilization.

Daly, Mary. 1973. *Beyond God the Father.* Beacon Press. Boston.

DHEW. 1979, June 18. Protection of human subjects: HEW support of human in vitro fertilization and embryo transfer. Report of the Ethics Advisory Board. *Federal Register.*

Edwards, R. G. and Patrick Steptoe. 1980. *A Matter of Life.* William Morrow and Co., Inc. New York.

Gaylin, Willard. 1974, Feb. On the borders of persuasion: a psychoanalytic look at coercion. *Psychiatry.* 37: 1–9.

Golbus, Mitchell, S., et al. 1974. Intrauterine diagnosis of genetic defects: results, problems and follow-up of one hundred cases in a prenatal genetic detection center. AJOG. 118(7): 897–905.

Harris, Muriel. 1978, Nov. 2. Louise: the test-tube miracle. *Nursing Mirror.*

Hays, H. R. 1964. *The Dangerous Sex.* G. P. Putnam's Sons. New York.

Kleiman, Dena. 1979, Dec. 16. Anguished search to cure infertility. *New York Times Magazine.*

Melrose, Julie. Preface to *The Harp That's Singing: Interviews with Feminist Writers.* Forthcoming.

Menning, Barbara Eck. 1977. *Infertility.* Prentice-Hall, Inc. Englewood Cliffs, New Jersey.

———. 1980, Oct. The emotional needs of infertile couples. *Fertility and Sterility.* 34(4): 313–319.

———. 1981. In defense of in vitro fertilization. In H. Holmes, B. Hoskins and M. Gross, eds., *The Custom-Made Child?* The Humana Press. Clifton, New Jersey.

Murche, John. 1978, July 27. Test-tube baby brings hope to childless women. *Daily Telegraph.*

Raymond, Janice. 1979. Fetishism, feminism and genetic technology. Paper given at American Association for the Advancement of Science meeting in Houston, Texas.

———. 1979. *The Transsexual Empire.* Beacon Press. Boston.

Rose, Hilary and Jalna Hanmer. 1976. Women's reproduction and the technological fix. In D. Barker and S. Allen, eds., *Sexual Divisions and Society: Process and Change.*

Rubin, Bernard. 1965, Aug. Psychological aspects of human artificial insemination, *Arch. Gen. Psychiat.* 13.

# *Babies, Heroic Experts, and a Poisoned Earth*

## Irene Diamond

Babies, once primarily dealt with within the world of women, are now the subject of theological proclamations, medical surveillance, and international policy. The possibilities posed by the so-called new reproductive technologies, which divide bodies into readily manipulable parts, have added new elements of commodification and sci-fi fantasy to the historic mysteries of human fertility. Yet, despite all the public and scholarly attention that surrounds the topic of baby-making, what is perhaps most remarkable about this debate is the fragmentary and partial nature of the discussion. ... Can ecofeminism provide a fuller picture of the issues than either feminism or ecology alone?

In the wake of the media drama over surrogate mothers and especially the fate of Baby M, which has framed the challenges in terms of the appropriateness or inappropriateness of contracts, it has become even more difficult to bring the contemporary restructuring of human procreation and birth into view. ... I want to argue that new technologies that assist with the seemingly benign tasks of helping infertile women have babies in their own bodies and of helping all mothers have "normal" babies pose profound threats to the dignity and well-being of human life itself.

The new opportunity of having experts provide information as to what kind of baby (what sex, what physical characteristics) a pregnant woman is likely to bear reshapes the experience of pregnancy at the same time that it devalues the lives of the living who may be of the "wrong" sex or chromosomal structure. This focus on the threats that hide within bodies enables us to look away from the threats to life that our culture has created. The biologist Ruth Hubbard, who has been an especially astute analyst of the toll of medical progress, notes, "As the world around us bcomes more hazardous and threatens us and our children with social disintegration, pollution, accidents, and above all nuclear war, it seems as though we seek shelter among the hazards that we are told lurk within us."[1] Moreover, the more we focus on the fertility problems of humans and ignore the ways in which humans are poisoning the Earth, the more we move toward a world where the complete and total control of baby-making by heroic experts is considered prudent and wise. Birth on a thoroughly poisoned Earth is likely to be so problematic that the choice of nonintervention will be totally lost. Machine-made babies will be the order of the day.

...

The push to regulate and monitor, which emerges in varying degrees from the expressed interests of medical researchers, lawyers, doctors, genetic counselors, and client-consumers, typically assumes that the birth of healthy babies is a function of equitably distributed diagnostic medicine. Access to the most advanced clinical techniques is the perceived critical issue. Some ethicists and legal scholars worry about how to settle complicated custody issues. Others concern themselves about appropriate rules to govern the use of laboratory-created human embryos. Within the confines of the debate there are differences of opinion. In discussions of the different procedures that accompany in vitro fertilization, for example, a few commentators, most especially spokespersons for the Catholic church, worry about the sanctity of human life. But, for the most part, the dominant discussion places its faith in the power of professional expertise to alleviate the individual trauma of infertility or the fear of malformed babies. The notion that the health of individual bodies is related to the health of the social body and the ecosystem that sustains all bodies recedes far into the background as heroic experts focus in on the microcomponents of baby-making.

...

... To understand the advance of technologies that appear to give individual women precise knowledge of their efforts to achieve or maintain healthy pregnancies, we cannot ignore the long-term historical forces that valorize predictability, control, and scientific evidence. Here we face a central paradox of contemporary feminism that I can only note. Although recent feminist scholars have profoundly criticized the presumed objectivity of scientific practice, feminism as an intellectual and social movement has its roots in the Enlightenment. That is, the ideals that feminism proclaims are themselves intimately entwined, indeed indebted, to the modern worldview that the phenomena of society and the natural world are proper objects for the exercise of human manipulation and control.

It is for this reason that, for many feminists, technologies that promise maximum individual choice and control with respect to the timing of reproductive decisions and the "products" of pregnancy are seen and applauded as enhancing women's freedom. ... This vision of individual freedom and technological modes of (re)production is fully implicated in the commodity logic of our society. When we consider the economic growth potential of this new colonization of procreation and birth it is little wonder that medical experts who help people have the babies they want are heralded as the harbingers of the new age.

...

In a society of isolated individuals where progress is measured in terms of scientific advance, experts' concern with the health of "populations" readily translates into complex forms of social control.[2] Whereas overt eugenics has usually taken the form of the sterilization of the "feebleminded" and those of "inferior" races, today the notion of the right of a child to be born healthy provides the impetus for monitoring the "correct" behavior of all pregnant women. "Quality" control is maintained through the complexities of normalization. Obstetricians now routinely advise women to take advantage of the best available tests lest the obstetrician be sued in the name of a future child. Maximizing access to prenatal screening is justified to funding bodies as a cost-savings device that will reduce the state's long-term medical costs.[3] The erosion of social commitment to babies and adults who require special support is particularly troublesome when we note that feminist advocates for persons with disabilities argue that, in many cases, the problem is not the disability but how people are treated because of it. These advocates question the whole medical view of disability as tragedy and ask further what the much heralded ability to conquer disabilities through encouraging women not to bear babies with disabilities means for the value of the lives of persons with disabilities.[4]

...

These are issues that are constantly on my mind. Yet after a new marriage, a miscarriage, and a diagnosis of fibroids, I found that I, too, wanted doctors and machines to provide answers and comfort. ... In discussing the issues with my husband, who was deeply drawn to the possibility of a child, I began to wonder about the difference between saving a fetus and more routine operations for a sick child. After miscarrying again, and becoming pregnant once more, my deep reservations about sonograms faded. I felt I needed to know if this fetus was still alive. ...

... After I miscarried and became pregnant again, I was 6 months older and found it somewhat more difficult to dismiss the numbers that seemed to be stacked against me. Whereas earlier I had concentrated on the risks of the procedure itself and thought how silly it would be to endanger a pregnancy I had been hoping for for 2 years, now I began to admit to myself that at my age, with two grown children, my desire for a child might not be strong enough to care for one with special needs. I was beginning to struggle with these new thoughts when the doctor asked about amnio. ... The tests now seemed reassuring if not necessary. ...

When the day for my amnio finally arrived I was feeling pretty good physically. I assumed my bouts of morning sickness and just plain sickness had passed because I had gotten past the difficult first trimester. The initial sonogram showed, however, that I was no longer pregnant—the fetus had died. In our initial shock and despair, it was somehow comforting to hear the geneticist tell me and my husband that given the three losses, it would be appropriate to test our genes for a transposed chromosome. If this were the case, my chances of giving birth to a normal baby were low, but even then we shouldn't be discouraged because with proper checking they had gotten other people successfully through pregnancies. On the way home, as I took note of my feelings, I thought, "How could I ever criticize a woman who chose in vitro fertilization?"

When I got home I realized that what the doctor had meant by "checking" was chorionic villi sampling, a diagnostic chromosome procedure similar to amniocentesis that can be done as early as 8 weeks rather than the 15 weeks for amnio. I knew that the test was still considered experimental in some places, but now I realized that if I got pregnant again, I might actually "choose" the less tested procedure to provide what I thought of as protection against another second-trimester miscarriage. I would want to know earlier that the pregnancy was doomed. Yet, I also realized that in a very real sense I had been blessed. What if the fetus had not died and I had had the amnio and been told that the chromosomes were not "normal"? Just that afternoon I had seen two children: a teenager in a wheelchair unable to hold his head up being fed by his mother, and a young boy about 12, who had that angelic look that some Down's syndrome children have, walking along very zestfully with an older brother or friend. Those two images within a half-hour of each other were a vivid reminder that prenatal testing does not tell how severe a child's problems will be. I had been spared from having to make a decision about life with a diagnostic category that did not distinguish between these children.

As the days passed, I became obsessed with trying to determine if our problems were a result of my husband's working in a nuclear submarine plant as a teenager and spending many summers swimming in the bay that adjoined the plant. (The knowledge that a childhood friend of his had given birth to a baby with cancer was additional impetus for concern.)[5] ...

I began this essay by asking whether ecofeminism could provide some greater clarity on the contemporary restructuring of procreation and birth. My own recent negotiation through the world of baby-making (which did not include clinics and lawyers' offices where alternative conception technologies are pursued) has impressed on me that there are no right or wrong answers for individual women. And I have no illusion that an ecological lens will somehow eliminate the pain of infertility or the anxiety of pregnant mothers for the health of their children. Indeed, the ethics of interconnectedness that I think we need to pursue is very different from the dominant instrumental ethic that assumes that the vulnerabilities of the body can be mastered and conquered.

Whereas this dominant masculinist ethic leads to dissecting human reproduction into ever more micro and more "manageable" parts, with the explicit goal of improving the operation of the perceived components, alternative ethics of interconnectedness would take heed of the intricate webs that link the birth and well-being of all animals—human as well as nonhuman—with the well-being of the Earth's ecosystems.[6] In a fragmented culture that is ambivalent if not fearful of women's bodies, where the language of liberation is wedded to entities with rights, and where dominant images increasingly stress the importance of "one's own child," it is tremendously difficult to comprehend ecosystemic and social webs, even those that are intuitively reasonable. Yet try we must, for the alternatives range from some combination of the poisoning of all life on Earth to more thoroughgoing mechanized control over more and more aspects of life.

It has been argued that in an economy built upon a growing trade in toxic materials, drugs, and radiation, babies are the best "canaries" we have—that pregnancy can provide a warning much like the canary did for coal miners.[7] Clusters of infertility, miscarriages, contaminated breast milk, and birth defects can be important signals. But increasing the use of prenatal screening, expanding the use of genetic screening in toxic workplaces, encouraging people to check before marriage about the compatibility of their genes, and making alternative reproduction technologies available can help hide those signals. The advantage of the latter, of course, is that the power of heroic experts is extended, the toxicities of late capitalism persist, and the poisoning of the Earth can continue. Thus, the challenge of transforming our relationships with each other and with the Earth is postponed.

## Notes

1. Ruth Hubbard, "Personal Courage Is Not Enough: Some Hazards of Childbearing in the 1980's," in Rita Arditti, Renate Duelli Klein, and Shelly Minden (eds.), *Test-Tube Women: What Future for Motherhood?* (London: Pandora Press, 1984), p. 343.

2. This new ability to monitor "health" before birth points to an expansion of the arenas for surveillance and regulation. For example, in a manual for physicians and genetic counselors, *Genetic Disorders and the Fetus* (New York: Plenum Press, 1986), p. 11, Aubrey Milunsky argues that "genetic counseling is best offered routinely and systematically prior to marriage."

3. In 1986, the state of California chose to launch a statewide alpha-feto-protein screening program even though the President's Commission for the Study of Ethical Problems recommended against routine screening. In arguing for the adoption of the program, the California Commissioner of Genetic Services emphasized the $3.7 million would be saved for Medi-Cal if 90 percent of the women found to be carrying severely deformed babies chose abortions. See Robert Steinbrook, "In California, Voluntary Mass Prenatal Screening," *Hastings Center Report* (October 1986): 4–7.

4. See, for example, Anne Finger, "Claiming All of Our Bodies: Reproductive Rights and Disabilities," and Marsha Saxton, "Born and Unborn: The Implications of Reproductive Technologies for People with Disabilities," in Arditti et al., *Test-Tube Women*, pp. 281–312.

5. See Rosalie Bertell, *No Immediate Danger* (London: Women's Press, 1985), for a discussion of the health effects of radiation exposure.

6. Tom Muir and Anne Sudar, "Toxic Chemicals in the Great Lakes Basin Ecosystem—Some Observations," (Burlington, Ontario, Canada: Water Planning and Management Branch, Inland Waters/Land Directorate, Ontario Region, November 1987), provides a valuable overview of ecosystem contamination as it affects human and nonhuman reproduction.

7. Erik Jansson, "The Causes of Birth Defects, Learning Disabilities, and Mental Retardation in Relation to Laboratory Animal Testing Requirements and Needs," *National Network to Prevent Birth Defects News* (June 14, 1988), argues that the child and fetus share a far greater susceptibility to toxic exposure "because rapidly dividing cells and migrating cells have been shown to be much more susceptible to radiation and toxins. Also, the child and fetus lack the enzymes in many cases to metabolize and excrete toxins."

# Access to In Vitro Fertilization: Costs, Care, and Consent

## Christine Overall

What would be a genuinely caring approach to the provision of procedures of so-called artificial reproduction such as in vitro fertilization (IVF)? What are appropriate and justified social policies with respect to attempting to enable infertile persons to have offspring? These urgent questions have provoked significant disagreements among theologians, sociologists, healthcare providers, philosophers and even—or especially—among feminists. ... (1) Some have suggested that access to IVF should be provided as a matter of right. (2) Some existing social policies and practices imply that access to IVF is a privilege. ... After evaluating ... these views, I shall offer a feminist alternative, describing what I think would constitute the caring provision of in vitro fertilization.

# The Right to Reproduce
# and the Right Not to Reproduce

Is there a moral *right* of access to in vitro fertilization? To answer that question requires consideration of the idea of a reproductive right. ...

It is necessary, first, to distinguish between the right to reproduce and the right *not* to reproduce.[1] ... The right not to reproduce means the entitlement not to be compelled to beget or bear children against one's will; the alternative to recognition of such a right is the acceptance of forced reproductive labour, or procreative slavery. To say that women have a right not to reproduce implies that there is no obligation of women to reproduce. The right not to reproduce is the entitlement not to be compelled to donate gametes or embryos against one's will, and the entitlement not to have to engage in forced reproductive labour. This right mandates access to contraception and abortion.

The right not to reproduce is distinct from the right to reproduce; that is, the right not to reproduce neither implies a right to reproduce nor follows from a right to reproduce. In my view, access to artificial reproduction cannot be defended by extension of the right not to reproduce.

The right to reproduce has two senses, the weak sense and the strong sense. The weak sense of the right to reproduce is a negative or liberty right: it is the entitlement not to be interfered with in reproduction, or prevented from reproducing. It would imply an obligation on the state not to inhibit or limit reproductive liberty, for example, through racist marriage laws, fornication laws,[2] forced sterilization, forced abortion, or coercive birth control programs. ...

In its strong sense, however, the right to reproduce as a positive or "welfare" right would be the right to receive all necessary assistance to reproduce. It would imply entitlement of access to any and all available forms of reproductive products, technologies and labour, including the gametes of other women and men, the gestational services of women and the full range of procreative techniques including in vitro fertilization, gamete intrafallopian transfer, uterine lavage, embryo freezing and sex preselection.

...

... There is good reason to challenge the legitimacy and justification of this right to reproduce in the strong sense. Recognizing it would shift the burden of proof on to those who have moral doubts about the morality of technologies such as IVF and practices such as contract motherhood, for it suggests that a child is somehow owed to each of us, as individuals or as members of a couple, and that it is indefensible for society to fail to provide all possible means for obtaining one. Recognition of the right to reproduce in the strong sense would create an active right of access to women's bodies and in particular to their reproductive labour and products. Thus, it might be used ... to imply an entitlement to obtain other women's eggs, and to make use of donor insemination and uterine lavage of another woman, all in order to maximize the chances of reproducing.[3] It would guarantee the entitlement to hire a contract mother, and force contract mothers to surrender their infants after birth.

This would constitute a type of slave trade in infants, and commit women to a modern form of indentured servitude. Finally, the right to reproduce in the strong sense might be used to found a claim to certain kinds of children—for example, children of a desired sex, appearance, or intelligence.

Exercise of the alleged right to reproduce in this strong sense could potentially require violation of some women's right not to reproduce. There is already good evidence, in both the United States and Great Britain, that eggs and ovarian tissue have been taken from some women without their knowledge, let alone their informed consent.[4] It is not difficult to imagine that recognizing a strong right to reproduce could require either a similar theft of eggs or embryos from some women, if none can be found to offer them willingly, or a commercial inducement to sell these products. It could be used as a basis for requiring fertile people to "donate" gametes and embryos. Even on a more ordinary level, recognition of a right to reproduce in the strong sense would seem to give men questionable rights over the reproductive products and labour of their female partners. Because of these implications—particularly the obligations that recognition of such a right would incur—I conclude that there is no right to reproduce in the strong sense. Even if some people willingly donate gametes, there is no *right* or entitlement on the part of the infertile that they should do so.

## Access to Artificial Reproduction as a Privilege

Access to methods of artificial reproduction such as in vitro fertilization cannot be justified by reference to an alleged right to reproduce in the strong sense. But while I am arguing that there is no right in the strong sense to IVF, such a claim does not of course imply that all use of IVF is thereby unjustified.

However, if appeal to such a right is abandoned, then it may seem that we are committed to holding that having children by means of artificial reproduction is necessarily a *privilege* that must be earned through the possession of certain personal, social, sexual, and/or financial characteristics. The provision of reproductive technology then appears to become a luxury service, access to which can be controlled by means of criteria used to screen potential candidates. Such limitations appear to be the price of sacrificing a right to reproduce in the strong sense.

And indeed, in actual practice, for processes such as IVF the criteria of eligibility have included such characteristics as sexual orientation—only heterosexuals need apply; marital status—single women are not usually eligible (unless they are part of an ongoing marriage-like relationship);[5] and consent of the spouse. Because IVF is costly, economic status and geographical location have also become, at least indirectly, criteria of eligibility. We can speculate that these are likely to lead to de facto discrimination against working-class women and women of colour.[6] Further criteria have also been used—for example, reproductive age, the absence of physical disabilities and characteristics such as "stability" and parenting capacities.[7] Some have also suggested or implied that infertility which is the result of the patient's own choices (for example, tubal ligation) should render the patient ineligible for IVF.

Should access to IVF be treated as a matter of privilege rather than right? Three arguments tell against this approach. First, persons who do not have fertility problems are not compelled to undergo any evaluation of their eligibility for parenthood. Moreover, some medical responses to infertility—for example, the surgical repair of damaged fallopian tubes—are undertaken without any inquiry into the patient's marital status, sexual orientation, or fitness for parenthood. If in vitro fertilization is classed as a medical procedure in the way that tubal repair is a medical procedure, then discrimination in access for the former and not for the latter is unjustified. The case of IVF seems to present an instance of discrimination on the basis of social criteria against people with infertility—and only certain kinds of infertility at that.

A second argument is the general difficulty of assessing the presence of some of the characteristics which have been assumed to be relevant for access to IVF. For example, for some women sexual orientation is a fluid and changing personal characteristic.[8] In addition, it is difficult to see how "stability" or aptitude for parenthood can be adequately measured, and there is likely to be a lot of disagreement about the appropriateness of criteria for evaluating these characteristics. One could also challenge the justification of allotting the assessment of these characteristics to IVF clinicians, who are not likely to have any better expertise than the rest of the population for making such evaluations.

Finally, it is essential to challenge the moral legitimacy of discrimination on the basis of characteristics such as sexual orientation and marital status. Such discrimination is founded upon false assumptions about the nature and abilities of single and lesbian women, and about the kind of mothering they can provide. While promoting good parenting practices is indisputably a worthwhile social goal, there is no evidence to suggest either that marriage and heterosexuality necessarily make women better mothers, or that the presence or a father is indispensable to childhood developmental processes. Nor do any research findings suggest that the ability to pay the enormous financial costs of IVF increases one's capacity to be a good parent.

…

Acceptance of these social barriers to accessibility is not the only alternative to claiming a right of access to IVF. Instead, it is important to critically evaluate screening processes for IVF, and to resist and reject practices of unjustified discrimination in access.

…

## Calling a Halt to Artificial Reproduction: Feminists

… [There] are criticisms expressed by some feminist scholars, scientists, and activists, criticisms that carry considerable empirical weight. For example, Canadian journalist Ann Pappert has investigated the sorry success record—perhaps more appropriately called a failure record—of IVF in Canada and the United States. She states: "Of the more than 150 IVF clinics in the United States, half have never had a birth, and only a handful have recorded more than five. Fifty percent of all U.S. IVF babies come from three clinics."[9] The success rate of the best IVF clinic in Canada is

13 percent; the majority of Canada's twelve IVF clinics have success rates of 8 percent or lower.[10]

The stressful and debilitating nature of the IVF experience for women has been powerfully documented by Canadian sociologist Linda Williams.[11] IVF's psychological costs include depression, anxiety and low self-esteem. But the physical suffering and health costs are even worse. They include the adverse effects of hormones such as Clomid, which are usually taken in large, concentrated doses to stimulate hyperovulation; repeated anaesthesia and surgery to extract eggs; the heightened risk of ectopic pregnancy; the development of ovarian cysts and of menstrual difficulties; and the early onset of menopause and an increased risk of some forms of cancer.

Moreover, while it is often said that the children "produced" through IVF are healthy, some recent studies in Australia dispute that claim. Rates of multiple pregnancy, spontaneous abortion, preterm delivery, perinatal death, birth defects and low birthweight are higher in IVF pregnancies than in other pregnancies.[12]

Because IVF represents an ongoing medical experiment on women and children, an experiment whose first success, Louise Joy Brown, is not yet fourteen years old, its long-term effects and risks are not known. Anita Direcks, a DES daughter from Holland, has written movingly about the parallels between the use of the synthetic hormone diethylstilbestrol (DES) allegedly to prevent miscarriage during the 1940s, 1950s and 1960s, and the use of in vitro fertilization, allegedly to alleviate infertility, during the 1970s and 1980s. Direcks writes:

> IVF is delivered by the same men who brought us DES, dangerous contraceptives, and other fertility-destroying technologies. One of the most important concerns I have in regard to IVF is the concern about the long-term effects of an IVF treatment for mother and child: the consequences of the hormonal treatment, the medium, and so on. ... IVF is an experiment on healthy women.[13]

> ...

As a result of considerations such as these, some feminists have called for a ban on further IVF research and practice. For example, Renate Klein and Robyn Rowland state, "IVF—in all its forms—must be ... abandoned. It is a failed and dangerous technology. And it produces a vulnerable population of women on which to continue experimentation."[14] FINRRAGE, the Feminist International Network of Resistance to Reproductive and Genetic Engineering, calls for resistance to "the development and application of genetic and reproductive engineering" and to "the take-over of our bodies for male use, for profit making, population control, medical experimentation and misogynous science."[15]

Feminists who would ban IVF depict those women who use it in a way entirely opposite to the picture painted by liberals who identify IVF access as a right. Far from being free and equal contractors in the reproductive marketplace, women are depicted as victims who are the incomprehending dupes of the scientific and medical systems. Whereas the rights advocates regard IVF as inevitably serving women's reproductive autonomy, advocates of a ban on IVF regard IVF as inevitably destroying it. Whereas the rights advocates claim, "Women want IVF," advocates of a ban on

IVF claim, "Women do not (really) want IVF," or, "Women's want for IVF is artificial."

> Does not this obsessive craving to have a child of one's own in many cases stem from an individual's sense of private property or the desire to have somebody around over whom one has substantial control for some years at least? Let us also face the questions that (a) is not this craving more created then [sic] natural and (b) does not the social pressure to fit to [sic] the image of "motherhood" put women in a more vulnerable position?[16]

But while many feminists have rightly stressed both the social construction of the desire for motherhood and the dangers and ineffectiveness of in vitro fertilization,[17] not all of them have been willing simply to attribute women's desire for IVF to false consciousness. Margarete Sandelowski suggests that:

> Feminists critical of the new conceptive technology and certain surrogacy and adoption arrangements suggest misguided volition on the part of infertile women, a failure of will associated not with causing infertility but with seeking solutions for it deemed hazardous to other women. … Beyond being politically useful as evidence for women's oppressive socialization to become mothers and their continued subservience to institutionalized medicine, infertile women occupy no more empathic place in many current feminist discussions than in the medical and ethical debates on reproductive technology feminists criticize.[18]

Sandelowski argues that some feminist theorists "equate women's desire for children with their oppression as women, viewing this desire and the anguish women feel when it remains unfulfilled as socially constructed rather than authentically experienced."[19] Thus, women's desires are discounted and their autonomy denied through the designation of socialization as the shaper and moulder of female selves.

…

… In fact, women's motives for seeking IVF are complex,[20] and it is important not to deny or underestimate the needs and experiences of infertile women.[21] It is, surely, inappropriate for feminists to claim to understand better than infertile women themselves the origins and significance of their desire for children. Even if the longing felt by infertile women is socially produced, it is nevertheless real longing. Furthermore, that longing cannot be assumed to extinguish women's autonomy. Women who are "trying everything" in order to obtain a baby are not necessarily less autonomous, less free from social conditioning, than women who gestate and deliver without technological intervention, nor less free than the feminists who call into question infertile women's motivations.

Sociologist Judith Lorber claims that consent to IVF is not a freely chosen act unless the woman is "an equal or dominant in the situation."[22] But if that is the criterion for freedom of choice, then almost no women make free choices, ever. I find philosopher Mary Anne Warren more plausible when she claims, "Freedom is not an all or nothing affair. We can rarely be completely free of unjust or inappropriate social and economic pressures, but we can sometimes make sound and appropriate decisions, in the light of our own circumstances."[23]

Radical feminist Janice G. Raymond has poured scorn on the kind of approach I advocate here, which she dismissively labels the "nuanced" approach to evaluating reproductive technologies.[24] This approach, she says, seeks to "limit the abuse [of women by reproductive technologies] by gaining control of some of these technologies, and by ensuring equal access for all women who need/desire them." The error here, she suggests, is in conflating need with desire, and then claiming that to oppose such needs/desires is to "limit women's reproductive liberty, options, and choices." In fact, however, "women as a class have a stake in reclaiming the female body—not as female nature—and not just by taking the body seriously—but by refusing to yield control of it to men, to the fetus, to the State. ..."[25]

My view, however, is that as feminists we can be extremely critical of the easy equation of need and desire, and of the social processes that create women's alleged "need" for babies and that require that that "need" be fulfilled through a biologically-related infant acquired in any way possible. We can also reject the facile claim that access to any and all reproductive services, products and labour, is indispensable to reproductive freedom. But it does not follow that feminists should protect women from these social processes and from acting on their own desires. We need not take women's desires as an unanalyzable and unrejectable given. But neither can we ignore or belittle what women say they feel. We can attack the manipulation of women's desires by current medical/scientific reproductive practices. But we can also resist the too-simple depiction of infertile women as nothing but dupes or victims.

...

The demand for an end to all use of IVF is an expression of a kind of feminist maternalism,[26] which seeks to protect the best interests of the women affected by IVF. I cannot agree with those who wish to ban IVF to protect women from the dangers of coercive IVF, any more than I can agree with so-called "pro-life feminists" who wish to ban abortion to protect women from the dangers of coercive abortions. It is not the role of feminist research and action to protect women from what is interpreted to be their own false consciousness. If, as Judith Lorber claims, women seeking IVF make "a patriarchal bargain" rather than a free choice,[27] then those women must be given the information and support they need in order to genuinely choose.

At this time, while women candidates are told something about the mechanical procedures for IVF, so far there is not much evidence that they are fully informed about the low success rates and the suffering and risks associated with IVF. The solution to the making of ideologically coerced choices is not always and necessarily the banning of the choices themselves, but education about that which is chosen.

Therefore, while I cannot support and endorse highly ineffective, costly and painful procedures such as IVF, until infertile women themselves, by the thousands, and especially those who seek and have sought IVF, call for the banning of artificial reproduction, I am uneasy about endorsing such a call by some feminists, any more than I would endorse a call for a ban on all interventionist hospital births in low-risk deliveries. I assume that when women are provided with complete information, real choices and full support with regard to artificial reproduction, they will be empowered to make reproductive decisions that will genuinely benefit themselves and their children. Based on my subjective impressions, from talking to women who have already rejected IVF, and to women who now have serious criticisms of IVF after trying it, it may well turn out that, when fully informed, women will reject in vitro fertilization at a much higher rate than they do now.

## A Feminist Alternative

Or they may not. It is therefore necessary to consider what a caring, feminist approach to the provision of in vitro fertilization would look like—an approach which is founded upon women's experiences, values and beliefs, which acknowledges the political elements of reproductive choices and practices, which seeks to minimize harm to women and children, and which recognizes and fosters women's dignity and self-determination. The caring provision of artificial reproduction services requires (a) truly informed choice and consent; (b) equal and fair access, unbiased by geographic, economic, or social criteria; (c) adequate record-keeping, follow-up and reserach; and (d) appropriate support systems for all participants. All of these services could be provided in free-standing women's reproductive health clinics, run on feminist principles, where the health care providers are primarily both responsible and responsive to their women clients.[28]

First, then, it is necessary to ensure that women—as individuals, not as part of a couple—entering and participating in infertility treatment programs make a genuinely informed choice and consent. Counselling should not be provided by the clinic itself, but by third parties who have no personal investment in persuading clients to use the clinic's services.

The notion of informed choice involves not merely telling women of the possible risks of the procedure, but discussion of the alternatives to in vitro fertilization.[29] It would also require open acknowledgement of the experimental status of the procedure. … Prospective patients must therefore be informed of IVF's unknowns, the short- and long-term risks, the possible benefits, the chances of success and failure, alternative approaches and treatments and pronatalist social pressures to procreate and other ways of responding to them. In particular, women who are offered in vitro fertilization for infertility in their male partners should clearly understand that they could become pregnant much more easily, safely and with lower risks if they made use of donor insemination.[30]

Second, it is essential to critically examine the artificial criteria, such as marital status, sexual orientation and ability to pay, that get in the way of women's fair access to reproductive technologies, with a view to dismantling those barriers that discriminate unjustifiably. …

Third, an adequate system of record-keeping should be established, to track the long-term effects of IVF on women and their offspring, and to ensure that any women who provide eggs for the program have genuinely chosen to do so, so that "egg-snatching" is eliminated. Moreover, donors should really be donors, not vendors; the commodification of reproductive products and services is morally unjustified. It is essential to resist the commercialization of reproduction and the spread of reproductive entrepreneurialism, the primary targets of which are likely to be poor women and women of colour. It would also be important to ensure thorough screening and long-term follow-up of donors of eggs and sperm, and to avoid too-frequent use of the same donors. The issue of control over and decision-making about so-called "spare" embryos, including those that are subject to cryopreservation, must also be faced. In addition, offspring of artificial reproduction need certain protections, in particular, access to information about their origins and the health status of their biological parents (if they were conceived using donor gametes), and knowledge of the life-long questions about and implications of IVF for their own health prospects.

Finally, participants and potential participants in IVF programs should be provided with support systems to enable them to evaluate fully their own reasons and goals for being in the program, and to provide assistance throughout the emotionally and physically demanding aspects of the treatment. It would be important that all counselling and group support not just function as a means of ensuring the patients' continued acquiescence, or eliminating those without the stamina to endure the ordeal,[31] but that it facilitate their active involvement and participation in their treatment.

I have tried to indicate what I think is a fair and caring approach to the justification of and access to in vitro fertilization. The approach that I have just sketched avoids, on the one hand, claiming access to artificial reproduction as a right in the strong sense, and on the other hand, making access to reproductive technology a privilege to be earned through the possession of certain personal, social, sexual and/or financial characteristics. Sweeping generalizations about the moral justification of all forms of artificial reproduction are on very uncertain ground: processes of artificial reproduction need to be evaluated individually, on their own merits, to determine which ones, if any, are genuinely valuable and worth supporting. ... Over the long term, certainly, the caring provision of artificial reproduction should also be coupled with research into the incidence and causes of and cures for infertility, and the elimination of iatrogenic and environmental sources of infertility, so that the apparent need for artificial reproduction is reduced. Ultimately, the genuinely caring provision of artificial reproduction will require a feminist reevaluation and reconstruction of all reproductive values, technologies and practices.

---

### Notes

1. Christine Overall, *Ethics and Human Reproduction: A Feminist Analysis* (Boston: Allen & Unwin, 1987), pp. 166–96.

2. Ethics Committee of the American Fertility Society, "The Constitutional Aspects of Procreative Liberty," in *Ethical Issues in the New Reproductive Technologies*, edited by Richard T. Hull (Belmont, CA: Wadsworth, 1990), p. 9.

3. From this point of view, then, IVF with donor gametes could be more problematic than IVF in which a woman and a man make use of their own eggs and sperm.

4. Genoveffa Corea, "Egg Snatchers," in *Test-Tube Women: What Future for Motherhood*, edited by Rita Arditti, Renate Duelli Klein and Shelley Minden (London: Pandora Press, 1984), pp. 37–51.

5. Gena Corea and Susan Ince report that in the United States in 1985, 42 out of the 54 clinics accepted only married couples. See their "Report of a Survey of IVF Clinics in the U.S.," in *Made to Order: The Myth of Reproductive and Genetic Progress*, edited by Patricia Spallone and Deborah Lynn Steinberg (Oxford: Pergamon Press, 1987), p. 140.

6. Judith Lorber, "In Vitro Fertilization and Gender Politics," in *Embryos, Ethics and Women's Rights: Exploring the New Reproductive Technologies*, edited by Elaine Hoffman Baruch, Amadeo F. D'Adamo, Jr. and Joni Seager (New York: Haworth Press, 1988), pp. 118–19.

7. There are comparable barriers to access to donor insemination. See, e.g., Deborah Lynn Steinberg, "Selective Breeding and Social Engineering: Discriminatory Policies of Access to Artificial Insemination by Donor in Great Britain," in Spallone et al., *Made to Order*, pp. 184–89.

8. See Rebecca Shuster, "Sexuality as a Continuum: The Bisexual Identity," in *Lesbian Psychologies: Explorations and Challenges*, edited by the Boston Lesbian Psychologies Collective (Urbana, IL: University of Illinois Press, 1987), pp. 56–71.

9. Ann Pappert, "In Vitro in Trouble, Critics Warn," *Globe and Mail*, February 6, 1988, p. A1. For a comparable discussion of IVF success rates in France, see Françoise Laborie, "Looking for Mothers You Only Find Fetuses," in Spallone et al., *Made to Order*, pp. 49–50.

10. Pappert, "In Vitro in Trouble," p. A14.

11. Linda S. Williams, "No Relief Until the End: The Physical and Emotional Costs of In Vitro Fertilization," in *The Future of Human Reproduction*, edited by Christine Overall (Toronto: Women's Press, 1989), pp. 120–38.

12. "What You Should Know About In Vitro Fertilization," in *Our Bodies ... Our Babies? Women Look at the New Reproductive Technologies* (Ottawa: Canadian Research Institute for the Advancement of Women, 1989); "Current Developments and Issues: A Summary," *Reproductive and Genetic Engineering*, 2, 3 (1989): 253.

13. Anita Direcks, "Has the Lesson Been Learned?: The DES Story and IVF," in Spallone et al., *Made to Order*, p. 163. For a discussion of the harmful effects of one hormone used in IVF, clomiphene citrate, see Renate Klein and Robyn Rowland, "Women as Test-Sites for Fertility Drugs: Clomiphene Citrate and Hormonal Cocktails," *Reproductive and Genetic Engineering: Journal of International Feminist Analysis*, 1, 3 (1988): 251–73.

14. Klein and Rowland, "Women as Test-Sites," p. 270.

15. "Resolution from the FINRRAGE Conference, July 3–8, 1985, Vallinge, Sweden," in Spallone et al., *Made to Order*, p. 211.

16. Sultana Kamal, "Seizure of Reproductive Rights? A Discussion on Population Control in the Third World and the Emergence of the New Reproductive Technologies in the West," in Spallone et al., *Made to Order*, p. 153.

17. See, e.g., Susan Sherwin, "Feminist Ethics and In Vitro Fertilization," in *Science Morality and Feminist Theory*, edited by Marsha Hanen and Kai Nielsen (Calgary: University of Calgary Press, 1987), pp. 265–84.

18. Margarete Sandelowski, "Failures of Volition: An Historical Perspective on Female Agency and the Cause of Infertility," *Signs: Journal of Women in Culture and Society*, 15, 3 (Spring 1990): 498.

19. Ibid.

20. Christine Crowe, " 'Women Want It': In Vitro Fertilization and Women's Motivations for Participation," in Spallone et al., *Made to Order*, pp. 84–93.

21. See Alison Solomon, "Integrating Infertility Crisis Counseling into Feminist Practice," *Reproductive and Genetic Engineering*, 1, 1 (1988): 41–49; and Naomi Pfeffer, "Artificial Insemination, In-Vitro Fertilization and the Stigma of Infertility," in *Reproductive Technologies: Gen-*

der, *Motherhood and Medicine,* edited by Michelle Stanworth (Minneapolis: University of Minnesota Press, 1987), pp. 81–97.

22. Judith Lorber, "Choice, Gift, or Patriarchal Bargain?" *Hypatia,* 4 (Fall 1989): 30.

23. Mary Anne Warren, "IVF and Women's Interests: An Analysis of Feminist Concerns," *Bioethics,* 2, 1 (1988): 40–41.

24. Janice G. Raymond, "Reproductive Technologies, Radical Feminist, and Social Liberalism," *Reproductive and Genetic Engineering: Journal of International Feminist Analysis,* 2, 2 (1989): 133–42.

25. Ibid., p. 135.

26. Deborah Poff, "Reproductive Technology and Social Policy in Canada," in Overall, *The Future of Human Reproduction,* p. 223.

27. Lorber, "Choice, Gift, or Patriarchal Bargain?," p. 24.

28. Vicki Van Wagner and Bob Lee, "Principles into Practice: An Activist Vision of Feminist Reproductive Health Care," in Overall, *The Future of Human Reproduction,* pp. 238–58.

29. Nikki Colodny, "The Politics of Birth Control in a Reproductive Rights Context," in Overall, *The Future of Human Reproduction,* p. 43.

30. Lorber, "Choice, Gift, or Patriarchal Bargain?" pp. 23–26.

31. Annette Burfoot, "Exploitation Redefined: An Interview with an IVF Practitioner," *Resources for Feminist Research/Documentation sur la recherche feministe,* 18, 2 (June 1989): 27.

# PART FIVE

# FAMILY VALUES

In the early 1990s, the expression "family values," as well as associated terms such as "intact family" and "traditional family," came to have a somewhat sinister ring for feminists in the United States. Conservative politicians used these expressions as codes for attacking the "values" of any woman who did not live in a male-"headed" household; they were especially critical of single mothers, who disproportionately included poor women, women of color, and lesbian women. Indeed, conservatives attributed a host of social ills to the lack of family values supposedly manifest in the lives of these women, ills ranging from poverty, to crime, to drugs, to poor school performance.

Feminists have responded to these right-wing attacks in a variety of ways. Some have proclaimed indignantly that households lacking an adult male may instantiate family values just as fully as households constituted by married couples; these feminists sometimes add that the nuclear family currently regarded as traditional or normative is a fairly recent historical invention and even now represents only a statistical minority of families in the United States. Other feminists have gone on the offensive, charging their critics themselves with abandoning family values, a sentiment succinctly summed up in the bumper sticker "Hate is not a family value." Still other feminists defiantly reject the male dominance that they regard as the overriding value distinguishing "traditional" male-headed families, a value expressed in such well-established family practices as incest, marital rape, wife battery, and "mistresses."

Whether feminists endorse family values obviously depends in part on the particular feminist in question and in part on what each takes family values to be. Regardless of the varying answers to these questions, the values that all feminists endorse are by definition feminist values. Even though the most salient of these is, of course, the value of ending women's subordination, many feminists argue that this ideal must be interpreted to include antiracist, antiheterosexist, egalitarian, and democratic values. Some feminists believe that these values can be instantiated in families constituted by married couples; others believe that in a male-dominant society heterosexual relationships can hardly sustain feminist values. What virtually no Western feminists accept, however, is that feminist values can be instantiated *only* within households constituted by heterosexual couples.

The readings in this part explore two different aspects of family values as these relate to childbearing and childrearing. The first set of readings focuses on the issue of contract child production, an issue most commonly discussed today in terms of so-called surrogate mothering. The authors debate the values instantiated in the practices of buying, selling, borrowing, and renting the means of human procreation. They consider questions such as the following: what value should be placed on the relationship between a birth mother and her child? A birth father and his child? Adoptive mothers or fathers and their children? These authors examine how genetics, history, and law enter into contemporary conceptions of the family and explore the ways in which these conceptions reflect concerns about personal identity, class, race, and gender. The second set of readings focuses on childrearing rather than child producing. The authors ask, why are women the primary caretakers of children? How far is femininity defined in terms of mothering? What is the relationship between mothering and women's subordination? What are the advantages and disadvantages of various childrearing arrangements with or without men?

## Contract Child Production

Contract mothering is the practice in which a woman is paid to gestate and bear a child with the deliberate intention that the other party to the contract, usually a married man, should be the social and legal parent of that child. The contract sets out the legal obligations on each side. Typically, the woman agrees to be inseminated with sperm chosen by the other party, usually his sperm; to refrain from sex with another partner until pregnancy is established; to accept certain restrictions on her conduct during pregnancy; and to relinquish the baby at birth. The other party agrees to cover the woman's medical expenses, to pay an additional sum to compensate for her inconvenience and health risks, and to accept custody of the child at birth.

Before we explore the moral issues raised by contract mothering, we should note two often overlooked points. First, any woman who conceives and bears a child is that child's birth mother; in ordinary speech she might be called the child's "natural" or even "real" mother. In the context of contract mothering, labeling her a "surrogate" mother is a rhetorical move that delegitimates her claims to a continuing relationship with the child. In fact, it is probably more in line with ordinary ways of thinking to regard the wife of the male contractor, the prospective adoptive mother or stepmother, as a surrogate mother. If the birth mother is a surrogate anything, she is a surrogate wife to the male contractor insofar as she is the bearer of his "legitimate" child. Second, the usual case of contract mothering requires little or nothing by way of reproductive technology. Although the pregnancy obviously may be initiated by ordinary heterosexual intercourse, even artificial insemination takes no special expertise and no equipment other than a syringe—or a turkey baster. It is true that a woman may also be paid to gestate the fertilized ovum of another woman, a practice called "full surrogacy," but given the current unreliability of in vitro fertilization, these cases are much less frequent. Thus, the moral issues raised by most cases of contract mothering are independent of those raised by sophisticated procreative technology.

Contract mothering is the contemporary version of practices that have existed in the West for centuries, even millennia. The book of Genesis (30:3) relates how Rachel, the infertile wife of Jacob, instructed her husband, "Behold my maid Bilah. Go in unto her; and she shall bear upon my knees, that I may also have children by her." Other cases are recorded of women friends and sisters bearing children for each other and even mothers for daughters. Frequently children have also been exchanged for a variety of economic and political, as opposed to emotional, reasons.

Given the long history of distinguishing between birth and social parents, it is worth asking why contract mothering has only recently become the focus of intense public controversy. It is also worth asking why the analogous practice of contract fathering—namely, the sale of sperm for artificial insemination—has so far received little moral scrutiny, even though it has been available since the 1930s. On the relatively few occasions when artificial insemination has been questioned, moreover, it has usually been in the context of challenging any technologically assisted means of limiting or facilitating procreation. Moral issues analogous to those typically raised about contract mothering, issues about buying and selling the means of human procreation and about relationships and responsibilities between birth parents and their children, have been largely ignored. This section, however, raises these questions about contract fathering as well as contract mothering.

The opening reading in this section offers a firsthand account of one woman's experience in applying to become a "surrogate" mother. In "Inside the Surrogate Industry," Susan Ince describes the perfunctory screening procedures, the high degree of control demanded over her life, and the insistence on her unquestioning obedience to the brokering agency's rules. Ince notes that so-called surrogate mothering may be conceptualized as the sale of services, the sale of an organ, or even the sale of a baby. She concludes that it most closely resembles prostitution but is in fact a new means by which men systematically exploit women, synthesizing the "brothel" and the "farming" models of exploitation. Ince urges feminists to oppose contract mothering because it both presupposes and reinforces women's subordination.

Christine T. Sistare's defense of contract mothering, "Reproductive Freedom and Women's Freedom: Surrogacy and Autonomy," places great moral weight on the individual freedom and autonomy of contract mothers, explicitly sidestepping deeper concerns about the nature of freedom and the structure of gender relations in capitalist societies. Sistare asserts that, although the historical subordination of women has been accomplished in large part through the mystification and control of our procreative capacities, changing social and technological conditions—many of them welcomed by feminists—have finally enabled women to benefit from these capacities. She argues that women's freedom to contract their gestational services is not outweighed either by possible harm to the offspring of contractual unions when they learn of their unconventional origins or by worries about women being enslaved through unfair contracts. She comments dryly that "a good surrogate contract could protect a woman from that fate more surely than most traditional maternal roles afforded to women past or present."

Sistare dismisses moral concerns about the exploitation of contract mothers by arguing that childbearing is no worse and often better than many of the other money-making alternatives currently open to women. The most extreme kinds of class and race exploitation are avoided because contractors buying procreative services prefer "surrogates" as similar as possible to themselves. Exploitation can further be avoided by intelligent regulation, including minimum wages. Legally recognizing so-called surrogacy arrangements will protect women better than driving such arrangements underground. Sistare concludes that the practice of contract mothering promotes feminist values: it reveals the true value of children, it enhances the parental role of fathers, it validates the separation of childbearing from childrearing, and it allows women to control and even capitalize on their procreative capacities.

Mary Gibson's article, "Contract Motherhood: Social Practice in Social Context," directly addresses a number of Sistare's arguments. Gibson argues that contract mothering exploits women economically by taking advantage of their economic vulnerability and also exploits them socially and psychologically by taking advantage of their limited social options and their internalized ideology of pronatalism and feminine altruism. Unusually, she suggests that the intended receiving parents are also exploited, though by the broker rather than the contract mother, and that the contracted-for infant is exploited by all the adults involved insofar as it is treated by all of them as a means to their own ends.

One type of exploitation is commodification, treating persons as things to be owned, exchanged, consumed, and used. Gibson argues that contract motherhood commodifies women, children, and the parent-child relationship. She believes that this would be morally wrong even if it did not directly harm those involved, but in fact, she argues, the child and the contract mother, those most vulnerable in the contract-mothering relation, suffer the psychological harm of alienation. Children's sense of security and identity is likely to be undermined by the knowledge that their birth mothers planned all along to relinquish them, and contract mothers' sense of self must inevitably be fragmented by the experience of having their intimate bodily processes monitored and controlled.

Sistare argues, like most feminist proponents of contract mothering, that prohibiting the practice would violate women's autonomy. Gibson responds that the conception of autonomy utilized by these feminists is inadequate and contends that a contract mother's refusal to relinquish her baby may itself be an exercise of moral autonomy. She concludes that commercial contract motherhood is morally unacceptable in principle and should be expressly prohibited, though unpaid private agreements may still continue.

The contrasts among the analyses offered by Ince, Sistare, and Gibson clearly illustrate the differences among three distinct conceptions of feminism. Ince's analysis, with its emphasis on men's exploitation of women's bodies, exemplifies a radical feminist approach, whereas Sistare's defense of individual women's freedom to enter contracts is classically liberal. Gibson is a socialist feminist who, unlike Sistare, considers contract motherhood, not primarily as a transaction between individuals, but as a social practice occurring in a social context where the dominant conception of family is shaped by values that are classist, racist, sexist, heterosexist, and pronatalist and in which children are regarded as the property of their parents. It is this conception of family, in Gibson's view, that creates the demand for contract mothering and this social context that is responsible for some of contract mothering's most morally troubling features. Gibson's ultimate objection to contract mothering is that it not only presupposes but also reinforces these morally unacceptable social structures and family values.

When feminist discussions of contract mothering refer to artificial insemination by a (usually unknown) donor (AID), they typically do so to legitimate contract mothering by likening it to a well-established practice widely regarded as morally unproblematic. Rather than simply assuming the moral neutrality of AID, Francie Hornstein goes further in offering an explicitly feminist justification for artificial insemination. In "Children by Donor Insemination: A New Choice for Lesbians," Hornstein argues that this practice makes it possible for women to take complete control over their procreative lives and provides a direct challenge to male-dominant and heterosexist family values.

Hornstein's own pregnancy resulted from a private, unpaid arrangement with a sperm donor and so avoids some of the ethical problems inherent in buying and selling the means of procreation. She does not inform the reader about the nature of the relationship, if any, between her own child and his or her father, but she does mention potential problems if donors wish to maintain relationships with the children they have fathered. In fact, many women who use artificial insemination seek to avoid these problems either by using a sperm bank or by having their donor sign a contract that not only frees him from responsibility for economic child support but also requires him to renounce any paternal rights to an ongoing relationship with the child.

It is precisely the requirement that birth mothers renounce all contact with their children that is central to Gibson's opposition to contract mothering. Gibson states explicitly that she has no principled objection to informal arrangements that would allow continuing relationships between birth mothers and their children, although she allows that practical difficulties could arise—as indeed they can in all family relationships. It is the same separation of biological from social parenting, rather than any "artificiality" in the process of conception, that Thomas W. Laqueur finds morally problematic in contract fathering.

In "The Facts of Fatherhood," Laqueur denies that there is any natural or biological basis for regarding mothers' connection with their offspring as deeper or stronger than fathers'. He asserts that fatherhood, like motherhood, is an "idea" or social construction owing less to biological facts than to the social meanings assigned to those facts through law, custom, sentiment, emotion, and the power of the imagination. Laqueur describes the intensity of his own emotional bond not only with his daughter but also with the imaginary child for whom he was asked to give sperm. He goes on to describe how biology is so far from playing a determining role in fatherhood that a woman who took paternal responsibility for her lover's child was legally recognized as its father.

Feminists have often criticized essentialist or biological determinist notions of motherhood; Laqueur reminds us that essentialist or biological determinist understandings of fatherhood are equally unwarranted. The practice of artificial insemination by a donor who will not be the social father of his child assumes that men are naturally alienated from their sperm; it is arguable that simply through its social acceptability the practice reinforces this alienation. In so doing, it encourages precisely that paternal irresponsibility that in other contexts has been a frequent target of feminist criticism.

Some feminists have drawn on the similarities between AID and contract mothering to legitimate contract motherhood—but, as Mary Gibson notes, the analogy may also work in the other direction by delegitimating AID. If contract mothering is unjustified in feminist terms, then the moral acceptability of buying and selling sperm must also come into question, as must contracts that require birth fathers to give up any claims to a relationship with their children. Feminists must ask what kinds of values inspire the search for individuals, female or male, who will participate in producing children with whom they will have no relationship and for whom they will take no responsibility. We must explore how these values may be implicated in legitimating racism, classism, and male dominance, not to mention children as property. Finally, we must question whether these are the values we wish to embody in our own—or anyone's—families.

## Valuing Alternative Families

In the expressions "contract mothering" and "surrogate mothering," "mothering" means giving birth to a child. In more common usage, however, mothering refers to childrearing rather than childbearing, to the daily work of attending to a child's physical and emotional needs. Institutions such as adoption and contract mothering clearly demonstrate that the labor of childbearing may be separated from that of childrearing. Nevertheless, the so-called traditional family values of Western Europe and North America prescribe that birth mothers normally be responsible for the daily welfare of their children, while fathers are responsible for paying the bills.

The second-wave Western feminists of the late 1960s and early 1970s were generally critical of these aspects of traditional family values. In her 1963 groundbreaking work, *The Feminine Mystique,* Betty Friedan complained bitterly about the boredom and frustration endured by suburban housewives with no one to talk to over three feet tall. Other feminists noted how the expectation that they should be primarily responsible for child care operated as a disadvantage for women in the labor market, creating an economic dependence on their husbands that made real the ideological value that the household should be headed by a man. Some feminists noted that, although men certainly benefited economically from the norm of women's mothering, they paid a considerable emotional cost for these benefits insofar as they tended to be alienated from their children, regarded primarily as a source of discipline by rebellious children and desperate mothers.

In addition to these unfortunate consequences for the individuals involved, some feminists also criticized traditional family values because of their broader social implications. Radical feminists charged that the nuclear family promoted a norm of heterosexuality, regarded as indispensable for maintaining male dominance, whereas Marxist and socialist feminists argued that the nuclear family fulfilled a variety of vital economic functions for capitalist society. These were said to include permitting the labor force to be much more mobile than would be possible under, for instance, an extended family system; maintaining aggregate demand at a higher level than would be reached if people lived in larger and more economical household units; accomplishing a great deal of socially necessary work, such as nursing and child care, without cost to the state; concealing real levels of unemployment, especially among women; providing a conduit for the transmission of capital to the next generation; and generally promoting capitalist values of competitive individualism and consumption.

By the late 1970s, some feminist theorists had identified women's mothering as a central mechanism maintaining female subordination. In *The Mermaid and the Minotaur* (1977), for instance, Dorothy Dinnerstein argued that women's exclusive responsibility for childrearing is the root of cultural misogyny because women become the ones who must introduce children to their "original and basic human grief"—that is, to "the loss of [the] infant illusion of omnipotence—the discovery that circumstance is incompletely controllable, and that there exist centers of subjectivity, of desire and will, opposed to or indifferent to one's own" (p. 60). Dinnerstein believed that the mother-rearing of children also explains the identification of women with nonhuman nature: because "the early mother's boundaries are so indistinct," we fail "to distinguish clearly between her and nature, we assign to each properties that belong to each other" (p. 108). In her 1978 book, *Mothering: Psychoanalysis and the Sociology of Gender,* Nancy Chodorow drew on neo-Freudian object relations theory to argue that women's responsibility for early child care results in the imposition of different character structures on girls and boys. Boys grow up preoccupied with separating themselves from others and from what is culturally associated with femininity; they are achievement oriented and emotionally closed to others. Girls, by contrast, grow up to be emotionally vulnerable, open to and even dependent on the approval of others. In the end, boys and girls become men and women who repeat the traditional sexual division of labor in childrearing and so perpetuate women's economic and psychological subordination.

Although many feminist theorists have seen mothering as integral to women's subordination, not all feminists have rejected it. On the contrary, a number of feminists have regarded mothering as a source of distinctively feminine values, which may not be feminist in themselves but which provide a source of moral insight on which feminists should draw. One of the best known of such theorists is Sara Ruddick, who argues that mothering can offer the basis for a feminist peace politics because it provides both motivation and methods for resolving conflicts nonviolently. Ruddick wishes to involve men in mothering in the hope that this will reduce their militarist proclivities, but other feminists who value mothering believe that men cannot be trusted with children and seek instead to seize mothering from male control.

Feminists thus have a variety of reasons for believing that women's subordination—not to mention capitalism, militarism, and the destruction of the environment—are perpetuated, if not generated, by family values that assign the primary responsibility for childrearing to mothers. Persuaded by one or more of these arguments, many Western feminists have sought alternatives to mothering in heterosexual nuclear families. The readings in this section describe some of the alternatives they have chosen and evaluate their successes and failures.

The section begins and ends with selections from Karen Lindsey, a longtime feminist activist who has rejected *motherhood,* though not necessarily *mothering.* In the opening article, "The Politics of Childlessness," first published in 1974 in the Boston women's liberation journal *The Second Wave,* Lindsey describes the pronatalist pressures she encountered when she decided to be sterilized, explaining how the desire for one's "own" children is socially created, especially in women, by the economic insecurities of capitalism and the lack of fulfilling alternatives for many women. Lindsey asserts that choosing to remain childless is both "a declaration against the patriarchal structure of the nuclear family" and "a rejection of reproductive sexuality as the only legitimate sexual base."

Diane Ehrensaft's 1980 article, "When Women and Men Mother," reports the experience of a small group of heterosexual couples who attempted shared parenting during the late 1960s and 1970s. Ehrensaft discovered that shared parenting was "easier said than done." Interestingly, she notes that many mothers are reluctant to give up power and control over their children, especially when their opportunities for fulfillment outside the home are still inferior to men's; she also reports that they may still suffer guilt for not being "real" mothers. Fathers assuming major responsibilities for child care receive mixed reactions: positive from the feminist counterculture, overwhelmingly negative from society at large. Overall, Ehrensaft asserts, women lose more than men from shared parenting—a surprising conclusion in light of many liberal feminist analyses that locate fulfillment in the world outside the home. (For example, Karen DeCrow's *The Young Woman's Guide to Liberation* has one chapter entitled "The Outer World Is Where the Fun Is.") Those who benefit most from shared parenting may be children, whose families are no longer tyrannies, to use the words of philosopher John Stuart Mill, and are more like crucibles of democracy.

The next article offers a strong challenge to Ehrensaft's insistence on the feminist necessity of involving men in child care. In "The Radical Potential in Lesbian Mothering of Daughters," Baba Copper believes that "for every well-fathered child, there are a million who were conceived irresponsibly or abandoned or raped or physically terrorized or emotionally denied by their fathers." She is also fiercely critical of "heteromothering," which she sometimes calls simply "mothering," claiming that heterosexual mothers, even "heterofeminists," teach female children to love everyone except themselves. Lesbian mothers, by contrast, "identify the mother/daughter dyad as *the* evolutionary crucible of society" and raise their daughters to be "freedom fighters."

Lindsy Van Gelder offers a less apocalyptic vision of lesbian mothering in "A Lesbian Family," describing a specific situation in which a child is parented successfully by her lesbian birth mother, her birth mother's lover, and her gay birth father. Van Gelder stresses the similarities, rather than the differences, between gay parenting and heteroparenting, and she does not claim that lesbian mothers enjoy a different kind of relationship with their daughters than heterosexual mothers enjoy with theirs. She does identify some difficulties specific to gay parenting, difficulties that result directly from heterosexist social and legal structures. Like the previous authors, Van Gelder sees alternative families not simply as individual solutions but also as contributions to social change. The arrangements she describes, however, are presented as one possible model among many rather than as a blueprint for domestic revolution.

Patricia Hill Collins's essay, "Black Women and Motherhood," traces the complex and sometimes contradictory meanings of motherhood for African American women. For African Americans, mothering in a fiercely racist society has been a source simultaneously of deep fulfillment and grinding oppression. African American men often have paid lip-service to the strength of Black mothers while failing to give adequate acknowledgment to the personal costs of mothering. Collins describes the dilemma faced by Black mothers who must teach their daughters to conform to systems of oppression so they may survive physically but who also seek to endow them with the spiritual strength necessary to resist oppression. These conflicting demands, coupled with the severe economic pressures on most Black mothers, often create strains in Black mother/daughter relationships. Nevertheless, Collins asserts, "most Black daughters love and admire their mothers and are convinced that their mothers truly love them."

One way in which African American women have coped with the difficulties of rearing children in conditions of extreme poverty has been by forming extended families that include "othermothers" as well as "bloodmothers," or birth mothers. Women are central in these extended families, and othermothers may include grandmothers, sisters, aunts, and cousins. Such women-centered networks may extend beyond the boundaries of biologically related individuals to include "fictive kin" and beyond them to neighbors and friends. These systems of community-based child care have enabled the survival of large numbers of children whose bloodmothers have been unable to care for them alone, and the existence of such systems is implicitly revolutionary insofar as it challenges the notion that children are private property. (This notion is crucial in creating the demand for contract parenting.)

For most African American women, the outer world is not at all "where the fun is," and many of them might well be thankful for the opportunity to stay home with their children. Instead, concern for the welfare of "their"—that is, all Black—children impels many Black women into political activism as an extension of their mothering. Respect for their work turns motherhood into a symbol of power in African American communities, and despite its high costs, mothering often becomes an experience that empowers African American women both personally and politically.

Ann Ferguson's article, "The Che-Lumumba School: Creating a Revolutionary Family Community," develops one socialist feminist ideal of a community facilitating egalitarian relationships for love and parenting. Such a community must, in Ferguson's view: eliminate childrearing inequalities between men and women, challenge the sexual division of labor, break down the possessive privacy of the couple and the parent-child relationship, equalize power as far as possible between adults and children, abandon normative heterosexuality, break down elitist attitudes about the superiority of mental and professional to manual work, deal with racism and classism, and introduce economic sharing and commitment. Ferguson describes the difficulties encountered by one school community attempting to practice these ideals, difficulties resulting from both external economic pressures and internalized reluctance on the part of some parents to deal with certain sensitive issues.

The title of the last article in this section, "Friends as Family: No One Said It Would Be Easy," might well be the epigraph for all contemporary feminism. Here Karen Lindsey describes the difficulties of establishing alternative families of friends in a social context where couples, especially heterosexual couples, are the norm. The absence of social formulae for permanent commitments to friends coupled with the lack of social and legal recognition for families outside the nuclear norm can create painful conflicts and disappointments as well as rich opportunities for intimacy and fulfillment.

In the context of a society that is deeply racist, sexist, heterosexist, and authoritarian, feminists have found it extremely difficult to establish families whose values are antiracist, antielitist, antiheterosexist, egalitarian, and democratic. We have discovered that conflicts and compromises are inescapable: with family members, with nonfamily members, and even within ourselves. Choosing between incompatible principles, weighing competing interests, and balancing the intensity of our socially constructed but nonetheless urgent emotional needs against the knowledge that fulfilling those needs may reinforce a social status quo we are deeply committed to changing provide feminists with a vivid sense that in the arena of family values, we are indeed living with contradictions.

### References

Nancy Chodorow. *Mothering: Psychoanalysis and the Sociology of Gender.* Berkeley and Los Angeles: University of California Press, 1978.

Karen DeCrow. *The Young Woman's Guide to Liberation.* Indianapolis: Bobbs-Merrill, 1971.

Dorothy Dinnerstein. *The Mermaid and the Minotaur: Sexual Arrangements and Human Malaise.* New York: Harper Colophon, 1977.

Betty Friedan. *The Feminine Mystique.* New York: Dell, 1974.

John Stuart Mill. *The Subjection of Women.* Arlington Heights, Ill.: Harlan Davidson, 1980.

Sara Ruddick. *Maternal Thinking: Toward a Politics of Peace.* Boston: Beacon Press, 1989.

# Inside the Surrogate Industry

## Susan Ince

...

This is not a nine-to-five job. It demands enormous commitment and understanding. It requires your total thought and consciousness, full-time, twenty-four hours a day.[1]

The job was for the key position in one of the 'growth industries' of the 1980s, and involved rigid application processes, including thorough medical examination, intelligence testing, psychological evaluation, and even genetic screening if indicated. I had just applied to become a surrogate mother.

From first reading the glowing newspaper reports and seeing the self-satisfied lawyers on television, I had been uneasy about the idea of a surrogate industry. I had played out lively and humorous 'what if' scenarios with friends, but had no substantive answers to the questions of proponents: what's wrong with it, if that's what the women want to do? Are you against them making money? Are you saying the industry should be regulated by the state? The questions were naggingly familiar, the same ones asked by apologists of the sex-buying industries, prostitution and pornography.

In order to get a first-hand look, I answered an advertisement placed in a local newspaper by a surrogate company considered reputable and established. Two weeks later, I met with the program's director and psychologist in their basement office on a street filled with small businesses and discount shops. The office looked newly occupied, and the director struggled with the unfamiliar typewriter and telephone system. Decorations included pictures of Victorian children; plump, white, and rosy-cheeked. Missing from sight were file cabinets, desks with drawers, and other standard office paraphernalia.

The director did most of the talking. I was touched by her stories of infertile couples—the woman who displayed the scars of multiple unsuccessful surgeries creating a tire-track pattern across her abdomen; the couple, now infertile, whose only biological child was killed by a drunk driver; the couples who tried in good faith to adopt an infant, and were kept on waiting lists until they passed the upper age limit and were disqualified. Stories like these, said the director, inspired her to offer a complete surrogate mother service to combine all the administrative, legal, and medical aspects of this modern reproductive alternative.

The screening and administrative procedures were outlined by the director as simple and proven successful. As a potential surrogate, I had to pass an interview with the director and psychologist, history and physical examination, and finally meet with a lawyer who would explain the contract before I signed to officially enter the program. Parents desiring surrogate services also had to pass screening by the director and psychologist, and pay $25,000 at contract-signing. Surrogate and purchasers never meet, although information about them is described so that both parties can determine if the match is acceptable. Complete anonymity is stressed as a benefit of going to this company instead of making private arrangements through a lawyer.

While pregnant, the surrogate receives approximately $200 to purchase maternity clothing, and is reimbursed 15¢/mile for transportation costs. It is her responsibility to enter the program with medical insurance that includes maternity benefits. The company will pay her medical and life insurance premiums and non-covered medical costs while she is in the program. After delivery of the baby to the father, the surrogate receives her $10,000 fee.

I tried to ask my many questions about the procedure in a curious and enthusiastic manner befitting a surrogate. The answers were not reassuring.

*What happens if you don't become pregnant?* Artificial insemination is tried twice a month for six months. If the surrogate has not conceived, she is then removed from the program and the father begins again with a different surrogate.

*And she receives no money for her participation?* 'No. Look at it this way. We pay all the fees and medical expenses. What has it cost you? Unless you start putting a value on your time.'

*What if she has a miscarriage?* Again, no money is paid to the surrogate. 'The father decides if he will take a chance again with her.' Then if the surrogate also wants to try again, there is a second attempt.

*What if the baby is born dead, or something is wrong with it and the father doesn't want it?* In this case, the surrogate has fulfilled her contract and is paid $10,000. 'We are not in the business of paying for a perfect baby. We are paying for a service rendered.' Possible fine-line distinctions between a late miscarriage (no fee to surrogate) and a stillborn premature baby (full fee paid) are made by the primary physician provided by and paid for by the company.

*What qualities are you looking for in a surrogate?* Ideally, they would like her to be married and to already have children. A healthy child provides 'a track record. It's as simple as that.' And the husband is a 'built-in support system.' They hastened to assure me, however, that there were exceptions (I am single with no children). 'Why, we just entered a single woman who had never been pregnant before. And the next couple that came in *demanded* a single donor. Things just always match up. It's a miracle!'

...

I was nervous two weeks later when I went to meet the psychologist who I thought would administer IQ tests and probe into my motivations to judge whether I was an acceptable surrogate. My plan was to offer no unsolicited information, but to tell the truth about all questions asked (except for my intention to become a surrogate). ... I was asked my name, address, phone number, eye color, hair color, whether I had any birth defects (no), whether I had children (no), whether I had relatives or friends in the area (yes, friends), whether I had a boyfriend (male friends, yes), whether I expected to someday marry, settle down, have babies and live happily ever after (no). He inquired as to my religious upbringing (Protestant) and began reminiscing about a college sweetheart ('Oh, I used to be so in love with a Protestant girl. ...') Ten minutes later, we got back on track and I was surprised to find he had no more questions. 'I just needed to be sure you're still positive 100 per cent. You are, aren't you?' Without a nod or a word from me, he continued, 'You seem like it to me.'

Because I was 'obviously bright,' there would be no IQ testing. I was never asked whether I had been pregnant before, whether I was under medical or psychiatric treatment, or how I would feel about giving up the baby. To lower costs and save time, the medical exam would take place after I had signed the contract, while a match was being made. The psychologist pronounced me 'wonderful' and 'perfect,' and I awaited my next call.

Soon the phone rang and the director solemnly said she had two serious questions to ask me. 'It's not easy but I think it's important for us to lay our cards on the table. ...' I gulped, thinking she was suspicious. 'I just want to ask you this straight up, right now, yes or no, are you going to have any trouble making appointments?' (I had rescheduled the last visit because of car trouble.) When I assured her that there would be no problem, she asked her second question. 'What are you going to do with the money?' This, I later heard her say, was asked of each surrogate to weed out those women who had frivolous motivations, such as 'buying designer jeans.' My answer was deemed acceptable, and screening was complete.

...

I decided to hear how th[e] independent company lawyer would explain the contract and our meeting was arranged. ... To my surprise the independent consultation was held within earshot of the director, who was called on by the lawyer to interpret various clauses of the contract, and who kept a record of questions I asked. ...

...

... Three areas were of greatest concern to me: the extensive behavioral controls over the surrogate, her precarious legal/financial position should something go wrong, and the ill-defined responsibilities of the company itself. Each of these was broached during this interview with what I hoped were sincere and non-threatening requests for clarification. Briefly, the rules governing surrogates' behavior are as follows (quotation marks indicate exact language of contract):

- *Sex:* The surrogate must abstain from sexual intercourse from two weeks before first insemination until a conception is confirmed.
  The surrogate must not engage in 'sexual promiscuity.'
- *Drug use:* The surrogate must not 'smoke nor drink any alcohol [*sic*] beverage from the time of initial insemination until delivery.'
  The surrogate must not use illegal drugs.

- *Medical:* The surrogate must keep all scheduled administrative, medical, psychological, counseling, or legal appointments arranged for her. These may be 'set by the physician in accordance with his schedule and, therefore, may not always be convenient for the surrogate mother.'
  The surrogate must use the services (medical, psychological, etc.) which are chosen and provided by the program.
  The surrogate must submit to all standard medical procedures and 'any additional medical precautions and/or instructions outlined by the treating physician.'
  The surrogate must furnish medical and psychological records to the company and the parents.

In general, any action that 'can be deemed to be dangerous to the well-being of the unborn child' constitutes a breach of contract which means the surrogate will forfeit her fee, and be subject to legal action from the buyers.

The company lawyer responded to my questions about these restrictions by denying their importance and reiterating the good will of all concerned. On alcohol— 'You're on the honor system. No one is going to care if you have a glass of wine now and then.' On sexual promiscuity—'Who cares? I don't know what that means. I don't know why that's in here.' When asked if there was a legal definition, he said, 'They just want to be sure who the father is. Intercourse doesn't hurt the baby, does it? Don't worry about it.'

I was worrying a lot, mostly about the company's complete control over the surrogate. There was no limit to the number of appointments that could be scheduled requiring the surrogate's participation. If she should become uncooperative, they could simply schedule more psychological visits. If they didn't want to pay her, they could schedule so many that she couldn't possibly keep them. The medical controls seemed particularly ominous: all standard procedures PLUS ANY OTHER precautions or instructions. This could include bedrest, giving up a job, etc. A medical acknowledgment attached to the main body of the contract advised that 'there are certain medical risks inherent in any pregnancy. Some of these may be surgical complications, such as, but not limited to, appendix and gall bladder.' Of course, these surgical complications would most likely arise from a cesarean delivery, major surgery which is not mentioned at all in conversation or contract. If the doctor should request one, the surrogate would have no contractual right to object.

Complications could also arise after birth. I learned that names of both surrogate and father would appear on the birth certificate, compromising promised anonymity, and that the certificate would only be destroyed several weeks, months, or years later when the child was adopted by 'the potential stepmother' (in the same way a new spouse can adopt a child if the former spouse wishes to relinquish her/his rights and responsibilities.) 'Why not right away?' I asked. The lawyer recommended a reasonable waiting period because an immediate adoption 'could be construed, by someone who wanted to construe it that way, as baby-selling.'

In fact, he elaborated, the baby-selling argument could also be used by a court to declare the entire contract illegal and void. It is acknowledged in the contract itself that its '*rights and liabilities may or may not be honored in a Court of Law should a breach arise*' The document further states that, in a lawsuit, it could be used to assist 'a court of competent jurisdiction in ascertaining the intention' of surrogate and parents.

If the surrogate breaches her contract, by abortion, by violation of rules, or by refusal to relinquish the child, the father may sue her for the $25,000 he paid into the program, plus additional costs. If the parents breach by refusal to accept delivery of the child or failure to pay medical expenses, the surrogate may sue them for her $10,000 fee, plus the expenses of child support or placing the child up for adoption. 'What about the company?' I asked. 'If something went wrong and I had to sue the parents, would they help me or pay my legal expenses?' 'No,' he replied. 'When the shit hits the fan you're on your own.' Indeed, each party is required to sign a 'hold harmless' clause which says that no matter what happens the company is not responsible. The lawyer explained this clause away as meaningless—everyone would, of course, sue everyone else if there should be a problem.

As we perused the contract, the lawyer discovered a new clause had appeared since his last consultation, the 'Amniocentesis Addendum' which stated that, should the treating physician request, the surrogate would submit to amniocentesis for prenatal diagnosis. If results were abnormal, she would consent to abortion at the parents' request. To my surprise, this clause out of the entire contract was worrisome to the lawyer. Why, he asked, should the surrogate abort at 20–4 weeks gestation and receive no fee, when she could carry the pregnancy to term and fulfill her contract regardless of the infant's condition? I was more concerned about what might be considered an abnormality sufficient to request abortion. What about a sex chromosome abnormality? What about just the 'wrong' sex? I was also concerned that this again allowed for the total discretion of the treating physician. Why was it left ambiguous in the contract when there is no legitimate indication for amniocentesis that couldn't be known before the pregnancy started? My suspicion was that it would always be requested, as an unacknowledged 'quality control' measure.

The lawyer called the director into the room, and asked about this clause's financial disadvantage to the surrogate. Any woman, she stated flatly, who would knowingly carry a defective fetus to term to cheat the parents out of $10,000 would not be acceptable to the program. Nevertheless, the lawyer suggested that I not sign until he spoke with the author of the contract, to suggest that a small fee be paid to the surrogate if there was such an unfortunate occurrence. My one request before signing was to see a copy of the parents' contract, to compare responsibilities, and to 'make sure they hadn't been promised something I couldn't fulfill.' The request was never honored.

The lawyer called the next day to say the Amniocentesis Addendum must remain as written. He paraphrased the company officials: 'The program works because it works the way it is. We cannot make big changes for the surrogate or the parents.' We arranged to meet a week later, after I had received the parents' contract, for final signing.

Before then, however, I was called by the director who had become concerned while listening in on my legal consultation. She admonished me for asking too many questions:

> The program works because it is set up to work for the couple. You have to weigh why you are participating in the program. For the money only, or to do the service of providing the couple with a baby. To be very frank, we are looking for girls with both those motivations. I felt after the last visit that this is a gal looking for every possible way to earn that money, and that concerns me. … We are playing with peoples' lives, with people who are desperately looking for a child. They have made an emotional investment … emotionally and in every other way that baby is not yours. … No contract is perfect for anyone, for anything.

She urged me to take an extra week before signing, and if I was still interested to arrange to be reevaluated by the psychologist.

…

The careful screening process was a myth. I encountered no evidence of real medical or psychological safeguards; just enough hurdles to test whether I would be obedient. The minimal questioning I did was labelled as selfish, dangerous, and unique in their experience. …

Anonymity was also a myth, since the father would know the city where I lived, my name from the birth certificate, and my physical characteristics from required baby pictures, from company files and medical and psychological reports. He would have visitation rights to the hospital nursery, and perhaps to the delivery room. Company files were said to be confidential, but it was acknowledged that they would be opened upon court order.

It is a myth that women are easily making large sums of money as surrogates. The director of this program acknowledges that the woman who goes through a lengthy insemination process may end up being paid less than $1.00/hour for her participation. To earn this sum, she is completely 'on-call' for the company. She may be required to undergo invasive diagnostic procedures, forfeit her job, and perhaps undergo major surgery with its attendant morbidity and mortality risks. Of course, should there be a miscarriage or failure to conceive, the surrogate receives no compensation at all.

…

Control by contract is a crucial element of this surrogate program, with power clearly in the hands of the company officials. Besides the explicit demands in the contract, an additional clause yielding staggering control to the company was brought to my attention by an unaffiliated lawyer I later consulted. She pointed out Item Nine in a list of rules for surrogates which reads: 'Surrogate mother and her husband must sign all documents provided by the (company) including but not limited to the surrogate mother agreement and contract', plus addendums listed. In essence, at any time I could be handed any new document and be obligated to sign it, no matter what its effect on my well-being or best interests.

…

There is a need for feminists to pay attention to the surrogate industry and to structure debate in feminist terms. There have, of course, been outspoken critics of the surrogate companies, but they have primarily questioned the industry's effect on traditional business dealings and family structure. For example, the only ethical issue raised in a lengthy *Wall Street Journal* article (Inman, 1982) was whether participants might be taking unfair advantage of insurance companies offering maternity benefits. Robert Francoeur, in his 1974 book *Utopian Motherhood,* (p. 102) envisioned a gloomy world in which so-called 'mercenary mothers' would jeopardize the traditional 'monogamous family structure.'

The metaphors of description and criticism are fascinating: Is the surrogate mother a prostitute, or is she instead a modern extension of the wet nurse? Is the surrogate arrangement like donating sperm, simply giving women the right to sell their reproductive capacity as men have done for years? Or is the arrangement more like building a house, where the father furnishes half the blueprint and materials and the labor is contracted out? Is it baby-selling? Or is it organ-selling, morally equivalent to allowing the needy to sell their kidneys to rich patients (Fletcher, 1983)? Each metaphor frames political/ethical discourse in different terms. Even the use of the term 'surrogate mothering,' or the more recently popular euphemism 'surrogate parenting,' begins by labeling the biological mother as artificial. Allowing the debate to be structured by the industry has slowed criticism from the feminist community. …

Our recognition of the problems of infertile women may also be delaying a strong feminist opposition to the surrogate industry. We must not only offer support to women in the painful emotional situation of being involuntarily childless, but we must examine its broader historical basis. The infertility was largely brought to us from the manufacturers of other types of reproductive control, birth control pills and IUDs. The same laws which make it difficult for many infertile women to adopt children will make the surrogate alternative equally unavailable unless she is part of a wealthy married heterosexual couple. Older children, children of color, and those with special needs will remain unadoptable, and the traditional patriarchal family system will remain intact.

In *Right-Wing Women* (1983), Andrea Dworkin has placed surrogate motherhood in the center of her elegant model of the systematic exploitation of women. In it, she describes the brothel model and the farming model. Simply stated, in the brothel model women are used efficiently and specifically for sex by groups of men. In the farming model, women are used by individual men, not so efficiently, for reproduction. The surrogate industry provides a frightening synthesis of both which

enables women to sell their wombs within the terms of the brothel model. Motherhood is becoming a new branch of female prostitution with the help of scientists who want access to the womb for experimentation and for power. A doctor can be the agent of fertilization; he can dominate and control conception and reproduction. Women can sell reproductive capacities the same way old-time prostitutes sold sexual ones but without the stigma of whoring because there is no penile intrusion. (pp. 181–2)

This system will become increasingly efficient with the refinement of other reproductive technologies such as embryo transplanting. As Genoveffa Corea points out
(1985), we are not far from being able to use a combination of artificial insemination
and embryo transplant to allow Third World women to become the prenatal carriers
of completely white children (at the same time that Depo-Provera and other exports
are compromising these women's ability to conceive their own children).

The language and process encountered in my experience within a surrogate company is consistent with the reproductive prostitution model described by Dworkin.
The surrogate is paid for 'giving the man what his wife can't.' She 'loves being pregnant,' and is valued solely and temporarily for her reproductive capacity. After she
'enters the fold' she is removed from standard legal protections and is subject to a variety of abuses. She is generally considered to be mercenary, collecting large un-
earned fees for her services, but the terms of the system are in reality such that she
may lose more permanent opportunities for employment, and may end up injured
or dead with no compensation at all. Even the glowing descriptions of the surrogates
sound remarkably like a happy hooker with a heart of gold.

The issue of prostitution has been a difficult one for feminists; so ancient and entrenched a part of the patriarchal system that it seems almost impossible to confront.
We must not now participate in a quiet liberal complicity with the new reproductive
prostitution. It is our challenge to pay attention to our feminist visionaries, and to
expose the surrogate industry during its formation.

---

### Notes

1. From the first telephone enquiry made by the author to the surrogate company.

### References

Corea, Genoveffa. 1985. *The Mother Machine.* Harper & Row, New York.
Dworkin, Andrea. 1983. *Right-Wing Women.* Perigee Books, New York.
Fletcher, John. 1983. Quoted in *Washington Post.* February 18: C-5.
Francoeur, Robert. 1974. *Utopian Motherhood.* A. S. Barnes, New York. p. 102.
Inman, Virginia. 1982. 'Maternity Plan.' *Wall Street Journal.* August 13: pp. 1, 8.

# Reproductive Freedom and Women's Freedom: Surrogacy and Autonomy

## Christine T. Sistare

...

... Most of the contributions to the debate over surrogacy seem to have centered on one or more of three issues. These are, in what I take to be ascending order of popularity:

1. whether there is any right [moral or legal] to have children, *i.e.,* to become parents; and whether or how that right might extend to third party involvement.
2. whether surrogacy violates accepted moral and legal prohibitions of baby-selling.
3. whether surrogacy inevitably involves or portends the exploitation of the women who act as surrogates by their contractors.[1]

It is worth noting that only one of these purportedly primary moral issues directly concerns the interests of the surrogate, and that it does so only *via* paternalistic intentions. In this paper, I want to address the debate over surrogacy from what I see as a neglected yet fundamental perspective: that of women's freedom. ... I will primarily treat of this freedom from the perspective of women who wish to become surrogates, but I will also attend to the freedom of all women as implicated in the surrogacy debate.

...

## Women's Freedom

I believe that a fundamental moral issue in the surrogacy debate is the nature and extent of women's freedom: their freedom to control their bodies, their lives, their reproductive powers, and to determine the social use of those reproductive capacities. This issue is fundamental both normatively and descriptively. That is, respect for women's personal freedom ought to be a guiding moral concern in resolving the debate, and recognition of the centrality of this issue is, I think, a basic source of the controversy and of much of its intensity.

I accept, as a premise, that women have often been manipulated and oppressed because of and through their reproductive capacities. The bearing of children is a biologically and socially important role, one which makes women valuable even when they seem least valued. The limitations which pregnancy itself imposes and the limitations which can be imposed through the mystification of reproduction, generally, and of maternity, in particular, have proven highly useful in the control of women. Such control has been enhanced insofar as women have internalized these limitations. Motherhood has been both pedestal and prison.

Now, however, there are social and technological contexts which provide a way for women to benefit through the free use of their reproductive powers. The social context, itself, is the result of the increased freedom of women in this society: the acceptance of childbearing and rearing by single mothers, the availability of contraception and abortion, independence from men through access to jobs and fulfillment without matrimony, the real possibility of life without husbands or children. The effect has been to place childbearing at a premium.[2]

...

... People who want a [genetically related] child but who cannot or will not provide for gestation can achieve their goal by arranging for a surrogate. Thus, women can demand payment for their service, their reproductive labors, and can do so in a way—really for the first time in our history—which greatly relieves them of the control of men and of traditional social constraints. Women need not accept marriage or some other promise of support without control as their payment. They need not provide access to their reproductive capacities on demand. They may make the arrangements they like and take their payment in unencumbered money. And that, I contend, is the deep source of the present controversy.

I take it to be a fundamental, if sometimes forgotten, principle of our common political morality that adults have a presumptive right to conduct their private lives and make important personal decisions without unwarranted interference by other individuals or by the law. This is the general liberal tendency of American thought. Surely, some right to primary control over one's body must be the necessary correlate.[3] The question which ought primarily to occupy us, therefore, is this: is there sufficient justification for society to deny to adult women the disposition of their reproductive capacities according to their own desires? Is there, perhaps, some weighty reason for refusing women the right to bear children under circumstances chosen or created by them [some reason which would not, similarly, license society either to prohibit or require sterilization of women who choose otherwise]?

## Freedom and the Body as Property

No doubt there are cogent arguments for social control over the disposition of individuals' bodies and their functions in some cases. One reason for overriding women's right to reproductive freedom which is pertinent to surrogacy might be that surrogacy amounts to no more than selling one's body and to treating the human body as property. This apparently reasonable concern seems to feature in the prohibition of slavery and has prompted recent restrictions on organ donation.

However, this is hardly sufficient as a general condemnation of surrogacy, since we do acknowledge the individual's right to primary control over her body, and since we certainly allow people to treat their bodies as property in a variety of ways: *e.g.,* the selling of blood, of antibodies, and (most apropos) of *sperm. A fortiori,* in our society, we permit people to sell their labor and even think well of them for it. In fact, the surrogate is more a laborer than a seller of body parts, since she really only sells her services while renting out her body. …

…

## Freedom and Consent

We might argue that women must be treated paternalistically in a legitimate sense because, with respect to surrogacy, there can be no truly informed or voluntary consent. Thus, in the current public debate we hear comments to the effect that "a woman can never consent to giving up a child because she can never know how she will feel after it is born." Of course, an obvious objection to this claim is that many people [men and women] seem to have given voluntary and informed consent to having their children adopted or to giving custody of their children to others. If such choices are said to be not really free, we must ask for the model of free choice, of consent, being promoted.

We can never know what it will feel like to do anything before the time of actual performance—certainly nothing likely to be fraught with strong emotions. Indeed, even if I have engaged in some type of conduct in the past, I cannot be *certain* as to how I will feel about a different instance of the same type of conduct in the future. If knowing how one will feel is a criterion of informed consent, there can never be such consent to any choice for the future. …

The operant but unavowed notion, here, is that maternity (or, perhaps, the feeling of Being-a-Mother) is such a primal, mystical experience that no one can appreciate its power to transport in advance of the moment. In the face of this notion, the genuine mystery is how we are to understand women who act as surrogates and do not regret doing so or women who choose to forfeit custody of their offspring.[4] Are all such women *monsters?* Surely it is not necessarily the case that to recognize the wonderful power of reproduction is to desire to keep all the products of it. We can and should value reproduction as both a capacity and an experience without mystifying it; what is naturally beautiful need not be regarded as preternatural to ensure appreciation.

… Neither a model of consent which precludes the possibility of consent nor the mystifying representation of maternal feeling as a primal urge too potent to admit of rational control can provide adequate grounds on which to *violate the right of all women* to be the dispositors of their own reproductive capacities. Women are not and should not be treated as a special subclass of adults by virtue of their reproductive capacities or their parental feelings. Such an interpretation is grossly insulting to women as well as *to men,* who are depicted as detached bystanders to an essentially female enterprise.

### Reproductive Freedom and Other Interests

Naturally, we must take account of interests other than the surrogate's interest in renting her reproductive services. Some critics of surrogacy argue that children born of surrogates may be disturbed when, in later life, they learn of the arrangement which brought them into the world. Now here is a curious argument. We know that such problems may arise in custody or adoption cases, as well, but I have never heard it suggested that children should not be adopted or that parents should be forced to retain custody of their offspring. There is something odd about the idea that it is better to not be born than to be born from one woman's body but raised by someone else. … Most importantly, that some children may have trouble dealing with their origins is not sufficient warrant for preemptive denial of freedom to all women. The probable harm just does not outweigh the fundamental interest of women in the control of their reproductive lives and the social use of their reproductive powers.

"Well then," we are told, "this fundamental interest will actually be impaired by surrogacy." Women will be enslaved by impossible contracts—forced to undergo unimagined indignities by ruthless baby-seeking males or heartless women unwilling to bear children themselves. Of course, the contractual worries are easily dealt with. The surrogate and the contractors agree upon her obligations, including prenatal care, on their obligations to her, and on stipulations for default according to a plan which is acceptable to all the parties. … A good surrogate contract could protect a woman from that fate more surely than most traditional maternal roles afforded to women past or present. Once again, we see that simple social intelligence and careful forethought will preclude most of the envisioned horrors of social change.

…

## Exploitation of Women

Much is made, in very loose terms, of the inevitable exploitation of women which will follow from socially and/or legally sanctioned surrogacy arrangements. The projected exploitation is framed, primarily, in class terms: poor women will be used as baby-gestators by the rich and sterile—or, worse yet, by the rich and vacuous whose obsessive concern for physical preservation and uninterrupted jet-setting will outweigh any inclination to become parents through most direct traditional means. So, we are told, "It will always be poor women who have babies and rich women who get them." Yet, if we inspect this farrago of complaints, we will see that the expected massive exploitation is neither very likely nor very different from a host of ways in which women [and men] are presently exploited with little or no legal interference.

To begin with, such trepidations fly in the face of what appears to be a deep cultural fixation with genetic or blood relationships. Indeed, the cross-cultural ubiquity of attention to biological links between parents and children suggests that there is some natural origin of our genetic narcissism. Innate or not, an obsessive determination to reproduce with as much genetic input as possible seems to be shared by persons of all classes. Even if the heartless, body-conscious women of the upper class have escaped this emotional investment in biologically exclusive reproduction, I suspect their male partners have not.

A surrogate could be employed, of course, only for gestation, with no genetic contribution. But, given the real class prejudices which can be expected to influence surrogate hirings, it hardly seems probable that wealthy persons will eagerly seek the services of women from impoverished or seriously disadvantaged backgrounds. Even the most inanely self-absorbed contractors will avoid the perceived risks of unhealthy or deficient children.[5] The reality of racial and ethnic prejudices must also be confronted in assessing the threat of exploitation: racially or ethnically privileged groups will not rush to have their children borne by members of despised minorities. These are ugly truths, but they must be acknowledged. Contractors will want their babies borne by surrogates with whom they themselves feel comfortable, and people typically feel most comfortable with others like themselves.

More to the point, the nature of the projected exploitation is obscure. This is a capitalist society. We do not, as a society, bemoan the fate of women who work as domestics or in truly degrading service and industrial jobs for minimum wages. Nor have we, as a society, envinced much concern with emotional strains on individuals when those strains were freely undertaken. Should awareness of the powerful emotions evoked by pregnancy and childbearing suddenly induce us to renounce our historical indifference to the emotional well-being of our fellows, we can simply stipulate that surrogate contracts will only be legally enforceable if the surrogate undergoes psychological screening, or has previously experienced pregnancy, etc.

It is just too difficult to see how being a self-employed surrogate, renting out one's reproductive capacity according to one's own determination, can be anything but an improvement on the opportunities presently available to many women. A surrogate may live in her own home, raise her own children, and be assured of good medical care. She can protect herself from the personal abuse and indignities which attend much of women's work in our society. She might pursue education or a career. Moreover, to guard against real rather than fantasized exploitation, we can impose legal minimum and maximum fees for surrogacy and apply the usual legal requirements to surrogate contracts. Ensuring that surrogates are paid well and treated well is the way to prevent their misuse, and this can be done through thoughtful regulation which both respects and protects all parties. We could start by limiting the role of lawyers and medical technicians so as to distribute payments in favor of the surrogates and away from these inessential third parties [typically white men].[6]

…

Other critics of surrogacy may express qualms about relations between classes because of a newly discovered aversion to capitalism as the culture of money. How ironic that those long-satisfied with our system and our culture should choose to refuse women an opportunity to enjoy the benefits of capitalism just when technology and social change have opened access to those benefits through women's special reproductive capacities. It is the sort of irony which ought to make us curious. We should wonder why there is this new fear of capitalist exploitation just when women have attained special access to the capitalist game—access not open to men and largely independent of traditional social controls.

The fact of the matter is that we, as a society, do not believe the best things in life are free. Cost is value and money is power. Unless and until our society and culture are radically altered, assuring women who act as surrogates full legal standing can only serve to prevent exploitation. We certainly do not want to drive surrogacy into a legal underground where exploitation can flourish. Nor should we forget that pinchbeck veneration of an idealized maternal role has always been a primary device for the very real exploitation and oppression of women. Women will best be protected when they are recognized as autonomous adults with full rights. That recognition cannot be won through either the mystification of Motherhood or a false idealization of our social values.

...

## Conclusion

I do not want to suggest that the surrogacy issue—or any of the social conundra arising from the new birth technologies—is a simple one. I doubt that the complex of issues and concerns involved can be perspicuously or fruitfully *reduced to* matters of the freedom of surrogates. I do not even think this complex can be reduced to a question of individual freedom, generally: the freedom of women and men playing any of the pertinent parts in surrogate arrangements or in society at large.

I do, however, believe that freedom—particularly the freedom of women to be the dispositors of their reproductive capacities and to control their lives—is a central consideration in this controversy. It is central normatively in that it ought to be taken account of and respected. I believe it is also central in the present waging of the debate, though it remains—as a consideration—very well hidden. I have tried to evince, here, the ways in which our fear of women's reproductive freedom informs much of the current opposition to surrogacy. I have attempted, as well, to disclose the way in which genuine concern for women and women's rights should inform our response to other social interests, values, and aims.

We can only hope that people will exercise their freedom wisely and with some degree of moral sensitivity. ...

...

... Social acceptance of surrogacy may prove beneficial in a number of ways. Consider, for example, how much the traditional panegyrics to Motherhood have really meant: seldom has any human social role been more honored in speeches and less rewarded in fact. Parenting, generally, has been more highly valued in word than in social reality, and Fatherhood has barely been recognized except as a form of property ownership.

Surrogacy advances the cause of loving parenting by enabling people who genuinely want to become parents to do so; thus, it both serves and validates the place of parenting in our lives. It very immediately discloses the value of children. And it may serve to enhance the role of fathers, both genetically and emotionally, as equal contributors to the process of bringing children into the world.

Finally, the acceptance and practice of surrogacy would reveal a meaningful respect for maternity. It would do so in the capitalist mode of paying well for what is deemed rare and precious. It would also encourage recognition that women—many women—really do enjoy the experiences of pregnancy and giving birth. I think that could be an important cultural lesson; for all our eulogizing of maternity as a social role, we don't seem to believe that women genuinely enjoy the childbearing process. Perhaps that doubt contributes to the conviction that normal women *must* want to keep the babies they bear: we can't imagine that anyone would endure, much less enjoy, the process of pregnancy and birthing except to become a parent. But even as we think this way, we recognize that it falsifies the experience of many women. Surrogacy permits women who find their basic reproductive capacity to be a source of joy to display that valuation through their free choice to exercise the capacity for the benefit of others and for themselves. Those who fear that maternity and women's reproductive role will be devalued by surrogacy ought to reconsider in light of this possibility. Here may be an instance of actions speaking more loudly and clearly than words.

---

## Notes

Many thanks are owed to Bill Schmitz, Steve Ross, Frank Kirkland, Gerry Press, John Lango, and an anonymous reader for comments on earlier drafts of this paper. ...

1. I recognize the standard criticisms of the terms "surrogate" and "surrogacy"—in particular, that they are persuasive by virtue of their very dispassionateness and by the implication that the person and role so designated are peripheral to the real (non-substitute) interests to be considered. Insofar as I am primarily addressing the freedom of surrogates, I obviously do not want to persuade in that direction (I don't suppose that "contractor"—for the other party to the contract—is a very attractive name for those who seek to become parents. Perhaps the lack of appeal will balance out.)

2. Unfortunately, an increase in the incidence of infertility and other childbearing problems has augmented the rarity and value of women able to bear children.

3. Note that the right to control over one's body claimed here is not to be regarded as an absolute right. It is also not to be pasted onto the abortion issue insofar as that involves any conflict of rights.

4. The majority of those who have served as surrogates appear to be happy with their role, describing it in terms of personal fulfillment and of contributing to the happiness of others. This is a fact which is curiously under-reported in the present debate. The little attention given to the perspective of the surrogate focuses on those few women who have been unhappy with the arrangement.

5. I suspect that it is just the inanely self-absorbed who will be most insistent on obtaining quality surrogates to bear their children.

6. My impression is that most of the calls for privatization—or, rather, continued non-regulation—of surrogacy come from those who presently benefit from the absence of legal control: *i.e.,* lawyers and fertility counselors. ...

# Contract Motherhood:
# Social Practice in Social Context

## Mary Gibson

### Social Context

...

As the practice of contract motherhood has emerged in our society, the most typical situation giving rise to it is that of a traditional, heterosexual married couple (the
intended receiving parents) who want to have one or more children but are unable to
because the wife is infertile, that is, unable to conceive and/or to sustain a pregnancy.
In the "standard" case, the contract mother is artificially inseminated with the sperm
of the intended receiving father, conceives, gestates, gives birth to an infant, delivers
the infant into the custody of the receiving couple, and renounces all rights to a parental relationship with the child.

Although infertility is by no means a necessary condition for contract motherhood,[1] many people regard the pain experienced by infertile couples as a compelling
reason to welcome, or at least permit, contract motherhood as a procreative option.
Indeed, there are some who would restrict it to such couples.[2] ...

... Many of the physical causes of infertility are directly or indirectly generated by
social conditions, practices, and institutions. ... Prevention of infertility wherever
possible is surely preferable to any after-the-fact response, and the measures needed
to address the causes ... would serve other socially desirable purposes as well: improving health education including sex education, providing access to health care,
holding manufacturers of drugs and devices liable for the harm they cause, strictly
enforcing informed consent procedures to prevent sterilization abuse, cleaning up
the environment and workplaces, and carrying out the social reorganization needed
to eliminate the barriers to combining paid work and family are all measures that
warrant the allocation of substantial societal resources. That they would also help to
prevent the pain of infertility is one important reason among many. At the same
time, it must be noted that "Pain is not an inevitable response to the fact of infertility
... a physical reality takes on significance in a particular social context."[3]

In this light, it is ironic that many of the features of our society that make contract
motherhood so very attractive to many people are the same features that make it so

morally and politically troubling. The features of our society that I have in mind are (1) the subordination of women, (2) class inequalities, (3) pronatalism, (4) a narrow, mystified conception of the family, (5) racism, (6) our market-oriented, contractarian conception of public personhood, and the relations and interactions among all of these. If these features were absent, contract motherhood might not be morally objectionable, but much if not all of its attractions would also be absent. This suggests that if there were a society in which contract motherhood would not be morally objectionable, the practice probably would not exist.

*Subordination of Women and Class Inequalities.* The subordination of women both within the family and outside of it means, among other things, that severely limited roles, opportunities, and resources are available to most women. The most meaningful and fulfilling activities available to many women are those involved in bearing and rearing children. For working class women, fewer avenues are open to other fulfilling endeavors than for "middle" or "upper" class women, who are likely to have access to challenging career (or volunteer) opportunities.[4]

Thus, when women's subordination and class inequalities are combined, it is not surprising that some working class women welcome the chance to be contract mothers. They can get paid for engaging in one of the most meaningful activities available to them. They can do it while staying home and caring for their other children (the ultimate "home work" or cottage industry). They can do it while working at another paid job, assuming that they don't lose the other job as a result of the pregnancy. They can, indeed must, do it even while reading, sleeping, eating, bathing, and making love. Thus it can be an attractive prospect for a woman who has few options and opportunities.

But these same factors, the subordination of women and class inequalities, are among those that make contract motherhood so morally and politically troubling. As the terms "surrogate mother" and "surrogate uterus" make clear, the practice reflects and reinforces a view of women as primarily suited for reproduction and of our role in reproduction as that of a vessel carrying a man's child.[5] Women are doubly demeaned by this view: first, we are reduced to our reproductive role, and second, the uniqueness and importance of that role are denied. This attitude not only demeans women, it also implicitly justifies and hence contributes to the restriction of roles and opportunities for women. In addition, it supports direct interference with the activities, and violation of the bodily integrity of women who are engaged in reproduction. Here I have in mind actions that have recently been taken against women who were not contract mothers: prohibition or restriction of abortions (including recent attempts by potential fathers to prevent pregnant women from obtaining abortions), forced fetal surgery, forced caesareans, and the arrest of a woman on charges of fetal abuse for disobeying her doctor's advice.[6]

There is a strong and arguably growing tendency for physicians and judges to regard a pregnant woman as simply "the fetal environment," and sometimes a hostile environment from which the fetus must be protected. Her interests in self-determination and bodily integrity may, on this view, be overridden by the interests of the fetus in life and wellbeing. This tendency would be even stronger in cases of contract motherhood, and stronger still for purely gestational contracts. (According to some proponents of contract motherhood, one of its advantages over adoption is the ability of the intended receiving parent(s) to "monitor the pregnancy.")[7]

The chance to bear children for others for a fee does nothing to break down the gender stereotyped roles and attitudes that so limit the options, opportunities and aspirations of women, especially working class women, in our society. If it had any effect at all, contract motherhood would tend to *reduce* pressures to open other avenues for working class women. If poor and working class women are to be paid for pregnancy, let it be for bearing and rearing *their* children, as in family allowances, not just for bearing children for the more affluent.

Thus class inequalities raise serious concerns about exploitation of the economic situation of poor women. These concerns will be examined in more detail in the discussion of exploitation, below. Let us now turn to explore some features of our society that make contract motherhood attractive to the intended receiving parents.

*Pronatalism, Narrow Conception of Family, and Racism.* Our pronatalist ideology combines with a narrow, rigid, mystified conception of the family and with the pervasive racism of our society to make contract motherhood more attractive to many would-be parents than alternatives, whether alternative routes to parenthood or alternatives to parenthood. In our pronatalist society, the desire for children is presumed to be universal, and parenthood is regarded as a normal and necessary developmental task. Those who do not conform are stigmatized, regarded as deviant, selfish, emotionally immature, psychologically maladjusted, sexually inadequate, and unhappy. Parenthood is considered not just a requirement for personal development and fulfillment, but also a religious, moral, and civic responsibility. The infertile not only face these attitudes in others, but, sharing this ideology, are subject to severe loss of self-esteem and potential psychopathology as a consequence of their inability to satisfy societal and personal expectations. The damage to self-esteem and risk of psychopathology are greatest for individuals whose self-identity is closer to the feminine stereotype than to androgeny or to the masculine stereotype. Although parenthood is considered normative for both men and women, it is considered more important for women.[8]

Thus pronatalism helps to explain not only why many people will go to great lengths to become parents, but also why infertile wives may feel especially inadequate and even guilty. ... Contract motherhood gives these wives the opportunity to allow their husbands to fulfill their biological and developmental "destinies" and to themselves become the social and in some cases the genetic mothers of their husbands' children. Pronatalism also seems to play a role in the motivation of contract mothers themselves. While most say they would not do it if they were not paid, many are moved by the real pain and the perceived emptiness of the lives of the infertile and feel good about being able to help fill that "void."[9]

When the social imperative of parenthood is combined with our society's narrow, mystified conception of the family, we can see why, despite the supposed universality of the desire or drive to procreate, pronatalism is actually restricted to married or stable heterosexual couples. Given the strength of pronatalist ideology, it is remark-

able that, not only are single persons and those in homosexual or non-couple relationships, the different, the disabled, and the very poor not socially required to have
children, *they* are regarded as selfish, immature, maladjusted, and irresponsible if
they *do* have children. Those who don't fit the "normal, healthy" family picture are
expected to suppress their desire to procreate for the sake of the (preferably nonexistent) children.[10]

Some feminists and others have welcomed alternative modes of reproduction as
offering expanded procreative choices for persons not in so-called "traditional" families, and perhaps helping in the long run to broaden the societal definition of the
family. I have serious reservations. First, although informal arrangements are carried
out employing reproductive practices that do not require special equipment or expertise, current professional practice is highly discriminatory. The fact that these restrictive views and attitudes appear to be widely shared by relevant professionals (reflected also in adoption policy) suggests that any regularizing of these practices
would, in our current social climate, almost certainly reflect and reinforce rather
than revise the rigid, narrow definition of the family.

My other reservations about welcoming alternative reproductive modes as enhancing the options of "nontraditional" families arise from concerns about contract
motherhood (and also, to some extent, about AID [artificial insemination by do-
nor]) whether commercial or unpaid, and whether the families are "traditional" or
not. People tend to want a child of their *own*, with "own" having many different, if
overlapping, meanings that are of differing importance to different people. One of
the things it seems to mean is that they want any "extra" parents (sperm donor, egg
donor, gestating mother) excluded from involvement in the life of the child. But I am
not sure that anyone should be expected to renounce all knowledge of and contract
with a child that is his or hers though not, in the exclusive sense, his or her *own*, or
that a child should be denied knowledge of and contract with any of her or his parents. I recognize that some people may prefer anonymity and no contact, but I question, first, whether such a preference at a particular time can or should be binding
for all time, and second, whether a child's right, need, or wish to know (or know
about) his or her parent should be denied because of the parent's preference.

The reasons for the social parents wanting to exclude the "extras" are, no doubt
many and varied. But, in the case of otherwise "traditional" families, a major factor
seems to me to be a desire to make the family structure as much as possible like the
mythical "normal" family consisting of breadwinning father, nurturing mother
(now possibly also a career woman/super-mom), and their genetic offspring (preferably, first a boy, then a girl) conceived, carried, and born the old-fashioned way.
Contract motherhood, if the contract mother is excluded, allows infertile couples to
come as close as possible to the "norm."[11] The exclusive, possessive quality of family
relationships involved in this conception of the family also contributes to a view of
children as the *property* of their parents. And this view of children is conducive to the
commodification of the child that is inherent in contract motherhood so long as the
contract includes the alienation of the child from the birth mother. In a society with
a broader, more open (and more realistic) conception of the family or of famil*ies*

there might be far more openness about the use of alternative modes of reproduction and far less urgency to exclude anyone. The term "collaborative reproduction," which I find misleadingly euphemistic when applied to contract motherhood in our society, might more accurately describe the practice that might exist in that sort of social context. To the extent that it might exist, I am suggesting, it would not be the same practice.[12] On the other hand, in such a society, other ways of becoming parents or of being significantly involved with children, or *not* being significantly involved with children might be far more attractive, so that such a practice might not exist at all. Thus pronatalism and our narrow conception of the family contribute both to the attraction of contract motherhood and to some of its morally troubling features. In addition, I would argue, although I don't have time to do so here, that both pronatalism and the "traditional" conception of the family reinforce and are reinforced by the subordination of women.[13]

The attempt to make one's family conform to the "traditional" family picture has racial implications as well. First, despite the Cosby show and the Jeffersons, the family in this picture is, unless otherwise specified, white; that is the "norm." Just as only women are thought of as being of a particular gender (men are just regular persons) so only people of color are thought to have race. But to think that white people's identities are not fundamentally shaped by race in a pervasively racist society is a serious mistake. No one can completely escape internalizing the racism as well as the sexism of our society. Hence, the desire to conform to the traditional family picture combined with the importance of race in all of our identities result in a very restricted view of "adoptable" children. At the same time, one does not have to be a bigot to regard transracial adoption in a racist society as problematic.[14] Thus I am not placing responsibility for all the children of color who need homes on the doorsteps of infertile white couples. I believe we, as a society, all share that responsibility, and in many cases the best way to carry it out may not be to take the children out of their communities but to provide the communities with the requisite resources (child-care, medical care, programs for those with physical or psychological disabilities, jobs, housing, and so on) to give them homes.

What I am saying is that racism in our society undeniably contributes to the fact that there are, on one hand many people who want desperately to be parents and on the other many children who need homes; yet it is difficult or impossible for them to fulfill each others' desires and needs. And this fact contributes to the pressure to create children by contract while other, existing, children languish in institutions or foster care, surely a morally troubling situation, even if one resists pointing fingers of blame. In a nonracist society with a more open conception of the family it is plausible to suppose that this situation would not exist.

Further, the desire for white infants plus the economic disparities associated with racial difference in our country and around the world, together with the feasibility of embryo transfer, make it all too likely that women of color will be hired to bear white babies. Again, in a non-racist society, this prospect might not be alarming, but in our society it is. And again, the same features that make it so likely are those that make it alarming.[15]

*Market-Oriented, Contractarian Conception of the Public Person.* There is a sharp contrast between our societal conception of the family and its members and the relations among them on one hand and our conception of individuals and the relations among them in the larger world outside the family. We have inherited from liberal political philosophy the notion that there is a clear distinction between the "private sphere" of the family and the "public sphere" of the marketplace and political life. The family is a "haven in a heartless world" and although in it "each man is king," it is the domain of women who provide nurture and sustenance to weary breadwinners and prepare the next generation for their appointed roles. The wife/mother is thought of as emotional, physical, dependent, and essentially self-less. She lives for and through her husband and children. By contrast, the public individual, the "normal healthy adult" is thought to be essentially rational (not physical and emotional) and *in*dependent. Free, equal, rational, autonomous individuals are thought to have no essential connections to one another. Each seeks to promote his or her own interests or conception of the good, and relations among these agents are voluntary, contractual ones.

Now a simple and inadequate feminist view (made even more simplistic here, with apologies) is that, if women are subordinated and stunted in their wife/mother role in the family, what they have to do is get out into the "public" world and learn to be more like men: independent, competitive, assertive, self-confident, and so on.[16] But neither of these conceptions, the dependent, emotional, nurturant, self-less wife/mother nor the independent, rational, competitive, market individual is either an attractive or a realistic conception of a person, whether man or woman. Yet contract motherhood, paradoxically and incoherently, combines the worst aspects of each. The disembodied, rationalistic, market-oriented conception of persons encourages us to think of our bodies and our physical capacities as property, appropriate for sale or rental in the market. Thus, women are seen as more autonomous if they recognize and exploit their marketable capacities that were hitherto exercised for free. They can rationally decide not to become emotionally involved, and even if they do, they should be able to honor a commitment made in a cooler moment. (Like much of traditional Western moral theory, this view denies the moral significance of the emotions and of embodiment.) On the other hand, the contract mother is often seen (and often sees herself) as making the ultimate sacrifice: she is self-less; she erases herself. In the words of one contract mother, "I'm only an incubator."[17] The rational, independent, self-interested market individual dissolves into the nurturant, subordinate, self-effacing, invisible woman. Does contract motherhood offer women increased self-determination and economic opportunity or increased subordination and exploitation?

## Exploitation

...

... Exploitation may take place along several different dimensions (economic, social, psychological) either alone or in combination. There can be various degrees or levels of vulnerability along each of these dimensions, and various degrees or levels of advantage taken along each. The severity of exploitation depends on all of these factors. A person or group may be exploited simultaneously by one or more other persons and/or groups in the same or different ways. Further, although it may be more reprehensible if done deliberately, exploitation need not be consciously intended by the exploiter. By the same token, the exploited need not necessarily *feel* exploited.

Let us now distinguish two forms of commercial contract motherhood arrangements, *brokered* and *paid private* forms, and ask, for whom do issues of exploitation arise under each of these forms, and how?

I propose that, in brokered contract motherhood, the broker exploits the contract mother at least economically (by taking advantage of the vulnerability resulting from her limited financial resources and security), but often also socially (by taking advantage of the vulnerability resulting from the restricted social roles and resources available to one in her combined gender and economic status),[18] and psychologically. The psychological exploitation can involve taking advantage of one or more of several possible vulnerabilities, for example, those resulting from the impacts on self-esteem of societal attitudes toward women and the economically insecure. As mentioned in the previous section, internalized ideologies of pronatalism and feminine altruism can constitute additional aspects of psychological vulnerability, especially for women whose other avenues to social recognition and achievement are extremely restricted. Further, significant percentages of women who apply to be contract mothers report feeling the need to "work through" previous experiences of loss through abortion, miscarriage, or relinquishment of a child for adoption. (I have seen nothing to indicate that the experience of losing yet another child through contract motherhood would be likely to help such a woman come to terms with her previous loss.) Finally, some interviews with contract mothers indicate that the attention they receive during the pregnancy from the intended receiving parents is a major motivating factor.[19] This suggests that a need for familial connections moves some women to engage in contract motherhood. These women are then subjected to a double loss upon the birth of the child, being cut off from both the child and the receiving parents.[20]

In addition, I contend that, in brokered contract motherhood, the broker exploits the intended receiving parent(s) economically and psychologically by taking advantage of the vulnerability resulting from the pain and impact on self-esteem of the experience of infertility in a pronatalist society with a narrow conception of the family. Further, in both brokered and paid private forms, the receiving parent(s) exploit the contract mother economically, and often in some or all of the additional social and psychological ways outlined above in connection with commercial brokers.

Finally, I suggest that all the adults involved (broker, if any, receiving parent(s) and contract mother) exploit the contracted-for infant by treating her or him as a mere means to their own ends.[21] The purposes of the parties may be legitimate: for example, on the part of the broker, to make a good living; on the part of the receiving parent(s) to have an infant to raise; on the part of the contract mother, to pay college tuition for herself or her other children, to work through feelings of loss, to experience familial connections, to "give the gift of experience life." But legitimate purposes do not justify the use of another person solely as a means to achieve those purposes.

Let us now consider some likely objections to the case outlined so far against contract motherhood on grounds of exploitation.[22] One common objection points to the fact that there are many dull, demeaning, risky, low-paid jobs in our society, many of them more obviously exploitative than contract motherhood, so why single out and ban the latter? But the fact that there exist in our society many exploitative relationships, including many jobs that ought not to exist in anything like their current form, is no reason to welcome, or even permit, the introduction of a new highly exploitative practice if we can prevent it.

Another objection denies that the practice is really exploitative. There are those who argue that, not only is it a boon to the infertile and others who might choose this reproductive option, it opens up potentially beneficial, even liberating, opportunities for women.[23] They argue that it is inconsistent, even hypocritical, to favor denying this option as long as there are women who would prefer it to the other options available to them. Some suspect that it is only because women have the market for this opportunity cornered that there is so much sentiment for restricting or banning it.

I agree that it would be hypocritical to oppose contract motherhood on grounds of exploitation if one were not at the same time actively committed to improving the circumstances of those for whom it would currently be a relatively attractive alternative. Further, as I have acknowledged above, it is a judgment call as to whether contract motherhood does, or would if widely practiced, open new opportunities for women and new possibilities for family structures or, on the contrary, serve to reinforce existing roles for and attitudes toward women and the existing narrow conception of the family. In my judgment, the latter is far more likely. I am acutely aware that people on both sides of the issue readily dismiss optimistic or pessimistic speculation by their opponents, while invariably engaging in it themselves. I see no alternative. We must concern ourselves with what kind of a society we are and would become if different policies were adopted, and there is some irreducible uncertainty involved.

Some proponents deny that even current commercially brokered contracts exploit contract mothers. This position is indefensible. Under the terms of Mary Beth Whitehead's (standard) contract drawn up by the Infertility Center of New York, she was to receive $10,000 upon delivery of a live child. That is less than half the minimum hourly wage for the time involved in a normal full-term pregnancy. She received no compensation for unsuccessful inseminations; she would receive no compensation if she miscarried in the first four months, and $1000 after four months in the event of miscarriage, stillbirth, or abortion mandated by William Stern.

Other proponents grant that currently the practice often is highly exploitative, but they argue that appropriate regulation could make it morally acceptable.[24] They propose requiring adequate compensation for all of the time involved and risks incurred. This requirement would more than double the minimum amount payable to contract mothers, raising once again the issue of access: the more expensive the practice for the receiving parent(s), the smaller the privileged group who will be able to avail themselves of this choice. That one class will provide women to bear children exclusively for members of another class is ensured.[25]

Another issue raised by the job-upgrade approach is the concern that much higher pay would constitute an undue inducement for women of limited means thus rendering their consent less than fully voluntary. It might be asked why this worry arises in the case and not, e.g., in those of domestic work, poultry work, retail sales, clerical work? I believe it clearly signals the recognition that to become a contract mother is an especially profound decision. If decent pay would constitute an undue inducement, it appears that the job of contract mother cannot be offered on morally acceptable terms: it will involve either direct economic exploitation or undue inducement. Moreover, might not the going $10,000 be a large enough sum to someone in financially difficult or insecure circumstances to constitute an undue inducement?

There seems to me to be at least two additional problems with this approach. One involves the question whether any monetary fee can fairly compensate not only for the process of becoming pregnant, carrying, sustaining and nurturing life that is thus enabled to develop, and laboring and giving birth to a child, but also for relinquishing that child for life. Some kinds of jobs cannot be made good jobs, and a decent society won't countenance them even if there are people willing to do them. I suggest that contract motherhood is such a job.[26]

The second problem arises from the fact, as I see it, that part of what a contract mother does is sell her child. That poor women or families in our society should find themselves faced with the option of selling a child in order to provide food, shelter, or education to other family members is both morally and legally repugnant. This aspect of contract motherhood raises most emphatically the issues of class division and exploitation. It also raises the closely related issue of commodification. ...

## Commodification

One way of treating people as mere means, and not as ends in themselves, is by treating them as commodities, things, property. Thus commodification of persons is, on the present account, a species of exploitation of persons.[27] I regard all commodification of persons, their capacities, and relationships as morally inappropriate. Commodities are things that are appropriately owned, exchanged, and consumed, used and used up, by persons. Persons are not property; we are not the sorts of entities that can, morally speaking, be owned, even by ourselves. We *are* ourselves; we don't *own* ourselves. Thus, in some respects, contract motherhood is not, to my mind, different in kind, as regards the commodification of human capacities and activities, from other low-paid, highly exploitative forms of wage labor.[28]

How, then, would I respond to the following challenge: "All of us who have jobs commodify our physical, intellectual, nurturant, and/or other capacities and skills. What is so different about commodifying women's reproductive capacity?" My answer has four parts: (a) the difference is one of degree, not of kind; (b) that people are inappropriately treated as commodities in some respects does not justify inappropriately treating them as commodities in other respects; (c) the commodification of women in our society goes far beyond that inherent in wage labor and both reflects and contributes to women's subordinate status, in particular, to the fact that women are not regarded and treated as whole persons; hence further commodification of women particularly should be resisted; and (d) women are not the only persons commodified by contract motherhood. Even if commodification of women's reproductive capacities is, or could be, morally and legally on a par with other forms of wage labor, commodification of contracted-for children is not. Here we have commodification of whole persons.

Commodification of the child in contract motherhood exacerbates commodification of the contract mother. For potential receiving parents will assess the suitability of applicants in terms of physical and other traits they hope will be passed on to the child.[29] Thus, not only are the woman's reproductive capacities on the market, her appearance (hair, eyes, nose, lips, skin tone, bone structure, height, weight, and so on), her eyesight, intelligence, talents, sense of humor and so forth are all actually or potentially on the market, valued not for the contribution they make to the person she is, but for their possible incorporation into the product of her reproductive activity.

...

## Alienation

When a whole person is treated by others as a commodity, to be owned, used, bought, and sold by them, not a party to the transaction, with no choice or voice in the decision, her or his personhood is denied and undermined. The person is, of course, still a person, but it must be extraordinarily difficult to develop and maintain a sense of oneself as a full person. ...

In addition, of course, the experience of adopted children must be taken into account. The feelings of abandonment, insecurity, and incomplete identity some adopted children experience are forms of alienation that must inform our assessment of the risks of harm imposed on contract children.[30] (Some AID children have also experienced difficulty dealing with their origins.)[31]

Some proponents of contract motherhood urge that surely these children will feel especially loved and wanted, knowing that their receiving parents went to such lengths to get them. This confidence is not borne out in the adoption case. The knowledge that one was planned and conceived to be relinquished by one's birthmother, does not seem likely to be more welcome or less apt to give rise to feelings of abandonment, insecurity, and incomplete identity than the thought that one's birthmother relinquished one reluctantly, as in the usual adoption case. Thus, in my view, commodification of children is wrong not only because if fails to respect them as ends in themselves but also because it imposes on them, unnecessarily and without their consent, significant risk of harm.[32]

We must also consider the potential alienating affects on other members of a contract mother's family in their relationship to her and the process of her pregnancy and childbirth, in their relationship to the fetus she carries and the baby to which she gives birth, and in their conceptions of themselves, their sense of wholeness, security, and connectedness within the family.[33] There are risks of harm here as well. And we must consider the potential alienation of the contract mother herself.

When we commodify aspects of ourselves, renting out or selling our human capacities, our bodies or portions thereof, we are said to fragment ourselves. We temporarily or permanently alienate aspects or portions of our persons. So it is when a worker sells her capacity to work, her labor power; so it is when a woman rents out her womb or her reproductive capacity.

This fragmentation is necessary if there is to be a self remaining to collect the rent or enjoy the proceeds of the sale. Otherwise, our whole self, our personhood, would be alienated in the transaction, as in indentured servitude or selling oneself into slavery. But the person or person-fragment that remains is diminished, and is further undermined when aspects of her self now in the domain of another are used to gain further control over her person.[34] So it is and will be when commercial brokers and receiving parents seek to monitor and control every aspect of the lives and medical care of contract mothers to get full benefit of the reproductive services they have bought and to ensure an undamaged, quality product, at the same time disempowering the woman, demeaning her personhood, her dignity, self-determination, and bodily integrity.

In fact, the fragmentation that permits a substantial self to remain sovereign, so to speak, while aspects of the person are commodified is largely illusory. A contract mother rents her womb or her reproductive capacity or sells her reproductive services. But a woman is pregnant with her whole self: physical, mental, and emotional. Her entire body is involved: nausea, swollen ankles, aching back, compressed organs, enlarged breasts, shortness of breath, and so on. If the fetus needs more calcium than her diet provides, the calcium comes from her teeth and bones. She is consciously aware of the progress of her pregnancy. She feels the fetus move inside her. But, as a contract mother, she is not to become emotionally involved with the life that is developing within her, not just contained by her, but an integral part of her. She contracts not to form a relationship with her fetus, and for her own good she had better not form one. Yet, as a conscientious contract mother, she is expected and expects herself to take every care for the wellbeing of the fetus, to be mindful of its needs and vulnerabilities just as she would a future child she intended to raise herself.

The separateness or separability of body, mind, and emotions presupposed by these contractual terms and expectations reflects the fundamentally fragmented nature of the conception of persons prevalent in our culture. The combination of attitudes toward herself, her pregnancy and her fetus that contract motherhood requires of a woman impresses me as perhaps the profoundest possible form of self-alienation. These attitudes are called for because, upon the birth of her child, she is expected to alienate that baby from herself completely and irrevocably.[35] These forms of alienation, I contend, are not only potentially harmful to contract mothers, but also pose significant threats to their autonomy, and ultimately to the autonomy of all women in our society.

## Autonomy

The conceptions of autonomy most prevalent in our culture presuppose the separation of mind, body, and emotions, the fragmentation of personhood, remarked just above. The autonomous self is conceived either as a purely rational self, with body and emotions irrelevant to its nature and to its autonomous decisions, or as divided against itself, with rationality winning out over base physicality and unruly emotion. In addition, autonomy so conceived presupposes separation from other persons, independence, unless a relationship is voluntarily entered into by mutual consent.

Such conceptions of autonomy seem to figure in the arguments of those proponents of contract motherhood who contend that prohibition or serious restriction of the practice would violate the autonomy of women. But these conceptions of autonomy are inadequate. Many feminists (and others) criticize such conceptions, and the liberal, contractarian moral theories in which they prominently figure, on grounds that can be labeled individualism, rationalism, voluntarism, and egalitarianism. The charge of individualism points to the realities of human interdependence and socialization as incompatible with the received conceptions of autonomy. The charge of rationalism questions the separation and privileging of the "purely" rational or intellectual over the emotional and embodied. The charge of voluntariness points to the pervasiveness and moral significance of relationships that are not chosen. And the charge of egalitarianism notes the pervasiveness and moral significance of relationships that are essentially unequal.

These criticisms must be taken seriously. We cannot, I think, deny that there can be nonintellectual springs of autonomous insight and action; we often do and should rely on feelings or gut reactions that we cannot even articulate, much less justify. We do not (or should not) want to say that the only autonomous response to nonvoluntary relationships is to avoid or extricate ourselves from them. Nor can we pretend that all relationships in which autonomous persons engage are or ought to be among adult peers who are equal in all relevant respects. I am one among many feminists and others currently working to develop a more adequate notion of autonomy, one that would not be subject to these criticisms. Since the job is far from done, if it can be done at all, its full implications for the contract motherhood debate cannot yet be drawn. But a few already seem clear.

For example, some feminists believe that respect for women's autonomy requires that women be able to make, in advance, a valid, enforceable contract to relinquish a child that is not yet conceived. Any other policy, they fear, would reinforce the notion that women are incapable of responsible decisionmaking. One feminist ethicist responds, writing of Mary Beth Whitehead's change of mind:

> She decided not to surrender her baby in part because of bodily experiences. She gave birth; she saw her newborn baby; she breast fed the infant. These physical experiences were among the factors that led Whitehead to conclude that she would not give her baby

up. ... Whitehead's behavior seems to confirm misogynist western cultural traditions. Women's perceived deeper ties to their bodies have been used as the rationale for disqualifying women as moral agents. ... However, the solution to this threat to women's standing as moral agents is not to insist that birth mothers be compelled to honor the contractual promises they made prior to birth. ... Rather, feminists and others need to challenge the view that disembodied, rational judgment is the moral ideal.[36]

I would add that the emotional response to physically seeing, holding, and nursing the infant, resulting in the realization that "I cannot sell my baby!" constitutes a moral insight and a moral imperative. To hold a woman to a decision made prior to this experience would be to deny, not uphold, her moral autonomy.

Other proponents of contract motherhood agree that any decision as profound as this one must be revocable up until the time of actual performance.[37] They advocate a waiting period after the birth of the child during which the birthmother may change her mind. They maintain that respect for the autonomy of potential contract mothers and for the procreative choice of potential receiving parents requires that we permit the practice with this proviso.

I doubt that an adequate conception of autonomy will support this position, but I cannot demonstrate that here. However, if I am correct about the commodification of contract children, I don't have to. Neither respect for autonomy nor respect for procreative choice can require that we permit the buying and selling of nonconsenting persons.

Earlier, I alluded to another threat to the autonomy of contract mothers. Presumably, self-determination in one's daily activities and in decisions concerning one's medical care and bodily integrity will be central features in any acceptable account of autonomy. Contractual provisions or judicial decisions that allow receiving parents and/or brokers to monitor and control the daily lives and medical decisions of contract mothers for the protection of the fetus would seriously undermine their autonomy. Some proponents of the practice actually advocate that such provisions be required. Others, however, recognize both direct violation of the autonomy of contract mothers and by extension of the policies, an increased threat to the autonomy of all pregnant women and even all fertile women. They suggest that contractual clauses of the sort in question be explicitly prohibited by statute. So motherhood contracts would be legal, but they could not contain any restrictions on the contract mother's activities or medical care nor any provisions for mandatory testing, monitoring, or treatment of the fetus during the pregnancy. I do not think this approach is viable for a couple of reasons.

First, other employees are often required not to smoke or drink, for example, while on the job. What could justify prohibiting such restrictions in the case of the job of contract mother? ...

Second, it might be that courts would not, in the end, uphold contract provisions or judicial orders requiring invasive medical procedures without the actual current consent of the contract mother. However, recent decisions in cases not involving contract motherhood are not reassuring, and as I suggested above, such decisions would be far more likely in cases where intended receiving parent(s) were seeking such orders for the protection of "their" future baby. Here again, the unequal social and economic resources available to the parties would be an important factor.

Thus, respect for women's autonomy does not entail permitting the practice of contract motherhood. Indeed, the practice poses several serious threats to women's autonomy.

## Conclusion

Taken together, the considerations, concerns and arguments offered above persuade me that, in our existing and foreseeable social context, the practice of commercial contract motherhood is morally and politically unacceptable. Moreover, no system of regulation can adequately address all of the compelling objections to the practice. … We saw repeatedly above that attempts to address one sort of objection by regulatory means inevitably exacerbated other concerns. For example, to address the exploitation objection by mandating higher pay for contract mothers would increase concerns both about the money constituting an undue inducement and about the high cost limiting access to the most affluent in a class stratified society. Addressing the exploitation and undue inducement objections by rejecting poor women as contract mothers discriminates against them, violates their autonomy, and denies what proponents insist is a relatively attractive occupational option to those in greatest need. Attempts to reduce the risks to all parties of the pains and possible lasting harms of broken or regretted agreements by mandating screening and counseling of potential contract mothers and intended receiving parents raise concerns about violation of autonomy and reproductive freedom and about discrimination against potential receiving parents not in traditional heterosexual couples. Attempting to prevent contract mothers from losing autonomy by restricting or prohibiting contractual provisions concerning their behavior while pregnant are themselves subject to the charge of paternalism and are unlikely to be legally sustainable. Further, administering any regulatory scheme would entail substantial expense, and it is difficult to see how government could justify expenditures to facilitate or regulate the creation of genetically related infants for those who want them, while existing children in need of homes might be placed if the resources were used to make it economically feasible for willing persons to take them in. In addition, if such resources were spent on the measures needed for *prevention* of infertility, they would more equitably benefit all who want to be parents, not just those who can afford the commercial fees (and, as we saw above, would serve other pressing social needs, as well.)

I conclude that commercial contract motherhood should be expressly prohibited. Commercial brokering should be a criminal offense. Paid private contracts should be void and unenforceable, and the parties subject to civil penalties.[38] Unpaid private agreements can be carried out legally under existing adoption law, but government should avoid promoting or endorsing the practice. (If it is carried out among strangers, the complete alienation of birthmother from child is still likely to be a common feature of the practice. Without governmental facilitation, it is more likely to be carried out among family and friends with some ongoing relationship possible.) Based on the degree of actual involvement with the fetus during pregnancy, there should be a strong presumption at the time of birth and for at least the first three months in favor of birthmother's custody in case of dispute, whether or not the birthmother is also the genetic mother. Finally, the measures outlined above for prevention of infertility should receive high social priority.

---

## Notes

An earlier version of this paper was presented at the American Philosophical Association Eastern Division meetings, Washington, DC, December 1988. I am deeply indebted to the commentator, Iris Young. ... I also want to thank the participants in the discussion at that session. I have benefitted from discussions with and comments by many people, including the participants in a faculty/guest discussion group that met regularly during the Spring 1988 semester at Rutgers, New Brunswick; participants in a graduate seminar on Feminist Ethics and Reproductive Practices I conducted at Rutgers in the Fall 1988 semester; the members and staff of the Task Force on Reproductive Practices of the New Jersey Commission on Legal and Ethical Issues in the Delivery of Health Care (the Task Force met approximately once a month from Spring 1988 through November 1990); participants in the Center for the Critical Analysis of Contemporary Culture, Rutgers University, 1988–89; and the participants in a presentation/discussion October 1990 in the Rutgers Philosophy Department's Colloquium series. The Rutgers University Research Council provided a grant that covered some photocopying and telephone costs associated with this project. Individuals (some in the above-mentioned groups and some not) I especially want to thank are Barbara Andolsen, Adrienne Asche, Sarah Boone, Martin Bunzl, Mary Sue Henifin, Nancy Holmstrom, Helen Holmes, Alison Jaggar, Howard McGary, Anne Reichman, Fadlou Shehadi, Lee Silver, Nadine Taub, Alan Weisbard, Bruce Wilshire, and Linda Zerilli.

1. Indeed, in the first case to receive widespread public attention, that of "Baby M," Elizabeth Stern, the intended receiving mother, was presumably not infertile, but had decided not to bear a child because she believed that she had multiple sclerosis and that pregnancy and childbirth would likely exacerbate her condition.

2. Others argue that there should be no restrictions on who can be a party to such a contract, just as there are no controls on who can become a parent by means of sexual intercourse.

3. Nadine Taub, "Surrogacy: A Preferred Treatment for Infertility?" *Law, Medicine & Health Care* 16 (Spring 1988) p. 90.

4. In all classes, domestic work and childrearing are regarded as primarily women's responsibilities (though more affluent women can often hire other women to do some of it). Some proponents and most opponents of contract motherhood see it as yet another way in which more privileged women can relegate some of "their" responsibilities to other women who have fewer options and opportunities.

5. Note, by the way, that if a fetus is deemed a person from the moment of conception (or at any time during pregnancy), the role of the gestating mother in the creation/development of the person it may become is completely denied (or correspondingly diminished).

6. See Eleanor J. Bader, "'Father's Rights'—What's Next?" *Guardian: Independent Radical Newsweekly*, June 1, 1988; Linda Kahn, "Fetus Died; Mother Prosecuted," *New Directions for Women*, 16 (January-February 1987); Jennifer Terry, "The Body Invaded: Medical Surveillance of Women as Reproducers," *Socialist Review*, 19 (July-September 1989) pp. 13–43.

7. Peter H. Schuck, "Some Reflections on the *Baby M* Case," *The Georgetown Law Journal*, 76:1793–1810, p. 1802.

8. Steven E. Perkel, "Infertility, Self-Esteem, Sex-Role Identity, Psychopathology, and the Social Meaning of Parenthood," Presentation to Task Force of Reproductive Practices of the New Jersey Commission on Ethical and Legal Problems in the Delivery of Health Care (hereafter, NJ Bioethics Comm TF), June 1, 1988. See also Deborah Gerson, "Infertility and the Construction of Desperation," *Socialist Review,* 19 (July-September 1989) pp. 45–64.

9. Adrienne Asche and Anne Reichman, NJ Bioethics Commission staff report to Task Force.

10. cf. Michelle Stanworth, "Reproductive Technologies and the Deconstruction of Motherhood," in *Reproductive Technologies: Gender, Motherhood and Medicine,* ed. Michelle Stanworth (Minneapolis: University of Minnesota Press, 1987).

11. Often the rationale for this quest on the part of receiving parents, adoptive parents, and parents of children conceived by AID is (a) that having "extra" parents in the picture would make childrearing decisions hopelessly complicated because of potential disagreements among the several parents, and (b) that it would introduce potential rivals for a child's affections. This rationale seems to ignore the fact that, even in the mythical "normal" family, there is more than one parent (both of whom have legal standing to make decisions on the child's behalf, which would not necessarily be the case for the "extra" parent). These two parents may disagree about important childrearing decisions and/or compete for a child's affections. In addition, there are generally an assortment of grandparents, aunts and uncles, child-care workers, teachers, close friends and neighbors any of whom may seek to participate in childrearing decisions and/or become (or be viewed) as rivals for a child's affections. When we consider as well the variety of blended families, joint custody arrangements, single parent families, gay and lesbian parent families, and so on, the notion of a "normal" family in which childrearing decisions are uncomplicated and affections unrivaled appears both unrealistic and an inadequate basis for severing all contact. (The threat to lesbian mothers of losing custody to an AID father is, however, very real in our heterosexist, patriarchal society.) There is an encouraging trend toward more openness in adoption; see Jeanne Warren Lindsay, *Open Adoption: A Caring Option* Buena Park, CA: Morning Glory Press, 1987).

12. According to anthropologist Catherine A. Lutz in *Unnatural Emotions* (Chicago: University of Chicago Press, 1988), on the Micronesian atoll of Ifaluk and neighboring islands, there is a practice that somewhat resembles, but is importantly different from each of the U.S. practices of adoption, (non-commercial) contract motherhood, and the informal extended family system in the African American community described by Carol Stack in *All Our Kin* (New York: Harper & Row, 1975). Nearly every household on Ifaluk has "adopted" children (Lutz, p. 132) and 40% of all children over five years of age are "adopted" (Lutz, p. 161). Children are offered for "adoption" by families with both parents living, for it is considered an act of generosity and caring to offer a child to a couple who "needs" one. Common reasons for "adoption" include "barren" marriages, the death of a child, and the desire to have children of both genders (important because of the complementarity of gender roles between brothers and sisters) (Lutz, pp. 132–3). It is a matter of course that contact and caring continue between adopted children and their biological parents.

13. cf. Martha E. Gimenez, "Feminism, Pronatalism, and Motherhood," in Joyce Trebilcot, ed., *Mothering: Essays in Feminist Theory* (Totowa, NJ: Rowman & Allanheld, 1984) pp. 287–314.

14. Adoption of Black children by white families is strongly opposed by the National Association of Black Social Workers (Statement by President William T. Merritt at Hearings of Senate Committee on Labor and Human Resources, June 25, 1985. National Association of Black Social Workers, 271 West 125th Street, New York, NY 10027).

15. It has been argued, in defense of contract motherhood, that racism itself would preclude this: "racially or ethnically privileged groups will not rush to have their children borne by members of despised minorities" (Christine T. Sistare, "Reproductive Freedom and Women's Freedom: Surrogacy and Autonomy," *The Philosophical Forum,* 14 [Summer 1988]: 227–240, p.

234). But, in addition to the advantage in potential custody disputes, note that slave owners and others had no objections to having their infants cared for and breast fed by members of despised minorities. Given the attitude, inherent in contract motherhood, that gestation is merely a service, any healthy woman should do just fine. ...

16. cf. Virginia Held criticizes such a view in "Non-contractual Society: A Feminist View" in Marsha Hanen and Kai Nielsen, eds. *Science, Morality & Feminist Theory* (*Canadian Journal of Philosophy* Supplementary Volume 13, 1987) p. 122.

17. Philip J. Parker, "Motivation of Surrogate Mothers: Initial Findings," *American Journal of Psychiatry* 140 (January 1983), 118. ...

18. Consider that Mary Beth Whitehead asked William Stern to recommend an attorney to represent her in the case that Stern had brought against her for custody of their child. For an incisive and insightful analysis of the class and gender biases at work in the testimony of the expert witnesses in the trial, see Michelle Harrison, "Social Construction of Mary Beth Whitehead," *Gender & Society* 1 (September 1987) pp. 300–311.

19. Adrienne Asche and Anne Reichman, "Surrogacy Matching Services: Field Trips," Staff Report to New Jersey Bioethics Commission New Reproductive Practices Task Force, December 7, 1988. ...

20. Unless they are permitted a continuing role in the life of the family. I have heard of one case in which a paid contract mother has a continuing relationship with the child and the receiving parents (conversation with Nadine Taub 12/88). It will become evident below, if it has not already, that I take the alienation of the birthmother from the contracted child as a central feature of contract motherhood in our society. Several, though not all, of my objections would be eliminated or mitigated if this feature were absent.

21. Since the infant does not yet exist, indeed, has not yet been conceived, at the time of the original contract, it is the *attitude* of the adults toward a possible child-to-be that is exploitative at that time. Actual exploitation awaits the birth of an actual child.

22. In the most general terms, it might be objected that the account of exploitation is so broad that, at least in a capitalist or profit-driven market society such as ours, virtually everyone exploits and is exploited by others most of the time. When people transact business in the marketplace, each is out simply to maximize his or her own returns and regards others merely as competitors or as means. It would seem to follow that either all of market society, not just contract motherhood, should be condemned or my account of exploitation is seriously flawed by being overly broad. Either way, the case against contract motherhood as exploitative fails to distinguish it from other practices widely regarded in our society as perfectly legitimate. But I do not agree that market relations are, in themselves, incompatible with treating others as ends in themselves (as well as means to one's own ends). That we officially recognize rules against fraud, coercion, misrepresentation, price-fixing, gouging, etc., is evidence that we regard respect for the personhood of others as constraining acceptable market behavior. At the same time, the degree, and it is substantial, to which participants in our society violate (often with impunity) standards of treatment required by full respect for personhood does constitute grounds for serious criticism of many aspects of our society.

23. e.g., Lori Andrews, "Alternative Modes of Reproduction," *Reproductive Laws for the 1990s: A Briefing Handbook,* ed. by Sherrill Cohen and Nadine Taub, (New Brunswick, NJ: Rutgers University, 1989); ... Laura Purdy, "Surrogate Mothering: Exploitation or Empowerment?" *Bioethics* 3 (January 1989) pp. 18–34; Sistare.

24. Proposed regulatory schemes are enormously varied and often mutually contradictory. Some, e.g., would provide a waiting period after birth when the contract mother could change her mind about relinquishing the child; others would require specific enforcement of the agreement to turn over the child so that the parties would know exactly what they were getting into. Some would prohibit any attempts to control the contract mother's behavior during pregnancy and childbirth; others would strictly regulate her behavior and give control over her medical care to the intended receiving parent(s) or the broker. Some would require careful

psychological screening and counseling. It would be a long and tedious job to consider and respond to all the possible permutations of these proposals. ...

25. Proponents of the practice who favor a free-market rather than regulatory approach respond to this concern with the assurance that, as the practice becomes more widespread and availability increases, the price will come down. This, of course, just intensifies the exploitative potential and raises again the prospect of super-exploitation of women of color and an international traffic in contract mothers (or their babies, if gametes, embryos and infants are transported instead of women).
...

26. Others would be gladiator, live organ and body-part source, and contract slave or indentured servant. (I would include on this list many jobs that currently exist in our society as well.)

27. For an interesting account of changes in the economic and sentimental value placed on children in the U.S. between the 1870s and the 1930s, see *Pricing the Priceless Child: The Changing Social Value of Children* (New York: Basic Books, 1985).

28. There are differences: 24 hours a day, no breaks, etc., that make it hard to take it seriously as a job that can be appropriately regulated in terms of existing labor law.

29. Some agencies show potential receiving parents albums with pictures of applicants *and their existing children.* Some hold gatherings where several potential receiving parents can meet and look over the available contract mother applicants.

30. David M. Brodzinsky, "Adjustment to Adoption: A Psychosocial Perspective," *Clinical psychology Review* 7 (1987) pp. 25–47.

31. Adrienne Asch, Report to Task Force on AID.

32. Contract children also bear increased risk of being rejected if they are born impaired.

33. See, e.g., Elizabeth Kane, *BirthMother* (New York: Harcourt Brace Jovanovich, 1988).

34. So it is when employers control every aspect of the work process to get full benefit of the labor power they have bought and to control the quality of the product, at the same time, fragmenting the work process, and thereby ignoring skills and disempowering the worker.

35. If neither commodification nor this total alienation of birthmother and child were involved, most of my objections to the practice would be eliminated. There would remain many potential difficulties, of course.

36. Barbara Andolsen, "Why a Surrogate Mother Should Have the Right to Change her Mind" in Herbert Richardson, ed., *On the Problem of Surrogate Parenthood: Analyzing the Baby M Case* (Lewiston, NY: Edwin Mellen Press, 1987) p. 50.

37. Suppose you had consented to be a kidney donor and then changed your mind; could they say "Sorry, you gave a valid consent; you were competent, informed, and not coerced; therefore, you must go through with it?"

38. The rationale for supporting criminal penalties for brokers but not for contract mothers or intended receiving parents is that the former promote the practice and profit from the commodification of some and the exploitation of all the others involved, while the latter act in response to personal vulnerability, pain and desperation.

# Children by Donor Insemination:
# A New Choice for Lesbians

## Francie Hornstein

…

My decision to conceive a child by donor insemination was a long time coming. It was nearly seven years between the time I first considered the possibility and when I began trying to get pregnant. The one recurring reservation in what had become a passionate desire to have children was my fear for how the children would cope with being from a different kind of family.

I knew I would be sorry if I never had children; sorry not only for giving up a part of life I really wanted, but for not making a decision that I believed was right. I felt I was as worthy of having children as any other person. To not have children simply because I was a lesbian would have been giving up on a goal that was very dear to me.

…

I first tried donor insemination in 1973, while I was working at the Feminist Women's Health Center in Los Angeles, I was unable to use the services of the sperm bank because they would only accept married women as candidates for insemination. It was difficult finding donors and I was absorbed in long hours of work in the women's health movement, so the work involved in my getting pregnant was shelved for a few years. With the help of my co-workers and the encouragement of my lover, I finally began trying to get pregnant in 1977.

I think it was significant that I was working at the Feminist Women's Health Center at the time I got pregnant. It seemed particularly fitting that the same women who developed the practice of menstrual extraction, a procedure which could be used for early abortion, also were among the pioneers in the practice of self-help donor insemination. We figured if we could safely help a woman end her pregnancy without the help of physicians and patriarchal laws, we could certainly help women get pregnant.

…

Finding donors was the most difficult part of the whole process for me. At the time I got pregnant, there was only one sperm bank in the city. It was owned and operated by a physician who had a private infertility practice and who was very conservative in selecting his clientele. He declined to make his services available to women who were not married, not to mention lesbians.

The only option open to us at the time was to find donors through our friends. I wanted to be able to give the children the option of knowing their father, so we preferred a situation in which the donor was known either to us or to a friend. Eventually, we were able to find donors.

The insemination itself was simple. All we had to do was have the donor ejaculate into a clean container, draw up the semen into a clean syringe (with the needle removed) and inject it into the vagina. We already knew how to do vaginal self-examination with a speculum, so we were familiar with the anatomy of the cervix, the opening of the uterus where the sperm needs to be put. Other women we later spoke with who didn't have access to medical supplies, such as syringes, improvised with common household items. A turkey baster, now synonymous with self-help insemination, works just fine. One innovative woman had her donor ejaculate into a condom, then she simply turned the condom inside-out in her vagina. Some women either insert a diaphragm or cervical cap to hold the semen near the cervix or they lie down for a half-hour or so after inserting the semen.

After our son was born, in the fall of 1978, my lover and I were asked to talk about our experiences at a variety of feminist conferences and programs. ... The majority of women we have met who have had children by donor insemination are lesbians, though there is now a growing number of single, heterosexual women who are choosing donor insemination as a way of getting pregnant. Some of these women prefer being single, but want to have children; others haven't yet met men they want to live with or have children with, but because of their age or other reasons, don't want to wait for marriage before having children.

Several feminist health groups have begun making donor insemination available to women who ordinarily would not be able to use the services of sperm banks. ...

...

One thing the feminist health services have in common with one another is their attempt to demedicalize the procedure of donor insemination. In most instances, physicians do not perform the insemination. Although the feminist health workers are willing to assist their clients who ask for their help, they prefer to provide the information so that women can do the insemination themselves, most often with the help of lovers or friends.

The intention on the part of feminist health services who provide donor insemination is less a desire to branch out into additional services but rather a strong political statement in support of a woman's right to make her own reproductive decisions. ... In discussing women's rights to make reproductive decisions, the positive impact of self-help donor insemination cannot be underestimated. But the practice does not exist in isolation and carries its fair share of potential problems and unanswered questions.

A woman deciding to have children on her own terms and without the inclusion of an on-site father is seen as attacking the traditional notion of a proper family. In spite of the fact that a large proportion of children end up living with their mothers

only, it remains more threatening to patriarchy for a woman to *choose* to set up such an arrangement than to merely end up that way as a result of divorce, desertion or death.
...

... We must all decide what to tell our children about their fathers. Our families, who may not share our feminist perspectives yet whose attachments we don't want to lose, often find it difficult to accept our lesbian families and our decisions to have children. Our children may well want to have contact or relationships with their fathers (in the event that they are known and can be located). We need to establish and protect the rights of partners of lesbians who may not be biological parents of the child, but who may be parents in every other sense of the word. And what do we do when a known donor who, after the baby is born, has a change of heart and wants more of a relationship with the child than was his original intention? These are all real issues that have and will continue to come up.
...

I think it is unwise and dishonest to gloss over many of the complex issues involved in donor insemination. Serious consideration and care must be taken for our children as they grow. Our children are not subjects in a social experiment but human beings with feelings whom we deeply love. There needs to be continuous support for mothers and for the rights of non-biological mothers who are part of the children's lives. We need to recognize the interests of the donors. But in the midst of trying to carve out new ways of doing things in an ethical way, we should also take joy in the fact that we have broken new ground. We have created new and important life choices for many people. We have taken back a little more of what is rightly ours—the chance to make decisions about how we will live our lives.

---

## Bibliography of Related Articles

Annas, George J. 1978. 'Artificial Insemination: Beyond the Best Interests of the Donor.' Hastings Center Report, August. A look at the legal aspects of donor insemination with emphasis on unanswered questions for the recipient of the sperm and for the child born as a result of the insemination.

'Artificial Insemination Packet.' 1981. Available from Lesbian Mother National Defense Fund, P.O. Box 21567, Seattle, Washington, 98111; $3. A collection of articles that cover the 'how to' medical and legal aspects of donor insemination.

Hitchens, Donna J. 1981. 'Lesbians Choosing Motherhood: Legal Implications of Donor Insemination.' Available from Lesbian Rights Project, 1370 Mission Street, San Francisco, CA. 94103; $1.50 incl. postage. An article describing the legal implications of donor insemination (custody, child support, visitation, and nomination of a guardian) with a focus on the special problems encountered by lesbians. The article discusses the benefits and risks of doing one's own insemination, using a known donor and entering into a contract with the donor. Also included are sample (1) donor-mother agreement; (2) nomination of a guardian for the child; (3) agreement for co-mothers; and (4) will provision for nominating a guardian.

Hornstein, Francie. 1974. 'Lesbian Health Care.' Available from the Feminist Women's Health Center, 6411 Hollywood Boulevard, L.A., CA. 90028. A first-person narrative outlining the issues of lesbian health care in the context of the feminist movement. Includes a section on options for lesbians who want children. Since this article was written in 1974, it is now more an interesting piece of history rather than an up-to-date monograph.

Kritchevsky, Barbara. 1981. 'The Unmarried Woman's Right to Artificial Insemination: A Call for an Expanded Definition of Family.' *Harvard Women's Law Journal*, 1. An excellent and comprehensive article on the legal implications of donor insemination. The only resource that pulls together cases and statutes on artificial insemination.

'Self-Insemination.' 1980. Available from the Feminist Self-Insemination Group, P.O. Box No. 3, 190 Upper Street, London, N1, United Kingdom; £2.00.

Stern, Susan. 180. 'Lesbian Insemination.' *Co-Evolution Quarterly*, Summer. Accounts of several lesbians conceiving by donor insemination and the gay men donating sperm to them.

Sutton, B. 1980. 'The Lesbian Family: Rights in Conflict Under the CH Uniform Parentage Act.' 10 *Golden Gate Law Review*, 1007. How the rights of a lesbian mother might be limited where there is a known donor. The first article that discusses the legal implications of artificial insemination for lesbians.

# The Facts of Fatherhood

## Thomas W. Laqueur

This essay puts forward a labor theory of parenthood in which emotional work counts. I want to say at the onset, however, that it is not intended as a nuanced, balanced academic account of fatherhood or its vicissitudes. I write it in a grumpy, polemical mood.

In the first place I am annoyed that we lack a history of fatherhood, a silence which I regard as a sign of a more systemic pathology in our understanding of what being a man and being a father entail. ...

Second, I write in the wake of Baby M and am annoyed with the neo-essentialism it has spawned. Baby M was the case of the decade in my circles, a "representative anecdote" for ancient but ageless questions in the late twentieth century. Like most people, I saw some right on both sides and had little sympathy for the marketplace in babies that brought them together. On the one hand Mary Beth Whitehead this ... ; on the other William Stern that ... The baby broker who arranged the deal was manifestly an unsavory character, the twentieth-century avatar of the sweatshop owners who in ages past profited unconscionably from the flesh of women. It was difficult not to subscribe to the doctrine that the baby's best interests must come first and it was by no means consistently clear where these lay. Each day brought new emotional tugs as the narrative unfolded on the front pages of every paper.

I was surprised that, for so many people, this transaction between a working-class woman and a professional man (a biochemist) became an epic prism through which the evils of capitalism and class society were refracted. It did not seem newsworthy to me that the poor sold their bodies or that the rich exploited their willingness to do so. What else would they sell? Malthus had pointed out almost two centuries ago that those who labored physically gave of their flesh and in the long run earned just enough to maintain and replenish it. So had Marx, who also identified women as the agents of social re-production.

...

I am, however, primarily interested in this case as the occasion for a return to naturalism. Feminism has been the most powerful de-naturalizing theoretical force in my intellectual firmament and, more generally, a major influence in the academic and cultural affairs that concern me. I regarded it as both true and liberating that "the idea that men and women are two mutually exclusive categories must arise out of something other than a nonexistent 'natural' opposition," and that "gender is a socially imposed division of the sexes."[1] A major strand of commentary on Baby M, however, rejects this tradition and instead insists that the category "mother" is natural, a given of the world outside culture. Phyllis Chesler, for example, in the major article of a special "Mothers" issue of *Ms* (May, 1988) argues that motherhood is a "fact," an ontologically different category than "fatherhood," which is an "idea." Thus, "in order for the *idea* [my emphasis] of fatherhood to triumph over the *fact* of motherhood," she says, "we had to see Bill as the 'birth father' and Mary Beth as the surrogate uterus." (Actually Chesler misstates the claims. Mary Beth has been, rightly or wrongly, called the "surrogate mother," not the "surrogate uterus." But since the point of the article seems to be that mother and uterus are more or less the same thing this may be an intentional prevarication.)

I resist this view for obvious emotional reasons: it assumes that being the "factual" parent entails a stronger connection to the child than being the "ideational" parent. (This assumption is widespread. During my daughter Hannah's five-week stay in the preemie nursery her caretakers, in the "social comments" column of her chart, routinely recorded my wife's visits to her incubator as "mother in to bond," whereas my appearances were usually noted with the affectively neutral "father visited.") While I do not want to argue against the primacy of material connection directly I do want to point out that it is not irrational to hold the opposite view and that, "in fact," the incorporeal quality of fatherhood has been the foundation of patriarchy's ideological edifice since the Greeks. In other words, simply stating that mothers have a greater material connection with the child is not to make an argument but to state a premise which historically has worked against Chesler's would-be conclusion. The Western philosophical tradition has generally valued idea over matter; manual labor for millennia was the great horizontal social divide. In other words, precisely because the mother's claim was "only" corporeal, because it was a matter of "fact," it was valued less.

I ... want to argue against [a] basic operating assumption [of this discourse]: the unproblematic nature of fact especially in relation to such deeply cultural designations as mother or father and to the rights, emotions, or duties that are associated with them. The "facts" of motherhood—and of fatherhood for that matter—are not "given" but come into being as science progresses and as the adversaries in political struggles select what they need from the vast, ever-growing storehouses of knowledge. The idea that a child is of one's flesh and blood is very old while its biological correlatives and their cultural importance depend on the available supplies of fact and on their interpretation.

... Laws, customs, and precepts, sentiments, emotion, and the power of the imagination make biological facts assume cultural significance. An Algonquin chief, confronted by a Jesuit in the seventeenth century with the standard European argument against women's promiscuity (how else would you know that a child is yours?), replied that he found it puzzling that whites could apparently only love "their" children, i.e., that only individual ownership entailed caring and affection.

Before proceeding I want to again warn my readers that some of my evidence and most of my passion arise from personal circumstance. I write as the father of a daughter to whom I am bound by the "facts" of a visceral love, not the molecular biology of reproduction. The fact of the matter is that from the instant the five-minute-old Hannah—a premature baby of 1430 grams who was born by Caesarean section—grasped my finger (I know this was due to reflex and not affection) I felt immensely powerful, and before the event, inconceivably strong bonds with her. ...

... [I also write] as the male member of a family in which gender roles are topsy turvy. Hannah early on announced that she would prefer being a daddy to being a mommy because mommies had to go to work—hers is a lawyer—while daddies only had to go to their study. ... I am far guiltier of the stereotypical vices of motherhood—neurotic worry about Hannah's physical and mental well being, unfounded premonitions of danger, excessive emotional demands, and general nudginess—than is Gail. In short, my experiences—ignoring for the moment a vast ethnographic and somewhat smaller historical literature—make me suspect of the naturalness of "mother" or "father" in any culturally meaningful sense.

...

The "fact" of motherhood is precisely the psychic labor that goes into making these [emotional] connections, into appropriating the fetus and then child into a mother's moral and emotional economy. The "fact" of fatherhood is of a like order. If a labor theory of value gives parents rights to a child, that labor is of the heart, not the hand. (The heart, of course, does its work through the hand; we feel through the body. But I will let the point stand in its polemical nakedness.)

While I was working as a volunteer in an old people's home I was attracted to, and ultimately became rather good friends with, a gay woman who was its director of activities. At lunch one day—she had alerted me that she wanted to discuss "something" and not just, as we usually did, schmooz—she asked whether I would consider donating sperm should she and her long-time lover decide, as they were on the verge of doing, to have a child. I was for her a generally appropriate donor—Jewish, fit, with no history of genetic disorders in my family. She was asking me also, she said, because she liked me. It was the first, and remains the only, time I had been asked by anyone, much less someone I liked, and so I was flattered and pleased.

I was also hesitant. My wife the lawyer raised serious legal difficulties with donating "owned" sperm, i.e., sperm that is not given or sold for anonymous distribution. I would remain legally liable for child-support for at least twenty-one years, not to speak of being generally entangled with the lives of a couple I liked but did not know well. (Anonymous sperm is alienated from its producer and loses its connection with him as if it were the jetsam and flotsam of the sea or an artisan's product in the marketplace. Semen, in other words, counts as one of these products of the body that can be alienated, like plasma and blood cells, and not like kidneys or eyes, whose marketing is forbidden.)

Legal issues, however, did not weigh heavily with me. The attractive part of the proposition—that I was being asked because of who I was and therefore that I was to be a father and not just a donor—also weighed mightily against it. A thought experiment with unpleasant results presented itself. I immediately imagined this would-be child as a version of Hannah, imagined that I could see her only occasionally and for short periods of time, imagined that her parents would take her back to their native Israel and that I would never see her again. Potential conflicts with my friend about this baby were almost palpable on the beautiful sunny afternoon of our lunch. In short, I was much too cathexed with this imaginary child to ever give up the sperm to produce her.

I recognize now, and did at the time, that my response was excessive. My reveries of fatherhood sprang from a fetishistic attachment to one among millions of rapidly replenished microscopic organisms—men make on the order of 400 billion sperm in a lifetime—swimming in an abundant, nondescript saline fluid. All that I was really being asked to do was to "produce" some semen—a not unpleasant process—and to give it to my friend so that *a* very, very tiny sperm—actually only its 4–5 micrometers long and 2.5 to 3.5 micrometers wide (c. 1/10,000 to 1/20,000 of an inch) head—might contribute the strands of DNA wafting about in it to her egg. Since we humans apparently share 95% of our genetic material with chimpanzees, the sperm in question must share a still higher percentage of base pairs with those of my fellow humans. In short, my unique contribution to the proposed engagement, that which I did not share with billions of other men and monkeys, was infinitesimally small. I was making a mountain out of much, much, much less than a molehill and not very much more than a molecule.

But this is as it should be. For much of history the problem has been to make men take responsibility for their children. Prince and pauper as circumstances required could easily deny the paternity that nature did so little to make evident. The double standard of sexual morality served to insure that however widely they sowed their wild oats the fruits of their wives' wombs would be unambiguously theirs. In fact, until very recently paternity was impossible to prove and much effort went into developing histo-immunological assays that could establish the biological link between a specific man and child. The state, of course, has an interest in making some male, generally the "biological father," responsible for supporting "his" children. In short, a great deal of cultural work has gone into giving meaning to a small bit of matter. ironically, now that tests make it possible to identify the father with about 100% accuracy, women—those who want children *without* a father—have considerable difficulty obtaining sperm free of filiation. History, social policy, imagination, and culture continue to encumber this cell with its haploid of chromosomes.

...

... The legal status of a sperm donor remains deeply problematic and, advises a National Lawyers Guild Handbook, those "consulted by a lesbian considering artificial insemination must be extremely careful to explain the ramifications of the various choices available to their clients."[2] Using a medically supervised sperm bank where the identity of the donor is unknown to the recipient is the most certain way to guarantee that the donor will not at some time in the future be construed as the father. Other possibilities include having a friend secure semen but keeping the source secret; using semen from multiple donors (not recommended because of possible immune reactions); using a known donor but having a physician as intermediary. Some lawyers recommend having the recipient pay the donor for his sperm and describing the transaction in an ordinary commercial contract of the sort with which the courts are familiar. And even if agreements between sperm donors and recipients are not predictably enforceable, lawyers suggest that the parties set down their understanding of their relationship as clearly as possible.

...

... Selling sperm at a price fixed by contract—the lawyer or sperm bank owner as de-blessing agent—would take off some of its paternal blush. Without such rites, a father's material claim in his child is small but his imaginative claims can be as endless as a mother's. Great care must be taken to protect and not to squash them.

Because fatherhood is an "idea," it is not limited to men. In a recent case litigated in Alameda County, California (Lofton v. Flouroy), a woman was, rightly in my view, declared to be a child's father, if not its male parent. Ms. Lofton and Ms. Flouroy lived together and decided to have a child. Lofton's brother Larry donated the required sperm but expressed no interest in having any further role in the matter. Ms. Lofton introduced her brother's semen into Flouroy with a turkey baster, Flouroy became pregnant, and in due course a baby was born. The "birth mother" was listed on its birth certificate as "mother," and L. Loften—Linda, not Larry, but who was to know?—was listed as "father."

Everything went well and the women treated the child as theirs until, two years later, they split up. The mother kept the child and there matters might have rested had not ... the State intervened. Flouroy applied for welfare benefits, i.e., aid to dependent children, and when asked by the Family Support Bureau to identify the father she produced, in a moment of unabashed concreteness, the turkey baster. The Bureau, not amused, did what it was meant to do and went after the "father" on the birth certificate—Linda, it was surprised to learn, not Larry. ... She welcomed the opportunity to claim paternity, did not dispute the claim and eagerly paid the judgment entered against her: child support, current and retroactive. She also demanded paternal visitation rights, which Ms. Flouroy resisted. Lofton then asked the court to compel mediation. It held that she was indeed a "psychological parent" and thus had standing to have her rights mediated. The other L. Lofton, Larry, makes no appearance in this drama.

Linda's claim is manifestly not biological nor even material. That she borrowed her brother's sperm or owned the turkey baster is irrelevant. What matters is that, in the emotional economy of her relationship with her lover and their child, she was the father, whatever that means, and enjoyed the rights and bore the obligations of that status. She invested the required emotional and imaginative capital in the impregnation, gestation, and subsequent life to make the child in some measure hers.

I hasten to add that I do not regard biology in all circumstances as counting for nothing. Women have claims with respect to the baby within them simply by virtue of spatial relations and rights to bodily integrity. These are not the right to be or not to be a mother as against the right to be or not to be a father, nor the claims of a person as against those of a non-person—the terms in which the abortion debate is usually put—but the right shared by all mentally competent adults to control and monitor corporeal boundaries, to maintain a body as theirs. Thus I would regard a court compelling a woman to bear a child against her will as a form of involuntary servitude however much its would-be father might wish for the child. And I would regard an enforced abortion as an even more egregious assault on her body. But this is not to acknowledge the "fact" of motherhood as much as the "fact" of flesh. History bears witness to the evils that ensue when the state abrogates a person's rights in her body.

The flesh does not make a mother's body an ahistorical font of motherhood and maternity. A writer who wants, but cannot herself have, a child and who finds surrogate motherhood morally unacceptable "cannot imagine" that "there are plenty of women now, the huge majority of surrogates who have, to hear them tell it, not suffered such a loss [as Mary Beth Whitehead's]."[3] While her empathic instincts extend easily to Whitehead she cannot, despite testimony to the contrary, conceive of a mother *not* feeling an instant and apparently unmediated bond to her child. Ms. Fleming cannot accept that feelings do not follow from flesh so that "surrogate mothers" who feel otherwise than they supposedly should must suffer, like un-class-conscious workers, from false consciousness.

...

What exactly are the facts of motherhood and what of significance ought to follow from them? For advocates of Mrs. Whitehead's, like Phyllis Chesler, her egg and its genetic contents are not especially relevant. She shares with Bill, a.k.a. Dr. Stern, the provision of chromosomes. The critical fact is therefore her nine months of incubation, which would remain a fact even if the fertilized egg she was bringing to term were others. Her claim, it appears, rests on labor, on her physical intimacy with the child within her, and would be just as strong if a second woman sought a stake in the child on the basis of her contribution of half its chromosomes.

I am immensely sympathetic to this view but not because of a fact of nature. Capitalist societies, as I suggested earlier, are not usually friendly to the notion that putting labor into a product entitles one to ownership or even to much credit. It is the rare company that gives its workers shares of stock. We associate a new production of *The Magic Flute* with David Hockney and not with those who sawed, hammered, and painted the sets; everyone knows that Walt Disney produced *Bambi* but only the "cognoscenti" could name even one of the artists who actually made the pictures. Having the idea or the plan is what counts, which is why Judge Sokoloff told Dr. Stern that in getting Melissa he was only getting what was already his. (The Judge should, of course, have said, "half his.")

I became so exercised by Baby M because Dr. Stern's claims have been reduced in some circles to his ownership of his sperm which, as I said earlier, amounts to owning very little. This puts him—all fathers—at a distinct material disadvantage to Mrs. Whitehead—all women—who contribute so much more matter. But, this essay has suggested, his claims, like hers, arise from the intense and profound bonding with a child, unborn and born, that its biological kinship might spark in the moral and affective imagination but which it does not entail.

The problem, of course, is that emotional capital does not accumulate steadily, visibly, and predictably as in a psychic payroll deduction plan. That is why, for example, it is unreasonable to demand of a woman specific performance on a surrogate mothering contract as if the baby were a piece of land or a work of art whose attributes would be well known to their vendor. A "surrogate mother," like a mother who offers to give up her baby for adoption to a stranger, must be allowed a reasonable time to change her mind and if she does, in the case of a surrogacy arrangement, be prepared to argue for her rights against those of the father.

Each parent would bring to such a battle claims to have made another person emotionally part of themselves. "Facts" like bearing the child would obviously be significant evidence but would not be unimpeachable, would not be nature speaking unproblematically to culture. While we can continue to look forward to continuing conflict over the competing claims of parents I suggest that we abandon the notion that biology—facts—will somehow provide the resolution. Neither, of course, will ideas alone in a world in which persons exist corporeally. The way out of the fact/idea dichotomy is to recognize its irrelevance in these matters. The "facts" of such socially powerful and significant categories as mother and father come into being only as culture imbues things, actions, and flesh with meaning. This is the process that demands our continued attention.

---

## Notes

1. Gayle Rubin, "The Traffic in Women: Notes on the 'Political Economy' of Sex," in Rayna Reiter, ed., *Toward an Anthropology of Women* (New York: Monthly Review Press, 1975) pp. 179–180.

2. Roberta Achtenberg, ed., *Sexual Orientation and the Law* (New York: Clark, Boardman, Co. Ltd., 1989) section 1–70.

3. Anne Taylor Fleming, "Our Fascination with Baby M," *New York Times Magazine*, March 29, 1987, p. 87. There were at the time of this article about one thousand known "surrogate mothers."

# The Politics of Childlessness

## Karen Lindsey

Before I got sterilized, at the age of 27, people told me I was crazy. I would ruin my life; I would regret my unalterable decision; I would feel like less of a woman. I would meet Mr. Right and my womb would start yearning to carry his child. After the terrible deed was done, I got another reaction: people kept asking me how I felt now that I had done it, and wasn't I worried about its effect on future relationships with men? The answers were disappointingly undramatic. I felt relieved that I had done it. Not ecstatic. Not despondent. Relieved. The dreary possibility that I might have to deal with an abortion or an adoption was gone: in a world of constant uncertainty, I had carved out one little piece of security for myself. As to how it would change my relationships with men, it wouldn't. I feel a moral obligation to tell any man I become involved with that I will never have children. Ten years ago, I felt the same obligation.

And here is the point that so easily gets missed by those who have trouble dealing with the concept of a childless woman getting sterilized. Sterilization is not the issue at all; it is only an act arising out of the real issue—the commitment to remain childless. This commitment scares people to death—scares them so much, in fact, that they often refuse to take it seriously until it is backed up by an unalterable act like sterilization. The very terminology of non-reproduction reflects a fear of dealing with childlessness: "family planning," "birth control." People who use contraceptives are not planning a family, they are planning, at least temporarily, *not* to have a family. They are not simply controlling birth; they are preventing it. If you plan to have a child in five years, you plan *not* to have one until then. But to emphasize that hints at the unthinkable possibility of choosing *never* to have children. This society persists in regarding childless people—especially women—as pathetic outcasts unable to have what they really want; and it reinforces this image by a system of rewards both tangible and mythological. The person who commits herself to childlessness by voluntarily ending her reproductive capacity flies in the face of the myth of womanly fulfillment through motherhood that patriarchy needs to sustain itself.

I don't mean, of course, to suggest that all women really want to be childless. But I do think that a lot more would choose that option if it were really open to them, if the kinds of emotional brainwashing and blackmailing built into the system didn't exist. I suggest that parenthood—by which I mean the commitment to assume the major responsibility in the rearing of a child or children—is a vocation similar to surgery, psychotherapy, social work, nursing. It requires an incredible amount of skill and a specific type of temperament that many people don't have. The lack of such skill is no more shameful than the inability to perform surgery or fix a drainpipe. Parenting is hard enough when both the skill and desire is there; when one or both are lacking, both parent and child are going to suffer, and suffer badly. ...

The old age argument is especially sinister. The idea of children as a kind of insurance policy against abandonment is a horrifying view of child-as-object: the obligation of a child to its parents becomes not the natural outgrowth of mutual caring but an end in itself. Since our society provides little care for its elderly, it is also a very real temptation. ... Capitalism, of course, thrives on such enforced insecurity. The old are provided for neither socially nor economically. The emotional blackmail is buttressed by stark economic threat: if you're old and haven't saved a fortune, you're going to have a grim existence indeed without a family to take care of you.

The capitalist ethic ... pervades the whole family mystique, (though it is not its sole source, and I think radicals who over-romanticize the extended biological family do the movement a great disservice, since such a family still emphasizes sex roles and the central importance of procreation). But the patriarchy does have its specific set of rules in capitalist America. Mothers who work, even if economically obliged to do so, are made to feel guilty for it, and women who play the housewife/mommy game when they are unhappy with it become the consumers who fill the empty spaces of their lives with toilet bowl cleaners and cosmetics, and give their children Pampers and expensive toys in place of the warmth they often cannot give. For both working mothers and housewives, the maintenance of a feeling of inadequacy is essential: without this low-key neurosis, they might begin to question their lives. Neurosis is built in to the capitalist foundation: a mentally healthy (not "adjusted") society would soon become a revolutionary one.

The most socially acceptable political argument for voluntary sterilization or childlessness has been population control, and it's one I don't buy. If I wanted children, I'd have them—maybe I'd have one or two instead of six or seven, but I'd have them. While population control *is* an important issue, it's dangerous to encourage women to find an altruistic excuse for a legitimately self-fulfilling decision. Control over one's own body and one's own life is the real political question: the assertion that there are options and that a woman has a right to choose among them is profoundly revolutionary. Choosing to remain childless (whether or not this decision is implemented surgically) has the same kind of political significance as open lesbianism: it is a declaration against the patriarchal structure of the nuclear family. (It is also, like lesbianism, a rejection of reproductive sexuality as the only legitimate sexual base and as such, calls down the same accusations of "unnatural"—you're not quite a woman if you don't have a man or a child or want one.) And, as it is essential that we question our own sexuality, it is also essential that we question our feelings about parenthood. To choose parenthood is a perfectly valid and decent decision, given the desire and skills for the job. Deciding not to have children may be a harder choice, but it is a necessary option, and it is important not only to respect those who have made it, but to work toward the creation of a society whose structures support such choices. But such a society presupposes an end both to sexism and economic oppression—the children of patriarchy. And these children, at least, can be counted on to serve their parent well.

# When Women and Men Mother

## Diane Ehrensaft

Ten years ago the women's movement put the traditional nuclear family on trial and declared it oppressive to women. Entrapment as housewives and mothers was targeted as key to female oppression. A prime focus, both theoretical and strategic, was to free women from their iron apron strings. Some women, particularly radical feminists, called for a boycott of women's involvement with marriage, men, or motherhood. Others demanded universal child care to free women from the home. Some opted for motherhood but no men. A minority of women within the movement, who were either already in nuclear families or still desired involvement with men and children, opted for a different solution in their own lives—the equal sharing of parenthood between mothers and fathers. Contrary to traditional heterosexual relationships in which men are reported to spend an average of twelve minutes a day on primary child care, this new model of parenting assumed that mothers and fathers would share the full weight of rearing their children.

. . .

### Shared Parenting in a Capitalist Context

Who is engaged in shared parenting? Any two individuals both of whom see themselves as primary caretakers to a child or children. As defined by Nancy Press Hawley, elements of shared parenting include: (1) intimacy, both between sharing adults and between adults and children; (2) care of the child in a regular, daily way; (3) awareness of being a primary caretaker or parent to the children; (4) ongoing commitment; and (5) attention paid to the adult relationship.[1] In addition to daily caretaking functions, we are talking about two individuals who fully share responsibility for the ongoing intellectual, emotional, and social development of the child.

…

… In theory shared parenting (1) liberates women from full-time mothering; (2) affords opportunities for more equal relationships between women and men; (3) allows men more access to children; (4) allows children to be parented by two nurturing figures and frees them from the confines of an "overinvolved" parent who has no other outside identity; (5) provides new socialization experiences and possibly a breakdown in gender-differentiated character structures in children; (6) challenges the myth buttressed by sociobiology that women are better equipped biologically for parenting and that women *are* while men *do;* (7) puts pressure on political, economic, and social structures for changes such as paternity and maternity leaves, job sharing, and freely available child-care facilities.

What, though, do we know about the actual implementation of shared parenting today? We have few models from the past, and few reports of present experiences. A woman writing about "Motherhood and the Liberated Woman" urges that "if women's liberation is to mean anything for people who have children or want to have them it must mean that fathers are in this, too. But in what ways it must change, my husband and I don't exactly know."[2] What can we conclude about the viability and political significance of shared parenting from the experience of those men and women who are trying to share "mothering"?

## The Dialectics of Pampers and Paychecks: The Sexual Division of Labor in Shared Parenting

### *Can Men Mother?*

In this argument, the word "mothering" is used specifically to refer to the day-to-day *primary* care of a child; to the consciousness of being *directly* in charge of the child's upbringing. It is to be differentiated from the once-a-week baseball games or twenty-five minutes of play a day that characterize the direct parenting in which men have typically been involved. In relationship to shared parenting, one mother aptly puts it as, "To a child Mommy is the person who takes care of me, who tends my daily needs, who nurtures me in an unconditional and present way. Manda has two mothers; one is a male, Mommy David, and the other a female, Mommy Alice."[3]

According to recent psychological studies, anyone who can do the following can "mother" an infant: provide frequent and sustained physical contact, soothe the child when distressed, be sensitive to the baby's signals, and respond to a baby's crying promptly. Beyond these immediate behavioral indices, psychoanalysts argue that anyone who has personally experienced a positive parent-child relationship that allowed the development of both trust and individuation in his or her own childhood has the emotional capabilities to parent. Much as sociobiologists would take issue, there is no conclusive animal or human research that indicates that female genitals, breasts, or hormonal structure provide women with any better equipment than men for parenting.[4] On the other hand, years in female-dominated parenting situations and in gender-differentiated cultural institutions can and do differentially prepare boys and girls for the task of "mothering."[5] And in adulthood social forces in the labor market, schools, media, etc. buttress these differential abilities. To understand what happens when two such differentially prepared individuals come together to parent, two issues have to be addressed: parenting and power, and the psychic division of labor in parenting.

## Power and Parenting

…

… We women who have shared parenting with men know the tremendous support and comfort (and luxury) of not being the only one there for our children. We see the opportunities to develop the many facets of ourselves not as easily afforded to our mothers or to other women who have carried the primary load of parenting. We watch our children benefit from the full access to two rather than one primary nurturing figure, affording them intimacy with both women and men, a richer, more complex emotional milieu, role models that challenge gender stereotypes. We see men able to develop more fully the nurturant parts of themselves as fathers, an opportunity often historically denied to men. And we develop close, open, and more equal relationships between men and women as we grapple with the daily ups and downs of parenting together. The quality of our lives no doubt has been improved immensely by the equalization of parenting responsibilities between men and women.

Yet we also know another side of the experience, that shared parenting is easier said than done. Because it has remained so unspoken, it is this latter reality I wish to speak to here, while urging the reader to keep in mind the larger context of the successes, the improvements in daily life, and the political import that accompany the shared parenting project.

> Men and women are brought up for a different position in the labor force: the man for the world of work, the woman for the family. This difference in the sexual division of labour in society means that the relationship of men as a group to production is different from that of women. For a man the social relations and values of commodity production predominate and home is a retreat into intimacy. For the woman the public world of work belongs to and is owned by men.[6]

While men hold fast to the domination of the "public sphere," it has been the world of home and family that is woman's domain. Particularly in the rearing of children, it is often her primary (or only) sphere of power. For all the oppressive and debilitating effects of the institution of motherhood, a woman *does* get social credit for being a "good" mother. She also accrues for herself some sense of control and authority in the growth and development of her children. As a mother she is afforded the opportunity for genuine human interaction in contrast to the alienation and depersonalization of the workplace:

A woman's desire to experience power and control is mixed with the desire to obtain joy in childrearing and cannot be separated from it. It is the position of women in society as a whole, their dependent position in the family, the cultural expectation that the maternal role should be the most important role for all women, that make the exaggerated wish to possess one's child an entirely reasonable reaction. Deprived and oppressed, women see in motherhood their only source of pleasure, reward, and fulfillment.[7]

It is this power and control that she must partially give up in sharing parenting equally with a father.

What she gains in exchange is twofold: a freedom from the confines of twenty-four-hour-a-day motherhood and the same opportunity as her male partner to enter the public world of work and politics, with the additional power in the family that her paycheck brings with it. But that public world, as Rowbotham points out, is controlled and dominated by men and does not easily make a place for women within it. The alteration in gender relations within the "shared parent" family is not met by a simultaneous gender reorganization outside the home. A certain loosening of societal gender hierarchies (e.g., the opening of new job opportunities for women) no doubt has prefigured and created the structural conditions that have allowed a small number of men and women to share parenting at this historical moment. But those structural changes are minor in contrast to the drastic alteration of gender relations and power necessary for shared parenting to succeed. So the world the sharing mother enters as she walks out her door will be far less "fifty-fifty" than the newly created world within those doors.

For men taking on parenting responsibilities, the gain is also twofold: he gains access to his children and is able to experience the pleasures and joys of child-rearing. His life is not totally dominated by the alienated relations of commodity production. He is able to nurture, discover the child in himself. But he, too, loses something in the process. First, in a culture that dictates that a man "make something of himself," he will be hard pressed to compete in terms of time and energy with his male counterparts who have only minimal or no parenting responsibility. ... Second, the sharing father is now burdened with the daily headaches and hassles of child care which can (and do) drive many a woman to distraction—the indelible scribble on the walls, the search for a nonexistent good child-care center, the two-hour tantrums, and so on. He has now committed himself to a sphere of work that brings little social recognition—I'm *just* a housewife and a mother.

In *shared* parenting, the gains and losses are not equal for men and women. Mom gives up some of her power only to find societally-induced guilt feelings for not being a "real" mother, and maybe even for being a "bad" mother. (Remember: for years she may have grown up believing she should and would be a full-time mommy when she was big.) The myth of motherhood remains ideologically entrenched far beyond the point when its structural underpinnings have begun to crumble. She is giving up power in the domestic sphere, historically her domain, with little compensation from increased power in the public sphere. Discrimination against women in the labor force is still rampant. She will likely have less earning power, less job opportunity, less creative work, and less social recognition than her male partner. When push comes to shove, she is only a *"working mother."* (There is yet no parallel term "working father").

The power dynamic for sharing fathers is quite different and more complicated. On one level he gains quite a bit of authority in the daily domestic sphere of child-rearing, a heretofore female domain. But by dirtying his hands with diapers he also removes himself from his patriarchal pedestal as the breadwinning but distant father, a position crucial to men's power in the traditional family. He now does the same "debasing" work as mama, and she now has at least some control of the purse strings. Nonetheless, as the second "mother" the father has encroached on an arena of power that traditionally belongs to women, while at the same time he most likely retains more economic and social power vis-à-vis mom in the public world of work and politics.

The societal reaction is also double-edged for the sharing father. Given the subculture that most current sharing parents come from, in his immediate circles dad often receives praise for being the "exceptional" father so devoted to his children or so committed to denying his male privileges. In challenging a myth so deeply embedded as motherhood, the man who marches with baby bottle and infant in arm can become quite an anti-sexist hero. But in the larger culture reactions are often adverse. A man who stays home to care for children is assumed by many to be either disabled, deranged, or demasculinized. One father, pushing his child in a stroller past a school on a weekday afternoon, was bemused by a preadolescent leaning out of the school window yelling, "Faggot, Faggot." Some time ago my grandmother, in response to my mother's praise of my husband's involvement with our children, snapped, "Well, of course, he doesn't work." But as pressures of shifting family structures increase, popular response is rapidly swinging in the sharing father's favor, at least among the middle classes; and the response to his fathering from his most immediate and intimate circles is most likely a positive or even laudatory one.

When the results are tabulated, the gains and losses for men and women are not comparable: women come out behind. …

…

## Physical vs. Psychic Division of Labor in Parenting

The tensions in shared parenting cannot, however, be reduced to power politics in personal relationships. External expectations, attitudes, and ideology collide with deeply internalized self-concepts, skills, and personality structures to make the breakdown of the sexual division of labor in parenting an exciting but difficult project. Often the sharing of *physical* tasks between mothers and fathers is easily implemented—you feed the baby in the morning, I'll do it in the afternoon; you give the kids a bath on Mondays, I'll do it on Thursdays. What is left at least partially intact is the sexual division of the *psychological* labor in parenting. There is the question, "Who carries around in their head knowledge of diapers needing to be laundered, fingernails needing to be cut, new clothes needing to be bought?" Answer: mother, because of years of socialization to do so. Vis-à-vis fathers, sharing mothers often find themselves in the position of cataloguer and taskmaster—We really should change the kids' sheets today; I think it's time for the kids' teeth to be checked. It is probable that men carry less of the mental load of parenting, regardless of mutual agreements to share the responsibility of parenting; this leaves the women more caught up in the psychic aspects of parenting.

...

## What Happens to the Children?

> *Jesse:* Daddy, Daddy, pick me up.
> **Daddy:** *No, Jesse, I'm cooking dinner.*
> **Mommy:** *Come on, Jesse, I can pick you up. I'm your mother.*
> *Jesse:* *No, Daddy's my mother.*
>
> (Unsolicited statement from a three-year-old son of shared parents)

In shared parenting situations that begin at the child's birth, both *mother* and *father* become equal in the child's eyes as individuals who provide primary care. In contrast to the female-raised infant, a mother and a father are equally internalized early in the child's life. The infant's sense of self is developed in relationship to two people, a man and a woman. This means that later individuation of self will also be from two people, both a mother and a father. In shared-parenting situations fathers are no longer abstractions or once-in-a-while idealized figures to the young child. They are as real and concrete as mothers in the child's eyes. And both girls and boys will have parallel struggles of individuation from like- and opposite-sex parents, albeit in different combination. They will have a parental interpersonal environment that is not gender-linked: both men and women will be available for strong emotional attachments. If different interpersonal environments for girls and boys in the family create different "feminine" and "masculine" personalities and preoccupations, an elimination of the different interpersonal environment through equal parenting by men and women should eliminate those personality differences.

But this is predicated on two assumptions: (1) that women and men are really equally involved in the parenting process; and (2) that families rather than the larger culture are the primal force in gender development. Concentrating first on the former assumption, we identified in the last section a tension that occurs in both men and women who attempt shared parenting at this moment in history, a tension that still draws women closer to the home and men further away from it. What might be the effects of these subtle (or sometimes not so subtle) tensions on the children's development of gender identity and concepts?

Because of ideological pressures, institutional barriers, and their own psychological preparation for motherhood, many women may experience much more inner turmoil than men in sharing parenting with another person and in balancing parenting with a non-parenting identity. This turmoil can influence the relationship between mother and child. Children now understand that mom does other things be-sides take care of them—she goes out in the world, can be an effective human being outside the family sphere: mommies can be anything (if the society and internalized norms will let them). Mommy can also have more "quality" interactions with the child because she is not suffocated or psychologically withered by twenty-four-hour imprisonment in child-care responsibilities. But mother is also under the strain of a great deal of ambivalence. After a frustrating day at work, where she spent half her day worrying about her child's day at school and the other half ill-treated by col-leagues, employers, or internalized lack of confidence, she comes home to find her daughter did indeed have a terrible day at school. (Father may have had an equally rotten day at work, but remember that he is probably carrying around less of the mental baggage of parenting). Mother vacillates between wanting her child to disap-pear, and wanting to quit her job immediately to be the kind of mother she ought to be. The child may experience some very schizoid qualities in mother, a dynamic in which mother draws her child close while at the same time she resents the child for the guilt the child induces in her. The child experiences the mother's drift into "tak-ing over," the competition with father for the parenting role which is still mother's most legitimate sphere of power, the "bossing" or directives to daddy who is just not as attuned to "mothering" as mommy. If mother herself cannot resolve how much of a mother she is going to be, her children may concurrently experience the parallel ambivalence—how much of a mommy is she? And what exactly is a woman's pri-mary identity in life?

Fathers, we have said, also feel a pull between their parenting and non-parenting identities. The child of the sharing father experiences intimacy and nurturance from a man. The child learns that Daddy, like Mommy, is a day-to-day real person in the family sphere. But if the child experiences resentment from the father for the sapping of an otherwise productive worklife, that child must integrate the male nurturance received with the negativity of experiencing oneself as a drain. Equally likely, the fa-ther, rather than expressing direct hostility, will at times slip off his fathering cape and do a psychological disappearing act. He simply makes himself less accessible to the child.

But relating to children involves more than the behavioral manifestations of con-flicts and ambivalences around parenting. There is also the laundry list of things daddies do with the kids vs. things mommies do with the kids. In my own observa-tion this varies so enormously from one shared-parenting family to another that it is near impossible to generate a common profile. But if I had to identify some salient differences that repeatedly appear, they would be as follows. Sharing mothers get more involved in their children's peer relations, worry more if their children are well-liked, spend more time talking to friends about their children, buy the children's clothes, wash dirty faces and comb hair more, and do more things *at home* with the kids. In contrast, sharing fathers take their kids on more outings, take more over-night trips away from home (often work-related), spend more time reading in the same room as the child, put kids' clothes on backwards, do not "fly off the handle" with the children as much, are able to distance themselves more from the children's squabbles and peer conflicts, and (sad but true), engage in more rough-and-tumble play with the kids. These differences accurately reflect the dynamics of a somewhat more involved mother and a more "balanced," but sometimes more distant father.

...

What effects do we see of these influences on the child of shared parenting? Superficially, sitting in a day-care center or classroom, you cannot easily pick out a shared-parented child in a crowd. They know that girls can be doctors and boys play with dolls, but so do a lot of other kids exposed to nonsexist education curricula. They know that mommies can go off to work in the morning, but so do children of single mothers or of working mothers in non-sharing two-parent households. Despite all conscious practices to the contrary at home, the girls may look as "fem" and the boys as "macho" as any of their non-shared-parented classmates. Influenced in the cognitive organization of their experience by the normative structures of the world around them, at preschool age they may look you straight in the eye and tell you only men can be lawyers (even though their own mother is a lawyer) or that mommies stay home and do all the cooking and daddies go off to work (even though daddy made meals all week while mom was off at a conference). In a society where more and more of a child's socialization experiences occur outside the home, societal norms and standards cannot help but organize a child's self-concept and organization of social experience.

...

We can speculate that children of shared parenting will develop a greater sense of trust in the world than children with only one primary parent. They grow up with a confidence that at least two, rather than one, persons can offer them basic nurturance and security. One could also predict that monogamy would not be as deeply ingrained. If monogamy is in part shaped in the child's psyche by the original mother-infant possessive dyad, breaking up the dyad with basic nurturing from another person conceivably shapes in the child a concept of love beyond a pas de deux. We can even predict an expanded notion of sexuality, perhaps a greater incidence of bisexuality. With primary care coming equally from women and men, and with individuation from both a father and a mother, rapprochement will also be toward a man and a woman for children of either sex. If gender becomes less of a central factor in who these children are, then sexuality may be more loosely tied to whether the object of love is male or female. But these are areas in which we must wait patiently for the children to grow to adulthood to unfold their own story.

Both the new right and left-wing critics of feminism condemn children growing up in anything but traditional nuclear families to a life of narcissism, neurosis, or psychopathy, stemming from the breakdown of authority in the family. What becomes confused in their argument is the differentiation between *authority* and *authoritarianism*. Children of shared parents indeed understand a hierarchy of responsibility and the "leadership" position of their parents in the family. What they do not experience is the unilateral power base of the patriarchal father who offers conditional love in exchange for unconditional submission. Because children of shared parents continually observe two adults democratically negotiating decision-making and division of responsibility in the home, they are presented with a new model of authority based on collectivity and flexibility rather than unchallenged power. Since two people fully share the parenting responsibility, one cannot simply criticize the other's parenting as a role foreign to him- or herself. The criticism comes within a joint endeavor in which they must mutually arrive at a parenting solution satisfying to both. Thus mutuality and consensus, rather than directives and compliance, further inform the child's internalization of democratic processes. In the actual parent-child interaction, the child learns quite early that authority does not lie in just one person's hands. There are always two, rather than one person, with whom the child can equally approach or consult on matters requiring parental decisions or guidance. Neither parent unilaterally holds the purse strings, manages the household, or enforces disciplinary actions. With authority more diffused than centralized, the child has more room to move as a meaningful participant in family decisions and functioning.

Shared parenting alters authority relations not only between parent and child, but between males and females. With all the qualifications noted above, shared-parenting families substitute "unisex" parenting for the "instrumental-emotional" gender division of traditional families. Girls and boys develop new understandings of equal authority among males and females. Even though all children in our culture have no doubt been affected by the Wonder Woman mystique, girls and boys of shared parents understand at a concrete level, not just in surreal fantasies, the strength and independence of women vis-à-vis men, the possibility of equality, rather than dominance-submission, in female-male relationships. This is often translated into peer relationships in which daughters are pugnacious, audacious, and stalwart in their interactions with boys and sons have a healthy respect and acceptance of the social power of girls.

While trust, democratic impulses, and balancing of social power between females and males may be outcomes for children of shared parents, a smothering from over-parenting is also possible. An ostensible advantage of shared parenting is that with two (or more) primary caretakers, one of the caretakers can comfortably take "time off," have space for oneself away from the children. The reality, however, is that shared parenting often leads to a consciousness of "on all the time" for both parents. From the point of view of the child, not just one parent but two parents are actively ego-involved in the child's development. Not just one but both parents tell the child to drag an umbrella to school on a rainy day. The potential for overprotectiveness, overinvolvement, or stifling of autonomy is obvious. Also, the implication for *two* parents now totally absorbed in parenting consciousness is potential "parent burn-out" not just by one, but by two people, leaving the child with two strung-out parents.

There is no doubt that children growing up in a shared-parenting household are exposed to a different socialization experience than children from other family structures. When daddy and only daddy can be mother, something crucial has changed. But we must wait to see what the *adult* personality outcomes of these children will be. In the reorganization of gender, the degree of reduction in the female-male division of psychological capacities can help us understand the significance of family structure and processes in producing gender. If female and male differences are indeed reduced in these people, compared to people who did not experience shared parenting, we will find validation for the primacy of family structure in gender development. If these children grow up with psychological capacities undifferentiated from families where parenting is more conventional, this will reflect either the greater primacy of extra-parental forces or the ineffectiveness of shared parents in successfully reorganizing gender-related parenting (or both). These experiences help us understand the ways in which reproduction, production, and ideology interpenetrate and can thus inform our strategy for transforming gender relations.

## Conclusion

… The new right has been built partly through addressing people's fears about the rapidly deteriorating quality of life. Recognizing people's concern for the future, particularly the well-being of their children, the new right offers reactionary programs which, retreating to old patriarchal forms, claim to save unborn offspring from murder, shield families from untoward homosexual influence, and put the dollar back in the family's pocket where it belongs. The left and the women's movement have to address the concerns that underlie these issues. Many of us have begun to look more closely at issues of family or personal life. Some have taken the tack of defending or rebuilding the family in the face of capitalist attack. Others of us feel wary of an approach which by uncritically "defending the family," tends to reproduce the romantic, antifeminist thrust of the new right. We need to demonstrate the ability of *new* social and family structures to provide the satisfactions that people legitimately long for—emotional and sexual intimacy, child-rearing by caring people, a sense of community.

In the latter context, shared parenting is an important political effort. It challenges an oppressive feature of the family—the universality of motherhood. Shared parenting frees women from the dual burden of paid and unpaid work, affords men access to the growth and development of children and children access to the growth and development of men, and helps to eliminate gender-linked divisions between males and females that reproduce the sex-gender system. But shared parenting must also be seen as only one aspect of the larger demand for new forms of personal life to replace the decaying traditional nuclear family and provide solutions to the problems of personal tension, violence, and loneliness experienced by so many. We need to restructure social responsibility for children so that not just mothers and fathers but also non-family-members have access to and responsibility for the care of children. What is labeled by many as a crisis of the family should more aptly be approached as a historical shift in family structure. In this period of flux, we can try to create and sustain a new fluidity between family and non-family for the responsibility of children, a greater involvement of men in this process, new kinds of authority relations between parents and children, and forms other than the traditional nuclear family in which people can choose to live. These goals necessitate addressing the interpenetration of reproduction, production, and ideology. These goals will not be achieved overnight. Yet we know much *can* be accomplished, and such efforts will be an increasingly important part of political and social life in the coming years.

---

## Notes

I want to thank Nancy Chodorow, Jim Hawley, Barry Kaufman, Gail Kaufman, Joanna Levine, Elli Meeropol, Robby Meeropol, David Plotke, Marcy Whitebook, and the SR West collective for their criticism and support in writing this paper.—D.E.

1. Nancy Press Hawley, "Shared Parenthood," in Boston Women's Health Collective, *Ourselves and Our Children* (New York: Random House, 1978). This framework differentiates shared *parenting* from shared *custody*, in which two parents, separated or divorced, share the children back and forth.

2. D. Baldwin, "Motherhood and the Liberated Woman," *San Francisco Chronicle*, 12 October 1978.

3. Alice Abarbanel, "Redefining Motherhood," in Louise Kapp Howe, ed., *The Future of the Family* (New York: Simon and Schuster, 1972), p. 366.

4. Cf. Ann Oakley, *Women's Work*, ch. 8, "Myths of Woman's Place, 2: Motherhood" (New York: Vintage, 1974); Wini Breines, Margaret Cerullo, and Judith Stacey, "Social Biology, Family Studies, and Antifeminist Backlash," *Feminist Studies*, February 1978, pp. 43–68.

5. Nancy Chodorow, *The Reproduction of Mothering: Psychoanalysis and the Sociology of Gender* (Berkeley: University of California Press, 1978).

6. Sheila Rowbotham, *Woman's Consciousness, Man's World* (Baltimore: Penguin, 1973), p. 61.

7. Oakley, *Woman's Work*, p. 220.

# The Radical Potential in Lesbian Mothering of Daughters

## Baba Copper

...

I am a lesbian mother to a lesbian daughter. I have moved from traditional to radical feminist lesbian midstream in my mothering process. My two married daughters reflect the "success" of the patriarchal mothering I did within a nuclear family; traditional socialization that more or less mirrored those values and practices my mother used with me. But my midlife switch has allowed me, as an old lesbian, to explore—

in practice as well as theory—active resistance to the ideology and institutions of heteromotherhood. I am extending and politicizing my mothering. I am making a connection between my radicalism and the lesbianism of my daughter.

Recently I sought out other mother/daughter dyads who are both lesbians. In carrying out this search, I discerned a suppressed anxiety surrounding the whole subject, resulting, I suspect, from the "congenital disease" theory of homosexuality promulgated by psychiatrists, and reinforced by the Gay Rights we-are-just-like-everybody-else defense against homophobia. The relationship my daughter and I share often appears invisible, even to our friends and lovers who see it as apolitical—a personal anomaly, threateningly different. Perhaps lesbians have not yet identified either the goals or the "rules" of heteropatriarchal mothering with sufficient clarity to be able to change them.

Why is there strong support among women for the separation between mothers and adult daughters? Why should they not remain close, expanding their ways of being together into adult-to-adult intimacy which provides mutual support and growth? Surely the separation of the daughter from the other is not an appropriate expectation to guide the behavior of two lesbians?

A tight mother/adult daughter bonding may be the ultimate patriarchal no-no. Therapists reinforce the definition of female maturity as a woman who has separated from, not bonded with her mother. There are the oft-repeated mother-in-law jokes which pressure married women to discard their mother as ally. Although loving relationships between traditional mothers and their heterosexual daughters are not unknown, most daughters value the distances which their lives have generated away from their mothers. Here is a rule of heteromothering worth breaking.

My lesbian daughter and I are exploring the mined territory of mother/adult daughter bonding. We do so without honor in the lesbian community. She suffers the indignity of derogatory comments from her peers, such as being told to "grow up" when she expresses yearning for my presence. I face the assumptions that my motherhood somehow defines my life, instead of being a small but important part of it.

...

My own experience, and my learnings from other lesbian mother/lesbian daughter dyads, indicate that something ... is happening between lesbians which merits attention. To extend and deepen the mother/daughter bond into adulthood did not seem a radical act to me, until I encountered the degree of opposition and misinterpretation which it evoked in other lesbians. I had assumed we were a threat to men, not to women-loving-women. Now I believe lesbians are fully as prejudiced toward mothers—any mothers—as any other segment of the population. The sooner lesbians detach from the heteromythology which clusters around motherhood, the better.

Although many mothers, hetero and lesbian, diligently study whatever expertise they can find on mothering as their bellies swell, probably half of what they do, once the hectic dance of mothering begins, are repetitions of the mothering they learned at a nonverbal level from their own mothers. Teaching little girls to cater to male supremacy—to serve and submit—have been the basic lessons of female survival.

Any woman who is herself adequately socialized by male standards, transmits some of this. Built into these unconscious patterns of communication between mother and daughter is content that lesbians will want to raise to a conscious level and judge with modern, politicized eyes.

Lesbians cannot look for satisfactory guidance from heterofeminists who write books about raising antisexist boys and liberated girls. These children are expected to be high achievers in a man's world without questioning the assumptions underpinning that goal. There is also a great deal of lyrical psychobabble by heterofeminists about the redemption of the human psyche possible through male mothering of infants. Theory needs some basis in evidence. No one has been denying fathers the joys of parenting. Some men have been successful fathers. But for every well-fathered child, there are a million who were conceived irresponsibly or abandoned or raped or physically terrorized or emotionally denied by their fathers. ...

There are issues important to lesbian mothers that heterofeminists do not address. First and foremost, we must acknowledge that the mothering of daughters is of primary importance to us. If women come first, then daughters come first. The next step in disengaging motherhood from male definitions is to identify the mother/daughter dyad as *the* evolutionary crucible of society. Any abuse by the adult males of the former family—daughter rape, or battery, or harsh labor exploitation—may diminish female autonomy in that family tree for generations. The mother teaches the next generation of mothers how to mother—how to transmit much of the societal information which humans share at an unconscious level.

...

Lesbian mothers are, almost without exception, themselves products of heteromothering. Lesbians raise their children within patriarchy, just like other women. However, the lesbian can make choices in relation to the degree of assimilation of her daughter into patriarchy, choices not possible to the heteromother, if she is willing to raise to a conscious level some of the unconscious roots of female subordination.

All mammals teach appropriate responses of submission to their young. ... In order to keep patriarchy functioning as a self-sustaining heterosystem, daughters must be taught to mistrust females and to attend/depend on males. Mothers teach daughters, even at a preverbal level, that their instinct of self-preservation is best served by the *absence* of female bonding, the *absence* of female-to-female entitlement. Mothers must also imprint their daughters with allegiance to patriarchal aesthetics. By example, mothers train their daughters to fear female aging, to find continual fault with their own bodies, to believe they must cash in on natural beauty or youth. Teaching daughters to be "attractive" and "successful" has been the innocuous justification for some of the most pernicious betrayals of daughters by mothers: footbinding; physical weakness and mental shallowness; cosmetic surgery and dieting; sexual ignorance; child brides, child prostitution, and child pornography; genital mutilation. Teaching daughters to succeed in the lifelong struggle to assimilate into a manmade hierarchy of female worth has always been a trap.

This subtle process and its woman-hating content is buried in the often harried day-to-day interactions between a mother and her daughters. Radical mothering means involving children in disloyalty to the culture the mother is expected to transmit at the expense of woman-bonding and female empowerment. Excavating the heteromyths buried in the transmitted information of daughter-rearing is the most important work of the lesbian radical mother. These heteromyths embody the unconscious informational chains between the generations of women that lesbians have the potential to break, if they will consciously accept the task.

The fact of lesbian existence as radical lesbians in patriarchy gives their mothering some clear advantages. For instance, lesbian mothers for the most part eschew that bedrock heteromyth which says a child needs a resident father in order to grow up whole. Lesbian mothering can enhance the development of female autonomy and self-love. Lesbian mothers may also have more motivation to imagine what might constitute positive female rights and role expectations for our daughters.

...

Another heteromyth which needs radical defusing is the notion that lesbian mothers must maintain neutrality in relation to the future sexual preference of their daughters. *Sexual preference* is not the issue. The reality underlying the myth is one we all know: female heterosexuality cannot be called a choice when it is compulsory in all cultures, everywhere. But we are lesbian, and it is a fundamental expression of self-love to want our daughters to grow up reflecting our woman-identified choices. Although many heteromothers have tried to force their daughters out of lesbianism, it is hard to imagine a lesbian mother who would deny choice to her daughter.

Radical mothering must also encompass many of the same struggles that conscientious heteromothers face. As all politically committed mothers have discovered, it is not enough to verbalize antiracist, antiageist, antilooksist sentiments to our children. In addition to talk, we must communicate by modeling the behavior we expect in them. This necessitates viewing one's lifestyle not as an extension of who-I-am but of who-I-want-them-to-learn-to-be. No mother succeeds in always being how she wants her children to be, but the radical mother structures her lifestyle so that her child has ample opportunity to see her trying. Lesbians do not hesitate to choose for our daughters when it comes to the prevention of childhood diseases, but we balk at inoculating them against assimilation into heterofemininity—into the addictive satisfactions of female normalcy.

We need to make some dramatic changes in the information usually shared with daughters. Daughters have been deprived *by their mothers* of knowledge of their orgasmic potential and the various ways of satisfying it, detailed knowledge of both the history and the current oppression of women worldwide, information about matrifocal civilizations and woman-defined women of the past, and revelations about their mothers' lives and sexuality. This suppression of information is a learned pattern of behavior passed from mother to daughter that teaches mistrust between women. Honor between women starts with honesty and with the determination to empower each other. Our children are the daughters of women who love women over men. Daughters of lesbians, like freedom fighters everywhere, need to be enlisted in infancy, and protected against heterofemininity by words and actions—not

for the mother's sake nor for the movement's sake—but for their own psychological well-being.
…

# *A Lesbian Family*

## Lindsy Van Gelder

Sarah is in most ways your basic five-year-old: a watcher of Charlie Brown videos, a reader of Richard Scarry books, a crayoner of cotton-puff clouds and fat yellow suns with Tinkertoy-spoke rays. Like every other piece of kindergarten artwork ever made, her portrait of "My Family" contains stick-figurey construction paper people, all holding hands and looking jolly. Except her family is a little different: there's Sarah, there's "Daddy," there's "Mom-my" … and there's Amy, Mommy's lover.

Sarah's "cubby" at school is special, too. While the other kids hang their windbreakers and lunch boxes next to photos of one parent, or two, Sarah has three. She takes this embarrassment of riches in stride—which is to say, without any embarrassment at all.

Not that she isn't a very savvy little girl about the precisely calibrated degrees to which the many adults in her life fit into the larger scheme of things. If you ask her about the members of her "whole" (i.e., extended) family, she will tick off various grandmothers and cousins on her fingers. "Francie [her biological mother's ex-lover and now best friend] is in my family, too," she adds. "But Richard [her father's new boyfriend] isn't *exactly* in my family … yet." The adults around her would probably say the same thing, in many more words.

… [Sarah's] biological mother, Nancy, had interviewed a dozen potential gay and straight sperm donors before she and Amy met Doug and his then-boyfriend. Unlike many lesbian couples who decide to have a child, Nancy has no particular quarrel with the notion that a parent of each gender is a desirable thing. But in the original scenario, the women weren't necessarily looking for anything much more enduring than a turkey baster deposit. They simply wanted someone they could point to on the day their daughter asked where Daddy was.

But something unexpected happened: a flowering of feeling that turned the American Gothic nuclear family progression on its head. Instead of two people meeting, falling in love, and having a baby, four people met, had a baby, and then became good friends.

In fact, their whole lives became entwined. At the time Nancy got pregnant, all the adults were entering their forties, both Amy and Doug were at career crossroads, and both couples were sick of the expense and hassle of living in New York City. The baby was both a symbol of the changes the adults were ready for and a catalyst to more. ... The men had moved to the Southwest, where Doug spent his childhood, and the women were talking about following. Although it wasn't part of their original agreement, Doug insisted on helping with Sarah's financial support. ... Recently, ... we found Amy, Nancy, Sarah, and their two cats living down the street from Doug in an adobe house with a yard full of mesquite trees. Amy and Doug have pooled their resources and opened a café. He does most of the cooking; she takes care of most of the business end. Nancy meanwhile teaches at a nearby college. All three contribute to Sarah's expenses, although Amy—because she lives with Sarah and has a more flexible schedule than Nancy—is the primary caregiver in terms of time at the moment.

"It confuses the hell out of people," Amy notes cheerfully. "People come into the restaurant, and they see that Doug and I are partners, and then they see this little kid running around after school relating to both of us. Not surprisingly, they assume that Doug and I are married—which, of course, we both hate. Usually, I sit them down and just explain the story." Some people still don't quite get it. "I'm thinking of having palm cards made up," she jokes, "Maybe like, *Good afternoon, you have entered a Strange Other World.*"

Amy, Nancy, and Doug are completely out of the closet in their dealings with the straight community. They grudgingly elected to use pseudonyms in this article only after Nancy's mother asked them to. Nancy's mother has told all her relatives that Sarah was born out of a liaison between Nancy and a married man. "Somehow that's better than being in a happy, committed, lesbian relationship," Nancy sighs.

"I think it behooves us to be out, and even to boast about it, to show that it can work," says Doug. For Sarah's sake, the adults tend to like to deal with the gay issue up front, where it can be defused if need be. "When it came time to get a pediatrician, all three of us marched in—we didn't want some situation later on where the doctor didn't realize that all of us were in on this. It's the same thing now that we've been looking at elementary schools for next year. At interviews our position is, 'This is our situation, and it's very important that Sarah get support on that if she needs it.'" At one school they considered, they got more than they asked for—several faculty members discreetly came out to them. ...

Sarah's parents have had some rough times, however. The biggest rupture in their lives occurred when Doug and his longtime boyfriend messily broke up two years ago. Aside from the immediate trauma, the women worried that Doug might find small-city gay single life intolerable and leave. "For a while he was dating someone here we weren't crazy about as stepdaddy material, either," they confide. Then Doug met Richard, an elementary school substitute teacher who loves children. The two men are about to start living together.

"It sounds crass, but part of my getting together with Richard is about Sarah," Doug says. "If I were 36, I probably would have cashed in my chips and left town. But at 46, I have different needs." In fact, Richard is now talking seriously with a lesbian woman—a close friend of Amy and Nancy's, as it happens—about adding another child to the extended family.

...

Not surprisingly, the adults in Sarah's life don't always agree. The funniest example was the time that Sarah snookered her father into buying her a "Wet 'n Wild Barbie," only mentioning once they were safely past the checkout counter that the item wouldn't be remotely welcome at her house. The crisis was resolved by keeping Barbie at Daddy's. There have also been many, many jokes about possible Birkenstocks and flannel shirts that one might add to Barbie's wardrobe. Sarah later made all the adults laugh when she bought her father his own Ken doll for his birthday. Of course, now that Doug has Richard, Sarah has Ken. She is not a dumb kid.

Doug and Richard have occasionally hinted that Sarah gets away with too much at Nancy and Amy's house, and the women have occasionally felt a financial pinch when Doug is casual about paying his share of the child support money on time. But the splits are minor, and they're by no means consistently Boys Versus Girls. Amy and Doug are currently pushing for Sarah to go to private or Episcopal parochial school next year; Nancy thinks "every justification for sending kids to private school sounds just like what white people in the South historically use as excuses. O.K., maybe the reading scores in the public schools are lower, but maybe it's because a lot of the kids are Mexican Americans who grew up bilingual. It doesn't necessarily mean the education is worse."

Nancy also strenuously objected to the "girls in skirts" dress code required by the school Doug and Amy favor—a rule Amy wasn't thrilled with either. The three parents brought it up with the administration and ascertained that if Sarah were to wear a nice blouse and a pair of dressy pants instead of a skirt, the school wouldn't object. "But she'll wear a dress anyway, because she likes them," Doug smirks. "She's very femme."

One of the worst parts of parenting for Amy and Nancy is that their schedules leave them very little time to be alone together. Nancy's teaching requires her to be out of the house several nights a week, as well as on Sunday, the one day the café is closed. Doug previously took care of Sarah on a fairly irregular basis, and he unabashedly notes: "I never thought I had to deal with her shitty diapers to bond with her. I wanted the fun parts." But when Nancy and Amy asked him if he would keep Sarah every Sunday night, he was glad to help.

"I told Doug I was asking him this as a personal favor, having nothing to do with his relationship to Sarah," Amy jokes. "I told him that as his friend that he works with, I'll be a lot happier, and therefore he'll be a lot happier. Now when I come in Monday morning, there's lots of leering, and lots of *gee, Sarah and I went to McDonald's last night—what did YOU guys do, hmmmm?*"

But Amy and Nancy are quick to note that almost all their minor difficulties—from scheduled sex to sporadic conflicts about child-raising—are typical of those encountered by all parents. "There's almost nothing so far that's wrong because we're gay," says Nancy, "and a lot of what's right is because we're gay." For one thing, there's no ancient sexual bitterness between Sarah's biological mother and father of the sort that mars so much postdivorce parental jockeying.

One gay problem is health insurance: none of them have it. "We've talked about supplying benefits here at the restaurant," says Doug, "but that would only help Amy and me. We have no legal relationship, in the eyes of the insurance companies, with Nancy and Sarah."

"There's also weird stuff you have to think about," says Amy. "Like, when Sarah goes to other kid's houses, sometimes the kids take a bath together. Her friends' parents seem to be cool about us, but it's still the sort of thing I'd think twice about doing, because you just know it would only take one asshole to turn Naked Kids in Lesbian Home into something really sordid and horrible."

But when you ask them all if there's anything they would do over differently, the answer is: not much. "I'm glad I did it with a father that I know, and not a sperm bank," says Nancy. When Sarah was an infant, Nancy did go through a spell of jealousy of Doug's relationship with their child. "I didn't want to share her with him; I hardly knew him," she admits. "Then I told myself to just cool out and think of what was best for Sarah." Nancy adds that she might be less enthusiastic if Doug were an absentee father. "There's this whole Daddy Thing; Daddy gets to be Daddy, and all that that represents, no matter what he does or doesn't do, and kids—all kids—just plug into that. But in fact, Doug *is* lovely with her."

Nancy and Amy have also been lucky in other ways. Seven or eight years ago, when they began their search for a donor, AIDS was an established fact, but it was less discussed than it is now. Despite urgings from their friends, the women thought it would be presumptuously rude to ask Doug to take an HIV test. Recently, Nancy was reading the New York *Times* and happened upon the name of another man she'd asked to be a donor—someone who inexplicably stopped taking her calls. Now there he was on the obit page, dead of AIDS.

Of all the adults in Sarah's life, Amy is the one in the most vulnerable position. She has no legal claim on Sarah if she and Nancy ever break up (although gay civil rights groups are fighting for the rights of nonbiological lesbian mothers who are thus left with no recourse). Nancy and Doug's wills specify that if they were to die, they would want Amy to have custody, but it's a wish that grandparents or even the state could challenge in court. "It's too devastating to think about," says Amy. "So I don't."

She also finds terminology a problem. "I'll be at the grocery store and some clerk will ask me if Sarah's mine. Well, she *is*, damn it, even if that's not what they meant. I periodically sit Sarah down to make sure she's okay with this stuff. Like I recently said to her, 'You know, I'm not your mother, but I'm sort of like your parent.' She nodded and said, 'Right. Mommy is my mother. But I *am* your daughter.'"

At the preschool Sarah currently attends, the other kids tend to announce "Your Amy is here to pick you up." There are several other children in Sarah's class who have gay parents, and in one of the more open families, the nonbiological mother also happens to be named Amy. It's becoming a sort of generic honorific: Sarah and her friend Rex both go off after school with their Amys.

Perhaps things will be more awkward when Sarah is older, the adults say. But perhaps they won't be. Or, more likely, they will be, but only because most teenagers
find *something* about their parents that's, like, totally gross. So far, so good.

Sarah's only recorded worry about the future is one that she shared with Nancy
one day when she was trying to figure out how she could be a doctor and stay home
with her own sick child. Nancy assured her that such things were eminently doable;
she herself could baby-sit. Sarah sighed with relief, her grown-up life secured.

"But," she suddenly asked, "where will I find a Daddy and an Amy?"

# Black Women and Motherhood

## Patricia Hill Collins

*Just yesterday I stood for a few minutes at the top of the stairs leading to a white doctor's of-
fice in a white neighborhood. I watched one Black woman after another trudge to the corner,
where she then waited to catch the bus home. These were Black women still cleaning somebody else's house or Black women still caring for somebody else's sick or elderly, before they
came back to the frequently thankless chores of their own loneliness, their own families. And
I felt angry and I felt ashamed. And I felt, once again, the kindling heat of my hope that we,
the daughters of these Black women, will honor their sacrifice by giving them thanks. We will
undertake, with pride, every transcendent dream of freedom made possible by the humility of
their love.*

—June Jordan 1985, 105

June Jordan's words poignantly express the need for Black feminists to honor our
mothers' sacrifice by developing an Afrocentric feminist analysis of Black motherhood. Until recently analyses of Black motherhood have largely been the province of
men, both white and Black, and male assumptions about Black women as mothers
have prevailed. Black mothers have been accused of failing to discipline their children, of emasculating their sons, of defeminizing their daughters, and of retarding
their children's academic achievement (Wade-Gayles 1980). Citing high rates of divorce, female-headed households, and out-of-wedlock births, white male scholars
and their representatives claim that African-American mothers wield unnatural
power in allegedly deteriorating family structures (Moynihan 1965; Zinn 1989). The
African-American mothers observed by Jordan vanish from these accounts.

White feminist work on motherhood has failed to produce an effective critique of elite white male analyses of Black motherhood. ... While white feminists have effectively confronted white male analyses of their own experiences as mothers, they rarely challenge controlling images such as the mammy, the matriarch, and the welfare mother and therefore fail to include Black mothers "still cleaning somebody else's house or ... caring for somebody else's sick or elderly." As a result, white feminist theories have had limited utility for African-American women (Joseph 1984).

In African-American communities the view has been quite different. As Barbara Christian contends, the "concept of motherhood is of central importance in the philosophy of both African and Afro-American peoples" (1985, 213). But in spite of its centrality, Black male scholars in particular typically glorify Black motherhood by refusing to acknowledge the issues faced by Black mothers who "came back to the frequently thankless chores of their own loneliness, their own families." By claiming that Black women are richly endowed with devotion, self-sacrifice, and unconditional love—the attributes associated with archetypal motherhood—Black men inadvertently foster a different controlling image for Black women, that of the "superstrong Black mother" (Staples 1973; Dance 1979). In many African-American communities so much sanctification surrounds Black motherhood that "the idea that mothers should live lives of sacrifice has come to be seen as the norm" (Christian 1985, 234).

Far too many Black men who praise their own mothers feel less accountable to the mothers of their own children. They allow their wives and girlfriends to support the growing numbers of African-American children living in poverty (Frazier 1948; Burnham 1985; U.S. Department of Commerce 1986, 1989). Despite the alarming deterioration of economic and social supports for Black mothers, large numbers of young men encourage their unmarried teenaged girlfriends to give birth to children whose futures are at risk (Ladner 1972; Ladner and Gourdine 1984; Simms 1988). Even when they are aware of the poverty and struggles these women face, many Black men cannot get beyond the powerful controlling image of the superstrong Black mother in order to see the very real costs of mothering to African-American women. ...

...

African-American women need an Afrocentric feminist analysis of motherhood that debunks the image of "happy slave," whether the white-male-created "matriarch" or the Black-male-perpetuated "superstrong Black mother." ...

...

## Bloodmothers, Othermothers, and Women-Centered Networks

In African-American communities, fluid and changing boundaries often distinguish biological mothers from other women who care for children. Biological mothers, or bloodmothers, are expected to care for their children. But African and African-American communities have also recognized that vesting one person with full responsibility for mothering a child may not be wise or possible. As a result, othermothers—women who assist bloodmothers by sharing mothering responsibilities—traditionally have been central to the institution of Black motherhood (Troester 1984).

The centrality of women in African-American extended families reflects both a continuation of West African cultural values and functional adaptations to race and gender oppression (Tanner 1974; Stack 1974; Aschenbrenner 1975; Martin and Martin 1978; Sudarkasa 1981; Reagon 1987). This centrality is not characterized by the absence of husbands and fathers. Men may be physically present and/or have well-defined and culturally significant roles in the extended family and the kin unit may be woman-centered. ...

Organized, resilient, women-centered networks of bloodmothers and othermothers are key in understanding this centrality. Grandmothers, sisters, aunts, or cousins act as othermothers by taking on child-care responsibilities for one another's children. When needed, temporary child-care arrangements can turn into long-term care or informal adoption (Stack 1974; Gutman 1976). Despite strong cultural norms encouraging women to become biological mothers, women who choose not to do so often receive recognition and status from othermother relationships that they establish with Black children.

In African-American communities these women-centered networks of community-based child care often extend beyond the boundaries of biologically related individuals and include "fictive kin" (Stack 1974). Civil rights activist Ella Baker describes how informal adoption by othermothers functioned in the rural southern community of her childhood:

> My aunt who had thirteen children of her own raised three more. She had become a midwife, and a child was born who was covered with sores. Nobody was particularly wanting the child, so she took the child and raised him ... and another mother decided she didn't want to be bothered with two children. So my aunt took one and raised him ... they were part of the family. (Cantarow 1980, 59)

Even when relationships are not between kin or fictive kin, African-American community norms traditionally were such that neighbors cared for one anothers' children. Sara Brooks, a southern domestic worker, describes the importance that the community-based child care a neighbor offered her daughter had for her: "She kept Vivian and she didn't charge me nothin either. You see, people used to look after each other, but now its not that way. I reckon its because we all was poor, and I guess they put theirself in the place of the person that they was helpin" (Simonsen 186, 181). Brooks's experiences demonstrate how the African-American cultural value placed on cooperative child care traditionally found institutional support in the adverse conditions under which so many Black women mothered.

Othermothers are key not only in supporting children but also in helping bloodmothers who, for whatever reason, lack the preparation or desire for motherhood. In confronting racial oppression, maintaining community-based child care and respecting othermothers who assume child-care responsibilities serve a critical function in African-American communities. Children orphaned by sale or death of their parents under slavery, children conceived through rape, children of young mothers, children born into extreme poverty or to alcoholic or drug-addicted mothers, or children who for other reasons cannot remain with their bloodmothers have all been supported by othermothers, who, like Ella Baker's aunt, take in additional children even when they have enough of their own.

...

Many Black men also value community-based child care but exercise these values to a lesser extent. Young Black men are taught how to care for children (Young 1970; Lewis 1975). ... Differences among Black men and women in attitudes toward children may have more to do with male labor force patterns. As Ella Baker observes, "my father took care of people too, but ... my father had to work" (Cantarow 1980, 60).

...

The entire community structure of bloodmothers and othermothers is under assault in many inner-city neighborhoods, where the very fabric of African-American community life is being eroded by illegal drugs. But even in the most troubled communities, remnants of the othermother tradition endure. Bebe Moore Campbell's 1950s North Philadelphia neighborhood underwent some startling changes when crack cocaine flooded the streets in the 1980s. Increases in birth defects, child abuse, and parental neglect left many children without care. But some residents, such as Miss Nee, continue the othermother tradition. After raising her younger brothers and sisters and five children of her own, Miss Nee cares for three additional children whose families fell apart. Moreover, on any given night Miss Nee's house may be filled by up to a dozen children because she has a reputation for never turning away a needy child ("Children of the Underclass" 1989).

... The resiliency of women-centered family networks illustrates how traditional cultural values—namely, the African origins of community-based child care—can help people cope with and resist oppression. By continuing community-based child care, African-American women challenge one fundamental assumption underlying the capitalist system itself: that children are "private property" and can be disposed of as such. Notions of property, child care, and gender differences in parenting styles are embedded in the institutional arrangements of any given political economy. Under the property model stemming from capitalist patriarchal families, parents may not literally assert that their children are pieces of property, but their parenting may reflect assumptions analogous to those they make in connection with property (J. Smith 1983). For example, the exclusive parental "right" to discipline children as parents see fit, even if discipline borders on abuse, parallels the widespread assumption that property owners may dispose of their property without consulting members of the larger community. By seeing the larger community as responsible for children and by giving othermothers and other nonparents "rights" in child rearing, African-Americans challenge prevailing property relations. It is in this sense that traditional bloodmother/othermother relationships in women-centered networks are "revolutionary."

## Mothers, Daughters, and Socialization for Survival

Black mothers of daughters face a troubling dilemma. On one hand, to ensure their daughters' physical survival, mothers must teach them to fit into systems of oppression. … On the other hand, Black daughters with strong self-definitions and self-valuations who offer serious challenges to oppressive situations may not physically survive. When Ann Moody became active in the early 1960s in sit-ins and voter registration activities, her mother first begged her not to participate and then told her not to come home because she feared the whites in Moody's hometown would kill her. Despite the dangers, mothers routinely encourage Black daughters to develop skills to confront oppressive conditions. Learning that they will work and that education is a vehicle for advancement can also be seen as ways of enhancing positive self-definitions and self-valuations in Black girls. Emotional strength is essential, but not at the cost of physical survival.

… Black daughters must learn how to survive in interlocking structures of race, class, and gender oppression while rejecting and transcending those same structures. In order to develop these skills in their daughters, mothers demonstrate varying combinations of behaviors devoted to ensuring their daughters' survival—such as providing them with basic necessities and protecting them in dangerous environments—to helping their daughters go further than mothers themselves were allowed to go.

…

Understanding this goal of balancing the need for the physical survival of their daughters with the vision of encouraging them to transcend the boundaries confronting them explains many apparent contradictions in Black mother-daughter relationships. Black mothers are often described as strong disciplinarians and overly protective; yet these same women manage to raise daughters who are self-reliant and assertive. …

African-American mothers try to protect their daughters from the dangers that lie ahead by offering them a sense of their own unique self-worth. Many contemporary Black women writers report the experience of being singled out, of being given a sense of specialness at an early age which encouraged them to develop their talents. My own mother marched me to the public library at age five, helped me get my first library card, and told me that I could do anything if I learned how to read. …

… For far too many Black mothers, the demands of providing for children in interlocking systems of oppression are sometimes so demanding that they have neither the time nor the patience for affection. And yet most Black daughters love and admire their mothers and are convinced that their mothers truly love them (Joseph 1981).

…

Othermothers often help to defuse the emotional intensity of relationships between bloodmothers and their daughters. In recounting how she dealt with the intensity of her relationship with her mother, Weems describes the women teachers, neighbors, friends, and othermothers she turned to—women who, she observes, "did not have the onus of providing for me, and so had the luxury of talking to me" (1984, 27). Cheryl West's household included her brother, her lesbian mother, and Jan, her mother's lover. Jan became an othermother to West: "Yellow-colored, rotund and short in stature, Jan was like a second mother. ... Jan braided my hair in the morning, mother worked two jobs and tucked me in at night. Loving, gentle, and fastidious in the domestic arena, Jan could be a rigid disciplinarian. ... To the outside world ... she was my 'aunt' who happened to live with us. But she was much more involved and nurturing than any of my 'real' aunts" (1987, 43).

June Jordan offers an eloquent analysis of one daughter's realization of the high personal cost African-American women can pay in providing an economic and emotional foundation for their children. In the following passage Jordan offers a powerful testament of how she came to see that her mother's work was an act of love:

> As a child I noticed the sadness of my mother as she sat alone in the kitchen at night. ... Her woman's work never won permanent victories of any kind. It never enlarged the universe of her imagination or her power to influence what happened beyond the front door of our house. Her woman's work never tickled her to laugh or shout or dance. But she did raise me to respect her way of offering love and to believe that hard work is often the irreducible factor for survival, not something to avoid. Her woman's work produced a reliable home base where I could pursue the privileges of books and music. Her woman's work invented the potential for a completely different kind of work for us, the next generation of Black women: huge, rewarding hard work demanded by the huge, new ambitions that her perfect confidence in us engendered. (1985, 105)

## Community Othermothers and Political Activism

Black women's experiences as othermothers provide a foundation for Black women's political activism. Nurturing children in Black extended family networks stimulates a more generalized ethic of caring and personal accountability among African-American women who often feel accountable to all the Black community's children.

...

... Black women frequently describe Black children using family language. In recounting her increasingly successful efforts to teach a boy who had given other teachers problems, my daughter's kindergarten teacher stated, "You know how it can be—the majority of children in the learning disabled classes are *our children*. I know he didn't belong there, so I volunteered to take him." In their statements both women use family language to describe the ties that bind them as Black women to their responsibilities as members of an African-American community/family.

...

Sociologist Cheryl Gilkes (1980, 1982, 1983) suggests that community othermother relationships can be key in stimulating Black women's decisions to become community activists. Gilkes asserts that many of the Black women community activists in her study became involved in community organizing in response to the needs of their own children and of those in their communities. The following comment is typical of how many of the Black women in Gilkes's study relate to Black children: "There were a lot of summer programs springing up for kids, but they were exclusive

... and I found that most of *our kids* were excluded" (1980, 219). For many women what began as the daily expression of their obligations as community othermothers, as was the case for the kindergarten teacher, developed into full-fledged actions as community leaders.

This community othermother tradition also explains the "mothering the mind" relationships that can develop between Black women teachers and their Black women students. Unlike the traditional mentoring so widely reported in educational literature, this relationship goes far beyond that of providing students with either technical skills or a network of academic and professional contacts. Bell Hooks shares the special vision that teachers who see our work in community othermother terms can pass on to our students: "I understood from the teachers in those segregated schools that the work of any teacher committed to the full self-realization of students was necessarily and fundamentally radical, that ideas were not neutral, that to teach in a way that liberates, that expands consciousness, that awakens, is to challenge domination at its very core" (1989, 50). Like the mother-daughter relationship, this "mothering the mind" among Blackwomen seeks to move toward the mutuality of a shared sisterhood that binds African-American women as community othermothers.

Community othermothers have made important contributions in building a different type of community in often hostile political and economic surroundings (Reagon 1987). Community othermothers' actions demonstrate a clear rejection of separateness and individual interest as the basis of either community organization or individual self-actualization. Instead, the connectedness with others and common interest expressed by community othermothers models a very different value system, one whereby Afrocentric feminist ethics of caring and personal accountability move communities forward.

## Motherhood as a Symbol of Power

Motherhood—whether bloodmother, othermother, or community othermother—can be invoked by African-American women as a symbol of power. Much of Black women's status in African-American communities stems not only from actions as mothers in Black family networks but from contributions as community othermothers.

Black women's involvement in fostering African-American community development forms the basis for community-based power. This is the type of power many African-Americans have in mind when they describe the "strong Black women" they see around them in traditional African-American communities. Community othermothers work on behalf of the Black community by expressing ethics of caring and personal accountability which embrace conceptions of transformative power and mutuality (Kuykendall 1983). Such power is transformative in that Black women's relationships with children and other vulnerable community members is not intended to dominate or control. Rather, its purpose is to bring people along, to—in the words of late nineteenth-century Black feminists—"uplift the race" so that vulnera-

ble members of the community will be able to attain the self-reliance and independence essential for resistance.

...

## The View from the Inside:
## The Personal Meaning of Mothering

Within African-American communities, women's innovative and practical approaches to mothering under oppressive conditions often bring power and recognition. But this situation should not obscure the costs of motherhood to many Black
women. Black motherhood is fundamentally a contradictory institution. African-
American communities value motherhood, but Black mothers' ability to cope with
race, class, and gender oppression should not be confused with transcending those
conditions. Black motherhood can be rewarding, but it can also extract high personal costs. The range of Black women's reactions to motherhood and the ambivalence that many Black women feel about mothering reflect motherhood's contradictory nature.

Certain dimensions of Black motherhood are clearly problematic. Coping with
unwanted pregnancies and being unable to care for one's children is oppressive. ...
Many Black women have children they really do not want. When combined with
Black community values claiming that good Black women always want their children, ignorance about reproductive issues leaves many Black women with unplanned pregnancies and the long-term responsibilities of parenting.

Ann Moody's mother ... did not celebrate her repeated pregnancies. Moody remembers her mother's feelings when her mother started "getting fat" and her boyfriend stopped coming by: "Again Mama started crying every night. ... When I heard
Mama crying at night, I felt so bad. She wouldn't cry until we were all in bed and she
thought we were sleeping. Every night I would lie awake for hours listening to her
sobbing quietly in her pillow. The bigger she got the more she cried, and I did too"
(Moody 1968, 46). To her children, Moody's mother may have appeared to be the stereotypical strong Black mother, but Ann Moody was able to see the cost her mother
paid for living with this controlling image.

Dealing with an unwanted pregnancy can have tragic consequences. ... In New
York, for example, during the several years preceding the decriminalization of abortions, 80 percent of the deaths from illegal abortions involved Black and Puerto Rican women (Davis 1981).

Strong pronatalist values in African-American communities may stem in part
from traditional Black values that vest adult status on women who become biological
mothers. For many, becoming a biological mother is often seen as a significant first
step toward womanhood. ... In spite of the high personal costs, ... an overwhelming
majority of unmarried Black adolescent mothers choose to keep their children
(Simms 1988). ...

Protecting Black children remains a primary concern of African-American mothers because Black children are at risk. Nearly 40 percent of all Black mothers receive

no prenatal care in the first trimester of pregnancy. One in every eight Black infants has a low birth weight, a factor contributing to an infant mortality rate among Black babies that remains twice that for white infants. During the first year of life Black babies die from fires and burns at a rate 4.5 times greater than that of white infants. The number of cases of pediatric AIDS has doubled between 1986 and 1989, and more than 75 percent of children with AIDS are Black or Hispanic, more than half of them the offspring of intravenous drug users ("Children of the Underclass" 1989, 27). An anonymous mother expresses her concern for Black children:

> I turn my eyes on the little children, and keep on praying that one of them will grow up at the right second, when the schoolteachers have time to say hello and give him the lessons he needs, and when they get rid of the building here and let us have a place you can breathe in and not get bitten all the time, and when the men can find work—because *they* can't have children, and so they have to drink or get on drugs to find some happy moments, and some hope about things. (Lerner 1972, 315)

To this mother, even though her children are her hope, the conditions under which she must mother are intolerable.

Black mothers also pay the cost of giving up their own dreams of achieving full creative ability. Because many spend so much time feeding the physical needs of their children, as Alice Walker queries, "when … did my overworked mother have time to know or care about feeding the creative spirit?" (1983, 239). Much of that creativity goes into dimensions of Black culture that are relatively protected from the incursions of the dominant group. Many Black women blues singers, poets, and artists manage to incorporate their art into their daily responsibilities as bloodmothers and othermothers. But for far too many African-American women who are weighed down by the incessant responsibilities of mothering others, that creative spark never finds full expression.

…

Despite the obstacles and costs, motherhood remains a symbol of hope for many of even the poorest Black women. One anonymous mother describes how she feels about her children:

> To me, having a baby inside me is the only time I'm really alive. I know I can make something, do something, no matter what color my skin is, and what names people call me. … You can see the little one grow and get larger and start doing things, and you feel there must be some hope, some chance that things will get better; because there it is, right before you, a real, live, growing baby. … The baby is a good sign, or at least he's *some* sign. If we didn't have that, what would be the difference from death? (Lerner 1972, 314)

Given the harshness of this mother's environment, her children offer hope. They are all she has.

Mothering is an empowering experience for many African-American women. Gwendolyn Brooks (1953) explores this issue of reproductive power in her novel *Maud Martha*. Maud Martha is virtually silent until she gives birth to her daughter, when "pregnancy and the birth of a child connect Maud to some power in herself, some power to speak, to be heard, to articulate feelings" (Washington 1987, 395). Her child serves as a catalyst for her movement into self-definition, self-valuation, and eventual empowerment. Marita Golden describes a similar experience that illustrates how the special relationship between mother and child can foster a changed definition of self and an accompanying empowerment:

> Now I belonged to me. No parents or husband claiming me. … There was only my child who consumed and replenished me … my son's love was unconditional and, as such, gave me more freedom than any love I had known. … I at last accepted mama as my name. Realized that it did not melt down any other designations. Discovered that it expanded them—and me. (1983, 240–41)

This special relationship that Black mothers have with their children can also foster a creativity, a mothering of the mind and soul, for all involved. It is this gift that Alice Walker alludes to when she notes, "and so our mothers and grandmothers have, more often than not anonymously, handed on the creative spark, the seed of the flower they themselves never hoped to see" (1983, 240).

But what cannot be overlooked in work emphasizing mothers' influences on their children is how Black children affirm their mothers and how important that affirmation can be in a society that denigrates Blackness and womanhood. In her essay "One Child of One's Own," Alice Walker offers a vision of what African-American mother-child relationships can be:

> It is not my child who tells me: I have no femaleness white women must affirm. Not my child who says: I have no rights black men must respect. It is not my child who has purged my face from history and herstory, and left mystory just that, a mystery; my child loves my face and would have it on every page, if she could, as I have loved my own parents' faces above all others. … We are together, my child and I. Mother and child, yes, but *sisters* really, against whatever denies us all that we are. (Walker 1979, 75)

---

### References

Aschenbrenner, Joyce. 1975. *Lifelines, Black Families in Chicago.* Prospect Heights, IL: Waveland Press.

Brooks, Gwendolyn. 1953. *Maud Martha.* Boston: Atlantic Press.

Burnham, Linda, 1985. "Has Poverty Been Feminized in Black America?" *Black Scholar* 16(2): 14–24.

Cantarow, Ellen. 1980. *Moving the Mountain: Women Working for Social Change.* Old Westbury, NY: Feminist Press.

"Children of the Underclass." 1989. *Newsweek* September 11, 16–27.

Christian, Barbara. 1985. *Black Feminist Criticism, Perspectives on Black Women Writers.* New York: Pergamon.

Dance, Daryl. 1979. "Black Eve or Madonna? A Study of the Antithetical Views of the Mother in Black American Literature." In *Sturdy Black Bridges: Visions of Black Women in Literature,* edited by Roseann Bell, Bettye Parker, and Beverly Guy-Sheftall, 123–32. Garden City, NY: Anchor.

Davis, Angela Y. 1981. *Women, Race and Class.* New York: Random House.

Frazier, E. Franklin. 1948. *The Negro Family in the United States.* New York: Dryden Press.
Gilkes, Cheryl Townsend. 1980. "'Holding Back the Ocean with a Broom': Black Women and Community Work." In *The Black Woman,* edited by La Frances Rogers-Rose, 217–32. Beverly Hills, CA: Sage.
_____. 1982. "Successful Rebellious Professionals: The Black Woman's Professional Identity and Community Commitment." *Psychology of Women Quarterly* 6(3): 289–311.
_____. 1983. "Going Up for the Oppressed: The Career Mobility of Black Women Community Workers." *Journal of Social Issues* 39(3): 115–39.
Golden, Marita. 1983. *Migrations of the Heart.* New York: Ballantine.
Gutman, Herbert. 1976. *The Black Family in Slavery and Freedom, 1750–1925.* New York: Random House.
Hooks, Bell. 1989. *Talking Back: Thinking Feminist, Thinking Black.* Boston: South End Press.
Jordan, June. 1985. *On Call.* Boston: South End Press.
Joseph, Gloria. 1981. "Black Mothers and Daughters: Their Roles and Functions in American Society." In *Common Differences,* edited by Gloria Joseph and Jill Lewis, 75–126. Garden City, NY: Anchor.
_____. 1984. "Black Mothers and Daughters: Traditional and New Perspectives." *Sage: A Scholarly Journal on Black Women* 1(2): 17–21.
Kuykendall, Eleanor H. 1983. "Toward an Ethic of Nurturance: Luce Irigaray on Mothering and Power." In *Motherhood: Essays in Feminist Theory,* edited by Joyce Treblicot, 263–74. Totowa, NJ: Rowman & Allanheld.
Ladner, Joyce. 1972. *Tomorrow's Tomorrow.* Garden City, NY: Doubleday.
Ladner, Joyce, and Ruby Morton Gourdine. 1984. "Intergenerational Teenage Motherhood: Some Preliminary Findings." *Sage: A Scholarly Journal on Black Women* 1(2): 22–24.
Lerner, Gerda, ed. 1972. *Black Women in White America: A Documentary History.* New York: Vintage.
Lewis, Diane K. 1975. "The Black Family: Socialization and Sex Roles." *Phylon* 36(3): 221–37.
Martin, Elmer, and Joanne Mitchell Martin. 1978. *The Black Extended Family.* Chicago: University of Chicago Press.
Moody, Ann. 1968. *Coming of Age in Mississippi.* New York: Dell.
Moynihan, Daniel Patrick. 1965. *The Negro Family: The Case for National Action.* Washington, DC: GPO.
Reagon, Bernice Johnson. 1987. "African Diaspora Women: The Making of Cultural Workers." In *Women in Africa and the African Diaspora,* edited by Rosalyn Terborg-Penn, Sharon Harley, and Andrea Benton Rushing, 167–180. Washington, DC: Howard University Press.
Simms, Margaret C. 1988. *The Choices that Young Black Women Make: Education, Employment, and Family Formation.* Working Paper No. 190, Wellesley, MA: Center for Research on Women, Wellesley College.
Simonsen, Thordis, ed. 1986. *You May Plow Here: The Narrative of Sara Brooks.* New York: Touchstone.
Smith, Janet Farrell. 1983. "Parenting as Property." In *Mothering: Essays in Feminist Theory,* edited by Joyce Trebilcot, 199–212. Totowa, NJ: Rowman & Allanheld.
Stack, Carol D. 1974. *All Our Kin: Strategies for Survival in a Black Community.* New York: Harper & Row.
Staples, Robert. 1973. *The Black Woman in America.* Chicago: Nelson-Hall.
Sudarkasa, Niara. 1981. "Interpreting the African Heritage in Afro-American Family Organization." In *Black Families,* edited by Harriette Pipes McAdoo, 37–53. Beverly Hills, CA: Sage.
Tanner, Nancy. 1974. "Matrifocality in Indonesia and Africa and among Black Americans." In *Woman, Culture, and Society,* edited by Michelle Z. Rosaldo and Louise Lamphere, 129–56. Stanford: Stanford University Press.
Troester, Rosalie Riegle. 1984. "Turbulence and Tenderness: Mothers, Daughters, and 'Othermothers' in Paule Marshall's *Brown Girl, Brownstones." Sage: A Scholarly Journal on Black Women* 1(2): 13–16.

U.S. Department of Commerce, Bureau of the Census. 1986. *Money Income and Poverty Status of Families and Persons in the United States: 1985.* Series P-60, No. 154, Washington, DC: GPO.

―――. 1989. *Money Income of Households, Families, and Persons in the United States: 1987.* Series P-60, No. 162. Washington, DC: GPO.

Wade-Gayles, Gloria. 1980. "She Who Is Black and Mother: In Sociology and Fiction, 1940–1970." In *The Black Woman,* edited by La Frances Rodgers-Rose, 89–106. Beverly Hills, CA: Sage.

Walker, Alice. 1979. "One Child of One's Own: A Meaningful Digression Within the Work(s)." *Ms.* 8(2), August: 47–50, 72–75.

―――. 1983. *In Search of Our Mothers' Gardens.* New York: Harcourt Brace Jovanovich.

Washington, Mary Helen, ed. 1987. *Invented Lives: Narratives of Black Women 1860–1960.* Garden City, NY: Anchor.

Weems, Renita. 1984. "'Hush. Mama's Gotta Go Bye Bye': A Personal Narrative." *Sage: A Scholarly Journal on Black Women* 1(2): 25–28.

West, Cheryl. 1987. "Lesbian Daughter." *Sage: A Scholarly Journal on Black Women* 4(2): 42–44.

Young, Virginia Heyer. 1970. "Family and Childhood in a Southern Negro Community." *American Anthropologist* 72(32): 269–88.

Zinn, Maxine Baca. 1989. "Family, Race, and Poverty in the Eighties." *Signs* 14(4): 856–74.

# The Che-Lumumba School: Creating a Revolutionary Family Community

## Ann Ferguson

Most of us have so completely absorbed the ideal of the patriarchal nuclear family—breadwinning husband, housewife, mom and children—that it comes as a shock to discover that only 15.9 percent of families in the U.S. meet the description.[1] This gap between reality and the ideal creates a crisis in values for most people. The needs for love, security and mutual aid in raising children that the family used to meet are no longer being met. We need to understand the causes of this crisis in order to explore possibilities for alternative structures for living, loving and parenting. The kind of structures I mean are not of the utopian sort … which cannot be achieved until after a socialist-feminist revolution. Instead, I will present some goals and ideas for creating what I call "revolutionary family-communities,"[2] communities that people can begin to set up right now. These communities will create a base for expressing in embryo some new egalitarian values of loving and parenting. Furthermore, they will at the same time provide us with the material support needed to continue to challenge the combined domination system of capitalist patriarchy.

...

## The Ideal of a Revolutionary Socialist-Feminist Family Community

My model of a revolutionary family community is a number of families and/or individuals who may live separately but who are united in a working network which constitute for them a self-conscious resistance community: a community which deliberately creates values which run counter to the dominant values of capitalist patriarchal culture. The community aims to provide a supportive structure for its children to learn revolutionary values and for its adults to eliminate habits and personality traits imposed by the dominant culture.

The overarching goal of the revolutionary family-community I propose is equality: that is, members should be economically, socially, psychologically and politically *equal* to the maximum extent possible. Different networks of families will have to develop practical procedures for equalizing members, and these procedures will vary depending on the extent of members' resources, the nature of their commitment to each other and the composition of the group.

Here are some basic goals for a socialist-feminist revolutionary family-community.

1. To eliminate childrearing inequalities between men and women in order to provide the structural base for men and women to be *equal nurturers* to the children and to each other as well as *equally autonomous*. This means challenging the male-as-autonomous, female-as-nurturer dichotomy.

2. To challenge the sexual division of labor. This involves reorganizing not only childrearing and other family maintenance tasks (cooking, car and house repair, etc.) but also whatever aspects of public life the family-community can control.

3. To break down the possessive privacy of the two primary sets of relationships in the American patriarchal family: the couple and the parent-child relationship. People in a revolutionary family-community have a joint responsibility both to build revolutionary values in their own couple and parent-child relationships, and also to *share in* responsibility for aiding all the couples and children in the community in these tasks. Other biological and social parents in the community must be seen as having rights and responsibilities in the upbringing and value formation of all the children. People must understand that unresolved conflicts in love relationships and in parent-child relationships divide and weaken the community as well. Thus, members have a commitment to the health and close ties of the community that is equal to their commitment to lover and children or parents.

4. To equalize power as far as possible between parents and children and, in general, between adults and children. There may indeed be biological limits to this process: from what we know about human development it would seem that children need to identify with adults to develop their core identity and values. Nonetheless,

there are structures which can give children more power and choice in the role-modeling process such as peer group collective learning situations, alternate social mothers and fathers, and a role in the decision-making and productive life of the community commensurate with abilities and age.

5. To eliminate the base for heterosexism in society which along with patriarchy and capitalism contributes to women's oppression. This means openly allowing gay persons, including gay mothers and fathers, into the revolutionary family-community. Single gay people should have the opportunity to have warm, loving roles as social parents, and thus break down the unique social privileges of access to a parent-child relationship now limited to biological parents.

6. To break down elitist attitudes about the superiority of mental and professional work to manual work.

7. To deal with racism and classism.

8. To introduce economic sharing in the family-community which allows members to develop a sense of commitment to each other.

In what follows, I shall present the outlines of one specific revolutionary family-community that I am a member of, the Che-Lumumba School Community.[3] I shall indicate the ways in which our community has successfully struggled to achieve some of the goals outlined and the problems that remain. Others hopefully will be able to take what lessons are relevant and modify them to suit their own potential family-community.

## The Che-Lumumba School
## Revolutionary Family-Community

The Che-Lumumba School is an alternative school for children from the ages of six to twelve. It has a political philosophy that involves active advocacy of Third World liberation struggles from a generally progressive or socialist viewpoint. It is a parent-teacher cooperatively-run school. The parents are students, teachers and community people connected to the Third World community in Amherst and centered around the University of Massachusetts. There are also non-parent student and community volunteers who help with the teaching. The number of children in the school during its eight-year existence has varied from two to thirteen and is presently seven. The parents hire a head teacher every year whom they pay with tuition money, based on what people can afford to pay, and money from benefits organized by parents.

Initially the school was started by several black nationalist parents who were graduate students at the School of Education.[4] These parents wished to provide an Afro-American self-defined education for their children as an alternative to the cultural whitewash and implicit racism of the public schools. The school subsequently broadened its base to include Hispanic parents and Third World members, then white parents with Third World children and, finally, a limited number of white children. The confusion over the political line of the school caused a succession of tensions which will be discussed later.

The political philosophy of the Che-Lumumba School currently emphasizes pride in traditional Third World cultures at the same time that it is dedicated to fight racism, sexism and classism by making the children aware of how the dominant culture is controlled in the interests of white male capitalists. The school represents a coalition of political interests rather than a unified set of priorities.

...

## Working Structure of the School and Socialist-Feminist Values

The following agreements are key to the organizational structure of the school:

Agreement 1: The parents are in control of all decisions as to content and form of the educational process.

Agreement 2: The children also have some weight in policy-making. There are regular joint children-parents' meetings in which the children say what they like and don't like about the school and parents discuss values with the children.

Agreement 3: All parents must do productive work involved with the continued existence and program of the school. Parents can either teach in the school an hour or two a week or serve on a committee.

What these agreements do in practice is the following: since both fathers and mothers are involved in teaching and since the school is like a supportive child-rearing community (school meetings are bi-weekly with children attending and pot-luck suppers), the child rearing inequalities between women and men are lessened. Children see men taking care of babies and nurturing children, and they see women in positions of authority. The children have supportive alternate role models in other parents of the same sex that they relate to regularly, which encourages the chances for autonomous development of strong personalities in boys and girls. The volunteer single student workers at the school are as involved in the decision-making and in the general community as the parents and children, so the children can see that one can be single and yet contribute to social parenting.

The destructive possessiveness of the parent-child relationship, typical of most nuclear families, is being challenged by the school, although this is a difficult area for everyone. The members are sensitive to criticisms about how they bring up their children. But everyone agrees that even simple family problems are also school and community problems. If Malik, reaching puberty, is obsessed with sexual interests and talks about this to the younger girls, Tanya gets upset, because her mother is very protective and has told her nothing about sex. It then takes a school meeting to decide parental policy on the degree of sex education and discussion of sex that should take place in the school.

...

A strong emphasis in the curriculum is on the history of workers' struggles in this country as well as studies of Third World socialist counties, problems of imperialism and so on. Children regularly visit factories, support strikes and march on picket lines. By meeting and identifying with workers in their community on strike, the children will have grounds to question the elitist assumption that intellectual labor is superior to manual labor.

## Problems and Limitations
## of the Che-Lumumba School-Community

Perhaps the most important problem that the school-community has faced in its nine-year history is its ongoing economic crisis. Foundations are simply not interested in funding a radical school with explicit socialist, anti-imperialist, anti-racist and anti-sexist values. The parents cannot pay tuition. Most are poor and overextended. The constant fundraising of the most labor intensive sort is exhausting. The school constantly hovers near bankruptcy, and the tension this engenders exacerbates political disagreements within the community.

The vagueness of the school's general stand against racism, sexism and classism has raised conflicts over relative priorities in attacking these issues. One example of such a conflict occurred around the issue of working class history and solidarity. Black nationalist parents could agree that the school should oppose classism. Nonetheless, they disagreed with an emphasis on working class struggles, particularly labor union struggles, on the grounds that many unions in American history have defended white workers' privileges at the expense of black workers. Guilt-tripping was used as a tactic to attack white Marxist parents' positions on these matters.

A similar problem occurred around the topic of sexism. Some of the parents were willing to agree to the general principle that the school should attack sexism, but balked when it came to educating the children about nitty gritty issues like the right of women to reproductive freedom. These parents did not want to process questions of male domination in the group or the special problems faced by single mothers. It was only when the three most vocal black nationalist parents left the community that this problem was resolved. Last year the older children had an intensive sex educational course where all these issues were discussed.

Most of the Third World women in the group do not define themselves as feminist. They worry that raising the issues of sexism will weaken their black or Hispanic community identification in favor of connections with the predominantly white feminist community. An important source of ambivalence about feminism is the existence of a strong lesbian separatist community in the Amherst-Northampton area, a community whose politics in practice are seen to exclude effective organizing around issues of racism, classism and imperialism.

Another important political disagreement has been the analysis of race. Members have felt a need to build a strong sense of black pride, of identification with African roots. The problem is that most of the children in the school are brown, and their parents white or mixed. The separatist tendencies of black nationalism tend to put strains on brown children who identify with both black and white communities and/or see themselves in the middle.

Although the group uses the techniques of criticism/self-criticism to deal with parent-child relationships, it has been wary of including discussions of the problems of couples. In part this is because members feel the right to privacy in this area, and in part because no one has been brave enough to start the process in the group by bringing up personal issues. This indicates a general problem for revolutionary family-communities. Groups will be loathe to deal with ingrained values which aren't obviously connected to the central work around which the families are focused.

Currently only one parent in the Che-Lumumba School-community is gay, and that person is a white lesbian feminist. The divisiveness in the school around feminist issues has made it politically difficult for this member to raise issues concerned with heterosexism. In part this is because her priority is feminist issues. Nonetheless, she has struggled privately with many of the members, including the children, around anti-gay attitudes as they arise.

Although the school collects tuition on a sliding scale, it has not dealt with more radical proposals for economic sharing, e.g. collective funds for clothes, food, to send children to summer camp or to help subsidize low income members for rent payments. Probably the major drawback to the idea of economic sharing in the school is that there really isn't much surplus to share. Economic sharing remains an important concept for those family-communities in which it could make a substantial difference to perceived class inequalities in the group.

Single mothers in the school have had an especially difficult situation. They were less likely to be able to attend as many school functions as other parents because of their "double shift" problem. Furthermore, many were not easily able to fully reciprocate shared childcare arrangements after school because of their demanding schedules. A higher proportion of children from these households involved school discipline problems, particularly among the boys. At first members tended to scapegoat these parents because of the extra responsibilities their membership placed on the others. Recently, however, the school-community has improved its consciousness by becoming more aware of the general problems single mothers face.

In conclusion, I would like to suggest another model of a revolutionary family-community that could be explored with differing intensities by those who have neither the resources nor the core of dedicated parents with common values to run an alternative community school. This is a community created with the help of a parents' support group, which might start out of a parent-teacher organization, a women's center or a community center. The parents' support group might begin as a support group for single parents or for Third World parents or for lesbian mothers or for socialist parents. Once the group is set up and meets regularly in consciousness-raising and mutual support sessions, members of the group may coalesce their values and decide on a more permanent commitment to a revolutionary family-community. We need to experiment in as many ways as possible and with as many communities as possible in creating revolutionary family-communities, structures we will need for the long haul ahead toward a socialist-feminist revolution.

---

### Notes

Acknowledgements: I want to thank Keitha Fine, Connie Kruger and Aylette Jenness for their valuable editorial help and content suggestions. Thanks secondly to the Che-Lumumba School for the model and for providing an important community for myself and my family. Finally, thanks to the socialist and feminist communities in Amherst for political values, theoretical frameworks and personal support.

1. All the statistics in this article are from the U.S. Statistical Abstract, 1977 as quoted in "Who is the Real Family?", *Ms.*, Aug. 1978. The 15.9 percent figure does not include couples who do not have children living with them, or families where the wife works part or full-time outside the home.

My general concept of "revolutionary family-community" is derived both from the examples of revolutionary communes in the first part of the Russian Revolution (cf. W. Reich, *The Sexual Revolution*, Simon and Schuster, N.Y., 1974) and from Gramsci's idea, in *The Prison Notebooks*, that revolutionaries should create counter cultural hegemonic structures to build support for revolutionary consciousness—a cultural revolution—before the economic and political revolution could occur.

3. [*Editor's note:* The Che-Lumumba School operated for several years in the late 1970s.]

4. The parents got the idea from a graduate class they took with Education Professor Gloria Joseph in which she stressed the importance of Black American parent cooperative schools as a means of community empowerment. With her help the students developed a model curriculum for such a school. When the class was over, some of the students decided to try out their model, and hence the Che-Lumumba School was born.

# Friends as Family: No One Said It Would Be Easy

## Karen Lindsey

Even when the alternative family is essentially decent, there can be problems. Creating alternatives to the traditional family isn't always easy. We are going against concepts we've been raised with, and we're stepping outside of the boundaries society has created for us. Because of this, we lack our own set of rules and roles, and we have to decide for ourselves, individually or together, what rules to make, what guidelines to follow.

Often, our guidelines are in direct conflict with the guidelines of the world outside. Sometimes there are legal prohibitions against living the lives we have defined for ourselves. Homosexuality remains, at least on the books, illegal. Many towns and cities have zoning ordinances limiting the number of unrelated individuals who can share a single household—in Belle Tere, California, only two unrelated individuals can live together in a single-family dwelling. Hence, people who are attempting to form communal or collective families in such areas are out of luck.

...

Sometimes it isn't the law that interferes with friendship families, but simply social attitudes. Almost everyone I spoke with had experienced minor hassles from nonfamilial friends, relatives, and strangers who couldn't deal with their unconventional families. Freelance writer Emily Prager wrote a poignant article in *Ms.* about her relationship with her friend Bill. Never lovers, she and Bill lived together for three years, but the relationship was far deeper than a conventional roommate arrangement. During the first year, both had recently ended their first serious love affairs. "We needed time to recover. Except for the hours we went to work, we mainly stayed home and licked our wounds."

Their friends were hostile to their arrangement. Some refused to believe that they weren't lovers; others who did believe it "felt that in a time when living together and sleeping together had just become acceptable, living together without sleeping together was distinctly perverse." But the two continued to maintain a close, warm bonding, going through their period of "recovery" together. When friends had parties, they went together—"running interference for each other."

In time, when they felt more open to forming new sexual or romantic relationships, their friends again put a damper on it: In spite of their insistence that they weren't a couple, their friends all assumed that they were lovers who weren't monogamous. It became impossible for either to meet potential mates.

It upset both of them. "We had established a home base, a family ... But what others could not understand was that this attachment did not preclude our having lovers." When Emily fell in love, the pressures became too strong; her new lover was horrified by her relationship with Bill. The relationship proved awkward, and Emily decided that she couldn't have "an all-encompassing love relationship" and still live with Bill. "We had managed to recreate the perfect adult childhood," she notes. "Security and love without sex, without risk. We were too entrenched to change it. We could only leave it behind." They soon moved into separate apartments, but remain a family: "We still spend Thanksgiving and Christmas together, and probably always will. We grew up together, Bill and I."[1]

In a sense, the saddest thing about Prager's story is her acceptance that such a relationship had to end—or at least to change form. Perhaps it did. But it's hard not to wonder whether she would have felt differently if Bill had been a brother—or a sister. How much did the definitions of their friends, of the world around them, create *their* definitions? Maybe they needed to live apart in order to be emotionally free to create important sexual relationships with other people. But in reading the article it's difficult to be convinced of that. The tone, the emphasis on friends' views of their relationship, suggest that their separation may not have been as much growth as capitulation. At the very least, the hassles that their friends put them through illustrate the difficulties of creating alternative families even in "liberated" circles.

But it's not only outside forces that cause problems when friends become, or try to become, family. The social concept of friendship as transient—a concept Christopher Lasch seizes on in his celebration of the mythical happy family of the past, *Haven in a Heartless World*—has a certain superficial appeal. Friends, we're told, make no demands on each other, have no major expectations of each other, make no major commitments to each other. Thus they can function as a relief from the demands and commitments involved in family or romantic relationships. But—and this Lasch conveniently ignores—when people begin to define friends as family, they usually lose that convenient, casual component of friendship. Depth in a relationship entails a loss of casualness: If someone is important, even necessary, in your life, then the interaction between you and that person becomes fraught with the same problems and uncertainties that characterize a romantic relationship, or a familial one.

But while there are social formulae for commitments to both family and lovers, there aren't any for commitments to friends. Your family—your parents, siblings, children—are yours for life. You may not be able to stand each other, but you belong to each other; there are certain obligations (often reinforced by law) that you have to each other. You don't even have to make a commitment; the commitment is made for you. With your spouse, you *do* make a commitment—but the commitment is clear. To have and to hold, for richer for poorer, till death do you part. However frequently that commitment fails, however obscured and confused it becomes in a supposedly "permissive" society, it retains at least its mythical power. The ideal you are expected to strive for is to love each other, to work through any problems you have, to live together for the rest of your lives.

But friendship commitments need to be defined by each of us for ourselves, and it can be terrifying. We want continuity, but what does continuity mean? Will you still love me tomorrow? Will you turn down a wonderful job because it's five hundred miles from where I live? If you have a new friend, will you get bored with me? Adolescents are allowed to ask these questions, but when they grow up, they are supposed to transfer all that intensity to a lover. What happens when we begin to transfer back—to reclaim the right to take friendship seriously?

...

... In the chosen family, as in the blood family, people sometimes die. "I had that happen to me one time," says Jane. ... "A friend who was family to me killed herself a couple of years ago, and that was preceded by a depression in which she wouldn't talk to anybody for six to eight weeks. Before that, there was a period when she'd say really scary things to me like 'everything is nothing' and 'nothing is everything.' She shut me and the other members of her family out. That loss—it might as well have been a member of my family of origin. In some ways my husband had a lot of trouble understanding what I was going through, because he just saw this person as a great friend, so he couldn't understand why six months later I'd hear somebody who sounded like her and get all teary-eyed ... It's been a year and half now, and just recently I drove through the town that she lived in, and the tears just started coming, and I had that feeling once again, 'Oh, yes, you don't get by this.'

"The more you make yourself that open, that vulnerable, that caring, to a large network of people, the greater the number of losses you must suffer in your life. And one of the things that bothers me about the intensity with which I approach these people is the intensity with which I have to deal with anything happening to them. When they are in crisis, in some profound way I have to be too. ...'"

Confusion over the extent of a commitment can create nearly as great a problem as loss. When people are clearly committed to their friendships, the question of what that commitment means can be a loaded one. I don't worry that my friend Kathy will forsake me for a lover, but I do wonder what the extent of her commitment is to me—and what the extent of my commitment is to her. I joke about it—"You can't move out of this neighborhood unless I go with you. If course, *I* can move any time I want." And Kathy laughs. But we know it's serious on some level; we both know that the mechanisms for creating continuity aren't there for us. We want commitment from each other, and we feel commitment to each other, but neither of us knows the parameters of that commitment beyond the present. We've both had bad experiences. One friendship of mine ended because the friend wanted more "family" than I did; with another, still-close friend, I'm constantly aware that I want more than she does, and that this is an ever-present undercurrent in our relationship. Who sees who as family, and what does family mean to each of the people involved?

...

When the relationships with friends involve children, there's another element of confusion to deal with. You are family with the offspring of somebody else, but what degree of authority, of input into the raising of the children, do you have? Again, there are no social guidelines. You're not a parent, or a stepparent, or a guardian. You're "just a friend." The deeper the involvement with the child, of course, the more difficult the problems. For people living communally, conflicts can become major. George and John, who have lived communally with their wives, the children of both couples, and several childless people for nine years, talked about some of the problems they've had. "John and Marcy and Berit and I used to have much more in common in the way we looked at childrearing, say two years ago, than we do now," George says. "The divergence has gotten to the point where it's a problem in the house, and so we're asking somebody from another house to come and do some conflict resolution to see if we can 'agree to disagree' in ways that are creative and mutually helpful rather than just being a tension producer. ...

In other communes, people have had to deal with the problems of being separated from children with whom they feel closely bonded. "I get freaked by Jan wanting to take Sam away," says a man quoted in Nell Dunn's *Different Drummer*. "That's a big disadvantage, this insecurity because Jan is his biological mother. It feels as if she can take my kid away."[2] "This seems to me to be a rock-bottom problem of this collective," says a member of a different commune, quoted in the same book. "The biological parents have power over the kids that the nonparents just don't have, although the nonparents are giving just as much in the way of care ... The nonbiological parents suffer from insecurity, the acute insecurity of having no legal power over *their* children."[3]

The problem can work the other way around as well: a child growing up in a commune may view *all* its members as parents, and be as devastated as any child of divorced parents when commune members decide to leave. Michael Weiss in *Living Together,* an account of the commune he, his wife, and their child lived in for several years, wrote of the effect on his son's life when two of the members decided to leave. Sobbing, the boy demanded to know if the couple was really leaving. When his mother told him that they were indeed planning to leave, he cried: "It's just like last year with Gil and Wendy … Communal living just isn't worth it if everybody keeps going away." "Shouldn't a kid feel that there are people he can depend on absolutely?" Weiss asks.[4]

Weiss didn't come up with an easy answer to this question—and indeed there are no easy answers. The effort to balance freedom with commitment is never an easy one, even among adults. In some relationships, the needs provide their own balance—when both (or all) the people involved need or expect the same degree of commitment and the same *form* of commitment. In others, the balance can be achieved through facing the problem, acknowledging the disparity of need, and working through it with each other as seriously as one would with a spouse or lover. But the confusions, the inequities, remain a given. Sometimes they are unresolvable, and the relationship ends. … Sometimes they're unresolvable and the relationship *doesn't* end—the people "agree to disagree" and accept the pain that accompanies the inequity. But these are problems that are organic to any relationship, not simply to nonbiological families. The difference is that we have fewer mechanisms to disguise them, fewer outside forces to define what we *should* give to each other and want from each other. In attempting to create bondings without bondage, we are forced to acknowledge and confront the conflicts within and among ourselves. Eternal vigilance is the price of personal, as well as political, freedom.

---

## Notes

1. Emily Prager, "Roommates, but not Lovers," *Ms.,* April 1979, pp. 16–19.
2. Nell Dunn, *Different Drummer* (New York: Harcourt Brace Jovanovich, 1977), p. 33.
3. Dunn, pp. 50–51.
4. Michael Weiss, *Living Together* (New York: McGraw-Hill, 1974), pp. 133–134.

# PART SIX

# THE PERSONAL

# AS POLITICAL

"The personal is political" was the distinctive slogan of 1960s radical feminism. It encapsulated significant differences between the second wave of Western feminism, on the one hand, and, on the other hand, both first-wave Western feminism and the two main contending political philosophies of the twentieth century, liberalism and Marxism.

A distinguishing feature of liberal political philosophy is its concern with protecting individuals from unwarranted governmental intrusion in their lives. This concern is expressed in liberal theory by a distinction between the public and private domains of human life: The public domain is the realm of the political, supposedly the proper arena of governmental regulation; the private domain, by contrast, comprises all those aspects of life that liberals believe should be exempt from governmental intervention. Not all liberals agree on just where the line between public and private life should be drawn, but one influential contemporary understanding of the private was summed up by former U.S. Chief Justice Warren Burger as follows: "This privacy right encompasses and protects the personal intimacies of the home, the family, marriage, motherhood, procreation and childrearing." Of obvious interest to feminists is that Burger's definition of the private sphere includes precisely those areas of life with which women are identified and to which we have often been confined. Indeed, Burger's definition is explicitly gendered in that it includes motherhood but not fatherhood.

Unlike liberalism, Marxist theory has not historically defended individual rights to privacy as a matter of political principle, but Marxism's primary theoretical and political focus has always been on the public spheres of economy and government rather than on what liberals call the personal spheres of the family and sexuality. Because Marxists have regarded so-called personal life as shaped by its economic and political context, they have often given priority to understanding and transforming that context rather than focusing directly on sexual or procreative issues.

The radical feminist insistence that the personal was political not only presented a direct challenge both to liberal theory and Marxist practice; it also contrasted sharply with the emphases of earlier Western feminism, which had focused primarily on winning such rights as the vote, education, property, and employment. Although the achievement of these rights obviously had implications for family life, and although some nineteenth- and early-twentieth-century feminists had actively promoted the availability of contraception, most earlier feminists stressed their sexual respectability. It was not until the late 1960s that issues of family life and especially sexuality came to the forefront of Western feminist concerns.

The radical feminists of the late 1960s were mostly white, middle-class, college-educated women. Some of them had been active in the National Organization for Women, founded in 1966 to combat discrimination against women in the areas of education and employment; others had participated in various New Left organizations of the 1960s, such as the free speech, civil rights, civil liberties, and antiwar movements. The New Left of the 1960s differed from the Marxist-Leninist Old Left in emphasizing Marx's earlier "humanistic" writings over his later, more economistic work. The New Left was antidogmatic and antiauthoritarian, preferring participatory to representative democracy, including the "democratic centralism" of Old Left groups such as the Communist Party USA. The New Left valued feelings and direct experience as bases for political action and opposed what it perceived as the sexual puritanism of the Old Left. Operating in a context of increasing sexual permissiveness, which often promoted sex outside marriage even for marital partners, New Left men tended to take for granted that their female comrades were willing and even eager to engage with them in sexual activity.

One way in which the New Left did resemble the old was in the low priority it gave to "the woman question." Although it certainly acknowledged the subordination of women, it assumed that this was something to be addressed "after the revolution." In the meantime, New Left women were expected to act as housekeepers or secretaries for the revolution, typing, operating mimeo and ditto machines, preparing food or coffee, cleaning up, and, of course, providing sexual services to the male leaders. One revealing slogan of the antiwar movement, "Chicks say 'Yes' to men who say 'No,'" promised sexual rewards to men who refused induction into the armed forces.

New Left men's assumptions about women shocked and profoundly disillusioned many idealistic and highly educated young women who were committed politically to racial equality and whose educational experience had led them to expect something closer to equality in their own personal lives. Coming together in consciousness-raising groups, these women developed critical perspectives on what they came to see as women's sexual exploitation. Their slogan "The personal is political" expressed a new awareness that their experiences of being sexually manipulated or coerced or valued only for their sexuality not only were common to most women but were also evidence of a pervasive system of male sexual power. Experiences such as rape, harassment, and even unsatisfying sexual interactions came to be seen less as problems to be solved by individual women than as manifestations of a shared subordination that required collective political solutions.

Analyzing "personal" problems in political terms was simultaneously comforting and disturbing to many feminists. On the one hand, it was reassuring to realize that many of their difficulties and disappointments were not a consequence of individual failings; on the other hand, the perception that significant political implications attached to hitherto personal decisions invested those decisions with a heavy burden of social as well as individual responsibility. One could no longer simply do what felt good or comfortable. Instead, one had to gauge the social consequences of one's decisions and question *why* certain things felt good or comfortable. Supposedly personal likes or desires were revealed as neither natural nor idiosyncratic but rather as socially constructed by systems of oppression.

Once feminists came to regard the personal as political, they subjected more and more aspects of daily life to moral and political scrutiny. What one ate, how one dressed, how one transported oneself or disposed of trash, and especially how one behaved sexually—all these became matters of moral and political import. This part of the book examines various feminist perspectives on several areas of what most nonfeminists still regard as personal life: sex, diet, clothing, and sport.

## Sexual Practice

"The Myth of the Vaginal Orgasm" is a classic radical feminist article dating from 1968. In it, Anne Koedt argues that the low incidence of orgasm experienced by women in heterosexual intercourse is due less to women's "frigidity" than to a male-dominant understanding of "the sex act." Heterosexual intercourse is well suited to producing orgasm in men but provides insufficient stimulation of the clitoris to bring most women to orgasm. Sexology's failure to emphasize that clitoral stimulation is indispensable for female orgasm comes, not from ignorance, but from a concern with promoting men's sexual interests. The myth of the vaginal orgasm not only devalues women's primary sexual organ but also, by portraying heterosexual intercourse as the paradigmatic sexual act, operates to delegitimate other practices that may be more satisfying to women, including lesbian practices. Koedt's challenge to heterosexual intercourse pioneered the feminist deconstruction of heterosexuality. Drawing on Koedt's analysis of intercourse as just one among many possible sexual practices, no more natural than any other and less satisfying to women than many, some later feminists came to portray heterosexual intercourse itself as a practice of male domination.

The next two articles develop the theme that heterosexuality is a social and even political construct rather than a manifestation of innate biological drives. In an extract from another classic article, "Compulsory Heterosexuality and Lesbian Existence," Adrienne Rich analyzes heterosexuality as both "a means of assuring male right of physical, economical, and emotional access" to women and a way of denying the historical significance of "the lesbian possibility." She suggests that heterosexuality is an institution imposed both by physical violence and false consciousness and introduces the idea of the *lesbian continuum,* which includes "a range—throughout each woman's life and throughout history—of woman-identified experience; not simply the fact that a woman has had or consciously desired genital sexual experience with another woman." Rich urges that lesbianism no longer be defined primarily in sexual terms; instead, she emphasizes the political dimension of women "sharing ... a rich inner life [and] ... bonding against male tyranny." She portrays lesbianism as being, "like motherhood, a profoundly *female* experience," quite unlike male homosexuality.

Coming out as lesbian has been particularly difficult for African American women because Black men, like white ones, have perceived lesbianism as a kind of disloyalty. In her article, "Scratching the Surface: Some Notes on Barriers to Women and Loving," Audre Lorde asserts that Black lesbianism is part of a long African as well as African American tradition and insists that it offers no real threat to the Black community. She argues that "horizontal hostility" between Black women and men is a foolish distraction from the "vertical" battle against racism.

That lesbianism is somehow connected with feminism is indisputable, though the precise nature of those connections is open to debate. Both feminism and lesbianism were encouraged by the nineteenth-century development of wage labor, which opened up the possibility of women living independently of men. In addition, the early-twentieth-century sexologists' invention of lesbianism as a distinct sexual pathology was at least in part a reaction to the perceived threat of women's economic and sexual independence—just as contemporary antifeminist "dyke baiting" expresses a similar fear. Although many lesbians have not been consciously feminist, just as many feminists have not been consciously lesbian, feminism and lesbianism both embody critiques of central aspects of femininity as it has been culturally constructed; moreover, the existence of each makes the other more threatening to male dominance. But in the 1970s and 1980s, feminists argued bitterly about whether the connections apparent at the level of social movements were also replicated in the lives of individual women: Were lesbians *better* feminists than nonlesbians? Were nonlesbians even feminists at all?

Marilyn Frye's article, "Virgin Women," addresses the question, Do you have to be a lesbian to be a feminist? Following what has by now become a well-established feminist tradition, Frye defines heterosexuality as a central institution set up to turn girls into women who are sexually subordinate to men. Although Frye is reluctant to assert categorically that engaging in male/female relationships that are not defined by male dominance is impossible, she herself cannot see how this possibility exists. Frye ends her essay by speculating about the nature of "Virgin" women who are capable of maintaining their feminist integrity while engaging in heterosexual connections with men. Such women refuse to put men before women, and they are stalwart marriage resisters. In conclusion, Frye asserts that feminists do not have to be lesbian but that they cannot be heterosexual in any standard patriarchal meaning of that word. "Lesbian or not, to embody and enact a consistent and all-the-way feminism you have to be a heretic, a deviant, an undomesticated female, an impossible being. You have to be a Virgin."

Confronting the extensive critiques of heterosexuality that feminists had developed by the mid-1980s, Christine Overall asks whether women may ever be said to choose heterosexuality and, if so, whether that choice may ever be justifiable in feminist terms. While acknowledging that heterosexuality in general is coerced, Overall argues that asserting the possibility of choosing lesbianism entails the corollary possibility that heterosexuality may also be chosen, even—or especially—by feminists. Overall makes an interesting distinction between heterosexual practice and the institution of heterosexuality, suggesting that even to pose heterosexual practice as a choice is to undermine heterosexuality as an institution. Despite the oppressiveness of contemporary heterosexuality as an institution, Overall believes that some heterosexual relationships can be valuable, partly because they may contribute to changing the institution itself. She notes that women's entire personality and political affiliation are not comprised by their sexual activity and concludes by suggesting that even women who engage in heterosexual practice may be part of what Rich calls the lesbian continuum.

Bisexuality is an issue with a complicated feminist history. It was endorsed in the late 1960s by some feminists as part of what was then promoted as the "liberated" androgynous personality, but androgyny soon fell into disfavor among feminists on the grounds that it incorporated, rather than rejected, traditional conceptions of masculinity and femininity as well as failing to address the real power disparities between men and women. Bisexuality came to be perceived as wishy-washy, a way of clinging to heterosexual privilege while refusing a wholehearted commitment to women. Karin Baker's article, "Bisexual Feminist Politics: Because Bisexuality Is Not Enough," reexamines bisexuality in the context of this history. She argues that although exclusive homosexuality presents a more outright challenge to compulsory heterosexuality, bisexuality offers a deeper challenge to the gender system. Both compulsory heterosexuality and the gender system play a key part in maintaining women's subordination, so both lesbianism and bisexuality are necessary for women's liberation, not to mention queer liberation. Baker asserts that bisexuals suffer a special type of oppression, one aspect of which is social invisibility, and that they need to form a distinct community uniquely capable of challenging rigid and dualistic systems of categorization.

Annie Sprinkle's article, "Beyond Bisexual," advocates a kind of pansexuality in which sex may be "a healing tool, ... a meditation, a way of life, and ... a path to enlightenment." Sprinkle's pro-sex attitude forms a striking contrast with the view presented by A Southern Women's Writing Collective, in "Sexual Resistance in Heterosexual Arrangements," which argues that sexuality is the root cause of women's political subordination. In circumstances of male supremacy, all sexual practices—not only heterosexual intercourse—are forms of eroticized dominance and submission; even if women sometimes experience these practices as joyous and liberating, they are in fact oppressive to women. A Southern Women's Writing Collective regards this as a conceptual truth that makes impossible individual exceptions. The collective asserts, *"If it doesn't subordinate women, it's not sex."* Because no individual solutions are possible, the collective advocates a practice of radical celibacy, a politically motivated resistance to sex based on a feminist analysis of compulsory sexuality. Radical celibacy should be practiced in a context of deconstructive lesbianism, which "aims to deconstruct or dismantle the practice of sexuality at the personal and experiential level ... [by attempting] to unweave the pattern of dominance and submission ... incarnated as sexuality in each of us."

The radical feminists of the 1960s regarded individual feelings and experiences as the only reliable bases for criticizing large-scale political theories. In the 1990s, by contrast, we find some radical feminists, such as A Southern Women's Writing Collective, using large-scale theoretical claims as the basis for political criticisms of individual feelings and experiences. Sandra Lee Bartky's article, "Feminine Masochism and the Politics of Personal Transformation," addresses the apparent war between (some) women's desires and (some) feminist principles. Using the example of sadomasochistic sexuality, which is overt in its eroticization of dominance and submission, Bartky argues that feminists must reject forms of sexual liberalism that refuse to recognize the inner conflict and shame experienced by a woman who produces fantasies of sexual humiliation even while she is committed politically to ending women's subordination. In opposition to what she calls sexual voluntarism, however, Bartky denies that women are invariably able to reshape their sexual desires. She concludes by suggesting that such women will simply have to find a way of living uneasily with the contradictions between sexuality and feminism.

This section concludes, as it began, with an article discussing a specific form of sexual practice, in this case, female ejaculation. Like Anne Koedt, Shannon Bell, in "Feminist Ejaculations," charges male sexologists with falsifying aspects of women's sexuality, but whereas Koedt accuses them of obscuring the role of the clitoris, Bell alleges that they have concealed women's capacity to ejaculate. Whereas Koedt portrays the clitoris as women's primary sexual organ, Bell asserts that women's sexual organ comprises the clitoris, urethra, and vagina together. Proper stimulation of this organ allows women to ejaculate, and Bell urges feminists to take control of ejaculation as a powerful body experience.

Previous sections of this book have shown how the sexualization of women in contemporary Western culture has meant that issues of sexuality are involved in many areas of feminist ethics. This section reveals some of the complexities of these issues as well as the depth of feminist disagreement concerning them.

## Consuming Animals

Nonhuman animals have always been integral to Western culture, which has used them, among other things, for food, transportation, clothing, entertainment, research, and companionship. A variety of rationales for the human domination of animals has been produced by Western thinkers, but it is only in comparatively recent times that any serious Western challenges to this domination have emerged. Some Western feminists now assert that the domination of nonhuman animals is linked with women's subordination. This section explores some of these alleged links.

The first article in this section, "Dismantling Oppression: An Analysis of the Connection Between Women and Animals," by Lori Gruen, asserts several connections between the subordination of women and the domination of nonhuman animals. Gruen argues that the categories "woman" and "animal" both function in male-dominant society to represent the dominated, submissive "other." Some feminist theoreticians speculate that male dominance originated when men turned against women the weapons used in hunting animals and simultaneously defined women, whose reproductive functions tended to exclude them from hunting, as part of nature rather than culture— like animals. Other feminists have suggested that the domestication of animals made evident the male role in reproduction as well as creating a conceptual model of females as breeders, a conception of women that came to predominate when the development of agriculture generated an increased need for labor. Women and nonhuman animals are also connected by male-dominant religions that have conceptualized both as parts of nature, simultaneously needed and feared by men. This view of women and nonhuman animals as parts of nature was secularized and reinforced by the rise of modern science, which treats both women and nonhuman animals as manipulable objects in scientific research. Gruen goes on to describe how animals are used in the production of cosmetics and furs, both of which are supposed to make women beautiful. Not all feminist theories are capable of articulating the connection between the subordination of women and the domination of nonhuman animals, but Gruen argues that this connection is clearly displayed in ecofeminism. She concludes by suggesting some ways in which an acceptance of feminist practices will contribute to the movement for animal liberation at the same time as a consistent feminism requires a refusal to treat "sentient individuals as objects to use and profit from."

The next two articles both advocate feminist vegetarianism but do so on different grounds. In "The Sexual Politics of Meat," Carol J. Adams argues that, in the Western tradition, meat has historically symbolized both male dominance and white dominance. To refuse meat is therefore symbolically to refuse collusion with both these systems of dominance. By contrast, in "Feminism and Vegetarianism," Lisa Martin advocates feminist vegetarianism on grounds that are neither symbolic nor animal focused. Instead, Martin argues that the economic and environmental consequences of meat production and consumption have disproportionately negative consequences for women. She concludes that there are strong feminist reasons to boycott the meat industry.

Gretchen Legler's article, "Hunting: A Woman's Perspective," offers a feminist defense of hunting. She asserts that hunting connects her with the natural world and offers insights about the fragility and importance of life. Although her hunting challenges the ancient Western stereotype of Man the Hunter, Legler insists that she does not hunt to become "one of the boys"; on the contrary, she believes that her attitude toward hunting is entirely distinct from masculinist perspectives. The article following hers, by contrast, argues that hunting is never justified, at least in industrialized nations. Andrée Collard and Joyce Contrucci criticize what they regard as the inconsistency and self-deception of those who assert that hunting expresses their connection with and love of nature. Hunting, in the authors' view, is "the *modus operandi* of patriarchal societies on all levels of life."

In "Some Doubts About Fur Coats," Slavenka Drakulic, a feminist from Yugoslavia, reflects on the meaning of fur coats to women from or in Eastern Europe. Although she acknowledges the animal suffering involved in making the coat, she is also sympathetic to the romantic dreams of women who have suffered a lifetime of material and aesthetic deprivation. As one of her friends remarks, perhaps First World ecological philosophy cannot be applied to Third World women.

The feminist slogan "The personal is political" has been extraordinarily powerful, both politically and theoretically, for feminists in the last half of the twentieth century. It has highlighted many systematic practices of male domination, practices defined previously as personal or private and thus exempted from moral and political scrutiny. The power of this slogan is nevertheless problematic if it is construed to mean that feminists should conform to rigid standards of conduct at every moment of their lives. In the 1990s, such construals of the notion that the personal is political have generated accusations that feminism imposes rules of "political correctness" that are totalitarian as well as dogmatic. Even though these accusations may often be motivated by personal defensiveness and/or antifeminism, it is true that feminist theory has not yet offered a systematic feminist reconceptualization of the notion of privacy. In the meantime, however, "feminist fascism" is not imminent, in part because feminists disagree so much among ourselves. In addition, as Drakulic's article illustrates, feminists increasingly recognize that facially similar social practices vary in meaning according to the social context, so that moral and political principles, even feminist principles, cannot be applied mechanically to all women.

# The Myth of the Vaginal Orgasm

## Anne Koedt

Whenever female orgasm and frigidity are discussed, a false distinction is made between the vaginal and the clitoral orgasm. Frigidity has generally been defined by men as the failure of women to have vaginal orgasms. Actually the vagina is not a highly sensitive area and is not constructed to achieve orgasm. It is the clitoris which is the center of sexual sensitivity and which is the female equivalent of the penis.

I think this explains a great many things: First of all, the fact that the so-called frigidity rate among women is phenomenally high. Rather than tracing female frigidity to the false assumptions about female anatomy, our "experts" have declared frigidity a psychological problem of women. Those women who complained about it were recommended psychiatrists, so that they might discover their "problem"—diagnosed generally as a failure to adjust to their role as women.

The facts of female anatomy and sexual response tell a different story. Although there are many areas for sexual arousal, there is only one area for sexual climax; that area is the clitoris. All orgasms are extensions of sensation from this area. Since the clitoris is not necessarily stimulated sufficiently in the conventional sexual positions, we are left "frigid."

Aside from physical stimulation, which is the common cause of orgasm for most people, there is also stimulation through primarily mental processes. Some women, for example, may achieve orgasm through sexual fantasies, or through fetishes. However, while the stimulation may be psychological, the orgasm manifests itself physically. Thus, while the cause is psychological, the *effect* is still physical, and the orgasm necessarily takes place in the sexual organ equipped for sexual climax—the clitoris. The orgasm experience may also differ in degree of intensity—some more localized, and some more diffuse and sensitive. But they are all clitoral orgasms.

All this leads to some interesting questions about conventional sex and our role in it. Men have orgasms essentially by friction with the vagina, not the clitoral area, which is external and not able to cause friction the way penetration does. Women have thus been defined sexually in terms of what pleases men; our own biology has not been properly analyzed. Instead, we are fed the myth of the liberated woman and her vaginal orgasm—an orgasm which in fact does not exist.

What we must do is redefine our sexuality. We must discard the "normal" concepts of sex and create new guidelines which take into account mutual sexual enjoyment. While the idea of mutual enjoyment is liberally applauded in marriage manuals, it is not followed to its logical conclusion. We must begin to demand that if certain sexual positions now defined as "standard" are not mutually conducive to orgasm, they no longer be defined as standard. New techniques must be used or devised which transform this particular aspect of our current sexual exploitation.

## Freud—A Father of the Vaginal Orgasm

Freud contended that the clitoral orgasm was adolescent, and that upon puberty, when women began having intercourse with men, women should transfer the center of orgasm to the vagina. The vagina, it was assumed, was able to produce a parallel, but more mature, orgasm than the clitoris. Much work was done to elaborate on this theory, but little was done to challenge the basic assumptions.

To fully appreciate this incredible invention, perhaps Freud's general attitude about women should first be recalled. Mary Ellman, in *Thinking About Women*, summed it up this way:

> Everything in Freud's patronizing and fearful attitude toward women follows from their lack of a penis, but it is only in his essay *The Psychology of Women* that Freud makes explicit ... the deprecations of women which are implicit in his work. He then prescribes for them the abandonment of the life of the mind, which will interfere with their sexual function. When the psychoanalyzed patient is male, the analyst sets himself the task of developing the man's capacities; but with women patients, the job is to resign them to the limits of their sexuality. As Mr. Rieff puts it: For Freud, "Analysis cannot encourage in women new energies for success and achievement, but only teach them the lesson of rational resignation."

It was Freud's feelings about women's secondary and inferior relationship to men that formed the basis for his theories on female sexuality.

Once having laid down the law about the nature of our sexuality, Freud not so strangely discovered a tremendous problem of frigidity in women. His recommended cure for a woman who was frigid was psychiatric care. She was suffering from failure to mentally adjust to her "natural" role as a woman. Frank S. Caprio, a contemporary follower of these ideas, states:

> ... whenever a woman is incapable of achieving an orgasm via coitus, provided the husband is an adequate partner, and prefers clitoral stimulation to any other form of sexual activity, she can be regarded as suffering from frigidity and requires psychiatric assistance. (*The Sexually Adequate Female*, p. 64.)

The explanation given was that women were envious of men—"renunciation of womanhood." Thus it was diagnosed as an anti-male phenomenon.

It is important to emphasize that Freud did not base his theory upon a study of woman's anatomy, but rather upon his assumptions of woman as an inferior appendage to man, and her consequent social and psychological role. In their attempts to deal with the ensuing problem of mass frigidity, Freudians embarked on elaborate mental gymnastics. Marie Bonaparte, in *Female Sexuality,* goes so far as to suggest surgery to help women back on their rightful path. Having discovered a strange connection between the non-frigid woman and the location of the clitoris near the vagina,

> it then occurred to me that where, in certain women, this gap was excessive, and clitoridal fixation obdurate, a clitoridal-vaginal reconciliation might be effected by surgical means, which would then benefit the normal erotic function. Professor Halban, of Vienna, as much a biologist as surgeon, became interested in the problem and worked out a simple operative technique. In this, the suspensory ligament of the clitoris was severed and the clitoris secured to the underlying structures, thus fixing it in a lower position, with eventual reduction of the labia minora. (p. 148.)

But the severest damage was not in the area of surgery, where Freudians ran around absurdly trying to change female anatomy to fit their basic assumptions. The worst damage was done to the mental health of women, who either suffered silently with self-blame, or flocked to psychiatrists looking desperately for the hidden and terrible repression that had kept from them their vaginal destiny.

## Lack of Evidence

One may perhaps at first claim that these are unknown and unexplored areas, but upon closer examination this is certainly not true today, nor was it true even in the past. For example, men have known that women suffered from frigidity often during intercourse. So the problem was there. Also, there is much specific evidence. Men knew that the clitoris was and is the essential organ for masturbation, whether in children or adult women. So obviously women made it clear where *they* thought their sexuality was located. Men also seem suspiciously aware of the clitoral powers during "foreplay," when they want to arouse women and produce the necessary lubrication for penetration. Foreplay is a concept created for male purposes, but works to the disadvantage of many women, since as soon as the woman is aroused the man changes to vaginal stimulation, leaving her both aroused and unsatisfied.

It has also been known that women need no anesthesia inside the vagina during surgery, thus pointing to the fact that the vagina is in fact not a highly sensitive area.

Today, with extensive knowledge of anatomy, with Kelly, Kinsey, and Masters and Johnson, to mention just a few sources, there is no ignorance on the subject. There are, however, social reasons why this knowledge has not been popularized. We are living in a male society which has not sought change in women's role.

## Anatomical Evidence

Rather than starting with what women *ought* to feel, it would seem logical to start out with the anatomical facts regarding the clitoris and vagina.

*The Clitoris* is a small equivalent of the penis, except for the fact that the urethra does not go through it as in the man's penis. Its erection is similar to the male erection, and the head of the clitoris has the same type of structure and function as the head of the penis. G. Lombard Kelly, in *Sexual Feeling in Married Men and Women,* says:

> The head of the clitoris is also composed of erectile tissue, and it possesses a very sensitive epithelium or surface covering, supplied with special nerve endings called genital corpuscles, which are peculiarly adapted for sensory stimulation that under proper mental conditions terminates in the sexual orgasm. No other part of the female generative tract has such corpuscles. (Pocketbooks; p. 35.)

The clitoris has no other function than that of sexual pleasure.

*The Vagina*—Its functions are related to the reproductive function. Principally, 1) menstruation, 2) receive penis, 3) hold semen, and 4) birth passage. The interior of the vagina, which according to the defenders of the vaginally caused orgasm is the center and producer of the orgasm, is:

> like nearly all other internal body structures, poorly supplied with end organs of touch. The internal entodermal origin of the lining of the vagina makes it similar in this respect to the rectum and other parts of the digestive tract. (Kinsey, *Sexual Behavior in the Human Female,* p. 580.)

The degree of insensitivity inside the vagina is so high that "Among the women who were tested in our gynecologic sample, less than 14% were at all conscious that they had been touched." (Kinsey, p. 580.)

Even the importance of the vagina as an *erotic* center (as opposed to an orgasmic center) has been found to be minor.

*Other Areas*—Labia minora and the vestibule of the vagina. These two sensitive areas may trigger off a clitoral orgasm. Because they can be effectively stimulated during "normal" coitus, though infrequently, this kind of stimulation is incorrectly thought to be vaginal orgasm. However, it is important to distinguish between areas which can stimulate the clitoris, incapable of producing the orgasm themselves, and the clitoris:

> Regardless of what means of excitation is used to bring the individual to the state of sexual climax, the sensation is perceived by the genital corpuscles and is localized where they are situated: in the head of the clitoris or penis. (Kelly, p. 49.)

*Psychologically Stimulated Orgasm*—Aside from the above mentioned direct and indirect stimulations of the clitoris, there is a third way an orgasm may be triggered. This is through mental (cortical) stimulation, where the imagination stimulates the brain, which in turn stimulates the genital corpuscles of the glans to set off an orgasm.

## Women Who Say They Have Vaginal Orgasms

*Confusion*—Because of the lack of knowledge of their own anatomy, some women accept the idea that an orgasm felt during "normal" intercourse was vaginally caused. This confusion is caused by a combination of two factors. One, failing to locate the center of the orgasm, and two, by a desire to fit her experience to the male-defined idea of sexual normalcy. Considering that women know little about their anatomy, it is easy to be confused.

*Deception*—The vast majority of women who pretend vaginal orgasm to their men are faking it to "get the job." In a new best-selling Danish book, *I Accuse,* Mette Ejlersen specifically deals with this common problem, which she calls the "sex comedy." This comedy has many causes. First of all, the man brings a great deal of pressure to bear on the woman, because he considers his ability as a lover at stake. So as not to offend his ego, the woman will comply with the prescribed role and go through simulated ecstasy. In some of the other Danish women mentioned, women who were left frigid were turned off to sex, and pretended vaginal orgasm to hurry up the sex act. Others admitted that they had faked vaginal orgasm to catch a man. In one case, the woman pretended vaginal orgasm to get him to leave his first wife, who admitted being vaginally frigid. Later she was forced to continue the deception, since obviously she couldn't tell him to stimulate her clitorally.

Many more women were simply afraid to establish their right to equal enjoyment, seeing the sexual act as being primarily for the man's benefit, and any pleasure that the woman got as an added extra.

Other women, with just enough ego to reject the man's idea that they needed psychiatric care, refused to admit their frigidity. They wouldn't accept self-blame, but they didn't know how to solve the problem, not knowing the physiological facts about themselves. So they were left in a peculiar limbo.

Again, perhaps one of the most infuriating and damaging results of this whole charade has been that women who were perfectly healthy sexually were taught that they were not. So in addition to being sexually deprived, these women were told to blame themselves when they deserved no blame. Looking for a cure to a problem that has none can lead a woman on an endless path of self-hatred and insecurity. For she is told by her analyst that not even in her one role allowed in a male society—the role of a woman—is she successful. She is put on the defensive, with phony data as evidence that she'd better try to be even more feminine, think more feminine, and reject her envy of men. That is, shuffle even harder, baby.

## Why Men Maintain the Myth

1. *Sexual Penetration Is Preferred*—The best physical stimulant for the penis is the woman's vagina. It supplies the necessary friction and lubrication. From a strictly technical point of view this position offers the best physical conditions, even though the man may try other positions for variation.

2. *The Invisible Woman*—One of the elements of male chauvinism is the refusal or inability to see women as total, separate human beings. Rather, men have chosen to define women only in terms of how they benefited men's lives. Sexually, a woman was not seen as an individual wanting to share equally in the sexual act, any more than she was seen as a person with independent desires when she did anything else in society. Thus, it was easy to make up what was convenient about women; for on top

of that, society has been a function of male interests, and women were not organized to form even a vocal opposition to the male experts.

3. *The Penis as Epitome of Masculinity*—Men define their lives primarily in terms of masculinity. It is a universal form of ego-boosting. That is, in every society, however homogeneous (i.e., with the absence of racial, ethnic, or major economic differences) there is always a group, women, to oppress.

The essence of male chauvinism is in the psychological superiority men exercise over women. This kind of superior-inferior definition of self, rather than positive definition based upon one's own achievements and development, has of course chained victim and oppressor both. But by far the most brutalized of the two is the victim.

An analogy is racism, where the white racist compensates for his feelings of unworthiness by creating an image of the black man (it is primarily a male struggle) as biologically inferior to him. Because of his position in a white male power structure, the white man can socially enforce this mythical division.

To the extent that men try to rationalize and justify male superiority through physical differentiation, masculinity may be symbolized by being the *most* muscular, the most hairy; having the deepest voice, and the biggest penis. Women, on the other hand, are approved of (i.e., called feminine) if they are weak, petite; shave their legs; have high soft voices.

Since the clitoris is almost identical to the penis, one finds a great deal of evidence of men in various societies trying to either ignore the clitoris and emphasize the vagina (as did Freud), or, as in some places in the Mideast, actually performing clitoridectomy. Freud saw this ancient and still practiced custom as a way of further "feminizing" the female by removing this cardinal vestige of her masculinity. It should be noted also that a big clitoris is considered ugly and masculine. Some cultures engage in the practice of pouring a chemical on the clitoris to make it shrivel up into "proper" size.

It seems clear to me that men in fact fear the clitoris as a threat to masculinity.

4. *Sexually Expendable Male*—Men fear that they will become sexually expendable if the clitoris is substituted for the vagina as the center of pleasure for women. Actually this has a great deal of validity if one considers *only* the anatomy. The position of the penis inside the vagina, while perfect for reproduction, does not necessarily stimulate an orgasm in women because the clitoris is located externally and higher up. Women must rely upon indirect stimulation in the "normal" position.

Lesbian sexuality could make an excellent case, based upon anatomical data, for the irrelevancy of the male organ. Albert Ellis says something to the effect that a man without a penis can make a woman an excellent lover.

Considering that the vagina is very desirable from a man's point of view, purely on physical grounds, one begins to see the dilemma for men. And it forces us as well to discard many "physical" arguments explaining why women go to bed with men. What is left, it seems to me, are primarily psychological reasons why women select men at the exclusion of women as sexual partners.

5. *Control of Women*—One reason given to explain the Mideastern practice of clitoridectomy is that it will keep the women from straying. By removing the sexual organ capable of orgasm, it must be assumed that her sexual drive will diminish. Considering how men look upon their women as property, particularly in very backward nations, we should begin to consider a great deal more why it is not in men's interest to have women totally free sexually. The double standard, as practiced for example in Latin America, is set up to keep the woman as total property of the husband, while he is free to have affairs as he wishes.

6. *Lesbianism and Bisexuality*—Aside from the strictly anatomical reasons why women might equally seek other women as lovers, there is a fear on men's part that women will seek the company of other women on a full, human basis. The recognition of clitoral orgasm as fact would threaten the heterosexual *institution*. For it would indicate that sexual pleasure was obtainable from either men *or* women, thus making heterosexuality not an absolute, but an option. It would thus open up the whole question of *human* sexual relationships beyond the confines of the present male-female role system.

---

### References

*Sexual Behavior in the Human Female,* Alfred C. Kinsey, Pocketbooks, 1953.
*Female Sexuality,* Marie Bonaparte, Grove Press, 1953.
*Sex Without Guilt,* Albert Ellis, Grove Press, 1958 and 1965.
*Sexual Feelings in Married Men and Women,* G. Lombard Kelly, Pocketbooks, 1951 and 1965.
*I Accuse (Jeg Anklager),* Mette Ejlersen, Chr. Erichsens Forlag (Danish), 1968.
*The Sexually Adequate Female,* Frank S. Caprio, Fawcett Gold Medal Books, 1953 and 1966.
*Thinking About Women,* Mary Ellman, Harcourt, Brace & World, 1968.
*Human Sexual Response,* Masters and Johnson, Little, Brown, 1966.

# Compulsory Heterosexuality and Lesbian Existence

## Adrienne Rich

… Whatever its origins, when we look hard and clearly at the extent and elaboration of measures designed to keep women within a male sexual purlieu, it becomes an inescapable question whether the issue feminists have to address is not simple "gender

inequality" nor the domination of culture by males nor mere "taboos against homosexuality," but the enforcement of heterosexuality for women as a means of assuring
male right of physical, economic, and emotional access.[1] One of many means of
enforcement is, of course, the rendering invisible of the lesbian possibility, an
engulfed continent which rises fragmentedly into view from time to time only to become submerged again. Feminist research and theory that contribute to lesbian invisibility or marginality are actually working against the liberation and empowerment of woman as a group.[2]

The assumption that "most women are innately heterosexual" stands as a theoretical and political stumbling block for feminism. It remains a tenable assumption
partly because lesbian existence has been written out of history or catalogued under
disease, partly because it has been treated as exceptional rather than intrinsic, partly
because to acknowledge that for women heterosexuality may not be a "preference" at
all but something that has had to be imposed, managed, organized, propagandized,
and maintained by force is an immense step to take if you consider yourself freely
and "innately" heterosexual. Yet the failure to examine heterosexuality as an institution is like failing to admit that the economic system called capitalism or the caste
system of racism is maintained by a variety of forces, including both physical violence and false consciousness. To take the step of questioning heterosexuality as a
"preference" or "choice" for women—and to do the intellectual and emotional work
that follows—will call for a special quality of courage in heterosexually identified
feminists, but I think the rewards will be great: a freeing-up of thinking, the exploring of new paths, the shattering of another great silence, new clarity in personal relationships.

I have chosen to use the terms *lesbian existence* and *lesbian continuum* because the
word *lesbianism* has a clinical and limiting ring. *Lesbian existence* suggests both the
fact of the historical presence of lesbians and our continuing creation of the meaning
of that existence. I mean the term *lesbian continuum* to include a range—through
each woman's life and throughout history—of woman-identified experience, not
simply the fact that a woman has had or consciously desired genital sexual experience with another woman. If we expand it to embrace many more forms of primary
intensity between and among women, including the sharing of a rich inner life, the
bonding against male tyranny, the giving and receiving of practical and political support, if we can also hear it in such associations as *marriage resistance* and the "haggard" behavior identified by Mary Daly (obsolete meanings: "intractable," "willful,"
"wanton," and "unchaste," "a woman reluctant to yield to wooing"),[3] we begin to
grasp breadths of female history and psychology which have lain out of reach as a
consequence of limited, mostly clinical, definitions of *lesbianism*.

Lesbian existence comprises both the breaking of a taboo and the rejection of a
compulsory way of life. It is also a direct or indirect attack on male right of access to
women. But it is more than these, although we may first begin to perceive it as a form
of naysaying to patriarchy, an act of resistance. It has, of course, included isolation,
self-hatred, breakdown, alcoholism, suicide, and intrawoman violence; we romanti-

cize at our peril what it means to love and act against the grain, and under heavy penalties; and lesbian existence has been lived (unlike, say, Jewish or Catholic existence) without access to any knowledge of a tradition, a continuity, a social underpinning. The destruction of records and memorabilia and letters documenting the realities of lesbian existence must be taken very seriously as a means of keeping heterosexuality compulsory for women, since what has been kept from our knowledge is joy, sensuality, courage, and community, as well as guilt, self-betrayal, and pain.[4]

Lesbians have historically been deprived of a political existence through "inclusion" as female versions of male homosexuality. To equate lesbian existence with male homosexuality because each is stigmatized is to erase female reality once again. Part of the history of lesbian existence is, obviously, to be found where lesbians, lacking a coherent female community, have shared a kind of social life and common cause with homosexual men. But there are differences: women's lack of economic and cultural privilege relative to men; qualitative differences in female and male relationships—for example, the patterns of anonymous sex among male homosexuals, and the pronounced ageism in male homosexual standards of sexual attractiveness. I perceive the lesbian experience as being, like motherhood, a profoundly *female* experience, with particular oppressions, meanings, and potentialities we cannot comprehend as long as we simply bracket it with other sexually stigmatized existences. Just as the term *parenting* serves to conceal the particular and significant reality of being a parent who is actually a mother, the term *gay* may serve the purpose of blurring the very outlines we need to discern, which are of crucial value for feminism and for the freedom of women as a group.[5]

As the term *lesbian* has been held to limiting, clinical associations in its patriarchal definition, female friendship and comradeship have been set apart from the erotic, thus limiting the erotic itself. But as we deepen and broaden the range of what we define as lesbian existence, as we delineate a lesbian continuum, we begin to discover the erotic in female terms: as that which is unconfined to any single part of the body or solely to the body itself; as an energy not only diffuse but, as Audre Lorde has described it, omnipresent in "the sharing of joy, whether physical, emotional, psychic," and in the sharing of work; as the empowering joy which "makes us less willing to accept powerlessness, or those other supplied states of being which are not native to me, such as resignation, despair, self-effacement, depression, self-denial."[6] ...

### Notes

1. For my perception of homosexuality as an economic institution, I am indebted to Lisa Leghorn and Katherine Parker, who allowed me to read the unpublished manuscript of their book *Woman's Worth: Sexual Economics and the World of Women* (London and Boston: Routledge & Kegan Paul, 1981).

2. I would suggest that lesbian existence has been most recognized and tolerated where it has resembled a "deviant" version of heterosexuality—e.g., where lesbians have, like Stein and Toklas, played heterosexual roles (or seemed to in public) and have been chiefly identified with male culture. ... Lesbian existence has also been relegated to an upper-class phenome-

non, an elite decadence (as in the fascination with Paris salon lesbians such as Renée Vivien and Natalie Clifford Barney), to the obscuring of such "common women" as Judy Grahn depicts in her *The Work of a Common Woman* (Oakland, Calif.: Diana Press, 1978) and *True to Life Adventure Stories* (Oakland, Calif.: Diana Press, 1978).

3. Mary Daly, *Gyn/Ecology: The Metaphysics of Radical Feminism* (Boston: Beacon Press, 1978), p. 15.

4. "In a hostile world in which women are not supposed to survive except in relation with and in service to men, entire communities of women were simply erased. History tends to bury what it seeks to reject" (Blanche W. Cook, "'Women Alone Stir My Imagination': Lesbianism and the Cultural Tradition," *Signs: Journal of Women in Culture and Society* 4, no. 4 [Summer 1979]: 719–720). The Lesbian Herstory Archives in New York City is one attempt to preserve contemporary documents on lesbian existence—a project of enormous value and meaning, working against the continuing censorship and obliteration of relationships, networks, communities in other archives and elsewhere in culture.

5. [A. R., 1986: The shared historical and spiritual "crossover" functions of lesbians and gay men in cultures past and present are traced by Judy Grahn in *Another Mother Tongue: Gay Words, Gay Worlds* (Boston: Beacon, 1984). I now think we have much to learn both from the uniquely female aspects of lesbian existence and from the complex "gay" identity we share with gay men.]

6. Audre Lorde, "Uses of the Erotic: The Erotic as Power," in *Sister Outsider* (Trumansburg, N.Y.: Crossing Press, 1984).

# Scratching the Surface: Some Notes on Barriers to Women and Loving

## Audre Lorde

**Racism:** *The belief in the inherent superiority of one race over all others and thereby the right to dominance.*

**Sexism:** *The belief in the inherent superiority of one sex and thereby the right to dominance.*

**Heterosexism:** *The belief in the inherent superiority of one pattern of loving and thereby its right to dominance.*

**Homophobia:** *The fear of feelings of love for members of one's own sex and therefore the hatred of those feelings in others.*

The above forms of human blindness stem from the same root—an inability to recognize the notion of difference as a dynamic human force, one which is enriching rather than threatening to the defined self, when there are shared goals.

To a large degree, at least verbally, the Black community has moved beyond the "two steps behind her man" concept of sexual relations sometimes mouthed as desirable during the sixties. This was a time when the myth of the Black matriarchy as a social disease was being presented by racist forces to redirect our attentions away from the real sources of Black oppression.

For Black women as well as Black men, it is axiomatic that if we do not define ourselves for ourselves, we will be defined by others—for their use and to our detriment. The development of self-defined Black women, ready to explore and pursue our power and interests within our communities, is a vital component in the war for Black liberation. The image of the Angolan woman with a baby on one arm and a gun in the other is neither romantic nor fanciful. When Black women in this country come together to examine our sources of strength and support, and to recognize our common social, cultural, emotional, and political interests, it is a development which can only contribute to the power of the Black community as a whole. It can certainly never diminish it. For it is through the coming together of self-actualized individuals, female and male, that any real advances can be made. The old sexual power relationships based on a dominant/subordinate model between unequals have not served us as a people, nor as individuals.

…

Increasingly, despite opposition, Black women are coming together to explore and to alter those manifestations of our society which oppress us in different ways from those that oppress Black men. This is no threat to Black men. It is only seen as one by those Black men who choose to embody within themselves those same manifestations of female oppression. For instance, no Black man has ever been forced to bear a child he did not want or could not support. Enforced sterilization and unavailable abortions are tools of oppression against Black women, as is rape. Only to those Black men who are unclear about the pathways of their own definition can the self-actualization and self-protective bonding of Black women be seen as a threatening development.

Today, the red herring of lesbian-baiting is being used in the Black community to obscure the true face of racism/sexism. Black women sharing close ties with each other, politically or emotionally, are not the enemies of Black men. Too frequently, however, some Black men attempt to rule by fear those Black women who are more ally than enemy. These tactics are expressed as threats of emotional rejection: "Their poetry wasn't too bad but I couldn't take all those lezzies." The Black man saying this is code-warning every Black woman present interested in a relationship with a man—and most Black women are—that (1) if she wishes to have her work considered by him she must eschew any other allegiance except to him and (2) any woman who wishes to retain his friendship and/or support had better not be "tainted" by woman-identified interests.

…

War, imprisonment, and "the street" have decimated the ranks of Black males of marriageable age. The fury of many Black heterosexual women against white women who date Black men is rooted in this unequal sexual equation within the Black community, since whatever threatens to widen that equation is deeply and articulately resented. But this is essentially unconstructive resentment because it extends sideways only. It can never result in true progress on the issue because it does not question the vertical lines of power or authority, nor the sexist assumptions which dictate the terms of that competition. And the racism of white women might be better addressed where it is less complicated by their own sexual oppression. In this situation it is not the non-Black woman who calls the tune, but rather the Black man who turns away from himself in his sisters or who, through a fear borrowed from white men, reads her strength not as a resource but as a challenge.

...

\*     \*     \*

Instead of keeping our attentions focused upon our real needs, enormous energy is being wasted in the Black community today in antilesbian hysteria. Yet women-identified women—those who sought their own destinies and attempted to execute them in the absence of male support—have been around in all of our communities for a long time. As Yvonne Flowers of York College pointed out in a recent discussion, the unmarried aunt, childless or otherwise, whose home and resources were often a welcome haven for different members of the family, was a familiar figure in many of our childhoods. And within the homes of our Black communities today, it is not the Black lesbian who is battering and raping our underage girl-children out of displaced and sickening frustration.

...

... Traditionally, Black women have always bonded together in support of each other, however uneasily and in the face of whatever other allegiances which militated against that bonding. We have banded together with each other for wisdom and strength and support, even when it was only in relationship to one man. We need only look at the close, although highly complex and involved, relationships between African co-wives, or at the Amazon warriors of ancient Dahomey who fought together as the King's main and most ferocious bodyguard. We need only look at the more promising power wielded by the West African Market Women Associations of today, and those governments which have risen and fallen at their pleasure.

In a retelling of her life, a ninety-two-year-old Efik-Ibibio woman of Nigeria recalls her love for another woman:

> I had a woman friend to whom I revealed my secrets. She was very fond of keeping secrets to herself. We acted as husband and wife. We always moved hand in glove and my husband and hers knew about our relationship. The villagers nicknamed us twin sisters. When I was out of gear with my husband, she would be the one to restore peace. I often sent my children to go and work for her in return for her kindnesses to me. My husband being more fortunate to get more pieces of land than her husband, allowed some to her, even though she was not my co-wife.[1]

On the West Coast of Africa, the Fon of Dahomey still have twelve different kinds of marriage. One of them is known as "giving the goat to the buck," where a woman of independent means marries another woman who then may or may not bear children, all of whom will belong to the blood line of the first woman. Some marriages of this kind are arranged to provide heirs for women of means who wish to remain "free," and some are lesbian relationships. Marriages like these occur throughout Africa, in several different places among different peoples.[2] Routinely, the women involved are accepted members of their communities, evaluated not by their sexuality but by their respective places within the community.

...

If the recent attack upon lesbians in the Black community is based solely upon an aversion to the idea of sexual contact between members of the same sex (a contact which has existed for ages in most of the female compounds across the African continent), why then is the idea of sexual contact between Black men so much more easily accepted, or unremarked? Is the imagined threat simply the existence of a self-motivated, self-defined Black woman who will not fear nor suffer terrible retribution from the gods because she does not necessarily seek her face in a man's eyes, even if he has fathered her children? Female-headed households in the Black community are not always situations by default.

The distortion of relationship which says "I disagree with you, so I must destroy you" leaves us as Black people with basically uncreative victories, defeated in any common struggle. This jugular vein psychology is based on the fallacy that your assertion or affirmation of self is an attack upon my self—or that my defining myself will somehow prevent or retard your self-definition. The supposition that one sex needs the other's acquiescence in order to exist prevents both from moving together as self-defined persons toward a common goal.

...

*             *             *

At a recent Black literary conference, a heterosexual Black woman stated that to endorse lesbianism was to endorse the death of our race. This position reflects acute fright or a faulty reasoning, for once again it ascribes false power to difference. To the racist, Black people are so powerful that the presence of one can contaminate a whole lineage; to the heterosexist, lesbians are so powerful that the presence of one can contaminate the whole sex. This position supposes that if we do not eradicate lesbianism in the Black community, all Black women will become lesbians. It also supposes that lesbians do not have children. Both suppositions are patently false.

...

Of the four groups, Black and white women, Black and white men, Black women have the lowest average wage. This is a vital concern for us all, no matter with whom we sleep.

As Black women we have the right and responsibility to define ourselves and to seek our allies in common cause: with Black men against racism, and with each other and white women against sexism. But most of all, as Black women we have the right and responsibility to recognize each other without fear and to love where we choose. Both lesbian and heterosexual Black women today share a history of bonding and strength to which our sexual identities and our other differences must not blind us.

### Notes

1. Iris Andreski, *Old Wives Tales: Life-Stories of African Women* (Schocken Books, New York, 1970), p. 131.
2. Melville Herskovits, *Dahomey,* 2 vols. (Northwestern University Press, Evanston, Illinois, 1967), 1:320–322.

# *Virgin Women*

## Marilyn Frye

... Every term in my feminism classes, a time comes when heterosexual women students articulate the question: Do you have to be a lesbian to be a feminist? I don't know how much other teachers of Women's Studies hear this question. My classroom is a situation which brings the connection between feminism and lesbianism to one's attention. I am a lesbian, I am "out" to my Women's Studies students, and I expose them to a great deal of wonderful and strong feminist thinking by feminists of many cultures and locales who are lesbians. In the classroom, this question signals our arrival at a point where newcomers to feminism are beginning to grasp that sexual acts, sexual desire, and sexual dread and taboo are profoundly political and that feminist politics is as much about the disposition of bodies, the manipulation of desire and arousal, and the bonds of intimacy and loyalty as it is about gender stereotypes, economic opportunity and legal rights. ... But what goes on in my class is clearly not the only thing that gives rise to this question.

One thing that leads students to ask this question is that they very commonly run into people who apparently believe that if you are a feminist you must be a lesbian.

I usually ask women in my Women's Studies classes if they have been called lesbians or dykes or been accused of being lesbian, and almost always a majority of them say they have. One woman was called a lesbian when she rejected the attentions of a man in a bar; another was called "butch" when she opened and held a door for a male friend; another was asked if she was a lesbian when she challenged a man's sexist description of another woman. A woman told a man that she did not want to have sex with him and he called her a lesbian. … A woman reports that her friends refer to her Women's Studies class as her "lesbian class"; several other women say some of their friends do that too.

The message of these exchanges is clearly that a woman who is feminist or does anything or betrays any attitude or desire which expresses her autonomy or deviance from conventional femininity is a lesbian. …

I want to suggest that this notion of a connection between feminism and lesbianism is *not* merely an *ad hoc* fiction invented by patriarchal loyalists to vilify feminism and intimidate feminists. … An intrinsic connection between feminism and lesbianism in a contemporary Euroamerican setting is just a historically specific manifestation of an ancient and intrinsic connection between patriarchal/fraternal social order and female heterosexuality. For females to be subordinated and subjugated to males on a global scale, and for males to organize themselves and each other as they do, billions of female individuals, virtually all who see life on this planet, must be reduced to a more-or-less willing toleration of subordination and servitude to men. The primary sites of this reduction are the sites of heterosexual relation and encounter—courtship and marriage-arrangement, romance, sexual liaisons, fucking, marriage, prostitution, the normative family, incest and child sexual assault. … The secondary sites of the forced female embodiment of subordination are the sites of the ritual preparations of girls and women for heterosexual intercourse, relations or attachments. I refer to training in proper deportment and attire and decoration, all of which is training in and habituation to bodily restriction and distortion; I refer to diets and exercise and beauty regimens which habituate the individual to deprivation and punishment and to fear and suspicion of her body and its wisdom; I refer to the abduction and seasoning of female sexual slaves; to clitoridectomy and other forms and sorts of physical and spiritual mutilation; all of which have no cultural or economic purpose or function if girls and women do not have to be ready for husbands and male lovers, pimps, johns, bosses and slavers. …

Lesbian feminists have noted that if the institution of female heterosexuality is what makes girls into women and is central to the continuous replication of patriarchy, then women's abandonment of that institution recommends itself as one strategy (perhaps among others) in the project of dismantling patriarchal structures. And if heterosexual encounters, relations and connections are the sites of the inscription of the patriarchal imperatives on the bodies of women, it makes sense to abandon those sites. And if female heterosexuality is central to the way sexism and racism are knit together in strange paradoxical symbiosis, it makes sense that non-participation in that institution could be part of a strategy for weakening both racism and patriarchy.

…

Commitment to the naturalness or inevitability of female heterosexuality is commitment to the power relations which are expressed and maintained by the institutions of female heterosexuality in patriarchal cultures around the world. …

Female heterosexuality is not a biological drive or an individual woman's erotic attraction or attachment to another human animal which happens to be male. Female heterosexuality is a concrete historical reality—a set of social institutions and practices defined and regulated by patriarchal kinship systems, by both civil and religious law, and by strenuously enforced mores and deeply entrenched values and taboos. Those definitions, regulations, values and taboos are about male fraternity and the oppression and exploitation of women. They are not about human warmth, fun, pleasure, deep knowledge between people. If any of the latter arise within the boundaries of these institutions and practices, it is because warmth, fun, pleasure and acknowledgement are among the things humans are naturally capable of, not because heterosexuality is natural or is naturally a site of such benefits.

So, is it possible to be a feminist without being a lesbian? My inclination is to say that feminism, which is thoroughly anti-patriarchal, is not compatible with female heterosexuality, which is thoroughly patriarchal. But I anticipate the following reply:

"To suppose that all relation, connection, or encounter of any passionate or erotic or genital sort or involving any sort of personal commitment between a woman and a man must belong to this patriarchal institution called 'female heterosexuality,' that it must be suffocated by this rubric, … to suppose that is to suppose we are all totally formed by history, social institutions and language. That is a kind of hopeless determinism which is politically fatal and is contradicted by your own presence here as a lesbian."

I agree that I cannot embrace any absolute historical, social determinism. The feminist lesbians' permanent project of defining ourselves and our passions and our communities is a living willful refusal of such determinism. But the free space of creation exists only when it is actively, aggressively, courageously, persistently occupied. Patriarchal histories and cultures mitigate against such space constantly, by coercion, by bribery, by punishment, and by shaping the imagination. What I am saying is that if you would have committed or occasional female/male connections—erotic, reproductive, home-making, partnership, friendship—which are not defined by your culture's patriarchal institutions of female heterosexuality, then you have to create the possibility of that. I am saying that as I see it that possibility *does not exist in patriarchal history and culture*. If it did, it would not be patriarchal.

…

The word "virgin" did not originally mean a woman whose vagina was untouched by any penis, but a free woman, one not betrothed, not married, not bound to, not possessed by any man. It meant a female who is sexually and hence socially her own person. In any universe of patriarchy, there are no Virgins in this sense, and hence Virgins must be unspeakable outlaws, outcasts, thinkable only as negations, their existence impossible. Radically feminist lesbians have claimed, and have been inventing ways of living out, positive Virginity, in creative defiance of patriarchal definitions of the real, the meaningful. The question at hand may be herstorical: Will anyone, can anyone manage to, invent and construct modes of living Virginity which include women's maintaining erotic, economic, home-making, partnering connections with men? What must be imagined here is females who are willing to engage in chosen connections with males, who are wild females, undomesticated females, thoroughly defiant of patriarchal female heterosexuality. Such females will be living

lives as sexually, socially and politically deviant and impossible as the lives undertaken by radically feminist lesbians. What must be imagined here is females who are
willing to engage in chosen connections with males, who are wild, undomesticated
females, creating themselves here and how.

*       *       *

In a way, it is not my place to imagine these wild females who have occasional and/or
committed erotic, reproductive, home-making, partnered or friendship relations
with males. The work and the pleasure of that imagining belong to those who undertake to invent themselves thus. But I do have a vivid, though partial, image of them.
It derives both from my own experience as an impossible being and from my intense
desire for alliance and sisterhood with women of my acquaintance who engage in relations with men in the patriarchal context but who also seem to me to have a certain
aptitude for Virginity. ... So I offer for your consideration a sketch of my image of
these wild women: (This is not a recipe for political correctness, and I am not legis-
lating: this is a report from my Imagination.)

These Virgins do not attire and decorate themselves in the gear which in their cultures signal female compliance with male-defined femininity and which would form
their bodies to such compliance. They do not make themselves "attractive" in the
conventional feminine modes of their cultures and so people who can ignore their
animal beauty say they are ugly. They maintain as much economic flexibility as they
possibly can to ensure that they can revert to independence any time economic partnership is binding them to an alliance less than fully chosen. They would no more
have sex when they don't expect to enjoy it than they would run naked in the rain
when they don't expect to enjoy it. Their sexual interactions are not sites where people with penises make themselves men and people with vaginas are made women.[1]

These Virgins who connect with men don't try to maintain the fictions that the
men they favor are better men than other men. When they are threatened by people
who feel threatened by them, they do not point to their connections with men as
soothing proof that they really aren't manhaters. They don't avail themselves of male
protection. They do not pressure their daughters or their mothers, sisters, friends, or
students to relate to men the ways they do so they can feel validated by the other
women's choices. They never consider bringing any man with them to any feminist
gathering that is not specifically meant to include men, and they help to create and
to defend (and they enjoy) women-only spaces.

These Virgins who connect with men are not manipulable by orchestrations of
male approval and disapproval, orchestrations of men's and children's needs, real or
fake. They are not capable of being reduced to conformity by dread or anxiety about
things lesbian, and are unafraid of their own passions for other Virgins, including
those who are lesbians. They do not need to be respectable.

These Virgins refuse to enter the institution of marriage, and do not support or
witness the weddings of others, including the weddings of their favorite brothers.
They are die-hard marriage-resisters. They come under enormous pressure to marry,
but they do not give in to it. They do not consider marriage a privilege. Not even the

bribe of spousal health insurance benefits lures them into marriage, not even as they
and their partners get older and become more anxious about their health and their
economic situations.

These Virgins have strong, reliable, creative, enduring, sustaining, ardent friendships with women. Their imagination and their politics are shaped more fundamentally by a desire to empower women and create friendship and solidarity among
women than by a commitment to appease, comfort or change men.

These Virgins who connect with men do not feel that they could be themselves
and be in closets; they are "out" as loose and noncompliant females, a very notice-
able phenomenon on the social and political scene. They make themselves visible,
audible, and tangible to each other, they make community and sisterhood with each
other and with lesbian Virgins, and they support each other in their wildness. They
frolic and make trouble together. They create ways to have homes and warmth and
companionship and intensity with or without a man included. They create value and
they create meaning, so when the pressures to conform to patriarchal female heterosexuality are great, they have a context and community of resistance to sustain them
and to engage their creative energies in devising new solutions to the problems conformity pretends to solve. ...

Are these beings I imagine possible? Can you fuck without losing your virginity? I
think everything is against it, but *it's not my call.* I can hopefully image, but the
counter-possible creation of such a reality is up to those who want to live it, if anyone
does.

*　　　*　　　*

...

"Do you have to be a lesbian to be a feminist?" is not quite the right question. The
question should be "Can a woman be heterosexual and be radically feminist?" My
picture is this: you do not have to be a lesbian to uncompromisingly embody and enact a radical feminism, but you also cannot be heterosexual in any standard patriarchal meaning of that word—you cannot be any version of patriarchal wife. Lesbian
or not, to embody and enact a consistent and all-the-way feminism you have to be a
heretic, a deviant, an undomesticated female, an impossible being. You have to be a
Virgin.

---

## Notes

1. These felicitous phrases are due to John Stoltenberg, *Refusing to Be a Man: Essays on Sex
and Justice* (Portland, Ore.: Breitenbush, 1989), *passim.*

# Heterosexuality and Choice

## Christine Overall

In one of my favourite cartoons, a young woman asks her tough and savvy feminist mother, 'Ma, can I be a feminist and still like men?' 'Sure,' replies the mother, 'Just like you can be a vegetarian and like fried chicken.' When I recounted this joke in an introduction to feminism course, my young female students were disturbed rather than amused. And this is not surprising. To some, the mother's reply may seem to be a reductio ad absurdum of combining feminism and heterosexuality. A good vegetarian, one might think, just does not like fried chicken; or she certainly *ought* not to like it. And if, in a moment of weakness, she does consume fried chicken, then she is either not a good, moral, consistent vegetarian, or, worse still, she is not a vegetarian at all. So also with the feminist. While many of my students hoped that it would be both logically and empirically possible to be a feminist and still like men, or even to love them, they also saw considerable tension in being both heterosexual and feminist. Some feminists who love men have expressed both doubt and guilt about the legitimacy of their lives, and some non-heterosexual feminists have encouraged those feelings. ...

Is, then, a 'feminist heterosexuality' possible?[1] To answer that question, it is necessary first to consider the nature of choice. If, as some feminists have argued, heterosexuality in women is coerced, it would seem that no woman chooses to be heterosexual. When there are not several recognized and legitimate options, when there are so many pressures to be heterosexual, and when failure to conform is so heavily punished, it is difficult to regard heterosexuality as the genuine expression of a preference. In fact, as one (heterosexual) woman remarked to me, given the damning indictment of heterosexuality which has been presented by some feminists, it might seem that any woman would be heterosexual only if it were *not* a choice.

But this is not all that can be said about the possibility of choosing heterosexuality. For, first, a single-minded focus on the coercive aspects of the heterosexual institution absolves heterosexual women of any responsibility for their sexual practice in a way that seems inappropriate, at least in the case of feminist women, who have had some opportunities to reflect upon the role of heterosexuality in patriarchal oppression. The idea that all heterosexual women (unlike non-heterosexual women) just can't help themselves and are somehow doomed to love and be attracted to men gives too much weight to the view of women as victims, and too little credit to the idea that women can act and make decisions on their own behalf. Moreover, it implicitly imputes to all heterosexual women a sort of false consciousness. Most such women will not see themselves as victims of coercion. Although they may not think of heterosexual practice as a choice they have made, they also do not necessarily feel like helpless victims of the heterosexual institution. But if no woman can choose to be heterosexual, then all heterosexual women either fail to correctly understand their own sexuality, or they can correctly understand their sexuality only by seeing themselves as helpless victims.

On the contrary, I would argue, it is a mistake to summarily dismiss *all* heterosexual women's experience as a failure to understand their own sexuality. Indeed, it is possible that some such women may

> have actively chosen, rather than fallen into, a life of heterosexual marriage and children … and that in their heterosexual relationships, they have control over their own sexuality and share equally in the enjoyment of and participation in their sexual relationships.[2]

I am not saying here only that some heterosexual women may lead exceptional lives in the sense that their relationship with their man (or men) is experienced as egalitarian and uncoercive; I am saying that there is an important sense in which a woman can genuinely and even sanely choose to be heterosexual, although the conditions and opportunities for that choice may be fairly rare. Beyond the claim that heterosexuality is innate (which seems to be an insufficiently grounded essentialist claim) and the claim that heterosexuality is coerced (which seems true in regard to the heterosexual institution as a whole) there is a third possibility: that heterosexuality is or can be chosen, even—or especially!—by feminists.

If it is possible to choose *not* to be heterosexual—and most radical feminists have argued that it is—then it is possible to actively choose to be heterosexual. To some degree, each of us is able to make ourselves into the kinds of sexual beings we are, through a process of interpretation and reinterpretation of our past and present experiences and of our feelings and emotions, and through active interaction with other persons, not just passive receptivity to their influence. By choosing one's heterosexuality I mean not merely acquiescing in it, or benefiting from heterosexual privilege, but actively taking responsibility for being heterosexual. Admittedly, most apparently heterosexual women never make, and never have an opportunity to make, such an active conscious choice. In what cases, then, might it be correct to say that a woman has genuinely chosen her heterosexuality? The following remark by Charlotte Bunch provides a crucial insight into the paradoxical answer to that question:

> Basically, heterosexuality means men first. That's what it's all about. It assumes that every woman is heterosexual; that every woman is defined by and is the property of men. Her body, her services, her children belong to men. If you don't accept that definition, you're a queer—no matter who you sleep with. …[3]

For a heterosexual woman, to start to understand the institution of heterosexuality and the ideology of heterosexism is already to start to leave standard heterosexuality behind. For part of what is customarily meant by the ascription of heterosexuality is its unconscious 'perfectly natural' character. Persons who are non-heterosexual never have the luxury of accepting their sexuality in this way. ...

... Marilyn Frye has pointed out that in discussions of sexual prejudice and discrimination one may often hear a statement such as 'I don't think of myself as heterosexual'—presumably said by a person who engages in heterosexual activity.[4] Heterosexuals ordinarily extend to others the somewhat dubious privilege of assuming that everyone is like them; since to be sexual is to be *hetero*sexual, '[t]he question often must be *made* to arise, blatantly and explicitly, before the heterosexual person will consider the thought that one is lesbian or homosexual.[5] On the other hand, such persons often perceive non-heterosexuals as being unnecessarily preoccupied with their sexuality, unable to stop talking about it and 'flaunting' it to the world. But, Frye suggests,

> Heterosexual critics of queers' "role-playing" ought to look at themselves in the mirror on their way out for a night on the town to see who's in drag. The answer is, everybody is. Perhaps the main difference between heterosexuals and queers is that when queers go forth in drag, they know they are engaged in theater—they are playing and they know they are playing. Heterosexuals usually are taking it all perfectly seriously, thinking they are in the real world, thinking they *are* the real world.[6]

The person whose sexual practice is heterosexual and who honestly and innocently states that she does not think of herself as heterosexual shows herself most clearly to be heterosexual in the standard sense. Paradoxically, then, for a woman to firmly and unambiguously affirm her heterosexuality may already be to begin to leave it behind, that is, to cease to be heterosexual in the unthinking unconscious way she once was: She ceases to participate wholeheartedly in the heterosexual institution, and begins the process of disaffiliation from it.[7] When that sort of reflection takes place, I believe, the woman is beginning genuinely to choose her heterosexuality; and she is choosing heterosexual practice without a concomitant endorsement of the heterosexual institution.

Of course, for such a woman, heterosexuality is still something which is enforced, in Rich's sense; that is, persistent cultural pressures strive to ensure her conformity, and deviance from heterosexuality is penalized, often severely. No amount of awareness of the heterosexual institution can, by itself, change the compulsory nature of heterosexuality, and disaffiliation by one woman will not rock the institution.

Nevertheless, that awareness can make a difference, for the previously unawarely heterosexual woman, in the dimensions of her own sexuality: She can begin the process of shaping her own sexuality, by making decisions and choices based upon an understanding of the power and the limits of the heterosexual institution. For she can explore her own personal history and determine how and when her sense of the erotic became separated from women and connected to men.[8] In so doing, she can no longer regard her heterosexual orientation as something over which she has no power or control, as something which just dominates her sexual feelings and practices. Instead, she can distinguish between sexual passion and attraction, on the one hand, and dependence, need, fear, and insecurity on the other. She can become aware of her feelings about women's and men's bodies, and discover whether and/or to what degree she has internalized a socially validated revulsion toward the female body. She can genuinely ask herself whether sexual activity with men is something she wants, or merely something in which she engages. (For, of course, we cannot assume that all women whose sexual practice is heterosexual also enjoy their sexual activities.)

If the answer is no, it is not something she wants, she then has the prospect of choosing to be non-heterosexual. On the other hand, if the answer is yes, she can, in a way, begin to come out as a heterosexual: not in the heterosexist fashion by which almost all heterosexuals, male and female, ordinarily mark their heterosexuality, but rather in terms of an informed and self-aware feminist evaluation of her life as a heterosexual,[9] renouncing as far as possible the privilege accorded by heterosexuality,[10] and recognizing both the different varieties of oppression non-heterosexuals undergo and also the affinities she shares with non-heterosexual women. She can support non-heterosexual women, validate their relationships, and refuse any longer to be complicitous in the erasures they often undergo. She thereby chooses to be heterosexual as a matter of sexual practice, but not as a matter of the exclusive heterosexist alignment or orientation of her life.

Nevertheless, although it may now seem that heterosexuality can be genuinely chosen by women, for some feminists the question may still remain whether it *ought* to be chosen, whether it is ever a good choice, a choice a feminist could responsibly make. … For any woman, heterosexual orientation seems to mean putting men, or at least a man, first. And even while rejecting the heterosexual institution, such a woman also still benefits from heterosexual privilege. Thus, no matter how idyllic her relationship, it seems to fail of its very nature to challenge the status quo, and to reinforce the apparent exclusive loyalty of a woman to her man. Together, the two persons in the relationship still appear to participate in and contribute to the perpetuation of an institution which is oppressive of women, particularly of non-heterosexual women and unattached women of any orientation, as well as of heterosexual women in abusive relationships.[11]

The foregoing observations appear to call into question the *legitimacy* of a woman's deliberately deciding to be heterosexual, and I have only very tentative responses to them. The first involves taking seriously the distinction between the institution of heterosexuality on the one hand, and on the other hand, specific heterosexual relations and the persons who become involved in them. This is the same sort of distinction made by Adrienne Rich in her discussion of motherhood. Rich has urged us to recognize that while motherhood itself is an oppressive institution, mothering particular children may be a delightful, worthwhile, valuable human activity.[12] Similarly, while heterosexuality is an oppressive institution, not all heterosexual relationships are valueless as a result. Glimpsing this possibility might also encourage feminists to make a distinction between what could be called the *institution* of manhood, on the one hand, and individual men on the other. …

... This answer, by itself, has of course all the weaknesses of any 'individual solution' to problems of oppression. For it depends upon a commitment of the man in the relationship not to avail himself of the power of his position. And so, it must be said, for a woman to actively choose to be heterosexual is an act of faith—faith first of all in the fundamental humanity of the men whom she chooses to love. By actively choosing to be heterosexual, a feminist woman is rejecting the view that male sexuality is inevitably and innately violent and exploitive, and that men are hopelessly fated to engage only in aggressive and oppressive relationships. Although members of the two sexes acquire very different roles, men just as much as women learn to participate in the heterosexual institution. And it is a lesson which men can reject. The heterosexual institution is a social artifact that can be changed, and men themselves may be the allies of women in changing it.

...

There are, moreover, degrees of heterosexuality. Heterosexual orientation need not mean the exclusion of loyalty to, attraction toward, and love for women. Women who are heterosexual can develop intimate relationships with women, and value them at least as much as they value their relationships with men. Adrienne Rich has spoken movingly of what she calls 'the lesbian continuum.' She defines it as

> [the full] range—through each woman's life and throughout history—of women-identified experience; not simply the fact that a woman has had or consciously desired genital sexual experience with another woman. [The lesbian continuum] embrace[s] many more forms of primary intensity between and among women, including the sharing of a rich inner life, the bonding against male tyranny, [and] the giving and receiving of practical and political support. ...[13]

Sometimes, unfortunately, the concept of the lesbian continuum is appealed to by some feminists rather prematurely as a way of foreclosing on confrontation and acrimony between heterosexual and non-heterosexual women. Nevertheless, provided the differences between heterosexual and non-heterosexual women in culture, experience, oppression, and privilege are not glossed over, the concept of the lesbian continuum is a powerful source of insight for women who have chosen to be heterosexual, and a reminder that they are not or need not be only heterosexual. So far, under patriarchal conditions, what women's sexuality is and can be has scarcely been explored; but in a non-patriarchal society there would be no limitations on life-promoting human relationships.

## Notes

1. The question is taken from the title of Angela Hamblin's article, 'Is a Feminist Heterosexuality Possible?,' in Sue Cartledge and Joanna Ryan, eds., *Sex and Love: New Thoughts on Old Contradictions* (London: The Women's Press 1983) 105–23.

2. Ruth Bleier, *Science and Gender: A Critique of Biology and Its Theories on Women* (New York: Pergamon Press 1984) 182–3. Cf. Ann Ferguson, 'Patriarchy, Sexual Identity, and the Sex-

ual Revolution,' in Nannerl O. Keohane, Michelle Z. Rosaldo, and Barbara C. Gelpi, eds., *Feminist Theory: A Critique of Ideology* (Chicago: University of Chicago Press 1982) 159.

3. Charlotte Bunch, 'Not For Lesbians Only,' in Charlotte Bunch et al., eds., *Building Feminist Theory: Essays From Quest* (New York: Longman 1981) 69.

4. Marilyn Frye, 'Lesbian Feminism and the Gay Rights Movement: Another View of Male Supremacy, Another Separatism,' in *The Politics of Reality: Essays in Feminist Theory* (Trumansburg, NY: The Crossing Press 1983) 147. Michael Ramberg has pointed out to me that to say 'I don't think of myself as heterosexual' could also mean 'I am not *only* heterosexual' or 'I will not always be heterosexual.'

5. Marilyn Frye, 'On Being White: Toward A Feminist Understanding of Race and Race Supremacy,' in *The Politics of Reality,* 116, her emphasis.

6. Marilyn Frye, 'Sexism,' in *The Politics of Reality,* 29, her emphasis.

7. Frye, 'On Being White,' 127.

8. Marilyn Frye, 'A lesbian Perspective on Women's Studies,' in Margaret Cruikshank, ed., *Lesbian Studies: Present and Future* (Old Westbury, NY: The Feminist Press 1982) 197.

9. See Katherine Arnup, 'Lesbian Feminist Theory,' *Resources for Feminist Research/Documentation sur la recherche féministe* 12 (March 1983) 55.

10. Amy Gottlieb, 'Mothers, Sisters, Lovers, Listen,' in Maureen Fitzgerald, Connie Guberman, and Margie Wolfe, eds., *Still Ain't Satisfied! Canadian Feminism Today* (Toronto: Women's Press 1982) 238–9.

11. See Leeds Revolutionary Feminist Group, 'Political Lesbianism: The Case Against Heterosexuality,' in *Love Your Enemy? The Debate Between Heterosexual Feminism and Political Lesbianism* (London: Onlywomen Press 1981) 5–10.

12. Adrienne Rich, *Of Woman Born: Motherhood as Experience and Institution* (New York: Bantam Books 1976).

13. Adrienne Rich, 'Compulsory Heterosexuality and Lesbian Existence,' in Catherine R. Stimpson and Ethel Spector Person, eds., *Women: Sex and Sexuality* (Chicago: University of Chicago Press 1980) 81.

# Bisexual Feminist Politics: Because Bisexuality Is Not Enough

## Karin Baker

...

... I believe that the struggles for queer liberation and women's liberation are intimately connected. ... I believe that bisexuals have a particular role to play in these struggles, a role that both overlaps and diverges from that of lesbians and gay men. I believe that, as a group, bisexuals need to focus more attention on examining what this role might be.

For example, bisexuals clearly challenge compulsory heterosexuality, as do lesbians and gay men, to the degree to which they relate sexually to the same sex. At the same time, bisexuals are not limited in their sexuality to a specific sex, and thus bisexuality challenges the gender system, which we associate with biological sex, in a way that lesbians and gay men do not. Gender is as much, if not more, a tool of women's and queer oppression as compulsory heterosexuality. Thus, the role that bisexuals can potentially play in subverting the gender system is indispensable to a radical social transformation. However, this potential can only come from a bisexuality that is consciously feminist.

## The Social Construction of Sexuality and Gender

Systems of oppression are often justified by an oppressor as being rooted in biology, as based in something biologically inherent to human nature. Feminists confront the deeply held cultural belief that women are inherently (biologically) inferior to men. The institution of compulsory heterosexuality rests on the concept that only heterosexual sex is "natural," leading to queer oppression.

In fact, it is clear that the traditional ideas described above, and others like them, are not biologically based, but rather are socially constructed, and any claims as to their biological basis are attempts to demonstrate their legitimacy.

Not only the concept of women's inferiority but our very category of gender itself is a social construction. Gender is a dual category system in which certain human traits are assigned to one biological sex, and certain traits to the other. Women and men are actually more alike than different, and most of our differences are social creations. The concept of the social construction of sexuality and gender plays a central role in the ideas I put forward here. By deconstructing these socially held attitudes, we can get at the basis of women's oppression and lesbian, bisexual and gay oppression, and work out a strategy for challenging them.

## Scientifically Proven or Socially Imposed Concepts?

Gender is the social construct applied to biological sex. Even where gender is recognized as socially variable, biological sex is often assumed to be a fixed and entirely definable category. This is not the case. One way to show this is to demonstrate how rigid the framework of this dual category system is compared to the biological realities. Women, for example, are recognized as physically smaller and weaker than men, and exceptions to this, cases in which women are larger and stronger, are ignored. Our system of categorization is not able to encompass the breadth of variation here.

Even chromosomes and hormones, seen as the basis for gendered behavior, can be demonstrated to have less to do with gender than social upbringing does. For example, individuals with male chromosomes will display social traits associated with females if they are raised to belong to that gender. Furthermore, it has been shown that perhaps as much as hormones govern behavior, behavior may influence hormone production. As one author on the subject has concluded, "no matter how detailed an investigation science has thus far made, it is still not possible to draw a clear dividing line between male and female."[1]

My point is not that there are not differences between groups our culture presently divides according to gender. Rather, these differences have been fetishized and made to fit into categories that are not as easily delineable as our usual culture framework makes them appear. Men are aggressive, it is said, so an aggressive woman is "mannish," because the categories must be maintained in spite of apparent contradictions.

I am not saying it is possible, or desirable, to go beyond any recognition of difference. My object is rather to point out that there are other ways of viewing difference, and an alternative I would advocate is a more flexible *continuum*, rather than forcing human traits into one or two opposing and inflexible categories.

Where does this all lead? Just as class oppression did not exist before human communities had divided into classes, women's separation and subordination make them appear inferior and this perception becomes a justification for their subordination, or economically, once women lose access to economic power they do not have the means to be economically powerful. Thus, the perception of women and men as belonging to separate and opposing genders is both a tool and a product of women's oppression.

## Tools of Oppression:
## Gender and Compulsory Heterosexuality

My position contrasts with much of lesbian feminist analysis which views *compulsory heterosexuality* as the basis for women's oppression. Heterosexual pairing is seen as a mechanism for the domination of women because it forces individual women into dependence on individual men while isolating women from each other. Given such a premise, the belief of some lesbian feminists is that lesbians are the true revolutionaries in the struggle for women's liberation. Lesbianism confronts the coercion of heterosexuality, avoids the domination within heterosexual pairing and, at the same time, brings women together.

There is no doubt that compulsory heterosexuality serves all the functions described above, and lesbianism most directly challenges this institution. My resistance is not to the conclusions of this analysis, but to what it leaves out.
...

## Bisexuality, Gender and Women's Oppression

Lesbianism *is* a challenge to compulsory heterosexuality. Bisexuality, however, has the potential to challenge the dual gender system, which oppresses women and queer people insofar as it is a foundation of compulsory heterosexuality.

Bisexuality fits in here in two ways, but the principle in both cases is the same: bisexuals blur the lines between categories often regarded as fixed and definable. First the strict dichotomy between homosexuality and heterosexuality gets blown. Bisexuals don't even fit into a clear-cut category because of the obvious variety of bisexual experience. Thus, bisexuality blurs the supposed duality of sexuality in a manner that is itself a challenge to other dual category systems, such as that of gender.[2]

In addition to this, bisexuality is not based on gender. Compulsory heterosexuality assumes a strictly defined gender system. Lesbian and gay relationships challenge gender by avoiding traditional gender roles. However, lesbian and gay sexuality is based on attraction to a specific gender to the same degree that heterosexuality is. By definition, both heterosexuality and homosexuality rely equally on a strictly defined gender system. Thus both uphold the present gender system, although compulsory heterosexuality has more to do with its perpetuation.

I believe that bisexuality has the potential to go beyond gender. True, there are bisexuals whose experience contradicts this to some extent. I have known some bis to say that they are attracted to women for the qualities culturally associated with this gender and to men for qualities identified as masculine. Even in such cases, however, sexual connections are possible with either gender and thus, to this degree, the gender system is challenged.

However, in many cases, including my own, bisexual people recognize that most, if not all, of which they find attractive in another has little to do with gender. In my case, I am attracted to people whose gender it is impossible for me to ignore, but my attraction for them involves many factors, none of which break down simply according to gender. I am attracted to people around whom I feel safe, individuals who seem to understand me better than most, who are straightforward, who can be supportive and nurturing, who are physically active and who "have some flesh on them." A few of these characteristics are more common with one gender, but they certainly aren't limited to that gender.

## Gender and Sexism: The Current Realities

...

It is the case that gender-blind bisexuality, if it lacks a feminist political analysis, is not a direct challenge to women's oppression. Bisexuality attacks sexism by subverting gender, but since the very manner in which it subverts gender is by ignoring it, it also ignores sexism. Unfortunately, sexism will continue in our present society, with the institutions that support it in place, even if we ignore it—more so in fact.

That means two things. On a personal level, any bisexual woman who chooses to be with a man faces sexism. From the outside, her relationship will be perceived as heterosexual relationships are seen—she becomes "his" woman. Within the relationship, with sexism as deeply embedded in our society as it is, there will be times when she will experience sexist dynamics with her lover. There are few men who will never fall back on male privilege when they feel threatened—for example, they may dismiss their lover's criticisms as "nagging" or wait for her to do the emotional processing necessary to smooth out a snag in the relationship.

On the level of broad social change, without lesbians women's options would be heterosexuality and bisexuality. In our social system based on the concept that women need men, neither of these orientations allows for the option that women can create lives without men. Thus, that aspect of compulsory heterosexuality that says that women need men is not challenged.

But we need to challenge this. We cannot leap from our present system to a nongendered, polysexual system of sexuality. It is necessary to confront sexism in all its institutionalized forms before we can go past it. Thus bisexuality itself is not enough. With compulsory heterosexuality still in place, even bisexual women will face strong social influences to be in relationships with men, and their power to avoid domination within these relationships will be relatively weak. Both gender and compulsory heterosexuality must be fought at the same time.

## The Central Role of Lesbians in Women's Liberation

We will not be able to say any woman has freely chosen to be with a man until all women are free not to be with men. For this reason, lesbianism must be an option. More directly than bisexuality, lesbianism is a challenge to compulsory heterosexuality. Thus, lesbians play a central role in the struggle for women's liberation and must remain a visible and distinct segment of this movement.

...

Clearly, lesbians and gay men also challenge gender. Heterosexual relationships are one of the main arenas for playing out gender roles. In contrast, within a relationship between lesbians, or gay men, traditional gender roles cannot be played out. Even cases in which gay men or lesbians take on approximations of traditional roles can never be the same in same-sex relationships as they are in opposite-sex relationships. In general, societal perceptions of lesbians and gay men indicate that their existence is a challenge to the system of gender. Men who are gay are seen as "effeminate," whereas lesbians are "mannish."

It follows then that, aside from avoiding gender-specific sexuality, bisexuals also challenge gender in their same-sex relationships by avoiding traditional gender roles, as lesbians and gay men do. They also confront compulsory heterosexuality in their same-sex relationships, as lesbians and gay men do. Lesbians and gay men, however, are a more outright and complete challenge to compulsory heterosexuality at least insofar as they confront that aspect of the institution that compels opposite-sex relations.

To summarize the above: lesbians and gay men directly challenge compulsory heterosexuality through their same-sex relationships and indirectly challenge gender through avoiding traditional gender roles within their relationships. Lesbians, specifically, confront the male supremacist belief that all women need men. Bisexuals directly challenge gender by avoiding gender-specific attraction and indirectly challenge compulsory heterosexuality and the acting out of gender roles through their openness to same-sex relationships. All of the above are necessary elements in the struggle for women's liberation and queer liberation.

## Bisexuals and Compulsory Heteromonosexuality

... Bisexuals are oppressed as bisexuals. One aspect of oppression, in my under-standing, is when a specific group is denied legitimacy by a socially upheld institu-tion.[3] The very invisibility of bisexual experience, which led my lesbian acquaintance to see bisexuals as sometimes a subset of the category "lesbian and gay," and some-times part of the straight world, is the basis for bisexual oppression.

In the process of exploring this idea, I developed a new perspective on the institu-tion of compulsory heterosexuality, which I had previously conceived of as oppres-sive *in its compulsion to other-sex relations and prohibition of same-sex relations*. Thus far in this paper I have written as though that were my underlying assumption. In fact, compulsory heterosexuality has two components (to do my own dichotomiz-ing): "hetero," and hidden within that, "mono." Bisexuals are sometimes affected by the first, and always by the latter. Without compulsory heterosexuality there would be no such thing as straight or queer. It is responsible for our current framework, which leaves no room for a sexuality that is not monosexual, no room for bisexuality.

If bisexuals are not bi-bashed, denied housing as bisexuals or subjected to overt forms of oppression, this is in fact a result of our invisibility, and that invisibility is, for the present, how we experience oppression. As we become more visible, our ex-periences of oppression will become more overt. A recent example of this is the scapegoating of bis in the AIDS crisis, which resulted from the fear of this murky cat-egory of people who blur the lines between "them" and "us," those who are innocent. This dynamic is clearly different from the type of stigma experienced by gay men as a result of AIDS.

## Bisexual Liberation

A bisexual politic as foundation for a bisexual liberation movement can confront the social framework that only allows for either/or. If explicitly feminist, it has a role to play in challenging gender, the basis for women's oppression. In a general sense, bi-sexuality challenges our system of categorization, which provides the basis for other forms of oppression: the division between "of color" and "white," as well as "wom-an" and "man," "queer" and "straight" and so on.

In the shorter term a bisexual feminist politic can form the basis for a group iden-tity upon which a bisexual community can be formed. Such a politic would create a framework for our common individual experiences. For the present, that which we have in common is harder to recognize than the shared experiences within each monosexual community. But, in fact, there are common threads within the bisexual experience. The achievement of a vibrant bisexual community would pose a signifi-cant and unique challenge to the dual gender system and the limitations inherent in compulsory heteromonosexuality. Our contribution might even go beyond this to challenge our entire oppressive social system, helping to break down the categories of identity on which much of it is based.

## Notes

1. Holly Devor, *Gender Blending: Confronting the Limits of Duality* (Bloomington, Indiana: Indiana University Press, 1989), p. 1.

2. One problem with the label "bisexual" is that the prefix "bi" assumes a dual gender system.

3. Economic oppression, where present, is something other than this, but it is not unrelated.

# *Beyond Bisexual*

## Annie Sprinkle

I started out as a regular heterosexual woman. Then I became bisexual. Now I am beyond bisexual—meaning I am sexual with more than just human beings. I literally make love with things like waterfalls, winds, rivers, trees, plants, mud, buildings, sidewalks, invisible things, spirits, beings from other planets, the earth, and yes, even animals.

I started out monogamous. Then I ended up with two lovers. At present I have many lovers. ... [One] is my beautiful lover, the sky.

The sky and I have a very special relationship, and we love each other very much. Sex with her is divine. Mostly we make love through my eleventh-floor Manhattan window. She calls to me when she is feeling tired, haggard, smoggy, lonely, or sometimes when she is feeling great and powerful and wants to celebrate. Or, I call to her when I need and want her, and she is always there for me. I breathe her air deeply into my lungs. She envelopes me, giving me lots of her sexual energy. It thrills me, turns me on, and overwhelms me. I give her all my love and lust. I have an orgasm—sometimes several. Maybe she has an orgasm too. Perhaps her rain is her arousal fluid and her thunder her orgasm. Often I cry because our sex together is so beautiful and nourishing. Our love is real. I feel it strongly.

Obviously, my concept of sex is "more expanded" than most people's. To me, sex is not about sticking a penis into a vagina (unless it's sex for procreation). Sex is about tapping into, building, sharing, and utilizing sexual *energy*. The genitals are simply an exquisitely perfect generator for that sexual energy. Whether the genitals are male or female, or whether there are no genitals at all, does not matter to me. It's about the energy. Since I have learned this I'm reaching whole new levels of sexual intensity, adventure, enjoyment, and satisfaction and have come to use sex for more than recreation and satisfying physical needs. I use sex as a healing tool, as a meditation, a way of life, and as a path to enlightenment.

...

### The Annie Sprinkle Sex Guidelines for the '90s: You Can Heal Your Sex Life—A 13-Step Program

1. *Honor your sexuality and realize its incredible value.* Sex can cure a headache, relieve stress and tension, help digestion, strengthen the heart, relieve menstrual cramps, help you sleep, wake you up, clear the mind, open you up to feelings, improve concentration, create life, burn unwanted calories, and cure depression. Research shows that just thinking about sex will strengthen your immune system. Sex can create intimacy with another human being, be an expression of love, bond people together, relieve loneliness, not to mention it can feel really good and be a hell of a lot of fun.

When our sexuality is repressed, violence results. We develop disease and disorder, tension, frustration, anxiety, drug and alcohol addiction, and a whole host of other destructive forces. This repression can come from outside of us through the pressures of society, or from within ourselves.

I'm not advocating that everyone run out and have lots of promiscuous sex. Simply allow your sexual energy to flow freely, pleasurably, guiltlessly through your body. You can be celibate and still honor and express your sexuality. Just lying in the sun or swimming, eating a meal, or walking down the street can be sexual.

2. *Do not judge yourself or others.* We are *all* at the right place at the right time in our sexual evolutions. Our sex lives, like all the parts of our lives, go through many phases. We learn from all of our experiences, including our mistakes. Allow others their own paths. Allow yourself your own path. ...

3. *Get rid of any last vestiges of sexual guilt and feelings that you don't deserve pleasure.* We are sexual beings. Enjoying sex is our birthright.

4. *Abstinence can be dangerous to your health.* The surgeon general tells us that abstinence is one form of safe sex, but it can really be outright dangerous. Using your own creative sexual energy celibately, for yourself, is one thing. You are honoring that energy and working with it for yourself. But abstinence—pushing your sexual feelings down and suppressing them because you think you shouldn't have them— can cause incredible anxiety, frustration, depression, disease, etc. If you like sex then don't give it up. It's too precious.

5. *Accept the fact that you are living in the AIDS era.* Stop complaining that sex isn't the way it used to be and that you hate condoms. Yes, you may need to mourn for the way it was, but then get over it and accept reality. Total acceptance of the AIDS era will release fear and frustration and bring awareness and compassion. Educate yourself on safe sex practices. Learn to love latex. ...

6. *Redefine your concept of sex.* Find new ways to make love, to be intimate, to enjoy and express our sexual feelings. Let go of old ideas of what sex is "supposed to be

like." Open your mind and heart and explore new territory. Be willing to be creative and experimental.

7. *Learn to focus on energy, not the way your bodies touch.* You can have an incredible, delirious sexual experience with someone without even touching, if you focus on the energy between you. It's like learning a new language. At first feeling energy will be subtle, but before long you will feel where the energy exists in your body, you will be able to move it around with the power of your thoughts and will. You can focus this energy to heal something in your body, send it to a sick friend for their healing, use the energy to pray, meditate, do magic, etc. ...

8. *Know that you can choose how you want to express your sexuality—self-lovingly or self-destructively.* ... The way I see it, there is junk sex, health sex, and gourmet sex. Junk sex is fast, very genitally focused, and not always very nourishing. It can even be harmful to your physical and emotional well-being. Health sex is healing and nourishing. Gourmet sex takes a lot of time to prepare and savor, as well as a certain amount of skill and knowledge. Try to make self-loving choices as to what kind of sex you have, but if you don't, then don't beat yourself up for it.

9. *Learn about your breath.* Sexual and orgasmic energy travel on the breath. Conscious breathing can make sex much more powerful and satisfying. In fact, orgasm is possible from breathing alone, without any touching. (Is this the safe sex of the future?) ...

10. *Take care of your body.* Eat well. Exercise. Pamper your body with long, hot baths with obscenely expensive toiletries.

11. *Visualize a safe and satisfying future for your sex life and the sex lives of people of future generations.* Our society is just in kindergarten when it comes to sex. There is so much more to learn, so much more potential. Past cultures, such as the ancient Taoists and Tantrics, some Native American tribes, some geisha, and the Sacred Prostitutes from ancient cultures like Sumeria and Mesopotamia, were far, far more developed.

12. *Make time for enjoying sex.* If you like sex, give yourself and others the gift of loving sensual and sexual pleasure. It's well worth the time. Throw away your TV if you have to.

13. *Make love to the earth and sky and all things and they will make love to you.* Open yourself up to the great web of energy that connects all things, become a channel for some of that ecstasy that's available just for the asking. Breathe it in, and you will be guaranteed many benefits. For one thing, you will find that perfect, ideal lover that you have been searching for for so long. That lover is yourself.

# Sex Resistance in Heterosexual Arrangements

## A Southern Women's Writing Collective

This paper was collectively produced by the women of A Southern Women's Writing Collective. In contrast to the pro-sex movement, we are calling ourselves Women Against Sex (WAS).[1] We are offering a theory which describes the practice of sexuality at the level of class interaction, struggle, and conflict; that is, at the political level. We take seriously the overwhelming statistics that scientifically document the harm done to women by men for sex. The statistic that most clearly shows the staggering amount of sexual assault or sexual harassment done against women is Diana E. H. Russell's findings from a random sample of 930 San Francisco households: only 7.8 percent of women reported experiencing *no* sexual assault or sexual harassment. (We must assume that the reported number of incidences were lower than actual experiences because we know that women frequently fail to recognize, name, or report abuse, including rape.) These sexual acts, done individually and one at a time, destroy women's lives, literally. They begin when we are infants, and never end, not even when we are corpses. Sex *is* what men say it is. It *means* what men say it means. Its practice is *how* men practice it. It is what has to remain in place no matter what. Otherwise, patriarchy will fall. As the systematic political practice of male supremacy—the concrete manifestation of male power over women—sex *is* our oppression. It is also how our oppression stays. Since we believe that the practice of sexuality politically subordinates women, we believe that the entire practice must be dismantled, taken apart, or deconstructed. Though we realize that many women, including WAS members, have had self-described affirmative sexual experiences, we believe that this was in spite of and not because the experiences were sexual. We also recognize that, as women in this patriarchal culture, we have not escaped the socially constructed dynamic of eroticized dominance and submission; that is, dominance and submission is *felt* in our bodies as sex and therefore "affirmative."

We believe that homosexuality, pedophilia, lesbianism, bisexuality, transsexuality, transvestism, sadomasochism, nonfeminist celibacy, and autoeroticism have the same malevolent relationship to conceptual and empirical male force as does heterosexuality. These activities represent only variations on a heterosexual theme, not exceptions. There is no way out of the practice of sexuality except *out*. All these erotic choices are also a part of sexuality as constructed by male supremacy. *We know of no exception to male supremacist sex.* The function of this practice permits no true metamorphoses; all gender permutations remain superficial. We therefore name intercourse, penetration, and all other sex acts as integral parts of the male gender construction which is sex; and we criticize them as oppressive to women. We name orgasm as the epistemological mark of the sexual, and we therefore criticize it too as oppressive to women.

We wish to emphasize that we are not attempting to describe or redescribe the lived sexual experiences of all women. We realize that these experiences are lived out in various ways, ranging from the joyous to the humiliating to the murderous. Though we believe that political reality "connects up" with each individual woman's personal experience and psychology, we do not believe there is any static formula that neatly captures this connection. We offer to the radical feminist community our beginning analysis of a practice—sexuality—which we believe is the root cause of women's political subordination.

The practice of sexuality is everything that makes socially possible the having of sex. That is, the practice of sexuality is everything that makes sex socially happen, that makes it socially real. The practice of sexuality includes gender roles, or social identification with femaleness and maleness; these roles function to make sex acts seem natural and inevitable, even though they are neither. Sex acts are central to the practice of sexuality; they are to sex what sex is to the subordination of women.

Historically, sex acts have included rape, marital rape, footbinding, fellatio, intercourse, autoeroticism, forced sex, objectification, child rape, incest, battery, anal intercourse, use and production of pornography, pimping and the use/abuse of [prostituted women], cunnilingus, sexual harassment, torture, mutilation, and murder—especially by dismemberment, strangulation, and stabbing. Sexual torture is known to be a military tool of genocide, targeting women most horribly; it functions to make war into a sexual experience. Forced breeding of black women and men under slavery, the rape of black women by white men, and the lynching primarily of black men are also understood to be sex acts perpetrated by white male supremacy shaped by racism.

Sex acts are those acts that men as a gender class have constructed as genitally arousing or satisfying. The medium of this construction is that of social meaning; the method of construction is material, and both meaning and method rely on male force.

Material conditions are (a) direct force used by men as a gender class against women as a gender class, and (b) preclusion of women's rightful options. Thus, the empirical conditions under which women's sexual desire is socially incarnated are the autonomy-denying conditions of direct force and preclusion used by men against women. These conditions which construct our desire produce a sexual desire which is nonautonomous or "unowned." The desire to act as one is forced to act becomes nonautonomous. Since there is no phenomenological difference between those desires produced by preclusion or force and those not so produced, introspection alone is a poor guide for discovering the nonautonomous nature of unowned desire.

We have learned that we cannot trust our feelings as the litmus test for the truth about sex because—although sex is experientially about feelings—it is about constructed, manipulated feelings. At the social level, the coercion that produces unowned desires can be experienced as coercion only if the process fails. If the incarnation of the desire is successful, the coercion can only be found by looking at the social conditions under which the desire was produced. This is why we base our analysis on our observations of sexuality as practiced under male supremacy, not on our feelings—good, bad, indifferent or rapturous—about patriarchal sexual practices.

Preclusion and force play another role, which is the medium of social meaning. They are the elements which subjunctively define sex acts. A sex act can be operationally defined as an act which, if a woman does not choose it, a male *qua* male would find it genitally arousing to force her. Thus, even if a woman is not empirically forced into a sex act, male arousal is nevertheless a response to the element of subjunctive force, which remains in all instances definitional. While a woman might evade empirical force, she literally cannot evade conceptual or definitional sexual force. This truth about sex, like all conceptual truth, is beyond the reach of individual choice, cleverness, privilege, or negotiating ability. It is for this reason that male force which defines sex is inescapable. For this reason, lesbians or people of other sexual preferences cannot escape or redefine sexual practice inside male supremacy. Thus, women are politically subordinated through sex, not because we do not ever choose it, but because the identity of what we choose is a function of male political power, power that valorizes and maintains itself through a process of genital arousal that is informed by the denigration and violation of women's autonomy and equality. Given this definition, genital arousal represents the literal incarnation of women's political subordination. It is politics made flesh.

Our study of pornography has made it clear that because the male is aroused through this medium of social meaning, pornography is as arousing as "real-life" sex. In both life and art, the male responds to the male-constructed meaning of woman. Thus the equation "pornography=sex" is literally true.

We believe that the practice of sexuality is entirely socially constructed by the power of men as a gender class. We do not believe it is either a curse of biology or a gift from God. Neither do we believe it is a joint-gender project of men and women. We believe the practice to be animated by an eroticized dynamic of male dominance and female submission. What makes this practice live and breathe, what sparks its social life, is class hierarchy or social top-bottomism. We believe that the function of this practice is to subordinate women to men. This dynamic and this function identify the practice at the political level. Any act informed by a practice without this dynamic and function—any act informed by a practice which did not subordinate women—would literally not be a sex act. More succinctly: *if it doesn't subordinate women, it's not sex.*

As far as we know, no act experienced as sexual is this "something else." The practice that could make this happen does not exist. In our feminist future, an act outwardly identical to a sex act *might* be informed by an entirely different practice. That act would not subordinate women. But that feminist future is not now and that different practice is not now. That is where we want to go/be after the defeat of male supremacy, after dismantling the practice of sexuality.

The sexual experience of most women occurs within heterosexual arrangements, and this experience is often lived out as an attempt to escape from the practice of sexuality. It is the experience of avoidance. ... Enough women have learned how to avoid becoming available so that mention of women's headaches is a male joke. So women do have headaches, and dress and undress in closets, deliberately gain or lose weight, become alcoholic, develop other drug dependencies, carefully orchestrate schedules, and attempt to shut down all communications that might hint at intimacy.

There are some feminists who seem to believe that these activities of sex avoidance represent the quaint subterfuges of a long-dead past—but they are wrong. This dismissive view may be a function of some social privilege that most ordinary women do not have. We believe the life of sex avoidance is the reality for many women in heterosexual arrangements.

Women's historical sex avoidance can, with feminist consciousness, become an act of *sex resistance*. The sex resister understands her act as a political one. Her goal is not only personal integrity for herself but political freedom for all women. She resists on three fronts: she resists male-constructed sexual "needs," she resists the misnaming of her act as prudery, and she especially resists the patriarchy's attempt to make its work of subordinating women easier by "consensually" constructing her desire in its own oppressive image.

The patriarchy attempts to reach *within* women to fuck/construct us from the inside out. This attempt assumes many forms, such as sex "education" and sex advice. ... Such advice ... never questions the practice of sexuality. ... The choice to avoid sex is never perceived as valid. ... The normalcy of such coercion of desire makes untrue the claim that our sexuality is our own. As long as the price of not choosing sex is what it presently is for any woman, sex is in fact compulsory for all women.

The compulsoriness of women's sexuality (not just heterosexuality) is hidden because it is sexual. We can try to expose this hidden force through thought, reflection, and action. ... We believe that we can begin by and through the processes which we have identified as (a) sexual resistance, (b) deconstructive lesbianism, and (c) radical celibacy to expose and perhaps even unmake or undo the sexualization that is our subordination.

Through collective and personal struggle, the desires that were socially incarnated in us in order to effect our subordination to men can be named and disowned. After all, if we can teach pigeons to play ping-pong, incarnating in them desires they never thought they had, perhaps we can teach ourselves to prefer a nonsexualized woman-identification to the desire for subordination and for self-annihilation that is the required content and social paradigm of our sexuality. Though political, structural conditions must change before the practice of sexuality can be eradicated, this should not stop us from politicizing the content of our own individual sexual lives. While we do not know to what extent changes in the practice of sexuality can be accomplished through collectively determined but individually initiated changes, we do know—sexually speaking—that business as usual is not liberating. The content of the sexual is the content of our subordination.

For women, sex acts have sometimes been sought out in love and through desire, and sometimes avoided and resisted with perhaps a nascent awareness of their antiwoman political function. The material arena for adult women's orientation to sexuality in general and sex acts in particular has usually been heterosexual. Our focus in this paper is on women in such heterosexual arrangements. We want to mention very briefly both deconstructive lesbianism and radical celibacy before discussing sex resistance in heterosexual arrangements.

At the practical level, we see deconstructive lesbianism as a transitional political choice. Deconstructive lesbianism aims to de-construct or dismantle the practice of sexuality at the personal and experiential level. It attempts to unweave the pattern of dominance and submission which has been incarnated as sexuality in each of us. At its most basic level, deconstructive lesbianism means being who we are as lesbians, but without sex. It represents a woman-centered attempt to say no to male force at all its levels, including the level we have all interiorized as sexual response. We believe that many lesbians in couples are living out deconstructive lesbianism at the present time, in fact, but not in theory. Unfortunately, this practice has been criticized as a problem rather than part of a solution. Named antisex (which it is), it has been seen as similar to the situation of the "frigid woman" with similar prescriptions recommended (pornography, for one) as a way to get back on track with dominance and submission. We hope that these lesbians will begin to think and write about their experiences in political terms.

Radical celibacy differs from celibacy—whether done by feminists or others—because it contains the analysis discussed in this paper about the condition of women under male supremacy and sees that our subordination turns on the continuation of the practice of sexuality. Radical celibacy understands that sex has to stop before male supremacy will be defeated. We believe that many women practice radical celibacy, perhaps without naming it, but knowing that it is key to their personal integrity and frequently as part of "sexual healing" after assault. We urge these women to speak out. Sex resisters can struggle and act within heterosexual arrangements to dismantle the dynamic through which men self-identify as the subordinators of women and women self-identify as the subordinated, meanwhile keeping other nonsexual, nonsubordinating aspects of relationships that have value for them.

Sex resistance is not to be understood as what has been traditionally known as celibacy, as that which lacks an articulated radical feminist analysis of the subordination of women. Although celibacy can and does have positive effects (e.g., lessening a particular woman's direct, personal sexual exploitation), celibacy must be transformed by a radical feminist consciousness to become politically meaningful. Sex resistance has a historical claim to feminist authenticity. It is what many women have done when demonstrating our claims to integrity, to self-possession of our own lives and bodies. It makes speech of women's silent refusal to validate and valorize male-constructed desire. Sex resistance has been misnamed and ridiculed by most men and some women as "prudery," "frigidity," and "sexual incompatibility." By performing the political act of sex resistance, the power imbalance is challenged and the practice of sexuality is exposed. We believe that acts of sex resistance can be part of the process of transition that will dismantle the practice of sexuality.

Radical celibacy together with deconstructive lesbianism and sex resistance are the only practical political choices for women oppressed under male supremacy.

In conclusion, our analysis claims that sex is compulsory for women because the price of not choosing it is social worthlessness and exclusion. There is no esteemed place—or even a socially neutral place—for the women who will not put out to someone at some time in some way. By male design, the relationships that ground our social sense of self and self-worth are a package deal—with love, security, emotional support, and sex all going together. Your value as a piece of ass becomes clear when you stop being that piece. The sex resister understands that beneath the label of "sexual incompatibility"—beneath that mystification—is the truth of the political equation: Woman equals her capacity as a cunt. The sex resister brings this hidden equation into view, dragging the entire practice of sexuality into the light of feminist scrutiny. The sex resister refuses to accept the package deal of male design. She demands the right not to be forced to follow the cultural precept that says: PUT OUT or GET OUT.

---

### Notes

1. Our analysis has evolved from our work as radical feminists in the antipornography movement. Specifically, our analysis reflects the realization that pornography *is* sex. We accept the definition of pornography as written in the Dworkin/MacKinnon Civil Rights Law (model) against pornography.

# Feminine Masochism and the Politics ∿ of Personal Transformation

## Sandra Lee Bartky

To be at once a sexual being and a moral agent can be troublesome indeed: no wonder philosophers have wished that we could be rid of sexuality altogether. What to do, for example, when the structure of desire is at war with one's principles? This is a difficult question for any person of conscience, but it has a particular poignancy for feminists. A prime theoretical contribution of the contemporary feminist analysis of women's oppression can be captured in the slogan "the personal is political." What this means is that the subordination of women by men is pervasive, that it orders the relationship of the sexes in every area of life, that a sexual politics of domination is as much in evidence in the private spheres of the family, ordinary social life, and sexuality as in the traditionally public spheres of government and the economy. The belief that the things we do in the bosom of the family or in bed are either "natural" or else a function of the personal idiosyncrasies of private individuals is held to be an "ideological curtain that conceals the reality of women's systematic oppression."[1] For the feminist, two things follow upon the discovery that sexuality too belongs to the sphere of the political. The first is that whatever pertains to sexuality—not only actual sexual behavior, but sexual desire and sexual fantasy as well—will have to be understood in relation to a larger system of subordination; the second, that the deformed sexuality of patriarchical culture must be moved from the hidden domain of "private life" into an arena for struggle, where a "politically correct" sexuality of mutual respect will contend with an "incorrect" sexuality of domination and submission.

A number of questions present themselves at once. What is a politically correct sexuality, anyhow? What forms would the struggle for such a sexuality assume? Is it possible for individuals to prefigure more liberated forms of sexuality in their own lives now, in a society still marked by the subordination of women in every domain? Finally, the question with which we began, the moral worry about what to do when conscience and sexual desire come into conflict, will look like this when seen through the lens of feminism: What to do when one's own sexuality is "politically incorrect," when desire is wildly at variance with feminist principles? …

# The Story of P.

If any form of sexuality has a *prima facie* claim to be regarded as politically incorrect, it would surely be sadomasochism. I define sadomasochism as any sexual practice that involves the eroticization of relations of domination and submission. Consider the case of P., a feminist, who has masochistic fantasies. If P. were prepared to share her secret life with us, this is what she might say:

> For as long as I can remember (from around age six …), my sexual fantasies have involved painful exposure, embarrassment, humiliation, mutilation, domination by Gestapo-like characters.[2]

P. regarded her fantasies as unnatural and perverse until she discovered that of all women who have sexual fantasies, 25 percent have fantasies of rape.[3] Indeed, much material which is often arousing to women, material not normally regarded as perverse, is thematically similar to P.'s fantasies. Many women of her mother's generation were thrilled when the masterful Rhett Butler overpowered the struggling Scarlett O'Hara and swept her triumphantly upstairs in an act of marital rape: "treating 'em rough" has enhanced the sex appeal of many a male film star ever since.[4] The feminine taste for fantasies of victimization is assumed on virtually every page of the large pulp literature produced specifically for women. Confession magazines, Harlequin romances, and that genre of historical romance known in the publishing trade as the "bodice-ripper" have sales now numbering in the billions, and they can be bought in most drugstores and supermarkets across the land. The heroes of these tales turn out to be nice guys in the end, but only in the end; before that they dominate and humiliate the heroines in small "Gestapo-like" ways. …

P. is deeply ashamed of her fantasies. … P. would be mortified if her fantasies were somehow to be made public. But she suffers a continuing loss of esteem in her own eyes as well. … P.'s psychic distress is palpable, for she feels obliged to play out in the theater of her mind acts of brutality which are not only abhorrent to her but which, as a political activist, she is absolutely committed to eradicating. She experiences her own sexuality as doubly humiliating; not only does the content of her fantasies concern humiliation but the very having of such fantasies, given her politics, is humiliating as well. Two courses of action seem open to someone in P.'s predicament; she can either get rid of her shame and keep her desire, or else get rid of her desire. I shall discuss each of these alternatives in turn.

## Sadomasochism and Sexual Freedom

Sadomasochism has been roundly denounced in feminist writing. … Feminists have argued that sadomasochism is one inevitable expression of a women-hating culture. It powerfully reinforces male dominance and female subordination because, by linking these phenomena to our deepest sexual desires—desires defined by an ideologically tainted psychology as instinctual—it makes them appear natural. To participate willingly in this mode of sexuality is thus to collude in women's subordination. No wonder, then, that the emergence of Samois has shocked and offended many in the feminist community. Samois is an organization of and for sadomasochistic women which describes itself both as "lesbian" and "feminist."

In several recent publications, members of Samois have tried to justify their sexual tastes against the standard feminist condemnation. Women like P. are urged to set aside shame, to accept their fantasies fully, to welcome the sexual satisfaction such fantasies provide and even, in controlled situations, to act them out. Most manifestations of sexuality are warped anyhow, they argue, so why the particular scorn heaped upon sadomasochism? Why are the acts of sadomasochistic women—"negotiated mutual pleasure"[5]—in which no one is really hurt worse than, e.g., conventional heterosexuality where the structure of desire in effect ties a woman erotically to her oppressor?[6] The critics of sadomasochism conflate fantasy and reality: Representations of violent acts should not be regarded with the same loathing as the acts themselves. Sadomasochism is ritual or theater in which the goings-on are entirely under the control of the actors; the participants are no more likely to want to engage in real acts of domination or submission than are the less sexually adventurous. Further, sadomasochism is liberatory, say its defenders, in that it challenges the sexual norms of the bourgeois family, norms still rooted to a degree in an older, more repressive sexual ethic that saw sexual acts as legitimate only if they were performed in the service of reproduction. Sadomasochism is the "quintessence of nonreproductive sex": its devotees have a "passion for making use of the entire body, every nerve fiber and every wayward thought."[7] ...

Finally, sadomasochism is defended on general grounds of sexual freedom. Here, three arguments are brought forward. First, since sex is a basic human need and the right to seek sexual satisfaction is a basic human right, it follows that sexual freedom, in and of itself, is an intrinsic good, provided of course that the sexual activity in question is consensual. Second, the feminist condemnation of sadomasochism is said to be sexually repressive, perpetuating shame and secrecy in sexual matters and discouraging sexual experimentation and the exploration of unfamiliar terrain. Third, anything less than a total commitment to sexual freedom is said to endanger the future of the women's movement by giving ground to the newly militant Right. In the wake of its crusade against pornography, so say the women of Samois, the contemporary women's movement has abandoned its earlier commitment to sexual freedom and taken up positions that are clearly reactionary. ...

How convincing is Samois's defense of sadomasochism? There is, first of all, some question whether the arguments they adduce are mutually consistent. It seems odd to insist that sadomasochistic practices are isolated and compartmentalized rituals which do not resonate with the rest of one's life activity and at the same time to claim that they can enhance the quality of ongoing real relationships, e.g., in the development of trust or the "clean" acting out of aggression. The claim that sadomasochism creates unique opportunities for the building of trust, while true in some sense, strikes me as peculiar. If someone—the "bottom"—allows herself to be tied helplessly to the bedpost, she must of course trust the one doing the tying up—the "top"—not to ignore whatever limits have been agreed upon in advance. If the bottom already knows her top and has reason to believe in her trustworthiness, how can this trust have come about except in the ordinary ways in which we all develop trust in intimate relationships? But if top and bottom are not well acquainted and the activity in question caps a chance meeting in a bar, the awarding of trust in such circumstances is an act of utter foolhardiness. ...

...

The most convincing defense of sadomasochism, no doubt, is the claim that since sexual satisfaction is an intrinsic good, we are free to engage in any sexual activities whatsoever, provided of course that these activities involve neither force nor fraud. But this is essentially a *liberal* response to a *radical* critique of sexuality and, as such, it fails entirely to engage this critique. ... One of the major achievements of contemporary feminist theory is the recognition that male supremacy is perpetuated not only openly, through male domination of the major societal institutions, but more covertly, through the manipulation of desire. Moreover, desires may be produced and managed in ways which involve neither force nor fraud nor the violation of anyone's legal rights. ... The imposition of masculinity and femininity may be regarded as a process of organizing and shaping desire. The truly "feminine" woman, then, will have "appropriate" sexual desires for men, but she will wish to shape herself, physically and in other ways, into a woman men will desire. Thus, she will aspire to a life-plan proper for a member of her sex, to a certain ideal configuration of the body and to an appropriate style of self-presentation. The idea that sexual desire is a kind of bondage is very ancient; the notion takes on new meaning in the context of a radical feminist critique of male supremacy.

...

The right, staunchly defended by liberals, to desire what and whom we please and, under certain circumstances, to act on our desire, is not an issue here; the point is that women would be better off if we learned when to refrain from the exercise of this right. A thorough overhaul of desire is clearly on the feminist agenda: the fantasy that we are overwhelmed by Rhett Butler should be traded in for one in which we seize state power and reeducate him. P. has no choice, then, except to reject the counsel of Samois that, unashamed, she make space in her psyche for the free and full enjoyment of every desire. Samois in effect advises P. to ignore in her own life a general principle to which, as a feminist, she is committed and which she is therefore bound to represent to all other women: the principle that we struggle to decolonize our sexuality by removing from our minds the internalized forms of oppression that make us easier to control.

In their enthusiasm for sexual variation, liberals ignore the extent to which a person may experience her own sexuality as arbitrary, hateful, and alien to the rest of her personality. Each of us is in pursuit of an inner integration and unity, a sense that the various aspects of the self form a harmonious whole. But when the parts of the self are at war with one another, a person may be said to suffer from self-estrangement. That part of P. which is compelled to produce sexually charged scenarios of humiliation is radically at odds with the P. who devotes much of her life to the struggle against oppression. Now perfect consistency is demanded of no one, and our little inconsistencies may even lend us charm. But it is no small thing when the form of desire is disavowed by the personality as a whole. The liberal is right to defend the value of sexual satisfaction, but the struggle to achieve an integrated personality has value too and the liberal position does not speak to those situations in which the price of sexual satisfaction is the perpetuation of self-estrangement.

Phenomenologists have argued that affectivity has a cognitive dimension, that emotions offer a certain access to the world. P.'s shame, then, is the reflection in affectivity of a recognition that there are within her deep and real divisions. Insofar as these divisions cannot be reconciled—the one representing stubborn desire, the other a passionate political commitment—there is a sense in which P. is entitled to her shame. Now this is *not* to say that P. *ought* to feel shame: Profound existential contradictions are not uncommon and our response to them may vary. But it seems equally mistaken to claim that P. ought not to feel what she feels. Her desires are not worthy of her, after all, nor is it clear that she is a mere helpless victim of patriarchal conditioning, unable to take any responsibility at all for her wishes and fantasies.

It is often the case that the less unwanted desires are acknowledged as belonging to the self and the more they are isolated and compartmentalized, the more psychic distress is minimized. The more extreme the self-estrangement, in other words, the less intense the psychic discomfort. P.'s shame and distress may well be a sign that she is *not* reconciled to her lack of inner harmony and integration and that she clings to the hope that the warring factions within her personality will still somehow be reconciled.

## The Strangest Alchemy: Pain into Pleasure

If P. is not well advised just to keep her desires, getting rid of them seems to be the obvious alternative. ...

...

Let us suppose that P., determined to bring her desires into line with her ideology, embarks upon a course of traditional psychotherapy, and let us further suppose that her psychotherapy is unsuccessful. As part of her political education, P. is now exposed to a radical critique of psychotherapy: Psychotherapy is sexist; it is authoritarian and hierarchical; it is mired in the values of bourgeois society. P. now resolves to consult a "politically correct" therapist, indeed, a feminist therapist. In order to bring our discussion forward, let us suppose that this second attempt is unsuccessful too, for in spite of its popularity there is evidence that therapy fails as often as it succeeds, whatever the theoretical orientation of the therapist.[8] P. is finding it no simple thing to change her desires. Ought she to try again? In a society with little cohesiveness and less confidence in its own survival, an obsessional preoccupation with self has come to replace more social needs and interests. For many people, there is no higher obligation than to the self—to get it "centered," to realize its "potentialities," to clear out its "hangups"—and little to life apart from a self-absorbed trek through the fads, cults, and therapies of our time. But how compatible is such a surrender to the "new narcissism" (the old "bourgeois individualism") with a serious commitment to radical reform? Few but the relatively privileged can afford psychotherapy anyhow, and the search for what may well be an unrealizable ideal of mental health can absorb much of a person's time, energy, and money. It is not at all clear that the politically correct course of action for P. is to continue in this way whatever the cost; perhaps she is better advised to direct her resources back toward the women's movement. She is, after all, not psychologically disabled; within the oppressive realities of the contemporary world, her life is richer and more effective than the lives of many other people, and she is reconciled to her life—in every respect but one.

## Paradise Lost and Not Regained: The Failure of a Politics of Personal Transformation

The view is widespread among radical feminists, especially among certain lesbian separatists, that female sexuality is malleable and diffuse and that a woman can, if she chooses, alter the structure of her desire. Here then is a new source of moral instruction for P., a source at the opposite pole from Samois. Without the help of any paid professional—for no such help is really needed—P. is now to pull herself up by her own psychological bootstraps.

The idea that we can alter our entire range of sexual feelings I shall call "sexual voluntarism." ... For the sexual voluntarist, individuals are thought to be blank tablets on which the culture inscribes certain patterns of behavior. Sexual norms are embedded in a variety of cultural forms, among them "common sense," religion, the family, books, magazines, television, films, and popular music. Individuals are "positively reinforced," i.e., rewarded, when they model their behavior on images and activities held out to them as normal and desirable, "negatively reinforced," i.e., punished, when their modeling behavior is done incorrectly or not done at all.

> If we come to view male-dominated heterosexuality as the only healthy form of sex, it is because we are bombarded with that model for our sexual fantasies long before we experience sex itself. Sexual images of conquest and submission pervade our imagination from an early age and determine how we will later look upon and experience sex.[9]

The masters of patriarchal society make sure that the models set before us incorporate their needs and preferences: All other possibilities become unspeakable or obscene. Thus, the pervasiveness of propaganda for heterosexuality, for female passivity, and male sexual aggressivity are responsible not only for ordinary heterosexuality but for sadomasochism as well. Sadomasochists reveal to the world, albeit in an exaggerated form, the inner nature of heterosexuality and they are stigmatized by the larger society precisely because they tear the veil from what patriarchal respectability would like to hide.[10] Sadomasochism is

> a conditioned response tot he sexual imagery that barrages women in this society. ... It is not surprising that women respond physically and emotionally to sadomasochistic images. Whether a woman identifies with the dominant or submissive figure in the fantasy, she is still responding to a model of sexual interaction that has been drummed into us throughout our lives.[11]

The language of these passages is graphic and leaves little doubt as to the theory of sexuality which is being put forward. Models of sexual relationship bombard us: they are drummed into our heads: the ideological apparatus of patriarchal society is said to condition the very structure of desire itself.

What is valuable in this view is the idea that sexuality is socially constructed. But are the voluntarists right about the mode of its construction? And those patterns of desire which may have been present in a person's psyche from the virtual dawn of consciousness: Are voluntarists perhaps too sanguine about the prospects of radically altering these patterns in adult life? ... Writing in *Signs*, Ethel Spector Person denies the ability of theories like this to account for sexual deviance; why it is, for example, that fully 10 percent of the American population is said to be exclusively homosexual, in spite of incessant bombardment by propaganda for heterosexuality.[12] Quite early in life, many people discover unusual sexual predilections which have been "modeled" for them by no one. "I thought I was the only one," such people say, when they "come out," enter psychoanalysis, or write their memoirs. Furthermore, deviance rarely goes unpunished: Punishments may range from a purely private embarrassment before the spectacle of one's own fantasy life to electric shock, the stake, or the concentration camp. Indeed, the history of sexual deviance, insofar as this history is known at all, is the history of the failure of massive negative reinforcement to establish an absolute hegemony of the "normal."

...

"Any woman can"—such is the motto of voluntarism. Armed with an adequate feminist critique of sexuality and sufficient will power, any woman should be able to alter the pattern of her desires. While the feminist theory needed for this venture is known to be the product of collective effort, and while groups of women—even, in the case of lesbian separatism, organized communities of women—may be waiting to welcome the reformed pervert, the process of transformation is seen, nonetheless, as something a woman must accomplish alone. How can it be otherwise, given the fact that no tendency within the contemporary women's liberation movement has developed a genuinely collective *praxis* which would make it possible for women like P. to bring their desires into line with their principles? ... A pervasive and characteristic feature of bourgeois ideology has here been introduced into feminist theory, namely, the idea that the victims, the colonized, are responsible for their own colonization and that they can change the circumstances of their lives by altering their consciousness. Of course, no larger social transformation can occur unless individuals change as well, but the tendency I am criticizing places the burden for effecting change squarely upon the individual, an idea quite at variance with radical feminist thinking generally.

One final point, before I turn to another mode of theorizing about sexuality—one not as subject to moralism and divisiveness. Those who claim that any woman can reprogram her consciousness if only she is sufficiently determined hold a shallow view of the nature of patriarchal oppression. Anything done can be undone, it is implied; nothing has been permanently damaged, nothing irretrievably lost. But this is tragically false. One of the evils of a system of oppression is that it may damage people in ways that cannot always be undone. Patriarchy invades the intimate recesses of personality where it may maim and cripple the spirit forever. No political movement, even a movement with a highly developed analysis of sexual oppression, can promise an end to sexual alienation or a cure for sexual dysfunction. Many human beings, P. among them, may have to live with a degree of psychic damage that can never be fully healed.

## Sex-prints, Microdots, and the Stubborn Persistence of the Perverse

The difficulties individuals experience in trying to propel themselves, through "will power" or various therapies into more acceptable modes of sexual desire may be due to a connection between sexuality and personal identity too complex and obscure to be contained within the simple schemas of determinism. Ethel Spector Person has suggested that the relationship between sexuality and identity is mediated not only by gender, but by what she calls the "sex-print." The sex-print is "an individualized script that elicits erotic desire," an "individual's erotic signature."[13] Because it is experienced not as chosen but as revealed, an individual script is normally felt to be deeply rooted, "deriving from one's nature," unchanging and unique, somewhat like a fingerprint. Person does not claim that one's sex-print is absolutely irreversible, only relatively so, in part because the learning of a sex-print is so connected to the process of identity formation. "To the degree that an individual utilizes sexuality (for pleasure, for adaptation, as the resolution of unconscious conflict) ... one's sexual 'nature' will be experienced as more or less central to personality."[14] In other words, what I take to be my "self" is constituted in large measure by certain patterns of response—to the events that befall me, to other people, even to inanimate nature. Thus, if someone asks me what I am like and I describe myself as aggressive, or ambitious, or fun-loving, I am naming certain modes of adaptation that capture who I am. Since sexuality is a major mode of response—a way of inhabiting the body as well as entering into relationships with others—patterns of sexual response may well be central to the structure of a person's identity.

...

The psychoanalyst Robert Stoller characterizes the individualized sexual script not as a "sex-print" but as a "microdot," a highly compressed and encoded system of information out of which can be read—by one who knows how to read it—the history of a person's psychic life. Stoller regards as central to a person's sexual scenario the history of her infantile sexual traumas and her concomitant feelings of rage and hatred. Of the various modes of adaptation and response that get inscribed in the sex-print or microdot,

> it is hostility—the desire, overt or hidden, to harm another person—that generates and enhances sexual excitement. ... The exact details of the script underlying the excitement are meant to reproduce and repair the precise traumas and frustrations—debasements—of childhood.[15]

...
Whatever the precise mechanisms involved in the formation of a sex-print, it seems clear to me that each of us has one and that feminist theorists have focused far too much on the larger and more general features of a scenario such as a person's sexual orientation and too little on its "details." Does a person favor promiscuity or monogamy, for example, sex with "irrelevant" fantasies or sex without them, sex with partners or her own or of another race? People with the "wrong" kind of sexual orientation suffer a special victimization in our society; nevertheless, less dramatic features of the sex-print may be quite as saturated with meaning and just as revelatory of the basic outlines of a personality; the fact, for example, that Portnoy desires only gentile women is not less important in understanding *who he is* than the fact that he desires women.

Stoller has written that the history of a person's psychic life lies hidden in her or his sexual script. This history and the meanings which compose it can sometimes be read out of someone's scenario but often as not, it is shrouded in mystery—as P., to her sorrow, has already learned. Is Portnoy's attraction to gentile women a manifestation of Jewish self-hatred? Or a feeble attempt to deceive the superego about the real object of desire, his mother—a Jewish woman? Or, by picking women with whom he has little in common, is Portnoy acting on a masochistic need to be forever unhappy in love? The pattern of Portnoy's desire may reflect a mode of adaptation to the conflict and pain of early life, to a buried suffering Portnoy can neither recover nor surmount.

Sexual desire may seize and hold the mind with the force of an obsession, even while we remain ignorant of its origin and meaning. Arbitrary and imperious, desire repels not only rational attempts to explain it but all too often the efforts of rational individuals to resist it. At the level of theory the lack of an adequate account of the mechanisms involved in sex-printing (and hence of sadomasochism) is a failure of *science;* at the level of personal experience, the opacity of human sexual desire represents a failure of *self-knowledge.*

## Instead of a Conclusion

P. will search the foregoing discussion in vain for practical moral advice. The way out of her predicament seemed to be the abandonment either of her shame or of her desire. But I have suggested that there is a sense in which she is "entitled" to her shame, insofar as shame is a wholly understandable response to behavior which is seriously at variance with principles. In addition, I have argued that not every kind of sexual behavior, even behavior that involves consenting adults or is played out in the private theater of the imagination, is compatible with feminist principles, a feminist analysis of sexuality, or a feminist vision of social transformation. To this extent, I declare the incompatibility of a classical liberal position on sexual freedom with my own understanding of feminism.

P.'s other alternative, getting rid of her desire, is a good and sensible project if she can manage it, but it turns out to be so difficult in the doing that to preach to her a feminist code of sexual correctness in the confident anticipation that she will succeed would be a futility—and a cruelty. Since many women (perhaps even most women) are in P.'s shoes, such a code would divide women within the movement and alienate those outside of it. "Twix't the conception and creation," writes the poet, "falls the shadow." Between the conception of a sexuality in harmony with feminism and the creation of a feminist standard of political correctness in sexual matters, fall not one but two shadows: first, the lack of an adequate theory of sexuality; the second the lack of an effective political practice around issues of personal transformation. The second shadow need not wait upon the emergence of the first, for to take seriously the principle of the inseparability of theory and practice is to see that a better theoretical understanding of the nature of sexual desire might well begin to emerge in the course of a serious and sustained attempt to alter it.

...

Those who find themselves in the unfortunate situation of P. are living out, in the form of existential unease, contradictions which are present in the larger society. I refer to the contradiction between our formal commitment to justice and equality on the one hand—a commitment that the women's movement is determined to force the larger society to honor—and the profoundly authoritarian character of our various systems of social relationships on the other. Those who have followed by "Story of P." will have to decide whether P. is in fact caught in a historical moment which we have not as yet surpassed or whether I have merely written a new apology for a very old hypocrisy.

## Notes

1. Alison Jaggar, *Feminist Politics and Human Nature* (Totowa, N.J.: Rowman and Allanheld, 1983), p. 122.

2. *Ms.,* July-August 1982, p. 35.

3. Maria Marcus, *A Taste for Pain: On Masochism and Female Sexuality* (New York: St. Martin's Press, 1981), p. 46. Needless to say, the having of a fantasy, every detail of which the woman orchestrates herself, is not like a desire for actual rape. ...

4. A recent history of women in Hollywood film sets out at some length the increasingly brutal treatment of women in the movies, movies made by men to be sure, but patronized and enjoyed by large numbers of women. See Molly Haskell, *From Reverence to Rape* (New York: Penguin Books, 1974).

5. Laura Lederer, ed., *Take Back the Night: Women on Pornography* (New York: William Morrow, 1980).

6. Janet Schrim, "A Proud and Emotional Statement," in Samois, ed., *What Color Is Your Handkerchief?* (Berkeley, Calif.: Samois, 1979), p. 24.

7. Pat Califia, "Feminism and Sadomasochism," *Heresies,* Vol. 12, p. 32.

8. See H. J. Eysenck, "The Effects of Psychotherapy: An Evaluation," *Journal of Consulting Psychology,* Vol. 16, 1952, pp. 319–324. For further discussion of this topic, see A. J. Fix and E. Haffke, *Basic Psychological Therapies: Comparative Effectiveness* (New York: Human Sciences Press, 1976).

9. Linda Phelps, "Female Sexual Alienation," in Jo Freeman, ed., *Women: A Feminist Perspective,* 2d ed. (Palo Alto, Calif.: Mayfield, 1979).

10. See Sarah Lucia Hoagland, "Sadism, Masochism and Lesbian-Feminism," in Linden et al., *Against Sadomasochism: A Radical Feminist Analysis* (Palo Alto, Calif.: Frog-in-the-Well Press, 1982).

11. Jeannette Nichols, Darlene Pagano, and Margaret Rossoff, "Is Sadomasochism Feminist?" in *Against Sadomasochism.* Many feminists, especially those in the anti-pornography movement, believe that men in particular will want to imitate the images of sexual behavior with which they are now being bombarded; this accounts for the urgency of these feminists' attack on male-oriented violent pornography. See Laura Lederer, ed., *Take Back the Night,* esp. Ann Jones, "A Little Knowledge," pp. 179 and 183, and Diana E. H. Russell, "Pornography and Violence: What Does the New Research Say?" p. 236.

12. Ethel Spector Person, "Sexuality as the Mainstay of Identity: Psychoanalytic Perspectives," *Signs,* Vol. 5, No. 4, Summer 1980, pp. 605–630.

13. Ibid., p. 620.

14. Ibid., p. 620.

15. Robert Stoller, *Sexual Excitement* (New York: Simon and Schuster, 1979), pp. 6 and 13.

# Feminist Ejaculations

## Shannon Bell

*For Gad, my partner in cum, with love.*

This text is about the ejaculating female body. How did it cum to be that male ejaculation has never been questioned, debated, analyzed; just accepted as a given feature of the male body and male sexuality? An odd question. Yet it is no more odd than what has actually happened to female ejaculation throughout history. There are two questions that have not been raised about female ejaculation, from its discussion by the early Greeks to the most recent. The first is how can women have control over ejaculation; the second, and more recent question, is: why have feminist voices failed to speak about and embrace female ejaculation?

These questions will be backgrounded while I trace the theorizations and writings on female ejaculation conducted by philosophers, physicians, and sexologists, and as recorded in the documentations kept by anthropologists. In Western philosophy and society female ejaculation has been framed five ways: as fecundity, sexual pleasure, social deviance, medical pathology, and as a scientific problem. These frames will become more defined during the discussion.

## Traces of Female Ejaculation in Patriarchal Texts

The expulsion of female fluids during sexual excitement was thought by a number of Greek and Roman doctors and philosophers to be a normal and pleasurable part of female sexuality, the debate evolving around whether female fluids were or were not progenitive. Aristotle argued against the general belief that female seed was produced by women; Hippocrates and Galen were the most well-known of those ancients who argued that women emit seed. Hippocrates (460–377 B.C.) advocated a "two semen" theory of generation based on the belief that both male and female fluids contributed to conception.[1]

In *The Generation of Animals,* Aristotle (384–322 B.C.) argued against the two semen theory of generation and connected female fluid with pleasure:

> Some think that the female contributes semen in coition because the pleasure she experiences is sometime similar to that of the male, and also is attended by a liquid discharge. But this discharge is not seminal ... The amount of this discharge when it occurs, is sometimes on a different scale from the emission of semen and far exceeds it.[2]

Galen, supporting the theory of female seed, made a distinction between female fluid that was procreative and female fluid that was pleasurable. He identified the source of pleasurable fluid as the female prostate.

> ... the fluid in her prostate ... contributes nothing to the generation of offspring ... it is poured outside when it has done its service ... This liquid not only stimulates ... the sexual act but also is able to give pleasure and moisten the passageway as it escapes. It manifestly flows from women as they experience the greatest pleasure in coitus ...[3]

Western scholars and doctors throughout the Middle Ages remained faithful to Hippocrates's and Galen's notion of female sperm, which came to them through Arab medicine. In fact, the theory of the female seed survived long after the Middle Ages.[4]

De Graaf, a seventeenth-century Dutch anatomist, in his *New Treatise Concerning the Generative Organs of Women,* outlined the Hippocratic and Aristotelian controversy over female semen. He sided firmly with the Aristotelians and denied the existence of female semen. In describing the pleasurable ejection of female fluid, De Graaf wrote: "it should be noted that the discharge from the female prostatae causes as much pleasure as does that from the male prostatae."[5] He identified the location and source of the fluid as the "ducts and lacunae ... around the orifice of the neck of the vagina and the outlet of the urinary passage [which] receive their fluid from the female 'parastate', or rather the thick membranous body around the urinary passage."[6] De Graaf also describes the fluid as "rush[ing] out," "com[ing] from the pudenda in one gush."[7]

...

Krafft-Ebing, in his mammoth study of sexual perversion, *Psychopathia Sexualis,* identified female ejaculation as the pathology of a small (albeit sexual) portion of a pathological group. Under the heading of "Congenital Sexual Inversion in Women," Krafft-Ebing discusses sexual contact among women, and contends that:

[t]he intersexual gratification among … women seems to be reduced to kissing and embraces, which seems to satisfy those of weak sexual instinct, but produces in sexually
neurasthenic females ejaculation.[8]

According to Krafft-Ebing ejaculation only occurs among women who suffer
neurasthenia—body disturbances caused by weakness of the nervous system. Krafft-
Ebing therefore relates female ejaculation to a nervous disability.

Perhaps this is to be expected from a Victorian sexologist; what is unexpected is
the manner in which this passage has been appropriated by a well-known lesbian
feminist historian, Shelia Jeffreys. Jeffreys, in *The Spinster and Her Enemies. Feminism and Sexuality 1880–1930*, marks female ejaculation as an "invention" of the male
imaginary: "There are … examples in the sexologicial literature of men's sexual fantasies about lesbian sexuality. Krafft-Ebing invented a form of ejaculation for wom-
en.[9]

Freud, in his analysis of Dora, followed the medical conventions of his time and
made a connection between Dora's hysterical symptoms and the secretion of female
fluids.

> The pride taken by women in the appearance of their genitals is quite a special feature of
> their vanity; and disorders of genitals which they think calculated to inspire feelings of
> repugnance or even disgust have an incredible power of humiliating them, of lowering
> their self-esteem, and of making them irritable, sensitive, and distrustful. An abnormal
> secretion of the mucous membrane of the vagina is looked upon as source of disgust.[10]

…

There have also been positive depictions of female ejaculation. The ejaculating female body can be found in the love discourse of two women at the margins of the patriarchal order; women who, according to Krafft-Ebing's contention, would have
been considered "neurasthenic," at least to him. Eleven years after the first publication of Dora, a love letter was written, by a triply bad girl, Almeda Sperry, who was a
lesbian prostitute anarchist, to a doubly bad girl Emma Goldman, an anarchist bisexual:

> Dearest, it is a good thing that I came away when I did … At this moment I am listening
> to the rhythm of the pulse coming in your throat. I am surging along with your life-
> blood, coursing in the secret places of your body. I cannot escape the rhythmic spurt of
> your love juices.[11]

Female ejaculation was marked a common and normal occurrence by Van de Velde
in his marriage manual, *Ideal Marriage: Its Physiology and Technique.* (1926).

> It appears that the majority of laymen believed that something is forcibly squirted (or
> propelied or extruded) or expelled from the woman's body in orgasm, and should so
> happen normally, as in the man's case.[12]

Female ejaculation was documented in passing by anthropologists. Two well
known anthropological studies, Malinowski's *The Sexual Life of Savages* (1929) and
Gladwin's and Sarason's *Truk: Man in Paradise* (1953), contain references to female
ejaculation. Malinowski notes that the Trobrianders use the same word, "momona,"

for both male and female discharge. Momona means "it squirts out the discharge."[13] Malinowski documents that the Trobrianders believe this discharge lubricates and increases pleasure. The Trukese, a matrilocal society where women are considered "domineering and assertive, sexually provoking and aggressive"[14] and where the female genitals are considered "in several respects intrinsically of more importance and interest than are the male genitals",[15] describe intercourse as

> ... a contest between the man and woman, a matter of the man restraining his orgasm until the woman has achieved hers. Female orgasm is commonly signaled by urination [sic] ... If the man ejaculates before this time he is said to have been defeated ...[16]

Anthropology has also revealed that female ejaculation is a part of the puberty rites of the Batoro of Uganda. The Batoro have a custom called "kachapati" which means "spray the wall." The older women of the village teach the younger females how to ejaculate when they reach puberty.[17]

Despite the descriptions of female ejaculation in medical, anthropological, philosophical, and popular literature from time to time throughout Western history, female ejaculation has been practically ignored until the late 1970s and 1980s.

## De-eroticizing Female Pleasure: Female Ejaculation and Sexual Science

The clearest and most complete description of the physiological process and anatomical structure of female ejaculation was published in *The International Journal of Sexology* (1950) by Grafenberg, a German obstetrician and gynecologist. In his "own experience of numerous women," Grafenberg observed that:

> An erotic zone always could be demonstrated on the anterior wall of the vagina along the course of the urethra ... Analogous to the male urethra, the female urethra also seems to be surrounded by erectile tissues ... In the course of sexual stimulation, the female urethra begins to enlarge and can be felt easily. It swells out greatly at the end of orgasm ... Occasionally the production of fluids is ... profuse ... If there is the opportunity to observe ... one can see that large quantities of a clear transparent fluid are expelled ... out of the urethra in gushes ...[18]

Despite Grafenberg's clear description, female ejaculation was ignored and/or denied by the dominant scientific discourses defining female sexuality from 1950–1978. Kinsey, Pomeroy, and Martin (1953), writing three years after Grafenberg, mention female ejaculation only to deny its existence.[19] Masters and Johnson (1966) note that "female ejaculation is an erroneous but widespread concept."[20] As recently as 1982, Masters, Johnson, and Kolondy continue to refer to female ejaculation as "an erroneous belief"[21] and suggest that the fluid could be the result of "urinary stress incontinence."[22]

Grafenberg's analysis remained in obscurity until Sevely and Bennett reintroduced it into sexological discourse in their review of the literature on female ejaculation, "Concerning Female Ejaculation and the Female Prostate" (1978) published in *The Journal of Sex Research*. Their review originated the contemporary debate among sex researchers, gynecologists, urologists, and sex therapists regarding the existence of female ejaculate and its source. This debate has focused on three areas of concern: efforts to prove that women do or do not ejaculate; analysis of the chemical composition of ejaculate to determine whether or not it is urine; and, the potential of ejaculation for constructing a new theory of sexuality.

. . .

Male sexologists still have an investment, perhaps an investment in holding onto a sexually privileged position where sexual activities revolve around their "spending" or "withholding" of ejaculate, in questioning whether women can ejaculate. Female ejaculation is, for some, a matter of belief, rather than a physiological response. Alzate, who conducted a clinical study of twenty-seven women, disregarded what he termed a subject's "emphatic" affirmation that she often ejaculated and discounted his recorded observation of her doing so, to claim that "the ignorance and/or confusion still prevalent among women about the anatomy and physiology of their sexual organs may make them mistake either vaginal lubrication or stress urinary incontinence for an "ejaculation."[23] There is a recurrent tendency for researchers to disregard, reinterpret, and overwrite women's subjective descriptions of ejaculation. Sex researchers Davidson, Darling, and Conway-Welch, in the most extensive social survey of a female population regarding their experience of ejaculation (1289 women responded), state that anecdotal data suggests that the physiological sensations associated with the expulsion of fluid are very similar to those physiological sensations associated with voiding of urine.[24] I was presenting a paper in a session on "Female Ejaculation" at the World Congress of Sexology in December 1989 in Caracas, Venezuela. I discussed representations of female ejaculation and showed slides of the ejaculating female body; a Spanish medical team showed vaginal photographs of the glands and ducts surrounding a woman's urethra. An older hegemonic male member of the audience, publically contended that "we have just seen pictures of this fluid shooting out of the female body and slides of its location but he would believe women ejaculated if one pathologist declared that they did."

. . .

Female ejaculation was legitimated and popularized for the first time in *The G Spot and Other Recent Discoveries About Female Sexuality* (1982). A large portion of the chapter "Female Ejaculation" is composed of self-reports from, and case vignettes of, female ejaculators. Some of the women had been diagnosed by their companions and by the medical profession as suffering from urinary incontinence. Other women depicted the act of ejaculation as an experience of pleasure and a regular part of their sexuality. The authors of *The G-Spot* suggest that because "female ejaculate can only serve one purpose: pleasure"[25] and that women have historically been absented from the realm of pleasure, the knowledge of ejaculation has not been accepted and socially appropriated by professionals or the public.

Josephine Sevely, *Eve's Secrets. A New Theory of Female Sexuality* (1987), has provided the most comprehensive study of female ejaculation. Her theory not only sexualizes the urethra but also emphasizes the simultaneous involvement of the clitoris, urethra, and vagina, which function as a single integrated sexual organ. The implications of Sevely's theory are threefold. First, a woman's sexual organ ceases to be fragmented into clitoris and vagina: it is an integrated whole composed of clitoris, ure-thra, and vagina. Second, this integrated whole is a multiplicity "full of things," all alive with sensation. The [w]hole is an active w[hole]; no more clitoral activity ver-sus vaginal passivity. Third, the "anatomical difference" between male and female genitals upon which phallocentric culture and society is premised is challenged by an alternative construction of anatomical symmetry. Both male and female bodies have prostate gland structures and both have the potential to ejaculate fluids during sex-ual stimulation. The female body, free from the limiting economy of the male psyche-libido, reveals physiological difference within anatomical symmetry. The fe-male body can ejaculate fluid from thirty-one ducts; with stimulation can ejaculate repeatedly; can ejaculate more fluid than the male body; and, can enjoy a plurality of genital pleasure sites; the clitoris, urethra, vagina, the vaginal entrance, the roof of the vagina, the bottom of the vagina, and the cervix.

## Feminism and Ejaculation

The ejaculating female body has not acquired much of a feminist voice nor has it been appropriated by feminist discourse. What is the reason for this lacuna in femi-nist scholarship and for the silencing of the ejaculating female subject? It has to do with the fact that the questions posed, and the basic assumptions about female sexu-ality, are overwhelmingly premised on the difference between female and male bod-ies: "the most visible difference between men and women, and the only one we know for sure to be permanent ... is ... the difference in body."[26] The most important pri-mary differences have been that women have the ability to give birth and men ejaculate. Women's reproductive ability has been emphasized as a central metaphor in feminist critiques of patriarchal texts and has been theorized into a "philosophy of birth" and an economy of (re)production. Feminists, in their efforts to revalorize the female body usually devalued in phallocentric discourse, have privileged some form of the mother-body as the source of écriture féminine: writing that evokes women's power as women's bodily experience. Mary O'Brien, for example, in *The Politics of Reproduction* (1981), provides a feminist model for interpreting masculinist political philosophy. O'Brien begins her project by posing the question: "Where does feminist theory start?" She replies: "Within the process of human reproduction. Of that pro-cess, sexuality is but a part."[27] O'Brien names her reappropriation and theorization of the mother-body as a "philosophy of birth." Luce Irigaray writes that "historically the properties of fluids have been abandoned to the feminine."[28] The fluids, re-appropriated in feminine sexual discourse and theorized by French feminist philoso-phers such as Luce Irigaray and Julia Kristeva, have been the fluids of the mother-body: fluids of the womb, birth fluids, menstrual blood, milk: fluids that flow. Ejaculate—fluid that shoots, fluid that sprays—has been given over to the male body. To accept female ejaculate and female ejaculation one has to accept the sameness of male and female bodies.

Contemporary feminism, however, has rejected sameness as being defined from the perspective of the male body, as conformity with the masculine mode. To avoid identification with a male phenomenon, women have suggested that the term "ejaculation" should not be used. I argue that the term should be kept while using the distinctive characteristics of female ejaculate to redefine and rewrite the meaning of the term: female ejaculate is not "spent"; with stimulation one can ejaculate repeatedly; and, a woman in control of ejaculation may ejaculate enormous quantities.

The second factor in feminists' failure to embrace ejaculation as a powerful body experience is their understandable concern regarding possible male control over female ejaculation in the context of a masculinist and heterosexual script in which ejaculation is presented as something men do to women's bodies. The Boston Women's Health Collective, editors of *Our Bodies, Our Selves* (1984), warn women that the G-Spot and female ejaculation could be "used to re-instate so-called 'vaginal' orgasms as superior" and could "becom[e] a new source of pressure" to perform.[29] Ehrenreich, Hess and Jacobs, in *Re-making Love. The Feminization of Sex* (1986) misconstrue the emphasis in *The G-Spot* on the urethra as a return to Freud's primacy of the mature vaginal orgasm. Ehrenreich et al, argue that Chapter Four of *The G-Spot*, "The Importance of Healthy Pelvic Muscles," which links strong pubococcygeus muscles (PC muscles) with ejaculation and G-Spot orgasms and provides case vignettes of women who discuss the merits of strengthening their PC muscles, encourages women to strengthen "the muscles that hold the penis in place."[30] In my experience these muscles do not in fact hold the penis in place; rather, they push it out and spray the ejaculate. The penis (if one is around) may then re-enter until the glands and ducts surrounding the urethra become so enlarged in size through stimulation that they expel the penis and spray again. Ehrenreich et al, also claim that "the acrobatics necessary to achieve the 'new' orgasm" privilege male-dominant sexual positions.[31] This criticism is odd since Ladas et al provide case vignettes of ejaculation in many different positions: woman on top, rear entry, man on top, partner using his/her hand, and woman using her own hand. They provide case histories from lesbians and note that "preliminary reports indicate that there may be a higher incidence of female ejaculation in the lesbian population than there is among heterosexual women.[32]

Female ejaculation is about power over one's own body. For many women who do experience ejaculation, however, it is a passive experience—something that happens, not a capacity and process they control. If feminists are going to appropriate and reclaim the female body, it is very important that women provide feminist scripts of the ejaculating body in *control* of ejaculation. ...

...

## Notes

1. Hippocrates, *De geniture*, eds. and trans. W.C. Lyons and J.N. Hattock, (Cambridge: Pembrooke Press, 1978), chap. 6 (7.478).

2. Aristotle, *De Generation Animalium*, trans. Arthur Platt, in *The Complete Works of Aristotle*, eds. J.A. Smith and W.D. Ross, (Oxford: The Claredon Press, 1912), II 728a.

3. Cited in Josephine Sevely, *Eve's Secrets. A New Theory of Female Sexuality*, (New York: Random House, 1987), p. 51.

536                                                                    *Sexual Practice*

4. Danielle Jacquart and Claude Thomasset, *Sexuality and Medicine in the Middle Ages,* trans. Matthew Adamson, (Great Britain: Polity Press, 1988), pp. 66–74.

5. Rainer de Graaf, *New Treatise Concerning the Generative Organs of Women* (1672), annot. trans. H.B. Jocelyn and B.P. Setchell, *Journal of Reproduction and Fertility,* Supplement 17, (Oxford: Blackwell Scientific Publications, 1972), p. 107.

6. Ibid., p. 141.

7. Ibid., p. 141.

8. Richard von Krafft-Ebing, *Psychopathia Sexualis,* trans. Franklin S. Klaf, (New York: Stein and Day, 1965), p. 265.

9. Shelia Jeffreys, *The Spinster and Her Enemies. Feminism and Sexuality 1880–1930,* (London: Routledge and Kegan Paul, 1985), p. 110.

10. Sigmund Freud, "Fragments of an Analysis of a Case of Hysteria" (1905), *The Standard Edition of the Complete Psychological Works by Sigmund Freud,* Vol. VII, trans. and ed. James Strachey, (London: The Hogarth Press and the Institute of Psycho-analysis, 1953), p. 84.

11. Candice Falk, *Love, Anarchy and Emma Goldman,* (New York: Holt Rinehart and Winston, 1984), p. 175.

12. T. Van de Velde, *Ideal Marriage: Its Physiology and Technique,* Second Ed., (London: Heinemann Medical Books), 1965, p. 138.

13. Bronislaw Malinowski, *The Sexual Life of Savages,* (New York: Harcourt Brace and World, 1929), p. 167.

14. Thomas Gladwin and Seymour B. Sarason, *Truk: Man in Paradise,* (New York: Wenner-Gren Foundation for Anthropological Research, Inc., 1956), p. 233.

15. Ibid., p. 253.

16. Ibid., p. 109.

17. Alice Ladas, Beverly Whipple, and John Perry, *The G Spot and Other Recent Discoveries About Human Sexuality,* (New York: Dell, 1983), pp. 74–75.

18. Cited in Sevely, pp. 85–86.

19. Alfred J. Kinsey, Wardell B. Pomeroy, and Clyde E. Martin. *Sexual Behavior in the Human Female,* (Philadelphia W.B. Saunders Co. 1953), pp. 634–5.

20. William H. Masters and Virginia E. Johnson, *Human Sexual Response,* (Boston: Little, Brown, 1966), p. 135.

21. William H. Masters, Virginia E. Johnson, and R.C. Kolodny, *Masters and Johnson on Sex and Human Loving,* (Boston: Little, Brown, 1982), p. 69.

22. Ibid., p. 70.

23. Heli Alzate, "Vaginal Eroticism: A Replication Study," *Archives of Sexual Behavior* 14 (1985): 530–33 and Heli Alzate and Zwi Hoch, "The 'G-Spot' and 'Female Ejaculation': A Current Appraisal," *Journal of Sex and Marital Therapy* 12 (1986): 217.

24. J.K. Davidson, Sr., C.A. Darling, and C. Conway-Welch, "The Role of the Grafenberg Spot and Female Ejaculation in the Female Orgasmic Response: An Empirical Analysis," *The Journal of Sex and Marital Therapy* 15 (1989): 120.

25. Ladas et al, p. 79.

26. Elaine Showalter, "Feminist Criticism in the Wilderness," *The New Feminist Criticism. Essays on Women, Literature and Theory,* ed. Elaine Showalter, (New York: Pantheon Books, 1985), p. 252.

27. Mary O'Brien, *The Politics of Reproduction,* (London: Routledge Kegan Paul, 1981), p. 8.

28. Luce Irigaray, *This Sex Which is Not One,* (New York: Cornell Press, 1985), p. 116.

29. The Boston Women's Health Collective, *Our Bodies, Our Selves,* (New York: Simon & Schuster, Inc., 1984), p. 171.

30. Barbara Ehrenreich, Elizabeth Hess, and Gloria Jacobs, *Re-Making Love, The Feminization of Sex,* (New York: Anchor Press, 1986), p. 185.

31. Ibid., p. 184.

32. Ladas et al, p. 84.

# Dismantling Oppression: An Analysis of the Connection Between Women and Animals

## Lori Gruen

Despite a growing awareness of the destructiveness of the human species and the precarious position in which such destruction puts all inhabitants of the earth, there as been shockingly little discussion of the fundamental forces that have led us to the brink. While multinational corporations and grassroots activists alike have stressed the urgency of a change in behavior, few have stressed the need for a serious change in attitudes and values. Those who do critically examine the underlying motivation for and psychology of destructive action tend to focus their attention on single issues, mimicking, in some ways, the very system at which their critique is aimed. Until recently this has been the trend among those engaged in the struggle for both women's and animal liberation.[1] ... Such exclusivity not only clouds the expansive nature of oppression, but also hinders the process of undermining such oppression and ultimately liberating all those oppressed.

The emerging discourse of ecofeminism attempts to take up the slack left by those who focus on various symptoms rather than the causes of oppression. In doing this, an often heterogeneous group of theorists have begun analyzing the connections between woman and nature and offering alternative conceptions of how we should live in the world. Whether theoretical, practical, or spiritual, ecofeminists call for a major shift in values. Ecofeminists of whatever variety (and there are many) are united in believing that it is immediately important that we each change our own perspectives and those of society from death-oriented to life-oriented—from a linear, fragmented, and detached mindset to a more direct, holistic appreciation of subjective knowing. How this shift is interpreted, however, varies tremendously within the ecofeminist literature. For present purposes, I want to suggest that any interpretation of an ecofeminist vision must ... not only analyze the joint oppression of women and nature, but must specifically address the oppression of the nonhuman animals with whom we share the planet. In failing to do so, ecofeminism would run the risk of engaging in the sort of exclusionary theorizing that it ostensibly rejects.

The categories "woman" and "animal"[2] serve the same symbolic function in patriarchal society. Their construction as dominated, submissive "other" in theoretical discourse (whether explicitly so stated or implied) has sustained human male dominance. The role of women and animals in postindustrial society is to serve/be served up; women and animals are the used. Whether created as ideological icons to justify and preserve the superiority of men or captured as servants to provide for and comfort, the connection women and animals share is present in both theory and practice. …

In this chapter I examine the connection between women and animals by discussing some of the various ways in which it is manifest in contemporary theory and in everyday life. This connection is not to be understood as a "natural" connection—one that suggests that women and animals are essentially similar—but rather a constructed connection that has been created by the patriarchy as a means of oppression. … I discuss [then] how an appreciation of the connection between women and animals and a renewed understanding of theories that advocate their liberation can enhance strategies of action for change.

## The Connection

The connection between woman and animal can be located in various strands of an elaborately constructed narrative. In the process of creating what Donna Haraway has referred to as "origin stories,"[3] anthropologists, in this case primarily white, middle-class men, have concocted theories of human cultural development and then attempted to convince themselves and others of the truth or essential nature of one or another of them. In this section, I briefly present four of these theoretical frameworks that serve to justify the oppression of women and animals. While these narratives appear to borrow from and reinforce one another, my presentation is not meant to be a reflection of some true, progressive history.

One of the more popular origin stories suggests that an evolutionary shift occurred as a result of the emergence of hunting behavior in male hominids.[4] According to this theory, the hunter's destructive, competitive, and violent activity directed toward his prey is what originally distinguished man from animal and thus culture from nature. This Myth of Man the Hunter was created by mid-twentieth-century Western minds (influenced by post–World War II political hostilities; the creation, use, and continuing development of nuclear weapons; and increased consumption in "advanced" Western societies); it defined a biologically determined being whose "natural" behavior served as the foundation of culture. It is hardly a coincidence that the act of killing was what established the superiority of man over animal and that the value of such behavior was naturalized and exalted. The myth thus serves not only to posit an essential difference between man and animal but also to elevate man because of his ability to systematically destroy animals.

Theoreticians, by creating a history in which man is separate from and superior to animals, establish a mechanism in which a separation from woman can be grounded. In this account of human social evolution, woman's body (being smaller, weaker, and reproductive) prevents her from participating in the hunt, and thus relegates her to the arena of non-culture. Woman's nonparticipation is conceived as naturally inferior. Her reproductive capacity and life-bearing activities stand in sharp contrast to the death-bringing activities that underlie culture.[5] Constructed in this way, human social evolution establishes the subservient status of woman and animals.

The second framework suggests that as the march of culture continued, nomadic hunting and gathering societies developed into stationary agrarian communities. The advent of agriculture brought with it a decrease in leisure time, the emergence of the process of domestication, and what can be understood as a further distancing of man from woman, animals, and nature. … As a result of an increased demand for laborers, women came to be thought of as breeders of a workforce. The need for more children to tend the land occurred at roughly the same time as the recognition of the mechanics of reproduction—a recognition that presumably was made possible by the domestication of animals. Once previously nomadic people settled down and began to cultivate the land, the domestication of animals, primarily sheep and goats, soon followed.[6] Before animals were domesticated, it would have been difficult to understand what role the male played in reproduction; observing animal mating may have clarified it. Thus, the domestication of animals, combined with the need for more laborers and the knowledge of how to create them, allowed for the further alienation and oppression of women. As Elizabeth Fisher suggests:

> … The keeping of animals would seem to have set a model for the enslavement of humans, in particular the large-scale exploitation of women captives for breeding and labor, which is a salient feature of the developing civilizations.[7]

The shift from nomadic existence to agricultural practices—practices founded on a belief that the natural world could be controlled and manipulated—permitted the conceptualization of animals as sluggish meat-making machines and reluctant laborers, and women as breeders of children.

The third framework, grounded in religious beliefs that developed with the rise of agriculture, also served as a source for separating man from woman and animals. Droughts, storms, and other natural conditions led to the devastation of crops, which in turn caused much suffering. Thus, nature was simultaneously the source of great fear and that which provided the means of survival. Woman, likened to the earth for her ability to bring forth life, was also feared. With the increased risks and uncertainties of the farming life came an intensified desire to dominate. This domination of both natural forces and women was often sought through "divine intervention." In order to enlist the help of the "gods," various rituals were devised. By removing themselves from the natural activities of daily life, men believed they would be in closer touch with the "supernatural" powers that would protect them from nature. In religious mythology, if not in actual practice, women often served as symbols for the uncontrollable and harmful and thus were sacrificed in order to purify the community and appease the gods.⁸ Animals too were sacrificed, and it has been suggested that many animals were first domesticated not as food sources but as sacrificial creatures. Religious belief can thus also be seen as a particularly pernicious construction of women and animals as "others" to be used.⁹

During the rise of industrialization, religion based on divine forces was complimented by a fourth framework structured on a belief system that centered on the empirical. The scientific revolution of the sixteenth century established what Carolyn Merchant describes as the "mechanistic world view,"¹⁰ a view that, in combination with the development of the "experimental method," laid yet another conceptual foundation for the manipulation of animals and nature. Domination and the imposition of order were formalized through the scientific objectification of reality. Objective scientists rely on an epistemology that requires detachment and distance. This detachment serves as justification for the division between active pursuer of knowledge and passive object of investigation, and establishes the power of the former over the latter. By devaluing subjective experience, reducing living, spontaneous beings to machines to be studied, and establishing an epistemic privilege based on detached reason, the mechanistic/scientific mindset firmly distinguished man from nature, woman, and animals.¹¹

The above-mentioned theoretical frameworks may be seen behind contemporary practices that involve, to varying degrees, the oppression and exploitation of women and animals. While not often explicitly recognized, the theories that separate man from animal and man from woman inform virtually every aspect of daily life. Such ways of constructing reality ground patriarchal conceptions of the world and its inhabitants. … With this in mind, I will now look at some of the ways in which the oppressive constructions of women and animals affect living beings.

## Exploitation in the Name of Scientific Progress

Between 17 and 70 million animals are killed in U.S. laboratories every year. Under the guise of scientific inquiry, dogs, cats, monkeys, mice, rats, pigs, and other animals are routinely suffocated, starved, shocked, blinded, burned, beaten, frozen, electrocuted, and eventually killed. …

Literally billions of dollars and countless animal lives have been spent in duplicative, often painful, and generally insignificant animal experiments. While much of the rhetoric employed to justify such experiments is cast in terms of altruistic researchers devoted to the promotion of human health and longevity, the bottom line is often obscured. Animal research in the United States is big business, and the currency is more than pain and suffering.

Large corporations make enormous profits selling specialized equipment (such as the Columbus Instruments Convulsion Meter), restraining devices, electrically wired cages, surgical implants, and decapitators. Animals themselves, mass produced by corporations such as Charles Rivers, are marketed as commodities that can be modified to consumer specifications. …

Reducing animals to objects devoid of feelings, desires, and interests is a common consequence of the scientific mindset by which those engaged in experimentation distance themselves from their subjects. Ordered from companies that exist to provide "tools" for the research business, animals' bodies are currently bought and sold in ways that are reminiscent of slave trading in the United States[12] or, more recently, Nazi experiments on women:

> In contemplation of experiments with a new soporific drug, we would appreciate your procuring for us a number of women. … We received your answer but consider the price of 200 marks a woman excessive. We propose to pay not more than 170 marks a head. If agreeable, we will take possession of the women. We need approximately 150. … Received the order of 150 women. Despite their emaciated condition, they were found satisfactory. … The tests were made. All subjects died. We shall contact you shortly on the subject of a new load.[13]

Conceiving of an experimental subject as an inferior, "subhuman" other—as a "specimen" meant to serve—lightens the burden of justifying the infliction of pain and death. Thus, current scientific practices motivate the cultivation of continued detachment.

The detachment is particularly acute in the area of contraceptive research, most of which is done on the female reproductive system. While the risks of childbirth are specific to females, the risks associated with contraception can be borne by either men or women. Yet is is primarily females, both human and nonhuman, who are subjected to risks in contraceptive research, which is controlled by male-dominated pharmaceutical companies. "Third World" women undoubtedly suffer the worst, in terms of both actual experimentation and the subsequent manipulation of reproductive choice.[14] Motivated by the desire for profit and the belief that women's bodies are legitimate sites of experimentation, U.S. contraceptive companies have a history of allowing dangerous drugs to be marketed even after animals have been harmed by them. … Upjohn, which manufactures Depo-Provera, found that the drug killed animals in laboratory tests, yet the company continued to market it overseas:

> Animal studies that [showed] Depo caused a significant incidence of breast tumors in beagle dogs and endometrial cancer in rhesus monkeys are downplayed as being irrelevant to humans since the test animals are inappropriate. … 'It's no use explaining about beagle dogs,' said one British doctor who had just injected a Bangladeshi immigrant, 'she's an illiterate peasant from the bush.'[15]

Because women and animals are judged unable to comprehend science and are thus relegated to the position of passive object, their suffering and deaths are tolerable in the name of profit and progress.

…

Often it is not literally women's bodies that are manipulated in laboratories but rather the body of "knowledge" created by Western scientists about women. Many animal experiments are designed to establish essential differences between men and women. Research on intelligence, aggression, competition, dominance, and the effect of various hormones on behavior serves to scientifically establish the lesser status of women.[16] Female animals stand in for human females in a number of experiments that would be too difficult to do with women.[17] One particularly chilling example of such research occurred at the University of Wisconsin Primate Research Center under the direction of Harry Harlow. In over two decades of research ostensibly designed to study affection, Harlow conducted numerous maternal deprivation experiments in which he separated baby monkeys from their mothers and placed the infants with what he called "monster mothers":

> Four surrogate monster mothers were created. One was a shaking mother which rocked so violently that the teeth and bones of the infant chattered in unison. The second was an air-blast mother which blew compressed air against the infant's face and body with such violence that the infant looked as if it would be denuded. The third had an embedded steel frame which, on schedule or demand, would fling forward and knock the infant monkey off the mother's body. The fourth monster mother, on schedule or demand, ejected brass spikes from her ventral surface, an abominable form of maternal tenderness.[18]

Harlow is also known for creating such horrors as the "well of despair," the "tunnel of terror," and living monster mothers who had been brought up in isolation and developed such anti-social behavior that they had to be forcibly tied down in "rape racks" in order to be mated. Harlow's work is objectionable not only because of the extreme cruelty inflicted on animals but also because of its reduction of love, affection, and companionship to manipulatable, reproducible variables that can be tinkered with by scientists. Commenting on Harlow's work, Donna Haraway suggests that "misogyny is deeply implicated in the dream structure of laboratory culture; misogyny is built into the objects of everyday life in laboratory practice, including the bodies of the animals, the jokes in the publications, and the shape of the equipment."[19]

Science, developed and conducted by white, middle-class Western men, has systematically exploited the bodies and minds of women and animals in a variety of ways. These practices, supported in part by a fallacious belief that objective science is value-free, are based on a conception of women and animals as different and lesser beings, beings whose suffering and death are justifiable sacrifices in the name of "progress."

## The Hygiene Fetish and the Great Cover-Up

Most research scientists plead that without animal experiments, human health and life expectancy would not be what they are today. Others argue that progress in these areas is largely the result of improvements in diet and sanitation. It is important to note, however, that advances in hygiene and the resulting decrease in disease have occurred primarily in the more affluent nations. In wealthy countries, billions of dollars are poured into research to find cures for the diseases of affluence, while diseases that we already know how to prevent and cure ravage poor communities, causing the suffering and death of millions. If researchers were really concerned about human health, alleviating the suffering of the poor would surely be one of the top priorities.

Hygiene has unarguably improved the health of those living in industrial societies, yet Western cultures have perverted the need for cleanliness in order to provide manufacturers with profits, subjugate women, and further distance man from nature. The proliferation of cleaning products and their subsequent marketing simultaneously perpetuate the notion that "dirt" and "natural odors" must be controlled and eliminated, and that it is women's job to do this. Thus, women have been placed at the boundary between nature, with its "contaminants," and civilized sterility. In addition to separating man from woman and nature, the production of cleaning products destroys the environment through the creation of toxic chemicals and contributes to the death of millions of animals.

Products ranging from oven cleaner to feminine deodorant spray are placed in every conceivable orifice of animals in order to test their toxicity. Two of the most common toxicity tests are the Draize eye irritancy test and the Acute oral toxicity test. In the former, a rabbit is placed in a restraining device while a substance (bleach, toilet bowl cleaner, air freshener, etc.) is placed in one of her eyes. The animal is then observed for eye swelling, ulceration, infection, and bleeding. The studies can last for as long as three weeks, during which time the eye may lose all distinguishing characteristics. At the end of the study the animals are killed and discarded. In oral toxicity tests, dogs, rats, and monkeys are forced to ingest various products. Often animals will display classic symptoms of poisoning—vomiting, diarrhea, paralysis, convulsions, and internal bleeding—but will be left to die "naturally." Cleaning products must also undergo tests in which the animals are forced to inhale lethal doses of chemicals; tests in which a particular substance is injected under the skin, into the muscle, or into various organs; and tests in which animals are forced to swim in a chemical bath, often drowning before the effect of the chemicals on the animal's system is determined. Ostensibly, these studies are designed to protect the consumer. However, the unreliable nature of such experiments and the difficulties associated with extrapolating data from one species to another make consumer protection doubtful. In addition, as we have seen with contraceptives, companies may determine that a particular product is highly dangerous but nonetheless release it. Animal experiments, regardless of their validity, cannot prevent accidental ingestion or dangerous exposure in humans. No matter how many animals die in attempts to determine the toxicity of furniture polish, for example, the effects on the child who drinks it will be the same.

These methods are also employed to test cosmetics, products primarily designed to mask women's natural appearance. Advertising for lipstick, eyeshadow, mascara, and the like suggests that women must be made up in order to conform to (male) standards of beauty. Contemporary culture constructs men as the lookers and women as the looked at. … By purchasing and using cosmetics, women become complicitous not only in their own reduction to the object of a gaze, but also in the suffering and death of animals.[20]

…

While women are covering up dirt and odors, masking their natural looks with cosmetic products, and enhancing their status and elegance by draping themselves in furs, animals are living and dying in terrible pain. The real cover-up, however, is the one perpetrated by industries that see both women and animals as manipulatable objects. Women are conditioned to believe that they must alter or disguise what is undesirable—nature—at great physical, psychological, and economic expense to themselves and at immeasurable cost to animals. The end result is an enormous profit by a few individuals and the perpetuation of the notion that the exploitation of women and animals is a legitimate means to such an end.

...

## Politics and Possibilities

The exclusionary nature of both animal liberation and feminist theory often manifests itself in practice. A number of years ago, I came across a booth of women in Grand Central Station in New York who were collecting signatures for a petition to ban pornographic material. Having just begun to think about the connection between the oppression of women and that of animals, I was quite interested in the cover of a *Hustler* magazine that these women were displaying. The particularly telling image was of a woman being put through a meat-grinder. I approached the women and explained my interest. I was immediately barraged with accusations challenging the sincerity of my feminist sensibilities and was dismissed. I continued to explain my belief that understanding the roots of oppression of all beings was an important way to undermine patriarchal exploitation, but my words fell on deaf ears. Marti Kheel conveyed to me a similarly structured experience, only this time the person who would not listen was an animal liberationist: "A man called me up from a noted animal rights organization requesting items for a garage sale. I was told that magazines such as *Playboy, Hustler,* etc. would be welcome. When I reproached him for promoting sexist literature, he accused me of not really caring about animals."[21] Although both of these incidents involved the sensitive topic of pornography, and thus emotions may have been high, feminists working to end the oppression of both women and animals encounter such experiences with remarkable regularity.

Exclusivity and inability to see beyond particular cases of oppression are not limited to personal encounters. Animal rights organizations are, for the most part, run by men, while the bulk of those working for them as employees and volunteers are women. Those organizations that are headed by women continue to adhere to the top-down authoritarianism so common to patriarchal institutions. Decisions are made by a select few, usually without the input of those who will be directly involved in carrying out the decisions. At conferences, demonstrations, and other media events, men are most often represented as the spokespeople and leaders of the movement. ... [Most of] those engaged in work for animal liberation have failed to examine the fundamental roots of oppression and as a result have incorporated oppressive practices into their struggle.[22]

Feminists, too, seldom see the practical connection between the liberation of women and that of animals. Few feminist gatherings are vegetarian, let alone vegan.[23] Often the decision to serve meat and other animal products is based on a reluctance to infringe on women's rights to choose or deference to the cultural traditions of women of color, for example. Such rationalizations … fail to recognize that cultural traditions are exactly those institutions at which legitimate feminist critiques are aimed. In an article that grapples with the question of "cultural imperialism" and the accusation that serving vegetarian food at feminist functions is racist, undermining the traditions of women of color, Jane Meyerding writes, "It is a contradiction for feminists to eat animals with whom they have no physical or spiritual relationship except that of exploiter to exploited. … I think concern for the lives of all beings is a vital, empowering part of feminist analysis, I don't think we can strengthen our feminist struggle against one aspect of patriarchy by ignoring or accepting other aspects."[24] By failing to take into account the plight of animals, feminists are acting out one of the deepest patriarchal attitudes. Ecofeminists argue that we need not and must not isolate the subjugation of women at the expense of the exploitation of animals. Indeed, the struggle for women's liberation is inextricably linked to abolition of all oppression.

Feminists can complement their work by adopting one of the most striking features of animal liberation practice—the immediate recognition of the consequences of individual action. Animal liberationists are deeply aware of how some of the most basic choices they make—what they eat, what they wear, what they purchase—directly affect the lives of animals. In their everyday practice, vegetarians and vegans live resistance. They simply do not contribute to the suffering of animals and the perpetuation of a system of oppression in this way. This refusal, rather than being antithetical to feminist concerns, in fact promotes them. For some feminists, such as the women at the Bloodroot Collective, taking direct action on behalf of animals was an outgrowth of their feminism:

> Our vegetarianism stems … from a foundation of thought based on feminist ethics: a consciousness of our connections with other species and with the survival of the earth. … Dependence on a meat and poultry diet is cruel and destructive to creatures more like ourselves than we are willing to admit—whether we mean turkeys and cows or the humans starved by land wasted for animal farming purposes to feed the privileged few.[25]

By refusing to consume the products of pain (not eating animals, not wearing leather, fur, and feathers, not using makeup and household products that have been tested on animals), feminists, like animal liberationists, can directly deny the legitimacy of a patriarchal system that treats sentient individuals as objects to use and profit from.

Similarly, animal liberationists can gain much, both personally and politically, by embracing feminist practices. Ironically, while animal liberation stresses individual responsibility for actions, most people interested in protecting animals abdicate a certain amount of responsibility by sending checks to large, wealthy organizations in the hope that these groups will act on their behalf. While particular issues often require the coordination of many different people and their respective talents (which certainly requires money), much animal abuse can be combatted in the home and local community. The hierarchical structure of animal protection organizations, coupled with often overstated claims of effectiveness, promotes a "follow-the-leader" mentality that devalues individual action. In contrast, feminist practice, which focuses on group decision making and consensus, strengthens the voice of every individual and allows for the often difficult development of cooperative action.

Both feminists and animal liberationists would do well to reflect upon how their inclusion of certain "others" is often accomplished at the expense of "other others." Animal liberation activists strive to set themselves apart from the "lunatic fringe," implicitly declaring that they are just as patriarchal as the next guy. Feminists all too often fail to consider the various ways in which oppression operates, particularly as it affects nonhumans, because, they proclaim, "We are not animals!" While the work of both feminists and animal liberationists has raised awareness of the oppressive conditions under which most women and animals live, and has often led to important reforms to improve, these lives, the roots of oppression remain intact.

Ecofeminist practice attempts to dig at these roots. Calling for a fundamental shift in values, ecofeminist practice is a revolt against control, power, production, and competition in all of their manifestations. Such practice embraces a "methodological humility,"[26] a method of deep respect for difference. In action, one must always operate under the assumption that there may be something happening that cannot be immediately understood. This is a particularly useful strategy for developing alliances between animal liberationists and feminists. Methodological humility suggests that there may not be one right answer to the problem of undoing patriarchal oppression. Making connections, between the various ways in which oppression operates and between those individuals who suffer such oppression, will allow all beings to live healthier, more fulfilling, and freer lives.

---

## Notes

*Acknowledgments:* I would like to express my gratitude to the following people who provided useful comments on earlier drafts of this work: Ken Knowles, Blueberry and Madeline, Laura Perez, Mary Richards, Ross Swick, Estelle Tarica, and especially Greta Gaard.

1. For the present purposes I will be focusing on the oppression of women and animals, but I believe that the type of analysis I am doing is not exclusive. A similar analysis could be done for oppression of all kinds, but it would be more appropriately accomplished by people of color, the infirm, the colonized, and so on, who are undoubtedly more able than I am to speak of their own oppression.

2. I would like to differentiate between the constructed category "woman" and individual "women," who have very different lives and experiences. When I seem to be speaking in more general terms, I do not mean to be overlooking differences between women and thus assuming a universal perspective, but rather am addressing the category. I have not figured out the best way to make this distinction explicit, but will use the term "woman" to indicate the constructed concept, as the text allows.

3. Donna Haraway, *Primate Visions: Gender, Race, and Nature in the World of Modern Science* (New York: Routledge, 1989), 5.

4. For one of the best discussions of the creation of the Myth of Man the Hunter, see Haraway, *Primate Visions,* chap. 6.

5. Some female anthropologists and other writers have attempted to reconstruct the history of early humans by emphasizing the important role women played in the development of culture. See, for example, Adrienne Zihlman, "Women as Shapers of the Human Adaptation," in *Woman the Gatherer,* ed. Frances Dahlberg (New Haven: Yale University Press, 1981). While this is an interesting approach, it ultimately legitimizes the enterprise of constructing essential and deterministic origins.

6. For an examination of some of the theories about how and why animals were domesticated, see Elizabeth Fisher, *Woman's Creation* (New York: McGraw-Hill, 1979), part 4.

7. Fisher, *Woman's Creation,* 197.

8. See, for example, Joan Banberger, "The Myth of Matriarchy: Why Men Rule in Primitive Society," in *Woman, Culture, and Society,* ed. Michelle Z. Rosaldo and Louise Lamphere (Stanford: Stanford University Press, 1974), 263–81.

9. For more on the way in which religion has served as a theoretical framework for oppression, see Mary Daly, *Beyond God the Father* (Boston: Beacon Press, 1973), and *Gyn/Ecology* (Boston: Beacon Press, 1978), and Marilyn French, *Beyond Power* (New York: Ballantine Books, 1985).

10. Carolyn Merchant, *The Death of Nature: Women, Ecology, and the Scientific Revolution* (San Francisco: Harper and Row, 1983).

11. For a more detailed critique of science from feminist perspectives, see my "Gendered Knowledge? Examining Influences on Scientific and Ethological Inquiries," in *Interpretation and Explanation in the Study of Animal Behavior: Comparative Perspectives,* ed. Dale Jamieson and Marc Bekoff (Boulder, Colo.: Westview Press, 1990), 56–73, and the references therein.

12. Marjorie Spiegel, *The Dreaded Comparison: Human and Animal Slavery* (Philadelphia: New Society Books, 1988).

13. Excerpted from letters from the I. G. Farben chemical trust to Auschwitz, as quoted in Bruno Bettelhiem, *The Informed Heart* (New York: Avon, 1971), 243. This example was brought to my attention by Jonathan Glover.

14. Betsy Hartmann, in her carefully researched work *Reproductive Rights and Wrongs: The Global Politics of Population Control and Contraceptive Choice* (New York: Harper & Row, 1987), writes that "in the contraceptive research business, the Third World has long been an important laboratory for human testing." She documents the ways in which many women are exploited and harmed as a result of population control pressures.

15. Ibid., 189–91.

16. See for example Hubbard, *Politics of Women's Biology* (New Brunswick, N.J.: Rutgers University Press, 1990), and Ruth Bleier, ed., *Feminist Approaches to Science* (New York: Pergamon Press, 1986), chap. 7.

17. One would like to say "too morally objectionable," but given the history of scientific use and abuse of "others," the difficulty undoubtedly lies in negative public opinion and illegality, rather than the experimenter's conscience.

18. Harry Harlow, *Learning to Love* (New York: Aronson, 1974), 38.

19. Haraway, *Primate Visions,* 238. …

20. Many women have suggested that there is an element of self-pleasure in the use of makeup. To examine this perspective here would take us too far afield. However, I would like to suggest that these women consider using cruelty-free cosmetics when they choose to make themselves up. Cruelty-free cosmetics can be purchased from the following distributors, who offer mail order catalogues: Vegan Street, P.O. Box 5525, Rockville, MD, 20855; Earthsafe Products, P.O. Box 81061, Cleveland, Ohio, 44181; A Clear Alternative, 8707 West Lane, Magnolia, TX, 77355; Pamela Marsen, Inc., P.O. Box 119, Teaneck, NJ, 07666; or ask your local grocer to start carrying cruelty-free products.

21. Personal correspondence, September 1990. See also Kheel, "Speaking the Unspeakable: Sexism in the Animal Rights Movement," *Feminists for Animal Rights Newsletter,* Summer/Fall 1985.

22. There are a few exceptions. A number of student organizations and Feminists for Animal Rights have recognized how oppressive theory often translates into oppressive practice and have conscientiously worked to combat both.

23. A "vegan" gathering is one in which no animal products are served. The fact that very few gatherings are vegan may be attributed to oversight or lack of awareness; in some cases, however, proposals to make feminist events cruelty-free have been rejected. ...

24. Jane Meyerding, "Feminist Criticism and Cultural Imperialism (Where Does One End and the Other Begin)," *Animals' Agenda* 2 (November-December 1982), 22–23.

25. Betsy Beavan, Noel Furie, and Selma Miriam, *The Second Seasonal Political Palate* (Bridgeport, Conn.: Sanguinaria Publishing, 1984), ix–x.

26. Uma Narayan develops this notion in a different context—namely, as a way in which white feminists and others can begin to bridge gaps that divide them from women of color. "Methodological humility," however, seems an appropriate strategy for ecofeminism as well. See "Working Together Across Difference: Some Considerations on Emotions and Political Practice," *Hypatia* 3 (Summer 1988): 31–47.

# The Sexual Politics of Meat

## Carol J. Adams

I left the British Library and my research on some women of the 1890s whose feminist, working-class newspaper advocated meatless diets, and went through the cafeteria line in a restaurant nearby. Vegetarian food in hand, I descended to the basement. A painting of Henry VIII eating a steak and kidney pie greeted my gaze. On either side of the consuming Henry were portraits of his six wives and other women. However, they were not eating steak and kidney pie, nor anything else made of meat. Catherine of Aragon held an apple in her hands. The Countess of Mar had a turnip, Anne Boleyn—red grapes, Anne of Cleaves—a pear, Jane Seymour—blue grapes, Catherine Howard—a carrot, Catherine Parr—a cabbage.

People with power have always eaten meat. The aristocracy of Europe consumed large courses filled with every kind of meat while the laborer consumed the complex carbohydrates. Dietary habits proclaim class distinctions, but they proclaim patriarchal distinctions as well. Women, second-class citizens, are more likely to eat what are considered to be second-class foods in a patriarchal culture: vegetables, fruits, and grains rather than meat. The sexism in meat eating recapitulates the class distinctions with an added twist: a mythology permeates all classes that meat is a masculine food and meat eating a male activity.

## Male Identification and Meat Eating

Meat-eating societies gain male identification by their choice of food, and meat textbooks heartily endorse this association. *The Meat We Eat* proclaims meat to be "A Virile and Protective Food," thus "a liberal meat supply has always been associated with a happy and virile people."[1] *Meat Technology* informs us that "the virile Australian race is a typical example of heavy meat-eaters."[2] Leading gourmands refer "to the virile ordeal of spooning the brains directly out of a barbecued calf's head."[3] *Virile: of or having the characteristics of an adult male,* from *vir* meaning *man.* Meat eating measures individual and societal virility.

Meat is a constant for men, intermittent for women, a pattern painfully observed in famine situations today. Women are starving at a rate disproportionate to men. Lisa Leghorn and Mary Roodkowsky surveyed this phenomenon in their book *Who Really Starves? Women and World Hunger.* Women, they conclude, engage in deliberate self-deprivation, offering men the "best" foods at the expense of their own nutritional needs. For instance, they tell us that "Ethiopian women and girls of all classes are obliged to prepare two meals, one for the males and a second often containing no meat or other substantial protein, for the females."[4]

In fact, men's protein needs are less than those of pregnant and nursing women and the disproportionate distribution of the main protein source occurs when women's need for protein is the greatest. Curiously, we are now being told that one should eat meat (or fish, vegetables, chocolate, and salt) at least six weeks before becoming pregnant if one wants a boy. But if a girl is desired, no meat please, rather milk, cheese, nuts, beans, and cereals.[5]

…

Most food taboos address meat consumption and they place more restrictions on women than on men. The common foods forbidden to women are chicken, duck, and pork. Forbidding meat to women in nontechnological cultures increases its prestige. Even if the women raise the pigs, as they do in the Solomon Islands, they are rarely allowed to eat the pork. When they do receive some, it is at the dispensation of their husbands. In Indonesia "flesh food is viewed as the property of the men. At feasts, the principal times when meat is available, it is distributed to households according to the men in them. … The system of distribution thus reinforces the prestige of the men in society."[6]

Worldwide this patriarchal custom is found. In Asia, some cultures forbid women from consuming fish, seafood, chicken, duck, and eggs. In equatorial Africa, the prohibition of chicken to women is common. For example, the Mbum Kpau women do not eat chicken, goat, partridge, or other game birds. The Kufa of Ethiopia punished women who ate chicken by making them slaves, while the Walamo "put to death anyone who violated the restriction of eating fowl."

Correspondingly, vegetables and other nonmeat foods are viewed as women's food. This makes them undesirable to men. The Nuer men think that eating eggs is effeminate. In other groups men require sauces to disguise the fact that they are eating women's foods. "Men expect to have meat sauces to go with their porridge and will sometimes refuse to eat sauces made of greens or other vegetables, which are said to be women's food."[7]

## Meat: For the Man Only

...

In technological societies, cookbooks reflect the presumption that men eat meat. A random survey of cookbooks reveals that the barbecue sections of most cookbooks are addressed to men and feature meat. The foods recommended for a "Mother's Day Tea" do not include meat, but readers are advised that on Father's Day, dinner should include London Broil because "a steak dinner has unfailing popularity with fathers."[8] In a chapter on "Feminine Hospitality" we are directed to serve vegetables, salads and soups. The New *McCall's* Cookbook suggests that a man's favorite dinner is London Broil. A "Ladies' Luncheon" would consist of cheese dishes and vegetables, but no meat. A section of one cookbook entitled "For Men Only" reinforces the omnipresence of meat in men's lives. What is for men only? London Broil, cubed steak and beef dinner.[9]

Twentieth-century cookbooks only serve to confirm the historical pattern found in the nineteenth century, when British working-class families could not afford sufficient meat to feed the entire family. "For the man only" appears continually in many of the menus of these families when referring to meat. In adhering to the mythologies of a culture (men need meat; meat gives bull-like strength) the male "breadwinner" actually received the meat. Social historians report that the "lion's share" of meat went to the husband.

...

Where poverty forced a conscious distribution of meat, men received it. Many women emphasized that they had saved the meat for their husbands. They were articulating the prevailing connections between meat eating and the male role: "I keep it for him; he *has* to have it." ... Women ate meat once a week with their children, while the husband consumed meat and bacon, "almost daily."

...

In situations of abundance, sex role assumptions about meat are not so blatantly expressed. For this reason, the diets of English upper-class women and men are much more similar than the diets of upper-class women and working-class women. Moreover, with the abundance of meat available in the United States as opposed to the restricted amount available in England, there has been enough for all, except when meat supplies were controlled. For instance, while enslaved black men received half a pound of meat per day, enslaved black women often found that they received little more than a quarter pound a day at times.[10] Additionally, during the wars of the twentieth century, the pattern of meat consumption recalled that of English nineteenth-century working-class families with one variation: the "worker" of the country's household, the soldier, got the meat; civilians were urged to learn how to cook without meat.

## The Racial Politics of Meat

The hearty meat eating that characterizes the diet of Americans and of the Western world is not only a symbol of male power, it is an index of racism. I do not mean racism in the sense that we are treating one class of animals, those that are not human beings, differently than we treat another, those that are, as Isaac Bashevis Singer uses the term in *Enemies: A Love Story:* "As often as Herman had witnessed the slaughter of animals and fish, he always had the same thought: in their behavior toward creatures, all men were Nazis. The smugness with which man could do with other species as he pleased exemplified the most extreme racist theories, the principle that might is right."[11] I mean racism as the requirement that power arrangements and customs that favor white people prevail, and that the acculturation of people of color to this standard includes the imposition of white habits of meat eating.

Two parallel beliefs can be traced in the white Western world's enactment of racism when the issue is meat eating. The first is that if the meat supply is limited, white people should get it; but if meat is plentiful all should eat it. This is a variation on the standard theme of the sexual politics of meat. The hierarchy of meat protein reinforces a hierarchy of race, class and sex.

Nineteenth-century advocates of white superiority endorsed meat as superior food. "Brain-workers" required lean meat as their main meal, but the "savage" and "lower" classes of society could live exclusively on coarser foods, according to George Beard, a nineteenth-century medical doctor who specialized in the diseases of middle-class people. He recommended that when white, civilized, middle-class men became susceptible to nervous exhaustion, they should eat more meat. To him, and for many others, cereals and fruits were lower than meat on the scale of evolution, and thus appropriate foods for the other races and white women, who appeared to be lower on the scale of evolution as well. Racism and sexism together upheld meat as white man's food.

… In his racist analysis, Beard reconciled the apparent contradiction of this tenet: "Why is it that savages and semi-savages are able to live on forms of food which, according to the theory of evolution, must be far below them in the scale of development?" In other words, how is it that people can survive very well without a great deal of animal protein? Because "savages" are

> little removed from the common animal stock form which they are derived. They are much nearer to the forms of life from which they feed than are the highly civilized brain-workers, and can therefore subsist on forms of life which would be most poisonous to us. Secondly, savages who feed on poor food are poor savages, and intellectually far inferior to the beef-eaters of any race.[12]

This explanation—which divided the world into intellectually superior meat eaters and inferior plant eaters—accounted for the conquering of other cultures by the English:

The rice-eating Hindoo and Chinese and the potato-eating Irish peasant are kept in subjection by the well-fed English. Of the various causes that contributed to the defeat of Napoleon at Waterloo, one of the chief was that for the first time he was brought face to face with the nation of beef-eaters, who stood still until they were killed.[13]

...

The word "cannibalism" entered our vocabulary after the "discovery" of the "New World." Derived from the Spaniards' mispronunciation of the name of the people of the Caribbean, it linked these people of color with the act. As Europeans explored the continents of North and South America and Africa, the indigenous peoples of those lands became accused of cannibalism—the ultimate savage act. Once labeled as cannibals, their defeat and enslavement at the hands of civilized, Christian whites became justifiable. ...

...

One cause of cannibalism was thought to be lack of animal protein. Yet most Europeans themselves during the centuries of European expansion were not subsisting on animal protein every day. The majority of cultures in the world satisfied their protein needs through vegetables and grains. By charging indigenous peoples with cannibalism (and thus demonstrating their utterly savage ways, for they supposedly did to humans what Europeans only did to animals) one justification for colonization was provided.

Racism is perpetuated each time meat is thought to be the best protein source. The emphasis on the nutritional strengths of animal protein distorts the dietary history of most cultures in which complete protein dishes were made of vegetables and grains. Information about these dishes is overwhelmed by an ongoing cultural and political commitment to meat eating.

...

## The Male Language of Meat Eating

Men who decide to eschew meat eating are deemed effeminate; failure of men to eat meat announces that they are not masculine. Nutritionist Jean Mayer suggested that "the more men sit at their desks all day, the more they want to be reassured about their maleness in eating those large slabs of bleeding meat which are the last symbol of machismo."[14] The late Marty Feldman observed, "It has to do with the function of the male within our society. Football players drink beer because it's a man's drink, and eat steak because it's a man's meal. The emphasis is on 'man-sized portions,' 'hero' sandwiches; the whole terminology of meat-eating reflects this masculine bias."[15] Meat-and-potatoes men are our stereotypical strong and hearty, rough and ready, able males. Hearty beef stews are named "Manhandlers." Chicago Bears' head football coach, Mike Ditka, operates a restaurant that features "he-man food" such as steaks and chops.

...

## Gender Inequality/Species Inequality

*The men ... were better hunters than the women, but only because the women had found they could live quite well on foods other than meat.*

—Alice Walker, *The Temple of My Familiar*[16]

What is it about meat that makes it a symbol and celebration of male dominance? In many ways, gender inequality is built into the species inequality that meat eating proclaims, because for most cultures obtaining meat was performed by men. Meat was a valuable economic commodity; those who controlled this commodity achieved power. If men were the hunters, then the control of this economic resource was in their hands. Women's status is inversely related to the importance of meat in non-technological societies:

> The equation is simple: the more important meat is in their life, the greater relative dominance will the men command. ... When meat becomes an important element within a more closely organized economic system so that there exist rules for its distribution, then men already begin to swing the levers of power. ... Women's social standing is roughly equal to men's only when society itself is not formalized around roles for distributing meat.[17]

Peggy Sanday surveyed information on over a hundred nontechnological cultures and found a correlation between plant-based economies and women's power and animal-based economies and male power. "In societies dependent on animals, women are rarely depicted as the ultimate source of creative power."[18] ...

Characteristics of economies dependent mainly on the processing of animals for food include:

- sexual segregation in work activities, with women doing more work than men, but work that is less valued
- women responsible for child care
- the worship of male gods
- patrilineality

On the other hand, plant-based economies are more likely to be egalitarian. This is because women are and have been the gatherers of vegetable foods, and these are invaluable resources for a culture that is plant-based. In these cultures, men as well as women were dependent on women's activities. From this, women achieved autonomy and a degree of self-sufficiency. Yet, where women gather vegetable food and the diet is vegetarian, women do not discriminate as a consequence of distributing the staple. By providing a large proportion of the protein food of a society, women gain an essential economic and social role without abusing it.

...
We might observe that the male role of hunter and distributer of meat has been transposed to the male role of eater of meat and conclude that this accounts for meat's role as symbol of male dominance. But there is much more to meat's role as symbol than this.

## "Vegetable": Symbol of Feminine Passivity?

Both the words "men" and "meat" have undergone lexicographical narrowing. Originally generic terms, they are now closely associated with their specific referents. Meat no longer means all foods; the word *man*, we realize, no longer includes *women*. Meat represents *the essence or principle part of something*, according to the *American Heritage Dictionary*. Thus we have the "meat of the matter," "a meaty question." To "beef up" something is to improve it. Vegetable, on the other hand, represents the least desirable characteristics: *suggesting or like a vegetable, as in passivity or dullness of existence, monotonous, inactive*. Meat is *something one enjoys or excels in*, vegetable becomes representative of someone who does not enjoy anything: a *person who leads a monotonous, passive, or merely physical existence*.

A complete reversal has occurred in the definition of the word vegetable. Whereas its original sense was to *be lively, active*, it is now viewed as dull, monotonous, passive. To vegetate is to lead a passive existence; just as to be feminine is to lead a passive existence. Once vegetables are viewed as women's food, then by association they become viewed as "feminine," passive.

Men's need to disassociate themselves from women's food ... has been institutionalized in sexist attitudes toward vegetables and the use of the word *vegetable* to express criticism or disdain. Colloquially it is a synonym for a person severely brain-damaged or in a coma. In addition, vegetables are thought to have a tranquilizing, dulling, numbing effect on people who consume them, and so we cannot possibly get strength from them. According to this perverse incarnation of Brillat-Savarin's theory that you are what you eat, to eat a vegetable is to become a vegetable, and by extension, to become womanlike.

...
The word vegetable acts as a synonym for women's passivity because women are supposedly like plants. Hegel makes this clear: "The difference between men and women is like that between animals and plants. Men correspond to animals, while women correspond to plants because their development is more placid."[19] From this viewpoint, both women and plants are seen as less developed and less evolved than men and animals. Consequently, women may eat plants, since each is placid; but active men need animal meat.

## Meat Is a Symbol of Patriarchy

In her essay, "Deciphering a Meal," the noted anthropologist Mary Douglas suggests that the order in which we serve foods, and the foods we insist on being present at a meal, reflect a taxonomy of classification that mirrors and reinforces our larger culture. A meal is an amalgam of food dishes, each a constituent part of the whole, each with an assigned value. In addition, each dish is introduced in precise order. A meal does not begin with a dessert, not end with soup. All is seen as leading up to and then coming down from the entrée that is meat. The pattern is evidence of stability. As Douglas explains, "The ordered system which is a meal represents all the ordered systems associated with it. Hence the strong arousal power of a threat to weaken or confuse that category."[20] To remove meat is to threaten the structure of the larger patriarchal culture.

Marabel Morgan, one expert on how women should accede to every male desire, reported in her *Total Woman Cookbook* that one must be careful about introducing foods that are seen as a threat: "I discovered that Charlie seemed threatened by certain foods. He was suspicious of my casseroles, thinking I had sneaked in some wheat germ or 'good-for-you' vegetables that he wouldn't like."[21]

Mary McCarthy's *Birds of America* provides a fictional illustration of the intimidating aspect to a man of a woman's refusal of meat. Miss Scott, a vegetarian, is invited to a NATO general's house for Thanksgiving. Her refusal of turkey angers the general. Not able to take this rejection seriously, as male dominance requires a continual recollection of itself on everyone's plate, the general loads her plate up with turkey and then ladles gravy over the potatoes as well as the meat, "thus contaminating her vegetable foods." McCarthy's description of his actions with the food mirrors the warlike customs associated with military battles. "He had seized the gravy boat like a weapon in hand-to-hand combat. No wonder they had made him a brigadier general—at least that mystery was solved." The general continues to behave in a bellicose fashion and after dinner proposes a toast in honor of an eighteen-year-old who has enlisted to fight in Vietnam. During the ensuing argument about war the general defends the bombing of Vietnam with the rhetorical question: "What's so sacred about a civilian?" This upsets the hero, necessitating that the general's wife apologize for her husband's behavior: "Between you and me," she confides to him, "it kind of got under his skin to see that girl refusing to touch her food. I saw that right away."[22]

Male belligerence in this area is not limited to fictional military men. Men who batter women have often used the absence of meat as a pretext for violence against women. Women's failure to serve meat is not the cause of the violence against them. Yet, as a pretext for this violence, meat is hardly a trivial item. "Real" men eat meat. Failing to honor the importance of this symbol catalyzes male rage. As one woman battered by her husband reported, "It would start off with him being angry over trivial little things, a trivial little thing like cheese instead of meat on a sandwich."[23] Another woman stated, "A month ago he threw scalding water over me, leaving a scar on my right arm, all because I gave him a pie with potatoes and vegetables for his dinner, instead of fresh meat."[24]

...

Men who choose not to eat meat repudiate one of their masculine privileges. The *New York Times* explored this idea in an editorial on the masculine nature of meat eating. Instead of "the John Wayne type," epitome of the masculine meat eater, the new male hero is "Vulnerable" like Alan Alda, Mikhail Baryshnikov, and Phil Donahue. They might eat fish and chicken, but not red meat. Alda and Donahue, among other men, have not only repudiated the macho role, but also macho food. According to the *Times,* "Believe me. The end of macho marks the end of the meat-and-potatoes man."[25] We won't miss either.

---

### Notes

1. P. Thomas Ziegler, *The Meat We Eat* (Danville, IL: The Interstate Printers and Publishers, 1966), pp. 5, 1.

2. Frank Gerrard, *Meat Technology: A Practical Textbook for Student and Butcher* (London: Northwood Publications, Inc., 1945, 1977), p. 348.

3. Waverley Root and Richard de Rochemont, *Eating in America: A History* (New York: William Morrow, 1976), p. 279.

4. Lisa Leghorn and Mary Roodkowsky, *Who Really Starves? Women and World Hunger* (New York: Friendship Press, 1977), p. 21.

5. Lloyd Shearer, "Intelligence Report: Does Diet Determine Sex?", summarizing the conclusions of Dr. Joseph Stolkowski, *Parade* 27 June 1982, p. 7.

6. Frederick J. Simoons, *Eat Not This Flesh: Food Avoidances in the Old World* (Madison: University of Wisconsin, 1961, 1967), p. 12. The quotation in the following paragraph is found in Simoons, p. 73.

7. Bridget O'Laughlin, "Mediation of Contradiction: Why Mbum Women do not eat Chicken," *Woman, Culture, and Society,* ed. Michelle Zimbalist Rosaldo and Louise Lamphere (Stanford: Stanford University Press, 1974), p. 303.

8. Sunset Books and Sunset Magazines, *Sunset Menu Cook Book* (Menlo Park, CA: Lane Magazine and Book Co., 1969), pp. 139, 140.

9. *Oriental Cookery* from ChunKing and Mazola Corn Oil.

10. Todd L. Savitt, *Medicine and Slavery: The Diseases and Health Care of Blacks in Antebellum Virginia* (Urbana and Chicago: University of Illinois Press, 1978), p. 91.

11. Isaac Bashevis Singer, *Enemies: A Love Story* (New York: Farrar, Straus and Giroux, 1972), p. 257.

12. George M. Beard, M. D., *Sexual Neurasthenia [Nervous Exhaustion] Its Hygiene, Causes, Symptoms and Treatment with a Chapter on Diet for the Nervous* (New York: E. B. Treat & Co., 1898, New York: Arno Press, 1972), pp. 272–78.

13. Ibid.

14. Quoted in "Red Meat: American Man's Last Symbol of Machismo," *National Observer* 10 July 1976, p. 13.

15. Marty Feldman, quoted in Rynn Berry Jr., *The Vegetarians* (Brookline, MA: Autumn Press, 1979), p. 32.

16. Alice Walker, *The Temple of My Familiar* (San Diego, New York: Harcourt Brace Jovanovich, 1989), p. 50.

17. Richard E. Leakey and Roger Lewin, *People of the Lake: Mankind and Its Beginnings* (New York: Doubleday & Co., 1978, New York: Avon Books, 1979), pp. 210–11.

18. Peggy Sanday, *Female power and male dominance: On the origins of sexual inequality* (Cambridge and New York: Cambridge University Press, 1981), pp. 65, 66.

19. From Hegel's *Philosophy of Right,* para. 166, p. 263, quoted in Nancy Tuana, "The Misbegotten Man: Scientific, Religious, and Philosophical Images of Women," unpublished manuscript.

20. Mary Douglas, "Deciphering a Meal," in *Implicit meanings: Essays in anthropology* (London: Routledge & Kegan Paul, 1975), p. 273.

21. Marabel Morgan, *Marabel Morgan's Handbook for Kitchen Survival: The Total Woman Cookbook* (New Jersey: Fleming H. Revell Co., 1980), p. 13.

22. Mary McCarthy, *Birds of America* (New York: Harcourt Brace Jovanovich, 1965, New York: New American Library, 1972), pp. 167, 180, 183.

23. R. Emerson Dobash and Russell Dobash, *Violence Against Wives: A Case Against the Patriarchy* (New York: The Free Press, 1979), p. 100.

24. Erin Pizzey, *Scream Quietly or the Neighbours will Hear* (Hammondsworth, England: Penguin Books, 1974), p. 35.

25. Editorial, *New York Times,* 17 August 1981.

# Feminism and Vegetarianism

## Lisa Martin

I will address the issue of whether vegetarianism is a feminist issue and, if so, what makes it a concern for feminists. My perspective is that the economic and environmental impacts of meat production and consumption make vegetarianism a feminist issue. The negative effects of the meat industry disproportionately affect women, thus making the boycotting of meat consumption, or vegetarianism, a feminist issue.

The first point that establishes vegetarianism as a feminist issue is the economic cost of meat production and its consequence for women. The amount of money that the government spends to subsidize the meat industry means that there is less money for social welfare programs that benefit women and children. Since women and children make up the largest percentage of the poor, the money used to support the meat industry instead of women is a feminist concern.

Three statistics stand out in regard to this issue of government subsidies to the meat industry versus money spent for programs to benefit women and children. The first statistic is that California subsidizes water to the meat industry in the amount of $24 billion a year; the state's budget for child welfare services is $425 million.[1] The second is that a government study of the grazing program in sixteen Western states showed that the subsidies to cattle ranchers for grazing on public lands resulted in a $52.3 million loss in revenues for the government.[2] The third statistic illustrates the enormity of money spent on government-subsidized water to the meat industry throughout the country: Without subsidized water to produce meat, the cheapest hamburger available would cost $35 per pound.[3]

While a tremendous amount of money is being spent to subsidize the meat industry, feminists are told that there isn't enough money for child care, health care, or any other program that would benefit women. If vegetarianism was the standard diet, this tax money could be used to fund programs more vital to women's needs and existence.

Another issue of the costs of the meat industry relates to the amount of resources consumed by the industry. The statistics on resource usage for meat production point out that 50 percent of all U.S. water is consumed in some phase of meat production.[4] Production of all meats, dairy products, and eggs accounts for one-third of all raw materials—that is, the resources used to feed, house, and process livestock and their products—consumed in the United States.[5] Additionally, foreign imports of oil could be cut by 60 percent if the United States adopted a vegetarian diet.[6] This inordinate consumption of resources by the meat industry means that there are less resources available to those who have less money and power. As these resources become more scarce, prices rise, and those most affected are the poor, of which women and children are the majority.

The environmental costs of meat production link vegetarianism to feminism. Meat production contributes a great deal to environmental degradation. The animals raised for consumption in this country produce 250,000 pounds of waste every second,[7] less than 50 percent of which is recycled because to do so is not economically feasible. Instead, this waste ends up in our water system. Fifty percent of our water pollution comes from the meat industry,[8] as well as more than three times as much harmful organic waste water pollution as all other industries combined.[9] This waste converts to ammonia and nitrates in the water and is responsible for rising levels of nitrates in both rural wells and city water supplies. Although it is not harmful to adults, it can cause serious brain damage or death to infants.[10]

The environmental issue connects vegetarianism to feminism in that women are disproportionately affected by the destruction of the environment. Women have less power in this society to affect what kinds of pollution will be produced, where it will be stored or dumped, and whether its production will be stopped. The result is that women have fewer options to escape from pollution's impact on their lives. Furthermore, since women are most often the caretakers of children, and children are more susceptible to illness from environmental pollution, women have the additional burden of caring for sick children.

Another environmental concern is the effect of the meat industry on the Third World. Since feminists are concerned about the subordination of women all over the globe, the ways in which the meat industry differentially affects women in the Third World connects vegetarianism to feminism. Since women are the majority of the world's farmers, the use of land to raise both livestock and livestock feed limits the availability of land for subsistence farming, hindering women's efforts to feed themselves and their families.

Fueled by the meat industry in this country, the rain forests of Central and Latin America are destroyed daily in an effort to create available land for grazing cattle and raising animal feed. Although this clearing of the land seems to indicate that there is more land available for the poor on which to grow crops, this is not the case. In Central America, more than 50 percent of all rural families are landless or own too little land on which to support themselves because the cattle industry has concentrated the land in the hands of the few.[11] In Brazil, the percentages are even greater, with 4.5 percent of the landowners controlling 80 percent of the land, while 70 percent of the rural population owns no land.[12] Women and their families are being displaced from the land that feeds them in favor of meat production.

Although the export of meat from Central America to the United States has decreased since 1980,[13] there has been an increase in the amount of grains grown in these countries specifically for cattle feed. In Mexico, more than one-third of all grain produced in the country goes to feed cattle.[14] Unfortunately, as the governments of these countries view it, cattle and feed exports are one of the few cash crops they can produce to get in on the global marketplace. The end result is that the poor and rural peoples of these countries suffer from higher prices for staple foods that are being displaced by the sorghum and soybeans needed for cattle feed.[15] Women and children exist at the bottom of this food pyramid.

Vegetarianism is also connected to feminism through the issue of women's health as it relates to the meat industry. Even though meat consumption affects the health of both men and women, the bias in the scientific community toward studying men as the physiological norm for both men and women means that health concerns specific to women regarding the consumption of animal products are understudied and largely unknown. One such health concern is osteoporosis. Statistics show that one in four women over the age of sixty-five has lost more than 50 percent of her bone mass.[16] The most frequently researched cause for osteoporosis is excess dietary protein, which creates a calcium loss from the body. Yet the advice given most women to ward off this condition is to consume more dairy products, which are high sources of protein.

Another health concern is the correlation between early onset of menstruation and higher incidences of breast cancer. Studies have shown that girls who eat meat have an earlier age (before thirteen) of menstruation onset than do vegetarian girls. Researchers have studied these differences and have determined that females with earlier onset of menstruation suffer four times higher rates of breast cancer than women who started menstruation later (after seventeen).[17] Women need more information and research done on the specific health problems they may be incurring by partaking of a meat-based diet.

Vegetarianism is in many ways a distinctly feminist issue. The negative effects of the meat industry on women from the economic, environmental, and health aspects point out the ways in which vegetarianism becomes a feminist concern.

---

### Notes

1. Judy Krizmanic, "Is a Burger Worth It?" *Vegetarian Times* (April 1990): 20.
2. Diane Harris, "Issues Awareness," *Vegetarian Living* (July-August 1992): 5.

3. John Robbins, *Diet for a New America* (Walpole, N.H.: Stillpoint Publishing, 1987), p. 367.

4. Ibid., p. 367.

5. Ibid., p. 374.

6. Ibid., p. 377.

7. Ibid., p. 372.

8. Krizmanic, "Is a Burger Worth It?" p. 21.

9. Robbins, *Diet for a New America*, p. 373.

10. Ibid.

11. Jeremy Rifkin, *Beyond Beef: The Rise and Fall of the Cattle Culture* (New York: Dutton, 1992), p. 192.

12. Ibid., p. 194.

13. Ibid., p. 192.

14. Ibid., p. 149.

15. Ibid., p. 148; Robbins, *Diet for a New America*, p. 364.

16. Robbins, *Diet for a New America*, p. 189.

17. Ibid., p. 266.

# Hunting:
# A Woman's Perspective

## Gretchen Legler

I started hunting seven years ago, surprising many of my friends and my family. Surprising my father, a veteran Rocky Mountain trout angler and one-time deer hunter, who said to me, "I didn't know you were interested in that sort of thing." Surprising many women I know, whose first reaction was, "What's a good feminist like you doing in a goose blind?"

I didn't know I was interested in hunting either, until I tried it with my husband, Craig Borck. I found I liked it, and every fall for seven years we have headed out again to Gooseberry Marsh, to Agassiz National Wildlife Refuge, to Thief Lake, to the logging roads around Blackduck, Minn., to hunt, to fill our freezer with ducks and venison, with geese and grouse, to eat well for the rest of the year.

Not being a man, and not coming from a hunting family, I wasn't raised on hunting, so I've been able to form my ideas about hunting in a space *relatively* free of cultural and family baggage; free of the idea, for instance, that hunting is not a woman's activity; free of the idea that success at hunting somehow translates into "manly" worthiness. And I have the luxury in my life of not having to hunt out of necessity. I can buy all the whole fryers and pot roast I want at the grocery store.

What I mean is that, although I wouldn't call what I do "hunting for fun," I *am* in a position of not being under any kind of cultural or economic pressure to hunt, or not to. I have chosen this activity. There is no reason for me to hunt except that I want to. There is one thing I am certain of, however, if I didn't hunt, I wouldn't eat meat. If I want to eat meat, I have to go and get it myself.

I don't have any women friends who hunt, but that is not because there aren't any others. I simply haven't sought them out. I should. … There *are* women who hunt, but not very many.

## Why Most Women Don't Hunt

There are lots of reasons women don't hunt, but these don't have anything to do with biology, with gender or with ability. They have to do with cultural conditioning and experience and obligations, both chosen and not chosen.

When men go out to hunt with their friends, women often are obligated to stay at home to be with children; to be in and take care of the domestic aspect of family life; a realm most women have a great deal more experience with than men. I don't have children, so, unlike many women, this hasn't been one of the hundred huge hurdles to my going out into the woods.

And women, typically, aren't initiated into hunting as boys are, by their fathers or male relatives and friends. I don't think we've gotten to a place yet in our culture where women can be introduced to hunting by other women, but wouldn't that be terrific? For most women, hunting has never been an activity that they felt invited to participate in.

## Male Perceptions

…

Another reason a lot of women don't hunt is that they feel like outsiders in what is largely a male community. The feeling of being an outsider can come from being hassled or harassed, or simply from a subtle sense of aloneness.

I've never had a truly bad experience, being a woman and being out there, in a goose blind or the duck marsh, but there have been plenty of times that I have felt uncomfortable, when there have been whispers and stares; men and their sons looking closely, trying to figure out, is it a woman or a boy? Stares that ask, "What are you doing here, lady?" And there have been plenty of stupid remarks. "Who said women can't shoot?" one guy said as I was carrying our geese away from the check-in station at Thief Lake Wildlife Management Area.

For all those reasons and more, hunting is still mostly a man's activity. But it shouldn't be.

## A Way of Life

I've made my own peace with hunting, finding that, instead of being antithetical to my views about the world, instead of being something I have to rationalize and apologize for, that hunting fits with the way I want to live. Hunting fits my life the same way that growing squash and tomatoes in my backyard garden does; the same way that harvesting wild grapes for jam and picking blueberries in the summer for pies all winter long does; the same way gathering mushrooms in the spring fits with my goal of living, somehow, in a way that is connected to the natural world.

...

## Personal Insights

I like hunting. I like being out in the fall, on a marsh at dawn, in a goose blind before light, hearing the geese wake up with their faraway, deep honking. I like listening to the swish of bird wings overhead. I like watching cranes fly over, hearing their musical cries. I like seeing a moose appear at the far end of a marsh, moving in the gold grass, like a dark, silent ghost. I like sitting quietly in a canoe, hidden by cattails, sitting so still sometimes that crackling ice on a cold day forms on the water around me, so still a muskrat comes up behind me, curious and unafraid.

I like being out. Out. Out in rain and cold and snow, and sometimes sun, and seeing the earth as many people seldom see it. And I like getting to know animals, getting to know them in a way I would never have a chance to know them if I didn't hunt, learning their habits; where deer sleep, that grouse come out to logging roads to eat clover and fill their crops with bits of gravel; what times of day the geese fly out to graze; how ducks' feathers lie across one another on their breasts and wings to make those beautiful designs. And I like eating wild things.

There is something about eating a duck or goose that you have shot yourself that gives you a kind of entre into a world non-hunters don't often enter. There is something about seeing a mallard, or a Canadian honker, alive, flying overhead, then holding it lifeless in your hand, gutting it, plucking it, wet feathers sticking to your fingers, then eating it by candlelight, that makes me feel I know some whole story about the world. When you eat a wild thing you have shot, there is a bridge that you cross, a bridge between your own body and the wild outside world.

...

## A Hunter's Place

Some hunters might think these ideas rather romantic; especially hunters who still hunt out of absolute necessity to feed themselves and their families. These ideas may seem romantic, too, to hunters who hunt for "manly camaraderie," who have only a vague interest in eating what they've shot or trapped, who don't like that "wild" taste of dark goose breast, whose ducks are passed along, instead, to friends who can take on the responsibility, the dirty job, of plucking and gutting, and who know how to cook a mallard so that it doesn't taste like mud or like leather.

And these ideas may seem romantic, or "womanish," to hunters who have been raised on hunting as a sport, where hunting is reduced to a game of skill and where you increase your chances of success through the purchase of increasingly sophisticated technical paraphernalia. In this game, the animal becomes a foe, an enemy of sorts, and your goal is to beat the animal, to beat nature.

Whenever I shoot something, take a life, I feel deeply the incredible power that gives me. But I have never felt that power the way a victor or a champion would. I simply have a deep sense of how easy it is to kill, how easily a life can be extinguished, and knowing that gives me a sense of the fragility of the world around me, the tenuousness of these animals' lives and of my own life, an understanding of the uneasy balance of the natural world.

…

---

# Shots in the Dark

## Andrée Collard with Joyce Contrucci

…

### Man's Oldest Profession

I have no sympathy for hunters. Their habit repels me as being senselessly brutal. Their language embarrasses me as sounding piteously immature. They remind me of irresponsible little boys driven to savagery out of boredom, a boredom so desperate that relief comes only from the thrill of hunting that culminates in the kill. Quite simply, hunters need to be 'turned on' to life. One of them expressed his inability to respond to nature unless he controlled/killed it when he said to me, 'Walking in the woods doesn't turn me on unless there's a purpose to it. Marking trees. Shooting deer. That's really living.' This middle-aged man, well-off, respectable-looking, and soft-spoken, makes a living from house-hunting, that is, from real estate, which he finds very dull. Hunting becomes the fix that enables the hunter to bear the humdrum of his unfeeling existence as a cog in the wheel of culture.

However my purpose is not to understand hunters but to situate hunting in the culture that spawned it. Hunting is the *modus operandi* of patriarchal societies on all levels of life—to support one level is to support them all. However innocuous the language may sound—we hunt everything from houses to jobs to heads—it reveals a cultural mentality so accustomed to predation that it horrifies only when it threatens to kill us all, as in the case of nuclear weapons. Underlying all this hunting is a mechanism that identifies/names the prey, stalks it, competes for it, and is intent on getting the first shot at it. This is blatantly done when the prey is named woman,[1] animal, or land but it extends to whatever phobia happens to seize and obsess a nation, whether this be another nation or a race other than that of powerholding groups.

Nature has been blamed for being either seductive (and dangerous) or indifferent to man. Siren-like, she beckons and invites hooks and guns in the same way women are said to lure men and ask for rape. Or, like the cold, uncaring 'bitch', nature does not respond to man's plight and must therefore be punished. Seduction and indifference are in the mind of the beholder who projects them in order to rationalise his acts and the rationalisation works because the culture approves it. We know that women want to be raped as much as deer and lions want to be shot and the earth, sea, and skies are asking to be gouged, polluted, and probed. …

… Those who cannot accept to be a *part* of the lifecycle must live in the realm of sadomasochistic fantasy and seek self-actualisation in violence. … Indeed *this* is the essence of hunting. It is an exercise of power on the part of one who feels overwhelmed, fragmented and frightened and it explains the pathetic urge to kill anything bold enough to be alive.

… A tradition that encourages us to free our bodies from the limitations of nature is one that plucks us from the web of life, leaving us stranded and longing for the very biophilic connections we are taught to repudiate. Blind to the inherent contradictions and delusions, man splits reality into discrete, self-contained and antagonistic categories—nature/culture, body/mind, emotion/reason—claims them all and calls himself healthy, whole and sound of mind. He is unruffled about the fact that he 'loves' animals, joins conservation societies, rescues abandoned dogs and cats *and at the same time* sinks hooks into fish and fires bullets into 'game', shoots rodents who occasionally munch vegetables in his backyard, condones the clubbing of baby seals to death, and the infliction of injury and excruciating pain on laboratory animals, hits rabbits, squirrels, hedgehogs, skunks, opossums by the thousands as they cross his highways, leaving them to their fate and, in an all-out war against 'the enemies of mankind', seeks to exterminate all manner of insects and 'lesser' life forms that threaten his comfort and possessions. It is the rare man who sees these acts as contradictions. He is even more rare who experiences them as conflicts. Such contradiction and delusion are cornerstones of the romantic tradition—a tradition which urbanely conveys sadomasochism into the realm of 'normal' human feelings and relationships by masking the brutality of 'love' grounded in the objectification of the 'love object'.

## The Hunt Romanticized

In simple terms, romanticism is a function of the idealisation process whereby brown paper is turned into holiday wrapping. A romantic removes the 'love object' from the reality of its being to the secret places of his mind and establishes a relationship of power/domination over it. There can be no reciprocity, no element of mutuality between the romantic lover and the 'love object'. The quest (chase) is all that matters as it provides a heightened sense of being through the exercise of power. Romantics engage in sadomasochistic games with their victims played against a background of obstacles, potentially threatening situations, and grandiose schemes. Since one cannot sustain the frenzy of feeling resulting from pursuit of an ideal—by definition, inaccessible—the romantic game point is death. The hunt, as epitomised in the idealisation of the chase, of the kill, of the hunter and of his victim, is the mainstay of romanticism.

...

## From the Romantic to the Real

Hunters often pose as conservationists who love nature, giving rise to yet another contradiction comfortably entrenched in this culture. In point of fact, hunters do not love nature as such but rather how they feel *in* nature as they stalk and kill her animals. Dependent for their thrills upon what nature 'provides', they therefore spend a considerable amount of money to ensure that conservation lands as well as fish and animal preserves are regularly stocked. They return compulsively to woods and lakes, rivers and fields, marshes and oceans, to live through the power of their rods and guns.

When rigorously challenged as to the morality of their predilections, hunters commonly resort to rationalisations that disguise their self-interest as 'concern' for animals and for other people. For example, 'deer would starve to death if hunters did not cull the herds', or 'bears would cause too much damage if not kept in check by hunters.' The deer's main natural predator is the wolf which hunters all but exterminated. As for marauding bears, it is human overpopulation and the 'need' to industrialise that is causing an expansion of *suburbia* into the 'wilderness', taxing the earth and all that lives on it. Thousands of innocent wild animals are forced from *their* habitats and then blamed and exterminated for damage *they* cause to human settlements. The deer did well when it was left alone. So did the bear.

Perhaps from the animal's point of view it is immaterial whether it is killed by the claws of a bear or by the bullet of a hunter. But it makes an enormous difference to the continuation and *quality* of life whether human beings kill like the bear or like the hunter. Bears do not kill gratuitously for 'pleasure', status, profit, power, masculinity. Hunters do. Bears kill because they have to eat what they kill in order to survive. The overwhelming majority of the 20.6 million 'registered' hunters in the United States do not kill for survival. Bears kill the weak. Hunters take the biggest and the best. Bears give back to the earth. Hunters give back nothing.

After he had witnessed a moose hunt, Henry David Thoreau wrote:

> This afternoon had suggested to me how base and coarse are the motives which commonly carry men into the wilderness. The explorers and lumberers generally are hirelings, paid so much a day for their labor, and as such they have no more love for wild nature than woodsawyers have for forests.[2]

Thoreau's experience of that hunt brought home to him the uniqueness of life, the rare and beautiful quality that is felt only by participating in 'the perfect success' of every part of nature. In other words, every part of nature is a gift in itself. For Thoreau the capacity to know the heart of the pine without cutting into it is to love the healing spirit of the wild without killing it. This contemplative, non-utilitarian, non-materialistic love of nature often passes as romantic because it is emotional and appears to ignore such realities of life as building houses and keeping warm. Thoreau's own attempt at self-sufficiency—for which he had to cut timber—did not prevent him from participating as fully as he could in the mystery of the wild.

Participation in nature is in diametric opposition to the romantic appetite for nature epitomised in the hunt, an appetite which consumes the object of its love and which is insatiable because based upon a neurotic need for power and control. Participation in nature is based upon a recognition of the reality that nature exists of, for, and by herself; that she is ordered by principles and forces which defy manipulation and harnessing; and that understanding of nature flows from the experience of her and not from the experiment upon her, from being with, not being over her. Participation in nature joins the lover and the loved in regenerative, mutually sustaining cycles of living and dying.

---

### Notes

1. The predictable inclusion of women in the ranks of man's rightful prey is easily seen in the fur industry which is keen on maintaining the connection between hunting, fur animals and women. Its advertisements degrade women because they invariably fuse animals and women in the same identity of prey, an identity that appeals to the hunter in man and the victim in woman. These ads tell the woman to take the bait (the fur coat) that will apparently bring the man to her feet. In reality she is the prey being brought down. She and the fur animal—one 'alive' and the other dead—are one and the same. After looking at dozens of these images it became obvious to me that the advertisers address not so much the woman who is lured into wearing the fur as the man whose money will buy it. Even when man does not actually hunt animals, his success is still reflected in the kill.

2. Henry David Thoreau, *The Maine Woods* (New York: Thomas Y. Crowell Co., 1961), pp. 156–7.

# Some Doubts About Fur Coats

## Slavenka Drakulic

Whether winter or summer, streetcar 14 never comes. They say it is because it was produced in Czechoslovakia. PRAHA, OBOROVY PODNIK, it says on a small metal plate inside. You know, a communist product—what can you expect from it? Our experience tells us that it can't stand either too much rain or too much sunshine; it runs only on nice days when the temperature is between 17 and 22 degrees Celsius and you are not in a hurry. But because it was December—the middle of winter—just before Christmas, drizzling, and incidentally I was in a hurry, number 14 was naturally nowhere in sight. Instead, in my sight was a lady, a lady in a splendid long fur coat—a silver fox, a wolf, a bear, or some other poor animal. Because of that coat, I couldn't miss her, even if I wanted to. There was a time when I'd wanted such a thing myself.

Years ago, I fell into the trap of buying a fur coat. It was winter and a cold wind was blowing from the harbor as I spotted it walking through the Church Street flea market in Cambridge, Massachusetts. It was an old-fashioned mink coat that caught my eye from a distance, like something from a thirties Hollywood movie. I knew it was just waiting for me, for the right alibi to buy it. It didn't take me long to make one up: it was so cheap, compared to the prices in my country, where you can't buy a second-hand fur and therefore new ones are very expensive. Perhaps I can finally afford it, I thought. I put it on. In the little mirror that a young woman held up for me, I didn't look like a sick, divorced, single mother, or an East European woman at all, but like the person I wanted to be. That's what I liked so much about it: it turned me instantly into another person.

I was very well aware that for that money—I remember it cost $90, but the woman reduced it to $75—I could buy books, something that I definitely needed much more. I also was aware that that had been my plan before I saw the coat. I was on my way to the Reading International Bookstore right there, at the corner of that very street. On the other hand, I knew that buying a fur coat for such an amount back home was absolutely out of the question; it would have cost me at least twice my monthly income. For a moment—but only a moment—I thought about the carefully composed book list in my purse—then I looked in the mirror again and took out $80. Somewhere at the back of my mind there was one last argument left. As if someone was whispering in my ear, I heard that tiny little voice: 'What about dead animals? Do you really want to wear their furs—you, the vegetarian, animal lover, ecologist?' As artificial fur was not yet in vogue and the animals in question were long dead, I simply ignored the weak voice of conscience in my head. It just couldn't match my whole Eastern European background, which was urging: Take it, take it, here's your chance.

I have worn the coat, forgetting the whole episode. It was while I was in New York in early 1989 that I remembered it again. Another episode reminded me of it. It happened in Beograd that winter, when a young girl, J. Simović, climbed onto bus number 26. It was cold and she had on an old mink coat. At eleven o'clock in the morning the bus was almost empty, only a few old people, a housewife or two, and two young couples. 'Where did you get your mink coat, pussycat?' asked one young man. 'Did your father buy it for you?' The girl didn't answer. She stood by the door, with her back to him. Then the four of them became more aggressive. They surrounded her, one took out his lighter, lit it, and grabbed her sleeve, as if he wanted to test whether it was a real fur or not. The girl withdrew, looking helplessly around the bus. But people in the bus—even the driver—pretended not to notice what was going on. Then the bus stopped and J. Simović was kicked out in the street. 'Out!' yelled one of the girls. 'If you can afford a mink coat, you can afford a taxi!'

I read this episode in an article from the newspaper *Politika* that a friend from Beograd sent me, as an example of what is going on back home: growing poverty and frustration, leading to the revival of the egalitarian syndrome. I noticed that the reporter chose to stress that the girl was wearing an *old* fur coat. What he meant by that, using it as an argument in her defense, was that she didn't deserve what happened to her because she wasn't really rich, she was as poor as the aggressors, and therefore she was not to blame. But by saying that, he justified the same logic of equal distribution of poverty that the two young couples from the bus used in molesting her. Yet the word 'old' in that context had more than one meaning: perhaps the fur coat was inherited? Then, if it belonged to her grandmother, it meant that she came from a prewar, wealthy bourgeois family—one more reason to be hostile toward her. But if the reporter, in his wish to protect the girl, wasn't accurate in his reporting, and she was wearing a *new* mink coat, then perhaps her father really did buy it for her. In that case, she was a daughter of a new class, the so-called, 'red bourgeoisie,' and again despised as a symbol. But in spite of a profound, decade-long indoctrination, much as it was hated, a fur coat was an object of envy at the same time. A fur coat, whether old or new, is a visible symbol of wealth and luxury everywhere—the only difference is that in Yugoslavia and Eastern Europe wealth and luxury were for a long time illegal (and they become illegal every time the country sinks into a deep economic and political crisis, when, for a moment, post-revolutionary egalitarianism replaces a real solution). And even those who would like to believe in egalitarianism must ask themselves why we have to be equal only in poverty.

That same winter my friend Jasmina from Zagreb visited New York, and one afternoon we went downtown for some windowshopping in SoHo. It was cold—five degrees below zero—and we were wandering around the stores. Due to the fact that we had no money, we were enjoying the expensive clothes just as someone would enjoy an exhibition of modern art. We had such a good feeling of detachment, like when you are looking at a Van Gogh painting: you love it, no matter that you know you won't be able to buy it in your lifetime. An American acquaintance advised Jasmina to go to the museums—MOMA or the Metropolitan—that she had not seen yet. 'Sure I will,' she answered, 'but we, too, have museums. It's the beautiful shops that we don't have, and I need to see them first.' We laughed at the prices, amusing ourselves by converting them into dinars. We browsed through delicate silk blouses and crazy, glittering evening dresses. We tried on Italian shoes, pretending that we were going to buy them, but they were just too little or too big or we wanted another, non-existent color, or … We loved playing these 'buying games,' choosing endlessly, behaving as if we could buy if only we wanted to, discovering an element of playfulness, of fun in consumerism.

Either that day was too cold—like the day in Cambridge—or else at some point Jasmina lost her sense of humor. As we entered the Canal Jean Company on Broadway at Canal Street, she stopped in the fur department, looking at the coats there as if she was drawn to them by some magic power. 'Look, Jasmina, you don't need a coat,' I tried to convince her, as if need has anything to do with buying, especially in New York. 'No, no, I'm just looking at how unbelievably cheap they are,' she answered, hesitatingly. It was all so familiar, her argument, her wish to have one … She was right, of course, they were cheap second-hand fur coats, ranging from $20 to about $100. And she didn't need one, she wanted one. She looked at me seriously. 'Why shouldn't I buy such a coat? You know I could never afford it back home.' By now, all the fun of our shopping spree was gone; I realized this was not a game anymore. She had on a $50 astrakhan that looked as if it was made for her. Her red lips, her pale face, her long curly brown hair looked gorgeous as she spun around in front of the mirror. 'You look lovely,' I admitted halfheartedly.

We stood there, amid racks and racks of coats—foxes, wolves, ermines, minks, real tigers, sheep—smelling of old fur, mothballs, dry-cleaning chemicals, and stagnant, unaired cupboards. And we both knew what it was about. This was an opportunity to buy something more than a simple fur coat: it was an opportunity to buy an image, a soft, warm wrapping that will protect you from the terrible vulgar gray Varteks or Standard konfekcija coats you have been wearing all your life, an illusory ticket to your dreams. While we could easily toy with expensive dresses or shoes, the affordable fur coat was just too big a challenge. Of course, I tried the same last argument that years ago hadn't worked with me: 'Remember a poster we saw in some English newspaper, a woman dragging her bleeding fur coat? It says: "It takes thirty dumb animals to make this coat, and only one to wear it," or something like that.' Jasmina stood still for a while, then she said: 'Yes, I remember, but I don't think that you can apply First World ecological philosophy to Third World women.' With that, she bought the astrakhan coat.

Her words made me remember a TV interview by an Italian journalist with Fidel Castro, back in 1987. Surprisingly enough, they touched on ecology. Castro said he won't let his people have one car each. It is simply not possible—not only for economical but for ecological reasons. There are too many cars in the world anyway, he said, the whole of Europe is suffocating in cars. I was sitting in a small rented apartment in Perugia. It was early evening, the air was still hot, and sweat was pouring down my temples. But as Castro uttered that sentence, I shivered with cold. At that very moment, I detected for the first time in his words a frightening totalitarian idea in ecology—or better, the totalitarian use of ecology. He was asking his people to give up a better standard of living, even before they tasted it, in order to save the planet, to renounce in advance something that was glorified as the idea of progress. It seemed to me that asking for post-consumer ecological consciousness in a poor, pre-consumer society was nothing but an act of the totalitarian mind. We do live on the same planet, I thought, as his voice faded away, but not in the same world. It is precisely the Third World people who have every right to demand that the Western European and American white middle class give up *their* standard of living and redistribute wealth so we can all survive. Otherwise, the Third World will have to pay the price for the 'development' and high standard of living of the First World in the way Castro proposed, and he definitely won't be the only one to blame.

For obvious reasons, Castro didn't mention furs in his interview, but the idea is the same, particularly because the ecological way of seeing the world is forced upon Third World people—in this case, women—in the name of 'higher goals,' a very familiar notion in the communist part of the world. And I can hardly think of anything more repulsive than that. So, what are women expected to do, when they see it as just an old ideological trick? Before they give up fur coats, they certainly want to have them, at least for a while; and I'm afraid that no propaganda about poor little animals will help before fur coats have become at least a choice.

This very winter I stumbled into the same situation again, this time not in New York and not with a friend, but in my own house with my mother. She had decided to buy a fur. She was saving money for it, calculating carefully where and how to buy it, and even found a shop that gives three months' credit. I felt like a character in a classic, well-rehearsed play. 'Mother,' I told her, in an over-rational, highly pedagogical tone of voice, 'you live on the coast, it's not even cold enough there.' Mother looked at me as if I were speaking a foreign language. And I was: there she was, an old lady now. Fifty years ago, she was a young beauty from a wealthy family who was to marry a factory owner's son. Then she met a partisan, Tito's warrior, 'a man from the woods,' as my grandfather used to say. Not only was he a People's Army officer, but he was hopelessly poor. But my mother married him against her parents' will, leaving her rich fiancé behind (not a bad move, in fact, because soon enough he wasn't rich anymore; his factory was nationalized by the same partisans and communists, 'men from the woods,' that my father belonged to). Her whole life she not only could not, but was afraid to buy a fur coat because of my father's true communist morals. Now he was dead. She was too old really to enjoy it. Nevertheless, she had decided to buy one. What right did I have to tell her not to? What did I know of her life, of her frustrations and renunciations—of the clothes bought with a monthly ration card, of her desire to be a woman, not just the sexless human being propaganda was teaching her to become. It seemed to me that I just couldn't find the right words and arguments to fight her will to buy a fur coat. I felt helpless—and guilty of the same desire, too. Sitting at the kitchen table, this is what she finally said: 'You know, I have wanted to buy a fur like this for forty years.' She said that as if it was the ultimate argument, the final judgment, her last word about it.

Standing at the streetcar stop and looking at the lady dressed in foxes (I finally recognized the fur), I remembered all those doubts about fur coats. I hardly noticed two teenagers, a boy and a girl of about fifteen, standing there, holding hands, and giggling. At first they whispered, pointing at the fox lady. Then they deliberately raised their voices. 'Just imagine,' the girl said, 'that this fur coat starts bleeding somewhere near the collar. Do you think the lady would notice?' The boy chuckled. 'Oh, yes, I'd like to see that—a tiny red stream of blood dripping from each animal that was killed to make this stupid coat.' She heard them—she must have, they wanted to be heard. But her face was stone. They were not egalitarian-minded, for sure; they were too well dressed for that. Even if they were the same age as the two couples in the Beograd bus, these kids were of an entirely different breed—a new breed around here, I dare say—real ecologists. Perhaps to them and their peers their ecological consciousness is a bigger sign of prestige than a fur coat. Perhaps they feel on more equal terms with the world. I admit I saw the future in them. But they were aggressive and I didn't like it, in spite of their concern for animals. On the other hand, perhaps they are too young to understand that human beings are an endangered species and that they too have a right to protection—particularly in some parts of the world. I hope they learn this soon.

# PART SEVEN

# FEMINISTS

# CHANGING THE WORLD

The last part of this book addresses two clusters of issues—militarism and environmentalism—that clearly have global implications. Traditionally, these have not been regarded as special concerns of women; indeed they have sometimes been seen as no concern of women's at all. It is even less common to consider the environment and militarism as raising *feminist* issues—that is, as linked in any way with women's subordination. Nevertheless, the following selections explore a variety of connections between militarism and the environment, on the one hand, and the subordination of women, on the other.

The introduction to this book notes that an extraordinarily large number of feminist controversies involve sexuality and procreation. Militarism and the environment appear, at first sight, to be exceptions to this rule since they seem to focus exclusively on the so-called public sphere. Where they affect women, they seem to do so in nonsexual and nonprocreative ways, treating women as workers, soldiers, or consumers, for instance, rather than as mothers or lovers. Ultimately, however, the apparent separation between private and public turns out to be illusory in the context of militarism and environmentalism, as in many other contexts. Most discussions of women, militarism, and the environment involve more than passing reference to women's sexual and procreative capacities.

## Militarism

The most obvious reason militarism has often been regarded as no concern of women's is that in the Western tradition, as in most others, soldiering is the quintessentially masculine activity. But even though warmaking is supposed to be exclusively men's business, women are indispensable to Western narratives of war. From the Trojan War to present-day conflicts, women are those for whom wars are fought, those whom brave male heroes must at all costs protect from the ravages of the enemy.

The Western mythology of war portrays women in wartime as relatively privileged. While men on the battlefield face discomfort, danger, and death, women remain behind the lines in relative safety and comfort, keeping the home fires burning. Many feminists have noted, however, that the privileges accorded to women by Western war narratives in fact are mostly illusory, especially in conditions of contemporary "total" war. War has always brought a suffering to women that is directly linked with our subordinate social status. Recognition of this suffering is already implicit in the idea that wars are fought to protect women: women need protection precisely because war brings us special danger, the danger of rape by enemy soldiers. This theme is evident in the earliest war narratives of the Western tradition. On the surface, the fact that the decade-long Trojan War was ignited by the abduction of Helen, owner of "the face that launched a thousand ships and burned the topless towers of Illium," may be interpreted as evidence of Helen's importance. A city was sacked and hundreds of men died in her name. In fact, however, the Trojan War narrative positions Helen as little more than an object over whom warring men contend. The treatment of women as spoils of war continues to the present day. Even as I write, Bosnian and Croation women are reportedly held by Serbian soldiers, their fellow citizens until a year ago, in "rape camps."

The subordination of women is reflected and reinforced in other ways by militarism. For instance, militarism has been a major contributor to the feminization of poverty in contemporary Western industrial nations because the state cannot afford both guns and butter. A high level of military spending means less money available for the social welfare programs on which women, more than men, depend; moreover, women benefit less than men from the employment opportunities created by weapons production because they tend to lack the scientific and technological credentials that would qualify them for the higher-paying jobs in those areas. Additionally, militarist states typically press women to have many babies, which is difficult to reconcile with equality of the sexes. In general, militaristic societies encourage a culture of masculine violence that reinforces women's subordination. Thus, there are a number of distinctively feminist reasons for opposing war and militarism.

Twentieth-century Western feminists have been highly ambivalent toward militarism. Feminists have noted strong connections between militarism and citizenship: in the eighteenth and nineteenth centuries, the rights of citizenship were limited to those considered capable of defending the nation, and many privileges continue to be extended to those who actually undertake this task. Soldiers with distinguished military records, including career officers such as Generals Dwight Eisenhower and Charles de Gaulle, frequently go on to high political office, and, in the 1992 U.S. presidential election, Bill Clinton's candidacy almost foundered on the fact that he had avoided service in the armed forces. Many contemporary feminists conclude that women's achievement of full citizenship requires our full participation in the military. Only this participation, they argue, will break the symbolic connections between heroism, political agency, and masculinity, on the one hand, and vulnerability, passivity, and femininity, on the other.

Other feminists want to reassert, rather than jettison, the gendered symbolism of war and peace. Although they accept the traditional association of war with masculinity, they argue that femininity should be associated less with vulnerability and passivity than with nurturing and active peacemaking. They argue that war is incompatible with traditional feminine values and conclude that women's participation in war is a betrayal of femininity as well as feminism. Women, they insist, should not seek heroism and political agency on the same terms as men. Instead, feminists should oppose militarism and promote nonviolent means of conflict resolution. These feminist goals may be advanced by drawing on a long tradition of peacemaking developed in the West by both feminist and nonfeminist women.

The first article, "The Protected, The Protector, The Defender," explores some of the political implications of the gendered Western mythology of war. Here Judith Hicks Stiehm argues that the exclusion of women from combat positions them as persons who must be protected—and who therefore are made dependent on their supposed protectors. As the persons protected, women's social power is limited, but they are able to enjoy the illusion that they bear no responsibility for the atrocities committed, often in their name, by male combatants. Conversely, men, who are positioned as women's protectors, seek to carry out this responsibility by controlling women's actions and may come to resent the women whose helplessness imposes the burden of protecting them. Gendered protective systems are oppressive to both sexes in different ways, but the psychological consequences of participating in them are so complicated that dismantling them will require "delicate management." Stiehm asserts that these systems must be dismantled because they reinforce women's subordination. In conclusion, she suggests that women, too, must accept the responsibility of being defenders, not least because it is utopian to expect men to give up war and become "womanly."

That men should become womanly is precisely the conclusion reached by the author of the next selection, Helen Michalowski. In "The Army Will Make a 'Man' Out of You," Michalowski explores the ways in which the military both exploits and reinforces prevailing ideologies of masculinity and femininity. To be a real man is to be a good soldier, and to be a good soldier is to be a sexually aggressive and violent man. Michalowski speculates that military training may encourage domestic violence, and she insists that, rather than advocating women's entry into the armed forces, feminists should teach men to nurture life.

Despite the pervasive ideological connections between militarism and masculinity, women in Western Europe and North America have a long tradition of military service. Cynthia Enloe's "'Some of the Best Soldiers Wear Lipstick'" illuminates various aspects of women's experience in the armed forces. Enloe describes how men have consistently perceived women soldiers as threats to prevailing conceptions of masculinity and have attempted in consequence to recast women soldiers in ways compatible with prevailing conceptions of femininity. She also explains what motivates many contemporary women to join the military—often a rejection of the available feminine roles as well as a (vain) attempt to avoid the racism of civilian life—and she looks at the rationalizations given for excluding women soldiers from combat. She suggests that this reflects the military's desire to utilize women's services, deprive them of equal opportunities for career advancement, and maintain the belief that war is ultimately men's domain.

In the light of Michalowski's and Enloe's essays, it is entirely unsurprising to read the information in the next selection, "Surprise! Rape in the Army," which reports the widespread occurrence of rape in that branch of the armed services. The rape of women soldiers by their comrades-in-arms indeed may seem overdetermined by the military's encouragement and sexualization of masculine aggression coupled with its resentment at women's entry into the "man's world" of the armed forces.

The next readings in this section shift their focus from women within the military to women outside it, especially women who oppose it. Gwyn Kirk, in "Our Greenham Common: Feminism and Nonviolence," describes British women's historic resistance to the stationing of cruise missiles at a U.S. army base on Greenham Common in England. In the late summer of 1981, a group of antimilitarist women set up a women's peace camp at one of the entrances to the base and established an oppositional presence that remained until the missiles were withdrawn a decade later. During the years of the existence of the Greenham Common Women's Peace Camp, it became a powerful symbol in British political life and an inspiration to antimilitarist feminists worldwide who set up many similar camps in Western Europe and North America. Although the Greenham women frequently engaged in the sabotage of military equipment, they adopted a feminist strategy of nonviolence toward people, which Kirk describes in terms of six principles: assertiveness, enjoyment, openness, support and preparation, flexibility of tactics, and resistance. It is instructive to consider how far these principles may be useful in guiding feminist opposition to other aspects of the status quo.

Kirk's article is followed by a brief piece, "Greenham Common and All That ... A Radical Feminist View," expressing concern about what the author, Lynn Alderson, perceives as the nonfeminist or even antifeminist implications of the Greenham Common protest. Alderson complains that the protesters deploy—and thus reinforce— traditional stereotypes of women as closer to nature than men, an association rationalized by women's motherhood, and notes that Greenham women are portrayed in the media as white, slender, and apparently heterosexual. She asserts that broad-based *feminine* opposition to militarism distracts women from such basic *feminist* issues as domestic violence and the underlying system of male dominance. She concludes by warning that a strategy of nonviolence will not necessarily protect women from police brutality. Alderson's article was written in 1983, near the beginning of the Greenham Common Women's Peace Camp. It is interesting to note that later Greenham protesters consciously challenged conventional norms of femininity and that, as media portrayals of them changed they experienced increased levels of police harassment and violence, much of it directed specifically at perceived lesbians.

Unlike Lynn Alderson, Sara Ruddick refuses to abandon all aspects of traditional femininity. She is particularly concerned with reclaiming mothering for feminist and antimilitarist politics. Throughout the 1980s, in a series of groundbreaking articles that finally issued in her book *Maternal Thinking: Toward a Politics of Peace,* Ruddick explored the ideals that she found implicit in maternal practice, presenting them as resources that could be utilized by those seeking to resolve conflicts by nonmilitary means. In the present selection, "Notes Toward a Feminist Maternal Peace Politics" (drawn from the concluding chapter of her book), Ruddick asserts that, even though the belief in maternal peacefulness is a myth, since mothers in fact have often supported wars, mothering nevertheless is a practice whose aims and strategies contradict those of war. She wishes to revise Western conceptions of mothering to actualize its potential as a public practice of peace.

Ruddick argues that such a transformation of mothering may draw on two political traditions. One is women's politics of resistance, which explicitly invokes its culture's symbols of femininity in opposing state policies. Although women's politics has often colluded with unjust regimes, women have also been moved to resistance precisely by their commitment to fulfilling their traditional obligations of feeding and caring for children. In their resistance, they "fulfill traditional expectations of femininity and at the same time violate them." The tradition of feminist politics, committed to solidarity with women in struggle, encourages mothers to expand their caring beyond their own children as well as to be suspicious of militarism. Some feminists have been contemptuous of mothering, but most feminists have been "sturdy allies" of mothers, and "by increasing mothers' powers to know, care, and act, feminism actualizes the peacefulness latent in maternal practice." Feminism has these transformative powers regardless of whether feminists are antimilitarist because, as the slogan says, "a feminist world is a peaceful world." Mothering and feminism strengthen each other and together are capable of generating a distinctively feminist politics of peace.

Ruddick's article is followed by " 'They Won't Take Me Alive,' " a moving letter written by Eugenia, a young mother and a Salvadoran guerrilla fighter. The letter was written to her husband just before Eugenia's death in battle. At first sight, Eugenia's commitment to armed struggle might appear to contradict Ruddick's claims of maternal peacefulness, but Eugenia's letter makes it clear that her commitment to "Revolution or death!" is inseparable from her commitment to a just future for her infant daughter, whom she hopes will also grow up to fight for social justice.

The final reading in this section is Barbara Omolade's "We Speak for the Planet." Omolade criticizes peace activists for so framing the problems of war and weaponry that their special implications for women of color are ignored. Women of color face daily violence and holocausts perpetrated by white men. Whether women of color reside in so-called Third World nations deliberately underdeveloped by neocolonialism or in the devastated inner cities of the United States, they live in a state of permanent and institutionalized war, the threats to their survival going far beyond those posed by nuclear weapons. The wars against women of color and their children are not only overtly militaristic; they are also economic and social. Omolade questions whether women of color can afford a commitment to feminist nonviolence, asserting that "all successful revolutionary movements have used organized violence." Rather than abandoning the rhetoric of war, she portrays women of color as warriors, but her conception of struggle goes beyond armed force to the nurturing of children and simple survival. True peace can come only with justice; therefore, women of color fight for total change, for "a new order in a world in which [they] can finally rest and love."

Omolade's work suggests that it is too simple for feminists either to advocate women's entry into existing armed forces or to dismiss completely violent means of conflict resolution. Instead, we need to understand the systemic causes of conflict, to rethink the nature of war and peace, and to reconceptualize both mothering and warriorship.

## Environmentalism

On the surface, the environment, like militarism, is not a gendered issue. Just as women, like men, may fight in war, so men, like women, depend on the nonhuman environment for survival. Like the Western symbolism of war, however, our symbolism of nature is clearly gendered. The explorers, pioneers, and scientists who "master" nature are coded symbolically as masculine, whereas nature "herself" is portrayed as female and the earth as maternal. This cultural symbolism reflects a variety of connections between the degradation of the environment and the subordination of women.

Not all feminists agree on the nature of these connections. Some feminists challenge traditional associations between women and nature, associations that suggest that women are simultaneously wilder and more passive than men, "stormier," less rational, and less fully human. Just as some feminists claim women's right to be soldiers, so they also assert women's right to be explorers and scientists, to participate with men in exploiting natural resources for the satisfaction of human—including women's—needs. Other feminists, by contrast, validate traditional associations between women and nature, claiming that women are more attuned to nature than men, more compassionate and nurturing, less exploitative, and less responsible for the contemporary degradation of the environment. Between these rather simplistic extremes lies a range of other positions, some of which are explored in the readings in this section.

The first article, Karen J. Warren's "Taking Empirical Data Seriously: An Ecofeminist Philosophical Perspective," explains why the degradation of the environment is a feminist issue. Environmental degradation has more adverse effects on women's lives than on men's—not because women are "naturally" more susceptible to environmental toxins, for instance, than men, but because women's subordination forces them to bear the primary impact of environmental degradation. This occurs, for instance, through social practices that require women to compensate for the depletion of natural resources by working even harder and to compensate for children's vulnerability to toxic environments by bearing more children. Already lacking in social power relative to men, women become the victims of environmental policies that further reinforce their subordination. Not all women, however, suffer the same degree of environmental victimization. Warren notes that poor women and women of color, together with their children, suffer disproportionately from the degradation of the environment and concludes that feminist concerns about the environment must include environmental racism and environmental ageism.

Marti Kheel's article, "From Healing Herbs to Deadly Drugs: Western Medicine's War Against the Natural World," asserts that contemporary Western allopathic medicine harms our bodies rather than healing them, in part because it constructs nature as a machine and healing as a war. The dominance of this "heroic" medical approach results from the suppression by upper-class men of an older Western tradition of lay healing that relied on herbs and was practiced by women. Kheel recommends a return to holistic methods of healing, which she sees as integral to the concerns of the movements for the environment, animal liberation, peace, and ecofeminism.

The following reading, by Vandana Shiva, looks at environmental degradation from the perspective of women in the Third World. This is a concern for Western feminists not only because environmental changes in one part of the world frequently have consequences in another but also because, according to Shiva, Third World environmental degradation results from Western policies of "development" that are simultaneously neocolonialist, racist, and patriarchal. In "Development, Ecology, and Women," Shiva examines how capitalist and patriarchal conceptions of growth, productivity, and development are simultaneously a source of ecological destruction and gender inequality. She denies that subsistence economies that satisfy basic needs through self-provisioning are poor since their inhabitants are not deprived, and she advocates a redefinition of growth, productivity, and development as categories linked to the production, rather than the destruction, of life.

Val Plumwood's article, "Conversations with Gaia," explores the implications of the feminine imagery, particularly maternal imagery, used so frequently by feminists who write about the environment. To the extent that this imagery retains patriarchal meanings, Plumwood argues that it is counterproductive both for nature and women. However, she suggests some ways in which the image of Gaia, Mother Nature, may be rethought so as to be capable of providing a symbol and rallying point for an alternative culture that challenges patriarchal conceptions of motherhood and deity. In conclusion, Plumwood remarks that no single model is likely to be capable of capturing the diversity and complexity of human relations with nature and suggests that varying models with different implications are likely to be useful for different contexts. One possibility is a model of kinship as used by Australian Aboriginal people. Plumwood thinks this model is especially useful because it includes the idea of reciprocity between human and nonhuman nature, with humans nurturing the earth as well as being nurtured by it.

In the first article in this section, Warren asserts that no single ecofeminist orthodoxy currently exists. One inspiration for ecofeminism may be bioregionalism, which places high value on "women's sphere," home and its close surroundings. In her "Searching for Common Ground: Ecofeminism and Bioregionalism," Judith Plant suggests that women's experience of working in the home may provide a resource from which men, too, may learn to live more harmoniously with humans and with nature. She insists, however, that the notion of home must be rethought by ecofeminists so that it is no longer conceptualized as "less than" the male world of politics, the intellect, and the market. In the following article, "Women, Home, and Community: The Struggle in an Urban Environment," Cynthia Hamilton also draws on the concept of home, showing how in 1986 it motivated the women of South Central Los Angeles to environmental activism. Addressing what Warren calls "environmental racism," Hamilton describes how the women of South Central Los Angeles came together to oppose a solid waste incinerator planned for the community. Although "no one thought much about environmentalism or feminism" in the beginning, the women's concern for home and children, the domain for which women have traditionally accepted responsibility, inspired them to highly effective political action. Like the Chilean and Argentinian Madres described by Sara Ruddick, the women of South Central Los Angeles provide yet another example of the feminist potential of the traditionally feminine.

Ellen O'Loughlin's article, "Questioning Sour Grapes: Ecofeminism and the United Farm Workers Grape Boycott," explains how a study of the United Farm Workers grape boycott can enrich ecofeminist understandings of the connections between apparently different forms of oppression. Specifically, she argues, the struggles of migrant, predominantly Latino, workers reveal the connections between the monoculture typical of large agribusiness farming practices and the abuse of both workers and land; between health concerns and economics in both production and consumption; and among race, gender, and class. That many farm worker women fight together with men and are concerned about men's as well as women's and children's health does not make their experience any less significant for ecofeminism.

The last three articles in this section all address the relationship between women's fertility and the nonhuman environment. In "Stealing the Planet," Jo Whitehorse Cochran records how Euro-Americans have decimated the indigenous people of North America not simply through war and disease but also through the forced sterilization of Native women. Cochran asserts that this violation of Native women's rights to own and control their own bodies, deliberately perpetrated by U.S. government physicians, constitutes the theft of Native women's procreative freedom and even of Native children. She links this forced sterilization with environmental concerns by concluding that, if a people is capable of stealing the children of another people, "it is only a small matter of time before they do the same to our mother, our grandmother, our planet."

The so-called population explosion is often identified as a major cause of environmental degradation. In "Reproductive Choices: The Ecological Dimension," Ronnie Zoe Hawkins asserts that, as a backup to contraception, abortion plays an important role in limiting the ecologically damaging effects of the human population in all parts of the globe. Confronting "pro-life" arguments against abortion, Hawkins maintains that a recognition of human connectedness with all other life on the planet reinforces the need for abortion. She concludes, "When the interests of life in this larger sense are taken into consideration, the prochoice position is the one most deserving of the adjective 'prolife.'"

Not all feminists share Hawkins's belief that population size and growth are among the primary causes of global environmental degradation. Moreover, some feminists are concerned that since women bear children—though never without the participation of men—a focus on limiting population may be used to justify targeting women of color in repressive, dangerous, and sometimes lethal interventions designed to control Third World fertility. (Some of these interventions are described in Part IV of this volume.) A recent statement by the international Committee on Women, Population, and the Environment challenges these practices on the grounds that they are both misdirected and unjust to women. The committee asserts that environmental degradation derives from a variety of causes, including economic inequality and militarism, and will not be halted by reducing population growth. It also argues that improving women's social, economic, and health status is the only morally acceptable way to limit population growth rates. The committee calls for an immediate end to all forms of discrimination against women and for an international commitment to providing the essential prerequisites for women's development and freedom.

Feminist writing about the environment reveals new aspects of issues already considered in this book, such as procreative freedom, militarism, and meat consumption. It also traces additional connections among these issues while showing how racism and the profit motive degrade the environment, in part by simultaneously exploiting and reinforcing women's subordination. Ecofeminists assert not only that the degradation of the environment is a feminist issue because it affects women first and worst; they also argue that processes of environmental degradation will not be halted or reversed until the subordination of women is ended. As they construe the ideal of ending women's subordination, however, it turns out to require much more than equality either in the sense of assimilation into existing political and economic institutions or in the sense of revalorizing the traditionally feminine. Most of the authors in this section are explicit in arguing for the necessity of rethinking male-dominant understandings of such master concepts as health, poverty, development, productivity, mothering, home, and life. Ecofeminism thus points beyond equality, as traditionally construed, toward a total transformation of Western institutions and ways of thinking.

# The Protected, the Protector, the Defender

## Judith Hicks Stiehm

### Introduction

This is not addressed to those who have a principled commitment to nonviolence. I have studied that position (Stiehm, 1972) and I respect it. What I do not respect and what I even fear is a position which accepts violence as effective, as necessary, and as appropriately exercised by men only. That view leads to a society divided into those who protect and those who are protected; it may stand if other societies are similarly divided. However, a society of defenders, a society composed of citizens equally liable to experience violence and equally responsible for exercising society's violence is, I think, stronger and more desirable. My argument, though, is admittedly comparative: 'this would be better'. I am reluctant to be superlative—to say: 'this would be best'.

...

### The Protected

A person who is protected may be quite safe from attack. She may be so because a protector effectively threatens or uses force on her behalf. She, however, does not use force; for that she is dependent on her protector. She is so because men have a near monopoly on the means of destruction—a means as fundamental to government as the means (1) of production (analyzed by Marxist theorists) and (2) of reproduction (analyzed by feminist theorists).

Because few women clamor for access to the means of destruction, it is well to bear these analogies in mind. Women are not presently denied access to the means of reproduction even if there is a certain amount of debate over the degree to which they should be able to control them. Also, most feminists argue the need for access to the means of production and hence to meaningful work. They do not argue that women should not work at all because work is unjustly organized, nor do they argue that women will accept and support the current system of work just because they participate in it. Indeed, women who work outside the home seem to be more interested in, knowledgeable about, and critical of society's arrangements for production than are those women who depend on the income of others for economic support.

In the same way I would argue that women (especially women who have been spared firsthand experience with war) will be more interested in, knowledgeable about, and critical of military policies and organizations if they are expected and even required to participate in them. After all, if one deplores dependency in the economic sphere, do not the same arguments compel one to reject it (dependency) in the military sphere?

...

Just who are the protected? Presumably all citizens who do not protect. While a detailed, comparative study of draft laws and their exemptions cannot be done here, there are certain groups which are generally excused from military service. They include: the young (who can later become protectors), the old (who may have been protectors), the highly valued (super-protectors like the President, his cabinet and his advisors), the despised (homosexuals), the distrusted (in the U.S. communists), and women (who seem to be simultaneously highly valued, despised and distrusted by male rule-makers).

Government officials raise, supply and command the military. They consider themselves protectors even if they are civilians. Their perception of the protected can be deduced from the rules they make. But what image do the protected have of themselves?

For individual men it must depend upon the reason (high value, disdain, distrust) they accept as controlling their assignment to the protected category. For women it is different because all are so assigned and all are so assigned solely because of their sex. Those who are not feminists may not wonder why they are so assigned. Or, they may be willing to accept an on-the-pedestal argument about being 'too valuable' without absorbing the equally prevalent arguments about women's ineffectiveness and unreliability. Other women simply give the service they are permitted to give. In uniform they work 'in the rear with the gear' or they care for the wounded or the files. As civilians they produce for the war (see Rosie the Riveter) or they 'keep the home fires burning'. Such tasks are important and those who do them are rightly proud. They do more than women usually do. It must be remembered, though, that they are not asked to contribute as men contribute. Those who remain civilians will not receive the post-war benefits given veterans, and those who don uniforms will be a protected, exempt-from-combat subset of the military. Their accomplishments will likely be forgotten and some doubt about their motives for joining the military will probably be expressed (Treadwell, 1954; chap. XI).

Feminists can respond to particular policies in a variety of ways but surely all are obliged to consider why it is that men do not want women to serve as soldiers. They must ask: why are women circumscripted instead of conscripted? Why are they forbidden to hurt or kill for their country? Does a principle support such a policy? Does it hold even in times of emergency and danger? Or is it only a sentiment indulged in peacetime and far from battle?

I suspect that the policy of attempting to protect women from becoming victims and of not asking them to become executioners is a conceit of foreign war or peacetime. Since World War II civilians have had little immunity. Wars, after all, are fought where people *live*. Both the bombs of Hiroshima and Nagasake (Ibuse, 1978) and the guns and grenades of Vietnam and El Salvador have been indiscriminate. The hard fact is that, try as he may, a protector often cannot give protection. A vivid reminder of this is one of the last acts of the U.S. military as it left Vietnam. In a final protective gesture a plane was filled with Vietnamese orphans to bring them to the U.S. The plane crashed.

Not only can the protector not always protect, sometimes women (like correspondents, medics and chaplains) do take on the role of executioner. Most women, though, rely on surrogate executioners. For the most part their wartime contribution is designed to make it more possible for a man to kill for them. By doing this some women may be hoping to maintain 'clean hands'. But to use an agent is not to absolve. In fact, those who are distant from slaughter may increase the likelihood of it occurring. This can happen in two ways. First, their distance makes it easier for women to ignore, to condone or even to support actions they would not take themselves. Thus they bless, they give permission for, or they accept men's most atrocious actions. Second, the pressure created by the burden of having to protect the distanced women, may lead men to do (and to justify) things *they* would not otherwise do—even in self-defense. ... I fear the division of society into the protected and the protectors offers the occasion for an immorality which would not exist in a society composed entirely of defenders who each bear an equal and similar responsibility and who are equi-distant from any acts of violence. Again, when combatants share equally in risk and deed there may be some limit to their behavior; conversely, the most murderous and unforgivable acts may require an 'on behalf' of justification.

Distance has another consequence. Those whose job it is to motivate men to violence know that one does not stress that the enemy is 'just like' us. In propaganda materials the enemy is dehumanized. He is referred to as an animal or evil incarnate. Nevertheless, soldiers sometimes do experience empathy with their enemy; and sometimes their respect for and identification with him can lead them to honor him—to honor him even over their own civilians! (Gray, 1959; pp. 4, 146). Ironically, soldiers may have more *need* to stereotype the enemy, but it is the protected (who never encounter him) who may be most *able* to stereotype him.

Women's distance from and their indirect responsibility for war also means that they are likely to be poorly informed about it. They are likely to think volunteers complete their enlistment, that equipment works and that intelligence reports are accurate. An experienced protector knows none of the above are true and he may, in fact, be more cautious than the protected about making any action commitments. Thus we must consider the possibility that the protected are readier to endorse the use of violence than are protectors (although the protector's code does require that he never hesitate to accept an assignment) (Betts, 1977).

Just as the protector knows more about war than the protected, it is possible he also knows or at least thinks more about the protected than that largely unselfconscious group thinks about itself. The protector draws recruits, supplies and authority from the protected and their civilian protectors, the government. He thinks about them. He also derives another crucial support from them, if Virginia Woolf is correct, for she argues in *A Room of One's Own* that women serve as 'magnifying mirrors' which show men at twice their natural size. Such mirrors, she claims, 'are essential to all violent and heroic action' (Woolf, 1957; pp. 35–36).

In sum, the protected are essential to the protector. They (ignorantly) endorse and justify. The negative power the protected have, though, is only nonviolent. It is rooted in refusal, in noncooperation, in sacrifice. It entirely lacks the power to compel. The question is: how does having access to violent power make the protector different from the protected?

## The Protector

Being the protector has its moments. Even in the 'Saigon Hilton' (A POW camp for U.S. servicemen) a prisoner wrote on the wall of his cell 'freedom—a feeling the protected will never know'. That judgement is now offered on a wall at the U.S. Air Force Academy for the instruction of young cadets. J. Glenn Gray, a gentle and reflective warrior of World War II, noted that civilians would be foolish if they were to ignore the feelings of unity, sacrifice and even ecstasy experienced by the combatant (Gray, 1959). In James' *The Moral Equivalent of War,* the positive attractions of war are systematically outlined. James concludes that a stable peace will have to offer men an equivalent excitement, challenge and satisfaction (James, 1943).

But it is also true that war is often awful and meaningless (Orwell, 1952; Keegan, 1977; Herr, 1978). Indeed, most men would prefer not to fight; those who are truly anxious to fire and return fire are few in number. Most men get into combat, into a position of great jeopardy, because they are (1) coerced and/or (2) progressively entrapped.

Experts seem to agree that the combat behavior of protectors is guided by (1) the desire to survive and (2) the wish not to be disgraced in the eyes of their immediate peers—their 'small group' (Moskos, 1970). This would seem to deny the importance of either high motive or distant audience. But it is commanders who get small groups into dangerous situations and it is they (those who command) who are conscious of being history-makers and of the need to perform for an audience (Keegan, 1977; pp. 112, 196, 283). The support of an admiring public is sought by most commanders. The danger and the possibility of a non-consenting public is understood by them. Moreover, they know that war requires not just majority support, but overwhelming support. Guerrillas are said to be able to wage successful war with the ratio as high as 10 to 1 against them; also, a substantial but small number of active resisters can wreak havoc in the most compulsory system.

But why do the men who are called upon to do the actual fighting do so? In large part it is because of coercion. In wartime men are drafted. They are punished if they refuse to serve. Their basic military training is highly compelling and intended to teach unquestioning obedience, compliance, submission, i.e. coercion is used to make coercion unnecessary. Still, at Waterloo cavalry were positioned behind the infantry to fire on them if they tried to run away and officers flogged cowardly enlisted men (Keegan, 1977; p. 324). Actually, Keegan says, what keeps men fighting is that it is *MORE* dangerous to run than to stand. In fact, he argues that the scale and impersonality of modern warfare impels 'more effectively than any system of discipline of which Frederick the Great could have dreamt'. In Vietnam, after all, where could one desert *to?*

Leadership, then can be described as the art of getting men into inescapable predicaments. It involves step-by-step ensnarement. It capitalizes on men's knowledge that the odds are against their serving in combat even if they are in uniform, and also on men's unwillingness to resist the preliminary or routine. But even when under pressure and with bold leadership men do refuse to fight (Rose, 1981; Keegan, 1977; p. 271). This makes it easier to understand why military trainers, leaders and even peers so often resort to a trump card—the manipulation of men's anxiety about their sexual identity.

Men are called to fight when they are young. They have undergone some preliminary training by watching popular films. Indeed, World War II films like *Patton* and *Bora Bora* are still shown to troops as 'motivation', and one war correspondent described troops' behavior as acting out movie roles they had seen (Herr, 1978). Again, troops are young. The average age of the U.S. serviceman is 25 years. This makes him vulnerable to assaults on his gender identity. Eighteen-year-olds don't always act like 'men'—often they are even uncertain as to how 'men' should act. If they are told by men that men do such and such, and if they are surrounded by men and *only* men are doing it, then they will probably believe what they are told. This should be especially likely when terms like 'ladies' or 'girls' are used as terms of derision. When this occurs, men tend to feel they must submit in order to prove they are men. Incidentally, it also makes them feel disdain for women. While it is hard to be certain about the exact meaning of the connection between men's sexuality and their participation in war, it is clear that such a connection exists. The saturation of military language with sexual words and the association of rape with war has been noted by Gray (1959; pp. 61–68). Brownmiller (1975) and many others. Herr describes the first worry of the wounded soldier as his balls (1978; pp. 39, 142), and Ibuse notes that Japanese men assumed that an Allied victory would mean the castration of Japanese men.

If it is difficult to get men to fight, and if attacks on men's sexuality are an important part of the training repertoire, military commanders may be right to resist women's military participation. At the same time self-regarding women may be wrong to leave the institution which manages legal violence as the exclusive domain of men. It is hard to know. Reports about the behavior of all-male groups make them sound unattractive; it appears they may also be dangerous. But do such groups change because women enter them? Legislatures don't seem to change much, but male-exclusivity has not been a part of legislative principle for some time, i.e. law-making institutions do not depend on women's absence as either a justification for or as a part of their ethic.

But is it fair to say the military *depends* on women's absence? Maybe.

First, the young draftees being trained for combat frequently come from the less privileged part of society. They have little reason to be self-regarding or appreciative of the society. But, by excluding all women these men can be taught to revel in the joy of being automatically superior to a full half of the population. They can learn to appreciate a society which expresses its appreciation of them. Second, the myth of substitutability must be considered. That myth says that while few *will* be, everyone in uniform *might* be called to combat. That myth is disproved when U.S. women wear uniforms because they are (currently) barred from combat. Their being in the service is justified by the essential duties they do and by the fact that most military personnel do not see combat anyway. This is rational, but it erodes the substitutability myth. It makes it glaringly evident that all who share the uniform do *not* share the risk. This may be especially embarrassing for the 'unmanly' men, i.e. those who do the military support jobs women also do. One can understand why *they* would prefer not to have women in uniform. In addition, when large numbers of military personnel are not in the combat pool the likelihood of having to go is increased for those who *are* in the pool. Women's presence may not change the odds much, but it makes it impossible for military men to believe the comforting myth that all soldiers are 'in it' together.

Perhaps the essential, the general thing about a protector is that he has dependents. Dependents represent both a burden and an expanded vulnerability. A successful attack on them is a demonstration of his failure. In addition, dependents can be unruly and draining. The protector cannot achieve status simply through his own accomplishment, then. Because he has dependents he is as socially connected as one who is dependent (Dodd, 1973). He is expected to provide for others. Often a protector tries to get help from and also to control the lives of those he protects—in order to 'better protect' them. In its most extreme form such protection assumes the form of *purdah*, female seclusion.

In the U.S. and in other countries as well, a variety of restrictions on women's work have been proposed and sometimes imposed for women's protection. Now these rules are seen by some as a way of segregating the work force. Women always work. They do so at home, as a labor reserve, and also in the market place. Outside the home, though, the particular jobs they hold are almost always different from and lower paid than men's. Indeed, in the women's sector wages are so low as to make it almost impossible for women to assume the role of provider—of economic protector. They are, then, almost as precluded from being protectors in the economic sphere as they are in the military sphere.

Earlier we noted that the protector was perceived by other protectors as a threat. Now we must ask whether or not the protector may be a threat to the very persons he is supposed to protect, i.e. is there a tendency for a protector to become a predator. Charlotte Perkins Gilman once told her 'natural protector', 'As a matter of fact, the thing a woman is most afraid to meet on a dark street is her natural protector' (Gilman, 1975; p. 72).

What are the ways protector and protected may relate to each other? In the classic protection racket an individual offers protection from an ambiguous foe (in fact, himself) for a price. In Vietnam and Angola peasants' lives have been disrupted and diminished when they were moved into 'strategic hamlets' for their protection. In an alliance separate members are said to achieve security through unity, yet the alliance's existence and the provocative behavior of some members may draw violence to other or all members. How does it happen that so many situations which are said to enhance safety end in decreased safety? Is it possible that the greatest threat to one's existence comes not from a vicious enemy but from one's own protector(s) who may (1) deliberately exploit one, (2) manipulate and harm one in the interests of better control or of guaranteed safety, (3) attract violence by organizing one's protection, and/or (4) turn on one? Many governments, after all, simply *are* the military, and even in many civilian governments the military represents the largest budget item.

Each of the possible relationships listed above occurs at one time or in one country or another. Those which involve rather naked exploitation with the excuse that one will be protected do not require further discussion. The protection is not accepted and both parties know the protected (the victim) would get out of the relationship if it were possible.

The problem of oppression derived from zealous efforts to achieve perfect safety are known to all teenage girls. The problem is that the potential victim is both more accessible and compliant than the marauder. Because the protector is embarrassed and frustrated by his failure to protect, he restricts his protectee instead.

Europeans are now asking whether or not the military protection offered by the U.S. increases or decreases their safety. To some degree Europeans are like women— they are dependent and without direct access to the (worst) means of destruction. They rightly ask whether massive 'defensive' weapons which generate or reflect a mirror image defense in the supposed threat don't lead to double jeopardy for them. They realize danger could come either from their own suspicious, anxious protector *or* from their suspicious, anxious threat.

One might even ask whether a protector does not sometimes simply destroy those he claims to protect, and if so, when? This query takes us beyond exploitation, and beyond analysis of a protection racket which offers no real protection but only a restraint from predation. It takes us beyond excessive control and mirror-image provocation. It takes us to incidents like that of U.S. soldiers burning a Vietnam village 'in order to save it'. It takes us to the acts of cult leaders who require group members not only to give up their property but to shave their heads, and ultimately to take new spouses designated by the leader. It takes us to the Rev. Jim Jones and the Guyana suicide/murders. These perversions in which protectees were disarmed, degraded and finally destroyed, may seem beyond comprehension. Possibly 'speed' (drugs) is a sufficient explanation, but such acts may also derive from the way the protector feels about the recipients of his protection.

When there is no real work or duty required of a protector the role is satisfying, it makes one proud. As role demands increase, and/or as the chances of fulfilling the role decrease, the practice of the role becomes less and less attractive. The protected become a nuisance, a burden, and finally a shame, for an unprotected protectee is the clearest possible evidence of a protector's failure. The dynamic may be something like this. As one gains ascendancy one gains dependents, as one gains dependents their requirements for protection increase. This is especially true when the dependents are drawn from groups which are desperately dependent. Then a well-ordered hierarchy in which valued goods and services are exchanged does not develop; instead, the protector becomes like Hobbes' *Leviathan*. He assumes the duty of directing all-without contract, consent, or stipulation. At this point he may begin to abuse his followers hoping to reduce their numbers; ironically he may then find that they are reinforced in their commitment to him. He may continually increase his abuse only to find that he is more closely bound to his protectees than ever. Thus the most wholly dependent protectees may be just the ones most likely to trigger a nihilistic impulse in their protector. Conversely, those best able to help their protector defend them may be the safest—not only from third parties but from the protector himself.

In sum, the relationship between protector and protected is always asymmetric. One has access to force and one does not. One has dependents, one is dependent. Both are difficult states, and a range of relationships between the two exist from benevolent to malevolent. Unfortunately, the form which exists at any particular time cannot be predicted solely on the basis of knowledge about the protector and the protected; outside forces are often crucial.

## The Defender

A defender has access to the means of destruction/protection. A defender is expected to be ready to share in all risks and roles society deems necessary for its safety. In a nation of defenders the roles of the protector and the protected cease to exist.

When women are defenders and no longer confined to the category of the protected they are able to shake off the disabilities which attend dependency: low esteem, low level of information, and little sense of responsibility. As defenders they should recognize that protection cannot be guaranteed, and that the protected's role of providing justification, applause and magnification for the feats of protectors is no longer appropriate.

Coercion and entrapment would likely continue in the recruitment, training and management of defenders. However, a male defender would be entirely freed of the coercion which is derived from the manipulation of his feelings about this 'manhood'. He would also be free of the burden of having able-bodied competent adults as dependents—a fact which must surely contribute to misogyny.

Is the equality and reciprocity implied in having defenders a possibility? To know one would have to examine patriarchy more closely. In addition to an understanding of the male-female dimension of patriarchy one would need to know more about the father-son, old-young dimension. Old men run governments; young men are used and tested by them especially through participation in the military. Analyses which dwell on the alliance of mother and son against war have created literature; unfortunately, it is the dynamic between fathers and sons (vs other fathers and sons) which has created what is commonly called history.

Trying to understand the essence of being protected, of offering protection and of sharing defense is intellectually useful because it disassociates gender issues from those concerning violence. Nevertheless, it *is* men who are the protectors and it is men who are the threat. It is also men who make the rules about the exercise of legitimate violence, and it is they who exact support, honor and reward from those they protect. (In the U.S. veterans receive preference for government jobs, for instance.) Further, even if it is not so disguised as the protection racket practiced by young thugs on small merchants, the protectors of one nation share an interest with the protectors of other nations in making protected populations feel threatened (Edelman, 1971; chap. 9). Bullying and aggressive talk by the U.S. government makes Russian citizens cooperate with their government; similarly Russian provocations make U.S. citizens less critical of their government. Both governments understand that it will not do to panic an opposing government. In his role as threat a protector does not usually want to provoke another's protected population so that the government actually falls, for a stable enemy is usually preferred to the chaos of a situation with no 'responsible' enemy.

In discussing protection one sometimes thinks in terms of invincible forces led by the likes of Patton or Napoleon. But defense does not require the ability to master all or even any other countries. It only requires that one be able to inflict enough discomfort or damage or be able to call on reliable others to assist in doing so, that it is not 'worth' attacking one. Similarly a nation that is unified, patriotic and steadfast does not require a Patton; it can resist even if its top leadership is removed, for a sense of responsibility permeates the citizens (Arendt, 1970). Defenders, must however, always be ready; one's will and capacity to respond will be tested and one day's demonstration will not hold for a second day.

## Conclusion

Even if women insist on becoming defenders of their states, they will soon learn that the problem of protection, of the relationship between protector and protected is not easily resolved. One reason is that whole states assume the role of protector vs other states. Thus some states totally lack access to weapons which will be used on their behalf. These states must accept their protector's definition of any threat and of the appropriate response. They must accept others' acting for them. They must accept the role of justifier of the protector's behavior—and still they must accept the fact that their protection cannot be guaranteed. Indeed they must acknowledge that the protector himself is sometimes jeopardizing.

In choosing a policy to remedy this situation it will be important to remember how coercive (as compared to voluntary) any protective system is. Also, one must realize that any undoing of the many stages of entrapment will require delicate management. Finally, understanding the responsibility for dependents felt by protectors and the deep involvement of the male ego is crucial to any thrust toward change.

The point is that while military calculation is portrayed as the epitome of rationality, there is much about it that is not only callous but casual. There is much that is irrational and symbolic as well as lethal. In one's consideration one must remember that one does not justify the protector's burden by examining it nor does one succumb to masculine scholarship by studying men—that happens only if men are taken as the norm.

…

The first protector, of course, is a mother. Her special relationship to the means of reproduction and men's envy of it may in fact, contribute to men's (non-reproducer's) offering physical protection to women (as a way of participating in reproduction (Rich, 1976; pp. 56, 101, 21, 27, 216). If this is true, it may be necessary to reflect upon what is a fair share of the means of production, reproduction and destruction simultaneously. As Rich says, if men are given the care of children (perhaps) they will have to cease being children—and, incidentally, perhaps they will cease to toy with the tools of destruction.

Finally, women often speak for peace at the same time that they accept protection. They seem to believe protection can be bought; they seem to assume government is a matter of reason and law and not also a test, a trial by ordeal in which relative potentials for force are assessed and accommodated (Nieburg, 1969). Women seem too often to ignore the fact that much 'successful' nonviolence is related to having (1) a potential for violence to renounce or (2) having someone else use or threaten force *for* one. All in all, though, the most important thing to remember may be that in relationship to men women have long practical unilateral disarmament. That relationship has been asymmetric but by no means fatal. Perhaps men can be persuaded to practice it vs each other, but can one really imagine appealing to the governments of the world with the slogan 'Come, be womanly!'?

---

### Note

Helpful criticism was offered by R. B. Fowler, Jessica Porter and Steven Wayne.

### References

Arendt, Hannah. 1970. *On Violence*. Harcourt, Brace and World, New York.
Betts, Richard. 1977. *Soldiers, Statesmen and Coldwar Crises*. Harvard University Press, Cambridge.
Brownmiller, Susan. 1975. *Against Our Will: Men, Women and Rape*. Simon and Schuster, New York.
Dodd, Peter. 1973. Family honor and the forces of change in Arab society. *Int. J. Middle East Stud.* 4, 40–54.
Edelman, Murray. 1971. *Politics as Symbolic Action*. Markham, Chicago.

Gilman, Charlotte Perkins. 1975. *The Living of Charlotte Perkins Gilman.* Harper, New York.

Gray, J. Glenn. 1959. *The Warriors.* Harper, New York.

Herr, Michael. 1978. *Dispatches.* Avon, New York.

Ibuse, Masuji. 1978. *Black Rain.* Kodansha, Tokyo.

James, William. 1943. The moral equivalent of war. *Essays on Faith and Morals.* Longmans, Green and Co., New York.

Keegan, John. 1977. *The Face of Battle.* Vintage Books, New York.

Moskos, Charles C. 1970. *The American Enlisted Man.* Russell Sage, New York.

Nieburg, Harold. 1969. *Political Violence.* St. Martin's, New York.

Orwell, George. 1952. *Homage to Catalonia.* Harcourt, Brace, New York.

Rich, Adrienne. 1976. *Of Woman Born: Motherhood as Experience and Institution.* Bantam, New York.

Rose, Elihu. 1981. The anatomy of mutiny. Unpublished.

Stiehm, Judith. 1972. *Nonviolent Power.* D.C. Heath, Lexington, Mass.

Treadwell, Mattie. 1954. *U.S. Army in World War II: Special Studies—The Women's Army Corps.* Department of the Army, Washington, DC.

Woolf, Virginia. 1957. *A Room of One's Own.* Harcourt, Brace and Jovanovich, New York.

# The Army Will Make a "Man" Out of You

## Helen Michalowski

. . .

Male children are set up to be soldiers. The military takes the attitudes and behaviors already developed in young males and hones them to a fine edge. The attitudes include being emotionally closed, preferring power over pleasure, and feeling superior to women. The behaviors include domination, aggression, and physical violence to oneself and to others.

The military prefers to work on young men who are still unsure of their individual identity and place in the world. … In basic training young men are isolated from everyone but people like themselves where they are totally under the control of drill sergeants who conduct a not so subtle form of brainwashing. [In basic training, the man is made an object, dehumanized, subjugated.]

**Steve Hassna, Army Drill Sergeant:** There's Joe Trainee doing what Joe does best— being dumb. And it's not the man's fault. But it is such a shock to his—to his whole being. You take that man, and you totally strip him, and then you make him like a big ball of clay, and you take and you make him a soldier. Whether he wants to be a soldier or not, you make him a soldier.

... They taught me in drill sergeant's [school], get the psychological advantage off the top. Remain on top; remain the aggressor. Keep the man in a state of confusion at all times, if you want to deal with him in that way, but do not let him get his thing together so he can retaliate in any way, you know what I mean? If in doubt, attack.

... I was gruff—I was gruff to the point where I was letting you know *I am in command.* You might as well strike anything in your mind, any feeling, that you are going to do anything but what I tell you. (Smith)

**Victor DeMattei, Army Paratrooper:** Basic training encourages woman-hating (as does the whole military experience), but the way it does it is more complex than women sometimes suppose. The purpose of basic training is to dehumanize a male to the point where he will kill on command and obey his superiors automatically. To do that he has to be divorced from his natural instincts which are essentially nonviolent. I have never met anyone (unless he was poisoned by somebody's propaganda) who had a burning urge to go out and kill a total stranger.

So how does the army get you to do this? First you are harassed and brutalized to the point of utter exhaustion. Your individuality is taken away, i.e., same haircuts, same uniforms, only marching in formation. Everyone is punished for one man's "failure," etc. You never have enough sleep or enough to eat. All the time the drill instructors are hammering via songs and snide remarks that your girl is off with "Jody." Jody is the mythical male civilian or 4F who is absconding with "your" girl, who by implication is naturally just waiting to leave with Jody.

After three weeks of this, you're ready to kill anybody. Keep in mind there is no contact with the outside world. The only reality you see is what the drill instructors let you see. I used to lie on my bunk at night and say my name to myself to make sure I existed. (Letter to Helen Michalowski, December 1978)

**Robert McLain, Marine:** Talk to anybody who was going through Marine Corps boot camp ... the dehumanizing process is just hard to describe. I wish somebody had a record of suicides that go on at these places ... [and] the beatings that go on daily. Boys are turned not into men, but beasts—beasts that will fight and destroy at a moment's notice, without any regard to what they are fighting or why they are fighting, but just fight. I have seen men fight each other over a drink of water when there was plenty for both of them. (Lifton)

...

During basic training, the man's insecurity about his own sexuality is manipulated so as to link sexuality with aggression and violence.

**Unnamed soldier:** ... I [was] very stirred, patriotically [and thought] that I someday was going to have to, might have to, do this ... That I would get my chance ... I remember questioning myself ... saying this may all be a pile of crap ... this stuff about patriotism and yet because of this indecision ... the confusion within myself, I said ... I don't think I'll ever be able to live with myself unless I confront this, unless I find out, because if I [do not] I'll always wonder whether I was afraid to do it ... I had the whole question of whether I was a man or not ... whether I was a coward. (Lifton)

**Wayne Eisenhart, Marine:** One of the most destructive facets of bootcamp is the systematic attack on the recruits' sexuality. While in basic training, one is continually addressed as faggot or girl. These labels are usually screamed into the face from a distance of two or three inches by the drill instructor, a most awesome, intimidating figure. During such verbal assaults one is required, under threat of physical violence, to remain utterly passive. A firm degree of psychological control is achieved by compelling men to accept such labels. More importantly, this process is used as a means to threaten the individual's sexual identity. The goals of training are always just out of reach. We would be ordered to run five miles when no one was in shape for more than two or were ordered to do 100 push-ups when they and we both knew we could only do 50. In this manner, one can be made to appear weak or ineffective at any time. At this point, the drill instructor usually screams something in your face like "You can't hack it, you goddamned faggot."

... Once the sexual identity was threatened, psychological control achieved, and sexuality linked with military function, it was made clear that the military function was aggression. The primary lesson of boot camp, towards which all behavior was shaped, was to seek dominance. Our mission was always "close with the enemy and destroy him." To fail in this, as in all else, was non-masculine. Aggression and seeking dominance thus was equated with masculinity. Recruits were brutalized, frustrated, and cajoled to a flash point of high tension. Recruits were often stunned by the depths of violence erupting from within. Only on these occasions of violent outbursts did the drill instructor cease his endless litany of "You dirty faggot" and "Can't you hack it, little girls." After a day of continuous harassment, I bit a man on the face during hand-to-hand combat, gashing his eyebrow and cheek. I had lost control. For the first time the drill instructor didn't physically strike me or call me a faggot. He put his arm around me and said that I was a lot more man than he had previously imagined. Similar events occurred during bayonet drill. In several outbursts I utterly savaged men. In one instance, I knocked a man off his feet and rammed a knee into his stomach. Growling and roaring I went for his throat. I was kicked off the man just before I smashed his voice box with my fist. In front of the assembled platoon the DI (drill instructor) gleefully reaffirmed my masculinity. The recruit is encouraged to be effective and to behave violently and aggressively. (Eisenhart, *J. of Humanist Psychology*)

Physical violence against troops is more central to basic training in the Marines than in other branches of the armed forces. All branches associate masculinity with insensitivity, invulnerability and violence—only more subtly.

**Wayne Eisenhart, Marine and Counselor:** ... In [Marine] boot camp, there was a Private Green who had a good deal of difficulty with the rigorous physical regime.

He was slender and light complexioned. Private Green was a bright, well-intentioned young man who had volunteered and yet lacked the composite aggressive tendencies thought to comprise manhood. Although not effeminate by civilian standards, he was considered so in boot camp. He was continually harassed and called girl and faggot. We began to accept the stereotyping of him as effeminate, passive, and homosexual.

While in the midst of a particularly grueling run, Private Green began to drop out. The entire platoon was ordered to run circles around him each time he fell out. Two men ran from the formation to attempt to carry him along. His eyes were glazed and there was a white foam all around his mouth. He was beyond exhaustion. He fell again as the entire formation of 80 men continued to run circles around him. Four men ran from the formation and kicked and beat him in an attempt to make him run. He stumbled forward and fell. Again he was pummelled. Finally four men literally carried him on their shoulders as we ran to the base area where we expected to rest. We were then told that, "No goddamned bunch of little girl faggots who can't run seven miles as a unit are going to rest." We were ordered to do strenuous calisthenics. Private Green, the weak, effeminate individual who had caused the additional exercises, was made to lead us without participating. He counted cadence while we sweated. Tension crackled in the air, curses were hurled, and threats made. As we were made to exercise for a full hour, men became so exhausted their stomachs cramped and they vomited. Private Green was made to laugh at us as he counted cadence. The DI looked at Private Green and said, "You're a weak no-good-for-nothing queer." Then turning to the glowering platoon he said, "As long as there are faggots in this outfit who can't hack it, you're all going to suffer." As he turned to go into the duty hut he sneered, "Unless you women get with the program, straighten out the queers, and grow some balls of your own, you best give your soul to God 'cause your ass is mine and so is your mother's on visiting day." With a roar, 60 to 70 enraged men engulfed Private Green, knocking him to the ground, kicking and beating him. He was picked up and passed over the heads of the roaring, densely packed mob. His eyes were wide with terror, the mob beyond reason. Green was tossed and beaten in the air for about five minutes and was then literally hurled onto a concrete wash rack. He sprawled there dazed and bleeding.

Private Green had almost been beaten to death in a carefully orchestrated ritual of exorcism. In him were invested those qualities most antithetical to the military ethos and most threatening to the sexual identity of the individual Marines. Masculinity is affirmed through aggression and completion of the military function. We had been ordered to run around Private Green in order to equate passivity and nonaggression with being a clear and present danger. (Eisenhart, *J. Humanistic Psychology*)

Basic training not only links sexuality with dominance, aggression and violence, it also teaches that the man's very survival depends upon maintaining these attitudes and behaviors. By associating qualities that are stereotypically considered common to women and homosexual men with all that is undesirable and unacceptable in the male recruit, misogyny and homophobia are perpetuated in the military and in society at large. It is understandable that it would take a long time and a lot of work for men to undo the effects of military training as it pertains to their own male self-image and these images of women and gays.

To my knowledge, no studies have been done to establish or refute a connection between military training/experience and violence against women; however, it seems reasonable to suspect such a connection. The purpose of basic training is to prepare men for combat. That experience certainly affects men in their relationships with other people, especially women.

...

**Wayne Eisenhart:** ... One young veteran I have worked with became completely impotent three years after discharge. Unable to maintain an erection during the last three attempts at intercourse, he was afraid to try again. At this time he purchased a weapon, a pistol, and began brandishing and discharging it. His sexuality was blocked by a frustrated idealized male role which could not tolerate intimacy. The means to affirm manhood was through face to face combat, aggressive behavior, and the seeking of dominance.

... [There] is a constant fear of being harmed by someone and a constant elimination of real or fantasized adversaries in order to maintain a feeling of adequacy and security. My personal experience directly validates this. Since I was not exposed to much combat in Vietnam, I can only conclude that this process originated for me in basic training.

Perhaps this can best be articulated if I share some observations concerning my own intrusive imagery. Generally these take the form of daydreams. They consist of brief, very violent, eye-gouging, throat-ripping fantasies revealing an underlying hypermasculine ideal. There is usually a woman involved and I am always dominant and inordinately violent in defeating some adversary. These brief images leave me with a feeling of power and supermasculinity. I usually find that my muscles tense during such imagery ...

As a civilian, one generally attempts to create a more authentic masculine self-image that cannot help but be influenced by the military experience. Constantly in social and sexual relationships I have found myself trying to be "heavy," feeling at times foolishly as if I were a caricature of myself. I have striven constantly to achieve dominance. In the past more so than now, I felt insecure sexually and had a very low tolerance for feeling threatened. Occasional outbursts of violence have shamed and frightened me. This all has cost me dearly in social relationships. (Eisenhart, *J. of Social Issues*)

...

**Steve Hassna:** ... A lot of times I'd wake up in the middle of the night and throw [my wife] out of bed and throw her behind the bunker. And start screaming. She was scared of me. She finally left me. Because I would get to the point where I was so pissed off, I'd tell her, "Don't do it again; don't push me." I didn't want to hurt nobody, but I'd get to the point where I can't relate to people no more and so I just snapped. I was going like this until I realized what it was that sent me to Vietnam, indoctrinated from childbirth, the whole thing, I stopped having these bad dreams. Because I could see it wasn't me that was fucked up, it was my government and my whole society that got me this way. (Smith)

**Robert Lifton, Psychologist:** Falling in love, or feeling oneself close to that state, could be especially excruciating—an exciting glimpse of a world beyond withdrawal and numbing, but also a terrifying prospect. A typical feeling, when growing fond of a girl [sic] was, "You're getting close—watch out!" The most extreme emotion of this kind expressed was:

"If I'm fucking, and a girl says I love you, then I want to kill her ... [because] if you get close ... you get hurt."

... It is possible that he and many others continue to associate the nakedness of sex with Vietnam images of grotesque bodily disintegration—as did Guy Sajer, with memories from the German Army experience of World War II: "As soon as I saw naked flesh [in a beginning sexual encounter] I braced myself for a torrent of entrails, remembering countless wartime scenes, with smoking, stinking corpses pouring out their vitals." (Lifton)

When people are divided into distinct sex roles, the function of the female is to give birth and nurture, while the function of the male is to kill and die. Powerful cultural myths support the idea that the purpose of the son is to be a blood sacrifice— [God the Father sacrifices Jesus the Son, Abraham prepares to sacrifice Isaac.]

There are some parallels between the oppression of women and men according to sex roles. The media/cultural hype is similar—women love being sex objects and men love getting their heads beaten, whether on a football field or a battlefield. The appeal to virtue is similar. Women sacrifice themselves to serving their family, while men sacrifice themselves to the Armed Service. The cover-up is similar. Until recently no one heard about rape or battered women, and no one ever talked about men who come back from war sound in body but emotionally disabled. And who ever talks about the physically disabled?

One wonders if there is a statistical difference between the incidence of women coming to women's shelters who associate with men having had military or paramilitary (police) experience and those who associate with men not having had this background. ...

...

For the last several years women have been recruited to the military in unprecedented numbers; not because the military has any great interest in "equality" for women, but because the male population ages 17–21 has declined by 15%. There is a great and urgent need to deepen and broaden the popular understanding that while women certainly have the right and capability to be soldiers, for women to become like men have been would not be a step toward anyone's liberation.

We have to redefine the word "service" so that it is neither forced nor armed. Rather than women being trained to kill, let men learn to nurture life.

## References

Eisenhart, Wayne. "Flower of the Dragon: An Example of Applied Humanistic Psychology," *Journal of Humanistic Psychology* 17, 1 (Winter 1977).

Eisenhart, Wayne. "You Can't Hack It Little Girl: A Discussion of the Covert Psychological Agenda of Modern Combat Training," *Journal of Social Issues* 31, 4 (1975).

Lifton, Robert J. *Home from the War: Vietnam Veterans, Neither Victims Nor Executioners* (New York: Simon and Schuster, 1973).

Smith, Clark, ed. *The Short-Timer's Journal: Soldiering in Vietnam*, No. 1. (Berkeley, CA: Winter Soldier Archive, 1980).

# *"Some of the Best Soldiers Wear Lipstick"*

## Cynthia Enloe

The word 'Amazon' is thought to be derived from the ancient Greek words *a mazon*—'breastless'.[1] According to legend, each Amazon seared off her right breast so it would not interfere with her use of the bow. Over the centuries Amazons came to represent a nation of women warriors. Their home territory moved from place to place depending on the teller, but always Amazons were portrayed as inhabiting a region just beyond the borders of the known world, and in this sense, their story is a variant of the familiar tale about a distant land where everything is done the wrong way round.

What is 'wrong' about the Amazons is not only that they are women who fight using military equipment and tactics, but that they live without men. They govern themselves and require heterosexual sex only periodically for the functional purposes of procreation. Male warriors have imagined Amazon women as a military challenge *and* a sexual challenge—or better, as a sexual challenge *because* they dare to present a military challenge. Amazons have been portrayed simultaneously as sexless and promiscuous. In myth, victory over the Amazons therefore entailed their defeat in battle followed either by rape or seduction.[2]

...

Like the Amazons, Joan of Arc has become as significant ideologically as historically in shaping our images of women and soldiering. Unlike the Amazons, Joan of Arc travelled with male soldiers. She joined the fifteenth-century male-dominated military campaign against Britain in the service of a male monarch, who in turn represented French nationalism. But though she was in the military, according to Vita

Sackville West, one of her many biographers, Joan 'had no respect for military strategy or obligations'.[3]

It was this illiterate peasant girl's clothes more than her soldiering *per se* that symbolised her defiance of patriarchal, ecclesiastical authority. To dare to dress as a man—this was an act that shook the foundations of the French social order. According to the trial records, Joan had

> Given up and rejected female dress, had her hair cut round ... wore a shirt, breeches, a doublet with hose attached by twenty laces, leggings laced on the outside, a short robe, to the knees, a cap, tight boots, long spurs, a sword, a dagger, a coat of mail, a lance and other arms ...[4]

Joan's judges declared that such attire was 'in violation of canon law, abominable to God and men, and prohibited by the actions of the Church under the penalty of anathema'.[5]

For her part, Joan of Arc expressed bemusement. She explained—not to her judges' satisfaction—that she had been told by God to dress in this manner and that she simply ran less danger of rape—on the battlefield and in the English prison—if she dressed as a man than if she dressed as a woman.[6]

The question of attire crops up repeatedly over the years as male officials have tried to figure out how to use women in armies without altering what it means to be a *soldier*, a *man* and a *woman*. If women are called upon to soldier, should the government issue them uniforms that declare their 'femininity', at the risk of emphasising their sexual otherness in an essentially masculine institution? Or should women soldiers wear uniforms designed to *hide* their sexual identity, to make them blend in with men, thus sacrificing whatever privilege males get from being soldiers and whatever protection women are supposed to get from their 'vulnerability'?

...

Ambivalence about the meaning of women-as-soldiers continues to plague military uniform and cosmetic designers. A woman in the present-day American army is instructed to keep her hair short enough so that it just reaches the collar of her uniform but *not* so short that it looks 'unfeminine'. Women in the US marines must tweeze their eyebrows in a regulation arch. An American army recruiting brochure reveals the military's ambivalence and institutional nervousness: below a colour photo of a pretty woman smiling out from under a camouflaged combat helmet is the caption, 'Some of the best soldiers wear lipstick'.

Many women have disguised themselves as men in order to be soldiers, but women have always assigned their own meanings to soldiering. ...

...

Lillian Faderman tells of numerous women who joined military forces disguised as men. Henrica Schuria served as a soldier under Frederic Henry, Prince of Orange, and fought in the Seige of Boisleduc. When she returned home she lived as a woman, but had sexual relationships with other women. When one of her liaisons was discovered she was subjected to a public whipping.[7] Similarly, in early eighteenth-century Germany, Catherine Margaretha Linck disguised herself as a man and fought as a soldier with four different armies—the Hanoverian, Prussian, Polish and Hessian. She ended her military service in 1717, but kept her disguise as a man so that, as a man, she could work as a cotton dyer. In this guise she also was able to marry another woman. Later, however, she was discovered, imprisoned and, in 1721, executed.[8]

One of the most celebrated women to disguise herself as a man in order to soldier was an American, Deborah Sampson. She fought with the rebels in the American Revolution. When found out, she was discharged but not punished, perhaps because her masquerade was taken to be a sign of patriotism. She was later treated as a popular heroine, though by that time she had married a neighbouring farmer and become a mother.[9]

One of the best-known folk heroes of the American Revolution was a woman who has come down to us in patriotic lore as 'Molly Pitcher'. Molly Pitcher is the heroic version of a camp follower. She is never portrayed in a man's uniform. She is always clearly identifiable as a woman and a civilian. According to legend, Molly Pitcher loaded and aimed or fired field artillery after her gunner husband collapsed from wounds.

However, historian Linda Grant DePaw's research has uncovered quite a different 'Molly Pitcher'.[10] She was not one woman—she was hundreds. They did not stand in the wings until their husbands collapsed. They were deliberately organised by General George Washington to serve as members of Continental Army gun crews. Their collective *nom de guerre* was derived from their relationship to the technology of eighteenth-century warfare. Artillery pieces of this era became too hot to fire if they weren't watered down between shots. It was the task of the Continental Army's 'Molly Pitchers' to carry water to the male gun crews in pitchers, or jugs. Using women to carry water to the guns, reasoned the manpower-short generals, would 'free men to fight'.

The Molly Pitchers were in combat. They were at the front. But the ideological construction of soldiering was so tightly bound to *masculinity* and to *combat,* that the Molly Pitchers' biographers presumed a woman couldn't be in combat and was at the front only by singular accident. The Molly Pitchers after all were ordinary women; it was only a mythical Amazon across some distant frontier or a Catherine Linck in deceptive masquerade who could be soldiering like male soldiers. The experience of the Molly Pitchers at the hands of male historians suggests that women will be used deliberately by manpower-short commanders, but only within an ideological framework that preserves for men the privileges that derive from soldiering.

...

Women were used in the first and second world wars only reluctantly. Furthermore, women were recruited into the military force only when recruitment of men from usually marginalised ethnic or racial groups wouldn't satisfy the generals' and admirals' manpower needs. As always, sexual ideologies and racial/ethnic ideologies operated simultaneously to determine who the government would use in its armed forces.

Once the war was over, women were demobilised as quickly as possible. Any Amazons were pushed back across the frontier of social imagination. The world was put right once more. War and peace were portrayed as distinct—war abnormal, peace normal. In 'normal' times women do not soldier.

...

## The Recruiter's Game: 'Skirts, Travel and Opportunity'

...

The armed forces are offering today's women ... not simply the chance to learn military skills or demonstrate patriotism. They are holding out to women a chance to leave stifling families, dead-end jobs and home towns, without sacrificing the security those institutions are presumed to give women.

Some women, in fact, join the military, that epitome of patriarchy, to avoid or delay entrance into that other patriarchal institution, marriage.

Helen is an ex-nun. Recently she has been trying to figure out why she joined a Catholic order at the age of 17. She has talked it over with a woman friend who enlisted in the army at about the same time. Helen says that she and her ex-army friend have discovered that their reasons were strikingly similar: 'To get away from home'; 'To find a safe place'; 'To be with other women'; 'To put off marriage and yet do something parents couldn't oppose'.[11]

To a woman walking past a recruiter's window, the choice may appear to be between a part-time job at the local Wimpy bar and getting married or enlisting as an army driver, travelling to Cyprus or Germany. British women soldiers are paid 2.5 per cent *less* than their male soldier counterparts, but that is far less than the gap in pay in the British civilian job market, in which women earn an average of only 69 per cent of men's weekly pay-cheques.

The thousands of women who are joining the military may be part of a deliberate government manpower strategy to expand the recruitment pool in a time of declining birth rates, but it would be a mistake to think of them as mere puppets on the ends of military strings. Women are trying to make individual choices in societies that are structured to limit those choices. Military recruitment strategies exploit those limitations by playing on women's desire to be independent and economically secure and to live and work closely with other women.

...

Not all women respond to the 'economic draft'. Brenda, an American black woman from Long Island, just outside New York City, wasn't young or unemployed or stifled by life in a small town when she was attracted by the military recruiter's message. She was a woman in her early twenties who had been a black student activist at her university but had decided to leave her studies for a while to take a job with one of the urban development corporations that started up in the early 1970s. One day as she was making her daily morning trip to work on the Long Island railroad, she spied an army recruiting poster. The opportunities being offered seemed an appealing change from what was becoming a less than stimulating job. Without telling any of her friends, who she was sure would try to talk her out of it, she went straight to the nearest army recruiter's office and signed up as an enlisted woman. The recruiter didn't tell her about the possibilities for officer training for someone with a university education. So, during the next six years, Brenda served as a clerk, nutritionist, and finally as race relations officer with the US forces in West Germany at a base with 17 women and 70,000 men.[12]

The appeals offered by military recruiters are most likely to connect with the private aspirations and needs of those women who have the fewest alternatives for education, income, and autonomy. In France, it is from regions where the textile industry—a major employer of women—is failing, that the French military has recruited the most women.[13] Similarly, in the US, black women in the military far exceed their proportion in American society as a whole.

This was not always so. Black women served in the American military before the 1970s, but in numbers far *below* their proportion in the civilian population because of official policies of exclusion and segregation. For instance, during the second world war the navy's and coast guard's women's corps, the WAVES and SPARS, refused to accept black women until 1944, late in the war; the US Marine Corps Women's Reserve excluded black women altogether. The Women's Army Corps enlisted 4,000 black women, but relegated most of them to jobs as cooks, bakers, laundry workers, hospital orderlies and waitresses. Only one black WACs unit, the 6888th Central Postal Battalion, was allowed to server overseas.[14] Why the reversal in the 1970s and 1980s?

This reversal is dramatic. While black women are approximately only 11 per cent of all American women, by June 1982 they comprised 25.7 per cent of all women in the armed forces combined and 42.5 *per cent of all enlisted women in the US army:*

- Women were 9 per cent of all US armed forces personnel
- Black men and women were 19.7 per cent of all US armed forces personnel
- Black women were 25.7 per cent of all US armed forces women
- Women were 9.5 per cent of all US *army* personnel
- Black men and women were 29.5 per cent of all US army personnel
- Black women were 25.7 per cent of all US army women
- Women were 7.9 per cent of all US *navy* personnel
- Black men and women were 11.1 per cent of all navy personnel
- Black women were 14.8 per cent of all US navy women
- Women were 4.3 per cent of all US *marines* personnel
- Black men and women were 19.7 per cent of all marines personnel
- Black women were 22.1 per cent of all US marines women
- Women were 11.1 per cent of all US *air force* personnel
- Black men and women were 14.7 per cent of all US air force personnel
- Black women were 17.9 per cent of all US air force women.[15]

Virtually all of the political discussion of the racial composition of, and racism in, the US military has concentrated on black men. Black women have been filed under the problem heading: 'women in the military'. Institutional racism as it affects black women soldiers has been treated as a non-issue. This is emphasised by the recent book title chosen by American black feminists: *All the Women Are White, All the Blacks Are Men, But Some of Us Are Brave.*[16]

The disproportionate numbers of black women voluntarily enlisting in the military in the 1980s as well as their political invisibility needs to be explained in order to make sense of how the current military recruitment strategies exploit women's frustrations and hopes. Black women—especially young black women—suffer some of the highest unemployment and underemployment rates in the American labour force. They, even more than white women, live in conditions which offer few options. When a black woman does find a waged job, her pay is likely to be even lower than a white woman's or a black man's pay. Education beyond secondary school is hard to afford. Perhaps this also explains why black women soldiers have *re*-enlisted at higher rates than their white women counterparts. Still, as the 1982 documentary film *Soldier Girls* revealed, black as well as white women have not endured the male-defined military discipline without resistance. Slowing down the forced march, or smiling into the face of an angry drill sergeant can serve as forms of resistance to a male-defined, white-controlled institution.

...

## The Anxious Scrutiny of Sexual Difference

In both world wars the contradiction between the need to mobilise women as soldiers and the need to prevent women's presence from undermining the military's legitimising image of manhood was softened somewhat by the very notion that the time was peculiar and finite: female recruitment was only 'for the duration'. In contrast, current recruitment is less time-bounded and thus more acutely contradictory. It is being carried out in order to compensate for long-term demographic changes in society and because of the long-term need of the armed forces to acquire soldiers with educational standards that match their ever more esoteric weaponry.

Lacking the finiteness and ideological peculiarity of wartime, a peacetime military force relying on women soldiers seems to have an exaggerated need to pursue more and more refined measures of sexual difference in order to keep women in their place. Western armed forces now conduct official studies of pregnancy, menstruation and 'upper body strength' in an almost desperate search for some fundamental, intrinsic (i.e. not open to political debate) difference between male and female soldiers. They search for a difference which can justify women's continued exclusion from the military's ideological core—combat. If they can find this difference, they can also exclude women from the senior command promotions that are open only to officers who have seen combat.

Women soldiers, not men soldiers, get pregnant. A pregnant soldier is likely to suffer morning sickness, her performance will not be up to standard; her comrades have to do extra work to compensate. A pregnant soldier who gives birth and takes time off, even if the law (as in most NATO countries) allows her to stay in the military, is the soldier/mother who, it is alleged, is likely to quit so she can devote her primary attention to child care. Thus, many military officials argue, it is not surprising that women recruits have a high 'attrition rate', that is, a high incidence of leaving the military rather than finishing their tours or re-enlisting.

Military pregnancy studies omit the fact that in the US military it is *male* soldiers who proportionately lose the most days of active duty—because of drug abuse, going AWOL (absent without leave), and as a consequence of disciplinary actions. Despite all their supposed 'frailties', women soldiers lose fewer days.[17] Furthermore, some American black women believe that one reason that black women soldiers have lower attrition rates in the US military than their white sisters is that black women soldiers are likely to have children for whom they are the sole source of support, and thus are less able to have the luxury of giving up a secure military salary than are those white women with no children or with a second income in their families.[18]

Military commanders hostile to having women in their units argue that a soldier who menstruates is likely to jeopardise her unit's mobility and thus its 'readiness'.[19] Military establishments commission studies of the consequences of menstruation. Such studies, of course, can draw on a whole mythology surrounding women's bleeding. But these studies [were] conducted with special enthusiasm by the US military in the 1980s, perhaps because it is the US military that is under the greatest pressure to expand its manpower in an era when the American government is increasingly involved in global conflict and when it faces declining birth rates in the societies of all its Western allies. The American studies—conducted by in-house Pentagon officials and, increasingly, by civilian social scientists under contract—are readily shared throughout NATO alliance.

Pregnancy and menstruation studies are ideological sandbags piled up to construct an essentialist barricade that many senior military policy-makers hope will protect their institution against the onslaught of 'feminisation'. Their goal is to create an ideological/political climate which allows them to *use* women as soldiers without being *threatened* by them. One half-step above these studies are those which measure men's and women's 'upper body strength'. This is such a frequently used term in American military bureaucratic lingo that it has been reduced to the shorthand, UBS.

Upper body strength differences may be a weak defence against women's feared intrusion into the military's inner sanctum, however. As women who have broken into American all-male fire-fighting departments have demonstrated, upper body strength can be developed; equipment and team procedures can be redesigned. Thus the question of UBS is not quite as impenetrable a defence against feminisation as menstruation or pregnancy. For the time being, though, it will do as a patriarchal military stop-gap.[20]

The reasoning goes like this: soldiers assigned to 'combat' must *lift* and *carry* heavy things and *pull* themselves over formidable obstacles. Therefore, every soldier assigned to a role that the military commander chooses to define as a 'combat' must have a certain minimal body strength. Moreover, presumably, it is too taxing on a military organisation to test every individual soldier's UBS; it has to use gross categories to sustain its division of labour. So, if it can be determined officially that women as a class have less UBS than men as a class, women soldiers can be excluded from any role that military officialdom places under the rubric of 'combat'.[21]

As these biological arguments are circulated among NATO governments and picked up by the media, they help to reproduce patriarchal sexist ideas in the society as a whole. If a menstruating woman soldier is imagined to jeopardise national security, what are the chances of any woman escaping the confines of biological determinism?

...

## 'Tooth to Tail'

Most of the public discussion of the role of women in the military has revolved around the concept of 'equal opportunity', rather than the concepts of militarisation and exploitation. This liberal interpretation of the issue has been generated by women's understandable anger in the face of exclusion from certain jobs and thus from the skills and social status they can bestow. Such an equal opportunity preoccupation, however, implies that the military is 'just one more employer', an employer that happens to measure success in terms of kill ratios rather than miles-per-gallon or rates of profit.

Yet even women who believe that armies are qualitatively different from Ford or IBM can gain valuable insight into militarism by exposing how the military creates and rationalises its internal sexual divisions of labour. First, such classification systems don't merely reflect the larger society's sexism, they help to perpetuate sexism in civilian society by backing it up with the State's authority. Second, the military periodically adjusts its sexual divisions of labour to meet current material and political challenges. These adjustments do not occur without setting up internal tensions and contradictions. By examining these contradictions, women opposed to militarism can gain a greater sense of their own power. They know they are confronting not an omniscient monolith but, instead, an often divided and confused institution.

In military lingo, the ratio between 'combat' personnel and 'support' personnel is the 'tooth to tail ratio'. The thousands of women who travelled with pre-industrial armies as camp followers showed how weighty the 'tail' of any military manoeuvre can be. In the latter half of the twentieth century there are trends that are making the tail an even more significant factor in military calculations. Military manpower strategists draw more and more on the modern camp followers, whether as uniformed decoders or as 'civilian' secretaries, computer programmers and social workers.

Between 1945 and 1977, the proportion of the total enlisted personnel to be found in the American army's combat arms (infantry, artillery, armoured and related trades) decreased from 39 per cent to 29 per cent. Similarly, in Canada's entire armed forces less than 20 per cent of non-officer personnel are in combat jobs.[22] The US military's much hearalded Rapid Deployment Force (designed especially for use in the Persian Gulf) is an ideal example of this 1980s model of a streamlined combat force dependent on a large and complex support establishment. Today's 'New Model Army' will deploy front line units that will be 'lean'—tightly *integrated, flexible, mobile,* and capable of *mobilisation* at a moment's notice.

. . . Just when 'combat', that centuries-old site for testing masculinity, seemed to be fading into oblivion to be replaced by high tech software and white collar technicians, it was suddenly revived—not so much in numbers of troops as in military prestige. Combat troop effectiveness is now being spoken of with a new sense of urgency and celebration just at the time when many military jobs are being made accessible to women. A new exclusiveness is being created around 'combat'. The so-called 'airland' military model is being idealised in Western Europe as well as in the US. It is praised as mobile, flexible, integrated and technologically sophisticated (e.g. using helicopters, gunships, backpacked 'smart' weapons, faster than ever armoured vehicles).

Implicitly, these attributes are seen to require a no-hassle, men-only organisation. The entrenched military notion of women and femininity is really a *package* of assumptions: women are distractions, women lack physical stamina, women are unaccustomed to complex technology, women require special facilities. Whether as wives, prostitutes or soldiers, women 'slow down the march'. No such drag will be tolerated in the go-anywhere combat units of the 1980s and 1990s.

Yet such wishful thinking on the part of military officials does not mean that women won't be needed. In fact, if combat can be ideologically protected against the onslaught of women, then women can be *more* usefully exploited than ever, in the military's expanding 'tail' section. For instance, the French military has cautiously begun recruiting women. Thus far its elite feels every confidence in the survival of the institution's masculine ethos and exclusively male combat core. But since its defeat in Algeria in the 1960s, the French military has stressed its nuclear, high tech development. This in turn has required a build-up of its 'tail' section. By 1981, only 2.7 per cent of the French military were women. But *50 per cent* of its computer operators were women.[23] Similarly, of all the four branches of the US military, the air force has the highest proportion of women. In large part this derives directly from the air force being the most technologically oriented of the services.[24]

. . .

As Commandant of the US marines, General Robert H. Barrow oversees the lowest per centage of women of all the four US services. But women marines are being trained with guns in boot camp alongside male recruits because, after all, the introduction of even a few women must not be allowed to dilute the marines' overall image as the 'toughest' soldiers. Thus it is important to General Barrow to draw the boundaries between 'front' and 'rear' sharply. There must be no confusion:

> War is man's work. Biological convergence on the battlefield would not only be dissatisfying in terms of what women could do, but it would be an enormous psychological distraction for the male who wants to think that he's fighting for that woman somewhere

behind, not up there in the same fox hole with him. It tramples the male ego. When you get right down to it, you've got to protect the manliness of war.[25]

...

Two criteria are referred to when officials try to delineate 'combat'. The first is the social space in which it occurs: is it the 'front'? Is it a relationship of direct, physical ('eyeball to eyeball') conflict? Thus a woman who is serving in the underground crew of an intercontinental missile in Kansas can be categorised as 'non-combat' although she may some day set off a weapon which will do far more destruction than any 'combat' infantryman with his rifle on the 'front'. This short of definition prompts military officials to perform intellectual acrobatics in their attempts to distinguish 'direct, physical conflict' from the more subtle sorts of conflict. It may come down to: if a woman—as a *soldier*—is close enough to an enemy male soldier to be raped and/or captured by him, she is in 'combat'—that is, where she shouldn't be for not only her sake, but for the sake of the men fighting at her side who will be distracted and demoralised by such a possibility.

Weaponry is the second, equally malleable criterion officials use when struggling to define and redefine 'combat'. A WRAF woman holding a hand gun is not equipped for 'combat'. An American woman marine or any woman trained in the use of rifle but not issued one as part of her post-boot camp job is not a 'combatant'. A woman sitting at the control panel of a nuclear warheaded missile, but who doesn't directly *control* or *physically* wield that missile in her hands, isn't in 'combat'.

...

---

## Notes

1. Robert Graves speculates that it is more likely that 'Amazon' derives from the Armenian word for 'Moon women'; Graves, *Greek Myths*, vol. 2, Harmondsworth, Penguin 1955, p. 355. I am indebted to Lois Brynes for sharing her research on the origins and evolution of the Amazon myths.

2. One of the most thorough accounts of the history of the Amazon myth is in Simon Shepherd, *Amazons and Warrior Women: Varieties of Feminism in Seventeenth-Century Drama*, New York, St. Martin's Press 1981.

3. Vita Sackville-West, *Saint Joan or Arc*, London, Cobden-Sanderson 1936, pp. 169, 181. More contemporary and scholarly investigations of Joan or Arc are: Frances Geis, *Joan of Arc: The Legend and the Reality*, New York, Harper and Row 1981; Marina Warner, *Saint Joan of Arc*, New York, Alfred A. Knopf 1981.

4. Quoted by Geis, *op. cit.* p. 192.

5. *Loc. cit.*

6. Geis, *op. cit.* p. 167, pp. 184ff., 204.

7. Lillian Faderman, *Surpassing the Love of Men*, New York, William Morrow 1981, pp. 53–54.

8. *Ibid.* pp. 51–52.

9. *Ibid.* p. 58–60.

10. Linda Grant DePaw, 'Women in combat: the revolutionary war experience', *Armed Forces and Society*, vol. 2, no. 21, Winter 1981, p. 216.

11. Helen Horigan, in conversation, Cambridge, Massachusetts, November 1982; she ... [wrote] about her experiences for a ... collection by and about lesbian ex-nuns: Rosemary Curb and Nancy Manahan (eds.), *Lesbian Nuns Breaking Silence*, Tallahasee, Florida, Naiad Press, 1985.

12. Conversation with Brenda Moore, ... a Ph.D. student at the University of Chicago, at 'Blacks in the Military Conference', Wingspread, Wisconsin, June 1982.

13. Michel Martin in *Armed Forces and Society*, vol. 8, no. 2, Winter 1982.

14. Lorraine Underwood, 'Minority women and the military', Women's Equity Action League (805 15th Street NW, Washington, DC 20005), June 1979. Also: *Black Women in the Armed Forces: A Pictorial History*, Hampton, Virginia, Hampton Institute, Carver Publishing 1975.

15. These figures are from the US Department of Defense Equal Opportunity Office, June 1982, supplied by the Equal Opportunity Office, Office of the Assistant Secretary of Defense (Manpower), 15 October 1982. Such figures are published in June and December of each year and are available to the public upon request.

16. Gloria T. Hull, Patricia Bell Scott and Barbara Smith (eds.), *All the Women Are White, All the Blacks Are Men, But Some of Us Are Brave: Black Women Studies*, Old Westbury, New York, Feminist Press 1982.

17. Major Robert L. Nabors, 'Women in the Army: do they measure up?', *Military Review*, October 1982, pp. 50–61. Nabors reveals the weakness in each of the standard official arguments for limiting women.

18. This interesting speculation was offered by Brenda Moore, during the 'Blacks in the Military Conference', Wingspread, Wisconsin, June 1982.

19. Nabors, *op. cit.*

20. Interestingly, many men who are firefighters define what they do as 'combat'. Karen Stabiner, 'The storm over women fire fighters', *New York Times Magazine*, 26 September 1982.

21. Judith Steihm has traced this argument. See her book on the introduction of women cadets into the US Air Force Academy in the 1970s: *Bring the Men and Women*, Berkeley, University of California Press 1981, pp. 147–77.

22. Franklin Pinch, 'Military manpower and social change', *Armed Forces and Society*, vol. 8, no. 4, Summer 1982, pp. 585–86.

23. Michel Martin, a French sociologist writing in *Armed Forces and Society*, vol. 8, no. 2, Winter 1982, p. 317.

24. I am grateful to Nina Gilden for describing to me the 'tooth-to-tail ratio' and for alerting me to the comparative differences among the services: in conversation, Worcester, Massachusetts, October 1981.

25. Michael Wright, 'The Marine Corps Faces the Future', *New York Times Magazine*, 20 June 1980, p. 73.

# Surprise!
# Rape in the Army

WASHINGTON, D.C.—Women in the U.S. Army are 50 percent more likely to be raped than civilian women, according to the records of the military itself.

A Freedom of Information Act request turned up Army records documenting cases from 1987 to 1991 of women soldiers raped while on active duty. The Army rate for 1990 was 129 rape cases per 100,000 women. The nationwide statistic for that year was 81 cases per 100,000.

The newly-released records also show that lower-ranking women were the target of sexual assault most often. Of the 484 rapes that the Army considered "confirmed" between 1987 and 1991, five women were officers and 479 were enlisted.

The Army defends its record by saying that commanders are being told to increase education on sexual assault and to pursue rape cases aggressively. What's more, and in a somewhat contradictory fashion, the Army claims that lack of consistent reporting measurements and differing demographics make comparisons between the Army and civilian rape rate unreliable.

Critics of the Pentagon, not to mention of militarism in general, point out that rape is even more underreported in the military than in the country as a whole. Women soldiers fear, quite reasonably, that the male-dominated command structure will not take reports seriously, and punish those women who do dare to take on men.

The Army disputes the claim that they are run by sexist, vindictive power-mad men. Said one Army spokesperson, "We take all these [rape allegations] very seriously. We vigorously investigate and take appropriate action. ... One rape is too many."

So sensitive, but still, it just begs the question, if one is too many, what are 484?

*—info. from detroit free press and s.r.*

*news compiled by fpe*

# Our Greenham Common:
# Feminism and Nonviolence

## Gwyn Kirk

> Living at Greenham seems like a challenge, an adventure. It makes few compromises
> with mainstream society, it is an alternative, an outdoor community of women. Living
> up against the fence means that there is no switching off—the terror is on our doorstep.
> We experience autumn, winter, spring and summer as we've never experienced them be-
> fore. ... From our alternative reality, the world from which we come looks pale and com-
> fortless. We have to transform it. Not by reforms, but by revolution.[1]

In August 1981 a small group of women organized a peace march from Cardiff
(South Wales) to Greenham Common, a virtually unknown U.S. Air Force base in
England, 125 miles away, as a protest against the decision made by the North Atlantic
Treaty Organization (NATO) to site ninety-six U.S. cruise missiles there. They arrived on September 5. Some decided to stay. Others had to go home, but more
women came, doubtless never imagining that what was soon called Greenham Common Women's Peace Camp would still be there more than eight years later, an inspiration to countless thousands of people in Britain and around the world.[2] In Britain,
*Greenham* has passed into everyday language, a term both complimentary and pejorative. It is a symbol of hope, a style of creative, nonviolent direct action, an organizational process, a network of women's peace groups, a politicizing experience, a certain kind of woman, a style of clothing. The word represents strength, courage,
imagination, persistence, confrontation, marginality, deviance, and stigmatization.
In the nearby town of Newbury many people call the camp women "the smellies." ...

Throughout the first winter (1981–1982) women lived relatively comfortably in
tents, caravans, and tipis, with a portacabin office and a large shelter for a communal
living room and meeting space. Nevertheless, Newbury District Council forbids any
structures on Greenham Common, and since these early months this regulation has
been rigorously enforced for long periods of time. Women have had to live out in the
open or at best take shelter under sheets of plastic, sleeping in Gortex sleeping bags
in the winter. At times they have lived in old vans or "benders"—small shelters made
from bent over branches covered with plastic tarps. They cook over open fires. There
is one cold water tap, no electricity, and no telephone. A major part of life at the
peace camp is taken up with sheer survival: tending fires, drying out bedclothes,

keeping food dry, ensuring that everything is compact and mobile so that if there is an eviction women can move their belongings in minutes—before the bailiffs destroy them.

...

Women have maintained an unbroken, round-the-clock presence, surviving the bad weather of nine winters, harassment, evictions, arrests, imprisonment, and attacks by vigilante groups. Looking through the fence, we can see the missile silos and the day-to-day military routine, never forgetting their dreadful purpose.

...

Some women have come to Greenham because it is a women's community. Others make the campaign against nuclear weapons their prime concern and downplay feminist issues. Thousands have been drawn to Greenham during the years, and many have been profoundly changed by their experiences. The peace camp extends and develops traditional peace protests and demonstrations because it is a women's action, protesting in original and creative ways. But more crucially it involves leaving home, literally and metaphorically, speaking out about our anger, fear, and hope— being independent women.

Greenham is down to earth, heroic, moving, hilariously funny, and jarring. It is visionary and utopian with a timeless quality that is both very old and prefigurative of a simple, peaceful, postnuclear society. The consumerism and false sophistication of the industrial world are largely irrelevant. Without clocks and regular schedules, time itself seems highly compressed and very drawn out. The basic living conditions and simplest technology, together with the close friendships and womanmade culture of songs and rituals, are reminiscent of preindustrial ways of living. They also anticipate a time when the earth's resources are truly shared, when people in industrialized nations will live more simply, recognizing that peace cannot be achieved at the expense of other people's poverty, illness, starvation, and oppression.

...

The history of the peace camp does not seem linear; rather, it seems more like a rhythmical process, ebbing and flowing as the tide. The original camp at Yellow Gate has moved from sites near the fence to sites near the main road and back again several times due to evictions. In March 1984 the road up to the base was widened in an attempt to move the women, in what was described at the time as the eviction to end all evictions. Since October 1984 there have been evictions almost every day, yet women are always there. The peace camps at the different gates develop and evolve. Some have closed several times and reopened. There are times of reflection and reassessment and a slow working toward the next development. There are times of bitter argument and division, times of rejuvenation and times of holding on.

In this chapter I look at Greenham as an example of feminist nonviolence.[3] ... I use Greenham in a broad sense to mean the peace camp and the many women's peace groups and projects associated with it. I have been involved in this network since February 1982 and have participated in many of the actions and discussions mentioned here, although I have not lived at the peace camp for any length of time. (I use "we" when describing actions I was involved in and "they" when discussing those I heard about or observed.) For me, as for so many others, Greenham has been an extremely important focus, forging, however falteringly, a distinctively feminist peace politics.

## Nonviolence as a Way of Life

I see nonviolence not just as the absence of violence but as a total approach to living, an ideal to aim for and a strategy for change. In Gandhi's words: "The first principle of nonviolent action is that of noncooperation with everything humiliating."[4] Nonviolence means refusing to support a system based on cynicism, greed, and utter contempt for human life. Nonviolence applies to how we relate to one another, how we spend our time and money, as well as how we conduct our campaigns. It involves a dignity and power that come from inner conviction; a belief in ourselves, our creativity, and intelligence; and a belief that people can change and grow. It is a commitment to openness, a celebration of life.

Nonviolence is not meekly turning the other cheek, nor is it a routine tactic—a mass demonstration on a Sunday (perhaps outside a government building where no one is at work) with civil disobedience on Monday for those who want to get arrested.[5] However sincere and inspiring these actions may be, this is a caricature of nonviolence as a philosophy of life.

Without questioning the "success" of violence, many people deride nonviolence as naive and utopian, assuming that it cannot be effective or that it will have to be abandoned when the "real struggle" begins. Yet we cannot achieve peace through violence. It is a fundamental contradiction in terms. We are saying that nonviolence is a possibility, that nations as well as individuals can settle differences without resorting to violence—and must, given the potential devastation of nuclear technology. We undermine our argument if we use violence ourselves. In saying this, I am not telling other people how to judge their own experiences. Some situations are so oppressive that violence may be the only option for immediate survival. But nonviolence is not simply a white, middle-class luxury, a privilege of so-called liberal democracies, as is sometimes made out. At root, it is truly oppositional.[6]

## A Feminist, Nonviolent Practice

There are important overlaps between feminism and nonviolence.[7] At Greenham, women have brought a challenging assertiveness to nonviolence by expressing themselves unequivocally in confronting the police and the military. Feminist nonviolence is strong, empowering, and fun. Nonviolent actions include singing and keening or being silent; decorating the fence surrounding the base with photos of our family and friends, children's drawings, toys, clothing, colored ribbons, balloons, prayers, and poems; growing tomatoes in a shopping cart so that they are instantly movable in an eviction; softly calling out names of women we want to remember alongside the fence at dusk; cutting the fence and getting onto the base; painting messages on the roads; obstructing cruise missile convoys, wearing a badge that says

"War is menstruation envy"; changing the sign R.A.F. Greenham Common to read OUR Greenham C<u>o</u>mm<u>o</u>n.

\*     \*     \*

On March 8, 1983, International Women's Day, a group of women handed out "peace pies"—small cakes, each with a message about peace—outside the Bank of England in London. They had posters linking the squandering of vast resources on weapons with famine and malnutrition, particularly in the Third World. This action had a gentle atmosphere. It is unusual to be given something nice by a stranger in the street, and the action generated constructive conversations about peace and disarmament with passersby. On May 24, 1983, International Women's Day for Disarmament, women at a supermarket made the point that as taxpayers each family spends £18 (approximately $30) a week on arms. They walked around the supermarket with two shopping trolleys, one full of cardboard bombs and missiles and the other with £18 worth of groceries. To highlight the government's war plans, another group hammered crosses into the lawn in a local park, designated as a mass burial ground in the event of war. Others held a "die-in," blocking traffic at a busy intersection for four minutes, the warning time we would get before a nuclear attack.

I want to discuss six principles of feminist nonviolence in some detail: assertiveness, enjoyment, openness, support and preparation, flexibility of tactics, and resistance.

## Assertiveness

As women we often respond to events rather than defining them from the outset, or we hold back from saying what we really believe. By contrast, the aim of nonviolent direct action is to make a strong, clear statement. This includes each woman's ideas and convictions, the means employed to make that statement, the action, and the ways of dealing with its immediate consequences. We set up the situation on our own terms and keep the initiative by not allowing anyone to undermine our resolve. We choose temporarily to set aside feelings of fear, nervousness, embarrassment, or anger. Nonviolent action feels very strong to the participants, with a powerful unity of thought and feeling.

This is an important contrast to how many people (including some feminists and some left-wing activists) see nonviolence—as passive, reactive, and self-denigrating. It is important to distinguish between the surface appearance—women lying down in the road, for example—and the underlying reason for it. Although we appear to be surrendering our bodies, we are in control. We make a conscious decision to take part, and we can choose to leave.

So much of patriarchal thinking involves false polarization, including the ostensible polarity of being aggressive or being a victim. A nonviolent approach shows the narrowness of this conceptualization. Trying to understand and communicate with people who are against us does not mean that we have to demean ourselves. Being nonviolent in an action does not mean making things easy for the police or letting their violence against us go unchallenged. If they hurt us, we can say so clearly and loudly.

By blockading the gates at Greenham, women confronted the men who were building the cruise missile silos with the reality of what they were building and the police with the reality of what they are "protecting." At the first full blockade (March 21–22, 1982) women yelled to the police who were dragging other women out of the road to stop being used by the U.S. military; to stop defending the U.S. Army against British women; to think for themselves. ...

## Enjoyment

Women's nonviolent action is celebratory and life affirming and expresses our power, creativity, and imagination. Singing, music, colorful decoration, costumes, and jokes are important elements. Sometimes actions are planned to celebrate a particular day or season: the spring equinox, the full moon, or Halloween.

Some people who come to nonviolent direct action from nonfeminist traditions and who see it as an expression of religious faith for which they are prepared to suffer are not always comfortable with women's assertiveness. Yet nonviolent action *is* a confrontation. It isn't nice, although the confrontation can sometimes be effected in a humorous way. On April 1, 1983, a group of women in costume went over the fence at Greenham for a picnic on the base—they were dressed as teddy bears, pandas, a jester, a witch, and a hot-pink rabbit. Before being arrested they were escorted by the police and the soldiers, stiff-backed in their dark uniforms and camouflage jackets, theoretically in control. Beside them the women lolloped along, skipping and hopping, thoroughly enjoying themselves. Some people active in the labor movement deride this kind of action as whimsical, frivolous, indulgent, yet women undermined the authority of the military much more effectively than by shouting slogans. It was also great fun—a good example of politics that enlivens and feeds the participants, as it must if we are to keep at it and not burn out.

...

## Openness

A commitment to openness is another important aspect of nonviolence. We have nothing to hide or be ashamed of. It is our business to make public and visible what goes on at military bases, weapons factories, and academic institutions doing military research. This does not mean asking police permission to do an action, or discussing details in public, with strangers, or on the phone (which may well be tapped). In planning the fence-cutting action of October 29, 1983, women from the peace camp worked out the main points and visited women's peace groups around the country to ask them to take part. The action was billed as a Halloween picnic, but women who were planning to participate knew that at four o'clock different groups would all start cutting down the fence.[8] When faced with the reality of the base, women are often prepared to take unanticipated risks at Greenham, but there should be no "hidden agendas" for actions. Each woman should know what is planned, so she can decide what part she wants to play and make the necessary preparations, practical and emotional.

As it happened, one thousand women cut down at least two miles of the fence in several sections. About one hundred fifty were arrested, although probably everyone had expected to be arrested. The police and military apparently thought women would invade the base (a good example of their logic being different from ours) and were waiting inside. We had agreed beforehand not to go onto the base, and neither the military nor the Ministry of Defense police have jurisdiction outside it. Most of them had to stand there and watch, shouting into their walkie-talkies, "They're cutting down the fence! They're cutting down the fence!" The civil police were hopelessly outnumbered on the outside, which explains why so few women were arrested. The police managed to confiscate some wire cutters, but most women hid their wire cutters in packs or under their coats to be used another time.

Openness with one another is important in a coordinated action like this and in small affinity groups, but it is not essential in looser situations. At the ten-day gathering of ten thousand women (September 20–30, 1984), groups at the different gates took whatever initiatives they chose—organizing meetings, workshops, vigils, and blockades of the gates and on the main road near the base and shaking the fence. Some women went into the nearby town of Newbury (mainly hostile to the peace camp) with signs on their backs saying who they were and why they supported the camp. The underlying assumption was that groups would not undermine each other's actions, and although this could not always be foreseen, it worked in practice.

…

### Support and Preparation

Although the focus of media attention is usually on those who do the blockading or who climb the fence, the support work is equally important to the success of the action. Taking care of each other by providing food and drinks; watching out for people who are cold, upset, or overtired; and giving moral support and encouragement are essential. So is explaining the action to passersby and reporters and buffering any hostility. In the event of arrests, we keep track of what is happening, note down the numbers of the arresting officers, and contact a lawyer. Someone also goes to the police station and waits until women are released. As blockaders, for example, we can only really concentrate on our roles when we know that others are there, watching, supporting, and ready to intervene if necessary.

The care that goes into planning women's actions is crucial. Detractors and supporters praised the organization for the December 1982 two-day action encircling and blockading the base. Women organized firewood, water, food, portable toilets, parking, road signs, and child care and arranged for lawyers to be there in case anyone was arrested. The planners produced a booklet with a map of the base, details of facilities, notes on nonviolence, legal information, and songs. About three thousand women who took part in the December 13 blockade registered with a coordinating group beforehand. Some women had been meeting together, and a few groups had already taken direct action. The majority had never done anything like it before. But each person had a role to play and was immediately involved in talking through possible consequences with others in small groups to make sure each woman felt confident.

No one is pressured to act in a way she feels uncomfortable with. Every woman must make certain that she is doing what is right for her, not what someone else thinks she ought to do. This is very important because in other contexts we all too often wait to be told what to do.

Because other people only see the result of an action, or the aspects the media deem significant, the planning and support work that make it successful are invisible except for those involved. Many actions may appear spontaneous when they are not. Sometimes at Greenham events are arranged very quickly, perhaps in a couple of hours. The women living at the camps are involved in a twenty-four-hour continuous action, with opportunities to talk things over, get to know each other, and sort out logistics. They often take actions together. Some people describe actions at Greenham as spontaneous, as if they happen as a reflex, without consideration or forethought. This seriously undervalues the thinking and attitudes that women bring to an action, which may not be explicit or obvious but which come from an accretion of experience and past conversations.

### Flexibility of Tactics

Nonviolent actions require imagination and flexibility if participants are to respond as a situation develops and keep up the pressure. It is clearly impossible to lay down rules about this. We may decide to finish an action if there seems nothing more to gain, rather than sitting it out until we are dragged away and perhaps arrested. On occasions it is useful for some people to get arrested to show that they are not intimidated. We hope this will increase publicity and support for the point we want to make. But it is never necessary to be arrested to prove our commitment. When getting arrested becomes fashionable, it is time to do something new to keep the confrontation alive. If the police are very angry, we may decide not to provoke them further and agree to move or leave. If they are casual or patronizing, we may continue to confront them. Humming, singing, chanting, or keening may seem appropriate and will reinforce our physical presence through noise. Sometimes complete silence may be better. Our goal is to recognize the dynamics of a situation and keep the initiative.

There is a danger that nonviolent actions such as blockades or die-ins may become a new orthodoxy that is incorporated into what is "allowed," as has happened with rallies and marches. Tactics such as refusing to move when cautioned by the police or going limp on arrest may become new rules people expect to follow, rather than choices to be made depending on the circumstances.

Unpredictability is also important. The authorities simply do not expect to be continually challenged in creative, nonviolent ways. We can always take them by surprise. There are potentially so many of us, and they cannot anticipate what we will decide to do next. In this sense we do not know our own strength.

## Resistance

Being nonviolent is no guarantee that no one will be hurt. During blockades at Greenham, police have dragged women and thrown them on the ground, thereby causing severe bruising and sometimes concussion. Some women have had their fingers, wrists, and arms broken by the police, their feet and hands stepped on. Once soldiers were ordered to pull barbed wire out of a woman's hands, knowing she was holding onto it and cutting her badly in the process. The soldiers have a wide repertoire of insults and threats, often sexual and particularly offensive. They are also authorized to shoot women who trespass on the base if they judged this the only way they can make an arrest, which gives the lie to the government claim that the missiles are there to protect *us*. Vigilantes have attacked women, throwing paint, bricks, maggots, and petrol onto their benders and setting fire to the bushes very close to the camps. These vigilantes drive round the base at night, hooting their car horns, waking women up, yelling abuse and insults. Women's car tires have been slashed and car windows broken. …

Perhaps the most insidious form of harassment is what the women call "zapping"—microwaves or ultrasound that the U.S. Air Force is beaming into the camps.[9] Zapping interferes with brainwave patterns. It is silent and invisible, but the effects are strong and immediate, ranging from mild headaches and drowsiness to bouts of temporary paralysis. Other symptoms are pressure in the ears, vaginal bleeding and miscarriage, burning skin, lack of concentration, depression, irritability, aggressiveness, lack of confidence, a sense of loneliness, panic in nonpanic situations, and loss of short-term memory.

… The government, military, medical profession, and the press have all either denied that zapping could be going on or refuse to take up the issue. They attribute women's symptoms to stress, hysteria, or a cynical attempt to grab the headlines. Of course, it would be extraordinary if the military admitted they were doing this to unarmed women!

…

Women at the peace camp are usually very short of sleep and often completely exhausted, yet they stay and continue to make a mockery of the security of the base (which provides no true security at all) by constantly challenging and resisting what is going on there. They often get into the base in small groups, sometimes night after night. They have planted seeds inside; spray-painted buildings and the long runway with peace messages; climbed into the control tower; driven a U.S. Air Force bus around inside the base; taken official documents from offices and made them public. Women have managed to get into the driving seat of a missile launcher. Once women spray-painted a Blackbird spy plane, ruining its sophisticated radar-proof protective coating. Another time they put a message through the internal base telephone demanding that all planes start taking food to Africa to feed the starving and that the death games stop immediately.

Since cruise missiles arrived at Greenham Common in November 1983, women at the peace camp have been more pressured and threatened than before. In turn they have stepped up their opposition and resistance. Whether they are arrested, whether they are charged, and what sentences they get have all varied considerably. Sometimes they have been thrown off the base, as the least embarrassing outcome for the military, which shows that the line between legality and illegality is not as clear-cut as it is made out to be. The authorities want to wipe out the protest, but they have to maintain some credibility in light of the alleged openness of liberal democracy, and sending women to jail has only made more want to be involved.

...

The nationwide campaign against cruise missiles in Britain has been a campaign of nonviolent direct action right from the start, with women playing a central role. By living outside the base they forced the issue of nuclear weapons and disarmament generally onto the public agenda so that it had to be discussed and debated. ...

Women's enduring presence at Greenham has been remarkably effective in raising awareness of the dangers of cruise missiles and has served as an ongoing forum for determined, powerful opposition to their deployment. As the Greenham experience shows, sustained nonviolent action as enormous potential for challenging the status quo and for empowering those who take part. Women at Greenham have brought a feminist consciousness to nonviolence, expanding and enriching it by incorporating elements of carnival and confrontation. This is what has kept their protest alive, oppositional, and uncoopted for so long.

---

## Notes

1. Barbara Harford and Sarah Hopkins (eds.), *Greenham Common: Women at the Wire* (London: Women's Press, 1984), p. 5.

2. Cruise missiles have been deployed in Britain against the will of the majority of people, as expressed in opinion polls, and without any meaningful parliamentary debate. The decision was taken by top NATO officials and involved only a tiny handful of British politicians. The campaign against cruise missiles is much broader than the Greenham network and includes peace camps outside U.S. Air Force Molesworth/Alconbury, the second cruise base; many local actions; lobbying, publicity campaigns, and massive demonstrations coordinated through the national Campaign for Nuclear Disarmament. Two hundred fifty thousand people protested cruise missiles in London in October 1983, the largest British demonstration since the campaign for women's suffrage. I refer to cruise missiles in Europe as U.S. missiles not *Euro*missiles, as they are often called in the United States. They are made in the United States, paid for by U.S. taxpayers, and under sole U.S. command in Europe. ... [In fact they have been withdrawn under the terms of the 1987 Intermediate-range Nuclear Force (INF) Treaty.]

3. ... Also see Harford and Hopkins, *Greenham Common: Greenham Women Against Cruise Missiles* (New York: Center for Constitutional Rights, 1984); Alice Cook and Gwyn Kirk, *Greenham Women Everywhere* (Boston: South End Press, 1983); Lynne Jones, ed., *Keeping the Peace* (London: Women's Press, 1983); Caroline Blackwood, *On the Perimeter* (New York: Penguin, 1985); Ann Snitow, "Holding the Line at Greenham," *Mother Jones* (February-March 1985), pp. 30–34, 39–44, 46–47. ...

4. Quoted in Pam McAllister, ed., *Reweaving the Web of Life* (Philadelphia: New Society Publishers, 1982), p. 118.

5. *Civil disobedience* (from H. D. Thoreau, *On the Duty of Civil Disobedience*) is a term we do not use in Greenham actions. We prefer the term *nonviolent direct action,* which is a much wider concept that is not defined in terms of the state and includes many activities that are not illegal.

6. Much nonviolent direct action has occurred in Third World countries or against highly authoritarian regimes. See accounts from India, Guatemala, and against the Nazis in Europe in Gene Sharp, *The Politics of Nonviolent Action,* (Boston: Extending Horizon Books, 1973) Parts 1, 2, and 3; Alice Partnoy, *The Little School: Tales of Disappearance and Survival in Argentina* (Pittsburgh: Cleis Press, 1986); Marilyn Thompson, *Women of El Salvador* (London: Zed Books, 1986). (In the United States, the civil rights and anti-Vietnam War movements were important nonviolent campaigns.)

7. See Feminism and Nonviolence Collective, *Piecing It Together: Feminism and Nonviolence* (Devon, England: Feminism and Nonviolence Collective, 1983); McAllister, *Reweaving the Web of Life;* Jane Meyerding, ed., *We Are All Part of One Another: A Barbara Deming Reader* (Philadelphia: New Society Publishers, 1984).

8. Some women thought cutting the fence was violent and thus did not participate. Others argued that the fence had no spirit and did not merit respect: It served a destructive purpose, protecting a first-use nuclear weapons base and enclosing former public common land. Many women saw cutting the fence as an act of liberation. They could see through a chain link fence and could be sure that no one would get hurt, unlike throwing stones through windows or bombing buildings. These women contended, however, that they were not arguing for indiscriminate destruction of property. The outer fence at Greenham has rolls of razor wire on top of it. In an earlier action women put several thicknesses of old carpet on top of the razor wire and climbed over without cutting the fence.

9. See Linda Pearson, "Greenham's Unwilling Guinea Pigs?" *Peace News,* no. 2253 (September 20, 1985), p. 8; Louis Slesin, "Zapped?" *The Nation,* March 14, 1987, p. 313; Joseph Regna, "Microwaves Versus Hope: The Struggle at Greenham Common," *Science for the People* (September-October 1987), pp. 21–23, 32. ...

# Greenham Common and All That ...
# A Radical Feminist View

## Lynn Alderson

I have some serious doubts and disagreements about the politics of the women's anti-nuclear campaigns and their compatibility with feminist politics and aims. I am writing as a radical feminist who has not been involved in the actions or the organisations, but I want to comment on the impressions which come through the media of these, and make one or two more general points also.

I understand that Greenham Common etc. claim to be women's campaigns and not feminist ones. What distresses me most about them is the image of women that is coming through as the symbol and justification of these movements. On the T.V. and in the newspapers I see women saying that they are here for the good of their families, that they are simply "ordinary" women who are deeply moved by the urgency of the situation, that they are "naturally" concerned to preserve life and defend their children, that if there was no nuclear threat, they could go on being nice, ordinary women and all would be O.K. I'm sure you can see from this the stereotyping of women which—granted, it is coming thro' the media—but is also deeply interwoven with the politics and tactics of the women's protest and perpetuated by many of the participants. I was disturbed to see a picture in the newspaper of a Greenham Common woman giving her blessing to the statue of 'Peace' outside the G.L.C. The statue looked like a '60's model, young, thin woman in shorts with long, straight hair (obviously white), holding a dove. The airforce base is "embraced" and covered with (mostly) baby clothes and pictures. All this is precisely the kind of protest that is expected of and allowed to women. It is the traditional voice of the poor woman left at home who can only use emotional appeals (on *others'* behalfs) to influence those that do have power. Popular press attitudes (the favourable ones!) take the view that they really must start to take some notice ... if the 'real' women have come out of their homes—they'd better be pacified again.

This 'ordinary' woman (and she is only 'real' if she is 'ordinary') is the heterosexual, white, married-with-children housewife—the appeal depends upon that image to be taken seriously. I know that feminists and lesbians, the childless and black do participate, but that's not the point here. Every time this 'ordinary' woman is held up, those of us who are not her are betrayed. The approved version of all women which feminists have been struggling to destroy is constantly reinforced. This is not accidental, it is crucial to the politics involved, that is, for the appeal to have credibility it must come from a respectable source. This reinforces the assumption that women should and mostly do conform to those stereotypes. It also implies that those who do conform are not oppressed other than by the possibility of nuclear war. Being women-only doesn't make the campaign a feminist one, on the contrary, the ideas behind this kind of organising are actually in opposition to feminist aims.

The idea that women are naturally non-violent, could not be responsible for wars and the development of nuclear technology, that is, wouldn't even if we had access to weapons and science; that it is a particular female characteristic to respect life—this is a dangerous one for us to hold. It goes along with some biological notion that we inherit our behaviour with our genitals or that we are protectors of life because we bear children and that this is right and proper. This is odd, both coming from women whose intention presumably is to influence men and/or those women who very definitely don't conform to this image. It is a self-contradictory position for the feminists who are involved, since it is precisely that polarised construction of masculinity and femininity which they analyse as, at least, partly responsible for the problems of the patriarchal development and use of nuclear power in the first instance.

How can you influence men if such matters originate in masculine biology? It would seem a losing battle either way.

It is highly suspect for women to be basing any claims on their supposed link with the natural. Yes, I too feel turned-on by small, furry animals and mountain scenery, however, I feel no particular affinity to the tapeworm, or the male of my own species if it comes to that. I would remind everyone that the smallpox virus is as natural as the panda, but no-one calls it an endangered species! The point is, that our idea of what's natural is highly selective and inconsistent. The point is that we shouldn't be using that as some given, unquestionable criterion. Surely we've learned our lessons about the way that the so-called natural has been used against us. To base a campaign on that kind of (largely unspoken), but strongly present feeling is not only double-think, but it is not in our interests as women and therefore likely to have reactionary rather than radical consequences.

Instead of being panicked or guilt-tripped into thinking that we have to save the world from imminent destruction it's important for us to consider what creates these situations. Instead of fighting repeated, rearguard actions which use all our resources and don't alter the balance of power, we should be working solidly against the underlying structure of patriarchy. Women's oppression is fundamental to maintaining the system which is the backbone of our oppressive, destructive society. It is not a secondary issue to be attended to 'after the revolution', or after you've saved the world. You can't do either without it. ...

...

# *Notes Toward a Feminist Maternal Peace Politics*

## Sara Ruddick

...

Maternal peace politics begins in a myth: mothers are peacemakers without power. War is men's business; mothers are outsiders or victims; their business is life. The myth is shattered by history. Everywhere that men fight, mothers support them. When powerful men have not discouraged them, women, and sometimes mothers, have fought as fiercely as their brothers. As feminists insist that women and men share fairly the burdens and pleasures of battle, many young women expect their lives to include, without contradiction, both fighting and mothering.

Yet the myth remains intoxicating. The contradictions between violence and maternal work is evident. Wherever there are wars, children are hurt, hungry, and frightened; homes are burned, crops destroyed, families scattered. The daily practice and long-term aims of women's caring labor are all threatened. Though mothers may be warlike, war is their enemy. Where there is peace, mothers engage in work that requires nonviolent battle, fighting while resisting the temptation to assault or abandon opponents. The connectedness of maternal nonviolence is symbolized in the relationship of a birthing woman to her infant and of the infant to her adoptive mother. Although mothers may not be peaceful, "peace" is their business. Despite clear historical evidence, the myth of maternal peacefulness survives.

. . .

## A Women's Politics of Resistance

A women's politics of resistance is identified by three characteristics: its participants are women, they explicitly invoke their culture's symbols of femininity, and their purpose is to resist certain practices or policies of their governors.

. . .

. . . A women's politics of resistance affirms obligations traditionally assigned to women and calls on the community to respect them. Women are responsible for their children's health; in the name of their maternal duty they call on the government to halt nuclear testing, which, epitomizing a general unhealthiness, leaves strontium-90 in nursing mothers' milk. If women are to be able to feed their families, then the community must produce sufficient food and sell it at prices homemakers can afford. . . .

Not all women's politics are politics of resistance. There are politics organized by women that celebrate women's roles and attitudes but that serve rather than resist the state. In almost every war, mothers of heroes and martyrs join together in support of military sons, knitting, writing, and then mourning, in the service of the military state. The best-known instance of women's politics is the organization of Nazi women in praise of *Kinder, Küche, Kirche.*[1] Today in Chile, a women's organization under the direction of the dictator Pinochet's wife celebrates "feminine power" (*el poder femenino*), which expresses itself through loyalty to family and fatherland.

A women's politics of *resistance* is composed of women who take responsibility for the tasks of caring labor and then find themselves confronted with policies or actions that interfere with their right or capacity to do their work. In the name of womanly duties that they have assumed and that their communities expect of them, they resist. This feminine resistance has made some philosophers and feminists uneasy. Much like organized violence, women's resistance is difficult to predict or control. Women in South Boston resist racial integration; mothers resist the conscription of their children in just wars.

. . .

Women's politics of resistance are as various as the cultures from which they arise. Of the many examples I could choose, I select one, the resistance of Argentinian and Chilean women to military dictatorship, specifically to the policy of kidnapping, imprisonment, torture, and murder of the "disappeared." The resistance of the Madres (mothers) of Argentina to its military regime and the similar, ongoing resistance of Chilean women to the Pinochet dictatorship politically exemplify central maternal concepts such as the primacy of bodily life and the connectedness of self and other. At the same time, these movements politically transform certain tendencies of maternal militarism such as cheery denial and parochialism.

...

> *To disappear* means to be snatched off a street corner, or dragged from one's bed, or taken from a movie theater or cafe, either by police, or soldiers, or men in civilian clothes, and from that moment on to disappear from the face of the earth leaving not a single trace. It means that all knowledge of the *disappeared* is totally lost. Absolutely nothing is known about them. What was their fate? If they are alive, where are they? What are they enduring? If they are dead, where are their bones?[2]

Nathan Laks describes the Argentinian protest that began in Buenos Aires in 1976:

> Once in power [in Argentina in 1976], the military systematized and accelerated the campaign of terror, quickly annihilating the armed organizations of the Left and the unarmed ones, as well as many individuals with little or no connection to either. The indiscriminate nature of the kidnapping campaign and the impunity with which it was carried out spread terror—as intended. Relationships among friends and relatives were shattered by unprecedented fear. Perfectly decent individuals suddenly became afraid even to visit the parents of a kidnap victim, for any such gesture of compassion might condemn the visitor to a terrible fate. In this terrorized society, a small organization of women, mothers and other relatives of kidnapped Argentines staged a stunning act of defiance. One Thursday afternoon they gathered in the Plaza de Mayo, the main square in Buenos Aires and the site of countless historic incidents beginning in 1810 with the events that led to Argentina's separation from the Spanish Empire. In the center of the Plaza de Mayo, within clear sight of the presidential palace, the national cathedral, and several headquarters of ministries and corporations, the Mothers paraded in a closed circle.[3]

The Madres met each other outside hospitals or prisons, where they took food and other provisions and looked for traces of the disappeared, or outside government offices, where they tried, almost invariably without success, to get some accounting of their loved ones' whereabouts. When they marched, the Madres wore white kerchiefs with the names of the disappeared embroidered on them. Often they carried lighted candles and almost always they wore or carried photographs of the disappeared. In Chile, women chained themselves to the steps of the capitol, formed a human chain to a mine, Lonquen, where a mass grave was discovered, and took over a stadium where disappeared people had been rounded up, later to be tortured and killed.

The Latin American women's movements are clearly politics of resistance. The women who engage in them court imprisonment and torture and in some cases have become "disappeared" themselves. Knowing what fearful things could happen to them, women in Chile trained themselves to name and deal with what they feared:

> If they were afraid of facing police, they were told simply to find a policeman and stare at him until they could see him as a man and not as a representative of the state. [They] circled police vans on foot, until these symbols of the regime appeared as just another kind of motor vehicle. ... The women also instructed one another how to deal with the tear gas ... to stop eating two hours before demonstrations, to dress in casual clothing, to take off makeup but to put salt on their cheekbones to keep teargas powder from entering their eyes, ... to carry lemon to avoid teargas sting and to get a jar with homemade smelling salts made up of salt and ammonia.[4]

The women talked among themselves about their terrors, found others who shared their fears, and marched with them in affinity groups. And thus they brought their bodies to bear against the state.

As in many women's politics of resistance, the Argentinian and Chilean women emphasize mothering among women's many relations. They are Madres, whether or not they are biological or adoptive mothers of individual disappeared; a later group is made up of Abuelas (grandmothers). Their presence and the character of their action, as well as the interviews they have given, invariably evoke an experience of mothering that is central to their lives, whatever other home work or wage labor they engage in. Repeatedly they remember and allude to ordinary tasks—clothing, feeding, sheltering, and most of all tending to extensive kin work. All these works, ordinarily taken for granted, are dramatically present just because they are interrupted; they are made starkly visible through the eerie "disappearance," the shattering mockery of a maternal and childlike "unchanging expectation of good in the heart."[5]

As these women honor mothering, they honor themselves. The destruction of the lives of their children, often just on the verge of adulthood, destroys years of their work; their loss and the impossibility of mourning it constitute a violent outrage against them. Yet there is something misleading about this way of talking. The women do not speak of their work but of their children; they carry children's photographs, not their own. The distinctive structuring of the relation between self and other, symbolized in birth and enacted in mothering, is now politicized. The children, the absent ones, are *not* their mothers, who have decidedly *not* disappeared but are bodily present. The singular, irreplaceable children are lost. Yet as the pictures the Madres carry suggest, the children are not, even in disappearance, apart from their mothers but, in their absence, are still inseparable from them.

For these Argentinian and Chilean women, as for women in most cultures, mothering is intuitively or "naturally" connected to giving birth. The Abuelas, especially, have made a political point of the emotional significance of genetic continuity. Since the fall of the military regime, one of their projects has been to form a genetic bank to trace the biological parentage of children adopted by people close to the ruling class at the time the military was in power. The insistence on genetic connection is one aspect of a general affirmation of the body. Indeed, the vulnerability, promise, and power of human bodies is central to this women's politics of resistance, as it is to maternal practice. ... Because they have suffered military violence—have been stripped naked, sexually humiliated, and tortured—children's bodies have become a locus of pain. Because the violation of bodies is meant to terrify the body itself becomes a place where terror is wrought. In resistance to this violation mothers' bodies become instruments of nonviolent power. Adorned with representations of bodies loved and violated, they express the necessity of love even amid terror, "in the teeth of all experience of crimes committed, suffered and witnessed."[6]

In their protests, these women fulfill traditional expectations of femininity and at the same time violate them. ... Women who bring to the public plazas of a police state pictures of their loved ones, like women who put pillowcases, toys, and other artifacts of attachment against the barbed wire fences of missile bases, translate the symbols of mothering into political speech. Preservative love, singularity in connection, the promise of birth and the resilience of hope, the irreplaceable treasure of vulnerable bodily being—these clichés of maternal work are enacted in public, by women insisting that their governors name and take responsibility for their crimes. They speak a "women's language" of loyalty, love, and outrage; but they speak with a public anger in a public place in ways they were never meant to do.

...

A woman's politics of resistance is not inherently a peace politics. Women can organize to sabotage peace treaties or to celebrate the heroes and martyrs of organized violence. During the Malvinas-Falklands war, Argentinian and English women sought each other out at a women's meeting in New York to denounce together their countries' militarism and imperialism. Yet during that same war, the Argentinian Madres were reported to use patriotic rhetoric to reinforce their own aims: "The Malvinas belong to us and so do our sons."

...

Whatever their militarist sentiments or rhetoric, the Argentinian and Chilean protests express to the world the ideals of nonviolence. ... The protesters did not set out to injure but to end injuring. None of their actions even risked serious, lasting physical damage. ... Like the maternal practice from which it grows, a women's politics of resistance may remain racial, tribal, or chauvinist; we cannot expect of women in resistance the rare human ability to stand in solidarity with all victims of violence. Yet if these Latin American protests are at all emblematic, they suggest that the peacefulness latent in maternal practice tends to be realized as participants act against, and therefore reflect on, violence itself.

## Feminist Politics

There is no litmus test for identifying a "feminist." ... When I speak of feminism I refer, minimally, to a politics that is dedicated to transforming those social and domestic arrangements that deliberately or unwittingly penalize women because of their sex. Second, whatever their other politics and interests, feminists focus seriously on the ways that gender—the social construction of masculinity and femininity—organizes political, personal, and intellectual life. The feminist assumption is that gender divisions of work, pleasure, power, and sensibility are socially created, detrimental to women and, to a lesser degree, to men, and therefore can and should be changed. Most important, though perhaps controversially, feminists are partisans of women,[7] fighting on their side, sometimes against, often with, men. As women, or in solidarity with them, feminists struggle against any social, racial, economic, or physical abuse that threatens women's capacity to work and to love.

This ... definition ... in no way commits feminists to antimilitarism. In many parts of the world, feminist women organize to procure arms in defense of themselves and their people. ...

...

... The feminist soldier heroine may be most perfectly represented by a young woman with a baby in her arms and a gun over her shoulder, although an armed girl dressed as and sometimes passing for a comely man is a close second. The many distinctly feminine, and often distinctly sexy, soldier heroines of exemplary spirit simultaneously domesticate violence, expand women's imaginative aggressiveness, and rewrite, in a manner titillating and scary, the sexual scripts of battle.

Whether or not feminists are militarist, feminist politics transforms maternal militarism. ...

... The confrontation of mothers and feminists—whether practical or psychological—is deeply beneficial to mothering. Although some feminists have indeed been guilty of contempt for mothers, no other movement has taken so seriously or worked so effectively to ensure women's economic and psychological ability to engage in mothering without undue sacrifice of physical health and nonmaternal projects. Organizing women workers, fighting for day-care centers, adequate health care, and maternal and parental leave, demanding birthgivers' right to participate in mothering as and when they choose—in these and many other struggles feminists have proved many times over that, as partisans of women, they are sturdy allies of mothers. In this practical support of mothers in their daily work the feminist transformation of maternal militarism is rooted.

Either because of their own experience of sexual prejudice and abuse or because they are heartened by particular feminist policies and fights on their behalf, many previously skeptical mothers become feminists. ...

...

... It is a feminist project to describe realistically the angers and ambivalences of maternal love. A feminist consciousness also requires mothers to look undefensively at women's social status and the political relations between men and women, which exact from mothers—even those who are men—unnecessary and unacceptable sacrifices of power and pleasures.

...

... Feminist habits of lucidity strengthen maternal nonviolence in distinctive ways. ...

...

... A feminist mother becomes increasingly clear-sighted about the violences she has suffered or inflicted and increasingly able to resist them. As she develops a critical stance toward violences that she previously accepted, she is also likely to become suspicious of the fantasies and theories that dominate organized, public violence. Myths of beastly males, alluring warriors, omniscient defense intellectuals, conspiracies, emergencies, and nuclear protection are all vulnerable to the lucid, knowing gaze. When conjoined with the commitment to protect, lucid, suspicious knowledge may in itself be sufficient to inspire a mother's resistance to militarist plans and "strategic defense initiatives" that threaten her children.

...

Unlike maternal thinking, which is rooted in particular passions and loyalties, feminism explicitly proclaims an ideal of solidarity and loudly rues its failures to implement the idea. ...

...

... The ideal of solidarity does not reflect an attitude feminists have to any or all women. Most obviously, the subjects of feminist solidarity are women who suffer abuse from individual men or from sexist and heterosexist institutions. Second, whatever their individual experiences, feminists tend to ally themselves politically with women who are abused—out of whatever combination of class, race, and sexual oppression—as birthgivers, mothers, or female kin. Solidarity extends indefinitely with different emphases depending on the feminist. But it does not extend to "women" in general, but rather to women in particular situations of struggle.

... Solidarity with women in struggle tends to undercut military loyalty to states. It eschews abstract labels of cause or party—"communist," "fascist," "democrat"—in favor of a closer look at what women actually suffer and how they act. Military loyalties require women and men to kill—or at least to pay for and train killers—in the name of abstract enmity. Feminist solidarity searches among these abstract enemies and allies to identify with women's culturally specific struggles to work, care, and enjoy, to think and speak freely, and to resist abuse.

...

... Any politics that does not make explicit claims about injustice to women will be seen by many feminists as diverting women's energies from feminist demands. Many feminists will be especially skeptical of a maternal antimilitarist politics that turns on women's identities as mothers, caretakers, kin workers, and shelterers. In drawing strength from women's work, this politics seems to ignore the exploitation of the workers and to reinforce a conception of women's responsibility that has boded ill for women themselves. Unlike a women's politics of resistance that proudly draws on traditional identities even as it transforms them, a feminist politics subjects all traditional womanly roles to critical reflection.

Nonetheless, despite these inevitable tensions I believe that feminists strengthen mothers' power to act whether as individuals, in mixed groups, or in a women's politics of resistance. ... Mothers who acquire a feminist consciousness and engage in feminist politics are likely to become more effectively nonviolent and antimilitarist. By increasing mothers' powers to know, care, and act, feminism actualizes the peacefulness latent in maternal practice. Feminism has these transformative powers whether or not feminists are antimilitarist. ...

... It is my belief that feminism is already conjoined with a peace politics that is marked by its double origins in women's traditional work and feminist resistance to abuse against women. ...

… Feminist peace activists offer peacemaking mothers resources, theoretical insights, psychological support, and solidarity in action. The direction is not only one way. Mothers strengthen even as they are strengthened by feminism, bringing to a collective peace politics distinctive habits of mind and principles of nonviolence honed by daily use.

…

---

### Notes

1. For a discussion of women's participation in (and occasional resistance to) the Nazi German government, see Claudia Koonz, *Mothers in the Fatherland: Women, the Family, and Nazi Politics* (New York: St. Martin's, 1987). Among the many virtues of this fascinating book is its tracing of the complex interconnections between women's separate spheres, the Nazi and feminist use of women's difference, and women's participation in but also disappointment in the Nazi state.

2. Marjorie Agosin, "Emerging from the Shadows: Women of Chile," *Barnard Occasional Papers on Women's Issues,* vol. 2, no. 3, Fall 1987, p. 12. I am very grateful to Temma Kaplan, historian and director of the Barnard College Women's Center, whose interest in "motherist" and grass-roots women's resistance movements inspired this section. Temma Kaplan provided me with material on the Madres and discussed an earlier draft of the chapter.

3. Nathan Laks, cited in Nora Amalia Femenia, "Argentina's Mothers of Plaza de Mayo: The Mourning Process from Junta to Democracy," *Feminist Studies,* vol. 13, no. 1, p. 10. …

4. Marjorie Agosin, Temma Kaplan, Teresa Valduz, "The Politics of Spectacle in Chile," *Barnard Occasional Papers on Women's Issues,* vol. 2, no. 3, Fall 1987, p. 6.

5. Simone Weil, "Human Personality," in *Simone Weil Reader,* ed. George A. Paniches (Mt. Cisco, N.Y.: Moyer Bell, 1977), p. 315.

6. Weil, "Human Personality," p. 315.

7. The phrase "partisans of women" is Terry Winant's in "The Feminist Standpoint: A Matter of Language," *Hypatia,* vol. 2, no. 1, Winter 1987.

# *"They Won't Take Me Alive"*

## Eugenia

…

Ana Maria Castillo Rivas, known as *Compañera* Eugenia, devoted ten of her thirty-one years to the Salvadoran revolution, developing from a student activist into a member of the FMLN leadership. Today she stands as an outstanding example of

the revolutionary woman in El Salvador. Not an idealized heroine, she is a woman who, like so many others in exceptional times, put her innate courage and intelligence at the service of her people. In looking at her life, we realize that in the final analysis all revolutions are made by human beings—by ordinary people who must call up extraordinary reserves of perseverance and courage. Often, revolutionary women must somehow raise a family while risking their lives in political activity. They struggle with doubt, with fear and with loneliness—as Eugenia's last letter to her husband poignantly illustrates.

Eugenia was born on May 7, 1950, the second of seven children in a large middle-class family. Her parents were anti-Somoza Nicaraguans who had resettled in El Salvador. Eugenia's father was a strict traditionalist, but made an effort to develop a social conscience in his children from the time they were small. At Catholic high school, Eugenia joined a group of students who regularly visited the slums and charity hospitals of San Salvador. As she cared for the swollen-bellied children of the shantytowns, she developed the commitment to social justice that would shape her life.

At eighteen, Eugenia went to Guatemala as a missionary and worked as a health educator with the Indians of Quetzaltenango. Deeply affected by the horrible exploitation and oppression that she witnessed there, Eugenia became even more determined to understand the causes of poverty and to find a solution to the suffering of her people.

...

While she was engaged in the practical work of organizing, Eugenia was also studying political and economic theory. After ten months of working with FECCAS [The Christian Federation of Salvadoran Peasants], she had come to the conclusion that there was only one road to true social change: revolutionary armed struggle. In February 1975, with Javier as her contact, she began to participate actively with the Popular Forces of Liberation (FPL), the revolutionary, political-military organization founded five years earlier.

Eugenia's assignment to train cadre took her all over the countryside of El Salvador. When speaking to male recruits, she stressed the importance of abolishing *machismo;* she encouraged these men to take on domestic responsibilities and to treat women as equals. She also organized groups of women and energetically promoted the participation of women in all aspects of political work. The fact that women in rural areas were so successfully integrated into the movement in spite of deeply ingrained *machismo* can be attributed to two factors: organizational principles which explicitly promoted equality, and the determined efforts of *compañeras* like Eugenia.

Javier and Eugenia were married in February of 1976. A few days later, the FPL assigned them new political and military responsibilities, and they both went underground. In December of 1976, Eugenia took an oath to become a full member of the FPL. She and Javier would spend the next five years in clandestinity, often separated from each other.

After almost two years of living and working underground, Javier was captured by the security forces. Eugenia faced the biggest crisis of her life. Her comrades recall that she cried often and worried constantly, but that she never let her sorrow affect the quality of her political work. On the contrary, during Javier's time in prison, she worked even harder than before. Finally, after he had endured four months of imprisonment and torture, national and international pressure forced the government to release Javier.

Javier and Eugenia had wanted a child from the time of their marriage but had decided to wait until they were more at ease with the difficulties of clandestinity. After Javier's release, the couple decided to have a child; they knew that this could well be a prolonged war and that the decision to have a child could not wait for peace. Cognizant of the risks, they saw creating a new life as an act of faith in the future. They felt certain that, even if they died, their organization would care for and protect their child. ...

During Eugenia's pregnancy the couple were separated, seeing each other only once or twice a week. Eugenia took no rest from her usual work and was promoted to the Central Command as Director of Work in Mass Organizations, the clandestine section that directed the FPL's work in the countryside. Her job as to reconstruct the FPL's network of clandestine contacts in rural areas, which had recently been broken up by the security forces.

Eugenia's daughter, Ana Patricia, was born in December of 1979. For the first year of her life, Ana Patricia lived with her mother in a safe house. Javier was deeply involved in military training at the time of the birth; he couldn't risk living with his family, but he came to see them as often as possible. Both Eugenia and Javier made a conscious effort to see that he participated as much as possible in Ana's care and education. ...

During 1980, Eugenia was assigned to the Political Commission of the FPL and given one of the most important tasks of the war: to formulate the structure of a party that could carry out and consolidate a revolution in El Salvador. …

This assignment was interrupted by the decision of the United Revolutionary Directorate of the FMLN to launch a general offensive on January 10, 1981. In December of 1980, a month of great preparations, the leaders of the FPL transferred Eugenia to the "Felipe Peña" Front in San Salvador. … As Chief of the Services Sector, Eugenia worked day and night to organize the logistics network that would stockpile and distribute food, medicine and clothing for the coming offensive. She also coordinated the numerous homemade arms workshops that would supply weapons for January 10.

During December, Eugenia and her daughter lived in a safe house, while Javier was on assignment outside of the country. Eugenia rushed to complete her work and to prepare herself to go to the front. Her letters to Javier during this period are full of love and concern for their daughter. She writes of her doubts about her ability to complete her new tasks, but always affirms her conviction that she has chosen the right course. Javier returned to El Salvador and on January 4, 1981, he and Eugenia met for a brief two hours. It was to be the last time they would see each other. The meeting was full of emotion for them both, as Eugenia said goodbye not only to Javier but also to Ana Patricia, who was leaving with him. Javier later remembered that Eugenia seemed to have a premonition of her own death. During their meeting she remarked several times that this might be the last time they would be together.

The next day, January 5, 1981, she wrote her final letter to Javier.

On January 10, the offensive began. By this time Eugenia was fully incorporated into the guerrilla leadership. … Her task was crucial: Return to San Salvador and organize the transport of arms from the capital to units fighting throughout the country. Arriving in San Salvador, she dispatched a pickup truck full of weapons on the 15th. But the *compañeros* were unable to make contact for the delivery, and the mission was unsuccessful. On the 16th, she dispatched the load again, but once more the comrades returned without delivering the arms.

Eugenia faced a decision—she knew this delivery was critical to the success of the offensive. She was not required to go on the mission herself, but she felt that its success was ultimately her responsibility. She believed that, as leader, it was her duty to identify the nature of the problems and to see that orders were carried out correctly. On January 17, 1981, she set out in the pickup with three other comrades. They took the road to Suchitoto and arrived without incident, although the highways were closely guarded by military and paramilitary patrols. But once again, no contact awaited them at the delivery site. Eugenia had no choice but to make the dangerous trip back to the capital. On the road between San Martín and Suchitoto, a van passed them and then turned around in pursuit. Another van, a paramilitary patrol, appeared in front of them, blocking the road. Eugenia and her comrades returned fire and attempted to escape, but all were killed.

"They'll never take me alive," Eugenia had often told Javier.

## Final Letter from Eugenia to Javier

*January 5, 1981*
*11 p.m.*

My love,

Today is January 5—I feel a great need just to talk to you for a while. There are so many thousands of things I want to tell you that they're all rushing together—words seem inadequate to express everything I feel.

My love, your visit yesterday went by so fast, but it made me so happy. You seemed even more handsome, there was something special about you. When you go, it always leaves such a void, such emptiness. I'm never satisfied with the time we have together.

Sweetheart, I will love you forever. Today I feel your presence in a special way—in me, in everything I do—my feeling for you is so strong. Every day I sense our love growing and deepening, growing like the rhythm of the war.

Gordo, I love you more every time I see you. You must know how much it hurts that I can't have you and our little girl here with me, by my side. Being apart from the two of you is so terrible for me, to come home today and not find her here, not to hear her laughter, her baby talk—it hurts me so much, sweetheart—but I get strength to go on from our people, from knowing that we're fighting for a just cause. I hope all this will be over soon, but there's really no way to tell. I love you both so much, but I've realized that the pain of our separation is small compared to the suffering of our people. We must keep up our courage and keep going. We must be willing to give of ourselves completely, without reservation; that is what I'm trying to do.

Sweetheart, yesterday I was pretty tense and that's why I wasn't able to tell you how much I love you, but you must know that I carry both of you very deep in my heart.

Today communication will be a problem. I know you'll be worried about me. I'll make every effort to be careful, but I must always try to be worthy of the fallen *compañeros* who live on in us, whom we honor through our actions.

I'll try to keep you informed—hope it's possible.

I was supposed to leave on the 7th but they say that the enemy captured "Sapo." The results are still unknown, we'll have to see how it goes. That's why the ones who were supposed to leave today didn't go. We might not be able to leave until the 7th. The enemy has really hit us hard. There's a lot of weaknesses and things that worry me, but anyway, onward.

I'm feeling a little weak, I haven't got much appetite. I hadn't eaten a thing for two days. Today I managed to eat something—I was thinking of you. If I don't eat, I'm not going to be strong enough, and I was starting to feel dizzy. I'll try to get my strength up. You're always on my mind, inspiring me.

The section I'm working in lacks organization and planning. It's a mess—and by the 7th everything has to be ready for us to settle over there. The work is pretty easy, I'm doing alright, but maintaining control is difficult. We'll see if I can pull it off. I'm constantly worried, but at least I feel better knowing I'm not the only one. It's confusing here, but like they say, let's get going and we'll sort things out on the road.

A great big kiss to the baby and all my love. I love her so much. I saw her picture today—she looks beautiful!

I'll take care of myself. But if something should happen, I love you forever—I'll always be with you. Make sure our daughter is brought up as a true revolutionary—I'm falling asleep—been sleeping very little lately—too much on my mind. I'll try to get a hold of myself.

There's a lot of surveillance around here, it's been really bad. We're constantly on guard. I'll be as careful as possible.

Sweetheart, I have to go now. I hope this letter reaches you. I will always love you—a big, big kiss. For you and the baby, everything I am and all my efforts to put into practice what you have shown me. I won't disappoint you.

Take care of yourselves. We'll see each other soon, I hope. Your absence digs deep into me. Just heard some commotion—I've got to go see what it is. Kisses—I love you. I hope this gets to you. I'm entrusting the baby to you. Take care of her, and please don't let her put dirt or poop in her mouth.

Write me if you can, or leave word with the baby's godmother, O.K.?

Kisses, kisses and more kisses. I love you sweetheart, forever and always …

I love both of you with all my heart.

Revolution or death—the people armed will triumph!

*Your gorda,*
Eugenia

---

# We Speak for the Planet

## Barbara Omolade

As women of color live and struggle, we increasingly realize that it's time for us to speak for earth and its future. We have heard the voices of white men who speak for earth and its future. When we look at the hunger, despair, and killings around us, we see what white men who speak for earth have done. Their weaponry and visions speak clearly of a future of more and more war.

…

Peace activists also fail to see people of color as initiators and creators and make assumptions about our limited abilities to work for peace and fundamental social change. Those opposed to nuclear weaponry and stockpiling project an equally disturbing politic and vision, which excludes people of color. The antiwar and antinuke organizers and their supporters have gathered millions to march and demonstrate against nuclear war and for a nuclear freeze as if only nuclear war threatens humankind. They have cleverly abstracted the technologies and apparatus of nuclear war and the existence of military conflict from the cultural and historical context that created that path in the first place.

... Many peace activists are ... blind to the constant wars and threats of war being waged against people of color and the planet by those who march for "peace" and by those they march against. These pacifists ... frequently want people of color to fear what they fear and define peace as they define it. They are unmindful that our lands and peoples have already been and are being destroyed as part of the "final solution" of the "color line." It is difficult to persuade the remnants of Native American tribes, the starving of African deserts, and the victims of the Cambodian "killing fields" that nuclear war is *the* major danger to human life on the planet and that only a nuclear "winter" embodies fear and futurelessness for humanity.

The peace movement suffers greatly from its lack of a historical and holistic perspective, practice, and vision that include the voices and experiences of people of color; the movement's goals and messages have therefore been easily coopted and expropriated by world leaders who share the same culture of racial dominance and arrogance. The peace movement's racist blinders have divorced peace from freedom, from feminism, from education reform, from legal rights, from human rights, from international alliances and friendships, from national liberation, from the particular (for example, black female, Native American male) and the general (human being). Nevertheless, social movements such as the civil rights–black power movement in the United States have always demanded peace with justice, with liberation, and with social and economic reconstruction and cultural freedom at home and abroad. The integration of our past and our present holocausts and our struggle to define our own lives and have our basic needs met are at the core of the inseparable struggles for world peace and social betterment.

> The Achilles heel of the organized peace movement in this country has always been its whiteness. In this multi-racial and racist society, no all-white movement can have the strength to bring about basic changes.
>
> It is axiomatic that basic changes do not occur in any society unless the people who are oppressed move to make them occur. In our society it is people of color who are the most oppressed. Indeed our entire history teaches us that when people of color have organized and struggled—most especially, because of their particular history, Black people—have moved in a more humane direction as a society, toward a better life for all people.[1]

Western man's whiteness, imagination, enlightened science, and movements toward peace have developed from a culture and history mobilized against women of color. The political advancements of white men have grown directly from the devastation and holocaust of people of color and our lands. This technological and material progress has been in direct proportion to the undevelopment of women of color. Yet the day-to-day survival, political struggles, and rising up of women of color, especially black women in the United States, reveal both complex resistance to holocaust and undevelopment and often conflicted responses to the military and war.

## The Holocausts

Women of color are survivors of and remain casualties of holocausts, and we are direct victims of war—that is, of open armed conflict between countries or between factions within the same country. But women of color were not soldiers, nor did we trade animal pelts or slaves to the white man for guns, nor did we sell or lease our lands to the white man for wealth. Most men and women of color resisted and fought back, were slaughtered, enslaved, and force marched into plantation labor camps to serve the white masters of war and to build their empires and war machines.

People of color were and are victims of holocausts—that is, of great and widespread destruction, usually by fire. The world as we knew and created it was destroyed in a continual scorched earth policy of the white man. The experience of Jews and other Europeans under the Nazis can teach us the value of understanding the totality of destructive intent, the extensiveness of torture, and the demonical apparatus of war aimed at the human spirit.

A Jewish father pushed his daughter from the lines of certain death at Auschwitz and said, "You will be a remembrance—You tell the story—You survive." She lived. He died. Many have criticized the Jews for forcing non-Jews to remember the 6 million Jews who died under the Nazis and for etching the names Auschwitz and Buchenwald, Terezin and Warsaw in our minds. Yet as women of color, we, too, are "remembrances" of all the holocausts against the people of the world. We must remember the names of concentration camps such as *Jesus, Justice, Brotherhood,* and *Integrity,* ships that carried millions of African men, women, and children chained and brutalized across the ocean to the "New World." We must remember the Arawaks, the Taino, the Chickasaw, the Choctaw, the Narragansett, the Montauk, the Delaware, and the other Native American names of thousands of U.S. towns that stand for tribes of people who are no more. We must remember the holocausts visited against the Hawaiians, the aboriginal peoples of Australia, the Pacific Island peoples, and the women and children of Hiroshima and Nagasaki. We must remember the slaughter of men and women at Sharpeville, the children of Soweto, and the men of Attica. We must never, ever, forget the children disfigured, the men maimed, and the women broken in our holocausts—we must remember the names, the numbers, the faces, and the stories and teach them to our children and our children's children so the world can never forget our suffering and our courage.

Whereas the particularity of the Jewish holocaust under the Nazis is over, our holocausts continue. We are the *madres locos* (crazy mothers) in the Argentinian square silently demanding news of our missing kin from the fascists who rule. We are the children of El Salvador who see our mothers and father shot in front of our eyes. We are the Palestinian and Lebanese women and children overrun by Israeli, Lebanese, and U.S. soldiers. We are the women and children of the bantustans and refugee camps and the prisoners of Robbin Island. We are the starving in the Sahel, the poor in Brazil, the sterilized in Puerto Rico. We are the brothers and sisters of Grenada who carry the seeds of the New Jewel Movement in our hearts, not daring to speak of it with our lips—yet.

Our holocaust is South Africa ruled by men who loved Adolf Hitler, who have developed the Nazi techniques of terror to more sophisticated levels. Passes replace the Nazi badges and stars. Skin color is the ultimate badge of persecution. Forced removals of women, children, and the elderly—the "useless appendages of South Africa"—into barren, arid bantustans without resources for survival have replaced the need for concentration camps. Black sex-segregated barracks and cells attached to work sites achieve two objectives: The work camps destroy black family and community life, a presumed source of resistance, and attempt t create human automatons whose purpose is to serve the South African state's drive toward wealth and hegemony.

. . .

Pacifists such as Martin Luther King, Jr. and Mahatma Gandhi who have used nonviolent resistance charged that those who used violence to obtain justice were just as evil as their oppressors. Yet all successful revolutionary movements have used organized violence. This is especially true of national liberation movements that have obtained state power and reorganized the institutions of their nations for the benefit of the people. If men and women in South Africa do not use organized violence, they could remain in the permanent violent state of the slave. Could it be that pacifism and nonviolence cannot become a way of life for the oppressed? Are they only tactics with specific and limited use for protecting people from further violence? For most people in the developing communities and the developing world consistent nonviolence is a luxury; it presumes that those who have and use nonviolent weapons will refrain from using them long enough for nonviolent resisters to win political battles. To survive, peoples in developing countries must use a varied repertoire of issues, tactics, and approaches. Sometimes arms are needed to defeat apartheid and defend freedom in South Africa; sometimes nonviolent demonstrations for justice are the appropriate strategy for protesting the shooting of black teenagers by a white man, such as happened in New York City.

Peace is not merely an absence of conflict that enables white middle-class comfort, nor is it simply resistance to nuclear war and war machinery. The litany of "you will be blown up, too" directed by a white man to a black woman obscures the permanency and institutionalization of war, the violence and holocaust that people of color face daily. Unfortunately, the holocaust does not only refer to the mass murder of Jews, Christians, and atheists during the Nazi regime; it also refers to the permanent institutionalization of war that is part of every fascist and racist regime. The holocaust lives. It is a threat to world peace as pervasive and thorough as nuclear war.

## Women of Color and Development

Women of color speaking from the underdeveloped countries and underdeveloped communities on the fringes of the so-called developed world are well aware that development has meant war and the violent reorganization of our cultures and our lands to produce the resources that will meet the needs, especially military, of multinational corporations and conglomerates. These include cash crops, precious ores and metals, and labor. The world economy is dominated by "11,000 transnational corporations whose production was estimated at $830 billion in 1976. Through their price manipulation they have caused the underdeveloped countries to lose between $50 and $100 billion a year."[2]

...

We speak for a planet whose merchants of war spend $515 billion per year on weapons and in which military expenditures in Third World countries increased from $33 billion in 1972 to $81.3 billion in 1981. These expenditures have risen from 8 percent of the world's expenditures to 16 percent in the last ten years.[3] Women of color represent the majority of the world's people—six-sevenths of whom are people of color and the majority of whom are women and girls—and we "do two-thirds of the world's work hours, receive a tenth of the world's income, and own less than a hundredth of the world's property."[4]

Under the guise of progress, development has robbed women of color of our former status in traditional societies. In these societies we were the primary agrarian work force. Our traditional roles as mother and wife were given high status, albeit in a patriarchal and sexist manner that often rendered these roles inhumanely burdened and unjustly discriminated against. Nonetheless, our primary role in agriculture and trade blunted the full impact of sexism and enabled us to accumulate wealth. In agrarian societies when single-crop, nonedible cash crops have taken over the most fertile lands, usually financed by multinational conglomerates, women farmers, particularly in Africa, have become marginalized, although we grow most of the food for domestic consumption.

When machines are introduced into our underdeveloped communities, we become further underdeveloped because we are denied access to these machines. Money and technology for farm expansion go to men. Mechanized farming uses male wage earners as its labor supply. Women must then farm with dated technology. Money and machines overpower the work of women of color worldwide while we prepare and serve food. We take care of children, the sick, and elderly. We sew garments. We care for shelter.

...

In developed countries, if women of color can find work at all, we work for the lowest wages, in the most labor-intensive areas of the economy. We also prepare and serve food and care for children, the sick, and the elderly. (Traditionally we worked for wages as domestics, caretakers, and lower echelon factory workers.) Women of color have been employed in public-sector jobs as buffers between the poor and powerless and the state. We work in welfare agencies, nursing homes, prisons, hospitals, and schools.

In the United States, Native American, Afro-American, Afro-Caribbean, Asian, Latin, and immigrant women from the Third World live at the bottom of all quality-of-life indicators. We recoil in horror as armies of the police occupy our neighborhoods and declare black and Hispanic men criminals to be shot on sight, with questions asked later. We watch the miseducation of our children and social workers' attempts to destroy the strengths of our families. The destruction of the black mind is an everyday occurrence. The continued existence of sweatshops and cash crops for illegal immigrants is an integral part of the U.S. economy. It is common for men to beg and for women to live out of shopping bags while young people live in abandoned buildings or on the streets. It is ordinary for there to be madness, murder, and mayhem in our daily lives. We live terrified, not only of ultimate war but of how we "gonna make it one more day, how we gonna keep on keeping on."

In an article entitled, "Peace, Disarmament and Black Liberation," Damu Imara Smith asks us to consider the following:

> As we lose in our fight for jobs with decent pay and stand in long unemployment lines, let us remember the MX missile, funded at a cost of $2.4 billion for FY 1983. As we lose our fight against dilapidated, rat infested slum housing, let us remember the 2.2 billion dollars for Phoenix and Sparrow air to air missiles. As we lose in our fight to put shoes on our children's feet and adequate clothes on their backs, let us remember the Pershing II missile. As we lose our struggle to put enough food on the table, let us think about the Minuteman 3 missiles. As we shiver in our homes and apartments this winter because we can't pay our utility bills, let us reflect on the Polaris and Poseidon missiles. As we witness plant closings, the resulting massive layoffs in our communities and the shutting down of day care centers, let us think about the SSN-688 nuclear attack submarine built at the cost of a whopping $900 million each! As we fall further into debt, let us remember the 5 year trillion dollar defense budget and the fact that all of the Pentagon's bills are paid while ours aren't. ... As we protest the myriad problems afflicting our communities and society, we should always link them with the military budget. We should make it clear to those who rule our society that we do understand how huge military expenditures affect our daily existence.[5]

Women of color are the present and historic victims of development and militarism. Our work has always represented the underpinnings of each society in which we reside. We make and maintain the life supports that everyone else depends upon, including the elite men who dominate the developed world, deciding when and where to militarily and socially wage war. But the work of women of color is invisible, and, when seen, it is devalued.

Our blood and our ancestor's blood have already been shed in continual war precipitated by the movement of a group of self-defined white men. They named themselves white and declared themselves superior to the darker-skinned people they encountered. They divided the world along racial lines and the biological distinctions of color. Military terrorism has become the method of world domination; capitalism, the method of social organization; and racism, the ideology and worldview that holds together the rational and cohesive system of exploitation and oppression they established and that we live under. Racism is an all-encompassing, economic, social, cultural, political, and military war against a group of people whose physical characteristics have been denigrated and used to divide and isolate them from others. Women of color in the developed and the undeveloped world have come to share the same condition and position regardless of different languages, cultures, and methods of colonization or domination. We are powerless victims, relentless toilers, stigmatized and dishonored by white men, white culture, and often our own men as well. We are victims of untold violence against our person, our children, and our communities. Therefore, we speak against all wars—economic, social, and political—for we and our children are often the first casualties.

...

## Women Warriors

Black and brown men said, "Hell no, we won't go!" White men joined them, white women were discovering their own power, and black and brown women warriors said, "Continue to struggle to free us all—to break our chains." Every demonstration, organizing effort, or act of defiance was surrounded by women who encouraged, urged, demanded *freedom,* with peace and love.

Rosa Parks refused to move and was jailed. Fannie Lou Hamer and Annelle Ponder were beaten in jail for daring to be citizens. Septima Clarke lost her job because she was a member of the National Association for the Advancement of Colored People. Teenage girls were hosed. Annie Pearl Avery snatched the menacing billy club from the hands of a southern sheriff. Old women were handcuffed and still they wouldn't stop.

The actions of these warriors were reflected in the refusal of Chicano women in lettuce fields to work, in the demands of Puerto Rican women in New York and San Juan for liberation, in the marches of Asian women, and in the protest by Native American women at Wounded Knee. And still they wouldn't stop. Everywhere there was space to say, "No!"—women of color hollered it, chanted it, and, if silenced, glared out our protest against all the evils and demons that limited and tied us down.

Our strength to "keep on keeping on" comes not from weapons but from the power of our prayers and visions—of peace, love, and freedom. Often we don't join *the* organization or the movement of men or of white women because our time, our moves, our ways are creatively complicated and cumbersome, woven ways of holding everything together around us. For underneath the conflicts between resistance and collaboration, the wholeness and connectedness of all things are understood by women warriors—for only if we survive, by any/all means available, can we resist. Women of color warriors are constant warriors who dig in bare earth to feed the hungry child, who pray for health at the bedside of the sick when there is no medicine, who fashion a toy to make a poor child smile, who take to the streets demanding freedom, freedom, freedom against armed police. Every act of survival by a woman of color is an act of resistance to the holocaust and the war. No soldier fights harder than a woman warrior for she fights for total change, for a new order in a world in which she can finally rest and love.

Everywhere women of color gather we realize a common concern, a common agenda for the planet, and a common practice to achieve the reality of liberation. We are sisters; at last we have found each other. For many women of color who have traveled and spoken with other women of color, sisterhood is a living reality.

...

... Our visions and our warriorship speak for and claim this planet, earth, for we have a precious covenant with our ancestors, our brothers, our sisters, and our progeny to "lay down the swords and shields" of the "masters of war," so we can "study war no more."

---

### Notes

1. Ann Braden, "A Call to Action," *Southern Exposure* (Waging Peace Issue) 10, no. 6 (November-December 1982), p. 3.

2. Fidel Castro, *The World Economic and Social Crisis* (Report to the Seventh Summit Conference of Non-Aligned Countries, Council of State, Havana, 1983), p. 142.

3. Ibid., pp. 203–204.

4. United Nations Decade on Women Report.

5. Damu Imara Smith, "Peace, Disarmament and Black Liberation," *Southern Exposure* 10, no. 6 (November-December 1982), p. 16.

# Taking Empirical Data Seriously: An Ecofeminist Philosophical Perspective

## Karen J. Warren

...

According to ecological ("eco-") feminists, there are important connections between the treatment of women, people of color, and the underclass, on the one hand, and the treatment of nonhuman nature, on the other hand. Ecological feminists claim that any feminism, environmentalism, or environmental ethic that fails to take these connections seriously is grossly inadequate.[1] Establishing the nature of these connections, particularly what I call "women-nature connections," and determining which are potentially liberating for both women and nonhuman nature are a major project of ecofeminist philosophy.

Here I focus on *empirical women-nature connections*. I suggest that from an ecofeminist philosophical perspective, it is important for all of us interested in finding solutions to environmental destruction, and the unjustified subordination of women and other subdominant groups, to take seriously these connections. By doing so, I hope to motivate and establish the practical significance of ecofeminist philosophy.

### Feminism and Feminist Issues

As I understand feminism, it is a movement committed to the elimination of male-gender power and privilege, or sexism. Despite differences among feminists, all feminists agree that sexism exists, is wrong, and ought to be changed. Anything is a feminist issue if it helps one understand sexism. ... According to ecofeminists, trees, water, animals, toxics, and nature language are feminist issues because understanding them helps one understand the status and plights of women cross-culturally. Consider why this is so.

641

# Ecofeminism

Just as there is not one feminism, there is not one ecofeminism or one ecofeminist philosophy. Ecological feminism has roots in the wide variety of different feminisms (e.g., liberal feminism, Marxist feminism, radical and socialist feminisms, Black and Third World feminisms). What makes ecofeminism distinct as a feminism is its insistence that nonhuman nature and naturism (i.e., the unjustified domination of nature) are feminist issues. Ecofeminist philosophy extends familiar feminist critiques of social "isms of domination" (e.g., sexism, racism, classism, heterosexism, ageism, anti-Semitism) to nature (i.e., naturism). According to ecofeminists, nature is a feminist issue. ...

# Trees, Forests, Forestry

In 1974, twenty-seven women of Reni in northern India took simple but effective action to stop tree felling. They threatened to hug the trees if the lumberjacks attempted to fell them. The women's protest, known as the Chipko (Hindi for "to embrace" or "hug") movement, saved twelve thousand square kilometers of sensitive watershed. This grass-roots, nonviolent, women-initiated Chipko movement also gave visibility to two basic complaints of local women: Commercial felling by contractors damages a large number of other trees, and the teak and eucalyptus monoculture plantations are replacing valuable indigenous forests.[2]

The Chipko movement is ostensibly about saving trees, especially indigenous forests.[3] But it is also about important women-nature connections: Trees and forests are inextricably connected to the rural and household economies governed by women, especially in Third World countries. So tree shortages are *also* about women. As a result of First World development decisions in India, multiculture species of trees have been replaced by monoculture species, primarily eucalyptus.

But eucalyptus is very unpopular among local women.[4] The reasons local women dislike eucalyptus plantations show *four* crucial respects in which trees, forests, and forestry are a feminist issue—that is, how understanding the empirical connections between women and trees improves one's understanding of the subordination of women. First, in the South (developing countries) women are more dependent than men on tree and forest products.[5] Trees provide five essential elements in these household economies: food, fuel, fodder, products for the home (including building materials, household utensils, gardens, dyes, and medicines), and income.

Second, women are the primary victims of environmental degradation and forest resource depletion.[6] This is because women must walk farther for fuelwood and fodder and must carry it all back themselves (e.g., without the help of animals). According to one estimate, women in New Delhi walk an average of ten kilometers every three or four days for an average of seven hours each time just to obtain firewood. As men increasingly seek employment in towns and cities, women must carry out men's former jobs plus the laborious tasks of collecting and processing forest products on degraded soils. The reduced availability of forest products for use as a source of income leaves women without income-producing alternatives. And new development projects have failed to adequately address the household technology needs of women.

Third, there are customs, taboos, legal obstacles, and time constraints that women face that men do not face. For example, among the Ibo, men own timber trees, women control the use of food trees, and women cannot inherit economic trees, although they have a right to be maintained from the proceeds of those trees owned by their parents.[7]

Last, trees, forests, and forestry are a feminist issue for *conceptual* reasons: Some key assumptions of orthodox forestry are male biased. Consider three such assumptions. One assumption of orthodox forestry is that *the outsider knows best:* The outsider has the requisite technical expertise to solve the problem of the lack of trees in Third World countries. But this assumption is false or problematic. It is the insider most inside the culture—the Chipko women of India, for example—who is the expert, who has what feminist foresters call "indigenous technical knowledge" (ITK) and feminist philosophers call "epistemic privilege" around forestry production. Because local women are the primary users of forest commodities in most developing countries, their "day-to-day, hands-on involvement with forestry goes far beyond that of many professionally trained foresters."[8] In a Sierra Leone village, for example, women were able to identify thirty-one products from nearby bushes and trees, whereas men could identify only eight.[9] Women's ITK grows out of their daily, felt, lived experiences as managers of trees and tree products.

A second assumption of orthodox forestry is that activities that fall outside the boundaries of commercial fiber production are less important. Yet these activities are precisely those that women engage in on a daily basis. Conceptually, the "invisibility" of what women do accounts for the mistaken assumption that the management and production policies of orthodox forestry are not gender biased. It also explains why many foresters "literally do not see trees that are used as hedgerows or living fence poles; trees that provide materials for basketry, dyes, medicines, or decorations; trees that provide sites for honey barrels; trees that provide shade; or trees that provide human food."[10] And because these foresters literally do not *see* these multiple uses of trees, they also often do not see a lot more—for example, that multiculture tree species are useful, that men and women may have very different uses for the same tree, or that they may use different trees for different purposes. This inability to see women's contributions is a "patriarchal conceptual trap" of orthodox forestry.

A third assumption of orthodox forestry is that it usually is better to have large-scale production using a small number of species than small-scale community-based forestry using a wide variety of species. The Chipko movement challenges this assumption. Since small-scale production reflects local priorities, involves multiple uses of many species of trees, and is responsive to the social reality of women's importance in agriculture and forest production, to threaten small-scale production is to threaten the livelihood and well-being of women. In summary, then, trees, forests, and forestry are (eco)feminist issues. Consider now other empirical examples.

# Water

Only 8 percent of the world's water supply is fresh or potable. Millions of humans have difficulty getting sufficient water necessary for survival, about five liters a day. In more than half the South, less then 50 percent of the population has a source of potable water or facilities for sewage disposal. The World Health Organization estimates that approximately 85 percent of all sicknesses and diseases in the South are attributable to inadequate water or sanitation and that as many as 25 million deaths a year are due to water-related illnesses. Every year 15 million children die before they are five; 4 million of these die from diarrhea and associated water-related diseases.[11]

In the South, women and children perform most of the water collection work.[12] Because of natural resource depletion, women must also walk farther for water (e.g., one to fifteen kilometers daily through rough terrain in Uttarakhand, India). Since women and children typically perform the water collection work, they experience disproportionately higher health risks in the presence of unsanitary water. Each year millions of people, predominately women, are affected by major illnesses acquired while drawing water—300 million people with malaria, 20–30 million with river blindness, and 270 million with elephantiasis.[13] Drinking water is often drawn from public bathing and laundering places, and the same water is frequently used as a public toilet.

Contaminated water is not just a problem of the South. In 1980, the United States produced 125 billion pounds of hazardous waste, enough to fill approximately three thousand Love Canals. In the mid-1970s, 90 percent of hazardous waste was being disposed of improperly. "These wastes have contributed to groundwater contamination on a local basis in all parts of the nation and on a regional basis in some heavily populated and industrialized areas. The [U.S.] House Subcommittee on Environment, Energy, and Natural Resources in 1980 listed 250 dump sites that present a great potential threat to drinking water supplies."[14] Groundwater is the drinking water source for nearly half the population of the United States. Yet according to 1991 estimates, one in six people in the United States drinks water contaminated by lead, a known cause of impaired IQ in children. Water, then, is an (eco)feminist issue.

# Food and Farming

It is estimated that women farmers grow at least 59 percent of the world's food and perhaps as much as 80 percent. Between one-third and one-half of the agricultural laborers in the Third World are women. Yet the gender division of labor typically puts men in charge of cash crops, while women manage food crops. Women in Africa produce more than 70 percent of Africa's food, typically without tractors, oxen, or even plows. According to Mayra Buvinic and Sally Yudelman, "As a rule, women farmers work longer hours, have fewer assets and lower incomes than men farmers do, and have almost as many dependents to support. The disparity is not due to lack of education or competence. Women farmers are poorer because their access to credit is limited. Without credit they cannot acquire productive assets, such as cattle, fertilizer or improved seeds, to improve the productivity of their labor."[15]

Consider the root crop cassava. It is critically important in parts of Africa in times of scarcity. Women do 70 to 80 percent of the growing and harvesting of cassava and 100 percent of the processing, which includes washing out the natural cyanide found in it (a process that takes eighteen five-hour days). Little money has been devoted to research on cassava or on the development of technologies that would increase the productivity of women farmers and the demand for and price of cassava.[16]

Women's agricultural roles are many: Women are farm owners and farm managers (with major decisionmaking responsibilities about production and most agricultural tasks), farm partners (who share responsibility for agricultural production, typically with another household member), farm workers (unpaid family laborers), and wage laborers (who work for a daily wage or are paid by output). Historically, a failure to realize the extent of women's contribution to agriculture (e.g., by First World development policies and practices) has contributed to the "invisibility of women" in all aspects of agricultural work (e.g., in ploughing, planting, caring for "livestock," harvesting, weeding, processing, and the storing of crops).

## Technologies

Often the technologies exported from the North to the South only exacerbate the problem of tree, water, and food shortages for women. In forestry, men are the primary recipients of training in urban pulp and commodity production plants and are the major decisionmakers about forest management, even though local women often know more about trees than local or outsider men. In agriculture, men are the primary recipients of training and access to machines, tractors, ploughs, and irrigation systems, even though women are the major food producers. In water systems, men are the primary recipients of training in the construction and use of water pumps, wells, filtering systems, and faucets, even though women are responsible for water collection and distribution tasks.

One striking example of so-called appropriate technologies—small-scale, simple, inexpensive, intermediate technologies made from local materials and labor, which are totally inappropriate for women—concerns women and food in Africa: "In Africa where sunshine is abundant but oil, coal and wood are scarce and expensive, a solar stove should really mean utmost happiness to women—or so some eager development theoreticians thought. Field tests then showed what every experienced expert [or local women] could have predicted: In the African bush, meals are prepared in the morning or in the evening when the sun has not yet risen or has already set. Furthermore: which cook wants to stand in the scorching sun? Finally: the nightly fire also has a group and therefore social function."[17] Thus, appropriate technology, when developed and carried out by men who lack a basic understanding of women's lives and work, results in the creation of solar stoves for women who cook before dawn and after dusk, maize shellers that take longer to do the job than when women do the shelling themselves, and pedal-driven grinding mills in areas where women are forbidden to sit astride. Technology is an ecofeminist issue.

## Toxics

Although neither sex is naturally more resistant to toxic agents and resistance appears to depend on the substance in question, there is strong evidence for the existence of gender-related differences in exposure to environmental toxic substances. Persistent toxic chemicals, because of their ability to cross the placenta, to bioaccumulate, and to occur as mixtures, pose disproportionately serious health threats to infants, mothers, and the elderly.

The household is also an important locus of environmental health hazards for women.[18] Women-headed households are a growing worldwide phenomenon, making up more than 20 percent of all households in Africa, the developed regions, Latin America, and the Caribbean. But "most workplace health standards tend to be based on criteria derived from the assessment of how *men* have responded in the historical past to pollutants."[19] Toxics are a gender issue; they are also a race and class issue.

## Environmental Racism

In the United States, Native American women face unique health risks because of the presence of uranium mining on or near Indian reservations. (The uranium is used for nuclear energy.) According to Lance Hughes, director of Native Americans for a Clean Environment, the Navajo, Zuni, Laguna, Cheyenne, Arapahoe, Ute, and Cree all report health problems from uranium mining on their land.[20] According to one report:

> A survey of households and hospitals on the Pine Ridge Reservation in South Dakota revealed that in one month in 1979, 38 percent of the pregnant women on the reservation suffered miscarriages, compared to the normal rate of between 10 and 20 percent. ... [There were] extremely high rates of cleft palate and other birth defects, as well as hepatitis, jaundice, and serious diarrhea. Health officials confirmed that their reservation had higher than average rates of bone and gynecological cancers.[21]

Navajo Indians are the primary work force in the mining of uranium in the United States. According to a 1986 report, "Toxics and Minority Communities," by the Center for Third World Organizing (Oakland, California), 2 million tons of radioactive uranium tailings have been dumped on Native American lands. Indian reservations of the Kaibab Paiute (northern Arizona) and other tribes are targeted sites for hazardous waste incinerators, disposal, and storage facilities.[22] Many tribes, "faced with unemployment rates of 80 percent or higher, are desperate for both jobs and capital."[23]

The issues facing women and men of color raise serious questions about environmental racism. In 1989, the United Church of Christ Commission for Racial Justice did a study entitled "Toxic Waste and Race in the United States."[24] The study concluded that race is a major factor in the location of hazardous waste in the United

States: Three out of every five African and Hispanic Americans (more than 15 million of the nation's 26 million African Americans and more than 8 million of the 15 million Hispanics) and more than half of all Asian Pacific Islanders and American Indians live in communities with one or more uncontrolled toxic waste sites. In the rural Southwest, 75 percent of the residents, most of whom are Hispanic, drink pesticide-contaminated water. The nation's largest hazardous waste landfill, receiving toxics from forty-five states, is in Emelle, Alabama, which is 79.9 percent African American. Probably the greatest concentration of hazardous waste sites in the United States is on the predominately African American and Hispanic South Side of Chicago. In Houston, Texas, six of eight municipal incinerators and all five city landfills are located in predominately African American neighborhoods.

There are hundreds of grass-roots environmental organizations and actions initiated by women and low-income minorities throughout the world. As Cynthia Hamilton claims:

> Women often play a primary role in community action because it is about things they know best. They also tend to use organizing strategies and methods that are the antithesis of those of the traditional environmental movement. Minority women in several urban areas [of the United States] have found themselves part of a new radical core of environmental activists, motivated by the irrationalities of capital-intensive growth. These individuals are responding not to "nature" in the abstract but to their homes and the health of their children. ... Women are more likely to take on these issues than men precisely because the home has been defined as a woman's domain.[25]

Environmental racism is a (eco)feminist issue.

## Environmental Ageism: Children

As the quote from Cynthia Hamilton suggests, the health of children is also a feminist environmental issue. The federal Centers for Disease Control in Atlanta, Georgia, document that lead poisoning endangers the health of nearly 8 million inner-city children, many of whom are African American or Hispanic. Countless more live with crumbling asbestos in housing projects and schools.[26] In the United States, more than seven hundred thousand inner-city children are suffering from lead poisoning (and the learning disabilities that result), 50 percent of whom are African, Hispanic, or Asian American.[27] In the United States, the National Resources Defense Council estimates that more than one-half of the lifetime risk of cancer associated with pesticides on fruit is incurred before age six.[28] Reproductive organ cancer among Navajo teenagers is seventeen times the national average.

Furthermore, women and children are seriously affected by poverty. In the United States, 78 percent of all people living in poverty are women or children younger than eighteen. In Australia, the proportion is 75 percent. Worldwide, the largest poverty group is women-headed households. The three elements that make up the major part of Third World disasters are deforestation, desertification, and soil erosion. The rural poor, a disproportionate number of whom are women and children, are the

primary victims of these disasters. The living conditions of women, people of color, the poor, and children, then, are an ecofeminist issue.
…

According to ecofeminism, empirical data help both to motivate and to establish the need for feminists, environmentalists, and philosophers—indeed, all of us—to think deeply about real-life connections not only between women and nature but also between people of color, children, the poor, and nature. These connections suggest why, from an ecofeminist philosophical perspective, we must take empirical data *very* seriously.

---

## Notes

An expanded version of this paper will appear as Chapter 1 in a book co-authored with Jim Cheney, *Ecological Feminism: A Philosophical Feminist Perspective on What It Is and Why It Matters* (Boulder, Colo.: Westview Press, 1993); and in Karen J. Warren, ed. *Ecological Feminism: Multidisciplinary Perspectives* (Bloomington: Indiana University Press, 1993).

1. For a selected bibliography of ecofeminist literature, see Carol J. Adams and Karen J. Warren, "Feminism and the Environment: A Selected Bibliography," *APA Newsletter on Feminism and Philosophy* (Fall 1991): 148–157.

2. *The State of India's Environment: 1984–1985; The Second Citizens' Report* (New Delhi: Center for Science and Environment, 1985), p. 94. The Chipko movement is especially noteworthy for its distinctively ecological sensitivity. This is clearly seen in the slogan of the Chipko movement: The main products of the forests are, not timber or resin, but "*soil, water,* and oxygen" (cited in Jayanta Bandyopadhyay and Vandana Shiva, "Chipko: Rekindling India's Forest Culture," *The Ecologist* 17, no. 1 [1987]: 35). For an excellent discussion of the Chipko movement and its effectiveness as a resistance strategy to "maldevelopment"—First World development policies and practices aimed primarily at increasing productivity, capital accumulation, and the commercialization of Third World economies for surplus and profit—see Vandana Shiva, *Staying Alive: Women, Ecology and Development* (London: Zed Books, 1988).

3. Trees and forests are disappearing at an alarming rate. India is losing 1.3 million hectares of forests a year, nearly eight times the annual rate put out by forest departments. Wood shortages are great and wood prices are high (*The State of India's Environment,* p. 49).

4. The replacement of natural forests in India with eucalyptus plantations has been justified on the grounds of increased productivity. But the productivity is in the area of pulpwood only: "What has been called the 'Eucalyptus controversy' is in reality a conflict of paradigms, between an ecological approach to forestry on the one hand, and a reductionist, partisan approach which only responds to industrial requirements on the other. While the former views natural forests and many indigenous tree species as more productive than eucalyptus, the reverse is true according to the paradigm of Commercial Forestry. The scientific conflict is in fact an economic conflict over *which* needs and *whose* needs are important" (*The State of India's Environment,* p. 33).

5. *Restoring the Balance: Women and Forest Resources* (Rome: Food and Agriculture Organization, with assistance from the Swedish International Development Authority, 1987), p. 4.

6. Louise Fortmann and Dianne Rocheleau, "Women and Agroforestry: Four Myths and Three Case Studies," *Agroforestry Systems* 9, no. 2 (1985): 37.

7. Louise P. Fortmann and Sally K. Fairfax, "American Forestry Professionalism in the Third World: Some Preliminary Observations on Effects," in *Women Creating Wealth: Transforming Economic Development,* selected papers and speeches from the Association of Women on De-

velopment Conference (Washington, DC, April 23–25, 1988), p. 107. Fortmann and Fairfax have taken their information from S.N.C. Obi, *The Law of Property* (London: Butterworths, 1963), p. 97.

8. Fortmann and Fairfax, "American Forestry Professionalism," p. 105.

9. Marilyn Hoskins, "Observations on Indigenous and Modern Agroforestry Activities in West Africa," in *Problems of Agroforestry* (Freiburg: University of Freiburg, 1982); cited in ibid., p. 105.

10. See Fortmann and Fairfax, "American Forestry Professionalism," p. 106.

11. See Marilyn Waring, "Your Economic Theory Makes No Sense," in *If Women Counted: A New Feminist Economics* (New York: Harper and Row, 1988), p. 257; and Lloyd Timberlake and Laura Thomas, *When The Bough Breaks … Our Children, Our Environment* (London: Earthscan Publications, 1990), p. 128. According to Waring, one-half of these children could be saved if they had access to safe drinking water.

12. Small-scale studies in Asia and Africa indicate that women and girls spend on average 5–17 hours per week collecting and carrying water (e.g., 17.5 hours in Senegal, 5.5 hours in rural areas of Botswana, and 43.5 hours on northern farms in Ghana; 7 hours in the Baroda region of India, 1.5–4.9 hours in Nepal villages depending on the ages of the girls, and 3.5 hours in Pakistan). See *The World's Women, 1970–1990: Trends and Statistics* (New York: United Nations, 1991), p. 75.

13. Joni Seager and Ann Olson, *Women in the World: An International Atlas* (New York: Simon and Schuster, 1986), section 25.

14. *New York Times,* September 20, 1980, p. 45; cited in Nicholas Freudenberg and Ellen Zaltzberg, "From Grassroots Activism to Political Power: Women Organizing Against Environmental Hazards," in Wendy Chavkin, ed., *Double Exposure: Women's Health Hazards on the Job and at Home* (New York: Monthly Review Press, 1984), p. 253.

15. Mayra Buvinic and Sally Yudelman, 24.

16. Ibid., p. 30. According to Buvinic and Yudelman, ibid., cassava illustrates four issues critical to understanding women's role in agriculture: (1) the extent of women's participation in food production and their contributions to food security, (2) the heavy demands farming places on women's time and labor, (3) the willingness of women to grow crops that have little or no economic payoff but that enable poor families to eat during periods of food scarcity, and (4) the general tendency to assign fewer resources to crops grown by women.

17. Helmut Mylenbusch, "Appropriate Technology—Fashionable Term, Practical Necessity, or New Social Philosophy?" *Development and Cooperation* 3 (1979): 18.

18. In her essay "The Home Is the Workplace: Hazards, Stress, and Pollutants in the Household," in Wendy Chavkin, ed., *Double Exposure,* pp. 219–224, Harriet Rosenberg claims that a rigid sexual division of labor in the household contributes to significant health and safety hazards for women who work in the home. (The data are based on U.S. households.) The work women do in the home includes housework, motherwork, and wifework. Product health hazards exist in most home cleaning products (e.g., drain and oven cleaners [lye], toilet bowl and window cleaners [ammonia], scouring powders, chlorine bleach, disinfectants, detergents, furniture polishes) and appliances (e.g., gas stoves that emit carbon monoxide, radiation leakage from microwave ovens, fluorescent lights). Furthermore, according to Rosenberg, the average household has about 250 chemicals that, if ingested, could send a child to the hospital. And the home has a full range of problematic chemicals (e.g., lead, asbestos, PCBs, formaldehyde, aerosols) used in household construction and insulation and in insecticides, pesticides, and herbicides.

19. Calabrese, p. 3.

20. Lance Hughes, "American Indians and the Energy Crisis: Interview with Lance Hughes," *Race, Poverty, and the Environment* 2, no. 2 (Summer 1992): 5, 17.

21. Freudenberg and Zaltzberg, "From Grassroots Activism to Political Power," 249.

22. On July 4, 1990, the *Minneapolis Star/Tribune* reported that members of the Kaibab Paiute reservation in northern Arizona were negotiating to bring about seventy thousand tons of hazardous waste each year to the reservation. An incinerator would burn the waste, and the ash would be buried on tribal land. The Paiute stand to reap $1 million a year from the waste-burning operation. The Kaibab Paiute and other tribes are torn between such economic gains and the integrity of their land and traditional ways.

23. *Christian Science Monitor*, February 14, 1991, p. 18.

24. *Toxic Wastes and Race in the United States: A National Report on the Racial and Socio-Economic Characteristics of Communities with Hazardous Waste Sites* (New York: Commission for Racial Justice, 1987).

25. Cynthia Hamilton, "Women, Home, and Community," *woman of power: a magazine of feminism, spirituality, and politics* 20 (Spring 1991): 43. (See also this volume.)

26. There are four specific areas in which children are physically more vulnerable than adults: food and water, home, schools, and outdoor play areas. Furthermore, characteristics unique to children, especially poor children and children of color, make them particularly vulnerable to environmental hazards. Poor children are more likely to live in neighborhoods with environmental hazards; poor families lack the financial resources to remove hazards from their home or purchase alternative, nonhazardous products; poor children are less likely to have access to health care for treatment; and the families of poor children often lack the necessary political clout to insist on the cleanup of hazards in the neighborhood. In homes and schools, hazardous products (e.g., cleaning products) and exposure to lead, radon, asbestos, and indoor air pollution (e.g., tobacco smoke, formaldehyde found in some carpeting, wallboard, and insulation) are particularly harmful to children since the same amount of exposure to children and adults is believed to produce higher concentrations in the smaller bodies of children. Outdoors, pesticides, harmful sun exposure, air pollution, and play in unsafe areas can result in serious health conditions in children (e.g., breathing certain kinds of asbestos fibers can increase the chance of developing chronic diseases; ground-level ozone-caused air pollution can cause respiratory problems such as shortness of breath, coughing). In Dana Hughes, "What's Gotten into Our Children" (Los Angeles: Children Now, 1990), pp. 3–5.

27. Hamilton, "Women, Home, and Community," p. 42.

28. Hughes, "What's Gotten into Our Children," p. 6.

# From Healing Herbs to Deadly Drugs: Western Medicine's War Against the Natural World

## Marti Kheel

Most people in the western world conceive of "alternative healing" as a deviation from the norm. Modern western medicine, by contrast, is typically viewed as the culmination of a long, steady march toward progress and truth. Through a collective lapse of memory, our culture seems to have forgotten that modern western medicine is a relatively recent phenomenon and that most of what is now called "alternative healing" has been practiced for thousands of years throughout the world. Ironically, the true "alternative" is modern western medicine which represents the greatest deviation in healing the world has ever known.[1]

At the heart of this deviation lies a dramatic transformation in our society's attitude toward the natural world. Along with this change there has been a drastic alteration in our conception of animals and of their role in helping humans to attain health. Perhaps, nowhere can this change be more clearly illustrated than in the changeover from one of the most ancient forms of healing to one of the most common forms of medicine today—namely, the shift from the use of healing herbs to the use of deadly drugs.

Herbal healing is considered by many to be the earliest form of healing.[2] It has been practiced by lay women healers for thousands of years and still remains the chief form of healing in most parts of the world. Women, in fact, have been the primary healers throughout history. According to World Health Organization figures, they still provide 95 percent of the world's health care needs.[3] Their practices have grown out of a rich tradition of holistic healing. Sadly, this tradition has been destroyed throughout much of the western world. Women "healers" now typically fill the ranks of the nursing profession where they play a role subordinate to the (male-dominated) "scientifically" trained medical elite. One of their chief functions is the dispensing of chemicals and drugs that only doctors are permitted to prescribe. Drugs—not herbs—have become the major treatment for the sick. And women have become the major consumers (and victims) of such drugs.[4]

In order to comprehend the transition from herbs to drugs and the transfer of power from women to men that accompanied it, we must understand the worldviews out of which both forms of healing evolved.[5] Herbal healing derives from a holistic worldview most fully expressed in matriarchal societies of the prehistoric world. These cultures regarded all parts of nature as interconnected aspects of a nurturing whole—the sacred Mother Earth. "Matter" (which derives from the same root word as "mother") was seen as a living being with a life force of her own. To use poultices, roots, and herbs was to trust in her healing energy and her vital force.

...

Healing was associated, in the early matriarchal cultures, with the life-giving capacities of women. The two main goddesses of healing, Hygea and Panacea, were also the names of the Great Goddess's milk-giving breasts.[6] Our own word "nurse" carries this age-old association with women's life-giving, nurturing powers.

For most of human history, lay women healers have seen nature as their ally. Working with the substances of the earth and the body's own healing energy, they have sought to fortify health, not attack disease. Lay women healers have prepared ointments, poultices, herbal teas and baths to relieve pain and to help restore the body to health. They have provided contraceptive measures, performed abortions, and eased the pain of labor. They have washed sores, set bones, massaged painful joints, and performed rituals and prayers. For many women, knowledge of herbal preparations has been as common as is the knowledge of cooking today.[7]

Just as herbal healing rests upon a holistic world view, modern drug-oriented medicine derives from dualistic ideas. Whereas the holistic perspective honors the healing energy of the body and of the earth, modern western medicine is founded upon a distrust of nature and nature's power to heal. The history of western medicine is that of a long protracted struggle to conquer and subdue the vital force of nature; it is the attempt to render her inert. Significantly, in patriarchal cosmologies, it is the *logos* or the *nous* (the "word" or the "mind") which gives birth to the world, not nature or the Goddess herself, as was formerly believed. Increasingly, the vital force of life, including the power to heal, is no longer seen to rest in "mere matter," (the body or the Earth), but rather in the "rational," "scientific" (male) mind.

...

The twin notions of conquering nature and of viewing nature as a machine have become the life-blood of modern western medicine. According to the modern, scientific viewpoint, disease reflects a failure in the body machinery. When disease strikes, it is the body's machinery that must be repaired. Whether the repair takes the form of surgery, a drug, or the replacement of "defective" body parts, such adjustments must be performed by those thought to have the necessary technology, expertise, and skill. The doctor and the doctor's tools alone can mend the failed machine.

Since the modern medical body is conceived as a machine, it is also thought to conform to Newtonian laws of cause and effect. Disease and ill health are thus seen to have a single, external "cause"—usually viruses, bacteria and other microorganisms. In order to restore health to the body, the offending agent need only be identified and rooted out. Typically, these enemy organisms are fought with chemical weapons forced from nature on another battlefront—the modern research laboratory.

This reductionistic view of the healing process has become so entrenched that it is difficult for many people to conceive of healing in any other way. And, yet, the concept of "one disease-one cure" (and one drug) is equally alien to the holistic view.[8] In the holistic tradition, only a single disease exists—namely, an imbalance or a lack of harmony with nature, whether within oneself or with the rest of the natural world.

Today, drugs have become the primary weapon employed by western medicine in its war against disease. Rather than trust in the healing power of nature—i.e., poultices, plants, and the body's own healing energy—western medicine prefers to respond to the "affront" of disease with an assault of its own. ... It is a war waged against the body and all of the natural world. Unable to trust in the healing power of nature, western medicine prefers to "penetrate nature" in order to produce "cures" of its own. Plants are no longer valued in and of themselves. Rather, the most powerful properties of plants must be isolated, extracted and then synthesized into chemicals and drugs. Nature is seen as a resource which is useful only when transformed by men's rational mind.

The human body has become the central battlefield in western medicine's war against disease. Thus, two of the weapons used in the "war" against cancer are nitrogen mustard and radiation, both weapons used during the last world wars. The terminology of warfare permeates the modern, medical world. Thus, we hear of the "war on cancer" declared by presidential decree in 1971. We hear, too, of "bombarding" cells with an arsenal of drugs and of "magic bullets" that "target" cancerous sites. Conversely, we often hear of our alleged enemies described as cancerous growths or other forms of disease. Most of all, we hear that the war *will* be won, provided, of course, that biomedical research scientists are given sufficient funds.

It should come as no surprise, however, that the "war on cancer" (and other diseases) has produced more victims than cures.[9] Indeed, the warfare mentality of western medicine has made medical casualties a routine part of our world. In the United States, prescription drugs have become a major cause of iatrogenic (doctor-induced) disease, causing more deaths each year than accidents on the road.[10] "According to the FDA, 1.5 million Americans had to be hospitalized in 1978 as a consequence of taking drugs (which were supposed to 'cure' them of something or other). And some thirty percent of all hospitalized people get further damaged by the therapy that is imposed on them. The number of people killed in the U.S. by the intake of drugs has been estimated at some 140,000 each year."[11] … Unfortunately, many drug "side effects" only appear after years of use, making it impossible to anticipate what such effects will be.

Meanwhile, the medical assault on our bodies is compounded by a chemical attack on another front—i.e., by the pesticides, additives and other chemicals and drugs that routinely pollute our water, food, and air. This massive chemical attack is wreaking untold damage on the "ecology" of our bodies and thus on our only genuine "defense" against disease—our body's natural immunological response.[12]

Faith in the medical profession has emerged largely unharmed by the prevalence of drug toxicity and drug abuse. On the contrary, most people now accord doctors the same reverence once reserved for priests delivering their sacraments to those who would be saved. And, yet, the veneration that today's doctors have come to expect as their due was only won through a long protracted struggle against all forms of healing that have not conformed to their own. The history of this battle takes us back many years.

…

Although it was the white, upper-class, male medical profession that, under the guise of science, ultimately wrested control from lay women healers, it was the church that initiated the first major blow. An estimated nine million people (mostly women) were executed or burned as witches between 1479 and 1735.[13] Interestingly, one of the titles for witches was "herberia," meaning "one who gathers herbs."[14] Often, the crime such women were accused of was literally their ability to heal. This attack by the church was, at once, directed against the Goddess-worshipping religion which embodied a reverence for all of the natural world and against the peasantry which lived by this tradition and passed its knowledge on.

In order to comprehend why healing should be considered a crime, it is necessary to understand the church's attitude toward women and all of the natural world. According to the church, the vital, healing force of nature resided not within the earth, but rather, within a male, sky God. Disease, illness, and even labor pains, were all expressions of God's will. Only church-approved individuals (mostly men with university training and the priests with whom they were obliged to consult) could work within "God's plan."

While the church was wielding its attack against lay women, the field of science was slowly developing ideas that would ultimately pose a far more serious challenge. The fields of physiology and chemistry, which evolved in part out of the herbal tradition, were subtly supplanting this tradition by subsuming it into a "science." The herbal tradition was not, however, fully usurped by science until many years later. Herbalism continued to be practiced throughout the countryside by lay women healers. Even up until the 1800s, most people consulted herbalists when sick. Drug preparations consisted primarily of "crude plants—i.e., ground up leaves, flowers and roots, or teas, extracts and tinctures of them. Medicine and botany were still intimately allied."[15] By the middle of the nineteenth century, at least in the United States and Europe, 80 percent of medicines used were still derived from plants. Today, less than 30 percent of the drugs used are plant-based.[16]

Only with the rise of the large pharmaceutical industries in the late nineteenth century and with the increased faith in science did the "regular" physicians successfully defeat the herbal, homeopathic, and other holistic traditions. The would-be medical profession saw in the rising pharmaceutical industry an opportunity to bolster its flagging reputation through an increased association with technology and science. To their good fortune, the pharmaceutical industry saw in the "regular" physicians an ideal vehicle for marketing their new drugs. The pharmaceutical industries, thus, began an all-out campaign (which has been continued to this day) to convince the "regulars" to prescribe their drugs. At the same time, the medical profession began an equally virulent drive to discredit the holistic practitioners (i.e., the "irregulars") for failing to fulfill the requirements of a "science." Thus, the fateful marriage between western medicine and science was sealed and the future course of western medicine was set.

...

Today's medical schools are living monuments to the victory of "science" over the earlier holistic worldview. Students now emerge from medical school with myriad courses in chemistry and physics but not a single course in the art of healing herbs. At most, the medical school graduate will have received one course in nutrition. He or she will enter the medical world with the faith of a true believer in the power of "science" (and drugs) to "cure."

The medical profession achieved ascendence over the holistic tradition largely because it was able to convince the public that their new drugs were the major factors in the elimination of infectious disease. The medical profession was, in fact, born of the germ/drug theory of disease on which it continues to thrive to this day. Although strong evidence suggests that most of the major infectious diseases declined most rapidly *before* the discovery of the much-touted vaccination programs and that there was no obvious change after the drugs were introduced,[17] the medical profession continues to proudly proclaim this "conquest" as its own. Careful studies, however, point to the decisive influence of environmental factors—improved nutrition and cleaner water and air.[18] Many of these improvements in health standards were the product of the Popular Health Movement of the 1830s and 1840s which was spearheaded by women.

Western medicine obstinately continues to deny the importance of environmental and lifestyle factors in the causation of disease. Even though it has been estimated that 80 percent or more of all cancers are attributable to environmental factors,[19] medical research continues to pour billions of dollars into finding magic (chemical) cures for this and other diseases. Approximately seventy thousand chemicals are presently in everyday use throughout the world with five hundred to one thousand new ones added to the list each year.[20] Our food is poisoned with pesticides and drugs and industries routinely pollute our water and our air. Research has also shown that meat-eating is a major cause of disease, not only due to the myriad chemicals and hormones that factory farm animals are forced to ingest, but also due to the high levels of protein, bacteria, cholesterol and fat that are found in meat.[21] And yet, the medical profession spends only a fraction of the health dollar on research into the prevention of disease.

One of the reasons for this skewed sense of priorities is that prevention is simply not a very dramatic thing to do. Western medicine is founded upon the notion of the heroic conquest of nature. To credit the environment or lifestyle with importance is letting nature steal the show. ...

...

Modern western medicine has sought to salvage disease from the untamed conditions of the natural world. Within the "controlled" setting of their laboratories, researchers have sought to replicate disease and to manufacture cures. But while medical scientists have been looking for "miracle" cures in their laboratories (apart from the natural world), the healing power of nature has continued to manifest itself throughout our lives. When we cut ourselves and our blood clots and our wound later heals with no outside help, we have seen its power at work. This regenerative life-force pervades every cell of our bodies. All of the various holistic or "alternative" practices attempt to affirm and work with this healing force. Different cultures have called it by a number of names. There is the *Prana* of India, the *Chi* of China and the *Ki* of Japan. The very word *physis*, from which our word "physician" derives, refers to both "Nature" and to this "vital force."

Although many of us have lost our connection to this healing power, it is one that nonhuman animals still retain. Animals *do,* ironically, have something to teach us, but it is not a knowledge that can be wrenched from their bodies behind laboratory walls. Many nonhuman animals know instinctively what to do when ill. For example, a "wild turkey during the rainy season force-feeds her young with leaves of the spice bush; a dog with a digestive problem chews upon the witch grass to produce vomiting; a bear feeds upon the fruit of rockberry with relish while fern roots become his healing agent; the wolf, bitten by a venomous snake, seeks out and chews snakeroot."[22] "Cats and dogs purge themselves with certain grasses and lie in wet mud (a source of natural 'antibiotic') in case of snake or insect bites or other irritations."[23] Wild animals will also naturally seek solitude and relaxation when ill.

...

... A number of commentators believe ... that many of the earliest herbal remedies used by humans were based on ... observations of animals in the wild. The American Indians, who watched bears closely in order to learn what they would eat both for food and for medicine, are a case in point.

...

Although western medicine's war against the body and against nature shows little sign of abating, significant signs of hope are also to be found. One source of hope can be seen in the growth of the animal liberation movement over the last ten years. Animal researchers compare the members of this growing movement to the Luddites who vainly smashed their machines in an attempt to forestall the modern, technological age. However, it is the very conception of animals as machines that the animal liberation movement seeks to destroy. The animal liberation movement, therefore, does pose one of the greatest challenges to the modern, technological age and to the mechanistic conception of life.

Other signs of promise can be found in the growth of the holistic health healing movement. This movement is encouraging not only because of the number of "alternative" health care practitioners who are emerging and the number of people who are now turning to such practitioners for their health care needs, but also because of the knowledge of holistic health care that has reached the public at large. More and more people are incorporating meditation, herbal supplements, yoga and other holistic practices into their daily lives; for the true role of a health care practitioner is not that of a mechanistic "curer" of disease, but rather that of a teacher who can guide us in working with the powers of the natural world.[24]

The wisdom of living in harmony with nature was possessed by our ancestors and is a heritage we would do well to reclaim. This wisdom embodies the principle of nonviolence so alien to modern western medicine in its war against the natural world. Holistic healing is a vital way in which we can honor this wisdom. By helping to integrate body, mind, instinct, and intuition, holistic healing enables us to live in harmony and ecological balance with all of the natural world. Along with the ecofeminist, environmental, and animal liberation movements, of which it is an integral part, holistic healing provides a formidable challenge to the violence perpetrated upon nature by the patriarchal mind. It is an antiwar protest of its own, helping to bring forth a world of peace and nonviolence for all living beings.

---

## Notes

1. For convenience, I have used the term "western medicine" to refer to the practice of "allopathy" which has become the orthodoxy of the medical world today. However, as I hope to show, western medicine is also heir to a rich tradition of holistic healing which it has yet to honor.

2. Barbara Griggs, *Green Pharmacy: A History of Herbal Medicine,* Viking Press, New York, 1982, p. 6.

3. Quoted in Monicao Sjoo and Barbara Mor, *The Great Cosmic Mother: Rediscovering the Religion of the Earth,* Harper and Row, San Francisco, 1987, p. 35.

4. Women constitute a disproportionately large share of the consumer drug market, particularly for mood-modifying and hormonally based drugs. (Kathleen McDonnel, ed., *Adverse Effects: Women and the Pharmaceutical Industry,* Women's Educational Press, Toronto, 1986, pp. 4–6).

5. For an in-depth history of women healers, see Dr. Kate Campbell Hurd-Mead, *A History of Women in Medicine from the Earliest Times to the Beginning of the Nineteenth Century,* The Haddam Press, Haddam, CT, 1938. Also see Barbara Ehrenreich and Deirdre English, *Witches, Midwives and Nurses: A History of Women Healers,* The Feminist Press, Old Westbury, NY, 1973, and Barbara Ehrenreich and Deirdre English, *For Her Own Good: 150 Years of Experts' Advice to Women,* Anchor Books, Garden City, NY, 1978.

6. Barbara Walker, *The Woman's Encyclopedia of Myths and Secrets,* Harper & Row, San Francisco, 1983, p. 420.

7. Griggs, op. cit., p. 89.

8. For an in-depth critique of western medicine's notion of specific aeriology, see Bernard Dixon, *Beyond the Magic Bullet,* Harper & Row, New York, 1978.

9. A recent comprehensive assessment of cancer research in the *New England Journal of Medicine* conceded that "we are losing the war on cancer." (John C. Bailes, III, and Elaine M. Smith, "Progress Against Cancer?," p. 314 (May 8, 1986: 1231).

10. E. W. Martin, Opening Statement, DIA/AMA/FDA/PMA Joint Symposium, "Drug information for patients," *Drug Information Journal,* II, Special Supplement, January 1977, 2S–3S.

11. Hans Reusch, *The Naked Empress,* Civis Publications, Milano, Italy, 1982, p. 12.

12. Evidence for the damage to our immune systems from this medical assault can be found in the unusual rate of increase of immune system related diseases as well as in the appearance of many new strains of drug-resistant bacteria. Thus, although penicillin originally was virtually always successful in treating gonorrhea, there are now strains of gonorrheal bacteria that are resistant to penicillin throughout the world and 90 percent of staphylococci infections no longer respond to it. (H. Smith, *Antibiotics in Clinical Practice,* Pitman Medical, London, 1977; Marc Lappe, *When Antibiotics Fail,* North Atlantic Books, Berkeley, 1986, p. xii).

13. William Woods, *A Casebook on Witchcraft,* G. P. Putnam & Sons, New York, 1974, p. 26.

14. Walker, op. cit., p. 1076.

15. Andrew Weil, *Health and Healing,* Houghton Mifflin Co., Boston, 1988, p. 97.

16. Richard Grossman, *The Other Medicines,* Doubleday and Co., New York, 1985, pp. 86–87.

17. See J. McKinlay and S. McKinlay, "The questionable contribution of medical measures to the decline of mortality in the United States in the twentieth century," *Milbank Memorial Fund Quarterly,* 1977, pp. 405–28. For research on England and Wales, see T. McKeown, *The Role of Medicine: Dream, Mirage, or Nemesis?* Oxford Press, Oxford, 1976.

18. Ibid.

19. John H. Knowles, M.D., "The Responsibility of the Individual," in *Doing Better and Feeling Worse: Health in the United States,* John H. Knowles, M.D., ed., Norton and Co., New York, 1977, p. 63.

20. U.S. International Trade Commission, Synthetic Organic Chemicals: United States Production and Sales, 1985, U.S. Government Printing Office, Washington, DC, 1986; The Number of Chemicals in Use from "The Quest for Chemical Safety," International Register of Potentially Toxic Chemicals Bulletin, May 1985; Number added annually from Michael Shodell, "Risky Business," *Science,* 1985, October 1985.

21. According to a report in "Diet and Stress in Vascular Disease," *Journal of the American Medical Association,* "A vegetarian diet can prevent 97 percent of our coronary occlusions."

(Vol. 176, No. 9, June 3, 1961, p. 806). For more on the health hazards of meat-eating (as well as its other adverse effects), see John Robbins, *Diet for a New America,* Stillpoint Publishing, Walpole, New Hampshire, 1987; and Barbara Parham, *What's Wrong with Eating Meat,* Ananda Marga Publication, Denver, CO, 1979.

22. Ben Charles Harris, *The Compleat Herbal,* Larchmont Books, New York, 1972. p. 23.

23. Ibid., p. 10.

24. According to ancient Chinese doctrine, sages did not treat those who were sick; they instructed those who were well, and they were paid for such advice. If the patient became sick, it was considered partly the doctor's fault and payments ceased. (Huang Ti, Nei Ching Su Wen, *The Yellow Emperor's Classic of Internal Medicine,* trans. Veith, I., Williams and Wilkins, Baltimore, 1949.)

### Other Sources

Armstrong, B., and R. Doll. "Environmental Factors and Cancer Incidence and Mortality in Different Countries with Special Reference to Dietary Practices." *International Journal of Cancer* 15 (1975).

Doll, R. "Prevention of Cancer: Pointers from Epidemiology." Nuffield Hospital Trust, London, 1967.

Epstein, "Environmental Determinants of Cancer." *International Journal of Cancer* 15 (1975).

Fulder, Stephen. *The Tao of Medicine: Oriental Remedies and the Pharmacology of Harmony.* Destiny Books, Rochester, VT.

Higginson, J. "Present Trends in Cancer Epidemiology." Proceedings of the Canadian Cancer Conference 8, 1969.

Higginson, J. "The Role of Geographical Pathology in Environmental Carcinogenesis." *Environmental Cancer.* Baltimore: Williams and Wilkins, 1972.

Melmon, L. "Preventable Drug Reactions—Causes and Cures." *New England Journal of Medicine* 284:1361, 1971.

# *Development, Ecology, and Women*

## Vandana Shiva

### Development as a New Project of Western Patriarchy

'Development' was to have been a post-colonial project, a choice for accepting a model of progress in which the entire world remade itself on the model of the colonising modern west, without having to undergo the subjugation and exploitation that colonialism entailed. The assumption was that western style progress was possible for all. Development, as the improved well-being of all, was thus equated with the westernisation of economic categories—of needs, or productivity, of growth. Concepts and categories about economic development and natural resource utilisation that had emerged in the specific context of industrialisation and capitalist growth in a centre of colonial power, were raised to the level of universal assumptions and applicability in the entirely different context of basic needs satisfaction for the people of the newly independent Third World countries. Yes, as Rosa Luxemberg has pointed out, early industrial development in western Europe necessitated the permanent occupation of the colonies by the colonial powers and the destruction of the local 'natural economy'.[1] According to her, colonialism is a constant necessary condition for capitalist growth: without colonies, capital accumulation would grind to a halt. 'Development' as capital accumulation and the commercialisation of the economy for the generation of 'surplus' and profits thus involved the reproduction not merely of a particular form of creation of wealth, but also of the associated creation of poverty and dispossession. A replication of economic development based on commercialisation of resource use for commodity production in the newly independent countries created the internal colonies.[2] Development was thus reduced to a continuation of the process of colonisation; it became an extension of the project of wealth creation in modern western patriarchy's economic vision, which was based on the exploitation or exclusion of women (of the west and non-west), on the exploitation and degradation of nature, and on the exploitation and erosion of other cultures. 'Development' could not but entail destruction for women, nature and subjugated cultures, which is why, throughout the Third World, women, peasants and tribals are struggling for liberation from 'development' just as they earlier struggled for liberation from colonialism.

The UN Decade for Women was based on the assumption that the improvement of women's economic position would automatically flow from an expansion and diffusion of the development process. Yet, by the end of the Decade, it was becoming clear that development itself was the problem. Insufficient and inadequate 'participation' in 'development' was not the cause for women's increasing under-development; it was rather, their enforced but asymmetric participation in it, by which they bore the costs but were excluded from the benefits, that was responsible. Development exclusivity and dispossession aggravated and deepened the colonial processes of ecological degradation and the loss of political control over nature's sustenance base. Economic growth was a new colonialism, draining resources away from those who needed them most. The discontinuity lay in the fact that it was now new national elites, not colonial powers, that masterminded the exploitation on grounds of 'national interest' and growing GNPs, and it was accomplished with more powerful technologies of appropriation and destruction.

Ester Boserup[3] has documented how women's impoverishment increased during colonial rule; those rulers who had spent a few centuries in subjugating and crippling their own women into de-skilled, de-intellectualised appendages, disfavoured the women of the colonies on matters of access to land, technology and employment.

The economic and political processes of colonial under-development bore the clear mark of modern western patriarchy, and while large numbers of women and men were impoverished by these processes, women tended to lose more. The privatisation of land for revenue generation displaced women more critically, eroding their traditional land use rights. The expansion of cash crops undermined food production, and women were often left with meagre resources to feed and care for children, the aged and the infirm, when men migrated or were conscripted into forced labour by the colonisers. As a collective document by women activists, organisers and researchers stated at the end of the UN Decade for Women, 'The almost uniform conclusion of the Decade's research is that with a few exceptions, women's relative access to economic resources, incomes and employment has worsened, their burden of work has increased, and their relative and even absolute health, nutritional and educational status has declined.'[4]

The displacement of women from productive activity by the expansion of development was rooted largely in the manner in which development projects appropriated or destroyed the natural resource base for the production of sustenance and survival. It destroyed women's productivity both by removing land, water and forests from their management and control, as well as through the ecological destruction of soil, water and vegetation systems so that nature's productivity and renewability were impaired. While gender subordination and patriarchy are the oldest of oppressions, they have taken on new and more violent forms through the project of development. Patriarchal categories which understand destruction as 'production' and regeneration of life as 'passivity' have generated a crisis of survival. Passivity, as an assumed category of the 'nature' of nature and of women, denies the activity of nature and life. Fragmentation and uniformity as assumed categories of progress and development destroy the living forces which arise from relationships within the 'web of life' and the diversity in the elements and patterns of these relationships.

The economic biases and values against nature, women and indigenous peoples are captured in this typical analysis of the 'unproductiveness' of traditional natural societies:

> Production is achieved through human and animal, rather than mechanical, power. Most agriculture is unproductive; human or animal manure may be used but chemical fertilisers and pesticides are unknown. ... For the masses, these conditions mean poverty.[5]

The assumptions are evident: nature is unproductive; organic agriculture based on nature's cycles of renewability spells poverty; women and tribal and peasant societies embedded in nature are similarly unproductive, not because it has been demonstrated that in cooperation they produce *less* goods and services for needs, but because it is assumed that 'production' takes place only when mediated by technologies for commodity production, even when such technologies destroy life. A stable and clean river is not a productive resource in this view: it needs to be 'developed' with dams in order to become so. Women, sharing the river as a commons to satisfy the water needs of their families and society are not involved in productive labour:

when substituted by the engineering man, water management and water use become productive activities. Natural forests remain unproductive till they are developed into monoculture plantations of commercial species. Development thus, is equivalent to maldevelopment, a development bereft of the feminine, the conservation, the ecological principle. The neglect of nature's work in renewing herself, and women's work in producing sustenance in the form of basic, vital needs is an essential part of the paradigm of maldevelopment, which sees all work that does not produce profits and capital as non or unproductive work. As Maria Mies[6] has pointed out, this concept of surplus has a patriarchal bias because, from the point of view of nature and women, it is not based on material surplus produced *over and above* the requirements of the community: it is stolen and appropriated through violent modes from nature (who needs a share of her produce to reproduce herself) and from women (who need a share of nature's produce to produce sustenance and ensure survival).

From the perspective of Third World women, productivity is a measure of producing life and sustenance; that this kind of productivity has been rendered invisible does not reduce its centrality to survival—it merely reflects the domination of modern patriarchal economic categories which see only profits, not life.

…

## Two Kinds of Growth, Two Kinds of Productivity

Maldevelopment is usually called 'economic growth', measured by the Gross National Product. Porritt, a leading ecologist has this to say of GNP:

> *Gross* National Product—for once a word is being used correctly. Even conventional economists admit that the hey-day of GNP is over, for the simple reason that as a measure of progress, it's more or less useless. GNP measures the lot, all the goods and services produced in the money economy. Many of these goods and services are not beneficial to people, but rather a measure of just how much is going wrong; increased spending on crime, on pollution, on the many human casualties of our society, increased spending because of waste or planned obsolescence, increased spending because of growing bureaucracies: it's all counted.[7]

The problem with GNP is that it measures some costs as benefits (e.g. pollution control) and fails to measure other costs completely. Among these hidden costs are the new burdens created by ecological devastation, costs that are invariably heavier for women, both in the North and South. It is hardly surprising, therefore, that as GNP rises, it does not necessarily mean that either wealth or welfare increase proportionately. I would argue that GNP is becoming, increasingly, a measure of how realwealth—the wealth of nature and that produced by women for sustaining life— is rapidly decreasing. When commodity production as the prime economic activity is introduced as development, it destroys the potential of nature and women to produce life and goods and services for basic needs. More commodities and more cash mean less life—in nature (through ecological destruction) and in society (through denial of basic needs). Women are devalued first, because their work cooperates with nature's processes, and second, because work which satisfies needs and ensures sustenance is devalued in general. … Feminism as ecology, and ecology as the revival of Prakriti, the source of all life, become the decentred powers of political and economic transformation and restructuring.

This involves, first, a recognition that categories of 'productivity' and growth which have been taken to be positive, progressive and universal are, in reality, restricted patriarchal categories. When viewed from the point of view of nature's productivity and growth, and women's production of sustenance, they are found to be ecologically destructive and a source of gender inequality. It is no accident that the modern, efficient and productive technologies created within the context of growth in market economic terms are associated with heavy ecological costs, borne largely by women. The resource and energy intensive production processes they give rise to demand ever increasing resource withdrawals from the ecosystem. These withdrawals disrupt essential ecological processes and convert renewable resources into non-renewable ones. A forest for example, provides inexhaustible supplies of diverse biomass over time if its capital stock is maintained and it is harvested on a sustained yield basis. The heavy and uncontrolled demand for industrial and commercial wood, however, requires the continuous overfelling of trees which exceeds the regenerative capacity of the forest ecosystem, and eventually converts the forests into non-renewable resources. Women's work in the collection of water, fodder and fuel is thus rendered more energy and time-consuming. (In Garhwal, for example, I have seen women who originally collected fodder and fuel in a few hours, now travelling long distances by truck to collect grass and leaves in a task that might take up to two days.) Sometimes the damage to nature's intrinsic regenerative capacity is impaired not by over-exploitation of a particular resource but, indirectly, by damage caused to other related natural resources through ecological processes. Thus the excessive overfelling of trees in the catchment areas of streams and rivers destroys not only forest resources, but also renewable supplies of water, through hydrological destabilisation. Resource intensive industries disrupt essential ecological processes not only by their excessive demands for raw material, but by their pollution of air and water and soil. Often such destruction is caused by the resource demands of non-vital industrial products. Inspite of severe ecological crises, this paradigm continues to operate because for the North and for the elites of the South, resources continue to be available, even now. The lack of recognition of nature's processes for survival *as factors in the process of economic development* shrouds the political issues arising from resource transfer and resource destruction, and creates an ideological weapon for increased control over natural resources in the conventionally employed notion of productivity. All other costs of the economic process consequently become invisible. The forces which contribute to the increased 'productivity' of a modern farmer or factory worker for instance, come from the increased use of natural resources. Lovins has described this as the amount of 'slave' labour presently at work in the world.[8] According to him each person on earth, on an average, possesses the equivalent of about 50 slaves, each working a 40 hour week. Man's global energy conversion from all sources (wood, fossil fuel, hydroelectric power, nuclear) is currently approximately $8 \times 10^{12}$ watts. This is more than 20 times the energy content of the food necessary to feed the present world population at the FAO standard diet of 3,600 cal/day. The 'productivity' of the western male compared to women or Third World peasants is not intrinsically superior; it is based on inequalities in the distribution of this 'slave' labour. The average inhabitant of the USA for example has 250 times for 'slaves' than the average Nigerian. 'If Americans were short of 249 of those 250 'slaves', one wonders how efficient they would prove themselves to be?'

In is these resource and energy intensive processes of production which divert resources away from survival, and hence from women. What patriarchy sees as productive work, is, in ecological terms highly destructive production. The second law of thermodynamics predicts that resource intensive and resource wasteful economic development must become a threat to the survival of the human species in the long run. Political struggles based on ecology in industrially advanced countries are rooted in this conflict between *long term survival options* and *short term over-production and over-consumption*. Political struggles of women, peasants and tribals based on ecology in countries like India are far more acute and urgent since they are rooted in the *immediate threat to the options for survival* for the vast majority of the people, *posed by resource intensive and resource wasteful economic growth* for the benefit of a minority.

In the market economy, the organising principle for natural resource use is the maximisation of profits and capital accumulation. Nature and human needs are managed through market mechanisms. Demands for natural resources are restricted to those demands registering on the market; the ideology of development is in large part based on a vision of bringing all natural resources into the market economy for commodity production. When these resources are already being used by nature to maintain her production of renewable resources and by women for sustenance and livelihood, their diversion to the market economy generates a scarcity condition for ecological stability and creates new forms of poverty for women.

## Two Kinds of Poverty

In a book entitled *Poverty: The Wealth of the People*[9] an African writer draws a distinction between poverty as subsistence, and misery as deprivation. It is useful to separate a cultural conception of subsistence living as poverty from the material experience of poverty that is a result of dispossession and deprivation. Culturally perceived poverty need not be real material poverty: subsistence economies which satisfy basic needs through self-provisioning are not poor in the sense of being deprived. Yet the ideology of development declares them so because they do not participate overwhelmingly in the market economy, and do not consume commodities produced for and distributed through the market *even though they might be satisfying those needs through self-provisioning mechanisms*. People are perceived as poor if they eat millets (grown by women) rather than commercially produced and distributed processed foods sold by global agri-business. They are seen as poor if they live in self-built housing made from natural material like bamboo and mud rather than in cement houses. They are seen as poor if they wear handmade garments of natural fibre rather than synthetics. Subsistence, as culturally perceived poverty, does not necessarily imply a low physical quality of life. On the contrary, millets are nutritionally far superior to processed foods, houses built with local materials are far superior, being better adapted to the local climate and ecology, natural fibres are preferable to man-made fibres in most cases, and certainly more affordable. This cultural perception of prudent subsistence living as poverty has provided the legitimisation for the development process as a poverty removal project. As a culturally biased project it destroys wholesome and sustainable lifestyles and creates real material poverty, or misery, by the denial of survival needs themselves, through the diversion of resources to resource intensive commodity production. Cash crop production and food processing take land and water resources away from sustenance needs, and exclude increasingly large numbers of people from their entitlements to food. 'The inexorable processes of agriculture-industrialisation and internationalisation are probably responsible for more hungry people than either cruel or unusual whims of nature. There are several reasons why the high-technology-export-crop model increases hunger. Scarce land, credit, water and technology are pre-empted for the export market. Most hungry people are not affected by the market at all. ... The profits flow to corporations that have no interest in feeding hungry people without money.'[10]

...

The economic system based on the patriarchal concept of productivity was created for the very specific historical and political phenomenon of colonialism. In it, the input for which efficiency of use had to be maximised in the production centres of Europe, was industrial labour. For colonial interest therefore, it was rational to improve the labour resource *even at the cost of wasteful use of nature's wealth*. This rationalisation has, however, been illegitimately universalised to all contexts and interest groups and, on the plea of increasing productivity, labour reducing technologies have been introduced in situations where labour is abundant and cheap, and resource demanding technologies have been introduced where resources are scarce and already fully utilised for the production of sustenance. Traditional economies with a stable ecology have shared with industrially advanced affluent economies the ability to use natural resources to satisfy basic vital needs. The former differ from the latter in two essential ways: first, the same needs are satisfied in industrial societies through longer technological chains requiring higher energy and resource inputs and excluding large numbers without purchasing power; and second, affluence generates new and artificial needs requiring the increased production of industrial goods and services. Traditional economies are not advanced in the matter of non-vital needs satisfaction, but as far as the satisfaction of basic and vital needs is concerned, they are often what Marshall Sahlins has called 'the original affluent society'. The needs of the Amazonian tribes are more than satisfied by the rich rainforest; their poverty begins with its destruction. The story is the same for the Gonds of Bastar in India or the Penans of Sarawak in Malaysia.

Thus are economies based on indigenous technologies viewed as 'backward' and 'unproductive'. Poverty, as the denial of basic needs, is not necessarily associated with the existence of traditional technologies, and its removal is not necessarily an outcome of the growth of modern ones. On the contrary, the destruction of ecologically sound traditional technologies, often created and used by women, along with the destruction of their material base is generally believed to be responsible for the 'feminisation' of poverty in societies which have had to bear the costs of resource destruction.

… The creation of inequality through economic activity which is ecologically disruptive arises in two ways: first, inequalities in the distribution of privileges make for unequal access to natural resources—these include privileges of both a political and economic nature. Second, resource intensive production processes have access to subsidised raw material on which a substantial number of people, especially from the less privileged economic groups, depend for their survival. The consumption of such industrial raw material is determined purely by market forces, and not by considerations of the social or ecological requirements placed on them. The costs of resource destruction are externalised and unequally divided among various economic groups in society, but are borne largely by women and those who satisfy their basic material needs directly from nature, simply because they have no purchasing power to register their demands on the goods and services provided by the modern production system. Gustavo Esteva has called development a permanent war waged by its promoters and suffered by its victims.[11]

The paradox and crisis of development arises from the mistaken identification of culturally perceived poverty with real material poverty, and the mistaken identification of the growth of commodity production as better satisfaction of basic needs. In actual fact, there is less water, less fertile soil, less genetic wealth as a result of the development process. Since these natural resources are the basis of nature's economy and women's survival economy, their scarcity is impoverishing women and marginalised peoples in an unprecedented manner. Their new impoverishment lies in the fact that resources which supported their survival were absorbed into the market economy while they themselves were excluded and displaced by it.

The old assumption that with the development process the availability of goods and services will automatically be increased and poverty will be removed, is now under serious challenge from women's ecology movements in the Third World, even while it continues to guide development thinking in centres of patriarchal power. Survival is based on the assumption of the sanctity of life; maldevelopment is based on the assumption of the sacredness of 'development'. Gustavo Esteva asserts that the sacredness of development has to be refuted because it threatens survival itself. 'My people are tired of development', he says, 'they just want to live.'[12]

The recovery of the feminine principle [as understood in Hindu cosmology] allows a transcendence and transformation of these patriarchal foundations of maldevelopment. It allows a redefinition of growth and productivity as categories linked to the production, not the destruction, of life. It is thus simultaneously an ecological and a feminist political project which legitimises the way of knowing and being that create wealth by enhancing life and diversity, and which delegitimises the knowledge and practise of a culture of death as the basis for capital accumulation.

## Notes

1. Rosa Luxemberg, *The Accumulation of Capital,* London: Routledge and Kegan Paul, 1951.

2. An elaboration of how 'development' transfers resources from the poor to the well-endowed is contained in J. Bandyopadhyay and V. Shiva, 'Political Economy of Technological Polarisations' in *Economic and Political Weekly,* Vol. XVIII, 1982, pp. 1827–32; and J. Bandyopadhyay and V. Shiva, 'Political Economy of Ecology Movements', in *Economic and Political Weekly,* forthcoming.

3. Ester Boserup, *Women's Role in Economic Development,* London: Allen and Unwin, 1970.

4. DAWN, *Development Crisis and Alternative Visions: Third World Women's Perspectives,* Bergen: Christian Michelsen Institute, 1985, p. 21.

5. M. George Foster, *Traditional Societies and Technological Change,* Delhi: Allied Publishers, 1973.

6. Maria Mies, *Patriarchy and Accumulation on a World Scale,* London: Zed Books, 1986.

7. Jonathan Porritt, *Seeing Green,* Oxford: Blackwell, 1984.

8. A. Lovins, cited in S.R. Eyre, *The Real Wealth of Nations,* London: Edward Arnold, 1978.

9. R. Bahro, *From Red to Green,* London: Verso, 1984, p. 211.

10. R.J. Barnet, *The Lean Years,* London: Abacus, 1981. p. 171.

11. Gustavo Esteva, 'Regenerating People's Space' in S.N. Mendlowitz and R.B.J. Walker, *Towards a Just World Peace: Perspectives From Social Movements,* London: Butterworths and Committee for a Just World Peace, 1987.

12. G. Esteva, Remarks made at a Conference of the Society for International Development, Rome, 1985.

# Conversations with Gaia

## Val Plumwood

The image of Gaia, often used to invoke an alternative to increasingly discredited western ways of viewing the biosphere, has helped to repopularize the notion of Mother Nature, until recently regarded as somewhat quaint. It is an image which appears to represent an extraordinary convergence of historical circumstances and currents—feminism, ecology, disillusionment with both rationalism and conventional religion and a search for new meaning, and alternative science in the form of Lovelock's Gaia hypothesis. This convergence may explain the extraordinary speed with which it has become popular. Clearly the seed has fallen on ground already prepared for it.

Perhaps that very ease of conquest is a reason for suspicion: one feels that a real break with tendencies so deeply rooted in our culture would have to be harder to win. Given the often demonstrated capacity of western culture to construct supposed alternatives which reproduce in subtle forms the old dynamics of power we are trying to escape, feminists are right to be suspicious and critical. But we should not dismiss the possibility too, that it draws on cultural roots which are old and deep, and which after 4000 years are still living and capable of putting forth green shoots, as resilient as the olive itself.

> Nobody knows how long it takes to kill an olive. Drought, axe, fire, are admitted failures. Hack one down, grub out a ton of mainroot for fuel, and the next spring every side root sends up shoots. A great frost can leave the trees leafless for years; they revive. Invading armies will fell them. They return through the burnt out ribs of siege machines.[1]

Gaia imagery raises for feminists a number of pressing questions. Does it involve a feminist recognition of female power and an environmental recognition of human dependence, or does it continue the backgrounding of nature and the feminine which has been so typical of the western tradition? Is the continued use of feminine imagery helpful, both for women and for nature? If the past use of feminine imagery and the assimilation of women to the sphere of nature has mainly served to intensify and reinforce their domination, can we now shed such meanings and give a new and liberatory significance to the feminization of nature? In a famous passage, Simone de Beauvoir writes of the ambivalence feminized nature inspires as both "the source of his being and the realm that he subjugates to his will and Idea; these forms now mingle and now conflict, and each of them wears a double visage."[2]

I shall argue in this paper that the Gaia imagery also points in two directions, has "a double visage," and must be treated with caution: Just to the extent that it retains patriarchal meanings, it is unhelpful both for nature and for women. However, there is some potential for the image of Gaia to provide a symbol and rallying point for an alternative culture which recognizes these problems. An examination of the issue here also points up some important but neglected aspects of western attitudes to nature and highlights some of the ways they need to change.

...

## Nature and Motherhood

As Ecofeminists have claimed, the backgrounding and instrumentalization of nature and women have run parallel. Systematic backgrounding and systematic devaluation are perceptually ingrained, forms of not noticing, not seeing. The way in which we background nature is evident in our treatment of it in a range of areas: for example, it is backgrounded in standard treatments of human history, where we never or rarely hear of ecological factors or natural limits as important factors in the decline and well-being of human social groups and civilizations, although they certainly have been.[3] It is backgrounded in standard economics where notoriously, no value is given to anything natural, or to resources as they stand before they acquire use value or before human labor is applied, and which takes no account of natural limits and treats ecological factors as "externalities." Similarly, the instrumental role of women does not usually need to be explicit, for it is written into women's role. Women need only be told to be women. Women are systematically backgrounded in many roles in both the public and the private sphere—as housewives,[4] as secretaries,[5] as colleagues and as workmates. Their labor in traditional roles is often systematically omitted from accounts in the economic system[6] and omitted from consideration when the story of what is important in human history and culture is told. Traditionally, women are "the environment"—they provide the environment and conditions against which male "achievement" takes place, but what they do is not itself accounted as achievement. Women are vulnerable to backgrounding even when they step outside their traditional roles, as the history of DNA research makes plain, but are most strongly backgrounded in their traditional roles and especially in their roles as mothers.

In fact, much of what has been wrong with western attitudes to nature may be captured in terms of parallel patriarchal attitudes to the feminine sphere and to the mother. If the dominant popular view has been one of nature as a nurturing mother,[7] this has not necessarily brought respect or love for either women or nature.[8] Within the Australian tradition for example, nature has often been viewed as the demonic mother, hostile and pitiless.[9] Patriarchy has never treated motherhood with unmixed respect.

If the model of nature is one of motherhood, it is the patriarchal conception of motherhood which has been, and mostly continues to be invoked, the conception of the mother as one who provides without cease; whose own needs, if they exist at all, always come second; whose value is determined by the child she produces; whose work is both expected, devalued and invisible, its real skill, importance and difficulty underestimated and defined into nature. They physical, personal and social skills she teaches the child are merely the background to real learning, which is defined as part of the male sphere.[10] The mother herself is background and is defined in relation to her child or its father, just as nature is defined in relation to the human as "the environment." And just as in western culture the human essence is defined in opposition to nature, so the mother's product, that which provides her raison d'etre and defines her essence—paradigmatically the male child—defines his masculine identity in opposition to her being, and especially her nurturance, expelling it from his own makeup and substituting domination and the reduction of others to instrumental status. He resists recognition of dependence, but continues to conceptually order his world in terms of a male sphere of free activity taking place against a female background of necessity.

The fact that the Gaian mother imagery has this background is not necessarily a reason for abandoning it so much as yet another good reason for seeing the liberation of women and the liberation of nature as intimately connected. From a feminist perspective, its use would be acceptable only if it does not reinforce an oppressive institution for women and respects feminist attempts to give a new meaning to motherhood. From an ecological viewpoint, Gaia would be a successful way to render nature just to the extent that it was able to render motherhood in terms of something other than traditional motherhood. For if we continue to think of nature along these traditional lines, we will be not only reinforcing women's oppression but reproducing many of the worst attitudes and traditions with respect to nature, however fashionably disguised in "Gaia" terminology. If the biosphere is a mother for humankind, she must be accounted not a passive, controllable and self-effacing provider but a powerful, potentially dangerous and stern mother, and one with no special concern for the fate of the most troublesome and arrogant of her numerous children, humankind.[11]

...

## Positive Aspects for Nature

Gaia partakes of many of the same complexities and ambivalences as motherhood itself. Motherhood is more than a prison for women; as many feminists have emphasized, it is also a potential source of alternative social relations and a key area of women's healing practice of connection to others.[12] Gaia similarly could provide much needed improvements in western ways of conceptualizing both women and nature. First, it seems that the concept could provide a way of recognizing nature, of asserting that the biosphere should not be viewed as an empty, dead mechanism, but as a living being which is a composite of living beings and with whom we must enter into dialogue. Thus, recognition of Gaia seems capable of providing an alternative to mechanistic ways of viewing nature. Second, through the stress on continuity and close kinship with the earth, recognition of Gaia could perhaps provide a corrective to the western tradition of stress on human discontinuity. Third, the recognition of Gaia as nurturer of all the species of the earth could help in countering human arrogance, the belief that humans are the chosen ones of evolution, rather than just some of Gaia's many children, and with no exclusive claim to the earth. Fourth, recognition of Gaia could provide a way to foreground the backgrounded sphere of reproduction and to recognize motherhood as a primary social relationship. It could also be an effective way to allow recognition of our primary human dependence on the biosphere for our basic physical being.

These four considerations would be valuable contributions to reworking our relationship to the earth. Unfortunately Gaia-as-mother, even if treated in ways liberatory for women, does not do many of these things with unqualified success. A conception of the earth as a living being with needs of its own with whom we must enter into dialogue could, I believe, be most valuable, and would certainly be a vast improvement over the belittling and commodified images of the globe as seen from space which are now used to sell everything from computers to armaments.[13] These images, which have proliferated remarkably recently, seem to be designed to reassure us that the earth really is a small and compassable object, easily manipulated and controlled through technology. But it is not clear that the Gaia concept as introduced by Lovelock successfully overcomes a reductionistic mechanism. Lovelock uses Gaia as a metaphor for a set of homeostatic mechanisms which yield a reductive understanding of life and teleology and operate through principles of physics and chemistry.[14] Lovelock is at pains to point this out and in fact distances himself from a less reductionist understanding of Gaia.[15] The concept of Gaia as a holistic, planetary being and as symbol of the mutuality and communicative exchange or dialogue we could experience with nature carries the danger of reproducing the rationalist tendency to deify the abstract and universal (this time as cosmic mother) at the expense of the particular, the daily, and the small-scale (all tendencies well-developed in deep ecology).[16] A cosmic conversation with the whole is not a substitute for and should not be allowed to drown out the diverse daily conversations we can have with the myriad particular beings who share this planet with us. Gaia can provide a way to recognize continuity, but so can other models which might in some respects be better. Gaia as mother provides a model which encourages recognition of our dependency on the biosphere, but in a way which perhaps does not allow sufficient and corresponding recognition of our own responsibility and power in relation to her. If Gaia was an appropriate image for peoples whose power in relation to the earth was less than our own, she may no longer be appropriate for modern industrial society.

Can Gaia provide symbolism which is empowering of women and the reproductive sphere generally? Plainly, only if the concept is used in non-patriarchal ways. We could try to retain the mother imagery and give it a new, liberatory meaning, one which does not identify women with motherhood, background motherhood, or treat it as a task just for women or restricted to the narrow confines of the nuclear family for its context or the human child for its object. The concept itself does not automatically empower women or nature, and remains dangerously open to co-option. In fact, I suspect that the mother model has been so powerful in western thought precisely because of its ambivalence. Thousands of years of patriarchal definition of the most basic human and animal relationship are not so easily shed.

…

## Alternative Models

… Given the diversity and complexity of our relations to nature, it seems unlikely that any single model will be adequate. We need a variety of models, and we need to think about the implications of all of them.

A highly flexible model which seems to capture some of the advantages of the mother model and which allows for the mother relation as an element is that of kinship. This model, for example as used by Australian Aboriginal people,[17] makes it possible to think of the earth in terms of a variety of close relations, including both mother and brother. It symbolizes human relations to the land in terms of these special relationships and others, and is most applicable to relationships to particular areas of land to which there is special attachment, or to a bioregionalist position. It allows that the earth, or particular parts of it, can be as essentially related to the self, as important a part of one's personal and social identity, and as deeply loved and grieved for if lost, as any human kin. Kinship has been the basis for a dialogue many tribal systems have heard but which the rationalist/scientific west has been long unable to hear. In Aboriginal ways of thinking about the earth, the model is to be taken literally, since the death of kin provides both a spiritual and a physical relation between the land and one's kin—past, present and future—via burial and return to the earth.[18]

We need a model for care and dialogue which enables us to recognize both our dependence on nature and also our reciprocal responsibilities and powers. On such a model we would not be free to order human lives and communities without recognition of these bonds and limits, as western liberal individualism encourages us to do. Kinship bonds do provide a good model for much of this. Ignoring the earth and the limits and responsibilities it places on us is in many ways like ignoring ties to kin, or to a wider human community, and could be regarded as a similar sort of moral failing.

The kinship model, like the mother model, acknowledges human continuity with nature, but also acknowledges human difference from nature. Depending on the particular kin relations involved, it may not stress human dependence or the power of nature as strongly as the mother model. But it allows both for greater responsibility and for the mother model where it is appropriate. It allows, too, for the reversal of the mother model; that we humans will ourselves sometimes need to adopt a mothering or nurturing relation with respect to nature, or to specific parts of it. This model of maternal care and compassion for the earth may in turn be problematic as a general model for relations to nature, because it takes as its paradigmatic relation one which carries a great deal of human power and which does not clearly allow in turn for the freedom or power of nature. But as the earth and its non-human inhabitants become increasingly wounded by human activities, this nurturing and healing relationship may, sadly, be the one we are most called upon to practice.

---

## Notes

1. From "To Kill an Olive" by Mark O'Connor, from *The Eating Tree* (Sydney: Curtis Brown, 1980).

2. Simone de Beauvoir, *The Second Sex: Vol. 1* (Four Square Books, 1961), p. 170.

3. It does not follow that they should be attributed as major or as reductive a role as they are given in some recent work. Paul Colinvaux, *The Fates of Nations* (Pelican Books, 1983). Presents a sort of converse ecological reductionism.

4. See Maria Mies, *Patriarchy and Accumulation on a World Scale* (London: Zed Books, 1986).

5. Rosemary Pringle, *Secretaries Talk: Sexuality, Power and Work* (Sydney: Allen and Unwin, 1988).

6. Marilyn Waring, *Counting For Nothing* (Allen and Unwin, 1988).

7. Carolyn Merchant, *The Death of Nature* (Wildwood House, 1980).

8. Marina Warner, *Alone of All Her Sex* (New York: Knopf, 1976).

9. Kay Schaffer, *Women and the Bush* (Cambridge: Cambridge University Press, 1988).

10. Jessica Benjamin, *The Bonds of Love* (London: Virago, 1988), especially chapter 1. See also Luce Irigaray, "One does not move without the other," *Refractory Girl* (March 1982), pp. 12–14.

11. J. E. Lovelock, *The Ages of Gaia* (Oxford University Press, 1989), p. 212.

12. See especially Sara Ruddick, *Maternal Thinking* (Boston: Beacon Press, 1989); Jean Baker Miller, *Towards a New Psychology of Women* (London: Penguin, 1979).

13. See Yaakov Jerome Garb, "The Use and Misuse of the Whole Earth Image," *Whole Earth Review* (no. 45 March 1985), pp. 18–25.

14. Lovelock (1989), p. 18.

15. Ibid., p. 215–218.

16. Val Plumwood, "Nature, Self and Gender: Feminism, Environmental Philosophy and the Critique of Rationalism" *Hypatia* (6[1] 1991); Jim Cheney, "The Neo-Stoicism of Radical Environmentalism" *Environmental Ethics* (1989) 11:293–325; "Ecofeminism and Deep Ecology," *Environmental Ethics* (1987), Vol. 9: 115–145.

17. Bill Neidjie, Allan Fox and Stephen Davis, *Kakadu Man* (Canberra: Mybrood P/L, 1986), and Bill Neidjie (ed. Keith Taylor), *Story About Feeling* (Wyndham: Magabala Books, 1989).

18. Bill Neidjie, op. cit. He writes: "Rock stays, earth stays. I die and put my bones in cave or earth. Soon my bones become earth. … My spirit has gone back to my country … my mother" (Kakadu Man p. 82). Elsewhere Bill Neidjie does not appear to privilege the image of the earth as mother over other views of the earth as a close relative, e.g., "Course your granny, your mother, your brother, because this earth, this ground, this piece of ground e grow you." (p. 30 *Story about Feeling*).

# Searching for Common Ground: Ecofeminism and Bioregionalism

## Judith Plant

...

## Ecofeminism: Its Values and Dimensions

Why does patriarchal society want to forget its biological connections with nature? And why does it seek to gain control over life in the form of women, other peoples, and nature? And what can we do about dismantling this process of domination? What kind of society could live in harmony with its environment? These questions form the basis of the ecofeminist perspective.

Before the world was mechanized and industrialized, the metaphor that explained self, society, and the cosmos was the image of organism. This is not surprising since most people were connected with the Earth in their daily lives, living a subsistence existence. The Earth was seen as female, with two faces: one, the passive, nurturing mother; the other, wild and uncontrollable. These images served as cultural constraints. The Earth was seen to be alive, sensitive; it was considered unethical to do violence toward her. Who could conceive of killing a mother, or digging into her body for gold, or mutilating her? But, as society began to shift from a subsistence economy to a market economy; as European cities grew and forested areas shrunk; and as the people moved away from the immediate, daily organic relationships that had once been their basis for survival, peoples' cultural values—and thus their metaphors—had to change. The image of Earth as passive and gentle receded. The "wrath and fury" of nature, as woman, was the quality that now justified the new idea of "power over nature." With the new technology, man (sic) would be able to subdue her.

The organic metaphor that once explained everything was replaced by mechanical images. By the mid-seventeenth century, society had rationalized the separation of itself from nature. With nature "dead" in this view, exploitation was purely a mechanical function, and it proceeded apace.

The new images were of controlling and dominating: having power over nature. Where the nurturing image had once been a cultural restraint, the new image of mastery allowed the clearing of forests and the damming and poisoning of rivers. And human culture that, in organic terms, should reflect the wide diversity in nature, was reduced to monoculture, a simplification solely for the benefit of marketing.

Since the subjugation of women and nature is a social construction, not a biologically determined fact, our position of inferiority can be changed. At the same time that we create the female as an independent individual, we can be healing the mind/body split.

Life struggles in nature become feminist issues within the ecofeminist perspective. Once we understand the historical connections between women and nature and their subsequent oppression, we cannot help but take a stand in the war against nature. By participating in these environmental standoffs against those who are assuming the right to control the natural world, we are helping to create an awareness of domination at all levels.

Ecofeminism gives women and men common ground. While women may have been associated with nature, they have been socialized to think in the same dualities as men have and we feel just as alienated as do our brothers. The social system isn't good for either of us! Yet, we *are* the social system. We need some common ground from which to be critically self-conscious, to enable us to recognize and affect the deep structure of our relations with each other and with our environment.

In addition to participating in forms of resistance, such as nonviolent civil disobedience in support of environmental issues, we can also encourage, support, and develop—within our communities—a cultural life that celebrates the many differences in nature and encourages thought on the consequences of our actions, in all our relations.

Bioregionalism, with its emphasis on distinct regional cultures and identities strongly attached to their natural environments, may well be the kind of framework within which the philosophy of ecofeminism could realize its full potential as part of a practical social movement.

## Bioregionalism: An Integrating Idea

Bioregionalism means learning to become native to place, fitting ourselves to a particular place, not fitting a place to our predetermined tastes. It is living within the limits and the gifts provided by a place creating a way of life that can be passed on to future generations. …

By understanding the limitations of political change—revolution—bioregionalists are taking a broader view, considering change in evolutionary terms. Rather than winning or losing, or taking sides, as being the ultimate objective, *process* has come to be seen as key to our survival. *How* we go about making decisions and how we act them out are as important as *what* we are trying to decide or do.

In evolutionary terms, a species' adaptation must be sustainable if the species is to survive. How can humans meet their requirements and live healthy lives? What would an ecologically sustainable human culture be like? It is in dealing with these questions that the bioregional movement and the philosophy of ecofeminism are very much interconnected.

Human adaptation has to do with culture. What has happened with the rise of civilization, and most recently with the notion of mass culture, is that what could be called bioregionally adapted human groups *no longer can exist*. It is difficult to imagine how society could be structured other than through centralized institutions that service the many. In our culture almost every city exists beyond its carrying capacity; diverse regions are being exhausted and ecologically devastated.

Becoming native to a place—learning to live in it on a sustainable basis over time—is not just a matter of appropriate technology, homegrown food, or even "reinhabiting" the city. It has very much to do with a shift in morality, in the attitudes and behaviors of human beings. With the help of feminism women especially have learned an intimate lesson about the way power works. We have painfully seen that it is the same attitude that allows violence toward us that also justifies the rape of the Earth. Literally, the images are the same. We also know that we are just as capable, generally speaking, of enacting the same kind of behavior.

The ideas of bioregionalism are being practiced all over the world—though they are rarely referred to as such. The name gives us common ground, however, like ecofeminism. But bioregionalism gives us something to practice and together they offer a *praxis*—that is, a way of living what we're thinking. Here we can begin to develop an effective method of sharing with our male friends the lessons we have learned about power, as well as our hopes and aspirations for an egalitarian society—a society that would be based on the full participation and involvement of women and men in the process of adaptation and thus in the maintenance of healthy ecosystems.

## Homing in on a New Image

One of the key ideas of bioregionalism is the decentralization of power: moving further and further toward self-governing forms of social organization. The further we move in this direction, the closer we get to what has traditionally been thought of as "woman's sphere"—that is, home and its close surroundings. Ideally, the bioregional view values home above all else, because it is here where new values and behaviors are actually created. Here, alternatives can root and flourish and become deeply embedded in our way of being. This is not the same notion of home as the bungalow in the suburbs of Western industrialized society! Rather, it is the place where we can learn the values of caring for and nurturing each other and our environments and of paying attention to immediate human needs and feelings. It is a much broader term, reflecting the reality of human cultural requirements and our need to be sustainably adaptive within our nonhuman environments. The word *ecology,* in its very name, points us in this direction: *oikos,* the Greek root of "eco," means home.

The catch is that, in practice, home, with all its attendant roles will not be anything different from what it has been throughout recent history *without* the enlightened perspective offered by feminism. Women's values, centered around life-giving, must be revalued, elevated from their once subordinate role. What women know from experience needs recognition and respect. We have had generations of experience in conciliation, dealing with interpersonal conflicts in daily domestic life. We know how to feel for others because we have practiced it.

At the same time, our work—tending to human physical requirements—has been undervalued. What has been considered material and physical has been thought to be "less than" the intellectual, the "outside" (of home) world. Women have been very much affected by this devaluation, and this is reflected in our images of ourselves and our attitudes toward our work. Men, too, have been alienated from child-care and all the rest of daily domestic life, which has a very nurturing effect on all who participate. Our society has devalued the source of its human-ness.

Home is the theater of our human ecology, and it is where we can effectively "think feelingly." Bioregionalism, essentially, is attempting to rebuild human and natural community. We know that it is nonadaptive to repeat the social organization that left women and children alone, at home, and men out in the world doing the "important" work. The *real work* is at home. It is not simply a question of fairness or equality; it is because, as a species, we have to actually work things out—just as in the so-called natural world—with all our relations. As part of this process, women and nature, indeed *humans* and nature, need a new image, as we mend our relations with each other and with the Earth. Such an image will surely reflect what we are learning through the study of ecology, what we are coming to understand through feminism, and what we are experiencing by participating in the bioregional project.

---

## Notes

A major source for this essay is Carolyn Merchant's *The Death of Nature* (New York: Harper & Row, 1979).

# Women, Home, and Community: The Struggle in an Urban Environment

## Cynthia Hamilton

In 1956, women in South Africa began an organized protest against the pass laws. As they stood in front of the office of the prime minister, they began a new freedom song with the refrain "now you have touched the women, you have struck a rock." This refrain provides a description of the personal commitment and intensity women bring to social change. Women's actions have been characterized as "spontaneous and dramatic," women in action portrayed as "intractable and uncompromising."[1] Society has summarily dismissed these as negative attributes. When in 1986 the City Council of Los Angeles decided that a 13-acre incinerator called LANCER (for Los Angeles City Energy Recovery Project), burning 2,000 tons a day of municipal waste, should be built in a poor residential, Black, and Hispanic community, the women there said "No." Officials had indeed dislodged a boulder of opposition. ...

Minority communities shoulder a disproportionately high share of the by-products of industrial development: waste, abandoned factories and warehouses, leftover chemicals and debris. These communities are also asked to house the waste and pollution no longer acceptable in White communities, such as hazardous landfills or dump sites. In 1987, the Commission for Racial Justice of the United Church of Christ published *Toxic Wastes and Race*. The commission concluded that race is a major factor related to the presence of hazardous wastes in residential communities throughout the United States. Three out of every five Black and Hispanic Americans live in communities with uncontrolled toxic sites; 75 percent of the residents in rural areas in the Southwest, mainly Hispanics, are drinking pesticide-contaminated water; more than 2 million tons of uranium tailings are dumped on Native-American reservations each year, resulting in Navajo teenagers having seventeen times the national average of organ cancers; more than 700,000 inner city children, 50 percent of them Black, are said to be suffering from lead poisoning, resulting in learning disorders. Working-class minority women are therefore motivated to organize around very pragmatic environmental issues, rather than those associated with more middle-class organizations. According to Charlotte Bullock, "I did not come to the fight against environmental problems as an intellectual but rather as a concerned mother. … People say, 'But you're not a scientist, how do you know it's not safe?' I have common sense. I know if dioxin and mercury are going to come out of an incinerator stack, somebody's going to be affected."

When Concerned Citizens of South Central Los Angeles came together in 1986 to oppose the solid waste incinerator planned for the community, no one thought much about environmentalism or feminism. These were just words in a community with a 78 percent unemployment rate, an average income ($8,158) less than half that of the general Los Angeles population, and a residential density more than twice that of the whole city. In the first stages of organization, what motivated and directed individual actions was the need to protect home and children; for the group this individual orientation emerged as a community-centered battle. What was left in this deteriorating district on the periphery of the central business and commercial district had to be defended—a "garbage dump" was the final insult after years of neglect, watching downtown flourish while residents were prevented from borrowing enough to even build a new roof.

The organization was never gender restricted but it became apparent after a while that women were the majority. The particular kind of organization the group assumed, the actions engaged in, even the content of what was said, were all a product not only of the issue itself, the waste incinerator, but also a function of the particular nature of women's oppression and what happens as the process of consciousness begins.

Women often play a primary part in community action because it is about things they know best. Minority women in several urban areas have found themselves part of a new radical core as the new wave of environmental action, precipitated by the irrationalities of capital-intensive growth, has catapulted them forward. These individuals are responding not to "nature" in the abstract but to the threat to their homes and to the health of their children. Robin Cannon, another activist in the fight against the Los Angeles incinerator, says, "I have asthma, my children have asthma, by brothers and sisters have asthma, there are a lot of health problems that people living around an incinerator might be subjected to and I said, 'They can't do this to me and my family.'"

Women are more likely than men to take on these issues precisely because the home has been defined and prescribed as a woman's domain. According to British sociologist Cynthia Cockburn, "In a housing situation that is a health hazard, the woman is more likely to act than a man because she lives there all day and because she is impelled by fear for her children. Community action of this kind is a significant phase of class struggle, but it is also an element of women's liberation."[2]

This phenomenon was most apparent in the battle over the Los Angeles incinerator. Women who had had no history of organizing responded as protectors of their children. Many were single parents, others were older women who had raised families. While the experts were convinced that their smug dismissal of the validity of the health concerns these women raised would send them away, their smugness only re-enforced the women's determination. ... None of the officials were prepared for the intensity of concern or the consistency of agitation. In fact, the consultants they hired had concluded that these women did not fit the prototype of opposition. The consultants had concluded:

> Certain types of people are likely to participate in politics, either by virtue of their issue awareness or their financial resources, or both. Members of middle or higher socioeconomic strata (a composite index of level of education, occupational prestige, and income) are more likely to organize into effective groups to express their political interests and views. All socioeconomic groupings tend to resent the nearby siting of major facilities, but the middle and upper socioeconomic strata possess better resources to effectuate their opposition. Middle and higher socioeconomic strata neighborhoods should not fall at least within the one mile and five mile radii of the proposed site.
>   ... although environmental concerns cut across all subgroups, people with a college education, young or middle aged, and liberal in philosophy are most likely to organize opposition to the siting of a major facility. Older people, with a high school education or less, and those who adhere to a free market orientation are least likely to oppose a facility.[3]

The organizers against the incinerator in South Central Los Angeles are the antithesis of the prototype: they are high school educated or less, above middle age and young, nonprofessionals and unemployed and low-income, without previous political experience. The consultants and politicians thus found it easy to believe that opposition from this group could not be serious.

...

The women in South Central Los Angeles were not alone in their battle. They were joined by women from across the city, White, middle-class, and professional women. ... These two groups of women, together, have created something previously unknown in Los Angeles—unity of purpose across neighborhood and racial lines. ...

This unity has been accomplished by informality, respect, tolerance of spontaneity, and decentralization. All of the activities that we have been told destroy organizations have instead worked to sustain this movement. For example, for a year and a half the group functioned without a formal leadership structure. The unconscious acceptance of equality and democratic process resulted practically in rotating the chair's position at meetings. Newspeople were disoriented when they asked for the spokesperson and the group responded that everyone could speak for the neighborhood.

...

The experts' insistence on referring to congenital deformities and cancers as "acceptable risks" cut to the hearts of women who rose to speak of a child's asthma, or a parent's influenza, or the high rate of cancer, heart disease, and pneumonia in this poverty-stricken community. The callous disregard of human concerns brought the women closer together. They came to rely on each other as they were subjected to the sarcastic rebuffs of men who referred to their concerns as "irrational, uninformed, and disruptive." The contempt of the male experts was directed at professionals and the unemployed, at Whites and Blacks—all the women were castigated as irrational and uncompromising. As a result, new levels of consciousness were sparked in these women.

The reactions of the men backing the incinerator provided a very serious learning experience for the women, both professionals and nonprofessionals, who came to the movement without a critique of patriarchy. They developed their critique in practice. In confronting the need for equality, these women forced the men to a new level of recognition—that working-class women's concerns cannot be simply dismissed.

Individual transformations accompanied the group process. As the struggle against the incinerator proceeded to take on some elements of class struggle, individual consciousness matured and developed. Women began to recognize something of their own oppression as women. This led to new forms of action not only against institutions but to the transformation of social relations in the home as well. … Children and husbands complained that meetings and public hearings had taken priority over the family and relations in the home. According to Charlotte Bullock, "My children understand, but then they don't want to understand. … They say, 'You're not spending time with me.'" Ironically, it was the concern for family, their love of their families, that had catapulted these women into action to begin with. But, in a pragmatic sense, the home did have to come second in order for health and safety to be preserved. These were hard learning experiences. But meetings in individual homes ultimately involved children and spouses alike—everyone worked and everyone listened. The transformation of relations continued as women spoke up at hearings and demonstrations and husbands transported children, made signs, and looked on with pride and support at public forums.

The critical perspective of women in the battle against LANCER went far beyond what the women themselves had intended. For these women, the political issues were personal and in that sense they became feminist issues. These women, in the end, were fighting for what they felt was "right" rather than what men argued might be reasonable. The coincidence of the principles of feminism and ecology that Carolyn Merchant explains in *The Death of Nature* (San Francisco: Harper & Row, 1981) found expression and developed in the consciousness of these women: the concern for Earth as a home, the recognition that all parts of a system have equal value, the acknowledgment of process, and, finally, that capitalist growth has social costs. …

In 2 years, what started as the outrage of a small group of mothers has transformed the political climate of a major metropolitan area. What these women have aimed for is a greater level of democracy, a greater level of involvement, not only in their organization but in the development process of the city generally. They have demanded accountability regarding land use and ownership, very subversive concerns in a capitalist society. In their organizing, the group process, collectivism, was of primary importance. It allowed the women to see their own power and potential and therefore allowed them to consolidate effective opposition. The movement underscored the role of principles. In fact, we citizens have lived so long with an unquestioning acceptance of profit and expediency that sometimes we forget that our objective is to do "what's right." Women are beginning to raise moral concerns in a very forthright manner, emphasizing that experts have left us no other choice but to follow our own moral convictions rather than accept neutrality and capitulate in the face of crisis.

The environmental crisis will escalate in this decade and women are sure to play pivotal roles in the struggle to save our planet. If women are able to sustain for longer periods some of the qualities and behavioral forms they have displayed in crisis situations (such as direct participatory democracy and the critique of patriarchal bureaucracy), they may be able to reintroduce equality and democracy into progressive action. They may also reintroduce the value of being moved by principle and morality. Pragmatism has come to dominate all forms of political behavior and the results have often been disastrous. If women resist the "normal" organizational thrust to barter, bargain, and fragment ideas and issues, they may help set new standards for action in the new environmental movement.

### Notes

1. See Cynthia Cockburn, "When Women Get Involved in Community Action," in Marjorie Mayo (ed.), *Women in the Community* (London: Routledge & Kegan Paul, 1977).
2. Cockburn, "When Women," p. 62.
3. Cerrell Associates, *Political Difficulties Facing Waste to Energy Conversion Plant Siting* (Los Angeles: California Waste Management Board, 1984), pp. 42–43.

# *Questioning Sour Grapes: Ecofeminism and the United Farm Workers Grape Boycott*

## Ellen O'Loughlin

Sour grapes. What an expression (on your face). Sour grapes are unexpected and unwanted. You pick a grape, bite through the skin to the fleshy fruit expecting sweetness. Perhaps you anticipate seeds, but more likely not (seedless reigns). Expecting sweetness, you are disappointed by the sour grape. Say "yuck" and spit it out if you can; if not, grimace and swallow. The grape is rejected. Is it bad? Or just not what you wanted? Not what you paid for? Were you deceived by the unblemished appearance of the fruit? Can you trust the next one?

Sour grapes: the expression refers to someone who is dissatisfied, holds a grudge, doesn't have a sense of humor, won't go along with the crowd, a sore loser. Sour is crabby, sullen, surly, as well as acerbic. Adjectives to put down, as well as to describe. Adjectives used to describe feminists, troublemakers. Sour grapes is an expression to describe something that leaves a bad taste in your mouth (another expression), in someone's mouth. ...

This chapter is about grapes. It's about attitudes, about people, about oppression, about resistance. About sour grapes in various forms. In this essay I plan to begin to explore the United Farm Workers' grape boycott from an ecofeminist perspective. Ecofeminism is a philosophy that, through analysis of the connectedness of the oppressions of women and nature, demonstrates the necessity of a connected liberation from domination. The UFW grape boycott is part of an activist-labor struggle in which women and environmental concerns are central. The boycott is an effort to connect the oppression of farm workers to health concerns of grape consumers and to free both from danger. This boycott against California table grapes demands from growers "the elimination of dangerous pesticides from all grape fields ... [a] joint testing program for poisonous substances in grapes sold in stores ... free and fair elections for farm workers, and good faith collective bargaining in the grape industry."[1] These issues, and others addressed by the UFW, such as clean air and water, sexual harassment, poverty, nondomination, and self-determination, are also ecofeminist topics. I am not saying that the UFW is ecofeminist; I wish, rather, to show that the movements share common concerns and can learn from each other. Through my interest in ecofeminism, I have been motivated to learn more about the UFW; in learning about the UFW, I am encouraged to think critically about ecofeminism.

...

The present UFW boycott, begun in 1984, continues the UFW's tradition of innovative organizing techniques. Originally a part of the wide demands for social justice that characterized much of the 1960s, the union has continued to forge a progressive path. Throughout its history the UFW has combined conventional labor demands for unionization with, for example, campaigns to get DDT and other dangerous pesticides out of the fields. In the 1970s the union was successful in organizing labor on farms and in vineyards. The conservative 1980s saw both the creation of a pro-management Agricultural Labor Relations Board in California and renewed political activity on the part of the UFW. Soliciting support from outside the fields, the UFW works with other labor organizations, with community and religious organizations, with school boards and city councils, and focuses on consumer health as well as labor conditions. Health, in the face of pesticide use, is an issue that transcends social boundaries and provides a unique space for communication and coalition.

Lin Nelson's "The Place of Women in Polluted Places" explains that "health as an ecological process is the visceral daily reality that forces us to face the crossroads at the end of the twentieth century."[2] The article looks at various ways in which women, ecology, and health are related. Some of the angles she looks at include environmental illness, reproductive hazards and fetal protection policies, mothers of children exposed to toxics, women as test objects, women polluters and women in complicity with polluters, activists and kitchen-table researchers. Nelson suggests that women have many places in our social ecology, places that we must explore.

If we recognize that women are in many places, we have little need for monolithic categories such as "woman." The concept of ecology can guide us in our attempts to see how our different places are connected. Ecology helps explain the various oppressions women face as a network, as a web, without ranking and without additive approaches. An ecologist cannot just add up the parts of a pond and think she is coming close to describing that ecosystem and how it functions. A fish in a pond and a fish in an ocean, looked at ecologically, must be understood as inhabiting different, maybe similar but not the same, places. Likewise, women are in different places: in pesticide-sprayed fields, in supermarkets, in agribusiness management. Women are also in different places in terms of class, race, sexuality, culture, and age. Whether I am in a field or an office, what I do there, my niche, is at least partially determined by the interconnection of societal environmental factors. My position when choosing whether or not to eat a grape at a friend's house is not the same as that of the worker who picked and packed that grape. But our positions are connected, and in more than one way. Furthermore, our respective positions are not determined simply by sex or sexism or women's relation to nature. If so, we'd be in the same place. Or that farm worker would have to be male (but then why do I seem to be in the better position?). Obviously there are many factors at work, intersecting in many ways. By using ecology as a model for understanding connections and diversity, ecofeminism can be transformative. Thinking ecologically thus helps me to include supporting the UFW grape boycott as a part of my understanding of ecofeminism and makes an examination of the boycott a critical educational opportunity for ecofeminism.

In her examination of women's many places, Nelson is particularly concerned with women who would not label themselves "ecofeminist" (probably never heard the term), "feminist," or "ecologist"—yet "without these women we would have no resistance and little knowledge about what ails us." Many farm worker women are these women; many UFW women are these women. The fact that they fight in association with men, are concerned about men's health too, certainly should not make their experiences, their knowledge, their leadership, less important to ecofeminism.

Nelson concludes that "we must not, and we must not let others, ghetto-ize environmental health as a 'women's problem'" and that "our sense of ecology must include where people spend most of their waking hours—the workplace." Certainly the UFW has been a leader in both of these areas. The UFW's focus on environmental health as a concern to both consumers and laborers, as well as their concern for men, women, and children in the fields and living near farms, is a strategy to counter ghettoization—whether by sex, ethnicity, or occupation. The focus of the grape boycott can be summarized as "Our concerns are yours too." The problem of pesticides does not stop at the harvest, does not affect only fieldhands. And, even more clearly, the UFW has been a leader in making the workplace part of ecology. From the earliest bans on DDT, Dieldren, and Aldrin (in 1970, years before the federal government acted), to the present campaign to ban Captan, Parathion, Phosdrin, Dinoseb, and methyl bromide, the UFW has been a leader in fighting for an ecologically safer and healthier workplace. Thus, ecofeminism can certainly learn from the UFW, as our literature says now what the union has demonstrated for years.

...

The UFW grape boycott asks consumers not to buy California table grapes until the growers agree to the elimination of dangerous pesticides from all grape fields, a joint testing program for poisonous substances in grapes sold in stores, free and fair elections for farm workers, and good-faith collective bargaining in the grape industry. The UFW brings together consumers and laborers, consumer and labor issues, with these three demands. ... Health concerns about pesticide oppression are the explicit connection that the UFW focuses upon to unify consumer and laborer.

The UFW film *The Wrath of Grapes* (1986) points out that the farm workers are the canaries for all of us. Just as canaries in cages were lowered into the ground so that their death from bad gases would warn miners that the mine was unsafe, so farm workers are indicators of the toxicity of pesticides. ...

...

... By incorporating information about resource and environmental pollution into the arguments about worker health, the UFW specifically allies itself with more conventional environmental and conservation causes. Again, this type of argument is meant to break down walls of classism and racism and evoke a true sympathy between farm workers and the rest of us.

*The Wrath of Grapes* and UFW newsletters publicize those central California valley towns where children, in the 1980s became the flags of cancer clusters. In McFarland, eleven children living within six blocks of each other were found to have cancer. In Fowler, a town of 3,000, there were seven children with cancer. More recently, a third community, Earlimart, was identified as yet another cluster site. Here the UFW believes the incidence of cancer is 1,200 times the "normal" rate.[3] With these stories of poisoned children, the UFW incorporates maternalism, and parentalism, into its multifaceted environmental politics, but as a partial strategy that does not exclude women, and men, in their other roles. As ecofeminists struggle with interpretations of the meanings of nurturance, the significance of reproduction, and the usefulness of metaphors such as "Mother Earth," we need to look around us for examples of how other groups have used maternalism and parentalism. In particular, we need to be able to fully integrate maternalism into our theories without making it the core of ecofeminism. ...

...

Agriculture is a primary category of internationalized capitalism, along with electronics, the sex trade, and handicrafts production.[4] Much U.S. food comes from exploitation of Third World people and land. Many of us became aware of where beef came from through concerns over the tropical rainforests. Other luxury foods, many of them fruits, are grown in huge plantations, from the Caribbean (continuing from the days of the African slave trade) to the Philippines. In the 1960s a lot of U.S. fruit companies moved south of the border, trying for a longer growing (and selling) season so Americans could eat (and buy) fresh strawberries in the winter. They were additionally motivated by the fact that "irrigation water, land, and labor were much cheaper in Mexico than in the United States. There were also fewer restrictions concerning the use of pesticides and fertilizers than in the United States. Even though most of the mechanical equipment had to be imported from the United States, it was the Mexican farm owner or manager who paid for this, not the fruit company."[5] The UFW negotiates a difficult path through this web of internationalized agriculture.

...

In "The Ecology of Feminism and the Feminism of Ecology," Ynestra King speaks of an ecofeminist belief in a "healthy, balanced ecosystem, including human and nonhuman inhabitants, [which] must maintain diversity." She explains further:

> Ecologically, environmental simplification is as significant a problem as environmental pollution. Biological simplification, i.e., the wiping out of whole species, corresponds to reducing human diversity into faceless workers, or to the homogenization of taste [e.g., no sour grapes] and culture through mass consumer markets. Social life and natural life are literally simplified to the inorganic for the convenience of market society.[6]

The connection between the monocultures in the fields and the monocultures in the stores is forged through the capitalist creation of faceless workers. In industrial capitalist agriculture this is especially clear in the case of seasonal farm workers. Not only are workers disempowered and faceless, but, if the system could have its way, workers would be bodyless during off-peak seasons. And so we must all listen to the farm workers who have been putting together the interests of the worker, the consumer, and the environment, symbolized and actualized most potently by pesticides. ... The exploitation of farm workers is clearly related to patterns of natural resource abuse. Farm workers' lives and bodies demonstrate the interconnections of ecology and social justice that ecofeminism seeks to understand.

In California (at least), the history of farm labor can be examined in terms of changing tides of exploitable immigrant labor that have been played against each other, sometimes to the benefit of one ethnic group over another, always to the benefit of the capitalist agricultural state system.[7] Today in California most farm workers are Chicano, as yesterday they were Chinese, Japanese, Mexican, Filipino, or white Dust Bowl refugees. The main concern of agriculturalists was always to have a large supply of cheap and amenable labor. If labor seemed to be gaining strength through labor movements or ethnic solidarity, business interests were threatened. The UFW came into being toward the end of the Bracero era (1942–1964), a period of government and agribusiness importation of Mexican labor to bring down and keep down farm workers' wages and ensure control. Just as big business plays American workers against their Third World counterparts by moving operations to cheap-labor free-trade zones, so agribusiness brought in floods of poor potential laborers to keep all farm labor cheap and under control. In fact, the *maquiladora* system of twin factories (officially known as the Border Industrialization Program) that now lines the Mexican–U.S. border began in 1965 as an incentive to the Mexican government to agree to the ending of the Bracero program.

The dangers to which farm workers are subjected, and which the UFW addresses, obviously include more than pesticide issues. The UFW is a labor organization confronting the fact that "farm workers are the poorest workers in America. Our members not only do the most dangerous work in the country ... they also receive the lowest wages." The UFW seems to downplay economic issues when going after public support, yet acknowledges them as baseline when, for instance, Cesar Chavez, organizer and leader of the UFW, says in the literature, "I'm sure I don't have to tell you that farm workers are the poorest workers in America." The farm worker force is poor, primarily people of color; the owners are increasingly wealthy, increasingly absentee.[8]

...

The UFW, with the leadership of Cesar Chavez and Dolores Huerta (the union's first vice president and chief contract negotiator), has always used nontraditional labor tactics to improve the lot of farm workers. ... Through the late 1960s and 1970s, [the union] concentrated on organizing the table grape segment of California agribusiness. The boycott of table grapes was built with boycott organizations and committees across the country. Help came from other unions, religious and civic organizations, and individuals. New York grape sales dropped 90 percent in the summer of 1968.[9] Chavez fasted, committing himself further to a "Gandhian nonviolent militance."[10] Anti-boycott activities included a sudden increase (from 555,000 to 2,167,000 pounds in a single year) in Defense Department purchases of grapes to ship to Vietnam.[11] In 1969 the union began to make the pesticide connection, getting increasing reports of worker illness from contamination and connecting this information to tests on grapes in stores that showed residues of Aldrin (later banned by the Food and Drug Administration as a carcinogen).[12]

The boycott is one of the alternative strategies used successfully by the UFW. The boycott, like the march, like the fast, has been used successfully many times in this century in struggles for social change. ...

...

The boycott is a more practical labor tool for the farm workers than the strike alone. The effectiveness of the strike tool for farm workers has often been undermined by the readily available pool of replacement workers and strikebreakers that agribusiness has used to undercut potential reforms. ... The boycott is also a more effective tool than the strike for the UFW because many farm workers cannot afford, financially or legally, to become involved in strikes. Because much of the work is seasonal, farm workers are under pressure to make as much money as they can when work is available. ...

Boycotts are feminist tools also. At the end of *Patriarchy and Accumulation on a World Scale,* ... Maria Mies includes a chapter entitled "Towards a Feminist Perspective of a New Society." This chapter deals with the question of activism, of feminist practice. In a discussion of intermediate steps, steps in which we begin to refuse our allegiance to and complicity with the existing destructive order, steps that begin to get us from here to there, Mies advocates boycotts as a path of conscientization that can "revive awareness of all exploitative relations in the commodities."[13] In so doing, boycotts can link the self-interest of the consumer to the exploitation of others and allow consumers to address their own role in exploitative systems. The generic "consumer" is a feminized position, a category still populated largely by women. ...

...

The more I listen to the UFW, the more I can taste the sour grapes, the more I become sour myself. The UFW exposes the *carrilla,* the pressure, growers use to force workers to meet unreasonable quotas by starting early and quitting late, by working through lunch and rest breaks, and by not going to the bathroom. Portable toilets often are not accessible, clean, or provided with toilet paper. The inconvenience is particularly problematic for women, but there is more than inconvenience involved. At least one farm worker was forced to abort her pregnancy because she had used some grape-packing paper that turned out to be treated with "medicine"—that is, pesticide—when there was no toilet paper available.[14] Many women are sexually harassed by foremen and can lose their jobs for resisting the boss's advances. Often workers have to give bribes to supervisors. In August 1989 the UFW sponsored a conference and speak-out about conditions. Five hundred came to share stories about *carrilla,* sexual harassment, poor sanitary conditions, and pesticides.[15] The Farm Worker Education and Legal Defense Fund and the UFW filed lawsuits in October 1989 on behalf of workers at several vineyards.[16]

These varied forms of systemic violence and exploitation on an everyday basis are symptomatic of a racist, classist, sexist society. ... Anzaldúa's poem *"sus plumas el viento"* tells of a farm worker and her lack of access to real choices; one section describes her situation:

> *Burlap sack wet around her waist,*
> *stained green from leaves and the smears of worms.*
> *White heat no water no place to pee*
> *the men staring at her ass.*
>
> *Como una mula,*
> *she shifts 150 pounds of cotton onto her back.*
> *It's either las labores*
> *or feet soaking in cold puddles en bodegas*
> *cutting      washing      weighing      packaging*
> *broccoli spears carrots cabbages in 12 hours      15*
> *double shift the roar of machines inside her head.*
> *She can always clean shit*
> *out of white folks' toilets—the Mexican maid.*
> *You're respected if you can use your head*
> *instead of your back, the women said.*
> *Ay m'ijos, ojala que hallen trabajo*
> *in air-conditioned offices.[17]*

This poem, with its objective and not-pretty picture of a female farm laborer's day, bluntly illustrates many reasons for women farm workers' involvement in the UFW.

From this vantage, ecology is not a concern for romanticized nature; it is about transforming drudgery into respected and healthful occupations.

... The issues farm workers are concerned about are ones we should all be concerned about: health, poverty, racism, working conditions, and pollution, as well as sexism. The UFW's grape boycott is not the solution to all these problems. But it is a good intermediate step worth the investment of ecofeminist time, energy, and interest. Because so many issues intersect within the oppressions faced by farm workers, we can begin to confront the many systems of domination that structure society through participating in the grape boycott and through studying acknowledged leaders like the UFW.

...

As an ecofeminist I need to know not only Rachel Carson's contributions to publicizing the dangers of DDT, but also that the United Farm Workers got the first bans on DDT, DDE, and Dieldren instituted in UFW-contracted fields. With guides to socially responsible investment and green consumption increasing in popularity, all people must acknowledge the UFW's leadership in developing these strategies for creating a better world. When I consider the variety of sponsors and supporters of the grape boycott—people of many races, religions, and organizations—I see further evidence that the UFW has a lot to teach about successful coalition politics. ... The UFW's commitment to uncovering and fighting oppression as a system of exploitative relationships has put it at the forefront of ecological politics. The grape boycott is an action we can all support and learn from as our struggle(s) to end oppression continue along many paths, through many fields. *Viva la Causa!*

\*          \*          \*

A sour grape is a prism. The UFW boycott holds the grape up high so the sun can stream through it and reveal the cross-currents of our society flavoring the fruit. See the glitter of industrial capitalism, the dust of degraded soils, the poverty of hardworking people, the shrinking spectrum of life. See the poisons flowing into the water, into the animals, and into our mouths.

Now put the grape to your eye and take a look at ecofeminism. What do you see? Is it easy to focus? Do you get only one picture? Hold the grape there for a minute and think about what you can see. Sure, everything looks different. Maybe you are getting multiple images when you try to focus on the woman/nature connection. Maybe the ecology you are seeing does not quite fit your old definition. Maybe you can see a little bit more.

---

### Notes

1. United Farm Workers, Summer 1989 fundraising letter, p. 2.

2. Lin Nelson, "The Place of Women in Polluted Places," in *Reweaving the World: The Emergence of Ecofeminism,* ed. Irene Diamond and Gloria Feman Orenstein (San Francisco: Sierra Club Books, 1990), 175.

3. UFW, "UFW Finds Cancer in Earlimart," *Food and Justice* 6 (November 1989): 3.

4. Maria Mies, *Patriarchy and Accumulation on a World Scale* (Atlantic Highlands, N.J., and London: Zed Books, 1986), 127.

5. Sonja Williams, *Exploding the Hunger Myths: A High School Curriculum* (San Francisco: Institute for Food and Development Policy, 1987), 106.

6. Ynestra King, "The Ecology of Feminism and the Feminism of Ecology," in *Healing the Wounds: The Promise of Ecofeminism*, ed. Judith Plant (Philadelphia: New Society, 1989), 20.

7. See, for example, Linda C. Majka and Theo J. Majka, *Farm Workers, Agribusiness, and the State* (Philadelphia: Temple University Press, 1982).

8. See, for example, Bruce W. Marion, *The Organization and Performance of the U.S. Food System* (Lexington, Mass.: D.C. Heath, 1986), 22–23, for statistics showing that 49 percent of U.S. farm production as of 1982 occurred on "larger than single family farms, with sales of at least $200,000," and that as of 1978 only one-third of U.S. farms were operated by their owners.

9. Majka and Majka, *Farm Workers, Agribusiness, and the State*, 188.

10. Ibid., 189.

11. Ibid., 193.

12. Ibid., 194.

13. Mies, *Patriarchy and Accumulation*, 224, 227. …

14. "Victims of Carrilla," *Food and Justice* (magazine of the United Farm Workers of America, AFL-CIO) 7 (January 1990): 5.

15. "Law Suits Expose Unsanitary, Slave-like Conditions in California Grape Fields," *Food and Justice* 7 (January 1990): 8.

16. "News from UFW," press release, October 25, 1989.

17. Anzaldúa, *Borderlands/La Frontera: The New Mestiza* (San Francisco: Spinsters/Aunt Lute, 1987), 117–18.

# *Stealing the Planet*

## Jo Whitehorse Cochran

I am a survivor of a race of peoples that have been brutally reduced to near extinction by the practice of forced or non-consensual sterilization of our women of child-bearing ages. Some time ago the Samish tribe in Washington State filed with the Department of the Interior a petition to place themselves as a tribe of people on the list of endangered species. Some folks laughed, thought it a good joke those "Indians" were playing on the government. Others thought it a good publicity stunt. I thought it was telling the truth. A voice rang in my head on the day I read the newspaper article about the Samish people. The voice was Paula Gunn Allen's, another Native woman; we had talked many times about genocide and the true meaning of it, and this practice to Native peoples the world over. Even though some men were sterilized, for the largest part sterilization abuse has been used against the women in Native America and across the world. Thereby leading Paula Gunn Allen to rename the practice gynocide—using the root gyn to signify women.

I have come to see this as a way of stealing the planet from those peoples who are indigenous to her. In the United States, because of war, disease-infested blankets in the early years of white colonization (1650–1875), and then through the later years (1875–1975) because of sterilization abuse the Native population in this country went from 14 million to below 1 million. In the 1984 census there were 1.4 million people in the United States who identified ourselves as Native. For hundreds of years, sterilization of the women of our tribes was performed by white doctors under orders of a white government. Sterilizations by the millions, done without consent, or with consent gotten under the anesthetic. Sterilization performed under the guise of other operations, for no other reason than a government wanting to control a population they deemed undesirable. If there is anger you read in these words, let it blaze, because the government has taken our children. When, in the 1970's, Congress ordered all Indian Health facilities to open their files and records for investigation on this matter what was found was incredible. Not a one of these white doctors over the years hid their work—it was documented, filed and logged—numbers, names, with consent, without consent. All in the name of going by government orders and quotas. All to destroy the Native community, family and tribe. And not to forget the destruction of each Native woman who was sterilized—those knowingly never to have children. And those without consent, unknowing—not knowing what was wrong with them. Or realizing too late when the drugs wore off and the pain of an operation, the bleeding of an operation that was perhaps for an arm or anywhere else in the body was coming from their wombs. No words for that kind of betrayal, that kind of murder. Some of these Native women already had children, but their rights to control and own their own bodies and choose to bear children or not was stolen. It is now easier to see as a Native woman that, once there is a people capable of stealing another people's children—it is only a small matter of time before they do the same to our mother, our grandmother, our planet.

# Reproductive Choices:
# The Ecological Dimension

## Ronnie Zoe Hawkins

While much has been said about the morality of choosing to abort a human fetus, too little attention has been given to the moral implications, from an environmentalist perspective, of deciding whether or not to add a new human life to the planet. In this essay I will argue that environmental considerations are relevant to the abortion debate and, conversely, that the abortion dispute ought to enter into a discussion of "feminism and the environment." I will speak from a perspective of concern for *life* in a broadly inclusive sense referring to the diversity of lifeforms on the planet, and will conclude that, when the ecological dimension of reproductive choice is considered, the term "prolife" might most properly undergo a dramatic change in usage.

## Environmental Considerations
## in the Abortion Debate: Population, Poverty,
## and Environmental Degradation

From a size of less than one billion throughout all our previous history, over the last two centuries the human population has shot up to somewhere between 5 and 6 billion people worldwide and is continuing to expand logarithmically. The median projection for stabilization is between 10 and 12 billion, roughly twice the present size, not to be attained before the end of the next century.[1] Estimates of the maximum number of people the planet's resources will support with intensive management vary widely,[2] and depend upon a variety of assumptions. The links between population growth, poverty, and environmental degradation, however, are becoming increasingly well documented, resulting in what has been called a "downward spiral"[3]—a growing number of poor people are forced to make a living on increasingly marginal land, with resultant deforestation, overgrazing, soil erosion, or an assortment of other environmental problems further exacerbating their poverty and often leading them to move on and repeat the process elsewhere. At least 1.2 billion people are presently estimated to be living in absolute poverty around the world, of which about half are thought to be trapped in such a self-reinforcing process.[4] Unequal access to land and resources, ill-conceived "development" schemes, local and national politics, and the international economic power structure may all contribute prominently to the maintenance of poverty worldwide, but continued population growth heightens the desperateness of the situation.

While the poor may seek to have large families as a way of coping with their immediate economic conditions, providing more hands to work and offering an increased chance that parents will be cared for in their old age, the long-term trade-off parallels that of employing ecologically damaging farming practices because of today's need to eat: tomorrow, the overall needs will be greater, while the resources for meeting them will be proportionately less. Women, bearing an increasingly large share of the burden of poverty, are increasingly seeking to limit their family size, but frequently, for institutional or social reasons, they are denied access to the means for doing so.[5]

## Population, Consumption, and the Toll of Nonhuman Life

Human beings are far from the only victims of the interaction between population growth and environmental degradation, however, and poor people are not the only actors in the ecological tragedy. As more and more land is radically altered to meet growing human needs and its biotic components are converted into resources for human use, nonhuman organisms are also affected by limitations on their growth, movements and interactions, deprivation of access to the necessities of life, and frequently loss of life itself. With destruction of habitats and fragmentation of populations, entire species are dwindling and disappearing as a result of human activities. In contrast to natural extinctions, which are relatively rare occurrences that are mitigated by the emergence of new species, anthropogenic, or human-caused, species extinctions are occurring at several hundred times the "natural" rate and, since they are the result of abrupt and often total destruction of habitats, are not offset by new speciation.[6] The changes are so enormous that conservation biologists, working within a "crisis discipline"[7] to stem the massive loss of species from the planet, have begun discussing a possible *end to evolution.* ...

...

## The Importance of Abortion in Population Limitation

If only for anthropocentric and even nationalistic or ethnocentric interests, many people will agree that some form of human population limitation is needed. Often, however, in the industrialized nations the population problem is construed as something "out there," a pressing issue for the Third World perhaps but of little relevance within a wealthy nation. Just as frequently, abortion is seen as isolatable from the larger picture, not an "acceptable method" of birth control. Those familiar with the empirical evidence relevant to these issues, however, present a different picture.

The population growth rate for what are referred to as the "less developed countries," while down from an earlier peak of 2.53% per year, is still about 2.33% when figures for China are excluded.[8] The median projection of a 10–12 billion maximum[9] is in large part dependent upon the optimistic assumption that, as these nations undergo the "demographic transition" from a state of high fertility and mortality to one where both rates are lower, the rate of overall population increase will fall substantially. In the process of making that transition, however, a large gap often develops between the death rate decline and the fall in birth rate, generating a great increase in absolute numbers before stabilization can be reached.[10] It is at this critical period of time, when smaller family sizes are becoming desirable but contraceptive use is unfamiliar or unavailable, that abortion plays a prominent and necessary role in fertility reduction, with abortion rates later declining as contraceptive use increases.[11] The abortion rates in Japan and in South Korea, for example, which underwent rapid transitions to a low birth rate during this century, rose when fertility was declining most sharply, then fell dramatically as the rate of contraceptive use gained. Without abortion, it is estimated that Korea's birth rate during the transition would have been 22% higher.[12] Since even small changes in the birth rate during this period will result in a substantial difference in ultimate population size, abortion has an important role to play in the long-term welfare of many "developing" nations.

While the populations of the "developed" nations are increasing at a lower rate (0.64% per year),[13] however, such countries should by no means be considered innocent of the toll being taken on the planet's living systems, even where numbers alone are considered. Estimates of the consumption of world resources and stress to the global environment generated per capita for citizens of the industrialized nations relative to those of the poorer countries have ranged from fifteen to more than one hundred times as great. ... The environmental toll taken by each new human born within the "developed" world will be very much greater than that of one born elsewhere. By the same token, those of us living in the industrialized nations can lower our overall destructive effect on the natural environment both by reducing the amount and nature of our consumption and by reducing the number of us that consume the planet's precious resources.

While efforts to diminish consumption and to restructure the global economic scheme can and should be advocated in light of this relation, so can a further slowing of our rate of population increase. And, while concerns about reducing environmental destruction may have heretofore played no more than a background role in the decision of most women that choose abortion in, for instance, the United States, one effect, however indirect, of the termination of a million and a half undesired pregnancies per year has been to reduce that toll, not insubstantially. Worldwide, figures for 1986 show that, while the total population increased by 82 million, an estimated 54 million abortions were performed, around 26 million in the industrialized nations and about 28 million in the poorer countries.[14] As a backup to contraception, abortion plays an important role in limiting the ecologically damaging effects of the human population in all parts of the globe.

## Relevance of the Abortion Issue to
## "Feminism and the Environment"

The above, drawing heavily on empirical material, is intended to illustrate the practical importance of ecological concerns to the abortion debate (as well as to discussions of birth control and population limitation). But it also suggests the theoretical importance of ecological concern to the abortion debate. The emerging position of *ecofeminism* can be seen to provide additional grounding for the "prochoice" stance.
...

...

Abortion has recently received attention as a problematic issue for ecofeminists: it has been viewed as a "masculine" response to unwanted pregnancy that "fails to respect the interconnectedness of all life,"[15] and as a choice that is difficult to reconcile with "an abstract pro-nature stance"[16] that would allow "natural" events such as pregnancy to run their course. However, if as [Val] Plumwood maintains, there is a need to reconceptualize both the concept of the human and the concept of nature,[17] part of meeting this challenge will lie in reconceiving ourselves as beings essentially of the natural world and yet beings whose nature it is to be active choosers of our own actions, responsible for their effects on each other and on other lifeforms, including the effects of our own reproductive activities. At the present time, recognition of our connectedness with all other life on the planet reinforces the need for abortion. When the interests of life in this larger sense are taken into consideration, the prochoice position is the one most deserving of the adjective "prolife."

---

### Notes

1. ... Paul Demeny, "The World Demographic Situation," in *World Population and U.S. Policy: The Choices Ahead,* ed. J. Manken (New York: W.W. Norton, 1986), 34–36.

2. Expectations range from the dire predictions of famine and social collapse early in the twenty-first century made in *The Limits to Growth* (D. Meadows et al, 1972), to the wild optimism foreseeing great improvement in life and environmental quality displayed in *The Resourceful Earth* (J. Simon and H. Kahn, 1984). ...

3. Alan B. Durning, *Poverty and the Environment: Reversing the Downward Spiral,* Worldwatch Paper 92 (Washington DC: Worldwatch Institute, 1989).

4. *Ibid.,* p. 45.

5. Surveys show ... that a majority in Latin America and Asia desire to limit their family size, and a growing number do so in the Middle East and Africa, though "the desire to maintain male dominance" on the part of the husband remains a major factor in keeping birth rates in Africa high. See Jodi L. Jacobson, *The Global Politics of Abortion,* Worldwatch Paper 97 (Washington DC: Worldwatch Institute, 1990), 22–37.

6. ... The present anthropogenic extinction event is "about 400 times that recorded through recent geological time and is accelerating rapidly," "the most extreme for 65 million years," since the end of the dinosaur era, and it is far more severe with respect to the loss of plant diversity; Edward O. Wilson, "The Biological Diversity Crisis," *Bioscience* 35 (1985): 703.

7. Michael Soule, "What is Conservation Biology?" *Bioscience* 35 (1985): 727.

8. Demeny, "The World Demographic Situation," pp. 38–39. The "more developed countries" include "Northern America, Europe, and the Soviet Union,, plus Japan, Australia, and New Zealand. All other areas are classified as LDCs [less developed countries]."

9. According to a recent report, the United Nations has now revised its population projections, renaming the former "high" and "middle" projections the new "middle" and "low" figures, with the median projection for stabilization now set at 14 billion people. See Virginia Abernethy, "Population Growth Curves, False Comfort?" *Population and Environment* 12 (1990): 97–98.

10. See George J. Stolnitz, "The Demographic Transition: From High to Low Birth Rates and Death Rates," in *Population: The Vital Revolution,* ed. R. Freedman (New York: Doubleday & Co., 1964), pp. 30–46.

11. Jacobson, *The Global Politics of Abortion,* p. 23.

12. *Ibid.*

13. Demeny, "The World Demographic Situation," pp. 38–39. It should be noted, however, that the United States has one of the highest rates of natural increase (0.8 percent per year) of the industrialized world (*1990 World Population Data Sheet,* Population Reference Bureau, Washington, DC) and that the U.S. birth rate has been increasing since mid-1987 (*Monthly Vital Statistics Report,* National Center for Health Statistics, Washington, DC, Nov. 13, 1990).

14. Population Crisis Committee, *Access to Birth Control: A World Assessment,* Population Briefing Paper No. 19 (October 1987), as reported in brief for Population-Environment Balance, et al., as *Amici Curiae,* Webster. ...

15. Celia Wolf-Devine, "Abortion and the 'Feminine Voice,'" *Public Affairs Quarterly* 3 (1989): 81–97.

16. Patricia Jangentowicz Mills, "Feminism and Ecology: On the Domination of Nature," *Hypatia* 6 (1991): 162–178.

17. See Val Plumwood, "Nature, Self, and Gender: Feminism, Environmental Philosophy, and the Critique of Rationalism," *Hypatia* 6 (1991): 3–27.

# Women, Population, and the Environment: Call for a New Approach

## The Committee on Women, Population, and the Environment

*We ... are troubled by recent statements and analyses that single out population size and growth as a primary cause of global environment degradation. We believe the major causes of global environment degradation are:*

- Economic systems that exploit and misuse nature and people in the drive for short-term and short-sighted gains and profits.
- War making and arms production which divest resources from human needs, poison the natural environment and perpetuate the militarization of culture, encouraging violence against women.
- The disproportionate consumption patterns of the affluent the world over. Currently, the industrialized nations, with 22% of the worlds' population, consume 70% of the world's resources. Within the United States, deepening economic inequalities mean that the poor are consuming less, and the rich more.
- The displacement of small farmers and indigenous peoples by agribusiness, timber, mining, and energy corporations, often with encouragement and assistance from international financial institutions, and with the complicity of national governments.
- The rapid urbanization and poverty resulting from migration from rural areas and from inadequate planning and resource allocations in towns and cities.
- Technologies designed to exploit but not to restore natural resources.

Environmental degradation derives thus from complex, interrelated causes. Demographic variables can have an impact on the environment, but *reducing population growth will not solve the above problems.* In many countries, population growth rates have declined yet environmental conditions continue to deteriorate.

Moreover, blaming global environmental degradation on population growth helps to lay the groundwork for the re-emergence and intensification of top-down, demographically driven population policies and programs which are deeply disrespectful of women, particularly women of color and their children.

In Southern countries, as well as in the United States and other Northern countries, family planning programs have often been the main vehicles for dissemination of modern contraceptive technologies. However, because so many of their activities have been oriented toward population control rather than women's reproductive health needs, they have too often involved sterilization abuse; denied women full information on contraceptive risks and side effects; neglected proper medical screening, follow-up care, and informed consent; and ignored the need for safe abortion and barrier and male methods of contraception. Population programs have frequently fostered a climate where coercion is permissible and racism acceptable.

Demographic data from around the globe affirm that improvements in women's social, economic and health status and in general living standards, are often keys to the declines in population growth rates. We call on the world to recognize women's basic right to control their own bodies and to have access to the power, resources, and reproductive health services to ensure that they can do so.

*National governments, international agencies and other social institutions must take seriously their obligation to provide the essential prerequisites for women's development and freedom. These include:*

1. Resources such as fair and equitable wages, land rights, appropriate technology, education, and access to credit.

2. An end to structural adjustment programs, imposed by the IMF, the World Bank and repressive governments, which sacrifice human dignity and basic needs for food, health and education to debt repayment and "free market", male-dominated models of unsustainable development.

3. Full participation in the decisions which affect our own lives, our families, our communities and our environment, and incorporation of women's knowledge systems and expertise to enrich these decisions.

4. Affordable, culturally appropriate, and comprehensive health care and health education for women of all ages and their families.

5. Access to safe, voluntary contraception and abortion as part of broader reproductive health services which also provide pre- and post-natal care, infertility services, and prevention and treatment of sexually transmitted diseases including HIV and AIDS.

6. Family support services that include childcare, parental leave and elder care.

7. Reproductive health services and social programs that sensitize men to their parental responsibilities and to the need to stop gender inequalities and violence against women and children.

8. Speedy ratification and enforcement of the UN Convention on the Elimination of All Forms of Discrimination Against Women as well as other UN conventions on human rights.

*People who want to see improvements in the relationship between the human population and natural environment should work for the full range of women's rights; global demilitarization; redistribution of resources and wealth between and within nations; reduction of consumption rates of polluting products and processes and of nonrenewable resources; reduction of chemical dependency in agriculture; and environmentally responsible technology. They should support local, national and international initiatives for democracy, social justice, and human rights.*

. . .

# About the Book and Editor

Some people believe that feminist ethics is little more than a series of dogmatic positions on issues such as abortion rights, pornography, and affirmative action.

This caricature was never true, but Alison Jaggar's *Living with Contradictions* is the first book to demonstrate just how rich and complex feminist ethics has become. Beginning with the modest assumption that feminism demands an examination of moral issues with a commitment to ending women's subordination, this anthology shows that one can no longer divide social issues into those that are feminist and those that are not.

*Living with Contradictions* does address many of the traditionally "feminist" issues. But it also includes issues not generally recognized as gendered, such as militarism, environmentalism, and the treatment of animals, demonstrating the value of a feminist perspective in these cases. And, far from reflecting any monolithic orthodoxy, the book shows that there is a rich diversity of views on many moral issues among those who share a feminist commitment.

Readers can sample a varied selection of papers and essays from books, journals, newspapers, and grassroots newsletters. Covering a wide range of moral issues, this collection refuses to offer simple solutions, choosing instead to reflect the complexities and contradictions facing anyone attempting to live up to feminist ideals in a painfully pre-feminist world.

Based on years of the editor's work in the field, imaginatively edited, and including generous introductions for students, this is the ideal text for introducing feminist perspectives into courses in ethics, social ethics, and public policy.

ALISON M. JAGGAR is professor of philosophy and women studies at the University of Colorado–Boulder. She was formerly Wilson Professor of Ethics at the University of Cincinnati and has also taught at the University of Illinois–Chicago, the University of California–Los Angeles, and Rutgers University, where she held the Laurie New Jersey Chair in Women's Studies. Her books include *Feminist Frameworks,* coedited with Paula Rothenberg (3d ed., 1993), *Feminist Politics and Human Nature* (1983), and *Gender/Body/Knowledge: Feminist Reconstructions of Being and Knowing,* coedited with Susan R. Bordo (1989). Currently she is working on a coauthored book entitled *Morality and Social Justice* (1994), and a book on feminist moral epistemology, *To-*

*ward a Feminist Conception of Practical Reason.* Jaggar was a founding member of the Society for Women in Philosophy and is past chair of the American Philosophical Association Committee on the Status of Women. She works with a number of feminist organizations and sees feminist scholarship as inseparable from feminist activism.

# Praise for LIVING WITH CONTRADICTIONS

"A beautifully balanced, carefully chosen, and timely set of selections, including many contemporary classics, on topics ranging from equality and work to militarism and environmentalism. The editor's introductory essay gives an excellent overview of current controversies in feminist ethics and is already enough to make the book worth having."

**—Claudia Card**
University of Wisconsin–Madison

"This is an anthology that professors will want to teach to their ethics, women's studies, political science, or sociology students as soon as possible. What most impresses about Jaggar's collection is how it enables readers not only to understand the diversity that characterizes feminist thought—the serious disagreements feminists have about the ideal family, good sex, meaningful work, and a humane society—but also to appreciate how intricate and tangled the connections are between one's personal morality and one's social ethics."

**—Rosemarie Tong**
Davidson College

"*Living with Contradictions* is sure to be much in demand for women's studies courses. For students in introductory courses, it will reveal deception in mainstream stereotypes of feminism and encourage self-directed thinking about feminist issues. For more advanced students, the book demonstrates the limitations of parochial feminism and inspires analyses that take account of the varieties of feminist experience."

**—Joyce Trebilcot**
Washington University–St. Louis

"A first-rate, exciting collection, which brings classical and cutting-edge feminist theorizing into fruitful dissent and dialogue. Poignant, passionate, and powerful, the voices speak to the most troubling and challenging issues at the center of the continuing struggle for the liberation of women, men, children, and the earth."

**—Kathryn Pauly Morgan**
University of Toronto

---

Alison M. Jaggar is professor of philosophy and women studies at the University of Colorado–Boulder. Her books include *Feminist Frameworks*, coedited with Paula Rothenberg (3d ed., 1993), *Feminist Politics and* ̶R̶3̶ ̶ ̶ ̶ ̶ ̶u̶r̶e̶ (1983), and *Gender/Body/Knowledge: Feminist Reconstructions* BLACKWELL'S ̶n̶o̶w̶i̶n̶g̶, coedited with Susan R. Bordo (1989).

For order and other information, please write to:

**WESTVIEW PRESS**
5500 Central Avenue • Boulder, Colorado 80301-2877
36 Lonsdale Road • Summertown • Oxford OX2 7EW

or use the enclosed inquiry card.

ISBN 0-8133-1776-2

9 780813 317762

90000